Developmental Pathways to Disruptive, Impulse-Control, and Conduct Disorders

Developmental Pathways to Disruptive, Impulse-Control, and Conduct Disorders

Edited by

Michelle M. Martel

University of Kentucky
Lexington, KY, United States

ELSEVIER

ACADEMIC PRESS
An imprint of Elsevier

Academic Press is an imprint of Elsevier
125 London Wall, London EC2Y 5AS, United Kingdom
525 B Street, Suite 1650, San Diego, CA 92101, United States
50 Hampshire Street, 5th Floor, Cambridge, MA 02139, United States
The Boulevard, Langford Lane, Kidlington, Oxford OX5 1GB, United Kingdom

Notices
Knowledge and best practice in this field are constantly changing. As new research and experience broaden our understanding, changes in research methods, professional practices, or medical treatment may become necessary.

Practitioners and researchers must always rely on their own experience and knowledge in evaluating and using any information, methods, compounds, or experiments described herein. In using such information or methods they should be mindful of their own safety and the safety of others, including parties for whom they have a professional responsibility.

To the fullest extent of the law, neither the Publisher nor the authors, contributors, or editors, assume any liability for any injury and/or damage to persons or property as a matter of products liability, negligence or otherwise, or from any use or operation of any methods, products, instructions, or ideas contained in the material herein.

British Library Cataloguing-in-Publication Data
A catalogue record for this book is available from the British Library

Library of Congress Cataloging-in-Publication Data
A catalog record for this book is available from the Library of Congress

ISBN: 978-0-12-811323-3

For Information on all Academic Press publications
visit our website at https://www.elsevier.com/books-and-journals

Publisher: Nikki Levy
Acquisition Editor: Dennis McGonagle
Editorial Project Manager: Karen Miller
Production Project Manager: Sujatha Thirugnana Sambandam
Cover Designer: Christian J. Belbow

Typeset by MPS Limited, Chennai, India

Dedication

For my father

Contents

List of Contributors

Theodore P. Beauchaine The Ohio State University, Columbus, OH, United States

Ilana S. Berman University of Arkansas, Fayetteville, AR, United States

Caroline L. Boxmeyer The University of Alabama, Tuscaloosa, AL, United States

Cassandra M. Brandes Northwestern University, Evanston, IL, United States

Jeffrey D. Burke University of Connecticut, Storrs, CT, United States

Anil Chacko New York University, New York, NY, United States

Julia E. Clark Department of Psychology, Louisiana State University, Baton Rouge, LA, United States

Cristina Crego University of Kentucky, Lexington, KY, United States

Victoria Dahl New York University, New York, NY, United States

Alex R. Dopp University of Arkansas, Fayetteville, AR, United States

Paul J. Frick Louisiana State University, Baton Rouge, LA, United States; Australian Catholic University, Banyo, QLD, Australia; Department of Psychology, Louisiana State University, Baton Rouge, LA, United States; Learning Sciences Institute Australia, Australian Catholic University, Banyo, QLD, Australia

Joseph Glicksohn Bar-Ilan University, Ramat Gan, Israel

Patrick Goh University of Kentucky, Lexington, KY, United States

Megan Granski New York University, New York, NY, United States

David J. Hawes The University of Sydney, Sydney, NSW, Australia

Morgan A. Hill University of Arkansas, Fayetteville, AR, United States

E. Parham Horn New York University, New York, NY, United States

Francesca Kassing The University of Alabama, Tuscaloosa, AL, United States

Shauna C. Kushner Toronto, ON, Canada

Rachel S. Lacks New York University, New York, NY, United States

Christine A. Lee University of Kentucky, Lexington, KY, United States

Rotem Leshem Bar-Ilan University, Ramat Gan, Israel

Michael D. Levy New York University, New York, NY, United States

Corey Lieneman West Virginia University, Morgantown, WV, United States

John E. Lochman The University of Alabama, Tuscaloosa, AL, United States

Michelle M. Martel University of Kentucky, Lexington, KY, United States

Tatiana M. Matlasz Louisiana State University, Baton Rouge, LA, United States

Heather M. McDonough-Caplan The Ohio State University, Columbus, OH, United States

Cheryl B. McNeil West Virginia University, Morgantown, WV, United States

Qshequilla P. Mitchell The University of Alabama, Tuscaloosa, AL, United States

Revital Naor-Ziv Bar-Ilan University, Ramat Gan, Israel

Holly E. Poore Emory University, Atlanta, GA, United States

Lauren B. Quetsch West Virginia University, Morgantown, WV, United States

Amrita Ramakrishnan New York University, New York, NY, United States

Emily L. Robertson Department of Psychology, Louisiana State University, Baton Rouge, LA, United States

Ari M. Romano-Verthelyi University of Connecticut, Storrs, CT, United States

Devon Romero The University of Alabama, Tuscaloosa, AL, United States

Allison B. Smith University of Arkansas, Fayetteville, AR, United States

Tess Smith University of Kentucky, Lexington, KY, United States

Jennifer L. Tackett Northwestern University, Evanston, IL, United States

Benjamin Thomas West Virginia University, Morgantown, WV, United States

Irwin D. Waldman Emory University, Atlanta, GA, United States

Thomas A. Widiger University of Kentucky, Lexington, KY, United States

Desireé N. Williford West Virginia University, Morgantown, WV, United States

Part I

Features and Assessment of Disruptive, Impulse-Control, and Conduct Disorders

Disruptive, impulse-control, and conduct disorders

1

Paul J. Frick[1,2] *and Tatiana M. Matlasz*[1]
[1]Louisiana State University, Baton Rouge, LA, United States, [2]Australian Catholic University, Banyo, QLD, Australia

Introduction

Symptoms of the most common mental health disorders have typically been conceptualized as falling into two broad dimensions in both adults (Krueger & Markon, 2006) and children (Lahey, Van Hulle, Singh, Waldman, & Rathouz, 2011). One dimension has been labeled as *overcontrolled, distress*, or *internalizing* and it includes symptoms of the emotional disorders such social withdrawal, anxiety, and depression. The second dimension has been labeled as *undercontrolled, disinhibited*, or *externalizing* and it includes various impulsive, hyperactive, substance use, disruptive, and aggressive behaviors. These two domains of psychopathology robustly form separate factors across various samples of different age groups supporting distinct patterns of covariation within individuals (i.e., phenotypic correlations; Lahey, Krueger, Rathouz, Waldman, & Zald, 2016). Research has also consistently supported that the specific patterns of behaviors (i.e., disorders) that can be subsumed under these two broad categories share a number of causal factors (Lahey et al., 2016). As a result, systems of classifying mental disorders that attempt to differentiate within these broad categories often result in high levels of co-occurring conditions or "comorbidities," such as the high rate of co-occurrence between hyperactivity and conduct problems that is found in samples of children and adolescents (Waschbusch, 2002). However, there is also evidence to support the contention that there are some unique causal processes that can lead to different disorders within these broad dimensions, making it important for causal theories to consider both the shared processes that increase risk for all disorders across the broad dimensions of psychopathology, as well as the specific processes that differentiate disorders within these overarching dimensions (Lahey et al., 2016).

The purpose of this book is to focus on these shared and unique causal factors related to the externalizing or disinhibited dimension of psychopathology and, even more specifically, on those disorders that are defined by disruptive behaviors. This specific form of externalizing psychopathology involves behavior that either violates the rights of others or brings the individual into conflict with society norms or authority figures (American Psychiatric Association, 2013). Thus, these disorders

Developmental Pathways to Disruptive, Impulse-Control, and Conduct Disorders.
DOI: https://doi.org/10.1016/B978-0-12-811323-3.00001-8

all involve potential harm to others. Further, persons who show significant levels of disruptive behavior are at risk for a host of significant problems in adjustment across the lifespan, including emotional, social, educational, occupational, and legal problems (Odgers et al., 2008). Given the harm to others and substantial risk for both current and future impairment in multiple life domains for persons who show significant disruptive behavior, it is not surprising that major systems for classifying mental disorders have all included syndromes or disorders defined by these behaviors.

Key issues in classifying disruptive behavior disorders

A brief history of classifying disruptive behavior disorders

One method for defining syndromes and disorders within this category has been based on factor analyses of items from rating scales that assess behavior problems in children and that define syndromes based on their observed pattern covariation across age, sex, and culture (Achenbach, Ivanova, & Rescorla, 2017). When this method is used with items defining the full range of externalizing behaviors, the findings consistently suggest that inattention and hyperactivity typically form separate dimensions from the disruptive behaviors (Rescorla et al., 2016). Further, the disruptive behaviors often factor into those that are (1) covert in nature and involve major violation of societal norms but do not involve a physical or verbal confrontation with a victim (e.g., theft, truancy, vandalism, substance use) or (2) overt in nature and involve verbal (e.g., defiant, angry, or oppositional behavior) or physical aggression (e.g., fighting, bullying, threats for harm) directed toward others (Burt, 2012; Frick et al., 1993). Importantly, this method for classifying disruptive behaviors explicitly endorses a dimensional approach for classifying people by defining a disruptive disorder as being a level of disruptive behavior that is past what is considered normative (e.g., 98th percentile) for the person's age and sex (Achenbach et al., 2017).

A second approach, and perhaps the dominant method for classifying externalizing disorders for both research and practice, has been the criteria published by the American Psychiatric Association in the Diagnosis and Statistical Manual of Mental Disorders (DSM; American Psychiatric Association, 2013). This system for classification was developed with the primary goal of defining persons in need of treatment, and thus emphasized distinctions between disordered and nondisordered individuals based largely on the level of impairment caused by the behavior (Kupfer, Kuhl, & Regier, 2013). Thus, in this approach, the primary consideration of whether a person was considered to show a disruptive behavior disorder was based more on whether the level of behavior caused impairments in the person's social, educational, or occupational adjustment rather than on whether the level was beyond a level that would be expected based on normative data.

Importantly, the distinctions within the externalizing disorders that have been made in the recent editions of the DSM have been at least partly based on the typical patterns of covariation among symptoms (Frick & Nigg, 2012). That is, the major externalizing disorders in childhood included in the most recent revisions of the DSM are Attention-deficit Hyperactivity Disorder (ADHD) defined by impairing levels of inattention, disorganization, impulsivity, and hyperactivity; Oppositional Defiant Disorder (ODD) defined by impairing levels of angry, defiant, and vindictive behaviors; and Conduct Disorder (CD) defined by impairing levels of behavior that violate the rights of others (aggression) or that violate important age-appropriate norms (destruction of property, deceitfulness or theft, serious violation of rules; American Psychiatric Association, 2013). Although these disorders have consistently been included in the DSM, the way that they have been conceptualized in terms of their relation to each other and to other forms of psychopathology has changed in recent editions of the manual.

Prior to the most recent edition of the DSM, ADHD, ODD, and CD were grouped together within a class of disorders labelled *Disorders Usually First Diagnosed in Infancy, Childhood, or Adolescence* (American Psychiatric Association, 1980, 1987, 1994, 2000). Besides these externalizing disorders, this section of the manual included diverse diagnoses such as Mental Retardation, Learning Disorders, Eating Disorders, Pervasive Developmental Disorders, and Tic Disorders. Thus, this grouping was not based on any consideration of shared etiology or any evidence for the frequency of co-occurrence among the symptoms of the disorders but was solely based on the presumed typical timing of onset. This method of grouping externalizing disorders changed in the DSM-5 based on several overarching goals for this edition of the manual (Kupfer et al., 2013).

First, one goal of the DSM-5 was to improve the manual's attention to important developmental considerations in the diagnostic criteria (Frick & Nigg, 2012). Specifically, the new edition of the manual had as its goal to promote a lifespan view of mental disorders, whereby continuities and changes in manifestations across development are considered for all disorders (Kupfer et al., 2013). Thus, a chapter grouping disorders based on timing of onset was not consistent with such a goal. Specifically, it ignored the fact that many disorders not included in this category often first manifested in childhood and adolescence, such as specific phobia (Kessler et al., 2007). Further, it minimized the importance of certain disorders included in this section when making diagnoses in adults, such as ADHD (Barkley, Murphy, & Fischer, 2010). Finally, it ignored the continuity in symptoms across certain disorders, most notably by placing two disorders both largely defined by antisocial behavior, CD and Antisocial Personality Disorder (APD), into two separate categories.

Second, DSM-5 had as a goal the aim of fostering a more dimensional approach to diagnosis. One way it attempted to do this was to organize disorders in ways that take into account common dimensions, such as shared risk factors or common symptom clusters (Frick & Nigg, 2012). For example, as noted above, there are rather extensive data to suggest that the symptoms of ODD, CD, and ADHD cluster around an overarching externalizing dimension that seems to share substantial genetic influences that are potentially reflective of shared problems in self-control (Lahey et al., 2011; Markon & Krueger, 2005). Thus, in the DSM-IV (American Psychiatric Association, 1994), these disorders were subdivided within the disorders first diagnosed in childhood in a category labelled, "Attention-Deficit and Disruptive Behavior Disorders." However, there is also evidence to suggest that some symptoms of ADHD, especially the inattention symptoms, cluster strongly with autistic symptoms, motor coordination, and reading problems (Frick & Nigg, 2012). Further, in terms of etiology, ADHD is associated with early appearing alterations or immaturities in neural development (Frick & Nigg, 2012). Thus, in terms of high levels of co-occurrence and their shared problems in self-control, ADHD could be placed with the disruptive behavior disorders, such as ODD and CD. However, in terms of high levels of co-occurrence and shared associations with alterations in neurological development, it could be placed with other neurodevelopmental disorders, such as learning disorders, motor disorders, and autistic spectrum disorders. The DSM-5 adopted the latter conceptualization, and thus ADHD was placed in the chapter entitled, "Neurodevelopmental Disorders," which has as their defining features that they manifest early in development and produce impairments in personal, social, academic, and occupational functioning (American Psychiatric Association, 2013). In contrast, ODD and CD were placed into a separate category of the Disruptive, Impulse-Control, and Conduct Disorders, which are defined by problems in the self-control of emotions and/or behaviors (American Psychiatric Association, 2013).

It is important to note that this grouping of the externalizing disorders is open to debate. That is, ODD and CD typically manifest early in development, often before the child enters grade school, and these disorders produce widespread impairment in the child's functioning, making these disorders similar to other Neurodevelopmental Disorders (Wakschlag et al., 2014). Similarly, ADHD is partly defined by problems in the self-control of emotions and behavior and, as a result, could be classified with the other diagnoses in the category of Disruptive, Impulse-Control, and Conduct Disorders. Further, although APD is still primarily listed with the other Personality Disorders in the DSM-5, it is cross-listed in this category to acknowledge the likely commonalities in both its manifestation (i.e., antisocial and aggressive behavior) and causes with CD.

In defining disorders in this category as all involving problems in the self-control of emotion and behaviors, the DSM-5 explicitly recognized that the causes of the problems in self-control can vary (1) across disorders included in the category and (2) among individuals with the same diagnosis (American Psychiatric Association, 2013). Further, the definition of Disruptive, Impulse-Control, and Conduct Disorders provided in the DSM-5 recognizes that disorders in other chapters of the DSM also involve problems in emotional and behavioral regulation but considers the disruptive disorders distinct by the problems in self-control being manifested primarily in behaviors that violate the rights of others or that bring the individual into significant conflict with societal norms or authority figures (American Psychiatric Association, 2013). This definition resulted in several other disorders being included in this category with ODD, CD, and APD. The first is Intermittent Explosive Disorder (IED) that is defined by impulsive aggressive outbursts involving either verbal or physical aggression that is out of proportion to any perceived provocation (American Psychiatric Association, 2013). Pyromania and Kleptomania are also included in this chapter, which focus on either deliberate firesetting or impulses to steal objects that are associated with tension or other forms of emotional arousal and that is relieved by setting fires or committing theft (American Psychiatric Association, 2013).

In summary, the category of Disruptive, Impulse-Control, and Conduct Disorders provides the primary grouping for the disruptive disorders in the DSM-5. In other chapters in this text, more extended discussions of these various disorders are provided that describe differences in their expression, in the potential causes for the problems in self-control that lead to these disorders, and in the response to treatment for persons with these disorders. These chapters also provide thoughtful critiques of the validity and usefulness of the DSM-5 method for classifying the disruptive disorders across the lifespan. However, in the rest of this introductory chapter, we provide a brief overview of each of the primary disorders included in this section of the DSM-5 and highlight a few critical issues that were considered when developing the diagnostic criteria that were included in the DSM-5.

Oppositional defiant disorder

Since the publication of the DSM-III (American Psychiatric Association, 1980), the two primary disruptive behavior disorders have been ODD and CD. Since that time, the basic characteristics of ODD have remained relatively unchanged and include a recurrent pattern of angry, irritable, argumentative, and vindictive behavior (American Psychiatric Association, 2013). Despite the long history of this disorder being in the DSM, there have been significant concerns raised about its usefulness as a diagnostic construct (Frick & Nigg, 2012). The first concern is that the oppositional and argumentative behaviors that form the criteria for this disorder are commonly displayed in normally developing children, especially at certain developmental periods, such early in preschool years (i.e., the terrible twos) and in adolescence (Wakschlag et al., 2007). The second concern is that ODD is frequently comorbid with a host of other disorders (Rowe, Maughan, Pickles, Costello, & Angold, 2002). As a result, concerns have been raised as to whether ODD overpathologizes a normative behavior pattern and that, unless it is accompanied by another disorder (e.g., ADHD, CD), is transient and benign and should not be considered as a separate disorder (Moffitt et al., 2008). In response to these issues, Frick and Nigg (2012) reviewed several studies testing the incremental utility of ODD in predicting problems in adjustment, after controlling for the most common co-occurring disorders (i.e., ADHD and CD). In studies controlling for co-occurring ADHD, children with ODD were still more likely to show CD, substance use, and emotional disorders both concurrently (Garland & Garland, 2001; Harpold et al., 2007) and predictively (Biederman, Petty, Dolan, et al., 2008; Biederman, Petty, Monuteaux, et al., 2008; Burke, Waldman, & Lahey, 2010). Further, in an epidemiological sample of 1420 children and adolescents ages 9–16, ODD predicted risk for diagnoses of anxiety and depression in adulthood (ages 19–21), even in the absence of CD (Rowe, Costello, Angold, Copeland, & Maughan, 2010). Thus, ODD appears to have diagnostic utility separate from other disorders and this supports maintaining the diagnosis of ODD as a separate clinical entity (Frick & Nigg, 2012).

Another issue related to the criteria for ODD concerns the best way to conceptualize and structure the symptoms that are used to make the diagnosis. That is, prior to the most current definition in the DSM-5, the symptoms of ODD included oppositional and defiant behaviors, as well as indicators of dysregulated negative affect (i.e., anger and irritability). These symptoms were all placed on a single list and the criteria required the presence of any four symptoms to meet the diagnostic threshold. However, factor analyses have supported a multidimensional conceptualization of the symptoms included in the criteria for ODD, with the angry–irritable mood symptoms forming a separate factor from the defiant–headstrong behavior symptoms across age, sex, and type of samples (Burke, Hipwell, & Loeber, 2010; Lavigne, Bryant, Hopkins, & Gouze, 2015; Leadbeater & Homel, 2015; Rowe et al., 2010). What is less clear from these analyses is the appropriate placement of the symptom "is often spiteful and vindictive," which does not consistently load with the other ODD symptoms and which may be more related to the severe conduct problems associated with CD (Stringaris & Goodman, 2009a). In addition, research generally suggests that all dimensions of ODD are associated with CD, but that the angry–irritable dimension is specifically related to emotional disorders (i.e., anxiety and depression), the defiant–headstrong dimension is more specifically related to ADHD, and the spiteful–vindictive symptom is related to indicators of callous and unemotional (i.e., lack of empathy and guilt) traits (Burke, Hipwell, & Loeber, 2010; Rowe et al., 2010; Stringaris & Goodman, 2009a, 2009b).

Thus, there is clear support for the contention that the ODD symptom list is multidimensional with meaningful differences in the symptoms based on both patterns of behavioral covariation and in their predictive validity for important outcomes. However, this evidence for the multidimensional structure of the symptoms needs to be interpreted in light of the fact that the symptoms tend to be highly intercorrelated, with correlations among the symptom domains typically ranging from 0.62 to 0.78 (Stringaris & Goodman, 2009a). Further, in a clinic-referred sample of boys ages 7–12 years, two clusters of ODD symptoms emerged with both clusters showing high rates of the argumentative and defiant behaviors but with only one cluster also showing high levels of angry and irritable mood. Thus, to reflect both lines of research (i.e., highly correlated but separable symptom domains), the DSM-5 criteria divided the symptoms of ODD into those related to angry–irritable mood (i.e., loses temper, touchy or easily annoyed, angry, and resentful), those reflecting argumentative and defiant behavior (i.e., argues with authority figures, defies or refuses request from authority figures; deliberately annoys others, blames others for mistakes), and the one symptom reflecting being spiteful or vindictive. However, the diagnostic threshold is still set at the presence of four or more symptoms across all three of these dimensions.

In addition to these changes in the criteria for ODD itself, another change was introduced into the DSM-5 to reflect the fact that a number of persons with ODD have significant levels of anger and irritability and those who show these problems regulating negative mood are at risk for developing mood disorders (Burke, 2012).

That is, the diagnosis of Disruptive Mood Dysregulation Disorder (DMDD) was added to the DSM-5 in the chapter of depressive disorders to capture children who have chronic, severe, persistent irritability defined by frequent temper outbursts and whose mood is chronically angry and irritable between these outbursts (American Psychiatric Association, 2013). This diagnosis was added to differentiate children with chronic patterns of irritable mood from those who show episodic patterns of abnormal mood states associated with bipolar or major depressive disorders (Carlson, 2016). However, as would be expected given the overlap between the symptoms of this new disorder and the mood symptoms included in the ODD diagnosis, almost all persons diagnosed with DMDD would also meet criteria for ODD (Freeman, Youngstrom, Youngstrom, & Findling, 2016; Mayes, Waxmonsky, Calhoun, & Bixler, 2016). The DSM-5 decision rules require such persons to be diagnosed with DMDD only. However, based on the research reviewed previously, they could also be considered as a subtype of ODD defined by severe problems in angry and irritable mood.

A final important issue that is reflected in the DSM-5 diagnostic criteria for ODD is related to variations in the pervasiveness of the symptoms. That is, prior definitions of ODD only required the symptoms to cause impairment in one situation, which raised concerns as to whether such situationally specific problems reflect developmentally normative problems in the parent–child relationship (Moffitt et al., 2008; Wakschlag et al., 2007). However, research suggests that when ODD is reported by parents at home only, it is still associated with significant problems in current and later adjustment (Drabick, Gadow, & Loney, 2007). However, there is also evidence to suggest that when the ODD symptoms are displayed in multiple settings, the level of impairment is greater than when they are displayed in only one (Frick & Nigg, 2012). Thus, the DSM-5 criteria for ODD maintained the minimal requirement of impairment being present in only one context but included a severity rating that considered symptoms that are confined to only one setting as indicative of a "mild" form of the disorder, whereas symptoms that are present in two settings are considered indicative of a "moderate" level of severity and symptoms in three or more settings are considered "severe."

Conduct disorder

Another disruptive behavior disorder that has been included in the most recent editions of the DSM is CD. CD is the prototypical disruptive behavior disorder because it is defined as a repetitive and persistent pattern of behavior which violates the rights of others or in which major age-appropriate societal norms or rules are violated (American Psychiatric Association, 2013). The symptoms of the disorder fall into four main dimensions:

1. aggression to people and animals,
2. destruction of property,
3. deceitfulness or theft, and
4. serious violations of rules.

CD is an important psychiatric disorder for a number of reasons. Specifically, it is highly related to criminal and violent behavior (Frick, Stickle, Dandreaux, Farrell, & Kimonis, 2005). Further, it is associated with a number of problematic outcomes across the lifespan. These outcomes include mental health problems (e.g., substance abuse), legal problems (e.g., risk for arrest), educational problems (e.g., school dropout), social problems (e.g., poor marital adjustment), occupational problems (e.g., poor job performance), and physical health problems (e.g., poor respiratory function) (Odgers et al., 2007, 2008). Even in a sample of young children (ages 4 and 5), CD predicted significant behavioral and educational difficulties 5 years later (Kim-Cohen et al., 2009). Thus, the importance of the diagnosis of CD for designating an impairing condition across the life span is well established. The key issue that has been the focus of much of the recent debate over classifying persons with CD has been how to best capture the great heterogeneity of persons with the disorder. That is, persons with CD can vary greatly in terms of the severity of the disorder, its course, and the potential causal processes leading to the disorder (Frick, 2016). As a result, there have been a number of different methods that have been proposed for classifying important subgroups of children with CD in the DSM.

One method for subtyping children with CD that has received substantial support from research (Frick & Viding, 2009; Moffitt, 2006) is the distinction between those in which the symptoms of CD emerge prior to adolescence (i.e., childhood onset) and those in whom the onset of CD coincides with the onset of adolescence (i.e., adolescent onset). The extensive research supporting this distinction can be summarized by a few key points. First, there are important differences in the life-course trajectory of the two groups. That is, children in the childhood-onset group often begin showing mild conduct problems as early as preschool or early elementary school, and their behavioral problems tend to increase in rate and severity throughout childhood and into adolescence (Frick & Viding, 2009). Further, the childhood-onset group is more likely to show aggressive behaviors in childhood and adolescence and is more likely to continue to show antisocial and criminal behavior into adulthood (Odgers et al., 2008). Second, the conduct problems in children with the childhood-onset subtype seem to be more strongly related to neuropsychological deficits (e.g., deficits in executive functioning), cognitive deficits (e.g., low intelligence), and temperamental/personality risk factors (e.g., impulsivity and problems in emotional regulation) (Frick & Viding, 2009; Moffitt, 2006). This group also is more likely to come from homes with greater family instability, more family conflict, and with parents who use less effective parenting strategies (Frick & Viding, 2009). In contrast, youth who show the adolescent-onset pattern of CD show higher levels of rebelliousness and are more rejecting of conventional values than other adolescents (Dandreaux & Frick, 2009; Moffitt, Caspi, Dickson, Silva, & Stanton, 1996).

The different outcomes and risk factors for the two subtypes of CD provide strong support for the clinical and theoretical importance of the childhood- and adolescent-onset distinction. As a result, a specifier for designating children with CD as showing either the childhood-onset (at least one symptom presents prior to age 10) or adolescent-onset (no symptoms present prior to age 10) type was included in the DSM-5 criteria for CD. However, there are several important limitations in this method of subtyping (Frick & Nigg, 2012). First, it is not firmly established what should be the exact age to differentiate childhood- and adolescent-onset groups or even if the distinction should be based on the child's chronological age, pubertal status, or some other method for assessing developmental level (Frick & Nigg, 2012). Further, there is evidence to suggest that any single age will be arbitrary and that the distinction between early and late onset should be considered continuous (Fairchild, van Goozen, Calder, & Goodyer, 2013). And finally, there is evidence to suggest that even within the childhood-onset type of CD, there is substantial variability in terms of severity, course, and putative causal processes (Fairchild et al., 2013; Frick, Ray, Thornton, & Kahn, 2014a).

In an effort to capture this heterogeneity within the childhood-onset CD, the DSM-5 included for the first time an additional specifier labelled "With Limited Prosocial Emotions" (American Psychiatric Association, 2013). This specifier is applied to persons who meet the criteria for CD and who show at least two of the following symptoms over an extended period (i.e., at least 12 months) and in multiple relationships and settings:

- lack of remorse or guilt,
- callous—lack of empathy,
- unconcerned about performance, and
- shallow or deficient affect.

In research, these symptoms have been labeled as the affective dimension of psychopathy (Hare & Neumann, 2008) or as callous—unemotional (CU) traits (Frick, 2012). The term "limited prosocial emotions" was chosen in an effort to promote its use in clinical settings by using a label with fewer pejorative connotations than the labels used in research (Frick et al., 2014a).

The research basis for including this specifier in the DSM-5 is reviewed in more detail in a later chapter. However, there is extensive research to support both the clinical and etiological importance for differentiating children with CD who do and do not show significant levels of CU traits. In terms of the clinical importance, youth who show serious conduct problems appear to show a more stable pattern of behavior problems, more severe aggression, and poorer response to treatment if they also show elevated CU traits (Frick et al., 2014a). Thus, this group appears to show a more severe and impairing pattern of CD. In terms of etiological importance, youth with CD who do and do not show significant levels of CU traits show very different genetic, cognitive, emotional, and social characteristics (Frick et al., 2014a). As a result, research that fails to consider these differences could lead to misleading and even erroneous conclusions about potential causal factors.

To illustrate this importance for causal theory, several studies have shown that children with serious conduct problems with and without CU traits show opposing emotional responses on neurological, physiological, and behavioral indices (Frick et al., 2014a). For example, using functional magnetic resonance imaging responses to fearful and calm faces in a sample of boys, Viding et al. (2012) reported that amygdala responses to fearful faces (relative to calm faces) were stronger in boys with conduct problems without elevated CU traits relative to boys without conduct problems, whereas the responses were weaker compared to controls in boys with conduct problems who were elevated on CU traits. Similarly, Fanti, Panayiotou, Lazarou, Michael, and Georgiou (2016) reported that on both physiological (i.e., startle reflex during fear imagery) and behavioral (i.e., ratings of fear and sensitivity to punishment) measures of fearfulness, children with chronic conduct problems who were high on CU traits showed weaker startle reflex and lower ratings of fear and punishment sensitivity, whereas those with conduct problems who were normative on CU traits showed enhanced physiological responses and higher behavioral ratings. For both studies, ignoring the differences among the two groups high on conduct problems would have obscured important associations between the child's emotional responses and their problem behavior and this would have led to erroneous conclusions on the potential importance of emotional responding for understanding the development of conduct problems.

Antisocial personality disorder

One lingering consequence of previous editions of the DSM separating disorders first evident in childhood from other disorders is that there are currently two diagnoses whose primary symptoms involve a disregard for or violation of the rights of others. That is, in addition to these symptoms being key to the DSM-5 definition of CD, they also form the criteria for APD (American Psychiatric Association, 2013). The primary difference is that for APD, like the other personality disorders, the behaviors must be relatively stable over time. That is, the diagnosis of APD is only used for individuals at least 18 years of age, who have shown a pervasive pattern of antisocial behavior since 15 years of age, and who met criteria for CD prior to age 15 (American Psychiatric Association, 2013). As a result, a person who has shown CD prior to age 15 has a change in diagnosis to APD at age 18, if his or her pattern of antisocial behavior persists. This example makes it clear that APD and CD are differentiated largely by the degree of persistence of the behavior and the age of the person being diagnosed and not by any changes in symptomology or by distinct etiological factors.

Consistent with this view of APD and CD being the same construct, there is evidence that the presence of CU traits designates both clinically and etiologically important subgroups of individuals with APD, similar to what was described previously for CD. That is, CU traits are one component of the larger construct of psychopathy that also includes a grandiose and manipulative interpersonal style and an impulsive and irresponsible pattern of behavior (Hare & Neumann, 2008). Further, the presence of psychopathic traits leads to a more severe, stable, and aggressive pattern of antisocial behavior within individuals with APD (Walters, 2003) and the presence of psychopathic traits designates a group of antisocial adults with distinct causal processes leading to their antisocial behavior (Blair, Mitchell, & Blair, 2005). Importantly, this link between CU traits and CD in children and psychopathy and APD in adults is largely conceptual, with little data directly testing the predictive relationship within the same individuals. In one notable exception, Lynam, Caspi, Moffitt, Loeber, and Stouthamer-Loeber (2007) reported that self-report of psychopathic traits, which included CU traitsat age 13 ($n = 250$), was significantly associated ($r = 0.31$, $P < 0.001$) with clinician ratings of psychopathic traits at age 24. Importantly, this stability coefficient included traits other than CU traits (e.g., impulsivity) when assessed in children. Also, this estimate was based on two different methods of assessing CU and psychopathic traits, which likely reduced the estimate of stability. However, this finding suggests that, while definitely not immutable, there is some level of stability from childhood to adulthood in the level of CU traits (see Frick, Ray, Thornton, & Kahn, 2014b for a more comprehensive review of research on the stability of CU traits across development).

Intermittent explosive disorder

Another disorder included in the DSM-5 in the chapter of Disruptive, Impulse-Control, and Conduct Disorders is Intermittent Explosive Disorder (IED).. IED is defined by discrete episodes of impulsive aggressive outbursts in response to minor psychosocial stressors, which result in verbal or physical assaultive acts toward others or serious destruction of property. The outbursts have a rapid onset, with little to no prodromal period, and are grossly out of proportion to the provocation (American Psychiatric Association, 2013). Individuals with IED often experience less severe outbursts, typically involving verbal or nondestructive property assaults, between the more severe outbursts (Coccaro, 2011). Although IED first appeared in the DSM in the third edition of the manual under the category "Disorders of Impulse Control Not Elsewhere Classified" (American Psychiatric Association, 1980), even earlier versions of the DSM included similar disorders characterized by impulsive aggression, such as Explosive Personality Disorder (American Psychiatric Association, 1968). Thus, the construct captured by IED has a long history of inclusion in the DSM. When IED was added to the DSM-III, its definition was very narrow and excluded individuals who displayed impulsive and aggressive behavior between outbursts as a way of differentiating people with IED from people with other chronic problems of impulse control, such as persons with APD (Coccaro, Kavoussi, Berman, & Lish, 1998; Coccaro, 2012). In both the DSM-IV and most recent DSM-5, the definition of IED did not explicitly exclude those with chronic problems of impulsivity but did explicitly state that the IED diagnosis can only be made after other disorders that might account for the aggressive outbursts could be ruled out, such as APD, CD, ADHD, and Borderline Personality Disorder.

Thus, one key consideration for the diagnosis of IED is whether it defines a unique and clinically important subgroup of individuals who show impulsive aggression but who are not adequately captured by other diagnostic categories that include disorders of conduct or impulse control (CD or APD; Coccaro, 2011, 2012) or disorders in which anger is a primary feature (ODD; Fernandez & Johnson, 2016). Another key issue with the diagnosis of IED is that while retrospective studies generally suggest that adults with IED typically start showing signs of the disorder in late childhood to adolescence (Coccaro, Posternak, & Zimmerman, 2005;

Coccaro, Schmidt, Samuels, & Nestadt, 2004; Kessler et al., 2006), there has been very minimal research on IED in children and adolescents. It is likely that the minimal research on IED prior adulthood is also related to concern over its independence from other disruptive behavior disorders. That is, IED clearly documents a clinically important category of behavior that results in significant distress and impairment to the person. However, there are a number of other diagnoses that can be used for children and adolescent who show angry outbursts and impulsive aggression (i.e., ODD, CD, and DMDD). In fact, as noted above, DMDD is also defined primarily by recurrent angry outbursts. However, unlike IED, DMDD requires that the person experience mood that is chronically angry and irritable between these outbursts (American Psychiatric Association, 2013). Thus, more research is needed to show what IED adds to these existing diagnoses in terms of its clinical and etiological utility, especially prior to adulthood.

Pyromania and kleptomania

This issue of whether a clinically significant behavior adds to existing diagnostic categories of Disruptive, Impulse-Control, and Conduct Disorders is also relevant to the diagnoses of Pyromania and Kleptomania that are also included in the DSM-5 (American Psychiatric Association, 2013). These disorders are defined by intentional firesetting and stealing, respectively, and both of which violate the rights of others and are included in the definition of CD and ASPD. Thus, it is important to consider whether these behaviors alone warrant consideration as separate disorders.

The disorder of Pyromania requires that the repeated firesetting is associated with tension or affective arousal prior to the act and some sort of relief or gratification during or following the act. Additionally, the individual must have a fascination or attraction to fire (American Psychiatric Association, 2013). Both of these requirements are unique to the criteria for this disorder and are not required by the symptom of firesetting that is part of the diagnosis of CD (Grant & Won Kim, 2007). However, research studying children who commit fires have suggested that they often report doing so for revenge, craving for sensation, and as an expression of anger (Räsänen, Hirvenoja, Hakko, & Väisänen, 1995), which are all motivations often associated with CD (Gannon & Pina, 2010). Similarly, the definition of Kleptomania requires that the person must feel tension prior to the theft and experience a sense of relief or gratification at the time of the theft (American Psychiatric Association, 2013), again differentiating this from the symptom of theft that is part of the criteria for both CD and APSD that is considered due to personal gain or as a form of rebellion (McElroy, Pope, Hudson, Keck, & White, 1991). However, again the research supporting the validity of this distinction, especially in children and adolescents, is limited (Kirsch, Simeon, Berlin, & Hollander, 2014).

The international classification of diseases

To this point, we have largely focused on the criteria for disorders included in the DSM-5 that has been published by the American Psychiatric Association for use by mental health professionals and to guide research (Kupfer et al., 2013). The other major classification system for disruptive and impulse-control disorders is the International Classification of Diseases (ICD) that is published by the World Health Organization (WHO). In contrast to the DSM, the ICD includes both mental health and medical disorders and is designed primarily for use by primary care providers in diverse public health settings (Kupfer et al., 2013). As a result, the ICD tends to focus more on broad description of disorders and does not typically include discrete symptom lists with specific diagnostic thresholds defined by a clearly defined number of symptoms. The most recently published version of the ICD is the 10th edition (ICD-10; World Health Organization, 1992) and was developed to be congruent with the criteria and the codes for mental disorders included in the DSM-IV (American Psychiatric Association, 1994). The new edition of the ICD, the 11th edition, is currently under development with the goal of enhancing congruence with the DSM-5 (Kupfer et al., 2013).

Like the earlier DSM-IV, the diagnoses of CD and ODD are included under the broad category of Behavioral and Emotional Disorders with Onset Usually Occurring in Childhood and Adolescence in the ICD-10 (World Health Organization, 1992). Within this category both ODD and CD exist in the same subheading of Conduct Disorders, with ODD and several subcategories of CD listed as possible subdivisions. The core symptoms for ODD and CD in the ICD-10 are very similar to those used by the DSM. Also, like the DSM, subtypes of CD include childhood- and adolescent-onset subtypes. However, unlike the DSM, the ICD-10 diagnosis of CD includes a conduct disorder confined to the family context, an unsocialized subtype (where the person is rejected by peers), and a socialized subtype (where peer relationships are normal; World Health Organization, 1992). Also, the ICD-10 includes "mixed disorders" that are given when the child's conduct problems co-occur with either anxiety or depression (Mixed disorders of conduct and emotions) or when they co-occur with symptoms of ADHD (Hyperkinetic conduct disorder). The ICD-10 does not have a specifier for CD that considers the presence of elevated CU traits. However, the revisions that are being considered for the upcoming ICD-11 does include an additional subtype of conduct disorders that would be similar to the DSM-5 specifier of "with Limited Prosocial Emotions" (Rutter, 2012).

The remaining DSM-5 Disruptive, Impulse-Control, and Conduct Disorders diagnoses are included under the broad heading of Disorders of Adult Personality and Behavior in the ICD-10. APD is listed under the subheading, Specific Personality Disorders, as Dissocial Personality Disorder. Similar to the DSM-5, the ICD-10 requires evidence of a stable pattern of antisocial behavior, encompassing behaviors that violate social norms and/or the rights of others. However, whereas the DSM-5 requires evidence of CD before age 15, the ICD-10 states that the presence of CD in childhood or adolescence may help the clinical picture but is not required for diagnosis. Pyromania, Kleptomania, and IED are included under the subheading of Habit and Impulse Disorders in the ICD-10, with similar criteria to those included in the DSM-5.

Summary

In summary, Disruptive, Impulse-Control, and Conduct Disorders refer to important forms of psychopathology that are associated with a host of problematic outcomes throughout the lifespan. Thus, it is not surprising that these disorders have been included in major classification systems for mental health conditions. While recent editions of these classification systems generally agree on the primary symptoms of ODD and CD, there is less consensus as to whether other disorders should be included in the same class (e.g., ADHD), whether or how to differentiate within these two disruptive disorders (e.g., childhood-onset vs adolescent-onset CD), and whether other disorders are needed to capture distinct patterns of disruptive behavior (e.g., IED, DMDD, Pyromania, Kleptomania) or to capture age-specific manifestations and levels of persistence in the disruptive behavior (e.g., APD). These important issues are the focus of the other chapters in this text, especially in terms of how they relate to causal theories and treatment.

References

Achenbach, T. M., Ivanova, M. Y., & Rescorla, L. A. (2017). Empirically based assessment and taxonomy of psychopathology for ages 1½-90 + years: Developmental, multi-informant, and multicultural findings. *Comprehensive Psychiatry*, *79*, 4–18.

American Psychiatric Association. (1968). *Diagnostic and statistical manual of mental disorders* (2nd ed.). Washington, DC: Author.

American Psychiatric Association. (1980). *Diagnostic and statistical manual of mental disorders* (3rd ed.). Washington, DC: Author.

American Psychiatric Association. (1987). *Diagnostic and statistical manual of mental disorders* (3rd ed., rev.). Washington, DC: Author.

American Psychiatric Association. (1994). *Diagnostic and statistical manual of mental disorders* (4th ed.). Washington, DC: Author.

American Psychiatric Association. (2000). *Diagnostic and statistical manual of mental disorders* (4th ed., rev.). Washington, DC: Author.

American Psychiatric Association. (2013). *Diagnostic and statistical manual of mental disorders* (5th ed.). Washington, DC: Author.

Barkley, R. A., Murphy, K. R., & Fischer, M. (2010). *ADHD in adults: What the science says*. Guilford Press.

Biederman, J., Petty, C. R., Dolan, C., Hughes, S., Mick, E., Monuteaux, M. C., & Faraone, S. V. (2008). The long-term longitudinal course of oppositional defiant disorder and conduct disorder in ADHD boys: Findings from a controlled 10-year prospective longitudinal follow-up study. *Psychological Medicine*, *38*, 1027–1036.

Biederman, J., Petty, C. R., Monuteaux, M. C., Mick, E., Parcell, T., Westerberg, D., & Faraone, S. V. (2008). The longitudinal course of comorbid oppositional defiant disorder in girls with attention-deficit/hyperactivity disorder: Findings from a controlled 5-year prospective longitudinal follow-up study. *Journal of Developmental and Behavioral Pediatrics*, *29*, 501–507.

Blair, J., Mitchell, D., & Blair, K. (2005). *The psychopath*. Blackwell Publishing.

Burke, J. D. (2012). An affective dimension within oppositional defiant disorder symptoms among boys: Personality and psychopathology outcomes into early adulthood. *Journal of Child Psychology and Psychiatry*, *53*, 1176–1183.

Burke, J. D., Hipwell, A. E., & Loeber, R. (2010). Dimensions of oppositional defiant disorder as predictors of depression and conduct disorder in preadolescent girls. *Journal of the American Academy of Child and Adolescent Psychiatry*, *49*, 484–492.

Burke, J. D., Waldman, I., & Lahey, B. B. (2010). Predictive validity of childhood oppositional defiant disorder and conduct disorder: Implications for the DSM-V. *Journal of Abnormal Psychology*, *119*, 739–751.

Burt, S. A. (2012). How do we optimally conceptualize the heterogeneity within antisocial behavior? An argument for aggressive versus non-aggressive behavioral dimensions. *Clinical Psychology Review*, *32*, 263–279.

Carlson, G. A. (2016). Disruptive mood dysregulation disorder: Where did it come from and where is it going. *Journal of Child and Adolescent Psychopharmacology*, *26*, 90–93.

Coccaro, E. F. (2011). Intermittent explosive disorder: Development of integrated research criteria for Diagnostic and Statistical Manual of Mental Disorders, Fifth Edition. *Comprehensive Psychiatry*, *52*, 119–125.

Cocarro, E. F., Kavoussi, R. J., Berman, M. E., & Lish, J. D. (1998). Intermittent explosive disorder-revised: Development, reliability, and validity of research criteria. *Comprehensive Psychiatry*, *39*(6), 368–376.

Coccaro, E. F., Posternak, M. A., & Zimmerman, M. (2005). Prevalence and features of intermittent explosive disorder in a clinical setting. *Journal of Clinical Psychiatry*, *66*, 1221–1227.

Coccaro, E. F., Schmidt, C. A., Samuels, J. F., & Nestadt, G. (2004). Lifetime and 1-month prevalence rates of intermittent explosive disorder in a community sample. *Journal of Clinical Psychiatry*, *65*, 820–824.

Coccaro, E. R. (2012). Intermittent explosive disorder as a disorder of impulsive aggression for DSM-5. *American Journal of Psychiatry*, *169*, 577–588.

Dandreaux, D. M., & Frick, P. J. (2009). Developmental pathways to conduct problems: A further test of the childhood and adolescent-onset distinction. *Journal of Abnormal Child Psychology*, *37*, 375.

Drabick, D. A., Gadow, K. D., & Loney, J. (2007). Source-specific oppositional defiant disorder: Comorbidity and risk factors in referred elementary schoolboys. *Journal of the American Academy of Child and Adolescent Psychiatry*, *46*, 92–101.

Fairchild, G., van Goozen, S. H., Calder, A. J., & Goodyer, I. M. (2013). Research review: Evaluating and reformulating the developmental taxonomic theory of antisocial behaviour. *Journal of Child Psychology and Psychiatry*, *54*, 924–940.

Fanti, K. A., Panayiotou, G., Lazarou, C., Michael, R., & Georgiou, G. (2016). The better of two evils? Evidence that children exhibiting continuous conduct problems high or low on callous–unemotional traits score on opposite directions on physiological and behavioral measures of fear. *Development and Psychopathology*, *28*, 185–198.

Fernandez, E., & Johnson, S. L. (2016). Anger in psychological disorders: Prevalence, presentation, etiology and prognostic implications. *Clinical Psychology Review*, *46*, 124–135.

Freeman, A. J., Youngstrom, E. A., Youngstrom, J. K., & Findling, R. L. (2016). Disruptive mood dysregulation disorder in a community mental health clinic: Prevalence, comorbidity and correlates. *Journal of Child and Adolescent Psychopharmacology*, *26*, 123–130.

Frick, P. J. (2012). *Conduct disorders and severe antisocial behavior*. Springer Science & Business Media.

Frick, P. J. (2016). Current research on conduct disorder in children and adolescents. *South African Journal of Psychology*, *46*, 160–174.

Frick, P. J., Lahey, B. B., Loeber, R., Tannenbaum, L., Van Horn, Y., Christ, M. A. G., ... Hanson, K. (1993). Oppositional defiant disorder and conduct disorder: A meta-analytic review of factor analyses and cross-validation in a clinic sample. *Clinical Psychology Review*, *13*, 319–340.

Frick, P. J., & Nigg, J. T. (2012). Current issues in the diagnosis of attention deficit hyperactivity disorder, oppositional defiant disorder, and conduct disorder. *Annual Review of Clinical Psychology*, *8*, 77–107.

Frick, P. J., Ray, J. V., Thornton, L. C., & Kahn, R. E. (2014a). Can callous-unemotional traits enhance the understanding, diagnosis, and treatment of serious conduct problems in children and adolescents? A comprehensive review. *Psychological Bulletin*, *140*, 1–57.

Frick, P. J., Ray, J. V., Thornton, L. C., & Kahn, R. E. (2014b). Annual research review: A developmental psychopathology approach to understanding callous-unemotional traits in children and adolescents with serious conduct problems. *Journal of Child Psychology and Psychiatry*, *55*, 532–548.

Frick, P. J., Stickle, T. R., Dandreaux, D. M., Farrell, J. M., & Kimonis, E. R. (2005). Callous–unemotional traits in predicting the severity and stability of conduct problems and delinquency. *Journal of Abnormal Child Psychology*, *33*, 471–487.

Frick, P. J., & Viding, E. (2009). Antisocial behavior from a developmental psychopathology perspective. *Development and Psychopathology*, *21*, 1111–1131.

Gannon, T. A., & Pina, A. (2010). Firesetting: Psychopathology, theory and treatment. *Aggression and Violent Behavior*, *15*, 224–238.

Garland, E. J., & Garland, O. M. (2001). Correlation between anxiety and oppositionality in a children's mood and anxiety disorder clinic. *The Canadian Journal of Psychiatry*, *46*, 953–958.

Grant, J. E., & Won Kim, S. (2007). Clinical characteristics and psychiatric comorbidity of pyromania. *The Journal of Clinical Psychiatry*, *68*, 1717–1722.

Hare, R. D., & Neumann, C. S. (2008). Psychopathy as a clinical and empirical construct. *Annual Review of Clinical Psychology*, *4*, 217–246.

Harpold, T., Biederman, J., Gignac, M., Hammerness, P., Surman, C., Potter, A., & Mick, E. (2007). Is oppositional defiant disorder a meaningful diagnosis in adults? Results from a large sample of adults with ADHD. *The Journal of Nervous and Mental Disease*, *195*, 601–605.

Kessler, R. C., Amminger, G. P., Aguilar-Gaxiola, S., Alonso, J., Lee, S., & Ustun, T. B. (2007). Age of onset of mental disorders: A review of recent literature. *Current Opinion in Psychiatry*, *20*, 359.

Kessler, R. C., Coccaro, E. F., Fava, M., Jaeger, S., Jin, R., & Walters, E. (2006). The prevalence and correlates of DSM-IV intermittent explosive disorder in the National Comorbidity Survey Replication. *Archives of General Psychiatry*, *63*, 669–678.

Kim-Cohen, J., Arseneault, L., Newcombe, R., Adams, F., Bolton, H., Cant, L., ... Matthews, C. (2009). Five-year predictive validity of DSM-IV conduct disorder research diagnosis in 4½–5-year-old children. *European Child and Adolescent Psychiatry*, *18*, 284–291.

Kirsch, J. L., Simeon, D., Berlin, H., & Hollander, E. (2014). Disruptive, impulse control, and conduct disorders: Intermittent explosive disorder, kleptomania, and pyromania. In Tasman, Kay, Lieberman, First, & Riba (Eds.), *Psychiatry, fourth edition* (pp. 1367–1393). New York, NY: Wiley.

Krueger, R. F., & Markon, K. E. (2006). Reinterpreting comorbidity: A model-based approach to understanding and classifying psychopathology. *Annual Review of Clinical Psychology*, *2*, 111–133.

Kupfer, D. J., Kuhl, E. A., & Regier, D. A. (2013). DSM-5—The future arrived. *Journal of American Medical Association*, *309*, 1691–1692.

Lahey, B. B., Krueger, R. F., Rathouz, P. J., Waldman, I. D., & Zald, D. H. (2016). A hierarchical causal taxonomy of psychopathology across the life span. *Psychological Bulletin*, *143*, 142–186.

Lahey, B. B., Van Hulle, C. A., Singh, A. L., Waldman, I. D., & Rathouz, P. J. (2011). Higher-order genetic and environmental structure of prevalent forms of child and adolescent psychopathology. *Archives of General Psychiatry*, *68*, 181–189.

Lavigne, J. V., Bryant, F. B., Hopkins, J., & Gouze, K. R. (2015). Dimensions of oppositional defiant disorder in young children: Model comparisons, gender, and longitudinal invariance. *Journal of Abnormal Child Psychology*, *43*, 423–439.

Leadbeater, B. J., & Homel, J. (2015). Irritable and defiant sub-dimensions of ODD: Their stability and prediction of internalizing symptoms and conduct problems from adolescence to young adulthood. *Journal of Abnormal Child Psychology*, *43*, 407–421.

Lynam, D. R., Caspi, A., Moffitt, T. E., Loeber, R., & Stouthamer-Loeber, M. (2007). Longitudinal evidence that psychopathy scores in early adolescence predict adult psychopathy. *Journal of Abnormal Psychology*, *116*, 155.

Markon, K. E., & Krueger, R. F. (2005). Categorical and continuous models of liability to externalizing disorders: A direct comparison in NESARC. *Archives of General Psychiatry*, *62*, 1352–1359.

Mayes, S. D., Waxmonsky, J. D., Calhoun, S. L., & Bixler, E. O. (2016). Disruptive mood dysregulation disorder symptoms and association with oppositional defiant and other disorders in a general population child sample. *Journal of Child and Adolescent Psychopharmacology*, *26*, 101–106.

McElroy, S. L., Pope, H. G., Hudson, J. I., Keck, P. E., & White, K. L. (1991). Kleptomania: A report of 20 cases. *The American Journal of Psychiatry*, *148*, 652–657.

Moffitt, T. E. (2006). Life-course persistent versus adolescence-limited antisocial behavior. In D. Cicchetti, & D. J. Cohen (Eds.), *Developmental psychopathology, 2nd edition, vol 3: Risk, disorder, and adaptation* (pp. 570–598). New York, NY: Wiley.

Moffitt, T. E., Arseneault, L., Jaffee, S. R., Kim-Cohen, J., Koenen, K. C., Odgers, C. L., ... Viding, E. (2008). Research review: DSM-V conduct disorder: Research needs for an evidence base. *Journal of Child Psychology and Psychiatry*, *49*, 3–33.

Moffitt, T. E., Caspi, A., Dickson, N., Silva, P., & Stanton, W. (1996). Childhood-onset versus adolescent-onset antisocial conduct problems in males: Natural history from ages 3 to 18 years. *Development and Psychopathology*, *8*, 399–424.

Odgers, C. L., Caspi, A., Broadbent, J. M., Dickson, N., Hancox, R. J., Harrington, H., ... Moffitt, T. E. (2007). Prediction of differential adult health burden by conduct problem subtypes in males. *Archives of General Psychiatry*, *64*, 476–484.

Odgers, C. L., Moffitt, T. E., Broadbent, J. M., Dickson, N., Hancox, R. J., Harrington, H., ... Caspi, A. (2008). Female and male antisocial trajectories: From childhood origins to adult outcomes. *Development and Psychopathology*, *20*, 673–716.

Räsänen, P., Hirvenoja, R., Hakko, H., & Väisänen, E. (1995). A portrait of the juvenile arsonist. *Forensic Science International*, *73*, 41–47.

Rescorla, L. A., Achenbach, T. M., Ivanova, M. Y., Turner, L. V., Althoff, R. R., Árnadóttir, H. A., ... Csemy, L. (2016). Problems and adaptive functioning reported by adults in 17 societies. *International Perspectives in Psychology: Research, Practice, Consultation*, *5*, 91.

Rowe, R., Costello, E. J., Angold, A., Copeland, W. E., & Maughan, B. (2010). Developmental pathways in oppositional defiant disorder and conduct disorder. *Journal of Abnormal Psychology*, *119*, 726–738.

Rowe, R., Maughan, B., Pickles, A., Costello, E. J., & Angold, A. (2002). The relationship between DSM-IV oppositional defiant disorder and conduct disorder: Findings from the Great Smoky Mountains Study. *Journal of Child Psychology and Psychiatry*, *43*, 365–373.

Rutter, M. (2012). Psychopathy in childhood: Is it a meaningful diagnosis? *The British Journal of Psychiatry*, *200*, 175–176.

Stringaris, A., & Goodman, R. (2009a). Three dimensions of oppositionality in youth. *Journal of Child Psychology and Psychiatry*, *50*, 216–223.

Stringaris, A., & Goodman, R. (2009b). Longitudinal outcome of youth oppositionality: Irritable, headstrong, and hurtful behaviors have distinctive predictions. *Journal of the American Academy of Child and Adolescent Psychiatry*, *48*, 404–412.

Viding, E., Sebastian, C. L., Dadds, M. R., Lockwood, P. L., Cecil, C. A., De Brito, S. A., & McCrory, E. J. (2012). Amygdala response to preattentive masked fear in children with conduct problems: The role of callous-unemotional traits. *American Journal of Psychiatry*, *169*, 1109–1116.

Wakschlag, L. S., Briggs-Gowan, M. J., Carter, A. S., Hill, C., Danis, B., Keenan, K., . . . Leventhal, B. L. (2007). A developmental framework for distinguishing disruptive behavior from normative misbehavior in preschool children. *Journal of Child Psychology and Psychiatry*, *48*, 976–987.

Wakschlag, L. S., Briggs-Gowan, M. J., Choi, S. W., Nichols, S. R., Kestler, J., Burns, J. L., . . . Henry, D. (2014). Advancing a multidimensional, developmental spectrum approach to preschool disruptive behavior. *Journal of the American Academy of Child and Adolescent Psychiatry*, *53*, 82–96.

Walters, G. D. (2003). Predicting institutional adjustment and recidivism with the psychopathy checklist factor scores: A meta-analysis. *Law and Human Behavior*, *27*, 541–558.

Waschbusch, D. A. (2002). A meta-analytic examination of comorbid hyperactive-impulsive-attention problems and conduct problems. *Psychological Bulletin*, *128*, 118–150.

World Health Organization. (1992). *The ICD-10 classification of mental and behavioural disorders: Clinical descriptions and diagnostic guidelines*. Geneva, Switzerland: World Health Organization.

Further Reading

Kolko, D. J. (2001). Efficacy of cognitive-behavioral treatment and fire safety education for children who set fires: Initial and follow-up outcomes. *Journal of Child Psychology and Psychiatry*, *42*, 359–369.

Lowenstein, L. F. (1989). The etiology, diagnosis and treatment of the fire-setting behaviour of children. *Child Psychiatry and Human Development*, *19*, 186–194.

Oppositional defiant disorder

2

Jeffrey D. Burke and Ari M. Romano-Verthelyi
University of Connecticut, Storrs, CT, United States

Oppositional defiant disorder (ODD) as a diagnostic category reflects a persistent manifestation of negativity and oppositional behavior and is comprised of the symptoms of losing temper, arguing, defying, annoying others, blaming others, being touchy, being angry, and being spiteful. Evidence emerging over the past two decades has helped to dramatically reshape theoretical and developmental models of ODD in multiple ways. As reviewed in this chapter, this evidence demonstrates that ODD has genetic influences, that it can be identified early in childhood, and that it persists into at least young adulthood. Research shows that ODD exerts pervasive negative influences on multiple aspects of development, among which are familial, peer, and other interpersonal interactions, the development of other psychopathology, and functioning in multiple contexts. An understanding of important distinctions in dimensions among symptoms has clarified the role of ODD in the development of both behavioral and affective disorders.

It might seem incongruous to suggest that substantial evidence has only relatively recently begun to accrue for a condition that is reliably identifiable very early in childhood, persists into adulthood, and exerts pervasive effects on multiple domains of functioning. Research on ODD has been delayed in part because the validity of the disorder has consistently been questioned. This includes concerns from the public at large (e.g., Kelland, 2012), where it has been described as a condition that risks "devaluating the seriousness of mental illness and medicalizing behaviors most people would consider normal [. . .]," and among researchers and clinicians as well (see Rey et al., 1988), who have expressed similar concerns. As recently as 2007, during the development of the Diagnostic and Statistical Manual of Mental Disorders, fifth edition (DSM-5), consideration was given as to whether ODD should be subsumed under the category of conduct disorder (CD) (Moffitt et al., 2008). In order to avoid continuing to make the same mistakes and further delaying new research that could address important persisting questions, some understanding of how ODD has been regarded in the past is necessary.

A brief history of ODD

Broadly speaking, the eight symptoms of the disorder have remained largely consistent since DSM-III-R [American Psychiatric Association (APA), 1987], with the

Developmental Pathways to Disruptive, Impulse-Control, and Conduct Disorders.
DOI: https://doi.org/10.1016/B978-0-12-811323-3.00002-X

exception that the DSM-III-R item of "often swears or uses obscene language" was dropped from the DSM-IV. An addition change in DSM-IV was the qualification of the frequency for each behavior; symptoms were required to have been present "often" in order to meet criteria. The duration of the presence of symptoms, 6 months or longer, has been consistent since the introduction of the disorder in DSM-III (APA, 1980).

Significant changes have been made to the diagnosis with DSM-5 (APA, 2013). Most substantial among these is the introduction of a subcategorization among the symptoms. The symptoms pertaining to losing temper, being angry, and being touchy fall into the category of Angry/Irritable Mood. The symptoms pertaining to arguing, defying, annoying, and blaming fall into the category of Argumentative/Defiant Behavior. Finally, the symptom of being spiteful and vindictive is the sole symptom in the category of Vindictiveness. The rationale for the introduction of these subcategories, and important diagnostic, clinical, and research implications, along with the controversies surrounding them, will be reviewed in more detail in the discussion of the dimensionality of symptoms below. An additional important, but more subtle change, with DSM-5 pertains to the modification of language to enhance the clinical application of symptoms to adults. This change will be reviewed in more detail in the discussion of developmental issues related to ODD below.

An important point regarding the historical and current definition of ODD is that it has consistently been regarded as a chronic, rather than episodic, disorder. This reflects an element of consistency between ODD as codified across versions of the DSM (APA, 1980) and the historical precursors to ODD. For example, "Oppositional Personality" (Group for the Advancement of Psychiatry, 1966) was said to describe children who "express their aggressiveness by oppositional patterns of generally passive character [...]. By the use of negativism, stubbornness, dawdling, procrastination and other measures, they covertly show their underlying aggressivity" (p. 242).

The DSM-III moved toward more objectively identifiable criteria, and the original description of "oppositional disorder" in DSM-III (APA, 1980) included five symptoms: violations of minor rules, temper tantrums, argumentativeness, provocative behavior, and stubbornness. The strong implication of a conceptual association, or even a continuity, with passive-aggressive behavior was still present. Specifically, for individuals aged 18 or older, the diagnosis of ODD could only be given if criteria for passive-aggressive personality disorder were not met. In these earlier incarnations of the disorder, the infusion of passive-aggressive elements may have contributed to a sense—which has persisted to a greater or lesser degree to the present—that ODD is a milder form of CD. That is, these children are motivated to aggress, but for some reason do not express this aggression directly, instead doing so passively.

More explicit on this point though was the hierarchical model imposed as part of the diagnostic framework. From DSM-III (APA, 1980, 2000) through DSM-IV-TR (APA, 2000), clinicians were prohibited from assigning the diagnosis of ODD if criteria for CD were met, and the text explicitly (e.g., in the DSM-IV; APA, 1994) stated that if criteria for CD are met, ODD criteria are likely to have been present as well. Based on evidence from studies of the development of these disorders as related but distinct, which will be reviewed in more detail below, this hierarchical structure of ODD and CD is no longer present (APA, 2013). Although the framework of ODD as the product of passive-aggressive behavior is inconsistent with the evidence base from a theoretical perspective, it may be worthwhile to retain the concept of ODD and CD being distinguished at least in part by individual variability in disposition to act with greater overt confrontation.

Prevalence rates

Contrary to frequent assertions that ODD pathologizes normative child behavior (e.g., Rey et al., 1988), studies of the prevalence rate of the disorder consistently generate estimates in the single digits, ranging as high as the mid-teens in some studies (e.g., from 1.1% to 13.3%; Maughan, Rowe, Messer, Goodman, & Meltzer, 2004). A systematic review of worldwide studies (Canino, Polanczyk, Bauermeister, Rohde, & Frick, 2010) resulted in an estimate of 3.3% and found that variations in prevalence were due to methodological, rather than cultural, differences. Retrospective reports yield an estimate of the lifetime prevalence of 10.2 (Nock, Kazdin, Hiripi, & Kessler, 2007).

Gender differences in prevalence rates

From childhood to early or mid-adolescence, ODD is more prevalent among boys than girls. A meta-analysis of gender differences in samples which roughly centered around middle childhood found that boys showed significantly, if somewhat modestly, higher rates of ODD (a ratio of 1.59 to 1) compared to girls (Demmer, Hooley, Sheen, McGillivray, & Lum, 2017). The authors noted that this gender difference is smaller than differences found for other disruptive behavior disorders [namely, CD and attention-deficit hyperactivity disorder (ADHD)] and also reported that the gender difference in ODD was evident only for samples from Western countries (Demmer et al., 2017). Given other evidence that culture does not explain disparate prevalence rates around the world (Canino et al., 2010), it is not clear why Western countries would show higher rates for boys than girls.

However, there may be developmental factors that differentially influence gender differences in ODD. A review (Boylan, Vaillancourt, Boyle, & Szatmari, 2007) found rates of ODD increasing for girls into adolescence. A study of symptom rates from adolescence into young adulthood found that differences between men and women across multiple time points were more often not significantly different from one another (Leadbeater & Homel, 2015). Similarly, the difference between men and women in regard to lifetime retrospective report was not significantly different (11.2% for men compared to 9.2% for women; Nock et al., 2007). It appears that the difference in prevalence rates between boys and girls is significant (but smaller than other behavioral disorders) in childhood and diminishes over time.

Onset and persistence

ODD has a typical onset in childhood and can be reliably distinguished from normative disruptive behavior as early as preschool (Keenan & Wakschlag, 2004). It is stable, showing persistence from early to middle childhood (Harvey, Youngwirth, Thakar, & Errazuriz, 2009), over time during middle childhood (Lavigne, Bryant, Hopkins, & Gouze, 2017), and from middle childhood into adolescence (Cohen, Cohen, & Brook, 1993). Trajectory analyses in a community sample of girls demonstrate stable high, moderate, and low severity level trajectories of ODD symptoms (Boylan et al., in press) from childhood into adolescence.

Historically, there was never a prohibition against assigning a diagnosis of ODD to an adult. However, adult ODD has been given very little empirical attention, and the course of ODD beyond childhood or adolescence, especially when that course did not include CD, is poorly understood (Burke, Waldman, & Lahey, 2010). When studied, evidence suggests that ODD may be reliably identified in adults (Harpold et al., 2007). Longitudinal studies show that the symptoms persist from adolescence into young adulthood (Leadbeater, Thompson, & Gruppuso, 2012) and that ODD through adolescence is associated with impairments in adulthood (Burke, Rowe, & Boylan, 2014). The DSM-5 (APA, 2013) includes changes to the wording of the symptoms that enhance the applicability of the symptoms to adults. For example, in prior versions of the text, the target of argument and defiance was given as "adults," implying that the symptoms themselves would not apply to adults. In DSM-5, this is changed to "authority figures," and specific mention is made that arguing with adults would meet criteria in the case of children or adolescents.

From a theoretical perspective, there is little reason to anticipate that ODD symptoms would spontaneously remit with the end of adolescence. However, further research is needed to identify the prevalence rates of ODD in adulthood, to confirm the presence of impairments associated with symptoms, and to further demonstrate persistence from adolescence into adulthood. Additionally, although the wording of the symptoms has been modified to enhance the applicability of symptoms to adults, it seems possible that adults would have fewer opportunities to defy or refuse to comply with directives from authority figures or to argue with authority figures. Whether additional changes to the existing symptoms, or the addition of new symptoms altogether, would improve identification is a question for which no evidence yet exists. Some initial evidence regarding the manifestation and persistence of ODD into adulthood is reviewed below, but much more study on the nature, prevalence, and impact of ODD in adulthood is greatly needed.

A dimensional model of ODD

The introduction of dimensional categories for symptoms of ODD in the DSM-5 is at this point supported by a substantial body of evidence. It is clear that one dimension reflects a chronically irritable manner of interacting with others. Approximately three dozen studies associate the items of *often being touchy and easily annoyed* and *often being angry* with this irritability dimension (see Evans et al., 2017 and Vidal-Ribas, Brotman, Valdivieso, Leibenluft, & Stringaris, 2016 for reviews). In about three-quarters of these studies (Evans et al., 2017), the symptom of *often loses temper* is also associated with the irritability dimension, whereas in the remaining one-quarter of studies, *often loses temper* is associated with a behavioral dimension, along with items such as *often argues* and *often actively defies* (e.g., Burke, Hipwell, & Loeber, 2010). Studies are inconsistent as to whether the remainder of the symptoms form one (e.g., Burke et al., 2014) or two (e.g., Aebi et al., 2010; Burke et al., 2010; Ezpeleta, Granero, de la Osa, Penelo, & Domenech, 2012; Herzhoff & Tackett, 2016; Lavigne, Bryant, Hopkins, & Gouze, 2014; Stringaris & Goodman, 2009b) additional dimensions. In studies that do find two additional dimensions beyond irritability, both represent aspects of behavior (e.g., headstrong or oppositional behavior vs antagonistic or hurtful behavior).

Chronic irritability

Irritability is associated either as a specific symptom or as a commonly associated feature with multiple disorders, such as generalized anxiety, depression in childhood, and bipolar disorder, as well as ODD. Irritability is also a common response to unpleasant or undesirable experiences and, as such, may arise secondary to the experience of other psychiatric disorders and their associated impairments.

An important distinction among the various instances of irritability across psychiatric disorders may be whether irritability is a chronic or episodic experience (Leibenluft, Cohen, Gorrindo, Brook, & Pine, 2006). In the context of depression, for example, irritable mood would represent atypical functioning on the part of the child and would be expected to remit in concert with the end of the depressive episode. Episodic irritability might be a core element of an episodic disorder, but it might also be epiphenomenal, arising secondary to the experience of a disorder and its impairments. Chronic irritability, on the other hand, would theoretically persist both before another disorder and subsequent to its remission. Thus, studies of the longitudinal precedence of irritability relative to other disorders provide important distinguishing information.

Given that ODD is a chronic condition, both in terms of its diagnostic definition and in regard to evidence for its persistence over time, the irritability dimension of ODD should also be expected to be chronic. Although limited empirical attention has addressed this question so far, evidence suggests that when the irritability dimension of ODD is present, it is also persistent over time (e.g., Boylan et al., in press; Leadbeater & Homel, 2015). In this chapter, unless irritability is specified as episodic, we use the term irritability to refer specifically to chronic irritability.

What does temper loss indicate?

As noted, the symptoms of often being angry and often being touchy consistently load on the chronic irritability dimension. Although losing temper often follows suit, in one-quarter of studies, it is placed on a behavioral dimension instead. This raises questions about how temper loss should be regarded and about the defining features of chronic irritability.

It is possible that differences arise from methodological factors. Specifically, some measures ask parents if their child loses his or her temper, whereas others ask whether the child has temper tantrums or outbursts. It is possible that these two phenomena are different; asking "have you lost your temper in the last month" may generate different responses that "have you had a temper tantrum in the past month." Further, it appears that there may be differences in respondents' connotations even when the queries are consistent. For example, Carlson, Danzig, Dougherty, Bufferd, and Klein (2016) found that although 20% of children in a community sample was reported by a parent to have lost their temper three or more times per week, only half of those were reported to have had a temper tantrum. This suggests that parents may be distinguishing between temper loss and temper tantrums. Additionally, they found that while most children (78.4%) in their community sample who engaged in tantrum behavior were reported to also show irritability, most (76.2%) children in their clinical sample who were described as having explosive outbursts were not reported to be irritable in between tantrums (Carlson et al., 2016). Determining whether temper loss and temper tantrums are part of the same phenomenon—perhaps as differing levels of intensity along a unidimensional scale—or whether they reflect different phenomena altogether could help to resolve inconsistencies in models of ODD dimensionality. Qualitative data on the connotations of temper loss and temper outbursts from varying informants may help to clarify why respondents endorse putatively similar temper-related items in ways that are more consistent with either behavioral or irritability symptoms of ODD.

How distinct are the ODD dimensions?

Despite the robust support for the distinctions between ODD dimensions of chronic irritability and at least one, if not two, additional behavioral symptom dimensions, the evidence so far does not support the proposition that irritability should be regarded as an entirely separate category from the rest of the symptoms of ODD. In the most comprehensive evaluation of the issue (Burke et al., 2014), five large community samples with five different measures of ODD symptoms were used to test a hierarchical set of models (see Fig. 2.1). These consisted of (1) a unidimensional structure, (2) separate specific and uncorrelated irritability and behavioral dimensions, (3) correlated specific dimensions, (4) a model with a general ODD factor and specific uncorrelated dimensions, and (5) a model with a general ODD factor and specific, correlated dimensions. The results supported model 5, with separate but correlated irritability and oppositional behavioral dimensions and a general ODD factor. In four of the five data sets, irritability was best modeled using the symptoms of loses temper, is often touchy, and is often angry, while in the remaining data set, the better fit was found for irritability identified by often touchy, often angry, and often spiteful (Burke et al., 2014). Given the superiority of model 5, and the poor fit of model 2 (which included uncorrelated separate irritability and

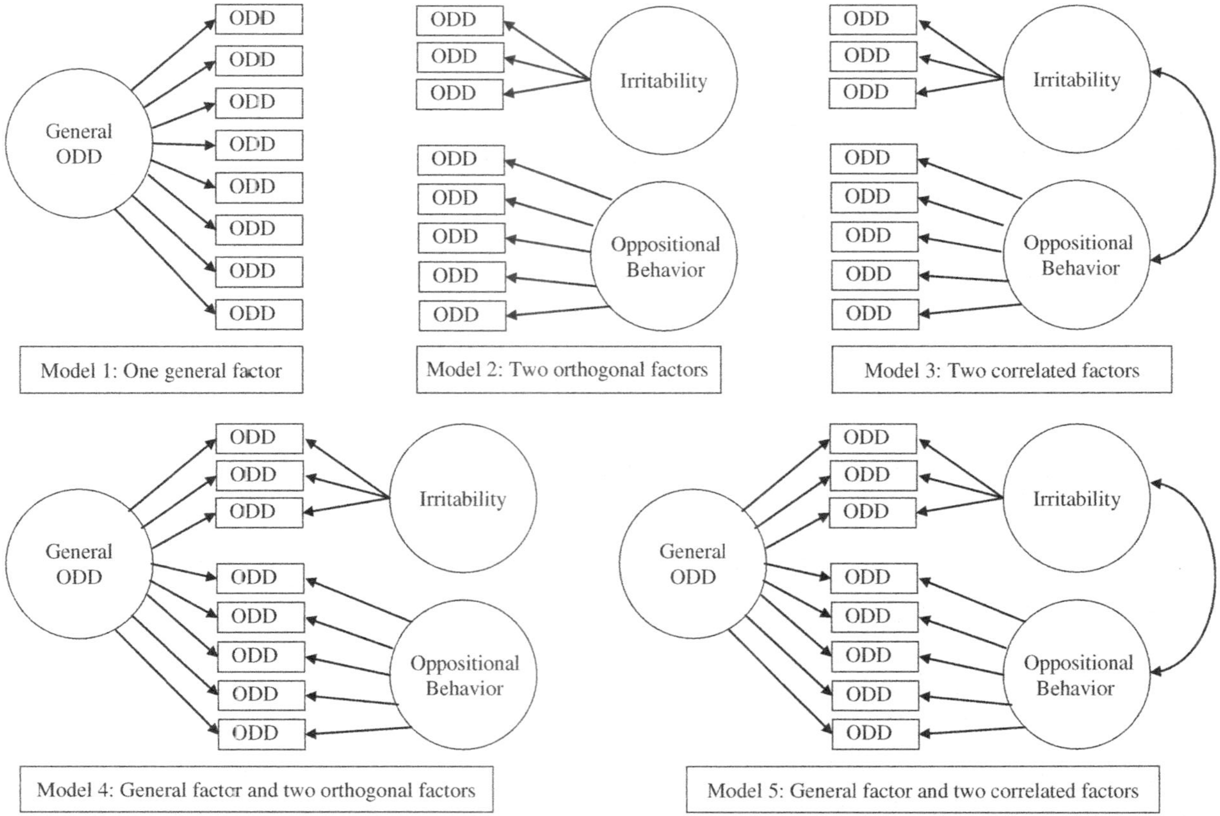

Figure 2.1 Unidimensional and multidimensional factor models of irritability and oppositional behavior among ODD.

oppositional behavioral dimensions), these results argue against completely parsing the irritability dimension from the remaining ODD behavioral symptoms.

Additional evidence inconsistent with the idea of separating irritability from the behavioral symptoms of ODD is found in other studies. In a trajectory analysis of girls in a community sample (Boylan et al., 2017), evidence supported distinctions between irritability, oppositional and antagonistic trajectories, but did not find evidence for individuals distinguished by elevated irritability alone. In a latent class analysis of the symptoms of ODD (Burke, 2012) using data from a sample of clinic-referred boys, evidence for a three class model was found (see Fig. 2.2). One class was low across all symptoms, a second class was elevated on the behavioral symptoms of ODD but low on the symptoms of being touchy, being angry, and being spiteful, and a third class elevated on both the behavioral and irritability symptoms. No class was found that was elevated on only the symptoms of the irritability dimension. Other studies, using latent class analysis in nonclinical samples, have found irritability-only latent classes (e.g., Aebi et al., 2016; Althoff, Kuny-Slock, Verhulst, Hudziak, & van der Ende, 2014; Kuny et al., 2013). Nevertheless, at present the preponderance of the evidence across studies, including clinical and community samples, suggests that the irritability and behavioral dimensions of ODD are highly correlated.

ODD dimensions and Disruptive Mood Dysregulation Disorder

In the DSM-5, the symptoms of chronic irritability are not only elements of an affective dimension of ODD, but they are also fundamental to the new diagnostic

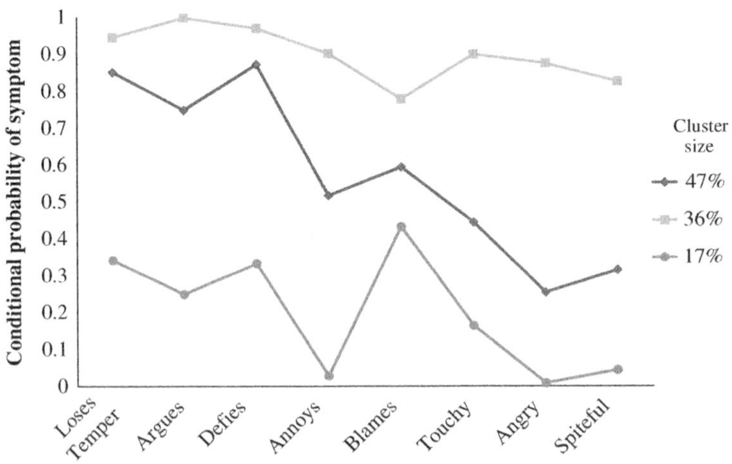

Figure 2.2 Latent classes of youth distinguished by ODD symptom probabilities in a clinical sample of boys between the ages of 7 and 12.

category of disruptive mood dysregulation disorder (DMDD). DMDD is defined by severe behavioral or verbal tantrum outbursts occurring three or more times per week, along with irritable or angry mood most of the day, nearly every day (APA, 2013). When it was introduced in DSM-5, there was essentially no empirical evidence evaluating DMDD. Instead, its support was based on studies of a different construct called severe mood dysregulation (SMD). These studies were designed to explore pediatric bipolar disorder, with the particular aim of reducing the false-positive identification of bipolar disorder among children. SMD (Brotman et al., 2006) was a broad construct that included symptoms of four other existing categories of psychopathology (ODD, ADHD, depression, and mania). The evolution of this construct to DMDD involved the paring down of symptoms to the ultimate focus on frequent temper outbursts and persisting angry or irritable mood. Because DMDD includes the same indicators (temper loss, anger, irritability) of the irritability dimension of ODD, the risk for overlap between ODD and DMDD was anticipated to be high.

On their face, the wording of the symptoms of DMDD suggests that it should identify individuals who fall at the high end of the severity distribution of irritability. In DMDD, temper loss appears in the form of aggressive behavior or verbal rages which occur three or more times per week, while the ODD item "often loses temper" does not specify the form of temper loss nor the frequency of temper loss beyond "often." DMDD requires that irritable or angry mood occurs "most of the day nearly every day," while irritability in ODD involves the symptoms "is often touchy or easily annoyed" and "is often angry and resentful." Given that ODD requires four symptoms, it is possible that someone might show only the three irritability symptoms and thus not meet criteria for ODD, but the wording of the symptoms of DMDD and irritability within ODD suggests the presence of the former would also mean the presence of the latter.

Indeed, since the introduction of DMDD, research has been consistent in finding that discriminating between DMDD and ODD is very difficult. Studies have typically found very high degrees of overlap between DMDD and ODD, such as 90% (Mulraney et al., 2016), 91% (Mayes et al., 2016), and 96% (Freeman et al., 2016). The DSM-5 addresses the anticipated high overlap between disorders by mandating that a diagnosis of ODD cannot be assigned if DMDD criteria are present. There is as of yet no good evidence to support the validity of cleaving severe chronic irritability from the rest of the irritability dimension or from the disorder of ODD altogether.

The development of the upcoming revision of the International Classification of Diseases (ICD) included a thorough consideration of the literature regarding the dimensions of ODD and DMDD (Evans et al., 2017; Lochman et al., 2015). This included the evidence for the high correlation between the dimensions and high overlap between DMDD, evidence to suggest that the presence or absence of irritability differentiates groups of children with ODD (Burke, 2012) who are at differential risk for affective disorders, and concerns about the level of empirical support for DMDD as a distinct and reliable diagnostic construct. Based on this evidence, the ICD-11 working group decided not to include DMDD as a diagnostic category

(Lochman et al., 2015). Instead, in order to reflect the clinical relevance of the irritability dimension of ODD and to be consistent with the evidence base, a diagnostic specifier of ODD with irritability will be included.

This decision also avoids a concerning oversight in the DSM-5. The DSM-5 (APA, 2013) prohibition against assigning a diagnosis of ODD if criteria for DMDD are met presents clinicians with a problem. The evidence base is robust to show that the behavioral symptoms of ODD denote a risk for persisting behavioral problems and for impairments associated with ODD. From a diagnostic perspective, since four of the eight symptoms of ODD are required to meet criteria, it is possible that even if the symptoms of being touchy, being angry, and losing temper go toward fulfilling criteria for DMDD, an individual could still meet criteria for ODD. Furthermore, evidence indicates that the presence of a subthreshold three symptoms of ODD and impairment is still associated with significant risk for persisting behavioral problems (Angold & Costello, 1996; Rowe, Maughan, Costello, & Angold, 2005). It is not clear how a clinician using the DSM-5 (APA, 2013) should represent the risks for future behavioral problems and other outcomes associated with ODD when criteria for DMDD are also met. Regardless, clinicians must ensure that they give attention in their treatment planning when behavioral symptoms of ODD are present, regardless of whether DMDD criteria are met or not. If using the ICD-11, clinicians will need to determine whether the specifier of ODD with irritability is appropriate for a given individual.

Dimensions of ODD and the comorbidity of ODD with other psychopathology

While evidence for separate dimensions of ODD symptoms is in and of itself interesting, the utility of knowledge regarding differences between the dimensions of irritability and oppositional behavior rests on whether this knowledge changes the prediction of risk. It is well established that ODD is commonly comorbid with multiple other behavioral and emotional disorders (e.g., Nock et al., 2007). In addition, longitudinal prospective analyses found that ODD showed developmental precedence relative to CD, depression, and anxiety, but not ADHD (Burke, Loeber, Lahey, & Rathouz, 2005). Similarly, in analysis using retrospective data, in cases of comorbidity with ODD, only ADHD was reported as having had an onset prior to ODD (Nock et al., 2007).

The role of ODD in the development of behavioral problems has never been controversial. As noted, ODD was historically regarded as so highly related to CD that the DSM (APA, 1994) presumed that if CD was present, ODD was also present. However, the strength of the prediction from ODD to later depression was more noteworthy. In a study of the prediction from childhood psychopathology to outcomes in adolescence and adulthood (Copeland, Shanahan, Costello, & Angold, 2009) not only was ODD strongly predictive of depression in later developmental periods, it was a stronger predictor of later depression than depression itself.

The dimensionality among the symptoms of ODD explains the robust prediction to both behavioral disorders and internalizing problems. In particular, the presence of irritability predicts specific risk for later depression and anxiety (Burke, 2012; Burke et al., 2010; Evans et al., 2017; Rowe, Costello, Angold, Copeland, & Maughan, 2010; Stringaris & Goodman, 2009a; Vidal-Ribas et al., 2016). Irritability has typically failed to predict later ADHD, CD, bipolar disorder (Evans et al., 2017; Vidal-Ribas et al., 2016), and borderline personality disorder (Burke & Stepp, 2012; Stringaris, Cohen, Pine, & Leibenluft, 2009), although there are some exceptions. For example, in a sample of adolescent male offenders (Aebi et al., 2016), the irritable dimension of ODD was associated with depressive disorders (DDs), anxiety disorders, CD, and suicidality, while the defiant and vindictive symptoms were also associated with depression and CD. In a community sample of girls (Burke et al., 2010), irritability predicted future CD for Caucasian girls but not for African American girls. Despite some nuances, the clear implication of the overwhelming bulk of the literature is that the irritability dimension robustly predicts depression and anxiety, while the behavioral dimension predicts behavioral problems.

If irritability is a reliable predictor of later depression across the life span, it may provide important warning of the risk for depression. It is evident that ODD typically emerges in childhood and can be distinguished from normative child behavior as early as preschool (Harvey et al., 2009; Keenan & Wakschlag, 2004). Additionally, the irritability dimension of ODD can be similarly identified as early as preschool (Dougherty et al., 2013). Given that depression tends not to emerge until early adolescence, irritability appears to be a potentially valuable predictor. The value of ODD, and of irritability in particular, in this prediction may be even greater if it is predictive not only of depression broadly, but of suicidality or suicidal ideation in particular. In fact, several studies have linked ODD with suicidal ideation and suicidal attempts. Among a clinical sample of boys and girls with ADHD, with a mean age of 8, ODD and sadness were strongly associated with suicidal ideation and attempts (Mayes et al., 2015). Additionally, the irritability dimension but not the behavioral dimensions of ODD were associated with suicidality in a sample of adolescent male offenders (Aebi et al., 2016).

Clinical utility of the dimensional model

In contrast to an entirely categorical approach, the dimensional framework (distinguishing irritability and behavioral symptoms) within ODD clearly improves clinical prediction with strikingly clear implications. ODD and its dimensions can be identified and distinguished from normative behavior in early childhood. The presence of the irritability dimension indicates a risk specific to later depression, anxiety, and suicidality. Regarding ODD as categorical and unidimensional and as hierarchically subsumed under CD dramatically impaired the full value of early assessment and intervention. Further, the impact of this framework on research, clinical practice, and prevention was substantial. Instead of understanding that chronic irritability within ODD, often identifiable in early childhood, placed children at risk for later depression, clinicians and researchers focused on the comorbid manifestation of CD and depression. Depressive conduct disorder (DCD) was proposed to represent a distinct diagnostic entity (Fleming et al., 1993; Puig-Antich, 1982), and although it was never included as a disorder in any version of the DSM, it was included as a disorder in the ICD-10 (World Health Organization, 1992).

Reviewing the literature from that time provides both clinical and theoretical guidance as well as a cautionary tale about the potential impact of a priori nosological decisions on research. For example, Simic and Fombonne (2001) compared symptom patterns and correlates between groups of children in a clinic setting as an evaluation of a diagnostic category of DCD. They contrasted children with CD, with DDs, and with DCD, ignoring ODD. Although the authors hypothesized that, when contrasting the DD group with the CD group, symptoms of depression would all be more prevalent among the DD group than the CD group, they found that the prevalence of one symptom, irritability, was significantly greater in the CD group. Further, they found that irritability was higher (albeit nonsignificantly) in the DCD group compared to the DD group. Additionally, they noted that the symptom of depressed mood was not reported among roughly one-quarter of the DCD group, and that in the majority of those cases, irritability was present (Simic & Fombonne, 2001). The authors also found that the DCD group had similar rates of suicidal ideation and higher rates of self-injurious behavior than the DD group (or the CD group) and higher rates of anxiety. Also noteworthy, children in the DCD group showed significantly less destructive behavior, lower levels of stealing, and lower levels of overt aggression.

Although the authors concluded that the results supported a DCD diagnosis, these results clearly suggest a central role of irritability in the comorbidity of CD and depression. Further, even though the analyses were cross-sectional, the relationships identified were consistent with a model in which an ODD irritability dimension explains the risk for later depression and anxiety (e.g., Burke & Loeber, 2010). Additionally, the distinctions observed by Simic and Fombonne (2001) in regard to irritability versus dysphoric mood are concordant with evidence (Stringaris, Maughan, Copeland, Costello, & Angold, 2013) that there may be differences between irritable depression and other types of depression.

Related dimensions

As noted above, the advantages of adopting a dimensional approach to research on ODD have led to dramatic improvements in models of developmental psychopathology. In that vein, the Research Domain Criteria (RDoC) approach of the National Institute of Mental Health (Cuthbert & Insel, 2013) offers the potential for even greater clarification of the relationships among ODD and other diagnostic constructs by evaluating cross-cutting dimensions, and in particular, irritability. Yet, there is some reason for concern, again due to a priori decisions that exert dramatic influence on the nature of ongoing research. This is due to the exclusion of irritability from the established RDoC constructs. The closest RDoC construct is frustrative nonreward.

It may be that there is no reason for concern, as on the one hand, it is easy to see an association between frustration and irritability. In fact, the construct of frustrative nonreward was originally developed as a means by which to examine the motivational processes associated with the experience of rats which, after being trained to anticipate a reward following a particular task, were presented with the absence of that expected reward (Amsel, 1958). More generally, it is common for people to report an undesirable emotional experience upon being stymied in their efforts toward a desired goal.

The inclusion of frustrative nonreward as one of the constructs of the RDoC has the advantage of encouraging researchers to employ established frustration paradigms. These are typically well suited to studies collecting biologically oriented measures (e.g., electroencephalogram (EEG) and functional magnetic resonance imaging (fMRI) studies) because of the ability to manipulate reward and nonreward experiences to generate frustration. It may be perfectly appropriate to draw conclusions about irritability using such methods if those same individuals who respond with elevated frustration to nonreward experiences are the same as those who have been identified as irritable in the aforementioned studies of risk for depression and anxiety. Accordingly, translational models have been advanced examining abnormalities in systems underlying reward and threat processing (Brotman, Kircanski, Stringaris, Pine, & Leibenluft, 2017).

On the other hand, irritability can be easily conceptualized as distinct from frustration. For example, the idiom, "I got up on the wrong side of the bed today" conveys a general unpleasant internal state that is explicitly not linked to an actual provocation or frustration. It may be that some people are more disposed than others to typically, or chronically, have such experiences. As above, chronic irritability has been proposed as distinct from episodic irritability (Leibenluft et al., 2006). If irritability is chronic as implied by such assessment methods, frustrative nonreward will be a valid measure only to the extent that those who react with elevated frustration to the experience of nonreward are also those who go through life with a persisting sense of general irritability. On the other hand, it may be that response to a frustrating event is distinct from chronic irritability. Perhaps, given two people who show the same high elevation in frustration subsequent to nonreward, one is able to engage regulatory resources in such a fashion as to reduce or eliminate any lasting effects. If this is the case, studies which equate irritability with frustration run the risk of including individuals who are not chronically irritable, at least, not in a manner consistent with the type of irritability that has been shown to increase the risk for depression and anxiety in longitudinal studies.

At present, it is not clear how chronic irritability and frustrative nonreward are related, but it is possible that chronic irritability is only a subset of frustrative nonreward or, perhaps less likely, that they are more completely independent. In either of these cases, extending the emerging literature on irritability as task-based frustration to evaluate associations involving chronic irritability would be misrepresentative of the experiences of youth with chronic irritability.

Risk factors

Much of the literature on risk factors pertaining to ODD is confounded by overlap between ODD and other disorders, rendering it difficult to discern whether a particular risk factor is specifically associated with ODD or is generally related to broader categories of psychopathology. This has been complicated by the nosological prohibition (APA, 1994) against assigning an ODD diagnosis when criteria for CD were present. Additionally, research has too often failed to account for preexisting ODD, often giving the impression that ODD is only an outcome of a risk factor without evaluating whether it has a causal or transactional relationship with a given risk factor.

Genetics

Studies have found evidence for genetic liability to ODD of approximately 40%–60% (Dick, Viken, Kaprio, Pulkkinen, & Rose, 2005; Rowe et al., 2008). Studies accounting for the co-occurrence of disorders also find specific genetic influences for ODD relative to other disorders (Dick et al., 2005; Lahey, Van Hulle, Singh, Waldman, & Rathouz, 2011; Rowe et al., 2008). At the same time, common genetic factors (Dick et al., 2005), such as a higher-order externalizing factor (Lahey et al., 2011), may explain overlap between ODD, CD, and ADHD.

Three studies have examined genetic factors related to the dimensions of ODD. These studies suggest that co-occurring irritability and depression and anxiety is associated with a common genetic component (Savage et al., 2015; Stringaris, Zavos, Leibenluft, Maughan, & Eley, 2012), whereas a behavioral dimension of ODD symptoms shared genetic linkage with delinquency. Another study used a series of Cholesky decompositions to model genetic and environmental influences on the general bifactor structure of ODD symptoms (Burke et al., 2014) and their association, in separate models, with CD, ADHD, depression, and anxiety. The results demonstrate that common genetic liabilities are shared between ODD dimensions and all disorders. However, irritability and defiant behavioral dimensions differed, in that irritability and internalizing disorders (depression and anxiety) shared common genetic factors not shared by defiant behavior. Conversely, defiant behavior and the externalizing disorders (ADHD and CD) shared common genetic factors independent of irritability (Waldman, Rowe, Boylan, & Burke, 2017). Although these results are in need of further replication, the research so far suggests that unique genetic factors are associated with the distinct phenotypic linkages between ODD dimensions and behavioral versus internalizing psychopathology.

ODD, temperament, and personality

Because it emerges early in life, is stable (i.e., persisting at least until early adulthood), and influences interactions with others, questions arise regarding whether temperament is a risk factor for ODD. A more fundamental question is whether ODD is distinct from measures of temperament or measures of personality. The context for these questions includes the fact that, as noted above, ODD itself emerged from a personality perspective ("oppositional personality"), and its early DSM iterations also linked ODD to personality, specifically to passive-aggressive personality disorder.

In a large British birth cohort study, measures of temperamental activity and emotionality, but not of shyness/sociability at 38 months of age both predicted ODD at 91 months of age (Stringaris, Maughan, & Goodman, 2010). Of particular interest, however, stronger and more specific associations were found when predicting ODD comorbid with other conditions. Specifically, temperamental emotionality predicted ODD comorbid with internalizing disorders (depression and anxiety disorders), whereas temperamental activity predicted ODD comorbid with ADHD (Stringaris et al., 2010).

In a clinical sample of boys, a latent class analysis of ODD symptoms at late childhood (ages 7–12) found three groups: ODD with irritability, ODD without irritability, and a group low on all symptoms of ODD. In prediction to personality measures at age 19, those in the ODD with irritability group showed significantly higher Neuroticism than those in either the ODD without irritability or the low ODD symptom groups (Burke, 2012). Yet, neither of the ODD classes (ODD with irritability and ODD without irritability) were significantly different from those in the low ODD symptom group in levels of age 19 Agreeableness, Conscientiousness, Extraversion, or Openness.

A more comprehensive investigation (Herzhoff, Smack, Reardon, Martel, & Tackett, 2017) of the relationship between personality and ODD used principal axis factor strategies to extract psychopathology scores [ODD, CD, ADHD, major depressive disorder (MDD), and anxiety] from parent and child structured clinical interview data and from mother and father Child Behavior Checklist (CBCL) data. A similar approach using data from the Inventory of Child Individual Differences and the Temperament in Middle Childhood Questionnaire was used to generate constructs reflecting Neuroticism, Agreeableness, and Conscientiousness. The authors found that comorbidity between ODD and CD was associated with scores on Neuroticism, Agreeableness, and Conscientiousness, comorbidity between ODD and ADHD was associated with Conscientiousness but not Agreeableness or Neuroticism, comorbidity between ODD and MDD was associated with Neuroticism and Agreeableness but not Conscientiousness, and comorbidity between ODD and anxiety was associated with Neuroticism and Agreeableness (Herzhoff et al., 2017).

Overall, comorbidities between ODD and externalizing disorders were associated with disinhibitory traits. The results involving Neuroticism are suggestive of potential clarification of the divergent comorbid associations involving the dimensions of ODD. Specifically, ODD was positively associated with Neuroticism, and after accounting for ODD, Neuroticism was negatively associated with CD. Furthermore, ODD and internalizing disorder comorbidities were particularly associated with high Neuroticism. In conjunction with evidence that the irritability dimension of ODD in childhood is predictive of Neuroticism in young adulthood (Burke, 2012), these findings suggest commonalities among irritability, internalizing disorders, and Neuroticism. Of additional importance was the finding of almost no differences between genders in associations between personality and ODD comorbidities, apart from ODD and anxiety comorbidities (Herzhoff et al., 2017). This adds to generally consistent evidence for a lack of differences between boys and girls in regard to the nature of the correlates of irritability, and perhaps to the lack of difference in the constituent elements of irritability between boys and girls.

Associations between measures of temperament (specifically surgency, negative affect, effortful control, and reactive control) and ADHD and ODD symptoms were also examined in a sample of 109 preschool age children (Martel, Gremillion, & Roberts, 2012). While at the bivariate level, most associations between psychopathology and temperament were significant, multivariate regressions found specific associations between ODD and negative affect, whereas surgency, effortful control, and reactive control were associated with ADHD symptoms (Martel et al., 2012). An additional study of this sample of preschoolers examined the association between measures of temperament and the separate dimensions of ODD symptoms (as specified in the DSM-5; APA, 2013). The results suggested that negative affect was associated with all three symptom domains (irritability, argumentative, and vindictive), whereas low agreeableness was associated only with irritability, and high surgency was associated with the argumentative and vindictive dimensions (Zastrow, Martel, & Widiger, 2016). Additionally, Neuroticism was not associated with any of the ODD dimensions. These results are intriguing given the aforementioned evidence pointing to associations between Neuroticism and ODD (Herzhoff et al., 2017), and the irritability dimension in particular (Burke, 2012). Further, the specificity of associations between irritability and mood disorders might suggest that negative affect should be specifically associated with irritability, but not with the behavioral dimensions of ODD. Whether these inconsistent results reflect developmental processes or measurement issues is not clear.

Overall, evidence from the study of personality and temperament holds some promise in helping to understand chronic irritability and the relationships between ODD dimensions and comorbid conditions. On the other hand, there is not yet sufficient consistency and clarity in the data to draw conclusions. It is possible that specific components within broader temperament or personality constructs are needed, just as a more granular focus allowed for the discrimination of ODD dimensions among the broader category of disruptive behavior disorders. As researchers look to improve conceptualizations of ODD in adulthood, or to flesh out nuances in the manifestation of chronic irritability, they may benefit from guidance found in the temperament and personality literature. It is clear that ODD works very well as a clinical diagnostic construct, in that it functions to identify subsets of individuals at risk for impairment, for distress and dysfunction, and for persistence in these features and difficulties over time. Understanding where this behavioral construct does and does not fit with traits identified in personality and temperament research may help to improve the prediction of the onset and persistence of ODD and to understand and mitigate its impact on function.

Parenting and family context

The historical view of ODD has been that it is the product of bad parenting or inadequate parent management (see Miller-Slough, Dunsmore, Ollendick, & Greene, 2016). This framework has undoubtedly contributed to broader perceptions that ODD is not a proper psychiatric diagnosis. However, research demonstrates conclusively that, not only is ODD caused by multiple factors beyond parenting, but that the relationship between ODD and parenting is more nuanced than simply seeing ODD as the outcome of bad parenting. Certainly, to be clear, a number of types of undesirable parenting behaviors and parenting qualities have been shown to predict increasing ODD (see Burke, Loeber, & Birmaher, 2002). However, it is crucial to rely on research that evaluates ODD and parenting behavior as transactions and tests bidirectionality in the relationship between the two.

Parental hostility

Parental hostility is among the most common parental qualities identified as particularly relevant to the development of ODD (Kolko, Dorn, Bukstein, & Burke, 2008; Lavigne, Dahl, Gouze, LeBailly, & Hopkins, 2015). It makes sense that if a parent were to treat a child with hostility, a portion of children would respond to that treatment with hostility, defiance, argument, anger, and irritability in return, even if those features were not part of the child's makeup prior to that experience. At the same time, it is reasonable to expect that if a parent were to experience chronic hostility, anger, and defiance from a child, a portion of parents would respond to that experience with their own hostility, fatigue, and withdrawal. Interpreting the direction of effects when measuring these relationships depends on where in the stream one begins measuring.

Research shows that parents find ODD to be among the most stressful types of psychopathology with which to cope (Bussing et al., 2003; Teagle, 2002), and ODD is a particularly strong predictor of parental divorce (Wymbs et al., 2008). Coping with chronic and severe child noncompliance and hostility is stressful. Making productive and positive parenting choices in the face of this behavior likely draws upon resources that themselves vary along a disposition. Given evidence of genetic liability to ODD, it may be that parents of children with ODD are themselves more likely to be challenged in the face of such stressors.

A more complex examination of the effect of parenting behaviors in the context of other risk factors was conducted by Lavigne, Gouze, Hopkins, and Bryant

(2016), who tested a cascade model of multiple domains of risk factors across ages 4 and 5 in predicting ODD at age 6. Not only did parental hostility, as well as family conflict more broadly, at age 5 predict ODD at age 6, but lower socioeconomic status at age 4 influenced ODD by contributing to family conflict at age 5. At the same time, when the autoregressive effects of ODD between ages 4, 5, and 6 were introduced into the model, they rendered the effects of other predictors in the model nonsignificant (Lavigne et al., 2016). That is, existing ODD was the strongest predictor of ODD at age 6 and was so explanatory that other factors were no longer predictive. Thus, it may be that factors such as parental hostility and family conflict existing prior to age 4 were causal in regard to ODD at age 4, but it is also possible that a child's disposition from earlier in childhood leads to problematic transactions with others, while also persisting as the best explanation for later ODD itself.

Coercive parent–child interactions

To evaluate the latter possibility, Burke, Pardini, and Loeber (2008) tested the bidirectionality of ODD and several parenting behaviors from childhood through late adolescence: supervision, communication, involvement, and a construct referred to as timid discipline, which reflected the degree to which parents withdraw from disciplinary practices due to their fears about the child's reaction. Controlling for existing levels of ODD, CD, and ADHD, only timid discipline predicted ODD symptoms over the following year, with parents who reported higher timid discipline in 1 year reporting higher ODD 1 year later. Conversely, higher levels of ODD in 1 year predicted increases in timid discipline, poorer involvement, and poorer communication in the following year. Thus, in those analyses, ODD was much more predictive of worsening parenting behaviors than the converse. Additionally, the only reciprocal relationships were found between ODD and timid discipline, supporting a specific transactional model between parenting and ODD that does not overtly involve hostility on the part of parents.

There is some evidence for gender differences in the relationship between parenting behaviors and ODD. In a representative community sample (Burnette, 2013), ODD symptoms at a mean age of 6 were predicted from parenting variables at a mean age of 4. Harsh parenting was associated with ODD symptoms for girls, but not boys, whereas emotional responsiveness (i.e., observations of positive interactions and feelings toward the child from the parent) was inversely associated with ODD for boys, but not girls. Acceptance (i.e., observed parental avoidance of expressing frustration or engaging in verbal or physical punishment) was associated with ODD for both boys and girls, as was self-reported violence between parents (Burnette, 2013). While these results are highly informative, it will be important to further evaluate whether parents are differentially responsive to ODD behaviors from boys compared to girls.

In regard to parenting and ODD, it is clear that coping with a child with ODD is a stressful challenge, and that maladaptive parenting can exacerbate problematic child behavior. Genetic evidence implies that parents of children with ODD may themselves struggle with ODD, which would complicate parenting behaviors.

Further research, particularly earlier in childhood, which examines multiple dimensions of parenting in transaction with child behaviors and in the context of other risk factors, is needed to improve the understanding of these complex processes.

ODD in the school context

The classroom is, after the home environment, the place in which children experience their most fundamental interactions. It provides challenges in the form of interactions with a variety of peers, interactions with new and different authority figures, and experiences in various settings with different rules and expectations for behavior. Research has indicated that the classroom may be an important environmental factor in the early expression of ODD symptoms and behaviors (de Zeeuw, van Beijsterveldt, Lubke, Glasner, & Boomsma, 2015). Transactions in this environment undoubtedly exert significant influence on social development, the development of self-regulation skills, and the experiences of successes and failures academically, athletically, and interpersonally. ODD is associated with poorer functioning in school settings (Greene et al., 2002). This is particularly true because so often teachers act as a key resource in identifying these symptoms and referring a child for evaluation and support.

Furthermore, ODD affects a child's interactions with his or her peers. The hostility, antagonism, arguing, and defiance they exhibit in schools increases the likelihood they will be rejected by their peers (Tung & Lee, 2014). They may be more likely to engage in bullying (Holmberg & Hjern, 2008; Turcotte Benedict, Vivier, & Gjelsvik, 2015; Verlinden et al., 2015). More so than a child with ADHD symptoms, boys with ODD in particular are more likely to engage in physical forms of bullying and victimization, particularly when there are also high levels of peer delinquency (Fite, Evans, Cooley, & Rubens, 2014).

Studies focusing on constructs broader than ODD alone have found that being able to socially and emotionally regulate oneself is an important predictor of future academic achievement, even after controlling for cognitive ability and family resources (Grolnick & Slowiaczek, 1994; Ladd, Birch, & Buhs, 1999; Normandeau & Guay, 1998; Raver & Zigler, 1997). Similarly, struggling with these skills has been found to put children at higher risk for academic failure and to predict the development of CDs and delinquency (Kellam et al., 1991; Patterson, Reid, & Dishion, 1992; Tremblay, Pagani-Kurtz, Mâsse, Vitaro, & Pihl, 1995). There may be an interaction between risk and environment in the form of disparities in available resources. Many times, the most at-risk children are taught by the most poorly trained teachers, who may not be well equipped to effectively manage classroom behavior or may not be exposed to effective strategies (Phillips, Voran, Kisker, Howes, & Whitebook, 1994; Stage & Quiroz, 1997; Webster-Stratton, Jamila Reid, & Stoolmiller, 2008). Further, children with behavior problems are more likely to be disliked by teachers and be disciplined through suspension and expulsion (Arnold, Griffith, Ortiz, & Stowe, 1998; Arnold et al., 1999; Campbell & Ewing, 1990; Carr, Taylor, & Robinson, 1991; Huffman et al., 2001). This results in the child getting even less opportunities for academic and social development, and thus makes them more likely to have worse relationships with school, their teachers, their peers, and learning in general (Bierman, Miller, & Stabb, 1987; Coie, 1990; Laird, Jordan, Dodge, Pettit, & Bates, 2001; Webster-Stratton et al., 2008).

ODD impairs interactions with peers and authority figures, increasing the challenges for school success. Additional research is needed that is specific to ODD within the context of other psychopathology to help discern which school-related impairments are due to ODD and which are due to comorbid conditions. It may be useful to develop treatment components that focus on school functioning and interpersonal skills for children with ODD. In addition, increasing the availability of school-based treatment models and teacher training modules may help to meet the needs of children with ODD in multiple contexts.

ODD and clinical issues

Although the eight symptoms of ODD have not changed markedly in a way that would affect assessment, the attention given to the role of symptoms of irritability in ODD has raised significant questions and has led to important differences between the DSM-5 (APA, 2013) and the upcoming ICD-11 (Evans et al., 2017; Lochman et al., 2015). It is now clear that clinicians must attend to the endorsement of the symptoms of often being angry, often being touchy, and often losing temper in the context of behavioral symptoms in making a diagnosis of ODD. From a prognostic perspective, as reviewed above, the presence of these symptoms strongly suggests an elevated risk for depression and anxiety in the future and may also suggest an elevated risk for suicidal ideation and self-harming behavior. Where assessment strategies use an abbreviated set of items as a screener, it will be important to ensure that these include the symptoms of chronic irritability in order to fully describe the future risks for both behavioral and affective problems. At the same time, clinicians must not lose sight of the prognostic relevance of the behavioral symptoms of ODD, which indicate a risk for CD, aggression, and antisocial behavior. Despite the implication in the DSM-5's prohibition of assigning a diagnosis of ODD when criteria for DMDD are met (APA, 2013), both ODD dimensions are prognostically important, albeit for differing types of conditions.

Unlike other disorders, such as ADHD, there is no requirement in the DSM-5 that ODD symptoms be evident in multiple settings (e.g., home, school, at work, or with peers) in order for criteria to be met. The manifestation of symptoms cannot be limited to interactions with siblings in order to meet criteria but could be limited to the home environment alone. However, a change from the DSM-IV to DSM-5 is the inclusion of a specifier of severity for ODD. A diagnostic specifier of "Mild" is indicated if symptoms of ODD are present in only one setting, "Moderate" if symptoms are present in two settings, and "Severe" if symptoms are present in three or more settings. It is not clear how well these designations are supported by empirical evidence, and clinicians likely can call to mind examples of ODD that parents would consider severe regardless of whether it was present in multiple contexts. In

DSM-III-R, there was a specifier for severity, but it was based on the number of symptoms present and not the number of settings in which symptoms were present.

Informant effects

A key persisting question regarding the assessment of ODD is the issue of differing informant ratings. It is true that parent, teacher, and child reports of ODD typically show low levels of agreement (Jensen et al., 1999; Munkvold, Lundervold, Lie, & Manger, 2009; Strickland, Hopkins, & Keenan, 2012). However, it must be noted that informant ratings for most disorders show similar inconsistency (e.g., Burke, Mulvey, & Schubert, 2015; De Los Reyes & Kazdin, 2005; Jensen et al., 1999). Inconsistent informant reports for ODD—as with other disorders—do not suggest that the disorder is not a valid disorder, nor that one or another of the informants is erroneous. Instead, it is likely that inconsistent informant reports result from differing contextual demands. Clinicians are best served by obtaining as much information about the child's behavior as possible. In regard to context, the DSM-5 specifies that ODD behaviors must be demonstrated in more than just interactions with siblings.

Assessment tools

The best method for making a diagnosis of ODD remains a careful clinical interview. Clinicians should obtain reports from as many informants as possible, recognizing that differing perspectives will lead to inconsistent reports. Clinicians should resolve inconsistent reports by integrating information across informants, rather than either requiring all criteria to be present by one informant or by discounting symptoms identified as present if not also reported by another.

Whether using a structured or unstructured clinical interview, clinicians should make sure that all symptoms are queried, particularly making sure to obtain enough information to assess whether both dimensions of oppositional and defiant behavior and chronic irritability are present. Symptom checklists provide useful information about the presence or absence of symptoms and may be valuable additions to the clinical interview. In addition, clinicians should take care to review the specific items being queried in a particular measure in order to ensure that they are carefully assessing the actual symptoms of ODD. As an example, the Child and Adolescent Symptom Inventory-5 (Gadow, 2015) queries each symptom in language similar to the DSM-5 (APA, 2013) and provides parents and clinicians with a four-point scale, from "never" to "very often" for each item. In addition, conversion to dichotomous symptoms is easy to do at a glance. The scale assesses other psychopathology, is relatively brief and easy for parents to complete, and is also available for teacher report.

As an example of the need for clinicians to be mindful of the specific items being addressed in a checklist, the CBCL (Achenbach & Rescorla, 2001) includes "DSM Oriented" subscales, one of which is "oppositional defiant problems." Of the five items in this subscale, three pertain to defiance or noncompliance. A fourth item assesses stubborn, sullen, and irritable in a single item, making it difficult to discern whether it best represents the behavioral dimension or the irritability dimension. A fifth item queries temper tantrums or having a hot temper. Given the apparent variability in the connotation of the actual ODD symptom of often losing temper, there is some reason to speculate that asking about temper tantrums or hot temper may not capture the same information. The CBCL ODD oriented subscale has been used in research contexts and may function as a screening method, but the items do not correspond directly to symptoms and do not sufficiently measure both the behavioral and irritability dimensions of ODD. For diagnostic purposes, clinicians should ensure that both the questions that they ask during clinical interviews and on checklists that they use are as precise in the assessment of DSM-5 symptoms as possible.

Treatment

Perhaps due to the past history of framing ODD as a less severe form of CD, as well as being a disorder of childhood, established treatments appropriate for ODD tend not to be specific to ODD and are most commonly validated for childhood populations. In addition, established treatments focus largely on the reduction of behavioral symptoms and less commonly on the reduction of irritability symptoms. Effective treatments include parent management training (PMT) skills, with a focus on the use of behavioral reinforcement practices to increase desirable behavior and extinguish undesirable behavior. Some treatment models, particularly those developed for older children, also include problem-solving skills training (PSST) components. Additional components of treatments may also include emotion regulation skills. Examples of established treatments for individual treatment include Parent–Child Interaction Therapy (Brinkmeyer & Eyberg, 2003), which focuses on direct instruction and practice in parent management, PSST and PMT (Kazdin, 2003), which include parent management training and the delivery of problem-solving skills to children, and Your Defiant Child (Barkley & Benton, 2013), which focuses on PMT and behavioral reinforcement. Other treatment models include the Incredible Years series of models for parents, teachers, and children (Reid, Webster-Stratton, & Hammond, 2003), which feature group-based treatment components. A group treatment model for parents and children with components for behavioral and emotion regulation training is the Stop Now and Plan program (Burke & Loeber, 2015).

There is value in the availability of treatments applicable to ODD in early childhood, given the potential that early intervention may reduce the risk for the development of depression, anxiety, and CD. On the other hand, established treatments for behavioral problems tend to conflate increasing age with an intensifying of the severity of conduct problems (e.g., increasing violence and delinquent behaviors). While the behavioral symptoms of ODD do indicate a risk for the development of such problems, approximately two-thirds of children with ODD never meet criteria for CD (Burke et al., 2010; Rowe et al., 2010) and conversely approximately half of children with CD do not have a history of ODD (Rowe et al., 2010). These are distinct disorders, and there remains a need for the validation of treatments specific to ODD, especially for adolescents who do not develop CD. Further, to our knowledge there are no treatments for ODD in adulthood.

Conclusions

ODD is a disorder that typically emerges early and often persists over time. It shapes a person's interactions with parents and family, peers and teachers, and romantic partners. The noxious and conflict-laden behavior involved generates stress, resentment, and rejection from others. When present in childhood, it is associated with parental stress and divorce and is both affected by and influential of poor parenting behaviors. Although boys are slightly more likely than girls to show ODD in childhood, gender differences in prevalence rates narrow during adolescence and adulthood. In addition to being associated with behavioral disorders, ODD is also predictive of anxiety, depression, and suicidality. Its relationship to affective disorders appears to be due to levels of chronic irritability. Further work is needed to address questions about chronic irritability, about the role of temper loss or temper outbursts in chronic irritability (or as an indicator of behavioral features of the disorder), and about how chronic irritability leads to affective and anxiety problems. Additionally, further research is needed to describe the manifestation of ODD in adulthood, to determine whether the current symptoms are sufficient to identify ODD, and to understand its persistence from adolescence and beyond young adulthood. Clinical assessment is best conducted using multiple informants, including a diagnostic interview and a symptom checklist. There are several well-established treatments for ODD behaviors in childhood, but few treatments for ODD independent of problems with aggression and delinquency in adolescence, and no treatments for ODD in adulthood.

References

Achenbach, T. M., & Rescorla, L. (2001). *Manual for the ASEBA school-age forms & profiles*. Burlington, VT: University of Vermont, Research Center for Children, Youth & Families.

Aebi, M., Barra, S., Bessler, C., Steinhausen, H. C., Walitza, S., & Plattner, B. (2016). Oppositional defiant disorder dimensions and subtypes among detained male adolescent offenders. *Journal of Child Psychology and Psychiatry, and Allied Disciplines*, *57*(6), 729–736. Available from https://doi.org/10.1111/jcpp.12473.

Aebi, M., Muller, U. C., Asherson, P., Banaschewski, T., Buitelaar, J., Ebstein, R., ... Steinhausen, H. C. (2010). Predictability of oppositional defiant disorder and symptom dimensions in children and adolescents with ADHD combined type. *Psychological Medicine*, *40*(12), 2089–2100. Available from https://doi.org/10.1017/S0033291710000590.

Althoff, R. R., Kuny-Slock, A. V., Verhulst, F. C., Hudziak, J. J., & van der Ende, J. (2014). Classes of oppositional-defiant behavior: Concurrent and predictive validity. *Journal of*

Child Psychology and Psychiatry, and Allied Disciplines, *55*(10), 1162–1171. Available from https://doi.org/10.1111/jcpp.12233.

American Psychiatric Association. (1980). *Diagnostic and statistical manual of mental disorders* (3rd ed.). Washington, DC: American Psychiatric Association.

American Psychiatric Association. (1987). *Diagnostic and statistical manual of mental disorders: DSM-III-R* (3rd ed.). Washington, DC: American Psychiatric Association.

American Psychiatric Association. (1994). *Diagnostic and statistical manual of mental disorders* (4th ed.). Washington, DC: American Psychiatric Association.

American Psychiatric Association. (2000). *Diagnostic and statistical manual of mental disorders: DSM-IV-TR* (4th ed.). Washington, DC: American Psychiatric Association.

American Psychiatric Association. (2013). *Diagnostic and statistical manual of mental disorders* (5th ed.). Arlington, VA: American Psychiatric Publishing.

Amsel, A. (1958). The role of frustrative nonreward in noncontinuous reward situations. *Psychological Bulletin*, *55*(2), 102–119.

Angold, A., & Costello, E. J. (1996). Toward establishing an empirical basis for the diagnosis of oppositional defiant disorder. *Journal of the American Academy of Child and Adolescent Psychiatry*, *35*(9), 1205–1212. https://doi.org/S0890-8567(09)63495-X [pii].

Arnold, D. H., Griffith, J. R., Ortiz, C., & Stowe, R. M. (1998). Day care interactions and teacher perceptions as a function of teacher and child ethnic group. *Journal of Research in Childhood Education*, *12*(2), 143–154.

Arnold, D. H., Ortiz, C., Curry, J. C., Stowe, R. M., Goldstein, N. E., Fisher, P. H., ... Yershova, K. (1999). Promoting academic, success and preventing disruptive behavior disorders through community partnership. *Journal of Community Psychology*, *27*(5), 589–598.

Barkley, R. A., & Benton, C. M. (2013). *Your defiant child: Eight steps to better behavior.* New York: Guilford Press.

Bierman, K. L., Miller, C. L., & Stabb, S. D. (1987). Improving the social behavior and peer acceptance of rejected boys: Effects of social skill training with instructions and prohibitions. *Journal of Consulting and Clinical Psychology*, *55*(2), 194.

Boylan, K., Rowe, R., Duku, E., Stepp, S., Hipwell, A. E., & Burke, J. D. (2017). Longitudinal profiles of girls' irritable, defiant and antagonistic oppositional symptoms: Evidence for group based differences in symptom severity. *Journal of Abnormal Child Psychology*, *45*(6), 1133–1145. Available from https://doi.org/10.1007/s10802-016-0231-z.

Boylan, K., Vaillancourt, T., Boyle, M., & Szatmari, P. (2007). Comorbidity of internalizing disorders in children with oppositional defiant disorder. *European Child and Adolescent Psychiatry*, *16*(8), 484–494. Available from https://doi.org/10.1007/s00787-007-0624-1.

Brinkmeyer, M.Y., & Eyberg, S.M. (2003). Parent-child interaction therapy for oppositional children. In A.E. Kazdin & J.R. Weisz (Eds.), *Evidence-based psychotherapies for children and adolescents* (pp. 204–223). New York, NY, US: Guilford Press.

Brotman, M. A., Kircanski, K., Stringaris, A., Pine, D. S., & Leibenluft, E. (2017). Irritability in youths: A translational model. *American Journal of Psychiatry*, *174*(6), 520–532, appi. ajp. 2016.16070839.

Brotman, M. A., Schmajuk, M., Rich, B. A., Dickstein, D. P., Guyer, A. E., Costello, E. J., ... Leibenluft, E. (2006). Prevalence, clinical correlates, and longitudinal course of severe mood dysregulation in children. *Biological Psychiatry*, *60*(9), 991–997. Available from https://doi.org/10.1016/j.biopsych.2006.08.042, S0006-3223(06)01136-X [pii].

Burke, J. D. (2012). An affective dimension within oppositional defiant disorder symptoms among boys: Personality and psychopathology outcomes into early adulthood. *Journal of Child Psychology and Psychiatry, and Allied Disciplines*, *53*(11), 1176–1183. Available from https://doi.org/10.1111/j.1469-7610.2012.02598.x.

Burke, J. D., Boylan, K., Rowe, R., Duku, E., Stepp, S. D., Hipwell, A. E., & Waldman, I. D. (2014). Identifying the irritability dimension of ODD: Application of a modified bifactor model across five large community samples of children. *Journal of Abnormal Psychology*, *123*(4), 841–851. Available from https://doi.org/10.1037/a0037898.

Burke, J. D., Hipwell, A. E., & Loeber, R. (2010). Dimensions of oppositional defiant disorder as predictors of depression and conduct disorder in preadolescent girls. *Journal of the American Academy of Child and Adolescent Psychiatry*, *49*(5), 484–492. Available from https://doi.org/10.1097/00004583-201005000-00009.

Burke, J. D., & Loeber, R. (2010). Oppositional defiant disorder and the explanation of the comorbidity between behavioral disorders and depression. *Clinical Psychology-Science and Practice*, *17*(4), 319–326. Available from https://doi.org/10.1111/j.1468-2850.2010.01223.x.

Burke, J. D., & Loeber, R. (2015). The effectiveness of the stop now and plan (SNAP) program for boys at risk for violence and delinquency. *Prevention Science: The Official Journal of the Society for Prevention Research*, *16*(2), 242–253. Available from https://doi.org/10.1007/s11121-014-0490-2.

Burke, J. D., Loeber, R., & Birmaher, B. (2002). Oppositional defiant disorder and conduct disorder: A review of the past 10 years, part II. *Journal of the American Academy of Child and Adolescent Psychiatry*, *41*(11), 1275–1293. Available from https://doi.org/10.1097/01.Chi.0000024839.60748.E8.

Burke, J. D., Loeber, R., Lahey, B. B., & Rathouz, P. J. (2005). Developmental transitions among affective and behavioral disorders in adolescent boys. *Journal of Child Psychology and Psychiatry*, *46*(11), 1200–1210.

Burke, J. D., Mulvey, E., & Schubert, C. (2015). Prevalence of mental health problems and service use among first-time juvenile offenders. *Journal of Child and Family Studies*, *24*(12), 3774–3781.

Burke, J. D., Pardini, D. A., & Loeber, R. (2008). Reciprocal relationships between parenting behavior and disruptive psychopathology from childhood through adolescence. *Journal of Abnormal Child Psychology*, *36*(5), 679–692. Available from https://doi.org/10.1007/s10802-008-9219-7.

Burke, J. D., Rowe, R., & Boylan, K. (2014). Functional outcomes of child and adolescent oppositional defiant disorder symptoms in young adult men. *Journal of Child Psychology and Psychiatry, and Allied Disciplines*, *55*(3), 264–272. Available from https://doi.org/10.1111/jcpp.12150.

Burke, J. D., & Stepp, S. D. (2012). Adolescent disruptive behavior and borderline personality disorder symptoms in young adult men. *Journal of Abnormal Child Psychology*, *40*(1), 35–44. Available from https://doi.org/10.1007/s10802-011-9558-7.

Burke, J. D., Waldman, I., & Lahey, B. B. (2010). Predictive validity of childhood oppositional defiant disorder and conduct disorder: Implications for the DSM-V. *Journal of Abnormal Psychology*, *119*(4), 739–751. Available from https://doi.org/10.1037/a0019708, 2010-19345-001 [pii].

Burnette, M. L. (2013). Gender and the development of oppositional defiant disorder: Contributions of physical abuse and early family environment. *Child Maltreatment*, *18*(3), 195–204. Available from https://doi.org/10.1177/1077559513478144.

Bussing, R., Gary, F. A., Mason, D. M., Leon, C. E., Sinha, K., & Garvan, C. W. (2003). Child temperament, ADHD, and caregiver strain: Exploring relationships in an epidemiological sample. *Journal of the American Academy of Child and Adolescent Psychiatry, 42*(2), 184–192.

Campbell, S. B., & Ewing, L. J. (1990). Follow-up of hard-to-manage preschoolers: Adjustment at age 9 and predictors of continuing symptoms. *Journal of Child Psychology and Psychiatry, 31*(6), 871–889.

Canino, G., Polanczyk, G., Bauermeister, J. J., Rohde, L. A., & Frick, P. J. (2010). Does the prevalence of CD and ODD vary across cultures? *Social Psychiatry and Psychiatric Epidemiology, 45*(7), 695–704. Available from https://doi.org/10.1007/s00127-010-0242-y.

Carlson, G. A., Danzig, A. P., Dougherty, L. R., Bufferd, S. J., & Klein, D. N. (2016). Loss of temper and irritability: The relationship to tantrums in a community and clinical sample. *Journal of Child and Adolescent Psychopharmacology, 26*(2), 114–122.

Carr, E. G., Taylor, J. C., & Robinson, S. (1991). The effects of severe behavior problems in children on the teaching behavior of adults. *Journal of Applied Behavior Analysis, 24* (3), 523–535.

Cohen, P., Cohen, J., & Brook, J. (1993). An epidemiological study of disorders in late childhood and adolescence--II. Persistence of disorders. *Journal of Child Psychology and Psychiatry, and Allied Disciplines, 34*(6), 869–877.

Coie, J.D. (1990). 13 Toward a theory of peer rejection. *Peer rejection in childhood*, 365.

Copeland, W. E., Shanahan, L., Costello, E. J., & Angold, A. (2009). Childhood and adolescent psychiatric disorders as predictors of young adult disorders. *Archives of General Psychiatry, 66*(7), 764–772.

Cuthbert, B. N., & Insel, T. R. (2013). Toward the future of psychiatric diagnosis: The seven pillars of RDoC. *BMC Medicine, 11*, 126. Available from https://doi.org/10.1186/1741-7015-11-126, 126-7015-11-126.

De Los Reyes, A., & Kazdin, A. E. (2005). Informant discrepancies in the assessment of childhood psychopathology: A critical review, theoretical framework, and recommendations for further study. *Psychological Bulletin, 131*(4), 483.

Demmer, D. H., Hooley, M., Sheen, J., McGillivray, J. A., & Lum, J. A. (2017). Sex differences in the prevalence of oppositional defiant disorder during middle childhood: A meta-analysis. *Journal of Abnormal Child Psychology, 45*(2), 313–325. Available from https://doi.org/10.1007/s10802-016-0170-8.

de Zeeuw, E. L., van Beijsterveldt, C. E., Lubke, G. H., Glasner, T. J., & Boomsma, D. I. (2015). Childhood ODD and ADHD behavior: The effect of classroom sharing, gender, teacher gender and their interactions. *Behavior Genetics, 45*(4), 394–408.

Dick, D. M., Viken, R. J., Kaprio, J., Pulkkinen, L., & Rose, R. J. (2005). Understanding the covariation among childhood externalizing symptoms: Genetic and environmental influences on conduct disorder, attention deficit hyperactivity disorder, and oppositional defiant disorder symptoms. *Journal of Abnormal Child Psychology, 33*(2), 219–229.

Dougherty, L. R., Smith, V. C., Bufferd, S. J., Stringaris, A., Leibenluft, E., Carlson, G. A., & Klein, D. N. (2013). Preschool irritability: Longitudinal associations with psychiatric disorders at age 6 and parental psychopathology. *Journal of the American Academy of Child and Adolescent Psychiatry, 52*(12), 1304–1313.

Evans, S. C., Burke, J. D., Roberts, M. C., Fite, P. J., Lochman, J. E., Francisco, R., & Reed, G. M. (2017). Irritability in child and adolescent psychopathology: An integrative review for ICD-11. *Clinical Psychology Review, 53*, 29–45.

Ezpeleta, L., Granero, R., de la Osa, N., Penelo, E., & Domenech, J. M. (2012). Dimensions of oppositional defiant disorder in 3-year-old preschoolers. *Journal of Child Psychology and Psychiatry*, *53*(11), 1128–1138. Available from https://doi.org/10.1111/j.1469-7610.2012.02545.x.

Fite, P. J., Evans, S. C., Cooley, J. L., & Rubens, S. L. (2014). Further evaluation of associations between attention-deficit/hyperactivity and oppositional defiant disorder symptoms and bullying-victimization in adolescence. *Child Psychiatry and Human Development*, *45*(1), 32–41.

Fleming, J. E., Boyle, M. H., & Offord, D. R. (1993). The outcome of adolescent depression in the Ontario Child Health Study follow-up. *Journal of the American Academy of Child and Adolescent Psychiatry*, *32*(1), 28–33, S0890-8567(09)64767-5 [pii].

Freeman, A. J., Youngstrom, E. A., Youngstrom, J. K., & Findling, R. L. (2016). Disruptive mood dysregulation disorder in a community mental health clinic: Prevalence, comorbidity and correlates. *Journal of Child and Adolescent Psychopharmacology*, *26*(2), 123–130.

Gadow, K. D. (2015). *The symptom inventories: An annotated bibliography*. Stony Brook, NY: Checkmate Plus.

Greene, R. W., Biederman, J., Zerwas, S., Monuteaux, M. C., Goring, J. C., & Faraone, S. V. (2002). Psychiatric comorbidity, family dysfunction, and social impairment in referred youth with oppositional defiant disorder. *American Journal of Psychiatry*, *159*(7), 1214–1224.

Grolnick, W. S., & Slowiaczek, M. L. (1994). Parents' involvement in children's schooling: A multidimensional conceptualization and motivational model. *Child Development*, *65* (1), 237–252.

Group for the Advancement of Psychiatry. (1966). *Psychopathological disorders in childhood: Theoretical considerations and a proposed classification* (No. 62). New York: Group for the Advancement of Psychiatry.

Harpold, T., Biederman, J., Gignac, M., Hammerness, P., Surman, C., Potter, A., & Mick, E. (2007). Is oppositional defiant disorder a meaningful diagnosis in adults? Results from a large sample of adults with ADHD. *The Journal of Nervous and Mental Disease*, *195*(7), 601–605. Available from https://doi.org/10.1097/NMD.0b013e318093f448, 00005053-200707000-00008 [pii].

Harvey, E. A., Youngwirth, S. D., Thakar, D. A., & Errazuriz, P. A. (2009). Predicting attention-deficit/hyperactivity disorder and oppositional defiant disorder from preschool diagnostic assessments. *Journal of Consulting and Clinical Psychology*, *77*(2), 349–354. Available from https://doi.org/10.1037/a0014638.

Herzhoff, K., & Tackett, J. L. (2016). Subfactors of oppositional defiant disorder: Converging evidence from structural and latent class analyses. *Journal of Child Psychology and Psychiatry*, *57*(1), 18–29.

Herzhoff, K., Smack, A. J., Reardon, K. W., Martel, M. M., & Tackett, J. L. (2017). Child personality accounts for oppositional defiant disorder comorbidity patterns. *Journal of Abnormal Child Psychology*, *45*(2), 327–335.

Holmberg, K., & Hjern, A. (2008). Bullying and attention-deficit–hyperactivity disorder in 10-year-olds in a Swedish community. *Developmental Medicine and Child Neurology*, *50*(2), 134–138.

Huffman, L.C., Mehlinger, S.L., Kerivan, A.S., Cavanaugh, D.A., Lippitt, J., & Moyo, O. (2001). Off to a good start: Research on the risk factors for early school problems and selected federal policies affecting children's social and emotional development and their readiness for school. Retrieved from: http://files.eric.ed.gov/fulltext/ED476378.pdf.

Jensen, P. S., Rubio-Stipec, M., Canino, G., Bird, H. R., Dulcan, M. K., Schwab-Stone, M. E., & Lahey, B. B. (1999). Parent and child contributions to diagnosis of mental disorders: Are both informants always necessary? *Journal of the American Academy of Child and Adolescent Psychiatry*, *38*(12), 1569–1579.

Kazdin, A. E. (2003). Problem-solving skills training and parent management training for conduct disorder. In A. E. Kazdin, & J. R. Weisz (Eds.), *Evidence-based psychotherapies for children and adolescents* (pp. 241–262). New York: Guilford Press.

Keenan, K., & Wakschlag, L. S. (2004). Are oppositional defiant and conduct disorder symptoms normative behaviors in preschoolers? A comparison of referred and nonreferred children. *The American Journal of Psychiatry*, *161*(2), 356–358.

Kellam, S. G., Werthamer-Larsson, L., Dolan, L. J., Brown, C. H., Mayer, L. S., Rebok, G. W., ... Wheeler, L. (1991). Developmental epidemiologically based preventive trials: Baseline modeling of early target behaviors and depressive symptoms. *American Journal of Community Psychology*, *19*(4), 563–584.

Kelland, K. (2012). New mental health manual is dangerous say experts. Reuters. Retrieved from http://www.reuters.com/article/us-mental-illness-diagnosis-idUSTRE8181WX20120209.

Kolko, D. J., Dorn, L. D., Bukstein, O., & Burke, J. D. (2008). Clinically referred ODD children with or without CD and healthy controls: Comparisons across contextual domains. *Journal of Child and Family Studies*, *17*(5), 714–734. Available from https://doi.org/10.1007/s10826-007-9186-6.

Kuny, A. V., Althoff, R. R., Copeland, W., Bartels, M., Van Beijsterveldt, C. E. M., Baer, J., & Hudziak, J. J. (2013). Separating the domains of oppositional behavior: Comparing latent models of the conners' oppositional subscale. *Journal of the American Academy of Child and Adolescent Psychiatry*, *52*(2), 172–183.

Ladd, G. W., Birch, S. H., & Buhs, E. S. (1999). Children's social and scholastic lives in kindergarten: Related spheres of influence? *Child Development*, *70*(6), 1373–1400.

Lahey, B. B., Van Hulle, C. A., Singh, A. L., Waldman, I. D., & Rathouz, P. J. (2011). Higher-order genetic and environmental structure of prevalent forms of child and adolescent psychopathology. *Archives of General Psychiatry*, *68*(2), 181–189.

Laird, R. D., Jordan, K. Y., Dodge, K. A., Pettit, G. S., & Bates, J. E. (2001). Peer rejection in childhood, involvement with antisocial peers in early adolescence, and the development of externalizing behavior problems. *Development and Psychopathology*, *13*(2), 337–354.

Lavigne, J. V., Bryant, F. B., Hopkins, J., & Gouze, K. R. (2014). Dimensions of oppositional defiant disorder in young children: Model comparisons, gender and longitudinal invariance. *Journal of Abnormal Child Psychology*, *43*(3), 423–439. Available from https://doi.org/10.1007/s10802-014-9919-0.

Lavigne, J. V., Bryant, F. B., Hopkins, J., & Gouze, K. R. (2017). Age 4 predictors of oppositional defiant disorder in early grammar school. *Journal of Clinical Child and Adolescent Psychology: The Official Journal for the Society of Clinical Child and Adolescent Psychology, American Psychological Association, Division 53*, 1–15. Available from https://doi.org/10.1080/15374416.2017.1280806.

Lavigne, J. V., Dahl, K. P., Gouze, K. R., LeBailly, S. A., & Hopkins, J. (2015). Multi-domain predictors of oppositional defiant disorder symptoms in preschool children: Cross-informant differences. *Child Psychiatry and Human Development*, *46*(2), 308–319. Available from https://doi.org/10.1007/s10578-014-0472-4.

Lavigne, J. V., Gouze, K. R., Hopkins, J., & Bryant, F. B. (2016). A multidomain cascade model of early childhood risk factors associated with oppositional defiant disorder symptoms in a community sample of 6-year-olds. *Development and Psychopathology*, *28*(4pt2), 1547–1562.

Leadbeater, B. J., & Homel, J. (2015). Irritable and defiant sub-dimensions of ODD: Their stability and prediction of internalizing symptoms and conduct problems from adolescence to young adulthood. *Journal of Abnormal Child Psychology*, *43*(3), 407–421.

Leadbeater, B., Thompson, K., & Gruppuso, V. (2012). Co-occurring trajectories of symptoms of anxiety, depression, and oppositional defiance from adolescence to young adulthood. *Journal of Clinical Child and Adolescent Psychology: The Official Journal for the Society of Clinical Child and Adolescent Psychology, American Psychological Association, Division 53*, *41*(6), 719–730. Available from https://doi.org/10.1080/15374416.2012.694608.

Leibenluft, E., Cohen, P., Gorrindo, T., Brook, J. S., & Pine, D. S. (2006). Chronic versus episodic irritability in youth: A community-based, longitudinal study of clinical and diagnostic associations. *Journal of Child and Adolescent Psychopharmacology*, *16*(4), 456–466.

Lochman, J. E., Evans, S. C., Burke, J. D., Roberts, M. C., Fite, P. J., Reed, G. M., de la Pena, F. R., Matthys, W., Ezpeleta, L., Siddiqui, S., & Elena Garralda, M. (2015). An empirically based alternative to DSM-5's disruptive mood dysregulation disorder for ICD-11. *World Psychiatry*, *14*(1), 30–33. Available from https://doi.org/10.1002/wps.20176.

Martel, M. M., Gremillion, M. L., & Roberts, B. (2012). Temperament and common disruptive behavior problems in preschool. *Personality and Individual Differences*, *53*(7), 874–879. Available from https://doi.org/10.1016/j.paid.2012.07.011.

Maughan, B., Rowe, R., Messer, J., Goodman, R., & Meltzer, H. (2004). Conduct disorder and oppositional defiant disorder in a national sample: Developmental epidemiology. *Journal of Child Psychology and Psychiatry*, *45*(3), 609–621.

Mayes, S. D., Calhoun, S. L., Baweja, R., Feldman, L., Syed, E., Gorman, A. A., & Siddiqui, F. (2015). Suicide ideation and attempts are associated with co-occurring oppositional defiant disorder and sadness in children and adolescents with ADHD. *Journal of Psychopathology and Behavioral Assessment*, *37*(2), 274–282.

Mayes, S. D., Waxmonsky, J. D., Calhoun, S. L., & Bixler, E. O. (2016). Disruptive mood dysregulation disorder symptoms and association with oppositional defiant and other disorders in a general population child sample. *Journal of Child and Adolescent Psychopharmacology*, *26*(2), 101–106.

Miller-Slough, R. L., Dunsmore, J. C., Ollendick, T. H., & Greene, R. W. (2016). Parent–child synchrony in children with oppositional defiant disorder: Associations with treatment outcomes. *Journal of Child and Family Studies*, *25*(6), 1880–1888.

Moffitt, T. E., Arseneault, L., Jaffee, S. R., Kim-Cohen, J., Koenen, K. C., Odgers, C. L., ... Viding, E. (2008). Research review: DSM-V conduct disorder: Research needs for an evidence base. *Journal of Child Psychology and Psychiatry*, *49*(1), 3–33. Available from https://doi.org/10.1111/j.1469-7610.2007.01823.x.

Mulraney, M., Schilpzand, E. J., Hazell, P., Nicholson, J. M., Anderson, V., Efron, D., & Sciberras, E. (2016). Comorbidity and correlates of disruptive mood dysregulation disorder in 6–8-year-old children with ADHD. *European Child & Adolescent Psychiatry*, *25* (3), 321–330.

Munkvold, L., Lundervold, A., Lie, S. A., & Manger, T. (2009). Should there be separate parent and teacher-based categories of ODD? evidence from a general population. *Journal of Child Psychology and Psychiatry*, *50*(10), 1264–1272.

Nock, M. K., Kazdin, A. E., Hiripi, E., & Kessler, R. C. (2007). Lifetime prevalence, correlates, and persistence of oppositional defiant disorder: Results from the national comorbidity survey replication. *Journal of Child Psychology and Psychiatry, and Allied Disciplines*, *48*(7), 703–713. https://doi.org/JCPP1733 [pii].

Normandeau, S., & Guay, F. (1998). Preschool behavior and first-grade school achievement: The mediational role of cognitive self-control. *Journal of Educational Psychology*, *90* (1), 111.

Patterson, G. R., Reid, J. B., & Dishion, T. J. (1992). *Antisocial boys: A social interactional approach*. Eugene, OR: Castalia.

Phillips, D. A., Voran, M., Kisker, E., Howes, C., & Whitebook, M. (1994). Child care for children in poverty: Opportunity or inequity? *Child Development*, *65*(2), 472–492.

Puig-Antich, J. (1982). Major depression and conduct disorder in prepuberty. *Journal of the American Academy of Child Psychiatry*, *21*(2), 118–128.

Raver, C. C., & Zigler, E. F. (1997). Social competence: An untapped dimension in evaluating Head Start's success. *Early Childhood Research Quarterly*, *12*(4), 363–385.

Reid, M. J., Webster-Stratton, C., & Hammond, M. (2003). Follow-up of children who received the incredible years intervention for oppositional-defiant disorder: Maintenance and prediction of 2-year outcome. *Behavior Therapy*, *34*(4), 471–491.

Rey, J. M., Bashir, M. R., Schwarz, M., Richards, I. N., Plapp, J. M., & Stewart, G. W. (1988). Oppositional disorder—fact or fiction. *Journal of the American Academy of Child and Adolescent Psychiatry*, *27*(2), 157–162. Available from https://doi.org/10.1097/00004583-198803000-00004.

Rowe, R., Costello, E. J., Angold, A., Copeland, W. E., & Maughan, B. (2010). Developmental pathways in oppositional defiant disorder and conduct disorder. *Journal of Abnormal Psychology*, *119*(4), 726–738. Available from https://doi.org/10.1037/a0020798, 2010-23724-004 [pii].

Rowe, R., Maughan, B., Costello, E. J., & Angold, A. (2005). Defining oppositional defiant disorder. *Journal of Child Psychology and Psychiatry, and Allied Disciplines*, *46*(12), 1309–1316. https://doi.org/JCPP1420 [pii].

Rowe, R., Rijsdijk, F. V., Maughan, B., Eley, T. C., Hosang, G. M., & Eley, T. C. (2008). Heterogeneity in antisocial behaviours and comorbidity with depressed mood: A behavioural genetic approach. *Journal of Child Psychology and Psychiatry, and Allied Disciplines*, *49*(5), 526–534. Available from https://doi.org/10.1111/j.1469-7610.2008.01834.x.

Savage, J., Verhulst, B., Copeland, W., Althoff, R. R., Lichtenstein, P., & Roberson-Nay, R. (2015). A genetically informed study of the longitudinal relation between irritability and anxious/depressed symptoms. *Journal of the American Academy of Child and Adolescent Psychiatry*, *54*(5), 377–384. Available from https://doi.org/10.1016/j.jaac.2015.02.010.

Simic, M., & Fombonne, E. (2001). Depressive conduct disorder: Symptom patterns and correlates in referred children and adolescents. *Journal of Affective Disorders*, *62*(3), 175–185, S0165032799002013 [pii].

Stage, S. A., & Quiroz, D. R. (1997). A meta-analysis of interventions to decrease disruptive classroom behavior in public education settings. *School Psychology Review*, *26*(3), 333–368.

Strickland, J., Hopkins, J., & Keenan, K. (2012). Mother-teacher agreement on preschoolers' symptoms of ODD and CD: Does context matter? *Journal of Abnormal Child Psychology*, *40*(6), 933–943.

Stringaris, A., Cohen, P., Pine, D. S., & Leibenluft, E. (2009). Adult outcomes of youth irritability: A 20-year prospective community-based study. *American Journal of Psychiatry*, *166*(9), 1048–1054. Available from https://doi.org/10.1176/appi.ajp.2009.08121849, appi.ajp.2009.08121849 [pii].

Stringaris, A., & Goodman, R. (2009a). Longitudinal outcome of youth oppositionality: Irritable, headstrong, and hurtful behaviors have distinctive predictions. *Journal of the American Academy of Child and Adolescent Psychiatry*, *48*(4), 404–412. Available from https://doi.org/10.1097/CHI.0b013e3181984f30, 00004583-200904000-00009 [pii].

Stringaris, A., & Goodman, R. (2009b). Three dimensions of oppositionality in youth. *Journal of Child Psychology and Psychiatry, and Allied Disciplines*, *50*(3), 216–223. Available from https://doi.org/10.1111/j.1469-7610.2008.01989.x, JCPP1989 [pii].

Stringaris, A., Maughan, B., Copeland, W. S., Costello, E. J., & Angold, A. (2013). Irritable mood as a symptom of depression in youth: Prevalence, developmental, and clinical correlates in the great smoky mountains study. *Journal of the American Academy of Child and Adolescent Psychiatry*, *52*(8), 831–840.

Stringaris, A., Maughan, B., & Goodman, R. (2010). What's in a disruptive disorder? temperamental antecedents of oppositional defiant disorder: Findings from the Avon longitudinal study. *Journal of the American Academy of Child and Adolescent Psychiatry*, *49*(5), 474–483. https://doi.org/00004583-201005000-00008 [pii].

Stringaris, A., Zavos, H., Leibenluft, E., Maughan, B., & Eley, T. C. (2012). Adolescent irritability: Phenotypic associations and genetic links with depressed mood. *American Journal of Psychiatry*, *169*(1), 47–54. Available from https://doi.org/10.1176/appi.ajp.2011.10101549.

Teagle, S. E. (2002). Parental problem recognition and child mental health service use. *Mental Health Services Research*, *4*(4), 257–266.

Tremblay, R. E., Pagani-Kurtz, L., Mâsse, L. C., Vitaro, F., & Pihl, R. O. (1995). A bimodal preventive intervention for disruptive kindergarten boys: Its impact through mid-adolescence. *Journal of Consulting and Clinical Psychology*, *63*(4), 560.

Tung, I., & Lee, S. S. (2014). Negative parenting behavior and childhood oppositional defiant disorder: Differential moderation by positive and negative peer regard. *Aggressive Behavior*, *40*(1), 79–90.

Turcotte Benedict, F., Vivier, P. M., & Gjelsvik, A. (2015). Mental health and bullying in the United States among children aged 6 to 17 years. *Journal of Interpersonal Violence*, *30*(5), 782–795.

Verlinden, M., Jansen, P. W., Veenstra, R., Jaddoe, V. W., Hofman, A., Verhulst, F. C., ... Tiemeier, H. (2015). Preschool attention-deficit/hyperactivity and oppositional defiant problems as antecedents of school bullying. *Journal of the American Academy of Child and Adolescent Psychiatry*, *54*(7), 571–579.

Vidal-Ribas, P., Brotman, M. A., Valdivieso, I., Leibenluft, E., & Stringaris, A. (2016). The status of irritability in psychiatry: A conceptual and quantitative review. *Journal of the American Academy of Child and Adolescent Psychiatry*, *55*(7), 556–570.

Waldman, I.D., Rowe, R., Boylan, K., & Burke, J.D. (2017). *External validation of a bifactor model of oppositional defiant disorder*. Unpublished manuscript.

Webster-Stratton, C., Jamila Reid, M., & Stoolmiller, M. (2008). Preventing conduct problems and improving school readiness: Evaluation of the incredible years teacher and child training programs in high-risk schools. *Journal of Child Psychology and Psychiatry*, *49*(5), 471–488.

World Health Organization. (1992). *International statistical classification of diseases and related health problems* (10th revision. ed.). Geneva: World Health Organization.

Wymbs, B. T., Pelham, W. E., Jr, Molina, B. S., Gnagy, E. M., Wilson, T. K., & Greenhouse, J. B. (2008). Rate and predictors of divorce among parents of youths with ADHD. *Journal of Consulting and Clinical Psychology*, *76*(5), 735.

Zastrow, B. L., Martel, M. M., & Widiger, T. A. (2016). Preschool oppositional defiant disorder: A disorder of negative affect, surgency, and disagreeableness. *Journal of Clinical Child and Adolescent Psychology: The Official Journal for the Society of Clinical Child and Adolescent Psychology, American Psychological Association, Division 53*, 1–11. Available from https://doi.org/10.1080/15374416.2016.1225504.

Further Reading

Lahey, B. B., Loeber, R., Burke, J., Rathouz, P. J., & McBurnett, K. (2002). Waxing and waning in concert: Dynamic comorbidity of conduct disorder with other disruptive and emotional problems over 7 years among clinic-referred boys. *Journal of Abnormal Psychology*, *111*(4), 556–567.

Wahler, R. G., Vigilante, V. A., & Strand, P. S. (2004). Generalization in a child's oppositional behavior across home and school settings. *Journal of Applied Behavior Analysis*, *37*(1), 43–51.

Conduct disorder: a neurodevelopmental perspective

3

Heather M. McDonough-Caplan and Theodore P. Beauchaine
The Ohio State University, Columbus, OH, United States

As currently defined in the *Diagnostic and Statistical Manual of Mental Disorders, fifth edition* (*DSM-5*; American Psychiatric Association, 2013), conduct disorder (CD) comprises "A repetitive and persistent pattern of behavior in which basic rights of others or major age-appropriate societal norms or rules are violated..." (p. 469). To meet DSM-5 criteria for CD, an individual must exhibit any 3 of 15 symptoms (e.g., initiates fights, is often truant from school) from a polythetic criterion set that spans four categories (aggression to people and animals, destruction of property, deceitfulness and theft, and serious rule violations). This yields 455 combinations of symptoms through which an individual could be diagnosed. To complicate matters further, specifiers are used to differentiate between (1) childhood versus adolescent onset, (2) normal versus limited prosocial emotional responding, and (3) level of severity. Given this diagnostic heterogeneity, two individuals with CD may present very differently, with significant implications for long-term course, prognosis, and treatment (e.g., Beauchaine, Zisner, & Sauder, 2017; Golmaryami & Frick, 2016; Moffitt et al., 2008). In this chapter, we focus primarily on more severe forms of CD, given space constraints. Readers who are interested in more lengthy reviews are referred to sources cited herein (e.g., Beauchaine & Hinshaw, 2016; Kimonis, Frick, & McMahon, 2014; Lahey & Waldman, 2017).

Historical context

Antisocial and related intemperate behaviors have been described throughout written history and were among the first childhood and adolescent syndromes to appear in the DSM (see Beauchaine & Hayden, 2016). The original DSM (American Psychiatric Association, 1952) included *conduct disturbance* as one of three adjustment reactions of childhood. The DSM-II (American Psychiatric Association, 1968) differentiated between two forms of conduct problems (CPs), including *group delinquent reaction* and *unsocialized aggressive reaction*. The former was defined primarily by associations with deviant peers and adoption of their values, whereas the latter was defined by hostility, disobedience, and overt aggression. The term *conduct disorder* was introduced in the DSM-III (American

Developmental Pathways to Disruptive, Impulse-Control, and Conduct Disorders.
DOI: https://doi.org/10.1016/B978-0-12-811323-3.00003-1

Psychiatric Association, 1980), which included four subtypes defined by quadrants formed by intersecting axes of socialization (socialized–unsocialized) and aggression (aggressive–nonaggressive).

Current diagnostic criteria appeared initially in the DSM-IV (American Psychiatric Association, 1994), which for the first time distinguished between life-course persistent and adolescent-onset CD. This distinction followed from the DSM-IV field trials (see Lahey et al., 1998), and a landmark review paper by Moffitt (1993). Moffitt proposed that those who begin delinquent behavior very early in life suffer from neuropsychological vulnerabilities that persist across development and eventuate in lifelong antisociality, whereas those who begin delinquent behavior in adolescence are likely to desist by early adulthood (Moffitt, 2003). This distinction, which has been largely upheld, undergirds the age of onset specifier in the DSM-5, which parses affected children and adolescents into those who engage in at least one criterion behavior before age 10 years versus those who engage in delinquent behaviors later in development. Children with early-onset CD, which we focus on for much of this chapter, typically engage in more intractable conduct (e.g., aggression, violence, criminality), and, as Moffitt suggested, are more likely to suffer from neurodevelopmental problems [e.g., prefrontal cortex (PFC) dysfunction], temperamental vulnerability (e.g., early life hyperactivity–impulsivity), and peer rejection (see, e.g., Moffitt & Caspi, 2001).

Prevalence and overview of societal costs

Many of those with early-onset CD develop antisocial personality disorder (ASPD) in adulthood (see Beauchaine et al., 2017; Robins, 1966). In fact, retrospective emergence of CD before age 15 is *required* to diagnose ASPD (American Psychiatric Association, 2013). Thus, continuity of externalizing behavior should be considered in any discussion of antisociality, as elaborated below (Beauchaine et al., 2017). Although prevalence rates of CD and ASPD are only 3%–6% among males and 1% among females (American Psychiatric Association, 2013; Kessler et al., 1994), about half of all property offenses and violent crimes are committed by affected individuals (e.g., Farrington, Ohlin, & Wilson, 1986). As a result, roughly half of incarcerated adult males in the United States meet criteria for ASPD (see Beauchaine, Klein, Crowell, Derbidge, & Gatzke-Kopp, 2009). Collectively, they account for over $70 billion in annual and federal corrections costs (Schmitt, Warner, & Gupta, 2010; Teplin, 1994)—a figure that omits the financial burden of crimes that led to incarceration.

Although often unacknowledged, about 1 in 20 males who suffer from ASPD eventually commits suicide. This rate is roughly 300 times that observed in the general population (Dyck, Bland, Newman, & Orn, 1988). Thus, CD and its developmental sequelae are major public health concerns for which improved understanding of etiology and formulation of more effective prevention and intervention programs are desperately needed. Unfortunately, research on prevention and treatment of CD does not receive levels of state and federal funding that many other psychiatric disorders garner (see, e.g., Insel, 2017). Likely reasons for this are complex and beyond the scope of this chapter. As we discuss below, however, prevention programs are most effective when delivered in childhood, before adolescents become embedded in multiple reinforcement systems that maintain antisocial behavior (e.g., deviant peer affiliations, the criminal justice system), and before problems with substance use emerge (see, e.g., Webster-Stratton & Taylor, 2001). In fact, effective prevention programs for 5-year olds who are on early-onset CD trajectories cost only 6%–12% of the cumulative 25-year economic burden of not intervening (Bonin, Stevens, Beecham, Byford, & Parsonage, 2011).

Sex differences

Given that far more children and adolescents with CD are male than female, much of the literature reviewed herein draws from male samples. There are a number of potential neurobiological explanations for observed sex differences, most of which are associated with general vulnerability to neurodevelopmental problems rather than CD per se (Kraemer, 2000). Males may be more vulnerable to many disorders in part because male fetal development is protracted compared with female fetal development, yielding more time for prenatal insults to accrue (Taylor, 1985). Furthermore, certain X-linked genes may confer differential vulnerability via complex interactions with environments. For example, the monoamine oxidase A (*MAOA*) gene, which is implicated in aggression in contexts of maltreatment (Caspi et al., 2002), responds differently to environmental insults among men versus women (Wong et al., 2010). Boys also exhibit more difficult temperaments and higher rates of attention-deficit hyperactivity disorder (ADHD) than girls, both of which predict future externalizing behavior, especially in high-risk environments (e.g., Barkley, 1995; Stringaris, Maughan, & Goodman, 2010). Finally, learning disabilities—which are often comorbid with early-onset CD (e.g., Moffitt, 2003)—are more common among boys than among girls (e.g., Wadsworth, DeFries, Stevenson, Gilger, & Pennington, 1992).

Social factors likely also contribute through interactions with biological predispositions. For example, boys with difficult temperaments affiliate with similar peers, who both model and reinforce antisocial behavior (Maccoby, 1986, 1990). In contrast, girls with externalizing problems are typically rejected by their peers and therefore get punished for their behavior (Keenan, Loeber, & Green, 1999). Sex effects on CD increase in puberty (Stattin & Magnusson, 1990), when (1) males and females undergo divergent hormonal maturation and (2) large sex differences in physical strength make aggressive behavior less likely to yield instrumental gains for girls.

Etiology as a multifactorial ontogenic process

As already noted, one cannot understand the etiology of CD without considering its development (Beauchaine & McNulty, 2013; Beauchaine, Shader, & Hinshaw, 2016). Although the DSM now subtypes CD based on age of onset (see above) and acknowledges links between CD in adolescence and ASPD in adulthood, it does not specify developmental relations between CD and other externalizing disorders, including ADHD, oppositional defiant disorder (ODD), and substance use disorders (SUDs). This is an important oversight because concurrent rates of comorbidity among externalizing disorders are exceedingly high and because many, if not most, individuals who present with early-onset CD follow a developmental trajectory that begins with ADHD very early in life and progresses to ODD, then early-onset CD, and eventually ASPD/SUDs (Beauchaine et al., 2017). This developmental trajectory has been recognized for many years (e.g., Loeber & Hay, 1997; Robins, 1978) and is subsumed into modern *ontogenic process* perspectives on externalizing psychopathology (Beauchaine & McNulty, 2013).

The ontogenic process perspective describes progression of and continuity in externalizing behavior as outcomes of complex longitudinal transactions between interdependent individual-level vulnerabilities (e.g., genetic, epigenetic, neural, allostatic) and equally interdependent contextual risk factors (e.g., coercive parenting, neighborhood violence/criminality, exposure to substances of abuse). Among children with early-onset CD who develop increasingly serious externalizing behavior into adolescence and adulthood, heritable, preexisting neurobiological vulnerabilities interact with environmental risk exposures to alter neuromaturation of prefrontal brain regions that subserve self-regulation (see Beauchaine et al., 2017). In fact, impulsive children and adolescents with CD often *seek out* environmental experiences such as delinquent peer affiliations and substance use (e.g., Button et al., 2007). These experiences both magnify their antisocial behavior and compromise neurodevelopment of frontal brain regions implicated in self-regulation (e.g., De Bellis et al., 2005; Dishion, McCord, & Poulin, 1999). Such self-reinforcing feedback systems make intervening late in development exceedingly difficult.

Core tenets of the ontogenic process perspective include (1) incorporation of neurodevelopmental mechanisms into models of early-onset CD (see above) and (2) consideration of interactive etiological influences at all relevant levels of analysis. These tenets are summarized in Fig. 3.1, which depicts longitudinal progression of externalizing behavior from preschool to adulthood. Development of early-onset CD and its comorbidities is represented along the *x*-axis, and levels of analysis, including environmental, syndromal, behavioral genetic, and molecular genetic, are represented along the *y*-axis. In sections to follow, we discuss current findings at each of these levels of analysis. We also consider neural vulnerabilities, which do not appear in Fig. 3.1. Notably, discussion of any single level of analysis could fill an entire chapter, so we present summaries herein. More comprehensive coverage can be found elsewhere (e.g., Beauchaine & Hinshaw, 2016; Beauchaine et al., 2017; Moffitt & Caspi, 2001).

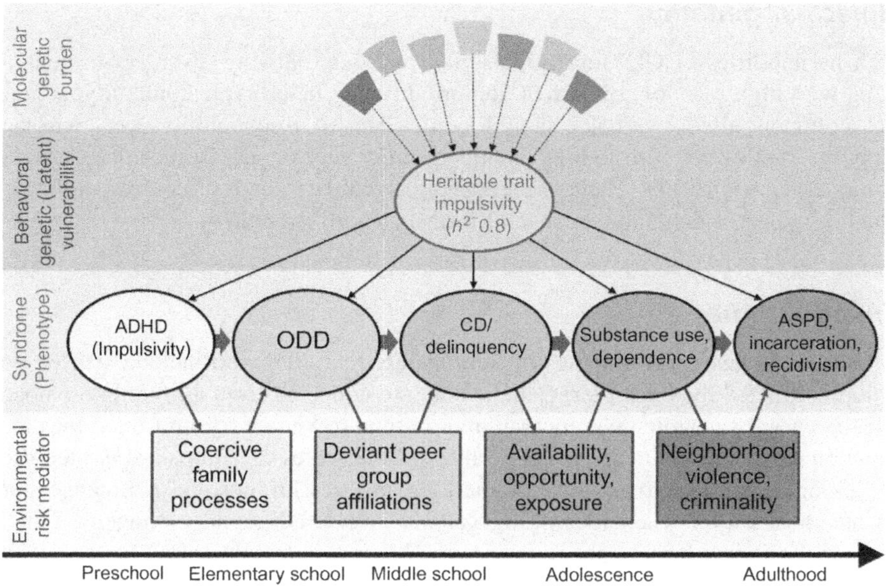

Figure 3.1 Ontogenic progression of externalizing behaviors, including early-onset conduct problems, from preschool to adulthood. Contemporary accounts of CD emphasize the complex, multifactorial, and interactive nature of vulnerabilities and risk factors across multiple levels of analysis.

Genetic vulnerabilities

Behavioral genetics

Twin and adoption studies demonstrate strong heritability coefficients for CD (e.g., Slutske et al., 1997). However, given etiological associations between CD and other externalizing disorders (see above and below), these heritability estimates tell an incomplete story. In fact, studies that account for common variance across externalizing disorders—rather than focusing on CD in isolation—reveal considerable shared heritability for ADHD, ODD, CD, SUDs, and antisociality (see, e.g., Dhamija, Tuvblad, & Baker, 2016; Krueger et al., 2002). As depicted in Fig. 3.1, a single, higher-order heritable factor (impulsivity) accounts for much of the covariation among first-order factors (disorders). In contrast, specific expressions of shared vulnerability (i.e., disorders themselves) are influenced strongly by environment (see Burt, 2009; Burt, Krueger, McGue, & Iacono, 2001; Krueger et al., 2002). Thus, although vulnerability to externalizing behavior is highly heritable, whether it progresses from ADHD to CD and related delinquent behaviors is dependent on environmental risk exposures, including maltreatment, deviant peer group affiliations, neighborhood violence, and substances of abuse (see Beauchaine & McNulty, 2013). We discuss each of these in a later section on environmental influences.

Molecular genetics

High heritabilities of CD, trait impulsivity, and externalizing disorders in general, along with high rates of concurrent comorbidity and heterotypic continuity, suggest that common allelic variants should confer shared vulnerability, yet twin and adoption studies tell us nothing about specific genes (see Beauchaine, Gatzke-Kopp, & Gizer, 2017). Rather, identifying candidate alleles requires *molecular genetic* studies, which come in several forms, as outlined below.

Linkage studies

In linkage studies, large samples of families are recruited who include at least two children affected by a disorder. Genetic data are collected from all family members, and searches for genetic markers that are proximal to known chromosomal locations are conducted. For example, the gene responsible for cystic fibrosis was identified by linking the disease to an allele on the long arm of Chromosome 7. Linkage studies are most useful when identifying genetic vulnerabilities to monogenic (single gene) and oligogenic (few gene) disorders. This is a major limitation for psychopathology research since psychiatric disorders are usually multifactorial (influenced by many genes). In fact, no single gene is necessary or sufficient for development of most forms of psychopathology (see Beauchaine & Constantino, 2017). Moreover, multifactorial genetic variabilities interact with one another and with environmental adversities across development to shape and maintain externalizing conduct (see Beauchaine & McNulty, 2013; Beauchaine et al., 2017). Nevertheless, linkage studies have provided some useful leads for psychiatric geneticists who study externalizing conduct. Consistent with the notion that externalizing disorders share common vulnerability, none of these genes are specific to CD.

Although a comprehensive review of molecular genetic studies is beyond the scope of this article, a few findings are noteworthy. Among these are studies linking both the dopamine (DA) receptor 2 (*DRD2*) and receptor 4 (*DRD4*) loci to externalizing personality traits (e.g., Hill, Zezza, Wipprecht, Xu, & Neiswanger, 1999). In addition, variation in the γ-aminobutyric (GABA) α_2 receptor subunit (*GABRA2*) gene on Chromosome 4—near the alcohol dehydrogenase gene cluster—has been linked to alcohol dependence (e.g., Reich et al., 1998). Notably, the *GABRA2* gene was later implicated in childhood CD symptoms and adult SUDs (Dick et al., 2006). Finally, several regions on Chromosome 3 have been linked to externalizing disorders. For example, the 3p13–p22.3 region on the short arm of Chromosome 3 has been linked to comorbid CD and cocaine use (Gelernter et al., 2005). Furthermore, the 3p26.2–q29 region of the long arm of Chromosome 3 has been linked to comorbid CD and ASPD (Ehlers, Gilder, Slutske, Lind, & Wilhelmsen, 2008), as well as co-occurring CD and drug dependence (Stallings et al., 2003, 2005). These regions contain several potential candidate genes, including the metabotropic glutamate 2 receptor gene (*GRM2*), cholecystokinin gene (*CCK*), neuroligin 1 gene (*NLGN1*), and several serotonin (5-HT) receptor genes (*HTR3C*, *HTR3D*, and *HTR3E*). Additional molecular genetic studies of these genes are discussed immediately below.

Association studies

In contrast to linkage studies, association studies compare variants of candidate genes among those with and without a given disorder. Most early association studies, which were conducted with smaller samples than modern genome-wide association studies (GWAS; see below), were theory-driven and therefore assessed allelic frequencies of genes that putatively affect neurotransmission in brain networks involved in expression of psychopathology. For example, since theories of ADHD have long implicated the midbrain DA system (e.g., Plichta & Scheres, 2014), many association studies compared allelic frequencies of genes that affect DA neurotransmission among those with and without the disorder (e.g., Li, Sham, Owen, & He, 2006). Given etiological connections between ADHD and other externalizing disorders (see above), many of these studies are relevant to CD. In addition, association studies of externalizing conduct have also evaluated genes that affect serotonergic, GABAergic, and glutamatergic systems.

As expected, many genes that affect DA neurotransmission (including interrelated processes of turnover, transport, reuptake, and metabolism) are associated with externalizing conduct. Although inconsistencies in the literature exist (see Gizer, Otto, & Ellingson, 2016), the DA receptor 4 and 5 genes (*DRD4*and *DRD5*), the DA transporter 1 gene (*DAT1*), *MAOA* gene, and the catechol-*O*-methyltransferase (*COMT*) gene have all been associated with externalizing behavior (e.g., DeYoung et al., 2010; Faraone & Mick, 2010; Gizer, Ficks, & Waldman, 2009). Although these genes perform different functions, all affect DA availability, and some are expressed differentially across functional subdivisions of the brain. For example, the *DRD2* gene, which is associated with externalizing personality traits (see above), is expressed heavily in the striatum (e.g., Jönsson et al., 1999), a midbrain structure implicated in trait impulsivity (see Beauchaine et al., 2017). Similarly, the *DAT1* (*SLC6A3*) gene—which is also expressed heavily in the striatum—is associated with vulnerability across the externalizing spectrum. Several studies have found associations between the 9-variable number tandem repeat (VNTR) and ADHD among children, as well as SUDs later in life (Hopfer et al., 2005; Todd et al., 2005; van der Zwaluw et al., 2009). Notably, some have proposed that *SLC6A3* vulnerability interacts with environmental adversities and other genetic liabilities to affect externalizing outcomes (e.g., Gizer et al., 2009). This is a good example of the complex, multifactorial nature of externalizing psychopathology, as discussed above.

In contrast to the *DRD2* and *DAT1* genes, which preferentially affect midbrain DA activity, the *DRD4* gene preferentially affects DA neurotransmission in the PFC, which is involved in top–down regulation of behavioral impulsivity and emotional lability (see Castellanos-Ryan & Séguin, 2016). Most who suffer from early-onset CD struggle in these domains (see Beauchaine, 2015). A 48-VNTR of *DRD4* exon 3 is associated with vulnerability to multiple externalizing disorders, including ADHD, comorbid ADHD and CD/ODD, and SUDs (e.g., Chen et al., 2011; Holmes et al., 2002; Kirley et al., 2004; Le Foll, Gallo, Le Strat, Lu, & Gorwood, 2009; Wu, Xiao, Sun, & Zou, 2012).

In addition, it has long been known that serotonergic networks both modulate DA circuits and subserve self-regulation and emotion regulation functions (see, e.g., Beauchaine, Neuhaus, Zalewski, Crowell, & Potapova, 2011; Hayes & Greenshaw, 2011; Herman & Balogh, 2012). Given this, it is unsurprising that genes involved in 5-HT neurotransmission also confer vulnerability to externalizing disorders, including CD. Three particularly important vulnerability alleles are the 5-HT transporter gene (5HTT/*SLC6A4*) and 5-HT receptor genes (*HTR1B*, *HTR2A*). Although these receptors are distributed throughout the central nervous system (CNS), *HTR1B* receptors are expressed preferentially in the striatum, whereas *HTR2A* receptors are expressed preferentially in the orbitofrontal cortex (OFC) (Dalley, Mar, Economidou, & Robbins, 2008; Dalley & Rosier, 2012). As outlined above, these brain regions are involved in behavioral impulsivity and self--regulation, respectively.

At this juncture, it is important to note that many of the findings summarized above are inconsistent, and all are of small effect size—a state of affairs that plagues psychiatric genetics research (see Beauchaine et al., 2017). Furthermore, taken together, effect sizes for all vulnerability alleles account for a limited portion of the high heritability of externalizing behavior. This phenomenon has come to be known as the "missing heritability" problem (Plomin, 2013), which likely derives in part from molecular genetic analyses of main effects, which do not account for complex interactions between genes and genes or between genes and environments. As outlined above, gene × gene and gene × environment interactions are central to progression of externalizing behavior and other forms of psychopathology (Beauchaine & McNulty, 2013). This point is illustrated by the highly cited finding by Caspi et al. (2002), who discovered that main effects of *MAOA* genetic vulnerability and child maltreatment accounted for little variance in juvenile or adult antisocial behavior. In contrast, interactive effects of genes and environment accounted for an impressive 65% of the variance in antisocial outcomes. Thus, those who incurred maltreatment *and* inherited the low *MAOA* activity genotype, which affects dopaminergic, serotonergic, and noradrenergic function, were at much higher risk for engaging in serious externalizing behavior than those who experienced maltreatment but did not inherit the vulnerability allele. This is a stark reminder that etiology is multifactorial and complex and cannot be reduced to either effects of genetic vulnerability or environmental adversity.

Although additional vulnerability alleles (e.g., *COMT*, *GABRA2*, *GRM7*) have been identified in traditional genetic association studies of externalizing disorders, we refer readers to recent reviews given space constraints (e.g., Arcos-Burgos, Vélez, Solomon, & Muenke, 2012; Gizer et al., 2016).

Genome-wide association studies

In GWAS, genetic markers are evaluated across the entire genome. Unlike traditional association studies, GWAS therefore do not require hypotheses about potential candidate genes. The trade-off, however, is that very large sample sizes—on the order of tens of thousands—are needed to balance statistical power with type I error rates (i.e., false positives). In essence, since so many statistical tests are run across the genome, corrections for family-wise type I error rates result in potentially large effects going undetected (type II errors or false negatives). Although strategies for addressing this problem are being developed (e.g., Tucker, Price, & Berger, 2014), it still limits discoveries from GWAS designs.

Although there are few GWAS of CD specifically, studies that focus on ADHD and ASPD are of interest given common etiological mechanisms, as outlined above. To date, GWAS have identified both cell adhesion protein genes and voltage-gated potassium channel genes in contributing to externalizing liability. Cell adhesion proteins facilitate cell binding and organization of synapses during neurodevelopment. Variants of the neurexin 1 (*NRXN1*) cell adhesion protein, which is involved in GABA and glutamate synapse formation, have been associated with ADHD in GWAS (Lesch, Timmesfeld, et al., 2008; Neale, Medland, Ripke, Asherson, et al., 2010; Yang et al., 2013). In addition, variants in the cadherin 13 (*CDH13*) and latrophilin 3 (*LPHN3*) cell adhesion genes have yielded GWAS signals for ADHD (Arcos-Burgos & Muenke, 2010; Lasky-Su et al., 2007; Lesch, Anney, et al., 2008; Neale, Medland, Ripke, Asherson, et al., 2010). Finally, variations of the catenin α_2 (*CTNNA2*) have been associated with both ADHD (Lesch, Timmesfeld, et al., 2008; Neale, Medland, Ripke, Anney, et al., 2010) and CD (Dick et al., 2008; Kendler et al., 2006).

Voltage-gated potassium channels affect repolarization efficiency of depolarized neurons, which influences neural excitability, neurotransmitter release, gene transcription, and neuroplasticity (e.g., Imbrici, Camerino, & Tricarico, 2013). GWAS show preliminary evidence of associations between voltage-gated potassium channel genes and externalizing disorders. For example, *KCNMA1* (potassium large conductance calcium-activated channel, subfamily M, α member 1) is associated with callous–unemotional (CU) traits among children (Viding et al., 2010). Such traits are implicated specifically in early-onset CD, as described below.

Structural variants

Structural variants are regions of DNA in which genes are duplicated (extra copies), deleted (missing copies), or translocated (rearranged copies). Some structural variants are inherited, whereas others arise *de novo* and are therefore not expressed by parents. Structural variants, which are often referred to as copy number variants (CNVs), can range between 50 base pairs (bp) and 1M bp (Girirajan, Campbell, & Eichle, 2011), but are often defined as regions of DNA that exceed 1k bp (National Center for Biotechnology Information, 2017). On average, members of the population carry seven CNVs, most of which are "silent." About 1% of the population carries a CNV of at least 1M bp. Research conducted in the last decade reveals that CNVs play etiological roles in several complex multifactorial disorders including externalizing psychopathology, particularly ADHD (e.g., Lesch et al., 2011). It is important to note, however, that no specific CNV is necessary for development of ADHD or any other externalizing disorder. Rather, CNVs interact with other genetic vulnerabilities, contributing an additional level of complexity to the multifactorial nature of etiology (see Beauchaine & Constantino, 2017).

Several CNVs that affect glutamate receptor genes, such as *GRM1*, *GRM5*, *GRM7*, and *GRM8*, have been associated with ADHD (Elia et al., 2010). Consistent with GWAS findings discussed above, CNVs that affect *CNTNAP2* and *CTNNA2* cell adhesion proteins are also implicated (Elia et al., 2010). Lesch et al. (2011) identified 17 CNVs that may be associated with ADHD, including 4 deletions and 13 duplications ranging in size from 110k to 3M bp. Among others, these affected the acetylcholine-metabolizing butyrylcholinesterase (*BCHE*) and glucose transporter 3 (*SLC2A3*) genes. Although there are no CNV studies of CD specifically, findings reviewed above are likely relevant to CD given developmental progression of externalizing behavior—a major theme of this chapter.

Epigenetics

Epigenesis refers to processes through which environmental experiences (e.g., trauma, prenatal insults, diet) alter gene expression. Thus, epigenetic effects on behavior are *experience-dependent*. Epigenetic changes in gene expression involve alterations in DNA structure that do not affect heritable DNA sequence (see, e.g., Mill, 2011). Epigenesis occurs through a number of mechanisms, most of which affect DNA methylation and chromatin structure. These mechanisms render previously inaccessible sections of DNA available for transcription by opening chromatin structure (*euchromatin*) or render previously accessible sections of DNA inaccessible for transcription by condensing chromatin structure (*heterochromatin*). Although long recognized as important for neurodevelopment, identification of epigenetic effects on behavior—including psychopathology—is somewhat recent.

Confirming epigenesis among humans is difficult since brain tissue is not directly accessible for assaying. However, research with animals reveals important prenatal effects that are likely homologous. In particular, the mesolimbic DA system of offspring is exquisitely sensitive to *maternal programming* effects, which are often exerted through epigenetic mechanisms (Gatzke-Kopp, 2011). Maternal programming occurs when experiences of mothers affect in utero neurodevelopment of their offspring—often in response to circulating stress hormones. Chronic exposure to stress during pregnancy alters in utero neurodevelopment and function of early maturing dopaminergic systems (e.g., Son et al., 2007), with effects that are often lifelong and have direct implications for impulsivity and self-control. In addition, prenatal exposure to neurotoxins (e.g., Fonnum & Mariussen, 2009), poor nutrition (e.g., Kuperstein, Eilam, & Yavin, 2008), and certain substances of abuse —particularly stimulants (e.g., Kubrusly & Bhide, 2010)—all affect midbrain DA responding (Gatzke-Kopp, 2011). Although immediate effects of such exposures typically hyperactivate midbrain DA neurons, long-term downregulation often ensues—a common neuroadaptation (see Mead, Beauchaine, & Shannon, 2010). As outlined below, deficient midbrain DA responding is a hallmark of externalizing disorders, including CD (see Beauchaine & McNulty, 2013).

One means of estimating epigenesis among humans is to measure methylation in blood. Although debate exists regarding the validity of this method for approximating CNS effects, several recent findings are worth noting. Zhang et al. (2013) reported increased methylation at receptor sites on the HTR1B serotonin receptor gene among alcohol-dependent participants who experienced early adversity (child abuse, death of a parent, exposure to violence). Of note, this 5-HT receptor gene is implicated in externalizing disorders (see above). In addition, individuals who experience child abuse exhibit increased 5-HT transporter methylation, which is associated with antisocial behavior following adversity (Beach, Brody, Dodorov, Gunter, & Philibert, 2011; Beach et al., 2013). Further epigenetic studies of externalizing disorders are critical toward understanding environmental influences on gene expression and resulting behavioral outcomes.

Neural vulnerabilities

Gene variants do not "cause" psychiatric disorders (or any behaviors) directly, but rather operate through indirect effects on neural, hormonal, and other neurobiological functions. In this section, we discuss relative contributions of subcortical and cortical vulnerabilities to externalizing behavior. In any such discussion, it is important to consider differing neurodevelopmental time courses for subcortical structures, which are volumetrically mature very early in life, versus cortical structures, which do not mature fully until early adulthood (e.g., Brain Development Cooperative Group, 2012; Casey, Jones, & Hare, 2008). This differential pattern of neurodevelopment has major implications for progression of impulsivity and ADHD to CD among those on the early-onset externalizing trajectory. According to neurodevelopmental models, vulnerability to externalizing behavior is driven more by subcortical vulnerability in early childhood, with cortical contributions taking on increasing importance in late childhood, adolescence, and adulthood (see Beauchaine et al., 2017). Although our presentation here is brief, more detailed accounts appear elsewhere (e.g., Beauchaine, 2015; Beauchaine, Zisner, & Hayden, in press; Casey et al., 2008).

Subcortical emotion generation mechanisms

As described above, trait impulsivity confers vulnerability to all externalizing disorders, beginning with development of ADHD as early as the preschool years (e.g., Beauchaine & McNulty, 2013). Trait impulsivity is defined by a consistent preference for immediate rewards over larger, delayed rewards, failures to plan ahead, and poor volitional control over behavior (see Neuhaus & Beauchaine, 2017; Sagvolden, Johansen, Aase, & Russell, 2005). When defined this way, trait impulsivity is captured well by DSM symptoms of hyperactivity–impulsivity and closely related constructs (see Beauchaine et al., 2017). Notably, these symptoms comprise a normally distributed personality trait that is problematic only when expressed in the extreme.

A voluminous literature links trait impulsivity to striatal hypo-responding to incentives. Hyperactive-impulsive children, adolescents, and adults exhibit blunted neural reactivity in mesolimbic structures—including the ventral striatum—while anticipating reward cues (e.g., Cubillo, Halari, Smith, Taylor, & Rubia, 2012; Plichta & Scheres, 2014). Consistent with the shared etiology perspective emphasized herein, this neural vulnerability is observed in all externalizing spectrum disorders, including CD, ASPD, and both active and remitted SUDs (e.g., Luijten, Schellekens, Kühn, Machielse, & Sescousse, 2017; Oberlin et al., 2012; Rubia, Smith, et al., 2009). Of note, blunted striatal responding is multiply determined by genetic liabilities, environmental influences, epigenetic factors, and neurohormonal modulators (see Beauchaine & Constantino, 2017; Gatzke-Kopp, 2011; Gizer et al., 2016).

Understanding how blunted striatal reactivity translates into impulsive behaviors requires that we consider the psychological state that neural hypo-responding imbues. The mesolimbic DA system, including the striatum, is a core neural substrate of approach motivation (see Neuhaus & Beauchaine, 2017). Accordingly, infusions of DA into mesolimbic structures induce pleasurable affective states (Berridge, 2003), and individual differences in DA expression correlate with positive affectivity (Ashby, Isen, & Turken, 1999). In contrast, low levels of striatal DA —as observed in CD and other externalizing disorders—are associated with discontentment and irritability (Laakso et al., 2003). As specified in reward-seeking models, these negative hedonic states motivate excessive approach behaviors, which temporarily upregulate mood through phasic DA neural firing (Zisner & Beauchaine, 2016). However, because phasic neural activity is transient, and of smaller magnitude among externalizing individuals than controls, frequent external reinforcers are sought, as manifested in behavioral biases toward approach observed in externalizing disorders (see Sagvolden et al., 2005).

Although subcortically generated approach emotions help to explain behavioral impulsivity, which characterizes all forms of externalizing psychopathology, striatal responding does not explain why some children never progress beyond ADHD, whereas others develop increasingly intractable comportment as they mature. As alluded to above, such progression is facilitated by cortical vulnerabilities that emerge over a more protracted time course and by environmental risk mediators that interact with neural vulnerabilities. We consider cortical vulnerabilities immediately below, before turning to environmental mechanisms in later sections.

Cortical emotion regulation mechanisms

As noted above, the human PFC, which includes several functional subdivisions, matures throughout childhood, adolescence, and young adulthood (Brain Development Cooperative Group, 2012; Casey et al., 2008). Among its many functions are volitional regulation of behavior and emotion. In fact, regulation of impulsivity is effected primarily through top–down orbitofrontal and dorsolateral prefrontal inhibition of striatal activity and reactivity (see Heatherton, 2011; Heatherton & Wagner, 2011). Although trait-impulsive individuals function adequately in society when they can exercise sufficient top–down regulation of behavior and emotion (Beauchaine, 2015), those who progress to CD, delinquency, and related behaviors exhibit both structural and functional compromises in PFC networks, as well as deficiencies in functional connectivity between prefrontal and striatal brain regions. Furthermore, adolescents with CD often engage in high-risk behaviors, such as alcohol and other substance use, that further compromise neuromaturation in the PFC and its interconnections, with adverse consequences for future self-regulation (e.g., Bava, Jacobus, Thayer, & Tapert, 2013).

Several studies demonstrate smaller cortical volumes among adolescent males with CD, particularly in the OFC (Huebner et al., 2008) and the anterior cingulate cortex (ACC) (Sauder, Beauchaine, Gatzke-Kopp, Shannon, & Aylward, 2012). Importantly, compromised PFC volumes appear to develop in the transition to adolescence and are not observed among younger children (De Brito et al., 2009). Functionally, adolescents with CD fail to recruit the anterior cingulate during extinction of previously rewarded behaviors and instead continue to recruit the striatum (Gatzke-Kopp et al., 2009). Finally, adolescents with CD exhibit reduced functional connectivity between cortical and striatal brain regions (Shannon, Sauder, Beauchaine, & Gatzke-Kopp, 2009). Together, these findings are consistent with (1) Moffitt's (1993) thesis of compromised executive function and IQ among those with early-onset CD and (2) the notion that CD arises at least in part from poor top–down regulation of subcortically generated impulses and emotions (Beauchaine, 2015; Beauchaine et al., 2017). As we review in later sections, neural maturation of the PFC is affected strongly by environmental adversity, which suggests that vulnerability to CD may be attenuated or potentiated by life experience.

Hormonal vulnerabilities

In addition to genetic and neural vulnerabilities, hormones and neurohormones contribute to externalizing liability. Here, we focus on testosterone and cortisol. Although other neurohormones, such as norepinephrine, are also relevant given their modulating effects on central DA and 5-HT systems (Stockmeier & Ordway, 2007), space constraints preclude comprehensive coverage. Interested readers are therefore referred elsewhere (e.g., Beauchaine et al., 2011).

Testosterone

Prenatally, exposure to testosterone renders males more active and rough-and-tumble in their play, more vulnerable to aggression and antisocial behaviors, and less empathic later in life than females (see, e.g., Chapman et al., 2006; Hines, 2006). Such findings are observed among both animals and humans. In fact, greater prenatal exposure to testosterone by the male versus female brain determines various sex differences in brain structure and function, some of which contribute to large sex differences observed in externalizing behaviors (see below) and other forms of psychopathology (e.g., Bao & Swaab, 2011). At 6–7 weeks in utero, the *Sry* gene on the Y Chromosome initiates development of gonads into testes among males. In turn, testes produce prenatal testosterone between gestational weeks 8 and 24. Nonhuman primate studies show that when macaques are dosed with testosterone prenatally, they exhibit rougher play as juveniles compared to controls (Hines, 2012). Animal studies such as these are invaluable because they rule out environmental effects (e.g., parenting) that are confounded with sex differences in testosterone exposure among humans.

A voluminous literature documents interspecies postnatal effects of circulating testosterone, and to an even greater extent testosterone reactivity to competition, on aggressive behavior (e.g., Carré & Olmstead, 2015). In both animals and humans, higher testosterone levels predict social dominance hierarchies, physical aggression, and provocative reactions to social status violations (see Mehta & Beer, 2010). Among adults, higher testosterone levels are associated with impulsive personality traits, criminality, and ASPD (e.g., Rasanen et al., 1999; Stalenheim, Eriksson, von Knorring, & Wide, 1998). It is important to note, however, that such associations are less consistent among children and adolescents with CD than among antisocial adults (e.g., Constantino et al., 1993) and instead develop over time. In fact, Row, Maughan, Worthman, Costello, and Angold (2004) found that developmental increases in circulating testosterone interacted with deviant peer affiliations to account for increases in antisocial behavior among boys ages 9–15 years. Recent findings suggest that testosterone may exert its effects through deficiencies in top–-down control of aggressive impulses by the OFC (Mehta & Beer, 2010).

Cortisol

Cortisol is produced by the limbic–hypothalamic–pituitary–adrenal axis—a major component of the human stress response system (see, e.g., Doom & Gunnar, 2013). Cortisol release following stress serves short-term supportive functions and long-term restorative functions, including conversion of protein and fats into energy and encouragement of food-seeking behaviors to replenish reserves depleted during active coping (Lupien et al., 2006). Although cortisol responses to stress vary across different forms of psychopathology and are moderated by early experience—most notably maltreatment—many children and adolescents with externalizing disorders including CD exhibit lower diurnal cortisol levels and blunted cortisol reactivity to social and pharmacological challenges (e.g., Beauchaine, Crowell, & Hsiao, 2015; Cicchetti & Rogosch, 2001; Fairchild et al., 2008). Importantly, Alink, Cicchetti, Kim, and Rogosch (2012) reported that maltreatment prospectively predicted lower cortisol levels across 1 year through low prosocial and disruptive/aggressive behavior. This suggests that compromised social functioning may play an important role in neuroendocrine dysregulation among externalizing children who were maltreated. Such findings provide yet another example of the complexity of externalizing etiology. Failure to account for maltreatment and other environmental risk mediators may help to explain null outcomes in other studies of cortisol–externalizing associations (e.g., Klimes-Dogan, Hastings, Granger, Usher, & Zahn-Waxler, 2001; Kryski, Smith, Sheikh, Singh, & Hayden, 2013).

Cognitive vulnerabilities

Although sometimes overlooked in an era in which neurobiological explanations of psychopathology are assigned priority over other mechanisms, cognitive vulnerabilities to CD have been recognized for many years. Foremost among these are hostile attributional biases and CU traits. Children with CD often interpret social behaviors of others as hostile, even when such behaviors are at worst ambiguous (e.g., Dodge & Pettit, 2003). Although such biases are often construed as maladaptive, they may instead reflect adaptive responses to local environments within which affected children are reared—especially contexts of abuse and neglect (cf. Pollak & Sinha, 2002). In fact, aggressive children often ignore current social cues and rely almost entirely on past experiences when evaluating intentions of others in social situations (Dodge & Tomlin, 1987). One interpretation is that aggressive children expect negative evaluations and reactions from peers so they attend selectively to negative cues (see Dodge, 1993). According to social information processing theory, hostile attributional biases drive aggressive social behavior among affected children and adolescents (see, e.g., Dodge, 1980; Dodge, Pettit, McClaskey, & Brown, 1986). Aggressive children up to 50% more likely than controls to interpret neutral behaviors as hostile (Dodge, 1980; Waas, 1988). In turn, hostile attributional biases correlate positively with CD symptoms (Dodge, Price, Bachorowski, & Newman, 1990), over-and-above effects of IQ, socioeconomic status (SES), and race. Perhaps more importantly, aggressive children often see their aggression as both tangibly and instrumentally rewarding and therefore evaluate it positively (Perry, Perry, & Rasmussen, 1986).

More recently, research on CU traits among those with CD has burgeoned given its importance in indicating severity and long-term course (Frick, Ray, Thornton, & Kahn, 2014). As a result, CU traits are now included as a diagnostic specifier in the DSM-5 (American Psychiatric Association, 2013). CU traits include lack of guilt, lack of empathy, and using others for personal gain (see Frick & White, 2008). These traits are stable from late childhood to early adolescence (Frick, Kimonis, Dandreaux, & Farrell, 2003) and predict adult psychopathy, controlling for childhood CPs and antisocial behaviors (Burke, Loeber, & Lahey, 2005). Thus, high CU traits are especially likely among children with early-onset CD who progress to later ASPD (Christian, Frick, Hill, Tyler, & Frazer, 1997; Frick, Stickle, Dandreaux, Farrell, & Kimonis, 2005). Notably, children with high CU traits exhibit a range of cognitive deficits that are not typical among control children or children with CD but low CU traits. These include punishment insensitivity (especially following reward; O'Brien & Frick, 1996; Pardini, Lochman, & Frick, 2003) and positive expectations of aggressive behavior (Pardini, Lochman, & Wells, 2004).

Environmental risk mediators

The genetic vulnerabilities reviewed above confer functional patterns of neural activity and reactivity that are associated with impulsivity and vulnerability to CD and other externalizing disorders. Beginning early in development, heritable mesolimbic DA dysfunction yields an aversive, irritable mood state that affected individuals attempt to avoid via reward-seeking behavior (hyperactivity–impulsivity). If frontal brain regions fail to mature, poor top–down regulation of emotion and behavior by the PFC potentiates subcortical vulnerabilities, facilitating progression of impulsivity to CD and other externalizing outcomes. As described below, adverse environments contribute to cortical dysregulation—as evidenced by their effects on PFC neuromaturation. In sections to follow, we review socioeconomic, family, neighborhood, and peer risk factors that facilitate progression along the externalizing spectrum (see Fig. 3.1).

Poverty/SES

Poverty exerts enduring, often lifelong effects on virtually all aspects of adaptive function (see Luby, 2015). Persistent poverty, defined by living below federal poverty level (FPL) for at least half of a child's life, is associated with 43% lower likelihood of completing college, 35% likelihood of teen pregnancy, 65% likelihood of inconsistent employment at ages 25–30, and 20% likelihood of being arrested by age 20 (Ratcliffe, 2015). It is therefore unsurprising that poverty predicts externalizing outcomes including CD (e.g., Santiago, Wadsworth, & Stump, 2011) and is a potent risk factor for violence, maltreatment, and other forms of trauma that alter neurodevelopment of brain regions implicated in impulse control, executive function, school readiness, and emotion regulation (see Blair & Raver, 2016; Santiago, Kaltman, & Miranda, 2012). In fact, children who are reared below FPL show a 7%–10% reduction in frontal brain volumes compared with children reared above FPL (Hair, Hanson, Wolfe, & Pollak, 2015). These findings have major implications for race disparities in mental health since 39% of Black children are reared in persistent poverty versus 4% of White children (Ratcliffe, 2015). Of course poverty does not exert effects on mental health directly, but rather operates through several interrelated mechanisms, some of which we consider below.

Family risk

As outlined above, child abuse, neglect, and other forms of maltreatment interact with neural and hormonal vulnerabilities to potentiate development of CD and other externalizing behaviors (e.g., Alink et al., 2012; Beauchaine et al., 2017). In the National Incidence Study of Child Abuse and Neglect, children from low SES families were five times more likely to incur maltreatment than their peers (Sedlak, et al., 2010). Notably, such effects are even larger in geographical locals with especially high income disparities (Eckenrode, Smith, McCarthy, & Dineen, 2013).

A number of family characteristics are associated with child maltreatment, and notably, many of these portend risk for CD even in the absence of obvious maltreatment. Most relate to parenting practices, which bidirectionally affect and are affected by children's externalizing behaviors (Pearl, French, Dumas, Moreland, & Prinz, 2014). As described many years ago in painstaking work by Patterson and colleagues, among families with a delinquent child, aggression and emotional lability are negatively reinforced via escape conditioning (e.g., Snyder, Schrepferman, & St. Peter, 1997). This occurs when parents and children escalate dyadic conflict because doing so terminates aversive interactions more quickly (Patterson, DeBaryshe, & Ramsey, 1989). Negative reinforcement of emotional lability and aggression occurs thousands of times throughout development and generalizes to peer groups and other socialization contexts (see Beauchaine & Zalewski, 2016). Of note, although coercive family processes are clearly bidirectional, impulsive children are more likely to evoke coercive parenting, which canalizes emotion dysregulation and aggression (O'Connor, Deater-Deckard, Fulker, Rutter, & Plomin, 1998).

In addition, parents of children with CD are less likely to engage in effective supervision (Frick et al., 1992) and more likely to engage in conflict with one another than other adults (Loeber, Farrington, & Stouthamer-Loeber, 1998). Parents of children with CD often struggle with their own impulse control problems and emotion dysregulation and paradoxically engage in lax parenting that is punctuated by overreactive outbursts (Lorber, 2012). Although data on fathers are sparse, paternal ASPD and SUDs portend risk for CD among offspring (Frick et al., 1992; Loeber, Green, & Keenan, 1995); yet, it is difficult to determine how much heredity versus environment accounts for such findings. In all likelihood, both are involved (Beauchaine & McNulty, 2013; Moffitt, 1993).

Peer and neighborhood risk factors

Impulsive children are much more likely to develop more serious externalizing behaviors—including CD—when reared in low SES neighborhoods that are high in violence and criminality. As reported by Lynam et al. (2000), who used extensive multimethod assessments, impulsive boys engage in more theft and violent crime—core symptoms of CD—when reared in poor neighborhoods. Such effects are either absent or attenuated in middle-class and high SES neighborhoods (see also Meier, Slutske, Arndt, & Cadoret, 2008). In addition to having greater opportunity to engage in crime, children reared in low SES neighborhoods are exposed to a higher density of deviant peers. This is important given strong links between deviant peer group affiliations and progression of delinquent behavior across late childhood and adolescence (e.g., Dishion et al., 1999; Loeber et al., 1995). Deviant peer affiliations and peer contagion are associated with growth in virtually all symptoms of CD, including truancy, substance use, and perpetration of aggression (e.g., Dishion & Tipsord, 2011).

Diagnosis and assessment

Diagnostic and Statistical Manual of Mental Disorders

In clinical settings, DSM-5 (American Psychiatric Association, 2013) criteria are typically used to assess mental disorders in the United States. For CD, both structured and unstructured interviews are common and are usually collected via parent reports given well-documented under-reporting of externalizing symptoms by affected children and adolescents (e.g., Sibley et al., 2010). The most common structured interviews include the Diagnostic Interview Schedule for Children (Shaffer, Fisher, Lucas, Dulcan, & Schwab-Stone, 2000) and the Diagnostic Interview for Children and Adolescents (Reich, Welner, & Herjanic, 1997). Both survey all DSM-5 symptoms and diagnostic features of CD. A common noninterview parent-report instrument that corresponds directly to DSM-5 criteria is the Child and Adolescent Symptom Inventory (Gadow & Sprafkin, 2016). This scale yields both diagnostic cutoffs and dimensional scores, which are useful given that externalizing outcomes are distributed continuously in the population and even subclinical symptoms can be impairing (see Beauchaine & Hinshaw, 2016; Beauchaine et al., 2017; Krueger & Tackett, 2016).

Despite widespread use, two limitations of the DSM are noteworthy. These include failure to consider (1) contextual influences and (2) developmental progression of externalizing behavior. When we ignore these influences, our understanding of etiology is incomplete. For many individuals, cultural and contextual risk factors are especially relevant to understanding CD symptoms (Richters & Cicchetti, 1993). For example, in certain threatening contexts, including high crime neighborhoods, "antisocial" behaviors are adaptive and may even be necessary for survival (see Mead et al., 2010). Similarly, child and adolescent immigrants from war-torn countries may engage in aggressive behaviors for previously adaptive purposes. In such cases, aggressive or delinquent behaviors do not warrant a diagnosis for CD unless they persist for some time in new contexts.

Although the DSM-5 recognizes stability in externalizing behavior by requiring a past CD diagnosis as a criterion for ASPD, considerably more continuity in externalizing behavior is often observed, as depicted by the heterotypic progression in Fig. 3.1 (Beauchaine & McNulty, 2013; Beauchaine et al., 2017). Unfortunately, unlike previous versions of the DSM, the DSM-5 moved ADHD from the disruptive behavior disorders section to the neurodevelopmental disorders section—a change the further obscures its etiological connections to CD and other externalizing disorders. Given space constraints, interested readers are referred elsewhere for further discussion of these and related issues (e.g., Beauchaine & Klein, 2017).

Empirically based taxonomies

In contrast to the DSM, empirically based taxonomies are largely *inductive* and therefore derive from empirical interrelations among symptoms, as assessed using factor analysis. The most commonly used empirically based taxonomy is the Achenbach System of Empirically Based Assessment (ASEBA; Achenbach, 2009), which includes the parent-report Child Behavior Checklist, the Teacher-Report Form (TRF), and Youth Self-Report. ASEBA scales reflect the long-recognized hierarchical latent structure of psychopathology whereby subsyndromes (e.g., anxiety/depression, aggression) load onto higher-order (i.e., broadband) *internalizing* and *externalizing* factors. The externalizing factor, which is comprised of attention problems and aggressive behavior in young children (with rule-breaking added for older children and adolescents), is directly relevant to assessing CD. Given that many externalizing behaviors present in the classroom, the TRF is useful for assessment purposes. Finally, behavior observations are often useful as a source of convergent diagnostic information and can be evaluated using the Direct Observation Form (McConaughy & Achenbach, 2004).

Empirically based taxonomies accommodate elevated scores within and across subsyndromes and higher-order factors, rather than forcing specific diagnoses over others. Instead, individuals can score high on a few or several scales, symptoms of which can be targeted for treatment. Finally, empirically based taxonomies are useful for capturing and assessing heterotypic continuity and shared etiology, which have implications for treatment.

Prevention/intervention

Although specific prevention and intervention strategies for treating CD are detailed in later chapters, here we provide a short summary of selected empirically supported programs. In doing so, we describe general principles for effective treatment and briefly summarize neurobiological mediators of treatment response. We begin with prevention before moving to intervention.

Prevention

As discussed above, high societal costs and treatment resistance of established CD are well documented (see, e.g., Beauchaine et al., 2009; Schmitt et al., 2010; Teplin, 1994). Given this state of affairs, the National Institute of Mental Health initiated the Fast Track prevention trail in the early 1990s [CPs Prevention Group (CPPG), 1992]. In following a developmental model of social factors that shape and maintain CD—as articulated and expanded upon herein—Fast Track components included parent training, home visits and case management, social skills training, tutoring, and teacher training for effective classroom management (see CPPG, 1992). A large sample ($n = 891$) of disruptive first grade children and their parents were enrolled and assigned to either prevention or control groups at the classroom level. Initial outcomes at the end of first grade indicated improved social and emotional skills, reduced CPs, improved parenting, and less disruptive behavior in the classroom (CPPG, 1999a, 1999b). By fourth and fifth grades, Fast Track yielded improved social cognition and social competence, decreased CPs at home, and decreased deviant peer affiliations (CPPG, 2004). Many of these gains were maintained through adolescence and adulthood. In fact, participants who received the intervention exhibited less psychopathology, fewer violent crime and drug convictions, and improved overall well-being compared with controls (CPPG, 2015). These findings are important for at least two reasons. First, they demonstrate that progression of CD can be halted for many children when appropriate mechanisms are targeted. Second, they demonstrate that prevention is far less costly than failing to intervene. As noted above, effective prevention programs for children in this age range who are on CD trajectories cost only 6%–12% of the cumulative 25-year economic burden of untreated CPs (Bonin et al., 2011). Since Fast Track, programs that incorporate similar components have proven efficacious in preventing progression to CD among younger children who are diagnosed with ADHD and ODD (Webster-Stratton, Reid, & Beauchaine, 2011, 2013).

Intervention

In addition to prevention, there are several effective treatment programs for established CD. Given that maintaining factors change from childhood (e.g., family coercion) to adolescence (e.g., peer groups, criminal justice involvement), successful interventions must be adjusted accordingly. We therefore discuss child and adolescent interventions separately.

Childhood

As alluded to above, effective interventions for child CPs target well-known environmental risk factors that maintain and promote aggressive and delinquent behavior. Major components of most effective child interventions therefore include child training, which targets problem solving, social skills, and emotion regulation; parent training, which targets consistency, positive interactions, coercion, and violence; and sometimes teacher training, which targets effective classroom management. A good example of this multicomponent approach is the Incredible Years series (IY; see Webster-Stratton & Hancock, 1998), which improves the quality of parent–child interactions, reduces harsh discipline, promotes academic and social skills, decreases classroom aggression, and improves children's social skills, anger management, and emotion regulation (e.g., Webster-Stratton, Rinaldi, & Reid, 2011). Importantly, IY intervention in late childhood yields sustained effects at long-term follow-ups (e.g., Webster-Stratton et al., 2013). For example, adolescents who complete the program in childhood exhibit lower—and indeed often normal—levels of substance use, sexual activity, and delinquency compared to national norms (e.g., Webster-Stratton et al., 2011).

Adolescence

When children with CD mature into adolescence, their coercive, aggressive, and delinquent behaviors become embedded in social reinforcement systems beyond the family and classroom. Among these reinforcement systems are peer groups, neighborhoods, and in many cases, the criminal justice system (see Dishion & Racer, 2013). The most effective interventions target all of these systems and are therefore more complex and more expensive than earlier intervention. Nevertheless, successful intervention in adolescence is still far cheaper than the economic costs of lifelong delinquency. According to a recent economic analysis, every $1 spent on multisystemic therapy (MST), described immediately below, saves taxpayers from \$10–\$24 compared with costs of persistent criminality (Klietz, Borduin, & Schaeffer, 2010).

MST, which usually lasts 4–6 weeks, targets parenting, delinquent peer group affiliations, adolescent's maladaptive social cognition, aggression, and academic/vocational goals, among other issues (see Henggeler & Borduin, 1990). Treatment teams are multidisciplinary and typically include masters-level therapists and caseworkers, clinical psychologists, and psychiatrists. Caseloads are kept small given the complexity and intensity of the intervention, which includes efforts to work with the criminal justice system to keep participants out jail and prison given high rates of recidivism once incarcerated. Therapist and caseworkers are available to participants at any time of day or night, 7 days a week. A recent meta analysis indicated two especially important findings (van der Stouwe, Asscher, Stams, Deković, & van der Laan, 2014). First, although MST reduces delinquent behavior, it is more effective for younger as opposed to older adolescents. This of course is consistent with the ontogenic process perspective, whereby increasingly intractable externalizing behaviors become canalized through complex, difficult to reverse interactive mechanisms (Beauchaine et al., 2017). Second, although MST reduces delinquency, psychopathology, substance use, and family dysfunction, it does not affect participants' social skills or social cognition. Earlier intervention may be needed to alter these outcomes.

Iatrogenesis

Iatrogenic effects occur when treatment either causes an adverse health condition or worsens an existing condition. When treating children and adolescents with CD in group settings, iatrogenic effects are well documented and occur through "deviancy training," whereby participants both model and reward one another's antisociality (see Dishion & Racer, 2013). Adolescents with externalizing problems who are treated in group settings often exhibit higher levels of delinquency than those who receive no treatment—an effect that persists across impressively long periods of time (Dishion et al., 1999). Contagion of delinquency should therefore be a primary concern when providing treatment for CD, as many intervention programs are delivered in group settings (Boxer, Guerra, Huesmann, & Morales, 2005).

Neurobiological mechanisms

Given (1) recognition that impulsive and delinquent behaviors have clear neurobiological substrates (see above) and (2) advances in neuroimaging, research has begun to address whether successful interventions improve and even normalize neural deficiencies observed among those who are acutely symptomatic. As we have noted elsewhere (e.g., Beauchaine et al., in press), since implicated subcortical structures (e.g., the striatum) mature very early in life, intervention effects are more likely to be observed in cortical brain regions (e.g., the ACC and OFC)—which exhibit neuroplasticity into adulthood (see above)—and in connectivity between cortical and subcortical structures. Consistent with these suppositions, evidence has begun to emerge linking interventions for impulsive and antisocial behavior to changes in PFC function (see Cornet, de Kogel, Nijman, Raine, & van der Laan, 2015). The few studies that exist report reduced activity in functional subdivisions of PFC and improved connectivity between cortical and subcortical structures (e.g., Rubia, Halari, et al., 2009; Woltering, Granic, Lamm, & Lewis, 2011). More effective top–down regulation of the subcortex by the cortex has also been reported (e.g., Regner et al., 2016), which likely reflects improved self-regulation and emotion regulation (see Lewis et al., 2008).

Conclusions and future directions

Conduct disorder—defined in the DSM-5 (American Psychiatric Association, 2013) as "A repetitive and persistent pattern of behavior in which basic rights of others or major age-appropriate societal norms or rules are violated. . ." (p. 469) —exacts tremendous costs on individuals, families, victims of property offenses and violent crimes, and societal institutions including the legal and criminal justice systems. Traditionally, CD has been treated as a distinct disorder in our diagnostic nomenclature, even though the research community has recognized for decades that males who develop ASPD almost invariably traverse a developmental pathway that begins in preschool with highly heritable hyperactivity–impulsivity (ADHD), and progresses to oppositionality (ODD), aggression and delinquency (CD), SUDs, ASPD, and incarceration and recidivism. In large part because ADHD, ODD, CD, SUDs, and ASPD are treated as separate disorders, distinct literatures—both basic and applied—have evolved for each. In this chapter and elsewhere, we argue that treating these disorders as distinct obscures their common etiologies and masks longitudinal pathways to CD, delinquency, and criminality (Beauchaine & Hinshaw, 2016; Beauchaine & McNulty, 2013; Beauchaine et al., 2017). We suggest further that externalizing behaviors are more accurately described along an *ontogenic developmental spectrum*. According to this perspective, progression of early-onset externalizing behavior is viewed as a product of interdependent individual-level vulnerabilities (e.g., genetic, epigenetic, neural) interacting with equally interdependent contextual risk factors (e.g., coercive parenting, deviant peer group affiliations, neighborhood criminality). This model is supported at behavioral genetic, molecular genetic, neural, and environmental levels of analysis.

A corollary of the ontogenic process perspective is that advanced externalizing behaviors—like end-state outcomes of all multifactorial diseases and traits—are difficult to reverse once established (see Beauchaine & Cicchetti, 2016). Over time, externalizing behaviors become embedded in an ever-expanding array of environmental reinforcement systems that not only maintain and magnify delinquency and criminality, but fundamentally alter structure and function of neural systems implicated in self-control and emotion regulation. Thus, the future of treatment is *prevention*, which, as outlined above, is far more effective than intervention, both behaviorally and economically. On the bright side, two generations of research have provided means of identifying highly vulnerable children, and very effective prevention programs exist. Somewhat discouragingly, however, few vulnerable children receive prevention services. Furthermore, those who receive treatment are typically identified only after CD emerges, at which time they are aggregated in group settings that often worsen the very behaviors being treated.

The general pattern described above, whereby multifactorial vulnerabilities respond better to early versus later intervention, is not unique to externalizing behavior. For example, both the research and treatment communities recognize the importance of early intensive intervention for autism spectrum disorder (ASD). For ASD, early intensive intervention often has profound, lifelong effects on adaptive function (e.g., Bernier & Dawson, 2016). In contrast to ASD, CD-related behaviors are often viewed pejoratively because they are thought to be volitional. It can therefore be difficult to convince the public, states, and funding agencies that CD is a mental health condition that requires investment to prevent. As a result, levels of funding for research on CD and delinquency have stagnated (see above). We find this particularly troubling given how many children, through no fault of their own, are reared in poverty (disproportionately children of color). As outlined above, a range of interactive influences that correlate with poverty potentiate heritable vulnerabilities among affected children. For many, these vulnerabilities might never coalesce into CD/delinquency in protective environments.

Following from this discussion, three major tasks for the future are to (1) create a public discourse in which those affected by poverty and other forms of adversity are no longer blamed for their predicaments, (2) counter the understandable reluctance of parents and educators to identify vulnerable children as "problems" very in life, so that (3) what we already know about early intervention might be applied for more children. These tasks are undoubtedly more difficult than the work that lies behind us. Hopefully we are up to the task.

Funding

Preparation of this chapter was supported by grant DE025980 from the National Institute of Dental and Craniofacial Research, and by the National Institutes of Health Science of Behavior Change (SoBC) Common Fund.

References

Achenbach, T. M. (2009). *Achenbach System of Empirically Based Assessment (ASEBA): Development, findings, theory, and applications*. Burlington, VT: University of Vermont Research Center for Children, Youth, and Families.

Alink, L. R. A., Cicchetti, D., Kim, J., & Rogosch, F. A. (2012). Longitudinal associations among child maltreatment, social functioning, and cortisol regulation. *Developmental Psychology*, *48*, 224–236.

American Psychiatric Association. (1952). *Diagnostic and statistical manual of mental disorders*. Washington, DC: Author.

American Psychiatric Association. (1968). *Diagnostic and statistical manual of mental disorders* (2nd ed.). Washington, DC: Author.

American Psychiatric Association. (1980). *Diagnostic and statistical manual of mental disorders* (3rd ed.). Washington, DC: Author.

American Psychiatric Association. (1994). *Diagnostic and statistical manual of mental disorders* (4th ed.). Washington, DC: Author.

American Psychiatric Association. (2013). *Diagnostic and statistical manual of mental disorders* (5th ed.). Arlington, VA: American Psychiatric Press.

Arcos-Burgos, M., & Muenke, M. (2010). Toward a better understanding of ADHD: LPHN3 gene variants and the susceptibility to develop ADHD. *Attention Deficit and Hyperactivity Disorders*, *2*, 139–147.

Arcos-Burgos, M., Vélez, J. I., Solomon, B. D., & Muenke, M. (2012). A common genetic network underlies substance use disorders and disruptive or externalizing disorders. *Human Genetics*, *131*, 917–929.

Ashby, F. G., Isen, A. M., & Turken, A. U. (1999). A neuropsychological theory of positive affect and its influence on cognition. *Psychological Review*, *106*, 529–550.

Bao, A.-M., & Swaab, D. F. (2011). Sexual differentiation of the human brain: Relation to gender identity, sexual orientation and neuropsychiatric disorders. *Frontiers in Neuroendocrinology*, *32*, 214–226.

Barkley, R. (1995). Sex differences in ADHD. *The ADHD Report*, *3*, 1–5.

Bava, S., Jacobus, J., Thayer, R. E., & Tapert, S. F. (2013). Longitudinal changes in white matter integrity among adolescent substance users. *Alcohol Clinical and Experimental Research*, *37*, E181–E189.

Beach, S. R. H., Brody, G. H., Dodorov, A. A., Gunter, T. D., & Philibert, R. A. (2011). Methylation of 5HTT mediates the impact of child sex abuse on women's antisocial behavior: An examination of the Iowa Adoptee Sample. *Psychosomatic Medicine*, *73*, 83–87.

Beach, S. R. H., Brody, G. H., Lei, M. K., Gibbons, F. X., Gerrard, M., Simons, R. L., ... Philibert, R. A. (2013). Impact of child sex abuse on adult psychopathology: A genetically and epigenetically informed investigation. *Journal of Family Psychology*, *27*, 3–11.

Beauchaine, T. P. (2015). Future directions in emotion dysregulation and youth psychopathology. *Journal of Clinical Child and Adolescent Psychology*, *44*, 875–896.

Beauchaine, T. P., & Cicchetti, D. (2016). A new generation of comorbidity research in the era of neuroscience and the Research Domain Criteria. *Development and Psychopathology*, *28*, 891–894.

Beauchaine, T. P., & Constantino, J. N. (2017). Redefining the endophenotype concept to accommodate transdiagnostic vulnerabilities and etiological complexities. *Biomarkers in Medicine*, *11*, 769–780.

Beauchaine, T. P., Crowell, S. E., & Hsiao, R. (2015). Post-dexamethasone cortisol, self-inflicted injury, and suicidal ideation among depressed adolescent girls. *Journal of Abnormal Child Psychology*, *43*, 619–632.

Beauchaine, T. P., Gatzke-Kopp, L. M., & Gizer, I. R. (2017). Genetic, environmental, and epigenetic influences on behavior. In T. P. Beauchaine, & S. P. Hinshaw (Eds.), *Child and adolescent psychopathology* (3rd ed., pp. 68–109). Hoboken, NJ: Wiley.

Beauchaine, T. P., & Hayden, E. P. (2016). Child and adolescent disorders. In J. C. Norcross, G. R. VandenBos, & D. K. Freedheim (Eds.), *American Psychological Association handbook of clinical psychology. Vol. IV: Psychopathology and health* (pp. 135–171). Washington, DC: Author.

Beauchaine, T. P., & Hinshaw, S. P. (Eds.), (2016). *The Oxford handbook of externalizing spectrum disorders*. New York, NY: Oxford University Press.

Beauchaine, T. P., & Klein, D. N. (2017). Classifying psychopathology: The DSM, empirically supported taxonomies, and the Research Domain Criteria. In T. P. Beauchaine, & S. P. Hinshaw (Eds.), *Child and adolescent psychopathology* (3rd ed., pp. 33–67). Hoboken, NJ: Wiley.

Beauchaine, T. P., Klein, D. N., Crowell, S. E., Derbidge, C., & Gatzke-Kopp, L. (2009). Multifinality in the development of personality disorders: A Biology × Sex × Environment interaction model of antisocial and borderline traits. *Development and Psychopathology*, *21*, 735–770.

Beauchaine, T. P., & McNulty, T. (2013). Comorbidities and continuities as ontogenic processes: Toward a developmental spectrum model of externalizing behavior. *Development and Psychopathology*, *25*, 1505–1528.

Beauchaine, T. P., Neuhaus, E., Zalewski, M., Crowell, S. E., & Potapova, N. (2011). Effects of allostatic load on neural systems subserving motivation, mood regulation, and social affiliation. *Development and Psychopathology*, *23*, 975–999.

Beauchaine, T. P., Shader, T. M., & Hinshaw, S. P. (2016). An ontogenic process model of externalizing psychopathology. In T. P. Beauchaine, & S. P. Hinshaw (Eds.), *The Oxford handbook of externalizing spectrum disorders* (pp. 485–501). New York, NY: Oxford University Press.

Beauchaine, T. P., & Zalewski, M. (2016). Physiological and developmental mechanisms of emotional lability in coercive relationships. In T. J. Dishion, & J. J. Snyder (Eds.), *The Oxford handbook of coercive relationship dynamics* (pp. 39–52). New York, NY: Oxford University Press.

Beauchaine, T. P., Zisner, A. R., & Hayden, E. P. (in press). Neurobiological mechanisms of psychopathology and treatment action. In T. H. Ollendick, S. W. White, & B. A. White (Eds.), *The Oxford handbook of clinical child and adolescent psychology*. New York, NY: Oxford University Press.

Beauchaine, T. P., Zisner, A., & Sauder, C. L. (2017). Trait impulsivity and the externalizing spectrum. *Annual Review of Clinical Psychology*, *13*, 343–368.

Bernier, R., & Dawson, G. (2016). Autism spectrum disorders. In D. Cicchetti (Ed.), *Developmental psychopathology. Vol. 3: Maladaptation and psychopathology* (3rd ed., pp. 81–115). Hoboken, NJ: Wiley.

Berridge, K. C. (2003). Pleasures of the brain. *Brain and Cognition*, *52*, 106–128.

Blair, C., & Raver, C. C. (2016). Poverty, stress, and brain development: New directions for prevention and intervention. *Academic Pediatrics*, *16*, S30–S36.

Bonin, E.-M., Stevens, M., Beecham, J., Byford, S., & Parsonage, M. (2011). Costs and longer-term savings of parenting programmes for the prevention of persistent conduct disorder: A modelling study. *BMC Public Health*, *11*, 803.

Boxer, P., Guerra, N. G., Huesmann, L. R., & Morales, J. (2005). Proximal peer-level effects of a small-group selected prevention on aggression in elementary school children: An investigation of the peer contagion hypothesis. *Journal of Abnormal Child Psychology*, *33*, 325–338.

Brain Development Cooperative Group. (2012). Total and regional brain volumes in a population-based normative sample from 4 to 18 years: The NIH MRI Study of Normal Brain Development. *Cerebral Cortex*, *22*, 1–12.

Burke, J. D., Loeber, R., & Lahey, B. B. (2005). Developmental transitions among affective and behavioral disorders in adolescent boys. *Journal of Child Psychology and Psychiatry*, *46*, 1200–1210.

Burt, S. A. (2009). Rethinking environmental contributions to child and adolescent psychopathology: A meta-analysis of shared environmental influences. *Psychological Bulletin*, *135*, 608–637.

Burt, S. A., Krueger, R. F., McGue, M., & Iacono, W. G. (2001). Sources of covariation among attention-deficit/hyperactivity disorder, oppositional defiant disorder, and conduct disorder: The importance of shared environment. *Journal of Abnormal Psychology*, *110*, 516–525.

Button, T. M. M., Corley, R. P., Rhee, S. H., Hewitt, J. K., Young, S. E., & Stallings, M. C. (2007). Delinquent peer affiliation and conduct problems: A twin study. *Journal of Abnormal Psychology*, *116*, 554–564.

Carré, J. M., & Olmstead, N. A. (2015). Social neuroendocrinology of human aggression: Examining the role of competition-induced testosterone dynamics. *Neuroscience*, *286*, 171–186.

Casey, B. J., Jones, R. M., & Hare, T. A. (2008). The adolescent brain. *The Year in Cognitive Neuroscience*, *1124*, 111–126.

Caspi, A., McClay, J., Moffitt, T. E., Mill, J., Martin, J., Craig, I. W., … Poulton, R. (2002). Role of genotype in the cycle of violence in maltreated children. *Science*, *297*, 851–854.

Castellanos-Ryan, N., & Séguin, J. R. (2016). Prefrontal and anterior cingulate cortex mechanisms of impulsivity. In T. P. Beauchaine, & S. P. Hinshaw (Eds.), *The Oxford handbook of externalizing spectrum disorders* (pp. 201–219). New York, NY: Oxford University Press.

Chapman, E., Baron-Cohen, S., Auyeung, B., Knickmeyer, R., Taylor, K., & Hackett, G. (2006). Fetal testosterone and empathy: Evidence from the Empathy Quotient (EQ) and the "Reading the Mind in the Eyes" test. *Social Neuroscience*, *1*, 135–148.

Chen, D., Liu, F., Shang, Q., Song, X., Miao, X., & Wang, Z. (2011). Association between polymorphisms of DRD2 and DRD4 and opioid dependence: Evidence from the current studies. *American Journal of Medical Genetics Part B: Neuropsychiatric Genetics*, *156B*, 661–670.

Christian, R. E., Frick, P. J., Hill, N. L., Tyler, L., & Frazer, D. (1997). Psychopathy and conduct problems in children: II. Implications for subtyping children with conduct problems. *Journal of the American Academy of Child and Adolescent Psychiatry*, *36*, 233–241.

Cicchetti, D., & Rogosch, F. A. (2001). The impact of child maltreatment and psychopathology on neuroendocrine functioning. *Development and Psychopathology*, *13*, 783–804.

Conduct Problems Prevention Research Group. (1992). A developmental and clinical model for the prevention of conduct disorders: The Fast Track Program. *Development and Psychopathology*, *4*, 509–527.

Conduct Problems Prevention Research Group. (1999a). Initial impact of the Fast Track prevention trial for conduct problems: I. The high-risk sample. *Journal of Consulting and Clinical Psychology*, *67*, 631–647.

Conduct Problems Prevention Research Group. (1999b). Initial impact of the Fast Track prevention trial for conduct problems: II. Classroom effects. *Journal of Consulting Clinical Psychology*, *67*, 648–657.

Conduct Problems Prevention Research Group. (2004). The effects of the Fast Track program on serious problem outcomes at the end of elementary school. *Journal of Clinical Child and Adolescent Psychology*, *33*, 650–661.

Conduct Problems Prevention Research Group. (2015). Impact of early intervention on psycho-pathology, crime, and well-being at age 25. *American Journal of Psychiatry*, *172*, 59–70.

Constantino, J. N., Grosz, D., Saenger, P., Chandler, D. W., Nandi, R., & Earls, F. J. (1993). Testosterone and aggression in children. *Journal of the American Academy of Child and Adolescent Psychiatry*, *32*, 1217–1222.

Cornet, L. J. M., de Kogel, C. H., Nijman, H. L. I., Raine, A., & van der Laan, P. H. (2015). Neurobiological changes after intervention in individuals with anti-social behaviour: A literature review. *Criminal Behaviour and Mental Health*, *25*, 10–27.

Cubillo, A., Halari, R., Smith, A., Taylor, E., & Rubia, K. (2012). A review of fronto-striatal and fronto-cortical brain abnormalities in children and adults with ADHD and new evidence for dysfunction in adults with ADHD during motivation and attention. *Cortex*, *48*, 194–214.

Dalley, J. W., Mar, A. C., Economidou, D., & Robbins, T. W. (2008). Neurobehavioral mechanisms of impulsivity: Fronto-striatal systems and functional neurochemistry. *Pharmacology, Biochemistry, and Behavior*, *90*, 250–260.

Dalley, J. W., & Rosier, J. P. (2012). Dopamine, serotonin, and impulsivity. *Neuroscience*, *215*, 42–58.

De Bellis, M. D., Narasimhan, A., Thatcher, D. L., Keshavan, M. S., Soloff, P., & Clark, D. B. (2005). Prefrontal cortex, thalamus, and cerebellar volumes in adolescents and young adults with adolescent-onset alcohol use disorders and comorbid mental disorders. *Alcoholism Clinical and Experimental Research*, *29*, 1590–1600.

De Brito, S. A., Mechelli, A., Wilke, M., Laurens, K. R., Jones, A. P., ... Viding, E. (2009). Size matters: Increased grey matter in boys with conduct problems and callous-unemotional traits. *Brain*, *132*, 843–852.

DeYoung, C. G., Getchell, M., Koposov, R. A., Yrigollen, C. M., Haeffel, G. J., Klinteberg, B., ... Grigorenko, E. L. (2010). Variation in the catechol-*O*-methyltransferase polymorphism associated with conduct disorder and ADHD symptoms among adolescent male delinquents. *Psychiatric Genetics*, *20*, 20–24.

Dhamija, D., Tuvblad, C., & Baker, L. A. (2016). Behavioral genetics of the externalizing spectrum. In T. P. Beauchaine, & S. P. Hinshaw (Eds.), *The Oxford handbook of externalizing spectrum disorders* (pp. 105–124). New York, NY: Oxford University Press.

Dick, D. M., Aliev, F., Wang, J. C., Grucza, R. A., Schuckit, M., Kuperman, S., ... Goate, A. (2008). Using dimensional models of externalizing psychopathology to aid in gene identification. *Archives of General Psychiatry*, *65*, 310–318.

Dick, D. M., Bierut, L. J., Hinrichs, A., Fox, L., Bucholz, K. K., Kramer, J., ... Foroud, T. (2006). The role of GABRA2 in risk for conduct disorder and alcohol and drug dependence across developmental stages. *Behavior Genetics*, *36*, 577–590.

Dishion, T. J., McCord, J., & Poulin, F. (1999). When interventions harm: Peer groups and problem behavior. *American Psychologist*, *54*, 755–764.

Dishion, T. J., & Racer, K. H. (2013). Development of adult antisocial behavior. In T. P. Beauchaine, & S. P. Hinshaw (Eds.), *Child and adolescent psychopathology* (2nd ed., pp. 453–488). Hoboken, NJ: Wiley.

Dishion, T. J., & Tipsord, J. M. (2011). Peer contagion in child and adolescent social and emotional development. *Annual Review of Psychology*, *62*, 189–214.

Dodge, K. A. (1980). Social cognition and children's aggressive behavior. *Child Development*, *51*, 162–170.

Dodge, K. A. (1993). Social-cognitive mechanisms in the development of conduct disorder and depression. *Annual Review of Psychology*, *44*, 559–584.

Dodge, K. A., & Pettit, G. S. (2003). A biopsychosocial model of the development of chronic conduct problems in adolescence. *Developmental Psychology*, *39*, 349–371.

Dodge, K. A., Pettit, G. S., McClaskey, C. L., & Brown, M. (1986). Social competence in children. *Monographs of the Society for Research in Child Development*, *51*. (2, Serial No. 213).

Dodge, K. A., Price, J. M., Bachorowski, J., & Newman, J. P. (1990). Hostile attributional biases in severely aggressive adolescents. *Journal of Abnormal Psychology*, *99*, 385–392.

Dodge, K. A., & Tomlin, A. (1987). Cue utilization as a mechanism of attributional bias in aggressive children. *Social Cognition*, *5*, 280–300.

Doom, J. R., & Gunnar, M. R. (2013). Stress physiology and developmental psychopathology: Past, present, and future. *Development and Psychopathology*, *25*, 1359–1373.

Dyck, R. J., Bland, R. C., Newman, S. C., & Orn, H. (1988). Suicide attempts in psychiatric disorders in Edmonton. *Acta Psychiatrica Scandinavia*, *77*, 64–71.

Eckenrode, J., Smith, E. G., McCarthy, M. E., & Dineen, M. (2013). Income inequality and child maltreatment in the United States. *Pediatrics*, *133*, 454–461.

Ehlers, C. L., Gilder, D. A., Slutske, W. S., Lind, P. A., & Wilhelmsen, K. C. (2008). Externalizing disorders in American Indians: Comorbidity and a genome wide linkage analysis. *American Journal of Medical Genetics Part B: Neuropsychiatric Genetics*, *156B*, 772–780.

Elia, J., Gai, X., Xie, H. M., Perin, J. C., Geiger, E., Glessner, J. T., ... White, P. S. (2010). Rare structural variants found in attention-deficit hyperactivity disorder are preferentially associated with neurodevelopmental genes. *Molecular Psychiatry*, *15*, 637–646.

Fairchild, G., van Goozen, S. H. M., Stollery, S. J., Brown, J., Gardiner, J., Herbert, J., & Goodyer, I. M. (2008). Cortisol diurnal rhythm and stress reactivity in male adolescents with early-onset or adolescence-onset conduct disorder. *Biological Psychiatry*, *64*, 599–606.

Faraone, S. V., & Mick, E. (2010). Molecular genetics of attention-deficit/hyperactivity disorder. *Psychiatric Clinics of North America*, *33*, 159–180.

Farrington, D., Ohlin, L., & Wilson, J. Q. (1986). *Understanding and controlling crime*. New York, NY: Springer-Verlag.

Fonnum, F., & Mariussen, E. (2009). Mechanisms involved in the neurotoxic effects of environmental toxicants such as polychlorinated biphenyls and brominated flame retardants. *Journal of Neurochemistry*, *111*, 1327–1347.

Frick, P. J., Kimonis, E. R., Dandreaux, D. M., & Farrell, J. M. (2003). The 4-year stability of psychopathic traits in non-referred youth. *Behavioral Sciences and the Law*, *21*, 713–736.

Frick, P. J., Lahey, B. B., Loeber, R., Stouthamer-Loeber, M., Christ, M. A., & Hanson, K. (1992). Familial risk factors to oppositional defiant disorder and conduct disorder: Parental psycho-pathology and maternal parenting. *Journal of Consulting and Clinical Psychology*, *60*, 49–55.

Frick, P. J., Ray, J. V., Thornton, L. C., & Kahn, R. E. (2014). Can callous-unemotional traits enhance the understanding, diagnosis, and treatment of serious conduct problems in children and adolescents? A comprehensive review. *Psychological Bulletin*, *140*, 1–57.

Frick, P. J., Stickle, T. R., Dandreaux, D. M., Farrell, J. M., & Kimonis, E. R. (2005). Callous-unemotional traits in predicting the severity and stability of conduct problems and delinquency. *Journal of Abnormal Child Psychology*, *33*, 471–487.

Frick, P. J., & White, S. F. (2008). Research review: The importance of callous-unemotional traits for developmental models of aggressive and antisocial behavior. *Journal of Child Psychology and Psychiatry*, *49*, 359–375.

Gadow, K. D., & Sprafkin, J. (2016). *Child and Adolescent Symptom Inventory-5*. Stony Brook, NY: Checkmate Plus.

Gatzke-Kopp, L. M. (2011). The canary in the coalmine: The sensitivity of mesolimbic dopamine to environmental adversity during development. *Neuroscience and Biobehavioral Reviews*, *35*, 794–803.

Gatzke-Kopp, L. M., Beauchaine, T. P., Shannon, K. E., Chipman-Chacon, J., Fleming, A. P., Crowell, S. E., . . . Aylward, E. (2009). Neurological correlates of reward responding in adolescents with and without externalizing behavior disorders. *Journal of Abnormal Psychology*, *118*, 203–213.

Gelernter, J., Panhuysen, C., Weiss, R., Brady, K., Hesselbrock, V., Rounsaville, B., . . . Kranzler, H. R. (2005). Genomewide linkage scan for cocaine dependence and related traits: Significant linkages for a cocaine-related trait and cocaine-induced paranoia. *American Journal of Medical Genetics Part B: Neuropsychiatric Genetics*, *136B*, 45–52.

Girirajan, S., Campbell, C. D., & Eichle, E. E. (2011). Human copy number variation and complex genetic disease. *Annual Review of Genetics*, *45*, 203–226.

Gizer, I. R., Ficks, C., & Waldman, I. D. (2009). Candidate gene studies of ADHD: A meta-analytic review. *Human Genetics*, *126*, 51–90.

Gizer, I. R., Otto, J. M., & Ellingson, J. M. (2016). Molecular genetics of the externalizing spectrum. In T. P. Beauchaine, & S. P. Hinshaw (Eds.), *The Oxford handbook of externalizing spectrum disorders* (pp. 149–169). New York, NY: Oxford University Press.

Golmaryami, F. N., & Frick, P. J. (2016). Callous-unemotional traits and the development of externalizing spectrum disorders. In T. P. Beauchaine, & S. P. Hinshaw (Eds.), *The Oxford handbook of externalizing spectrum disorders* (pp. 360–374). New York, NY: Oxford University Press.

Hair, N. L., Hanson, J. L., Wolfe, B. L., & Pollak, S. D. (2015). Association of child poverty, brain development, and academic achievement. *JAMA Pediatrics*, *169*, 822–829.

Hayes, D. J., & Greenshaw, A. J. (2011). 5-HT receptors and reward-related behavior: A review. *Neuroscience and Biobehavioral Reviews*, *35*, 1419–1449.

Heatherton, T. F. (2011). Neuroscience of self and self-regulation. *Annual Review of Psychology*, *62*, 363–390.

Heatherton, T. F., & Wagner, D. D. (2011). Cognitive neuroscience of self-regulation failure. *Trends in Cognitive Science*, *15*, 132–139.

Henggeler, S. W., & Borduin, C. M. (1990). *Family therapy and beyond: A multisystemic approach to treating the behavior problems of children and adolescents*. Pacific Grove, CA: Brooks/Cole.

Herman, A. I., & Balogh, K. N. (2012). Polymorphisms of the serotonin transporter and receptor genes: Susceptibility to substance abuse. *Substance Abuse and Rehabilitation*, *3*, 49–57.

Hill, S. Y., Zezz, N., Wipprecht, G., Xu, J., & Nesiwanger, K. (1999). Linkage studies of D2 and D4 receptor genes and alcoholism. *American Journal of Medical Genetics*, *88*, 676–685.

Hines, M. (2006). Prenatal testosterone and gender-related behaviour. *European Journal of Endocrinology*, *155*, S115–S121.

Hines, M. (2012). Sex and sex differences. In P. Zelaxo (Ed.), *Oxford handbook of developmental psychology* (Vol. 1, pp. 164–201). New York, NY: Oxford University Press.

Holmes, J., Payton, A., Barrett, J., Harrington, R., McGuffin, P., Owen, M., ... Thapar, A. (2002). Association of DRD4 in children with ADHD and comorbid conduct problems. *American Journal of Medical Genetics*, *114*, 150–153.

Hopfer, C. J., Timberlake, D., Haberstick, B., Lessem, J. M., Ehringer, M. A., Smolen, A., & Hewitt, J. K. (2005). Genetic influences on quantity of alcohol consumed by adolescents and young adults. *Drug and Alcohol Dependence*, *78*, 187–193.

Huebner, T., Vloet, T. D., Marx, I., Konrad, K., Fink, G. R., Herpertz, S. C., & Herpertz-Dahlmann, B. (2008). Morphometric brain abnormalities in boys with conduct disorder. *Journal of the American Academy of Child and Adolescent Psychiatry*, *47*, 540–547.

Imbrici, P., Camerino, P. C., & Tricarico, D. (2013). Major channels involved in neuropsychiatric disorders and therapeutic perspectives. *Frontiers in Genetics*, *4*, 76.

Insel, T. R. (2017). *The anatomy of NIMH funding*. Downloaded from https://www.nimh.nih.gov/funding/funding-strategy-for-research-grants/the-anatomy-of-nimh-funding.shtml.

Jönsson, E. G., Nöthen, M. M., Grünhage, F., Farde, L., Nakashima, Y., Propping, P., & Sedvall, G. C. (1999). Polymorphisms in the dopamine D2 receptor gene and their relationships to striatal dopamine receptor density of healthy volunteers. *Molecular Psychiatry*, *4*, 290–296.

Keenan, K., Loeber, R., & Green, S. (1999). Conduct disorder in girls: A review of the literature. *Clinical Child and Family Psychology Review*, *2*, 3–19.

Kendler, K. S., Kuo, P.-H., Webb, B. T., Kalsi, G., Neale, M. C., Sullivan, P. F., ... Prescott, C. A. (2006). A joint genome-wide linkage analysis of symptoms of alcohol dependence and conduct disorder. *Alcoholism: Clinical and Experimental Research*, *30*, 1972–1977.

Kessler, R. C., McGonagle, K. A., Zhao, S. Y., Nelson, C. B., Hughes, M., Eshlemen, S., ... Kendler, K. S. (1994). Lifetime and 12-month prevalence of DSM-III-R psychiatric disorders in the United States—Results of the National Comorbidity Survey. *Archives of General Psychiatry*, *51*, 8–19.

Kimonis, E. R., Frick, P. J., & McMahon, R. J. (2014). Conduct and oppositional defiant disorders. In E. J. Mash, & R. A. Barkley (Eds.), *Child psychopathology* (3rd ed., pp. 145–179). New York, NY: Guilford.

Kirley, A., Low, N., Mullins, C., McCarron, M., Daley, G., Waldman, I., ... Hawi, Z. (2004). Phenotype studies of the DRD4 gene polymorphisms in ADHD: Association with oppositional defiant disorder and positive family history. *American Journal of Medical Genetics Part B: Neuropsychiatric Genetics*, *131B*, 38–42.

Klietz, S. J., Borduin, C. M., & Schaeffer, C. M. (2010). Cost-benefit analysis of multisystemic therapy with serious and violent juvenile offenders. *Journal of Family Psychology*, *24*, 657–666.

Klimes-Dogan, B., Hastings, P. D., Granger, D. A., Usher, B. A., & Zahn-Waxler, C. (2001). Adrenocortical activity in at-risk and normally developing adolescents: Individual differences in salivary cortisol basal levels, diurnal variation, and responses to social challenges. *Development and Psychopathology*, *13*, 695–719.

Kraemer, S. (2000). The fragile male. *British Medical Journal*, *321*, 1609–1612.

Krueger, R. F., Hicks, B. M., Patrick, C. J., Carlson, S. R., Iacono, W. G., & McGue, M. (2002). Etiologic connections among substance dependence, antisocial behavior, and personality: Modeling the externalizing spectrum. *Journal of Abnormal Psychology*, *111*, 411–424.

Krueger, R. F., & Tackett, J. L. (2016). The externalizing spectrum of personality and psychopathology: Empirical and quantitative alternative to discrete disorder approaches.

In T. P. Beauchiane, & S. P. Hinshaw (Eds.), *The Oxford handbook of externalizing spectrum disorders* (pp. 79–89). New York, NY: Oxford University Press.

Kryski, K. R., Smith, H. J., Sheikh, H., Singh, S. M., & Hayden, E. P. (2013). HPA axis reactivity in early childhood: Associations with symptoms and moderation by sex. *Psychoneuroendocrinology*, *38*, 2327–2336.

Kubrusly, R. C., & Bhide, P. G. (2010). Cocaine exposure modulates dopamine and adenosine signaling in the fetal brain. *Neuropharmacology*, *58*, 436–443.

Kuperstein, F., Eilam, R., & Yavin, E. (2008). Altered expression of key dopaminergic regulatory proteins in the postnatal brain following perinatal n-3 fatty acid dietary deficiency. *Journal of Neurochemistry*, *106*, 662–671.

Laakso, A., Wallius, E., Kajander, J., Bergman, J., Eskola, O., Solin, O., ... Hietala, J. (2003). Personality traits and striatal dopamine synthesis capacity in healthy subjects. *American Journal of Psychiatry*, *160*, 904–910.

Lahey, B. B., Loeber, R. F., Quay, H. C., Applegate, B., Shaffer, D., Waldman, I., ... Bird, H. R. (1998). Validity of DSM-IV subtypes of conduct disorder based on age of onset. *Journal of the American Academy of Child and Adolescent Psychiatry*, *37*, 435–442.

Lahey, B. B., & Waldman, I. D. (2017). Oppositional defiant disorder, conduct disorder, and juvenile delinquency. In T. P. Beauchaine, & S. P. Hinshaw (Eds.), *Child and adolescent psychopathology* (3rd ed., pp. 449–496). New York, NY: Oxford University Press.

Lasky-Su, J., Banaschewski, T., Buitelaar, J., Franke, B., Brookes, K., Sonuga-arke, E., ... Faraone, S. V. (2007). Partial replication of a DRD4 association in ADHD individuals using a statistically derived quantitative trait for ADHD in a family-based association test. *Biological Psychiatry*, *62*, 985–990.

Le Foll, B., Gallo, A., Le Strat, Y., Lu, L., & Gorwood, P. (2009). Genetics of dopamine receptors and drug addiction: A comprehensive review. *Behavioral Pharmacology*, *20*, 1–17.

Lesch, K.-P., Anney, R. J. L., Neale, B. M., Franke, B., Zhou, K., Maller, J. B., ... Faraone, S. V. (2008). Genome-wide association scan of the time to onset of ADHD. *American Journal of Medical Genetics Part B; Neuropsychiatric Genetics*, *147B*, 1355–1358.

Lesch, K.-P., Selchl, S., Renner, T. J., Jacob, C., Nguyen, T. T., Hahn, T., ... Ullmann, R. (2011). Genome-wide copy number variation analysis in ADHD: Association with neuropeptide Y gene dosage in an extended pedigree. *Molecular Psychiatry*, *16*, 491–503.

Lesch, K.-P., Timmesfeld, N., Renner, T. J., Halperin, R., Röser, C., Nguyen, T. T., ... Jacob, C. (2008). Molecular genetics of adult ADHD: Converging evidence from genome-wide association and extended pedigree linkage studies. *Journal of Neural Transmission*, *115*, 1573–1585.

Lewis, M. D., Granic, I., Lamm, C., Zelazo, P. D., Stieben, J., Todd, R. M., ... Pepler, D. (2008). Changes in the neural bases of emotion regulation associated with clinical improvement in children with behavior problems. *Development and Psychopathology*, *20*, 913–939.

Li, D., Sham, P. C., Owen, M. J., & He, L. (2006). Meta-analysis shows significant association between dopamine system genes and attention deficit hyperactivity disorder (ADHD). *Human Molecular Genetics*, *15*, 2276–2284.

Loeber, R., Farrington, D. P., & Stouthamer-Loeber, M. (1998). *Antisocial behavior and mental health problems: Explanatory factors in childhood and adolescence*. Mahwah, NJ: Erlbaum.

Loeber, R., Green, S. M., & Keenan, K. (1995). Which boys will fare worse? Early predictors of the onset of conduct disorder in a six-year longitudinal study. *Journal of the American Academy of Child and Adolescent Psychiatry*, *34*, 499–509.

Loeber, R., & Hay, D. (1997). Key issues in the development of aggression and violence from childhood to early adulthood. *Annual Review of Psychology*, *48*, 371–410.

Lorber, M. (2012). The role of maternal emotion regulation in overreactive and lax discipline. *Journal of Family Psychology*, *26*, 642–647.

Luby, J. L. (2015). Poverty's most insidious damage: The developing brain. *JAMA Pediatrics*, *169*, 810–811.

Luijten, M., Schellekens, A. F., Kühn, S., Machielse, M. W. J., & Sescousse, G. (2017). Disruption of reward processing in addiction: An image-based meta-analysis of functional MRI studies. *JAMA Psychiatry*, *74*, 387–398.

Lupien, S. J., Ouellet-Morin, I., Hupbach, A., Tu, M. T., Buss, C., Walker, D., . . . McEwen, B. S. (2006). Beyond the stress concept: Allostatic load—A developmental biological and cognitive perspective. In D. Cicchetti, & D. Cohen (Eds.), *Developmental psychopathology* (2nd ed., pp. 578–628). Hoboken, NJ: Wiley.

Lynam, D. R., Caspi, A., Moffitt, T. E., Wikström, P. H., Loeber, R., & Novak, S. (2000). The interaction between impulsivity and neighborhood context in offending: The effects of impulsivity are stronger in poorer neighborhoods. *Journal of Abnormal Psychology*, *109*, 563–574.

Maccoby, E. E. (1986). Social groupings in childhood: Their relationship to prosocial and antisocial behavior in boys and girls. In D. Olweus, J. Block, & M. Radke-Yarrow (Eds.), *Development of antisocial behavior in boys and girls* (pp. 263–284). New York: Academic Press.

Maccoby, E. E. (1990). Gender and relationships: A developmental account. *American Psychologist*, *45*, 513–520.

McConaughy, S. H., & Achenbach, T. M. (2004). *Manual for the test observation form for ages 2-18*. Burlington, VT: University of Vermont, Center for Children, Youth, & Families.

Mead, H. K., Beauchaine, T. P., & Shannon, K. E. (2010). Neurobiological adaptations to violence across development. *Development and Psychopathology*, *22*, 1–22.

Mehta, P. H., & Beer, J. (2010). Neural mechanisms of the testosterone–aggression relation: The role of orbitofrontal cortex. *Journal of Cognitive Neuroscience*, *22*, 2357–2368.

Meier, M. H., Slutske, W. S., Arndt, S., & Cadoret, R. J. (2008). Impulsive and callous traits are more strongly associated with delinquent behavior in higher risk neighborhoods among boys and girls. *Journal of Consulting and Clinical Psychology*, *117*, 377–385.

Mill, J. (2011). Epigenetic effects on gene function and their role in mediating gene-environment interactions. In K. S. Kendler, S. R. Jaffee, & D. Romer (Eds.), *The dynamic genome and mental health* (pp. 145–171). New York, NY: Oxford University Press.

Moffitt, T. E. (1993). Adolescence-limited and life-course-persistent antisocial behavior: A developmental taxonomy. *Psychological Review*, *100*, 674–701.

Moffitt, T. E. (2003). Life-course-persistent and adolescence-limited antisocial behavior: A 10-year research review and a research agenda. In B. B. Lahey, T. E. Moffitt, & A. Caspi (Eds.), *Causes of conduct disorder and juvenile delinquency* (pp. 49–75). New York, NY: Guilford.

Moffitt, T. E., Arseneault, L., Jaffee, S. R., Kim-Cohen, J., Koenen, K. C., Odgers, C. L., . . . Viding, E. (2008). Research review: *DSM-V* conduct disorder: Research needs for an evidence base. *Journal of Child Psychology and Psychiatry*, *49*, 3–33.

Moffitt, T. E., & Caspi, A. (2001). Childhood predictors differentiate life-course persistent and adolescence-limited antisocial pathways among males and females. *Development and Psychopathology*, *13*, 355–375.

National Center for Biotechnology Information. (2017). *Overview of structural variation*. Retrieved from https://www.ncbi.nlm.nih.gov/dbvar/content/overview/.

Neale, B. M., Medland, S., Ripke, S., Anney, R. J., Asherson, P., Buitelaar, J., . . . IMAGE II Consortium Group. (2010). Case-control genome-wide association study of attention-deficit/hyperactivity disorder. *Journal of the American Academy of Child and Adolescent Psychiatry*, *49*, 906–920.

Neale, B. M., Medland, S., Ripke, S., Asherson, P., Franke, B., Lesch, K. P., . . . Psychiatric GWAS Consortium: ADHD Subgroup. (2010). Meta-analysis of genome-wide association studies of attention-deficit/hyperactivity disorder. *Journal of the American Academy of Child and Adolescent Psychiatry*, *49*, 884–897.

Neuhaus, E., & Beauchaine, T. P. (2017). Impulsivity and vulnerability to psychopathology. In T. P. Beauchaine, & S. P. Hinshaw (Eds.), *Child and adolescent psychopathology* (3rd ed., pp. 178–212). Hoboken, NJ: Wiley.

O'Brien, B. S., & Frick, P. J. (1996). Reward dominance: Associations with anxiety, conduct problems, and psychopathy in children. *Journal of Abnormal Child Psychology*, *24*, 223–240.

Oberlin, B. G., Dzemidzic, M., Bragulat, V., Lehigh, C. A., Talavage, T., O'Connor, S. J., & Kareken, D. A. (2012). Limbic responses to reward cues correlate with antisocial trait density in heavy drinkers. *Neuroimage*, *60*, 644–652.

O'Connor, T. G., Deater-Deckard, K., Fulker, D., Rutter, M., & Plomin, R. (1998). Genotype–environment correlations in late childhood and adolescence: Antisocial behavior problems and coercive parenting. *Developmental Psychology*, *34*, 970–981.

Pardini, D., Lochman, J., & Wells, K. (2004). Negative emotions and alcohol use initiation in high-risk boys: The moderating effect of good inhibitory control. *Journal of Abnormal Child Psychology*, *32*, 505–518.

Pardini, D. A., Lochman, J. E., & Frick, P. J. (2003). Callous/unemotional traits and social-cognitive processes in adjudicated youths. *Journal of the American Academy of Child and Adolescent Psychiatry*, *42*, 364–371.

Patterson, G. R., DeBaryshe, B. D., & Ramsey, E. (1989). A developmental perspective on antisocial behavior. *American Psychologist*, *44*, 329–335.

Pearl, A. M., French, B. F., Dumas, J. E., Moreland, A. D., & Prinz, R. (2014). Bidirectional effects of parenting quality and child externalizing behavior in predominantly single parent, under-resourced African American families. *Journal of Child and Family Studies*, *23*, 177–188.

Perry, D. G., Perry, L. C., & Rasmussen, P. (1986). Cognitive social learning mediators of aggression. *Child Development*, *57*, 700–711.

Plichta, M. M., & Scheres, A. (2014). Ventral–striatal responsiveness during reward anticipation in ADHD and its relation to trait impulsivity in the healthy population: A meta-analytic review of the fMRI literature. *Neuroscience and Biobehavioral Reviews*, *38*, 125–134.

Plomin, R. (2013). Missing heritability, polygenic scores, and gene–environment correlation. *Journal of Child Psychology and Psychiatry*, *54*, 1147–1149.

Pollak, S. D., & Sinha, P. (2002). Effects of early experience on children's recognition of facial displays of emotion. *Developmental Psychology*, *38*, 784–791.

Rasanen, P., Hakko, H., Visuri, S., Paanila, J., Kapanen, P., Suomela, T., & Tiihonen, J. (1999). Serum testosterone levels, mental disorders and criminal behaviour. *Acta Psychiatrica Scandinavica*, *99*, 348–352.

Ratcliffe, C. (2015). *Child poverty and adult success*. Low-income Working Families Initiative. Downloaded from http://www.urban.org/sites/default/files/publication/65766/2000369-Child-Poverty-and-Adult-Success.pdf.

Regner, M. F., Saenz, N., Maharajh, K., Yamamoto, D. J., Mohl, B., Wylie, K., ... Tanabe, J. (2016). Top-down network effective connectivity in abstinent substance dependent individuals. *PLoS One*, *11*, e0164818.

Reich, D., Edenberg, H. J., Goate, A., Williams, J. T., Rice, J. P., Van Eerdewegh, P., ... Begleiter, H. (1998). Genome-wide search for genes affecting the risk for alcohol-dependence. *American Journal of Medical Genetics*, *81*, 207–215.

Reich, W., Welner, Z., & Herjanic, B. (1997). *Diagnostic Interview for Children and Adolescents-IV (DICA-IV)*. North Tonawanda, NY: Multi-Health Systems, Inc.

Richters, J. E., & Cicchetti, D. (1993). Mark Twain meets DSM-III-R: Conduct disorder, development, and the concept of harmful dysfunction. *Development and Psychopathology*, *5*, 5–29.

Robins, L. N. (1966). *Deviant children grown up*. Baltimore, MD: Williams and Wilkins.

Robins, L. N. (1978). Sturdy childhood predictors of adult antisocial behaviour: Replications from longitudinal studies. *Psychological Medicine*, *8*, 611–622.

Row, R., Maughan, B., Worthman, C. M., Costello, E. J., & Angold, A. (2004). Testosterone, antisocial behavior, and social dominance in boys: Pubertal development and biosocial interaction. *Biological Psychiatry*, *55*, 546–552.

Rubia, K., Halari, R., Cubillo, A., Mohammad, A. M., Brammer, M., & Taylor, E. (2009). Methylphenidate normalises activation and functional connectivity deficits in attention and motivation networks in medication-naive children with ADHD during a rewarded continuous performance task. *Neuropharmacology*, *57*, 640–652.

Rubia, K., Smith, A., Halari, R., Matukura, F., Mohammad, M., Taylor, E., & Brammer, M. J. (2009). Disorder-specific dissociation of orbitofrontal dysfunction in boys with pure conduct disorder during reward and ventrolateral prefrontal dysfunction in boys with pure ADHD during sustained attention. *American Journal of Psychiatry*, *166*, 83–94.

Sagvolden, T., Johansen, E. B., Aase, H., & Russell, V. A. (2005). A dynamic developmental theory of ADHD predominantly hyperactive/impulsive and combined subtypes. *Behavioral and Brain Sciences*, *28*, 397–419.

Santiago, C. D., Kaltman, S., & Miranda, J. (2012). Poverty and mental health: How do low-in-come adults and children fare in psychotherapy?. *Journal of Clinical Psychology*, *69*, 115–126.

Santiago, C. D., Wadsworth, M. E., & Stump, J. (2011). Socioeconomic status, neighborhood disadvantage, and poverty-related stress: Prospective effects on psychological syndromes among diverse low-income families. *Journal of Economic Psychology*, *32*, 218 230.

Sauder, C., Beauchaine, T. P., Gatzke-Kopp, L. M., Shannon, K. E., & Aylward, E. (2012). Neuroanatomical correlates of heterotypic comorbidity in externalizing male adolescents. *Journal of Clinical Child and Adolescent Psychology*, *41*, 346–352.

Schmitt, J., Warner, K., & Gupta, S. (2010). *The high budgetary cost of incarceration*. Retrieved from http://www.cepr.net/documents/publications/incarceration-2010-06.pdf.

Sedlak, A. J., Mettenburg, J., Basena, M., Petta, I., McPherson, K., Green, A., & Li, S. (2010). *Fourth National Incidence Study of Child Abuse and Neglect (NIS-4): Report to Congress*. Washington, DC.: U.S. Department of Health and Human Services.

Shaffer, D., Fisher, P., Lucas, C., Dulcan, M., & Schwab-Stone, M. (2000). NIMH Diagnostic Interview Schedule for Children, version IV (NIMH DISC-IV): Description, differences from previous versions, and reliability of some common diagnoses. *Journal of the American Academy of Child and Adolescent Psychiatry*, *39*, 28–38.

Shannon, K. E., Sauder, C., Beauchaine, T. P., & Gatzke-Kopp, L. (2009). Disrupted effective connectivity between the medial frontal cortex and the caudate in adolescent boys with externalizing behavior disorders. *Criminal Justice and Behavior*, *36*, 1141–1157.

Sibley, M. H., Pelham, W. E., Molina, B. S. G., Waschbusch, D. A., Gnagy, E. M., ... Biswas, A. (2010). Inconsistent self-report of delinquency by adolescents and young adults with ADHD. *Journal of Abnormal Child Psychology*, *38*, 645–656.

Slutske, W. S., Heath, A. C., Dinwiddie, S. H., Madden, A. F., Bucholz, K. K., Dunne, M. P., ... Martin, N. G. (1997). Modeling genetic and environmental influences in the etiology of conduct disorder: A study of 2682 adult twin pairs. *Journal of Abnormal Psychology*, *106*, 266–279.

Snyder, J., Schrepferman, L., & St. Peter, C. (1997). Origins of antisocial behavior: Negative reinforcement and affect dysregulation of behavior as socialization mechanisms in family interaction. *Behavior Modification*, *21*, 187–215.

Son, G. H., Chung, S., Geum, D., Kang, S. S., Choi, W. S., Kim, K., & Choi, S. (2007). Hyperactivity and alteration of the midbrain dopaminergic system in maternally stressed male mice offspring. *Biochemical and Biophysical Research Communications*, *352*, 823–829.

Stalenheim, E. G., Eriksson, E., von Knorring, L., & Wide, L. (1998). Testosterone as a biological marker in psychopathy and alcoholism. *Psychiatry Research*, *77*, 79–88.

Stallings, M. C., Corley, R. P., Dennehey, B., Hewitt, J. K., Krauter, K. S., Lessem, J. M., ... Crowley, T. J. (2005). A genome-wide search for quantitative trait loci tat influence antisocial drug dependence in adolescence. *Archives of General Psychiatry*, *62*, 1042–1051.

Stallings, M. C., Corley, R. P., Hewitt, J. K., Krauter, K. S., Lessem, J. M., Mikulich, S. K., ... Crowley, T. J. (2003). A genome-wide search for quantitative trait loci influencing substance dependence vulnerability in adolescence. *Drug and Alcohol Dependence*, *70*, 295–307.

Stattin, H., & Magnusson, D. (1990). *Pubertal maturation in female development*. Hillsdale, NJ: Erlbaum.

Stockmeier, C. A., & Ordway, G. A. (2007). Interactions of norepinephrine with other neurotransmitter systems: Anatomical basis and pharmacology. In G. A. Ordway, M. A. Schwartz, & A. Frazer (Eds.), *Brain norepinephrine: Neurobiology and therapeutics* (pp. 53–67). New York, NY: Cambridge University Press.

Stringaris, A., Maughan, B., & Goodman, R. (2010). What's in a disruptive disorder? Tempera-mental antecedents of oppositional defiant disorder: Findings from the Avon Longitudinal Study. *Journal of the American Academy of Child and Adolescent Psychiatry*, *49*, 474–483.

Taylor, D. (1985). Developmental rate is the major differentiator between the sexes. *Behavioral and Brain Sciences*, *8*, 459–460.

Teplin, L. A. (1994). Psychiatric and substance abuse disorders among male urban jail detainees. *American Journal of Public Health*, *84*, 290–293.

Todd, R. D., Huant, H., Smalley, S. L., Nelson, S. E., Wilcutt, E. G., Pennington, B. F., ... Neuman, R. J. (2005). Collaborative analysis of DRD4 and DAT genotypes in population-defined ADHD subtypes. *Journal of Child Psychology and Psychiatry*, *46*, 1067–1073.

Tucker, G., Price, A. L., & Berger, B. (2014). Improving the power of GWAS and avoiding confounding from population stratification with PC-select. *Genetics*, *197*, 1045–1049.

van der Stouwe, T., Asscher, J. J., Stams, G. J. J. M., Deković, M., & van der Laan, P. H. (2014). The effectiveness of multisystemic therapy (MST): A meta-analysis. *Clinical Psychology Review*, *34*, 468–481.

van der Zwaluw, C. S., Engels, R. C. M. E., Buitelaar, J., Verkes, R. J., Franke, B., & Scholte, R. H. J. (2009). Polymorphisms in the dopamine transporter gene (SLC6A3/DAT1) and alcohol dependence in humans: A systematic review. *Pharmacogenomics*, *10*, 853–866.

Viding, E., Hanscombe, K. B., Curtis, C. J. C., Davis, O. S. P., Meaburn, E. L., & Plomin, R. (2010). In search of genes associated with risk for psychopathic tendencies in children: A two-stage genome-wide association study of pooled DNA. *Journal of Child Psychology and Psychiatry*, *51*, 780–788.

Waas, G. A. (1988). Social attributional biases of peer-rejected and aggressive children. *Child Development*, *59*, 969–992.

Wadsworth, S. J., DeFries, J. C., Stevenson, J., Gilger, J. W., & Pennington, B. F. (1992). Gender ratios among reading-disabled children and their siblings as a function of parental impairment. *Journal of Child Psychology and Psychiatry*, *33*, 1229–1239.

Webster-Stratton, C., & Hancock, L. (1998). Training for parents of young children with conduct problems: Content, methods, and therapeutic processes. In J. M. Briesmester, & C. E. Schaefer (Eds.), *Handbook of parent training* (2nd ed., pp. 98–152). New York: Wiley.

Webster-Stratton, C., Reid, M. J., & Beauchaine, T. P. (2011). Combining parent and child training for young children with attention-deficit/hyperactivity disorder. *Journal of Clinical Child and Adolescent Psychology*, *40*, 191–203.

Webster-Stratton, C., Reid, M. J., & Beauchaine, T. P. (2013). One-year follow-up of combined parent and child intervention for young children with ADHD. *Journal of Clinical Child and Adolescent Psychology*, *42*, 251–261.

Webster-Stratton, C., Rinaldi, J., & Reid, M. J. (2011). Long-term outcomes of Incredible Years Parenting program: Predictors of adolescent adjustment. *Child and Adolescent Mental Health*, *16*, 38–46.

Webster-Stratton, C., & Taylor, T. (2001). Nipping early risk factors in the bud: Preventing substance abuse, delinquency, and violence in adolescence through interventions targeted at young children (0-8 years). *Prevention Science*, *2*, 165–192.

Woltering, S., Granic, I., Lamm, C., & Lewis, M. D. (2011). Neural changes associated with treatment outcome in children with externalizing problems. *Biological Psychiatry*, *70*, 873–879.

Wong, C. C., Caspi, A., Williams, B., Craig, I. W., Houts, R., Ambler, A., … Mill, J. (2010). A longitudinal study of epigenetic variation in twins. *Epigenetics*, *5*, 516–526.

Wu, J., Xiao, H., Sun, H., & Zou, L. Q. (2012). Role of dopamine receptors in ADHD: A systematic meta-analysis. *Molecular Neurobiology*, *45*, 605–620.

Yang, L., Neale, B. M., Liu, L., Lee, S. H., Wray, N. R., Ji, N., … Hu, X. (2013). Polygenic transmission and complex neuro developmental network for attention deficit hyperactivity disorder: Genome-wide association study of both common and rare variants. *American Journal of Medical Genetics Part B: Neuropsychiatric Genetics*, *162B*, 419–430.

Zhang, R., Miao, Q., Wang, C., Zhao, R., Li, W., Haile, C. N., … Zang, X. Y. (2013). Genome-wide DNA methylation analysis in alcohol dependence. *Addiction Biology*, *18*, 392–403.

Zisner, A., & Beauchaine, T. P. (2016). Midbrain neural mechanisms of trait impulsivity. In T. P. Beauchaine, & S. P. Hinshaw (Eds.), *The Oxford handbook of externalizing spectrum disorders* (pp. 184–200). New York, NY: Oxford University Press.

Further Reading

Beauchaine, T. P., Webster-Stratton, C., & Reid, M. J. (2005). Mediators, moderators, and predictors of 1-year outcomes among children treated for early-onset conduct problems: A latent growth curve analysis. *Journal of Consulting and Clinical Psychology, 73*, 371–388.

McMahon, R. J., Wells, K. C., & Kotler, J. S. (2006). Conduct problems. In E. J. Mash, & R. A. Barkley (Eds.), *Treatment of childhood disorders* (3rd ed., pp. 137–268). New York, NY: Guilford.

Antisocial–psychopathic personality disorder

4

Cristina Crego and Thomas A. Widiger
University of Kentucky, Lexington, KY, United States

Many externalizing problems occur within a circumscribed period of a person's life. It might be for an extended period of time, but at least not sustained throughout the person's life. However, some externalizing problems can be lifelong, evident in childhood and throughout adulthood. As such, these problems could be inherent to one's personality.

Everybody has a personality, which is a person's characteristic manner of thinking, feeling, behaving, and relating to others. According to the American Psychiatric Association (APA), some persons have a personality disorder. The authoritative statement for what constitutes a personality disorder is provided within the APA's Diagnostic and Statistical Manual of Mental Disorders (DSM), the current edition of which is DSM-5 (APA, 2013; the prior version was DSM-IV; APA, 1994). As stated in DSM-5, it is "when personality traits are inflexible and maladaptive and cause significant functional impairment or subjective distress [that] they constitute Personality Disorders" (APA, 2013, p. 647).

The personality disorder which is most strongly and commonly linked to externalizing problems is the antisocial, as it includes such traits as disinhibition and antagonism (Kotov et al., 2017; Krueger & Markon, 2014). Evident within the DSM-5 diagnostic criteria for antisocial personality disorder (ASPD) are externalizing problems (e.g., aggressiveness, criminal acts, impulsivity, irritability, recklessness, and irresponsibility; APA, 2013). DSM-5 ASPD is also understood under the alternative name of "psychopathy" (Crego & Widiger, 2015). Psychopaths are "social predators who charm, manipulate, and ruthlessly plow their way through life .... Completely lacking in conscience and feeling for others, they selfishly take what they want and do as they please, violating social norms and expectations without the slightest sense of guilt or regret" (Hare, 1993, p. xi). The distinctions between ASPD and psychopathy are discussed later in this chapter, within the section on alternative conceptualizations.

One real life example of an antisocial–psychopath was Clyde Barrow (Hare, 1993; Widiger & Crego, in press). As an adolescent, Clyde was an indifferent student. He hated school and dropped out at the age of 16, subsequently taking a variety of low-paying jobs which he also failed to perform in any credible manner. He was repeatedly irresponsible, negligent, and lax. He soon began to rely on his criminal activities to make money. He was a violent criminal who traveled the central

Developmental Pathways to Disruptive, Impulse-Control, and Conduct Disorders.
DOI: https://doi.org/10.1016/B978-0-12-811323-3.00004-3

United States in the early 1930s with his gang (and girlfriend, Bonnie Parker) boldly and impulsively stealing cars and robbing small stores, rural gas stations, and small town banks, killing most anyone who attempted to thwart, threaten, or arrest him. He would at times simply capture and then release persons when he felt it was safe to do so, but he would not hesitate to kill a policeman or a civilian if he felt it was necessary for the completion of his crime. His criminal gang is believed to have killed at least nine police officers, as well as several civilians, the latter attempting to keep him from stealing their hard-earned property. It is perhaps noteworthy that the "take" from his robberies was often quite small, consistent with the impulsivity and lack of planning.

Clyde was also rather charming and engaging interpersonally, contributing to his popularity among persons he met and the general public who followed his exploits. He was at times glamourized by the popular press and within subsequent media portrayals (e.g., the movie, *Bonny and Clyde*, directed by Arthur Penn). However, he also had a severe temper and viscous pleasures. As a child, he would wring the necks of chickens just to watch them suffer or break the wings of birds to watch them struggle to fly (Traherne, 2000). He never showed any remorse for his murders and thefts. His own life ended quite early, at the age of 25, when he was ambushed by the police on a rural road, who, perhaps understandably, did not want to take any chances of risking their own lives in making an arrest (found in his car were automatic rifles, sawed-off semiautomatic shotguns, assorted handguns, and several thousand rounds of ammunition).

Psychopathy is one of the more heavily researched and intriguing personality disorders as some of the most famous, or perhaps infamous, criminals, real or imagined, have been considered to be psychopathic (e.g., Dexter, Ted Bundy, Tony Soprano, Kenneth Bianchi, Jeffrey MacDonald, Hannibal Lector, Bernie Madoff, Henry Hill; Hare, 1993; Widiger & Crego, in press). Considered in this chapter will be alternative conceptualizations of psychopathy, its forensic assessment, comorbidity, etiology, pathology, course, and treatment.

Alternative conceptualizations of ASPD and psychopathy

A longstanding and ongoing debate in the scientific literature is how to best characterize ASPD and/or psychopathy. The description of ASPD within DSM-5 (APA, 2013) has considerable authority, given that all mental health centers must use the APA diagnostic manual. However, the scientific community has generally preferred an alternative description provided by Hare's (2003) Psychopathy Checklist Revised (PCL-R). DSM-5 ASPD and PCL-R psychopathy are very convergent models. The only real substantive difference is that the PCL-R includes such additional traits as glib charm, arrogance, and lack of empathy. However, the PCL-R places relatively more emphasis on personality traits, such as exploitation, manipulation, aggression, criminal activity, impulsivity, and irresponsibility, whereas the APA diagnostic criteria place relatively more emphasis on behavioral indicators of these same traits to facilitate the obtainment of reliable diagnosis within clinical practice (Lilienfeld, 1994).

The emphasis on behavioral indicators, including criminal acts, has contributed to an excessive diagnosis of ASPD within prison settings. Approximately 40%–50% of male prisoners (some studies report even higher values) will meet the criteria for ASPD. The percent for PCL-R psychopathy is considerably lower (i.e., 20%). Within the community, approximately 5% of men and 1% of women would meet the criteria for ASPD, whereas it appears that only 1% of men and 0.5% of women would meet criteria for PCL-R psychopathy (Hare, Neumann, & Widiger, 2012). This differential prevalence rate is typically attributed to the DSM-5 Section II emphasis on overt behavioral features (Hare, 2003). However, it may also though simply reflect different cutoff points that are used for the DSM-5 ASPD criteria versus the PCL-R (Widiger & Crego, in press).

DSM-5 ASPD/psychopathy

It was the intention of the DSM-5 Personality Disorders Work Group to shift the diagnosis of ASPD toward the concept of psychopathy. This was explicitly evident in the proposal to change the name from "antisocial" to "antisocial/psychopathic" (Skodol, 2012). However, the primary basis for diagnosing antisocial/psychopathy proposed for DSM-5 was to be through a clinician's subjective impression of a patient matched to a two-paragraph narrative description rather than using an explicit set of diagnostic criteria, the preferred method for diagnosing all of the other mental disorders within the diagnostic manual. In addition, the source for this prototype narrative was not the PCL-R (Hare, 2003). It was instead the psychodynamic prototype narratives of Westen, Shedler, and Bradley (2006). No reference was in fact made to the seminal contributions of Hare (2003) or Cleckley (1941) in the presentation of the rationale and empirical support for the proposal (Blashfield & Reynolds, 2012; Hare et al., 2012).

The prototype narrative proposal was eventually withdrawn due to inadequate empirical support for both its reliability and validity (Widiger, 2011; Zimmerman, 2011). It was replaced by another novel approach to diagnosis, referred to as a "hybrid" model, combining psychodynamically oriented deficits in the sense of self and interpersonal relatedness (Skodol, 2012) with maladaptive personality traits obtained from a five-domain dimensional trait model (Krueger et al., 2011), including the five domains of negative affectivity, detachment, psychoticism, antagonism, and disinhibition.

The psychodynamically oriented self/interpersonal proposed deficits (APA, 2013) concerned identity (e.g., egocentrism), self-direction (e.g., goals focused on personal gratification), empathy (e.g., lack of concern for feelings and sufferings of others), and intimacy (e.g., incapacity for mutually intimate relationships). The seven maladaptive traits from the five-domain trait model were manipulativeness, deceitfulness, callousness, and hostility from the domain of antagonism, as well as irresponsibility, impulsivity, and risk-taking from the domain of disinhibition. There were (initially) no traits from the domains of negative affectivity or detachment. The hybrid model proposal though was also eventually rejected, again due to the absence of empirical support for its reliability or validity (Skodol, Morey, Bender, & Oldham, 2013). In the end, DSM-5 retained the DSM-IV criterion set for ASPD for its official diagnosis (within Section II of DSM-5) and provided the hybrid model in an appendix to DSM-5 for proposals needing further study (APA, 2013, Section III).

The initial list of traits included within the hybrid model proposal did actually align quite well with the DSM-IV criterion set for ASPD (Lynam & Vachon, 2012), and there is a considerable body of research to support the validity of the trait list to cover the DSM-IV ASPD criterion set (Miller, 2012, 2013; Miller, Lyman, Widiger, & Leukefeld, 2001; Rojas & Widiger, 2017). However, Lynam and Vachon (2012) did note that the trait list failed to cover the additional traits of Hare (2003) PCL-R psychopathy that were not included within DSM-IV, such as arrogance and glib charm. As indicated by Blashfield and Reynolds (2012), "Cleckley and Hare are well-known authors who defined how psychopathy is currently conceptualized; neither was referenced in the DSM-5 rationale" (p. 826).

After the final posting on the DSM-5 website, further revisions were made to the trait list for ASPD in a last-minute effort to represent psychopathy. However, the revisions were not made to align ASPD closer to the PCL-R of Hare (1986, 2003). They were made instead to align ASPD to psychopathy as defined by the more recently developed models of Lilienfeld and Widows (2005) and Patrick, Fowles, and Krueger (2009), more specifically, to include traits of fearlessness and boldness. In addition, they were apparently unable to simply add the traits of fearlessness and boldness to the 25-trait list. Therefore, they suggested that "high attention-seeking and low withdrawal capture the social potency (assertive/dominant) component of psychopathy, whereas low anxiousness captures the stress immunity (emotional stability/resilience) component" (APA, 2013, p. 765). Crego and Widiger (2014) subsequently indicated that high attention-seeking and (reverse-keyed) social-withdrawal are only weakly related to boldness, and reverse-keying anxiousness does not actually suggest the presence of fearlessness. An absence of maladaptive anxiousness is most likely to suggest simply the presence of a normal placid composure rather than the opposite and more extreme trait of fearlessness.

The quandary of fearlessness and boldness

The proposed traits of fearlessness and boldness have in fact been the focus of considerable discussion and debate (Lilienfeld, Patrick, et al., 2012; Lynam & Miller, 2012; Miller & Lynam, 2012). For many years, the predominant conceptualization and assessment of psychopathy within the scientific and clinical psychology literature has been provided by the PCL-R semistructured interview (Hare, 2003), and nowhere within the PCL-R is there an explicit reference to boldness or fearlessness (nor is there any reference to fearlessness or boldness within the DSM-5 Section II ASPD). Fearlessness and boldness are relatively new additions to the conceptualization and assessment of psychopathy provided by the Triarchic Model of Psychopathy (TriPM) by Patrick et al. (2009), the Psychopathic Personality

Inventory (PPI-R) by Lilienfeld and Widows (2005), and the Elemental Psychopathy Assessment (EPA) by Lynam et al. (2011). Studies have compared the assessment of psychopathy by the TriPM, the PPI-R, and the EPA, with traditional measures of psychopathy and ASPD, and a consistent finding has been a lack of correlation of the traditional measures with either fearlessness or boldness (Crego & Widiger, 2014; Malterer, Lilienfeld, Neumann, & Newman, 2010; Poy, Seggara, Esteller, Lopez, & Molto, 2014; Stanley, Wygant, & Sellbom, 2013). In sum, whether to include fearlessness and boldness in conceptualization of ASPD–psychopathy remains an ongoing point of dispute (Lilienfeld, Patrick, et al., 2012; Lynam & Miller, 2012; Miller & Lynam, 2012). However, informing this debate is how psychopathy is understood from the perspective of the five-factor model (FFM) and by Cleckley (1941).

Characteristics of psychopathy from the perspective of the FFM

As with all the personality disorders, the personality traits associated with psychopathy can be captured by the FFM of general personality structure (Lynam & Widiger, 2007; Widiger & Lynam, 1998). The FFM is the predominant dimensional model of general personality structure within psychology (John, Naumann, & Soto, 2008). The FFM has amassed a substantial body of empirical support (Widiger, 2017) and covers virtually every maladaptive and adaptive trait identified within the English language (De Raad & Mlačić, 2017) and included within most any measure of normal and abnormal personality (O'Connor, 2002, 2005). The FFM consists of the five broad domains of neuroticism (vs emotional stability), extraversion (vs introversion), openness (vs closedness), agreeableness (vs antagonism), and conscientiousness (Costa & McCrae, 2017). Within each domain are more specific facets (six per domain as identified by Costa & McCrae, 1992). For example, within the domain of agreeableness versus antagonism are the facets of trust versus suspiciousness, straightforwardness versus deception and manipulation, altruism versus exploitation, compliance versus aggressive opposition, modesty versus arrogance, and tendermindedness versus tough-minded callousness. The five-domain dimensional trait model included within Section III of DSM-5 is closely aligned with the FFM (APA, 2013, p. 773).

Miller et al. (2001) surveyed psychopathy researchers, asking them to describe a prototypic psychopath in terms of the 30 facets of the FFM on a 1–5 point scale (1 = extremely low; 5 = extremely high). Table 4.1 provides their description. This description included all of the traits of antagonism (e.g., exploitation, callousness, arrogance, aggression, and manipulation), along with traits of extraversion (excitement-seeking, assertiveness, and boldness), low neuroticism (lack of anxiousness and glib charm), high neuroticism (angry hostility and impulsivity), and low conscientiousness (rashness, immorality, disinhibition, and irresponsibility). In other words, the researchers considered the prototypic psychopath to be bold (i.e., high in assertiveness and excitement-seeking) and fearless (low in anxiousness and vulnerability). The Miller et al. description also characterized the prototypic psychopath as being high in competence, but Miller et al. suggested this might have been perceived competence rather than actual competence.

Table 4.1 FFM profile of prototypic and Cleckley psychopath

FFM facet	Prototypic psychopath[a]	Average Cleckley psychopath[b]
Neuroticism		
Anxiousness	1.5	2.0
Angry hostility	3.9	2.8
Depressiveness	1.4	1.8
Self-consciousness	1.1	1.7
Impulsivity	4.5	4.1
Vulnerability	1.5	1.9
Extraversion		
Warmth	1.7	2.2
Gregariousness	3.7	3.5
Assertiveness	4.5	3.5
Activity	3.7	3.6
Excitement-seeking	4.7	4.0
Positive emotions	2.5	2.9
Openness		
Fantasy	3.1	3.3
Aesthetics	2.3	2.5
Feelings	1.8	2.3
Actions	4.3	3.8
Ideas	3.5	3.5
Values	2.9	2.4
Agreeableness		
Trust	1.7	2.0
Straightforwardness	1.1	2.1
Altruism	1.3	1.7
Compliance	1.3	1.8
Modesty	1.0	1.8
Tender-mindedness	1.3	1.7
Conscientiousness		
Competence	4.2	2.3
Order	2.6	2.1
Dutifulness	1.2	1.6
Achievement	3.1	1.7
Self-discipline	1.9	1.5
Deliberation	1.6	1.7

[a]Adapted from Miller, J. D., Lyman, D. R., Widiger, T. A., & Leukefeld, C. (2001). Personality disorders as extreme variants of common personality dimensions: Can the Five Factor Model adequately represent psychopathy? Journal of Personality, 69, 253–276.

[b]Adapted from Crego, C., & Widiger, T. A. (2016a). Cleckley's psychopaths: Revisited. Journal of Abnormal Psychology, 125, 75–87.

Psychopathy as conceptualized by Cleckley

It is evident that most psychopathy researchers and theorists pay homage to the conceptualization of psychopathy by Cleckley (Crego & Widiger, 2016a). "The modern clinical conception of psychopathy has been shaped primarily by the writings of Hervey Cleckley" (Lilienfeld, Watts, Smith, Berg, & Latzman, 2015, p. 596). "Most contemporary conceptualizations [of psychopathy] are linked, at least in part, to the work of Cleckley (1941) and his book *The Mask of Sanity*" (Salekin, 2002, p. 80). "Cleckley's classic treatise, *The Mask of Sanity* ... served as the foundation for modern conceptualizations and measures of psychopathy" (Patrick et al., 2009, p. 915). "Perhaps no major psychological disorder is so clearly identified as originating from the work of one scholar as is psychopathy" (Skeem, Polaschek, Patrick, & Lilienfeld, 2011, p. 99). Indeed, PCL-R psychopathy has been favored over DSM ASPD in large part because it was considered to be more consistent with Cleckley psychopathy (Crego & Widiger, 2015; Lilienfeld, 1994). "We wished to retain the essence of psychopathy embodied in Cleckley's work" (Hare, 1986, p. 15).

Patrick et al. (2009) has suggested that boldness is consistent with the Cleckley (1941) description, and therefore it was an error on the part of Hare (2003) not to include boldness within the PCL-R. More specifically, Patrick et al. suggested that four of Cleckley's (1941) 16 criteria for psychopathy are indicators of positive adjustment: superficial charm and good intelligence; absence of delusions or irrationality; absence of nervousness; and low incidence of suicide. However, absence of delusions, irrationality, nervousness, and suicide might be better understood as exclusionary criteria of clinical dysfunction, rather than the presence of a superior psychological adjustment (Hare & Neumann, 2008). In addition, absence of delusions, absence of suicide, and good intelligence would not appear to actually imply "a capacity to remain calm and focused in situations involving pressure or threat, an ability to recover quickly from stressful events, high self-assurance and social efficacy, and a tolerance for unfamiliarity and danger" (Patrick et al., 2009, p. 926).

Crego and Widiger (2016a), however, explored whether the traits of boldness and fearlessness were nevertheless evident within the original Cleckley (1941) case histories of prototypic psychopaths. Cleckley presented 15 detailed case histories to serve as illustrative cases of psychopathy, which he in turn used to derive his criterion set. Crego and Widiger coded each of the 15 cases with respect to 33 potential traits of psychopathy, including boldness, fearlessness, unconcern, self-assured, and invulnerable, all of which received high ratings in at least 70% of the cases. In sum, most of Cleckley's psychopaths were indeed fearless and bold.

Each of the Cleckley psychopaths was also rated in terms of the 30 facets of the FFM, using the same instrument that was used in the work of Miller et al. (2001). Table 4.1 also provides the mean FFM profile for the 15 Cleckley psychopaths. It is evident that the Cleckley FFM profile is closely consistent with the Miller et al. FFM description of the prototypic psychopath. The primary exceptions are the obtainment low scores on all facets of conscientiousness by the Cleckley psychopaths. The Cleckley psychopaths were indeed lax, irresponsible, negligent, incompetent, and rash (much of which appears to be true for Clyde Barrow).

Fearlessness and boldness as adaptive personality strengths

The FFM and Cleckley perspectives on psychopathy support the inclusion of traits of fearlessness and boldness. However, an additional concern regarding TriPM boldness, PPI-R fearless-dominance, and EPA invulnerability is that, within these measures, the traits of fearlessness and boldness are adaptive personality strengths (Lynam & Miller, 2012; Miller & Lynam, 2012). If fearlessness is included perhaps it should be a problematic fearlessness, contributing, for example, to a failure to be appropriately concerned about the negative consequences of risky, dangerous, and/or criminal behavior. If charm is included it should perhaps be one that is superficial and slick. The charm of a psychopath can be initially instrumental and advantageous in his (or her) seductions, cons, and frauds, but perhaps it should also be ultimately exposed for its insincerity, shallowness, and superficiality. A personality disorder is defined in DSM-5 as "an enduring pattern of inner experience and behavior that ... *leads to distress or impairment*" (APA, 2013, p. 645, our emphasis). What makes a personality disorder a disorder is the presence of maladjustment, not adaptive high functioning.

The inclusion of adaptive traits within a conceptualization and/or assessment of psychopathy can also be problematic to the extent that they have a substantial impact on the assessment, or they are considered out of the context of the maladaptive traits. For example, Lilienfeld, Waldman, et al. (2012) suggested that Theodore Roosevelt, John F. Kennedy, and Ronald Regan were psychopathic presidents, not because they were exploitative, callous, or ruthless, but because they were bold. Lilienfeld, Waldman, et al. reported no meaningful relationship between presidential success and any aspect of PCL-R psychopathy, including what has been considered the core PCL-R traits of selfish, callous, and remorselessness. Lilienfeld, Waldman, et al. did make it clear that they were not suggesting that these presidents were actual psychopaths; they did not have all of the traits of psychopathy. However, they were stating that their success was due in part to the presence of psychopathic traits, which then clearly implies that the presidents were, to a meaningful degree, psychopathic. It would perhaps be more accurate and potentially less misleading to state that these presidents were successful because they were bold, not because they were psychopathic.

It is intriguing to suggest "that the hero and the psychopath may be twigs off the same genetic branch" (Lykken, 1995, p. 29), but the hero and the psychopath will have substantially different personality profiles. Lykken suggested that fearlessness is the cardinal trait of psychopathy, a trait from which all of the other traits of psychopathy arise, including even the traits of antagonism and disinhibition. An alternative view is that the psychopath and the hero share just the one trait of fearlessness, as heroes are unlikely to be high in the traits of antagonism and low in conscientiousness. Adopting Lykken's metaphor, heroes and psychopaths are perhaps best understood to be occupying very different genetic branches, as the psychopathic traits of high antagonism (e.g., manipulative, duplicitous, exploitative, aggressive, and deceptive) and low conscientiousness (e.g., irresponsible, hedonistic, lax, and rash), clearly integral to the conceptualization of psychopathy

(Cleckley, 1941; Hare, 2003; Miller et al., 2001), will not be evident in most heroes and these traits occupy quite different genetic branches within the structure of personality (Jarnecke & South, 2017; Yamagata et al., 2006). In sum, it would appear accurate to describe a psychopath as feeling bold, fearless, and invulnerable (certainly this was true for Clyde Barrow), but perhaps it should reflect a dysfunctional, potentially harmful and risky fearlessness (Crego & Widiger, 2015).

Successful psychopathy

A variant of psychopathy that has long been of theoretical and clinical interest has been the successful psychopath (Hall & Benning, 2006; Lilienfeld, Watts, & Smith, 2015). Successful psychopaths are, in theory, individuals who have the core traits of psychopathy and have largely succeeded in their exploitations of others. Existing research on psychopathy has often sampled from prison populations. A prison does provide a compelling setting for the study of psychopathy, as clearly many criminals will be psychopathic. There would certainly be more psychopaths within a prison setting than within a psychiatric, student, or general community sample. However, one might also consider prisoners to represent, to a large extent, unsuccessful psychopaths, given that their exploitations were detected and they are now incarcerated, perhaps for a very extended period of time. In contrast, there could be psychopathic lawyers, professors, businessmen, and politicians who have not committed crimes that warranted arrest or have successfully avoided detection (Cleckley, 1941; Hare, 2003). There is quite a bit of anecdotal reference to successful psychopaths within business, politics, and the law (e.g., Babiak & Hare, 2006; Dutton, 2012; Stevens, Deuling, & Armenakis, 2012), but relatively little systematic research.

One view is that the success of these psychopaths is obtained from the traits of fearlessness and boldness (Lilienfeld, Watts, & Smith, 2015). Given that these traits are defined and/or assessed as adaptive rather than maladaptive, they would indeed be associated with successful life outcomes (e.g., Lilienfeld, Latzman, Watts, Smith, & Dutton, 2014). As noted earlier, Lilienfeld, Waldman, et al. (2012) suggested that the success of some presidents was due to the trait of boldness. However, also noted earlier, these presidents did not have other traits of psychopathy, such as callous exploitation and disinhibition, and would not actually be considered to be psychopaths.

A difficulty with empirically studying psychopathy within leading professions is obtaining a willingness of the successful psychopaths to participate in research. One is unlikely to obtain sufficient cooperation from a psychopathic lawyer or professor to complete a battery of self-report inventories. However, it is reasonable to expect that these persons will be known to others who would be willing to participate in such a study. Mullins-Sweatt, Glover, Derefinko, Miller, and Widiger (2010) surveyed attorneys, forensic psychologists, and clinical psychology professors. They were provided with a brief description of psychopathy (i.e., the quotation from Hare, 1993, provided in the second paragraph of this chapter) and were asked if they personally knew of any such person and, most importantly, knew of such a person who was largely successful in his or her psychopathic endeavors.

Twenty-five of the attorneys, 58 of the professors, and 81 of the forensic psychologists indicated that they did indeed know personally someone who would be characterized as a successful psychopath. Narrative descriptions of these psychopaths were consistent with the presence of what one would consider to be psychopathy. The participants also completed a 15-trait rating form to document quantitatively the presence of the core traits of psychopathy. Indicators of success included "a top notch police detective," "dean from a major university," "successful retail business," "made large sum of money and was mayor for three years," "managerial position in government organization," "full professor at two major universities," and "endowed professor with numerous federal grants" (Mullins-Sweatt et al., 2010, p. 556).

The participants also described the successful psychopath in terms of the FFM. Their descriptions were quite consistent across the three professions, and the traits that distinguished these successful psychopaths from a prototypic psychopath were being high rather than low in traits of conscientiousness. Prototypic psychopaths are considered to be irresponsible, lax, and negligent, and it is quite likely that these traits of low conscientiousness have contributed to their criminal arrests, whereas traits of high conscientiousness contribute to a successful psychopathic career. This is consistent with a large body of research to indicate that low conscientiousness is associated with occupational and academic failure, as well as criminal arrest (Ozer & Benet-Martinez, 2006).

One might question whether it would be accurate to describe the persons as being psychopaths, given that they were high rather than low in conscientiousness. They would certainly be inconsistent with the Cleckley (1941) psychopaths (Crego & Widiger, 2016a). However, the successful psychopaths did have such principal traits of psychopathy as callousness, dishonesty, low remorse, exploitativeness, and arrogance. These traits from the FFM domain of antagonism would appear to represent the core or key traits of psychopathy (Lynam & Miller, 2015; Miller & Lynam, 2015). The traits of disinhibition are also important and do contribute to the harmful, dangerous qualities of a psychopath (Widiger & Lynam, 1998), but they may also contribute to a likelihood of being careless, lax, or reckless that would lead to failure or even arrest and conviction.

A person who was unquestionably psychopathic was Ted Bundy. Bundy was a serial murderer. He was responsible for at least 30 homicides committed in seven states between 1974 and 1978. He was handsome, charming, bold, and engaging and would use his glib charm to entice his female victims into his car, where he would bludgeon them into submission. He once called himself "the most cold-hearted son of a bitch you'll ever meet" (Hare, 1993, p. 23). Samuel and Widiger (2007) surveyed clinicians as to the FFM profile of Ted Bundy, and it is noteworthy that his profile closely paralleled the FFM profile of a successful psychopath, with all of the traits of antagonism, neuroticism, and extraversion, coupled with high conscientiousness. Bundy was described as being highly competent, orderly, achievement striving, and deliberate. These are traits that boded well for the ability to become a successful serial murderer for so many years.

In sum, it is important to keep in mind that psychopathy is a constellation of traits, not all of which will be present in every case. There will be some persons who have all of the traits of psychopathy, but not all cases will be prototypic cases. Prototypic psychopathy includes traits of low conscientiousness (e.g., lax, irresponsible, and negligent), but an intriguing variation would be psychopathic persons characterized by high conscientiousness (e.g., competent, achievement-striving, and deliberate) that would perhaps be even more dangerous than the prototypic case.

Forensic assessment

There are quite a few alternative instruments for the forensic assessment of both psychopathy and ASPD (Gacono, 2016; Rojas & Widiger, in press-b). Many clinicians, particularly within the United States, would prefer, or would perhaps even need, to use a measure of DSM-5 Section II ASPD rather than psychopathy, given that ASPD remains the official diagnosis within the authoritative APA nomenclature. Medical, disability, and forensic settings within the United State are typically required to use the diagnostic nomenclature of the APA (2013). However, in Canada, many forensic psychologists prefer the PCL-R, and this is true as well for a portion of forensic psychologists within the United States (Hare & Neumann, 2008; Hare et al., 2012); DSM-5 ASPD and PCL-R psychopathy are highly convergent constructs (Crego & Widiger, 2015), but they are not precisely equivalent. Clinicians within forensic settings, such as a prison, would be advised to recognize that DSM-5 ASPD does probably over diagnose this disorder within populations predominated by a criminal history (Crego & Widiger, 2015; Hare, 2003).

The PCL-R (Hare, 2003) has been the predominant measure of the construct of psychopathy for many years. "The enormous increase in theory and research on psychopathy over the past two decades owes much to the development and adoption of the PCL-R as a common metric for assessing the disorder" (Hare & Neumann, 2008, p. 218). Some have even referred to the PCL-R as "the gold standard in psychopathy research" (Vitacco, Neumann, & Jackson, 2005; Westen & Weinberger, 2004, p. 599). Indeed, the PCL-R has in fact been the only semistructured interview for the assessment of psychopathy for many years. It is generally preferable for there to be multiple alternative measures, allowing for the ability to consider whether any particular finding is due to an idiosyncratic aspect of the assessment (Rojas & Widiger, in press-b). At least with respect to semistructured interview assessments, this has not been feasible, given the predominance of the PCL-R. Some have come to question the reliance on the PCL-R for psychopathy research (Cooke, Michie, Hart, & Clark, 2005). There is now though an alternative semistructured interview for psychopathy, the Comprehensive Assessment of Psychopathic Personality (CAPP), that purportedly relies less heavily on criminal behaviors for its assessment (Cooke & Logan, 2015). Empirical studies comparing the PCL-R with the CAPP are now emerging (e.g., Pedersen, Kunz, Elsass, & Rasmussen, 2010).

There are many alternative self-report measures of psychopathy (and many alternative semistructured interviews for ASPD; Rojas & Widiger, in press-b). The PCL-R has been preferred over self-report measures in part because it would seem paradoxical to rely on the self-report for a syndrome that explicitly involves dishonesty, manipulativeness, and deceit. Self-report measures would not appear to be problematic though within research contexts in which there is little motivation for respondents to be deceitful. However, it would likely be naïve to rely on a self-report measure within a forensic setting in which there is an invested interest or benefit on the part of the respondent not to appear psychopathic (Kelsey, Rogers, & Robinson, 2015). In addition, very few self-report measures, and none of the more recently developed self-report measures of psychopathy, have validated cutoff scores for interpretation.

One of the major strengths of the PCL-R is its success in risk assessment, prediction of violence, and prediction of criminal recidivism (Hare & Neumann, 2010; Hare et al., 2012). A PCL-R assessment has often been integral for a forensic parole hearing. "Perhaps the PCL-R *saves* lives . . .because it helps to keep very dangerous people in prison" (Hare, 2003, p. 16, emphasis in original). However, concerns have also been raised with respect to a potential tendency of a PCL-R assessment to be unable to identify whether the person is no longer psychopathic (DeMatteo & Edens, 2006). The PCL-R assessment relies heavily on the history of exploitative, selfish, deceitful, and manipulative (e.g., criminal) acts. Indeed, this is one of the strengths of the measure as the prevalence, nature, and severity of the past criminal behavior are instrumental in predicting future criminal behavior (Corrado, Vincent, Hart, & Cohen, 2004; Leistico, Salekin, DeCoster, & Rogers, 2008). But, to the extent that an assessment is largely historical, there is little room to recognize actual personality change. Of course, this is not a concern that would be unique to the PCL-R. What is apparent is that further work and research is needed with respect to the validity of any personality measure to identify actual change, particularly when the person is within an incarcerated setting, providing a heavily restricted and controlled environment that does not allow much room for the expression of psychopathic traits.

Comorbidity

Of course, like many other forms of psychopathology, including externalizing psychopathology, ASPD—psychopathy does not often occur alone. In fact, ASPD co-occurs with other externalizing disorders (such as substance use) most, if not all, of the time. Therefore, a comprehensive assessment of ASPD—psychopathic PD will also consider the most commonly comorbid disorders which include narcissistic personality disorder (NPD), substance use disorders, and problems with criminality (Widiger & Crego, in press).

Narcissistic personality disorder

NPD is another personality disorder included within DSM-5 (APA, 2013). NPD involves a pervasive pattern of grandiosity (in fantasy or behavior), need for admiration or adulation, and lack of empathy (APA, 2013). Its primary diagnostic criteria include a grandiose sense of self-importance; preoccupation with success, power, brilliance, or beauty; a belief that one is special and can only be understood by high-status individuals; a demand for excessive admiration; a strong sense of entitlement; an exploitation of others; lack of empathy; and arrogance. There is a substantial body of research on narcissism (Miller, Widiger, & Campbell, 2010; Pincus & Lukowitsky, 2010), although, surprisingly, NPD was actually slated for deletion from DSM-5 (Skodol, 2012).

Narcissism has a theoretical and clinical literature that is quite independent of psychopathy. Nevertheless, there have also long been cross-references within both literatures (Widiger & Crego, in press). For example, psychodynamic views of narcissism suggest that many features of psychopathy are apparent within narcissistic persons (Kernberg, 1998). Antisocial and psychopathic tendencies are in fact conceptualized as being on a continuum with narcissism, with both involving a motivation to dominate, humiliate, and manipulate others. Kernberg (1970), a theorist of narcissism, had suggested that "the antisocial personality may be considered a subgroup of the narcissistic personality" (p. 51). Hart and Hare (1998), theorists of psychopathy, suggested conversely that "psychopathy can be viewed as a higher-order construct with two distinct, albeit related facets, one of which is very similar to the clinical concept of narcissism" (p. 429).

Some of the features of NPD are explicitly suggestive of psychopathy, notably a grandiose sense of self-importance and arrogant, haughty behaviors (akin to psychopathic arrogant self-appraisal); lack of empathy; and interpersonal exploitation. It has even been intimated that NPD is closer to Cleckley's (1941) conception of psychopathy than is ASPD (Hare, Hart, & Harpur, 1991; Harpur, Hart, & Hare, 2002).

Consideration was given in the development of DSM-IV ASPD (APA, 1994) to include additional features of PCL-R psychopathy, in particular glib charm, arrogance, and lack of empathy (Widiger & Corbitt, 1995). However, a significant concern with this proposal was that these features were also central to the diagnosis of NPD. Their inclusion would have markedly increased the diagnostic co-occurrence of ASPD with NPD. The authors of the NPD criterion set (Gunderson, Ronningstam, & Smith, 1991) considered the antisocial and narcissistic personality disorders to be qualitatively distinct conditions and argued that revisions should help differentiate between the disorders rather than further increase their overlap. The final decision for DSM-IV was to at least acknowledge that glib charm, arrogance, and lack of empathy are included within other conceptualizations of ASPD and that their inclusion within the criterion set would likely increase the validity of the assessment of ASPD within prison and other forensic settings (APA, 1994).

Substance use disorders

The comorbidity of substance use disorder with ASPD and psychopathy is substantial (Widiger & Crego, in press). These are both externalizing disorders that are characterized in large part by disinhibitory, reckless, and indulgent behavior (Krueger et al., 2002). Alcohol and/or drug use are even included within the diagnostic criteria for ASPD and/or psychopathy. For example, driving while intoxicated is listed as a potential indicator of the "reckless disregard" criterion for ASPD, and one of Cleckley's (1941, 1976) criteria for psychopathy was "fantastic and uninviting behavior with drink." Many other behaviors that would count toward a diagnosis of ASPD and/or psychopathy—such as thefts, deception, conning, poor work history, and recklessness—could be due, at least in part, to a history of dyscontrolled drug usage. In the development of DSM-III, DSM-III-R, and DSM-IV, it was suggested that an exclusion criterion be added to ASPD to disallow the diagnosis when the behaviors involved substance usage (Widiger & Corbitt, 1995). However, this exclusion criterion has never been added because the differentiation between ASPD and substance dependence is facilitated by the requirement for evidence of conduct disorder in childhood. The presence of conduct disorder prior to the age of 15 will often date the onset of ASPD prior to the onset of a substance-related disorder, making it unlikely that the adult antisocial acts involving substance-related behaviors are secondary to an adult substance-related disorder. The PCL-R includes two similar diagnostic criteria (i.e., early behavior problems and juvenile delinquency), but, in contrast to DSM-5 ASPD, the PCL-R does not require the childhood antecedents to be evident for the diagnosis of psychopathy (Hare, 2003).

Differentiation between ASPD and substance use disorder is more complicated if the onset and course of the substance usage are congruent with the onset and course of the ASPD behaviors. However, if both have been evident prior to the age of 15 and persist thereafter into adulthood, it may then be clinically meaningless to differentiate them. Both disorders would likely be present. Persons with ASPD can develop a substance use disorder, and a substance use disorder can contribute to the development of ASPD (Widiger & Crego, in press). In such cases, it might be useful to recognize that both warrant recognition and treatment.

Criminal behavior

The relationship of criminality to psychopathy warrants particular consideration, as the extent to which psychopathy should be diagnosed on the basis of criminal and/or antisocial behavior has been hotly debated (Hare & Neumann, 2008, 2010; Skeem & Cooke, 2010). A longstanding criticism of the DSM-III through DSM-IV is that the ASPD criterion sets placed too much emphasis on criminal behavior. Hare (1986), for example, suggested that DSM-III ASPD was unable to identify psychopathic persons who lacked a criminal history because it purportedly relied heavily on criminal behavior for its diagnosis. "DSM-III has difficulty in identifying individuals who fit the classic picture of psychopathy but who manage to avoid early or formal contact with the criminal justice system" (Hare, 1986, p. 21). This charge is somewhat ironic, as Skeem and Cooke (2010) eventually suggested that the PCL-R suffers from the same limitation by placing too much emphasis on criminal history for its diagnosis. "The two-factor model [of the PCL-R] poorly identifies this 'great majority of psychopaths' who escape contact with the legal system or simply express their psychopathic tendencies in a manner that does not conflict with the law" (Skeem & Cooke, 2010, p. 435).

The criticism of DSM-III was perhaps overstated given that most of the DSM-III diagnostic criteria in fact made no explicit reference to criminal activity (referring instead to poor work history, irresponsible parenting, relationship infidelity, aggression, lack of planning, and financial irresponsibility). On the other hand, it was certainly true that the DSM-III and DSM-III-R ASPD criterion sets identified considerably more persons with ASPD within prison settings than would be identified as psychopathic using the PCL-R (Hare, 2003; Hare et al., 2012).

As suggested from the DSM-IV ASPD field trial (Widiger et al., 1996), criminal behavior is not a particularly useful indicator of psychopathy within prison or forensic settings, the primary settings for the majority of PCL-R research. The reason is rather clear, in that criminal behavior is universal within a prison population. In contrast, adult criminal behavior is more specific to persons who are psychopathic within routine clinical settings. The DSM-IV (now DSM-5) diagnostic criteria for ASPD were presented in a descending order of diagnostic value (Gunderson, 1998). Adult criminal behavior is listed first because it is the most useful criterion within general clinical settings (Widiger & Corbitt, 1995).

Criminal behavior has long been closely associated with psychopathy. "The clinical concept of psychopathy is linked inextricably to criminal behavior, and in particular to criminal violence" (Hart, 1998, p. 355; but for an alternative view, see Skeem & Cooke, 2010). Psychopathy is a diagnostic concept that was developed in part to help understand and explain criminal behavior (Hare & Neumann, 2008). Many studies have indeed indicated that psychopathy as defined by the PCL-R has been successful in identifying a particularly callous, dangerous, and remorseless subset of criminals who repeatedly engage in particularly heinous, brutal, and exploitative acts (Hare et al., 2012).

As noted by Patrick (2006), "without exception, all the individuals represented in [Cleckley's] case histories engage in repeated violations of the law-including truancy, vandalism, theft, fraud, forgery, fire-setting, drunkenness and disorderly conduct, assault, reckless driving, drug offences, prostitution, and escape" (p. 608). As expressed by Cleckley (1976), "not only is the psychopath undependable, but also in more active ways he cheats, deserts, annoys, brawls, fails, and lies without any apparent compunction" (p. 343). In sum, "there is no question that Cleckley considered persistent antisocial deviance to be characteristic of psychopaths" (Patrick, 2006, p. 608).

However, it is also worth noting though that very few of Cleckley's psychopaths were cruel, angry, hostile, callous, aggressive, or even just mean (Crego & Widiger, 2016a). They were exploitative, duplicitous, dishonest, unempathic, insincere, and manipulative, but not in any particularly vicious or brutal manner. None of Cleckley's psychopaths committed murder or rape, let alone serial murder or serial rape (Patrick, 2006). These are not the psychopaths that are typically portrayed in the media or clinical literature, such as Clyde Barrow, Ted Bundy, Kenneth Bianchi, or Henry Hill, who committed many severe crimes of violence (Lilienfeld & Arkowitz, 2007; Widiger & Crego, in press). This is not to suggest that a serial murder, such as Ted Bundy (Samuel & Widiger, 2007), is not accurately described as being psychopathic, but the cruel, heinous, depraved, and barbarous acts of such persons are not at all evident in the psychopaths of Cleckley (Crego & Widiger, 2016a; Skeem et al., 2011). Their antisocial acts were, for the most part, petty, if not even pointless. The Cleckley psychopaths were not persons pursuing a productive criminal career, having successfully worked their way up in organized crime. Their antisocial acts were said by Cleckley to be "inadequately motivated"; that is, often with no apparent benefit or value. The Cleckley psychopath with the highest score on inadequately motivated antisocial behavior was Tom, who "wandered more or less aimlessly, sometimes shooting at a [farmer's] chickens, setting fire to a rural privy . . . or perhaps loitering about a cigar store or a poolroom, reading the comics, throwing rocks at squirrels in a park, perpetuating small thefts or swindles" (Cleckley, 1955, p. 91).

Although it is not difficult to imagine a psychopathic person without a criminal record or even a criminal history, it is perhaps difficult to imagine a psychopathic person not having a history infused with unethical, predatory, and other disreputable acts. Skeem and Cooke (2010) made a distinction between criminal and antisocial behavior. "Criminal" behavior is sanctioned by the legal system, whereas "antisocial" behavior is more inclusive, involving "behavior that defeats the interests of the social order" (p. 435). "Snakes in suits" (i.e., psychopathic persons in business, law, or other white collar professions; Babiak & Hare, 2006) may not in fact break many laws, but they will significantly bend, massage, and work the rules to an unfair, self-serving advantage. Although Skeem and Cooke were quite critical of including criminal behavior within an assessment of psychopathy, they did feel that "some antisocial behavior seems inherent to the interpersonal and affective core of psychopathy (e.g., noncriminal manipulative behavior)" (p. 435). Indeed, it is difficult to imagine a person being exploitative, callous, selfish, unremorseful, egocentric, deceitful, and manipulative but not engaging in any significant unethical and/or antisocial behavior (Hare & Neumann, 2008).

Etiology

Given the tremendous costs to society (and the psychopath) of this personality disorder, understanding its etiology would go far in developing some form of prevention. Twin, family, and adoption studies have provided substantial support for a genetic contribution to the etiology of the criminal, delinquent tendencies of persons meeting criteria for ASPD, accounting for approximately 50% of the variance in antisocial behavior (Waldman & Rhee, 2006; Werner, Few, & Bucholz, 2015). Exactly what is inherited in ASPD and psychopathy, however, is not really known

(Glenn & Raine, 2014). Most likely ASPD and psychopathy involve independent genetic contributions to the disinhibitory, antagonistic, assertive, and fearlessness traits (Jarnecke & South, 2017).

Numerous environmental factors have also been implicated for ASPD (Crego & Widiger, 2016b; Werner et al., 2015). Shared, or common, environmental influences account for 15%–20% of variation in antisocial behavior (Rhee & Waldman, 2002). Not surprisingly, shared environmental factors such as low family income, poor parental supervision, single-parent households, inner city residence, rearing by antisocial parents, delinquent siblings, parental conflict, harsh discipline, and neglect have all been implicated (Farrington, 2006). Nonshared environmental influences (30%) comprise the remaining variance not accounted for by the genetic (50%) or shared environmental (20%) influences. Nonshared environmental factors may include delinquent peers, individual social and academic experiences, or sexual, physical abuse (Moffitt, 2005).

The interactive effects of genetic and environmental influences though are difficult to tease apart, confusing what the estimates of variance accounted for in antisocial behavior mean in terms of causation. For example, a person with a genetic disposition for antisocial behavior will likely elicit experiences and responses that can in turn contribute to the development of antisocial behavior, such as interpersonal relationship problems, academic difficulties, and excellent, harsh, and/or inconsistent discipline from parental figures. The person genetically disposed to antisocial behavior will create an environment that will further reinforce antisocial behavior. In addition, antisocial individuals will receive their genes from antisocial parents who may have also modeled delinquent and irresponsible behavior. It can then be quite difficult to disentangle what is really genetic and what is really environmental. Studies that explicitly address these issues though have found that environmental factors continue to play an important part in the etiology of antisocial behavior beyond simply the genetic factors. For instance, after controlling for the genetic component of physical maltreatment, Jaffee, Caspi, Moffitt, and Taylor (2004) reported that the environmental etiological effect of physical maltreatment remained.

In sum, the etiology of ASPD–psychopathy appears to be the result of gene–environment interactions. No single gene or environmental event is likely to be the sole cause, consistent with the view that the syndrome is a constellation of traits, each with its own independent etiology (Crego & Widiger, 2015; Lilienfeld, Watts, & Smith, 2015). The development of this syndrome is the result of a series of events (e.g., physical abuse, neglect) and experiences (tough urban environment) that interact with fundamental dispositions (e.g., disinhibition and antagonism), the impact of which accumulates over time.

Underlying pathology

The symptoms of a mental disorder are presumably due to an underlying pathology, such as a cognitive, emotional, and/or neurophysiological deficit. Researchers have devoted much of their careers in an effort to discover and/or articulate the specific pathology of psychopathy (e.g., Cleckley, 1941; Hare, 1993; Lykken, 1995). However, with the recognition that psychopathy is a multifaceted syndrome of independent traits (e.g., antagonism, low conscientiousness, fearlessness, and excitement-seeking), there is unlikely to be a specific pathology (Lilienfeld, Watts, Smith, Berg, et al., 2015; Widiger & Lynam, 1998). Brain imaging findings implicate abnormalities in prefrontal, limbic, and paralimbic structures, including the orbital frontal cortex, ventromedial prefrontal cortex, anterior superior temporal gyrus, insula, anterior and posterior cingulate, amygdala, and parahippocampal gyrus (Stratton, Kiehl, & Hanlon, 2015). Raine (in press) speculates that the prefrontal, amygdale, striatal regions provide three core aspects of ASPD dysfunction, namely a lack of self-control (prefrontal), low avoidance of punishment (amygdala), and excessive approach to rewarding stimuli (striatum).

Cleckley (1941) had suggested that the psychopathic individual suffered from a "superego lacunae" or a "semantic dementia," a deficit of conscience or, more generally, a deficient processing of feelings and emotions. Laboratory research has provided support for this theoretical model in studies assessing the psychopath's autonomic reaction to emotional words and fearful images (Blackburn, 2006; Crego & Widiger, 2016b). This deficit may represent aspects of antagonism, deficits that reflect feelings of a cold-hearted callousness, an indifference to the concerns and suffering of others, and a lack of remorse.

Cognitive functioning deficits have also been implicated. The psychopath's notorious failure to accurately anticipate negative consequences suggests to some a cognitive deficit (Hamilton, Racer, & Newman, 2015; Hiatt & Newman, 2006). Existing research indicates that the psychopath experiences deficits of attention and response modulation (Gao, Glenn, Schug, Yang, & Raine, 2009). According to this research, psychopaths continue to engage in behaviors that are initially interpreted as positively reinforcing, even when additional information is presented indicating substantial overall costs (Newman & Lorenz, 2003). This deficit might relate to the broader trait of low constraint or disinhibition, albeit this has not been tested. In any case, a limitation of this model is that it does not appear to explain a substantial proportion of psychopathic behavior.

Many psychophysiological deficits have also been associated with psychopathy, including for example a low level of physiological arousal and/or fear response (Fowles & Dindo, 2006). Support for this hypothesis has included abnormally low physiological responses (reduced skin conductance) to a conditioned stimulus paired with electric shock, indicating that the psychopath may not develop the expected anticipatory arousal from threat of physical punishment. Additional autonomic arousal assessments include low resting heart rate levels and startle response deficits (Derefinko & Widiger, 2016). This research would be consistent with and supportive of low levels of FFM anxiousness. Some distress-proneness (FFM anxiousness or neuroticism), along with attentional self-regulation (FFM constraint or conscientiousness), may be necessary for the development of feelings of guilt and a moral conscience. Normal levels of neuroticism may promote the internalization of a conscience by associating wrongdoing or misbehavior with distress and anxiety (Fowles & Kochanska, 2000; Kochanska & Kim, 2014).

In sum, consistent with the research on etiology, there is unlikely to be a single pathology. As noted earlier, ASPD–psychopathy is a syndrome, a constellation of traits, each having its own distinct underlying pathology. The response modulation deficits suggested by Hiatt and Newman (2006) might underlying the traits of disinhibition, the deficits in empathy suggested by Hare (2003) concerning the traits of antagonism, and the low physiological fear arousal concerning the domain of low neuroticism (Lynam & Widiger, 2007; Widiger & Lynam, 1998).

Course

ASPD–psychopathy is essentially a lifelong condition that is evident within childhood, albeit as yet not fully developed, and remains largely present throughout adulthood, consistent with all personality disorders (APA, 2013). Many clinicians and researchers though have been uncomfortable in diagnosing personality disorders within childhood, given the implication that they would be labeling a child with a largely lifelong condition. However, ASPD is the personality disorder for which there is a clear childhood variant: conduct disorder. Conduct disorder, an externalizing disorder of childhood, includes aggression to people and/or animals (e.g., bullying, fights), destruction of property, deceitfulness (lying or stealing), and serious rule violations. Conduct disorder is clearly a childhood variant of ASPD. In fact, one is required to document evidence for features of conduct disorder when diagnosing ASPD (APA, 2013). Approximately 40% of children who meet criteria for conduct disorder (particularly if there is an early age of onset) grow up to meet criteria for ASPD. In addition, DSM-5 now includes a specifier for conduct disorder for the presence of limited prosocial emotions; more specifically, lack of remorse or guilt, callous lack of empathy, unconcern about performance, and/or shallow or deficient affect (APA, 2013). These additional traits are clearly extending the concept of adult psychopathy to children with a particularly severe form of conduct disorder (Barry et al., 2000; Frick, Ray, Thornton, & Kahn, 2014), a proposal presaged by Lynam (1996) years ago.

Consistent with all personality disorders, there are also compelling data to indicate that ASPD is a relatively chronic disorder which persists throughout adulthood, although research does suggest that as the person reaches middle to older age, the frequency of criminal acts decreases. Nevertheless, the core personality traits may remain largely stable (Hare et al., 2012).

Psychopaths are typically quite comfortable in their skin, even though the psychopathic traits cause considerable trouble for them. As noted earlier, the life of a psychopath is at times glamorized and can be very appealing at a young age. Henry Hill was a member of the New York City Mafia; more specifically, the Lucchese crime family. His life story was portrayed in the highly successful Martin Scorsese movie, *Goodfellas*. As an adolescent, Hill famously stated, "At the age of twelve my ambition was to be a gangster" (Pileggi, 1985, p. 13). However, the exciting psychopathic lifestyle can come with a heavy cost. Although psychopaths are clearly dangerous to others, they are also actually dangerous to themselves. The prognosis for their future is not good. Psychopathic persons have a very difficult time maintaining employment; their relationships are unstable; they are at risk of serious injury and even death; and many spend a considerable amount of time imprisoned (Hare et al., 2012).

Indeed, the outcome for the three psychopaths identified earlier within this chapter illustrates well the not uncommon, unhappy ending. The movie *Goodfellas* ends with Henry Hill entering a witness protection program, avoiding a very long imprisonment by informing on most everyone else within his crime family. Subsequently, Hill was divorced by his wife, disavowed by his two children (Hill & Hill, 2004), and arrested again numerous times (often for drug-related crimes), contributing to a removal from the witness protection program. The life course for Ted Bundy ended even worse, with an execution by electric chair. As indicated earlier, Clyde Barrow died as a young adult, ambushed in a hail of gunfire (Traherne, 2000).

Treatment

Very few psychopaths, or persons with ASPD, seek treatment for their personality disorder. If they are in treatment, it is most likely due to the presence of a substance use disorder, or an effort to avoid or limit incarceration. ASPD is considered to be the most difficult personality disorder to treat (Gunderson & Gabbard, 2000; Hare et al., 2012). Individuals with ASPD can be seductively charming and may declare a commitment to change, but they often lack sufficient motivation. Their declarations of desire to change might even be dishonest. They will also fail to appreciate the future costs associated with antisocial acts (e.g., imprisonment and lack of meaningful interpersonal relationships) and may stay in treatment only as required by an external source, such as a parole. Studies have indicated that outpatient therapy is not likely to be successful, although the extent to which persons with ASPD are entirely unresponsive to treatment may have been somewhat exaggerated (Salekin, 2002). Rather than attempt to develop a sense of conscience in these individuals, therapeutic techniques should perhaps focus on rational and utilitarian arguments against repeating past mistakes. These approaches would focus on the tangible, material value of prosocial behavior (Young, Klosko, & Weishaar, 2003). Motivation interviewing might also be useful (Miller & Rollnick, 2012). Residential programs that provide a carefully controlled environment of structure and supervision, combined with peer confrontation, have been recommended and earlier in the life the better (Crego & Widiger, 2016b). However, it is unknown what benefits may be sustained after the ASPD individual leaves this environment. If a weekend, 2-week, or even 3-month environmental intervention can change behavior, then a return of the person to a tough, urban environment, with close friends still engaging in antisocial acts, would also likely return the person to his or her antisocial lifestyle.

Conclusions

Psychopathy is personality syndrome consisting of a constellation of maladaptive (and perhaps adaptive) personality traits. The core traits are antagonistic (i.e., callousness, exploitativeness, manipulativeness, deceitfulness, lack of empathy, and aggression), coupled with traits of low conscientiousness (laxness, irresponsibility, and rashness), high extraversion (assertiveness, boldness, and excitement-seeking), high neuroticism (angry hostility), and low neuroticism (fearlessness and glib charm). Psychopathy may indeed represent the most dangerous and lethal combination of traits that characterize a person. However, although psychopathic persons pose a considerable threat to others, they are also harmful to themselves, as their lives are replete with loss, impairment, and failure, including imprisonment and at times even death. Psychopathy, particularly as assessed by the PCL-R, has established itself as an important clinical construct, especially within forensic-correctional settings. Psychopathy was among the first disorders of personality to be recognized and continues to generate substantial social, clinical, and public interest. There are many areas of dispute within the psychopathy research literature (e.g., whether it should include such traits as fearlessness and boldness and whether these traits are adaptive strengths; the difficulty in identifying a specific etiology or pathology; and the optimal or most accurate assessment instrument). However, these debates are also an indication of how important, active, and lively is the investigation of psychopathy and how further work is urgently needed on its etiology, pathology, and treatment. Future research might be most effective if it is focused on the individual components of the disorder rather than the full syndrome.

References

American Psychiatric Association. (1994). *Diagnostic and statistical manual of mental disorders* (4th ed.). Washington, DC: American Psychiatric Association.

American Psychiatric Association. (2013). *Diagnostic and statistical manual of mental disorders* (5th ed.). Washington, DC: American Psychiatric Association.

Babiak, P., & Hare, R. D. (2006). *Snakes in suits: When psychopaths go to work*. New York, NY: Regan Books/Harper Collins Publishers.

Barry, C. T., Frick, P. J., DeShazo, T. M., McCoy, M., Ellis, M., & Loney, B. R. (2000). The importance of callous–unemotional traits for extending the concept of psychopathy to children. *Journal of Abnormal Psychology*, *109*(2), 335–340.

Blackburn, R. (2006). Other theoretical models of psychopathy. In C. Patrick (Ed.), *Handbook of psychopathy* (pp. 35–57). New York, NY: Guilford Press.

Blashfield, R. K., & Reynolds, S. M. (2012). An invisible college view of the DSM-5 personality disorder classification. *Journal of Personality Disorders*, *26*, 821–829.

Cleckley, H. (1941). *The mask of sanity*. St. Louis, MO: Mosby.

Cleckley, H. (1955). *The mask of sanity* (3rd ed.). St. Louis, MO: Mosby.

Cleckley, H. (1976). *The mask of sanity* (5th ed.). St. Louis, MO: Mosby.

Cooke, D. J., & Logan, C. (2015). Capturing clinical complexity: Towards a personality-oriented measure of psychopathy. *Journal of Criminal Justice*, *43*(4), 262–273.

Cooke, D. J., Michie, C., Hart, S. D., & Clark, D. (2005). Searching for the pan-cultural core of psychopathic personality disorder. *Personality and Individual Differences*, *39*, 283–295.

Corrado, R. R., Vincent, G. M., Hart, S. D., & Cohen, I. M. (2004). Predictive validity of the Psychopathy Checklist: Youth Version for general and violent recidivism. *Behavioral Sciences & the Law*, *22*, 5–22.

Costa, P. T., & McCrae, R. R. (1992). *Revised NEO Personality Inventory (NEO PI-R) and NEO Five-Factor Inventory (NEO-FFI) professional manual*. Odessa, FL: Psychological Assessment Resources.

Costa, P. T., & McCrae, R. R. (2017). The NEO inventories as instruments of psychological theory. In T. A. Widiger (Ed.), *The Oxford handbook of the five factor model* (pp. 11–37). New York, NY: Oxford University Press.

Crego, C., & Widiger, T. A. (2014). Psychopathy, DSM-5, and a caution. *Personality Disorders: Theory, Research, and Treatment*, *5*, 335–347.

Crego, C., & Widiger, T. A. (2015). Psychopathy and the DSM. *Journal of Personality*, *83*, 665–677.

Crego, C., & Widiger, T. A. (2016a). Cleckley's psychopaths: Revisited. *Journal of Abnormal Psychology*, *125*, 75–87.

Crego, C., & Widiger, T. A. (2016b). Personality disorders. In J. Maddux, & B. Winstead (Eds.), *Psychopathology: Foundations for a contemporary understanding* (4th ed., pp. 218–236). Mahwah, NJ: Lawrence Erlbaum Associates, Inc.

DeMatteo, D., & Edens, J. F. (2006). The role and relevance of the Psychopathy Checklist-Revised in court: A case law survey of US courts (1991-2004). *Psychology, Public Policy, and Law*, *12*, 214–221.

De Raad, B., & Mlačić, B. (2017). The lexical foundation of the Big Five factor model. In T. A. Widiger (Ed.), *The Oxford handbook of the five factor model* (pp. 191–216). New York, NY: Oxford University Press.

Derefinko, K. J., & Widiger, T. A. (2016). Antisocial personality disorder. In S. H. Fatemi, & P. J. Clayton (Eds.), *The medical basis of psychiatry* (4th ed., pp. 229–245). Totowa, NJ: Humana Press.

Dutton, K. (2012). *The wisdom of psychopaths: What saints, spies, and serial killers can teach us about success*. New York, NY: Macmillan.

Farrington, D. P. (2006). Family background and psychopathy. In C. J. Patrick (Ed.), *Handbook of psychopathy* (pp. 229–250). New York, NY: Guilford Press.

Fowles, D. C., & Dindo, L. (2006). A dual-deficit model of psychopathy. In C. J. Patrick (Ed.), *Handbook of psychopathy* (pp. 14–34). New York, NY: Guilford Press.

Fowles, D. C., & Kochanska, G. (2000). Temperament as a moderator of pathways to conscience in children: The contribution of electrodermal activity. *Psychophysiology*, *37*, 788–795.

Frick, P. J., Ray, J. V., Thornton, L. C., & Kahn, R. E. (2014). Can callous-unemotional traits enhance the understanding, diagnosis, and treatment of serious conduct problems in children and adolescents? A comprehensive review. *Psychological Bulletin*, *140*, 1–57.

Gacono, C. B. (Ed.), (2016). *The clinical and forensic assessment of psychopathy. A practitioner's guide* (2nd ed.). New York, NY: Routledge.

Gao, Y., Glenn, A. L., Schug, R. A., Yang, Y., & Raine, A. (2009). The neurobiology of psychopathy: A neurodevelopmental perspective. *Canadian Journal of Psychiatry*, *54*, 813–823.

Glenn, A. L., & Raine, A. (2014). *Psychopathy: An introduction to biological findings and their implications*. New York, NY: New York University Press.

Gunderson, J. G. (1998). DSM-IV personality disorders: Final overview. In T. A. Widiger, A. Frances, H. A. Pincus, R. Ross, M. B. First, W. Davis, & M. Kline (Eds.), *DSM-IV sourcebook* (Vol. 4, pp. 1123–1140). Washington, DC: American Psychiatric Association.

Gunderson, J. G., & Gabbard, G. O. (Eds.), (2000). *Psychotherapy for personality disorders*. Washington, DC: American Psychiatric Press.

Gunderson, J. G., Ronningstam, E., & Smith, L. (1991). Narcissistic personality disorder: A review of data on DSM-III-R descriptions. *Journal of Personality Disorders*, *5*, 167–177.

Hall, J. R., & Benning, S. D. (2006). The "Successful" Psychopath: Adaptive and subclinical manifestations of psychopathy in the general population. In C. J. Patrick (Ed.), *Handbook of psychopathy* (pp. 459–478). New York, NY: Guilford Press.

Hamilton, R. K., Racer, K. H., & Newman, J. P. (2015). Impaired integration in psychopathy: A unified theory of psychopathic dysfunction. *Psychological Review*, *122*, 770–791.

Hare, R. D. (1986). Twenty years experience with the Cleckley psychopath. In W. H. Reid, D. Dorr, J. I. Walker, & J. W. Bonner, III (Eds.), *Unmasking the psychopath* (pp. 3–27). New York, NY: W.W. Norton.

Hare, R. D. (1993). *Without conscience. The disturbing world of the psychopaths among us*. New York, NY: Pocket Books.

Hare, R. D. (2003). *Hare Psychopathy Checklist Revised (PCL-R). Technical manual*. North Tonawanda, NY: Multi-Health Systems.

Hare, R. D., Hart, S. D., & Harpur, T. J. (1991). Psychopathy and the DSM-IV criteria for antisocial personality disorder. *Journal of Abnormal Psychology*, *100*, 391–398.

Hare, R. D., & Neumann, C. S. (2008). Psychopathy as a clinical and empirical construct. *Annual Review of Clinical Psychology*, *4*, 217–246.

Hare, R. D., & Neumann, C. S. (2010). The role of antisociality in the psychopathy construct: Comment on Skeem and Cooke (2010). *Psychological Assessment*, *22*, 446–454.

Hare, R. D., Neumann, C. S., & Widiger, T. A. (2012). Psychopathy. In T. A. Widiger (Ed.), *Oxford handbook of personality disorder* (pp. 478–504). New York, NY: Oxford University Press.

Harpur, T. J., Hart, S. D., & Hare, R. D. (2002). Personality of the psychopath. In P. T. Costa, & T. A. Widiger (Eds.), *Personality disorders and the five factor model of personality* (2nd ed., pp. 299–324). Washington, DC: American Psychological Association.

Hart, S. D. (1998). Psychopathy and risk for violence. In D. J. Cooke, A. E. Forth, & R. D. Hare (Eds.), *Psychopathy: Theory, research, and implications for society* (pp. 355–373). Dordrecht, The Netherlands: Kluwer.

Hart, S. D., & Hare, R. D. (1998). Association between psychopathy and narcissism: Theoretical reviews and empirical evidence. In E. F. Ronningstam (Ed.), *Disorders of narcissism. Diagnostic, clinical, and empirical implications* (pp. 415–436). Washington, DC: American Psychiatric Press.

Hiatt, K. D., & Newman, J. P. (2006). Understanding psychopathy: The cognitive side. In C. J. Patrick (Ed.), *Handbook of psychopathy* (pp. 156–171). New York, NY: Guilford Press.

Hill, G., & Hill, G. (2004). *On the run: A Mafia childhood*. New York, NY: Time Warner Book Group.

Jaffee, S. R., Caspi, A., Moffitt, T. E., & Taylor, A. (2004). Physical maltreatment victim to antisocial child: Evidence of an environmentally mediated process. *Journal of Abnormal Psychology*, *113*, 44–55.

Jarnecke, A. M., & South, S. C. (2017). Behavior and molecular genetics of the five factor model. In T. A. Widiger (Ed.), *The Oxford handbook of the five factor model* (pp. 301–318). New York, NY: Oxford University Press.

John, O. P., Naumann, L. P., & Soto, C. J. (2008). Paradigm shift to the integrative Big Five trait taxonomy: History, measurement, and conceptual issues. In O. P. John, R. R. Robins, & L. A. Pervin (Eds.), *Handbook of personality. Theory and research* (3rd ed., pp. 114–158). New York, NY: Guilford Press.

Kelsey, K. R., Rogers, R., & Robinson, E. V. (2015). Self-report measures of psychopathy: What is their role in forensic assessments. *Journal of Psychopathology & Behavioral Assessment*, *37*, 380–391.

Kernberg, O. F. (1970). Factors in the treatment of narcissistic personalities. *Journal of the American Psychoanalytic Association*, *18*, 51–85.

Kernberg, O. F. (1998). Pathological narcissism and narcissistic personality disorder: Theoretical background and diagnostic classification. In E. F. Ronningstam (Ed.), *Disorders of narcissism. Diagnostic, clinical, and empirical implications* (pp. 29–52). Washington, DC: American Psychiatric Press.

Kochanska, G., & Kim, S. (2014). A complex interplay among the parent–child relationship, effortful control, and internalized, rule-compatible conduct in young children: Evidence from two studies. *Developmental Psychology*, *50*, 8–21.

Kotov, R., Krueger, R. F., Watson, D., Achenbach, T. M., Althoff, R. R., Bagby, M., … Zimmerman, M. (2017). The Hierarchical Taxonomy of Psychopathology: A dimensional alternative to traditional nosologies. *Journal of Abnormal Psychology*, *126*, 454–477.

Krueger, R. F., Eaton, N. R., Clark, L. A., Watson, D., Markon, K. E., Derringer, J., … Livesley, W. J. (2011). Deriving an empirical structure of personality pathology for DSM-5. *Journal of Personality Disorders*, *25*, 170–191.

Krueger, R. F., Hicks, B. M., Patrick, C. J., Carlson, S. R., Iacono, W. G., & McGue, M. (2002). Etiologic connections among substance dependence, antisocial behavior, and personality: Modeling the externalizing spectrum. *Journal of Abnormal Psychology*, *111*, 411–424.

Krueger, R. F., & Markon, K. E. (2014). The role of the DSM-5 personality trait model in moving toward a quantitative and empirically based approach to classifying personality and psychopathology. *Annual Review of Clinical Psychology*, *10*, 477–501.

Leistico, A. M. R., Salekin, R. T., DeCoster, J., & Rogers, R. (2008). A large-scale meta-analysis relating the Hare measures of psychopathy to antisocial conduct. *Law and Human Behavior*, *32*, 28–45.

Lilienfeld, S. O. (1994). Conceptual problems in the assessment of psychopathy. *Clinical Psychology Review*, *14*, 17–38.

Lilienfeld, S. O., & Arkowitz, H. (2007). What "psychopath" means. *Scientific American Mind*, *18*, 80–81.

Lilienfeld, S. O., Latzman, R. D., Watts, A. L., Smith, S. F., & Dutton, K. (2014). Correlates of psychopathic personality traits in everyday life: Results from a large community survey. *Frontiers in Psychology*, *5*, 740.

Lilienfeld, S. O., Patrick, C. J., Benning, S. D., Berg, J., Sellbom, M., & Edens, J. F. (2012). The role of fearless dominance in psychopathy: Confusions, controversies, and clarifications. *Personality Disorders: Theory, Research, and Treatment*, *3*, 327–340.

Lilienfeld, S. O., Waldman, I. D., Landfield, K., Watts, A. L., Rubenzer, S., & Faushingbauer, T. R. (2012). Fearless dominance and the U.S. presidency: Implications of psychopathic personality traits for successful and unsuccessful political leadership. *Journal of Personality and Social Psychology*, *103*, 489–505.

Lilienfeld, S. O., Watts, A. L., & Smith, S. (2015). Successful psychopathy: A scientific status report. *Current Directions in Psychological Science*, *24*, 298–303.

Lilienfeld, S. O., Watts, A. L., Smith, S., Berg, J. M., & Latzman, R. D. (2015). Psychopathy deconstructed and reconstructed: Identifying and assembling the personality building blocks of Cleckley's chimera. *Journal of Personality*, *83*, 593–610.

Lilienfeld, S. O., & Widows, M. R. (2005). *Psychopathic personality inventory—Revised professional manual*. Lutz, FL: Psychological Assessment Resources, Inc.

Lykken, D. T. (1995). *The antisocial personalities*. Hillsdale, NJ: Erlbaum.

Lynam, D. R. (1996). Early identification of chronic offenders: Who is the fledgling psychopath? *Psychological Bulletin*, *120*, 209–234.

Lynam, D. R., Gaughan, E., Miller, J. D., Miller, D., Mullins-Sweat, S., & Widiger, T. A. (2011). Assessing the basic traits associated with psychopathy: Development and validation of the Elemental Psychopathy Assessment. *Psychological Assessment*, *23*, 108–124.

Lynam, D. R., & Miller, J. D. (2012). Fearless dominance and psychopathy: A response to Lilienfeld et al. *Personality Disorders: Theory, Research, and Treatment*, *3*, 341–353.

Lynam, D. R., & Miller, J. D. (2015). Psychopathy from a basic trait perspective: The utility of a five-factor model approach. *Journal of Personality*, *83*, 611–626.

Lynam, D. R., & Vachon, D. D. (2012). Antisocial personality disorder in DSM-5: Missteps and missed opportunities. *Personality Disorders: Theory, Research, and Treatment*, *3*, 483–495.

Lynam, D. R., & Widiger, T. A. (2007). Using a general model of personality to identify the basic elements of psychopathy. *Journal of Personality Disorders*, *21*, 160–178.

Malterer, M. B., Lilienfeld, S. O., Neumann, C. S., & Newman, J. P. (2010). Concurrent validity of the Psychopathic Personality Inventory with offender and community samples. *Assessment*, *17*, 3–15.

Miller, J. D. (2012). Five-factor model personality disorder prototypes: A review of their development, validity, and comparison with alternative approaches. *Journal of Personality*, *80*, 1565–1591.

Miller, J. D. (2013). Prototype matching and the five-factor model: Capturing the DSM-IV personality disorders. In T. A. Widiger, & P. T. Costa (Eds.), *Personality disorders and the five-factor model of personality* (3rd ed., pp. 249–268). Washington, DC: American Psychological Association.

Miller, J. D., & Lynam, D. R. (2012). An examination of the Psychopathic Personality Inventory's nomological network: A meta-analytic review. *Personality Disorders: Theory, Research, and Treatment*, *3*, 305–326.

Miller, J. D., & Lynam, D. R. (2015). Understanding psychopathy using the basic elements of personality. *Social and Personality Psychology Compass*, *9*, 223–237.

Miller, J. D., Lyman, D. R., Widiger, T. A., & Leukefeld, C. (2001). Personality disorders as extreme variants of common personality dimensions: Can the Five Factor Model adequately represent psychopathy? *Journal of Personality*, *69*, 253–276.

Miller, J. D., Widiger, T. A., & Campbell, W. K. (2010). Narcissistic personality disorder and the DSM-V. *Journal of Abnormal Psychology*, *119*, 640–649.

Miller, W. R., & Rollnick, S. (2012). *Motivational interviewing* (3rd ed.). New York, NY: Guilford Press.

Moffitt, T. E. (2005). The new look of behavioral genetics in developmental psychopathology: Gene-environment interplay in antisocial behaviors. *Psychological Bulletin*, *131*, 533–554.

Mullins-Sweatt, S. N., Glover, N. G., Derefinko, K. J., Miller, J. D., & Widiger, T. A. (2010). The search for the successful psychopath. *Journal of Research in Personality*, *44*, 554–558.

Newman, J. P., & Lorenz, A. R. (2003). Response modulation and emotion processing: Implications for psychopathy and other dysregulatory psychopathology. In R. J. Davidson, K. Scherer, & H. H. Goldsmith (Eds.), *Handbook of affective sciences* (pp. 1043–1067). New York, NY: Oxford University Press.

O'Connor, B. P. (2002). A quantitative review of the comprehensiveness of the five-factor model in relation to popular personality inventories. *Assessment*, *9*, 188–203.

O'Connor, B. P. (2005). A search for consensus on the dimensional structure of personality disorders. *Journal of Clinical Psychology*, *61*, 323–345.

Ozer, D. J., & Benet-Martinez, V. (2006). Personality and the prediction of consequential outcomes. *Annual Review of Psychology*, *57*, 401–421.

Patrick, C. J. (2006). Back to the future: Cleckley as a guide to the next generation of psychopathy research. In C. J. Patrick (Ed.), *Handbook of psychopathy* (pp. 605–617). New York, NY: Guilford Press.

Patrick, C. J., Fowles, D. C., & Krueger, R. F. (2009). Triarchic conceptualization of psychopathy: Developmental origins of disinhibition, boldness, and meanness. *Development and Psychopathology*, *21*, 913–938.

Pedersen, L., Kunz, C., Elsass, P., & Rasmussen, K. (2010). Psychopathy as a risk factor for violent recidivism: Investigating the *Psychopathy Checklist Screening Version* (PCL: SV) and the *Comprehensive Assessment of Psychopathic Personality* (CAPP) in a forensic psychiatric setting. *International Journal of Forensic Mental Health*, *9*, 308–315.

Pileggi, N. (1985). *Wiseguy*. New York, NY: Simon Schuster Pocket Books.

Pincus, A. L., & Lukowitsky, M. R. (2010). Pathological narcissism and narcissistic personality disorder. *Annual Review of Clinical Psychology*, *6*, 421–446.

Poy, R., Seggara, P., Esteller, A., Lopez, R., & Molto, J. (2014). FFM description of the triarchic conceptualization of psychopathy in men and women. *Psychological Assessment*, *26*, 69–76.

Raine, A. (in press). Antisocial personality as a neurodevelopmental disorder. *Annual Review of Clinical Psychology*.

Rhee, S. H., & Waldman, I. D. (2002). Genetic and environmental influences on antisocial behavior: A meta-analysis of twin and adoption studies. *Psychological Bulletin*, *128*, 490–529.

Rojas, S.L., & Widiger, T.A. (2017). Coverage of the DSM-IV-TR/DSM-5 Section II personality disorders with the DSM-5 dimensional trait model. *Journal of Personality Disorders, 31(4), 462–482.*

Rojas, S.L., & Widiger, T.A. (in press-b). Personality disorders. In J. Hunsley & E. J. Mash (Eds.), *A guide to assessments that work*. New York, NY: Oxford University Press.

Salekin, R. T. (2002). Psychopathy and therapeutic pessimism: Clinical lore or clinical reality? *Clinical Psychology Review*, *22*, 79–112.

Samuel, D. B., & Widiger, T. A. (2007). Describing Ted Bundy's personality and working toward DSM-V. *Independent Practitioner*, *27*, 20–22.

Skeem, J. L., & Cooke, D. J. (2010). Is criminal behavior a central component of psychopathy? Conceptual directions for resolving the debate. *Psychological Assessment*, *22*, 433–445.

Skeem, J. L., Polaschek, D. L., Patrick, C. J., & Lilienfeld, S. O. (2011). Psychopathic personality bridging the gap between scientific evidence and public policy. *Psychological Science in the Public Interest*, *12*(3), 95–162.

Skodol, A. E. (2012). Personality disorders in DSM-5. *Annual Review of Clinical Psychology*, *8*, 317–344.

Skodol, A. E., Morey, L. C., Bender, D. S., & Oldham, J. M. (2013). The ironic fate of the personality disorders in DSM-5. *Personality Disorders: Theory, Research, and Treatment*, *4*, 342–349.

Stanley, J. H., Wygant, D. B., & Sellbom, M. (2013). Elaborating on the construct validity of the Triarchic Psychopathy Measure in a criminal offender sample. *Journal of Personality Assessment*, *95*, 343–350.

Stevens, G. W., Deuling, J. K., & Armenakis, A. A. (2012). Successful psychopaths: Are they unethical decision-makers and why? *Journal of Business Ethics*, *105*, 139–149.

Stratton, J., Kiehl, K. A., & Hanlon, R. E. (2015). The neurobiology of psychopathy. *Psychiatric Annals*, *45*, 186–194.

Traherne, J. (2000). *The strange history of Bonnie and Clyde*. New York, NY: Cooper Square Press.

Vitacco, M. J., Neumann, C. S., & Jackson, R. L. (2005). Testing a four-factor model of psychopathy and its association with ethnicity, gender, intelligence, and violence. *Journal of Consulting and Clinical Psychology*, *73*, 466–476.

Waldman, I. D., & Rhee, S. H. (2006). Genetic and environmental influences on psychopathy and antisocial behavior. In C. J. Patrick (Ed.), *Handbook of psychopathy* (pp. 205–228). New York, NY: Guilford Press.

Werner, K. B., Few, L. R., & Bucholz, K. K. (2015). Epidemiology, comorbidity, and behavioral genetics of antisocial personality disorder and psychopathy. *Psychiatric Annals*, *45*, 195–199.

Westen, D., Shedler, J., & Bradley, R. (2006). A prototype approach to personality disorder diagnosis. *American Journal of Psychiatry*, *163*, 846–856.

Westen, D., & Weinberger, J. (2004). When clinical description becomes statistical prediction. *American Psychologist*, *59*, 595–613.

Widiger, T. A. (2011). A shaky future for personality disorders. *Personality Disorders: Theory, Research, and Treatment*, *2*, 54–67.

Widiger, T. A. (Ed.), (2017). *The Oxford handbook of the five-factor model*. New York, NY: Oxford University Press.

Widiger, T. A., Cadoret, R., Hare, R., Robins, L., Rutherford, M., Zanarini, M., . . . Frances, A. (1996). DSM-IV antisocial personality disorder field trial. *Journal of Abnormal Psychology*, *105*, 3–16.

Widiger, T. A., & Corbitt, E. M. (1995). Antisocial personality disorder in DSM-IV. In W. J. Livesley (Ed.), *The DSM-IV personality disorders* (pp. 103–126). New York, NY: Guilford Press.

Widiger, T.A., & Crego, C. (in press). Psychopathy and DSM-5 psychopathology. In C.J. Patrick (Ed.), *Handbook of psychopathy* (2nd ed.). New York, NY: Guilford Press.

Widiger, T. A., & Lynam, D. R. (1998). Psychopathy from the perspective of the five-factor model of personality. In T. Millon, E. Simonsen, M. Birket-Smith, & R. D. Davis (Eds.), *Psychopathy: Antisocial, criminal, and violent behaviors* (pp. 171–187). New York, NY: Guilford Press.

Young, J. E., Klosko, J. S., & Weishaar, M. E. (2003). *Schema therapy: A practitioner's guide*. New York, NY: Guilford Press.

Yamagata, S., Suzuki, A., Ando, J., One, Y., Kijima, N., Yoshimura, K., Ostendorf, F., Angleitner, A., Riemann, R., Spinath, F. M., Livesley, W. J., & Jang, K. L. (2006). Is the genetic structure of human personality universal? A cross-cultural twin study from

North America, Europe, and Asia. *Journal of Personality and Social Psychology*, *90*, 987–998.

Zimmerman, M. (2011). A critique of the proposed prototype rating system for personality disorders in DSM-5. *Journal of Personality Disorders*, *25*, 206–221.

Part II

Risk Markers of Externalizing Problems

Negative affect

5

Cassandra M. Brandes[1], Shauna C. Kushner[2], and Jennifer L. Tackett[1]
[1]Northwestern University, Evanston, IL, United States, [2]Toronto, ON, Canada

Traits reflecting self-regulatory capacity and the experience of negative emotions have been primarily associated with externalizing psychopathology (Tackett, 2006). Disinhibition, or effortful control from a temperament perspective, or conscientiousness from a personality perspective, is the primary higher-order trait that has most often linked to externalizing problems across the life span (Eisenberg, Spinrad, & Eggum, 2010; Nigg, 2006; Tackett, 2006, 2010). Effortful control has approximate analogs in other temperament/personality models such as conscientiousness and constraint. Effortful control/conscientiousness is a broad trait that reflects characteristics such as impulsivity, norm-governed behavior, and intrapersonal self-regulation. A related aspect of this trait, sensation-seeking, and risk-taking, will be discussed in Chapter 8, Sensation seeking and risk-taking.

The other higher-order trait that is often connected with externalizing problems at younger ages is negative emotionality/neuroticism (Eisenberg et al., 2010; Nigg, 2006; Tackett, 2006), the subject of the current chapter. Negative emotionality/neuroticism typically includes a propensity to experience negative affect including sadness, anxiety, and irritability. One important trait for understanding adult externalizing disorders is (dis)agreeableness, which often does not have a direct analog in child temperament/personality models (De Pauw, 2017). Importantly, some aspects of agreeableness (such as compliance) tend to covary with effortful control, whereas other aspects of (dis)agreeableness (such as antagonism) tend to covary with negative emotionality in childhood. Therefore, (dis)agreeableness is important to examine in relation to negative emotionality and externalizing disorders.

The current chapter will first discuss personality measures of neuroticism and temperament measures of negative emotionality, or negative affectivity (NA), including subfacets and superordinate structure, across development. Next, linkages between NA broadly defined and externalizing disorders will be reviewed. Finally, etiological links and models of NA and externalizing disorders will be covered. Finally, important future directions will be explicated.

Personality measures of neuroticism

Personality researchers have broadly defined neuroticism as characteristic individual differences in one's tendency to experience negative emotions such as anxiety, sadness, and anger (e.g., Caspi, Roberts, & Shiner, 2005). People who are highly neurotic are often thought of as moody, high-strung, irritable, or self-conscious. This trait was one of the first to be identified in early trait models (Allport &

Developmental Pathways to Disruptive, Impulse-Control, and Conduct Disorders.
DOI: https://doi.org/10.1016/B978-0-12-811323-3.00005-5

Odbert, 1936; Cattell, 1943; Eysenck, 1967), demonstrates cross-cultural validity (John & Srivastava, 1999; Tackett et al., 2012), and is present in nearly every current measure of adult and child personality (Tackett & Lahey, 2017). Additionally, neuroticism is an important determinant of life outcomes; it demonstrates the most robust cross-sectional and longitudinal associations with mental and physical health of any trait in the five-factor model (Mroczek, Spiro, & Turiano, 2009; Ormel et al., 2013).

Neuroticism, like other personality traits, has been studied most extensively in adults, though it manifests very early in life (Tackett et al., 2012). Child neuroticism shows moderate stability over the lifespan, including early in development (Caspi et al., 2005; Tackett, Lahey, et al., 2013). However, neuroticism in childhood differs from adult neuroticism (Soto & Tackett, 2015), and its measurement in youth is still in early stages. Top-down approaches to the assessment of child neuroticism involve the adaptation of existing adult personality measures for use with children (Soto, John, Gosling, & Potter, 2008). Bottom-up measurement approaches, however, have used naturalistic, free descriptions of children (primarily obtained from interviews with parents in which they describe their children) to construct a developmentally calibrated framework for the trait in childhood (e.g., Halverson et al., 2003; Mervielde & De Fruyt, 1999).

Both approaches provide distinct advantages and disadvantages (Soto & Tackett, 2015). Notably, childhood measures of neuroticism are weighted more by characteristics of irritability and fear, some of which overlap with disagreeableness (for irritability markers), with less emphasis on the internal experiences of sadness and self-consciousness that are more prominent in adult measures (Tackett et al., 2012). These measurement issues may contribute to the findings that, while childhood neuroticism reliably predicts adult neuroticism, levels of stability are often lower for neuroticism, relative to other five factor model traits (Caspi et al., 2005; McCrae et al., 2002; Soto & Tackett, 2015). While we may interpret these fluctuations in mean-level neuroticism as changes in emotional experience and maturity between developmental stages, we may also be observing measurement differences and limitations.

Temperament models of negative affectivity

Temperament is another approach to the categorization of early individual differences that largely grew independently of child personality taxonomies and measures. Temperament traits are often defined in terms of reactivity to stimuli, are observable from infancy and are theoretically situated in a biologically based framework (Rothbart, Ahadi, & Evans, 2000). Indeed, temperament has been posited as the biological foundation of adult personality—early individual differences that emerge prior to mature personality traits.

There are three main traditions within the temperament literature; each with its own structure of traits. However, the most popular taxonomy of temperament delineates three higher-order dispositional factors (De Pauw & Mervielde, 2010; Rothbart et al., 2000). This model, particularly promoted by Rothbart and colleagues, is composed of the traits surgency/extraversion, effortful control/constraint, and NA/negative emotionality. Though temperament and personality have traditionally been studied as distinct constructs, recent research indicates that these models and their respective measures overlap substantially in the variance captured (e.g., Tackett, Kushner, De Fruyt, & Mervielde, 2013). In this framework, neuroticism is most closely aligned with the temperament trait NA /negative emotionality.

NA is characterized by the tendency to react negatively to environmental stimuli. Children high in NA exhibit a pattern of frustration, sadness, and fear in response to new or stressful circumstances (Rothbart & Bates, 2006). These children are generally perceived as difficult, fussy, or irritable. NA has often been thought to precede neuroticism, providing the biological foundation for the more psychologically complex personality trait (hypothetically; Rothbart et al., 2000). Aside from the substantial conceptual similarity between these constructs, neuroticism and NA are related to many of the same outcomes such as poorer mental health and relationship quality (Buil, van Lier, Brendgen, Koot, & Vitaro, 2017; Jeronimus, Riese, Oldehinkel, & Ormel, 2017; Rothbart & Bates, 2006; Tackett, Kushner, et al., 2013; De Clercq, De Fruyt & Widiger, 2009).

However, temperament and personality constructs do not completely overlap, and each makes unique contributions to the prediction of negative life outcomes (Tackett, Kushner, et al., 2013; Tackett, Kushner, Herzhoff, Smack, & Reardon, 2014). The assumption that NA underlies neuroticism has become less well-accepted in the time since temperament's origination in infant studies. In more recent years, temperament measures have been adapted for developmental periods up to adolescence, when the Big Five are reliably observable (John et al., 1994; Tackett et al., 2012). Personality measures, on the other hand, have also been created or empirically adapted down for children as young as three years of age (Halverson et al., 2003; Soto et al., 2008).

Studies of the temporal stability of NA across developmental periods yield mixed results. Some studies of temperament find that NA has moderate rank-order stability over the lifetime (Howland, Armeli, Feinn, & Tennen, 2017; Putnam, Rothbart, & Gartstein, 2008), though others have found only weak associations between developmental epochs. Likewise, adult neuroticism has shown only modest correlations with child NA (McCrae et al., 2000), though this convergence is stronger between teens and adults (Farrell, Brook, Dane, Marini, & Volk, 2015). Contributing to this confusion, there are few longitudinal studies of temperament constructs across the lifespan, and interpretation of the extant findings is unclear.

While the same three higher-order temperament factors are used across age groups, the lower-order traits comprising these factors in temperament measures do not have complete overlap between developmental stages (De Pauw & Mervielde, 2010). This is partly due to a tendency for temperament measures to map on to fairly circumscribed age ranges, which creates challenges in measuring the same trait over longer timespans. Therefore, it is unclear whether the correlation between child NA and adult neuroticism reflects the developmental course of a single, core individual difference or simply the association between two related constructs. More research is needed on the stability and change of NA across development to clarify its developmental course.

The lower-order structure of neuroticism/NA

In children, higher-order personality traits are composed of several lower-order facets, much as they are in adults (Tackett et al., 2012). However, there is little consensus on the number and character of these facets, in children as in adults. Due to the relatively fewer studies on the structure of child personality relative to adults, this uncertainty holds especially for child neuroticism (De Pauw, 2017). Though research on this topic has been limited, it suggests that neuroticism has a simpler structure in children than adults (De Pauw & Mervielde, 2010). Whereas adult neuroticism reflects a large repertoire of complex negative emotions such as insecurity, shame, and rumination, there is some indication that neuroticism/NA in children is composed of just a few foundational components, described later. Using parental free-descriptions as well as laboratory observations of children, foundational studies into the measurement of neuroticism/NA seem to converge on this point.

Using the lexical approach historically central to adult personality research (c.f. Goldberg, John, Kaiser, Lanning, & Peabody, 1990; Mervielde and De Fruyt (1999) derived a five-factor personality structure from parental free-descriptions of children. This structure closely parallels the adult Big Five, and the resulting measure —the Hierarchical Personality Inventory for Children (HiPIC)—has been validated across early, middle, and late childhood samples. The five higher-order traits in the HiPIC can be further broken down into 18 more narrowly defined facets of personality. One common model of adult neuroticism encompasses six lower-order facets (Costa & McCrae, 1992), in contrast to the HiPIC, which captures only two lower-order traits: Anxiety and Self-Confidence (or lack thereof). In this model, highly neurotic children would be described as "quick to worry about things" and "quick to doubt his/her own capabilities." While these anxious traits are found in all measures of child neuroticism/NA, other measures capture additional indicators of trait negative emotionality.

Another commonly used measure of child personality is the Inventory of Child Individual Differences (ICID), a measure which also follows the Five Factor Model of personality (Halverson et al., 2003). The ICID is also validated across ages spanning childhood and adolescence, and it measures 15 personality facets which are subsumed by the five higher-order traits. Of these, three lower-order traits index neuroticism—Fearful/Insecure, Negative Affect, and Shy. Among several differences between the HiPIC and ICID models of neuroticism, a notable one is the inclusion of an irritability dimension in the ICID. As measured by the ICID, Negative Affect includes patterns of angry and tempestuous behavior (e.g., description of a child as "moody" or "quick-tempered"). Whereas the HiPIC construes neuroticism as primarily anxiety, fearfulness, and negative self-evaluation (the latter of which is not particularly well-captured by the ICID), other outward expressions of negative emotional states (e.g., anger, frustration, irritability, and antagonism) are included in the ICID, which is also commonly incorporated in temperament models of neuroticism/NA/negative emotionality.

As temperament measures typically invoke a developmentally specific approach, NA is measured somewhat differently in different age group. Because of this, there are as many temperament facet structures as there are developmental epochs (Rothbart & Bates, 2006). In very young children, NA is characterized by fear, frustration/irritability, sadness, and falling reactivity (or the speed with which the child recovers from emotionally arousing events). In middle childhood, common temperament scales propose five facets of trait NA: Anger-frustration, fear, sadness, discomfort, and (low) soothability. Discomfort and soothability describe reactivity patterns that generally do not appear in adult disposition research. Respectively, they are the tendency to react strongly to aversive physical stimuli and to be easily calmed by caregivers after a negative experience. In adolescent temperament measurement, NA includes frustration, fear, and depressed mood facets.

In comparison to common models of child neuroticism, there is much more outwardly directed negative emotional content in NA across all measures. Further, the dimensions of sadness and depressed mood capture an individual's tendency toward misery and rumination, which few empirically valid child personality measures assess. While the reliability of this particular facet of NA has yet to be fully tested, temperament's unique contributions to the measurement of trait negative emotionality suggest its usefulness in examining child NA (and perhaps neuroticism) from multiple angles.

While there is not consensus among child personality researchers as to how many facets of neuroticism/NA exist in youth, the pattern of results suggests that there are at least two consistent elements: Irritability and fear (Caspi et al., 2005). These facets, corresponding to outwardly and inwardly directed negative affect, are consistently recovered in both bottom-up and top-down research in child dispositions. The existence of these lower-order dimensions of neuroticism/NA draw further support in their conceptual correspondence to the dichotomy between externalizing and internalizing psychopathology in children (Oldehinkel, Hartman, De Winter, Veenstra, & Ormel, 2004). The irritability facet of neuroticism/NA also overlaps substantially with (or is best positioned in the interstitial space between neuroticism and) dis/agreeableness and, therefore, may be most relevant to studies of neuroticism/NA linkage with externalizing disorders, although this idea remains understudied.

Hierarchical structure of neuroticism/NA

While the Big Five structure of personality traits is arguably the most commonly used framework for disposition research, some scientists argue that different levels of analysis may be more useful for different research questions. By iteratively decomposing two, three, four, and five factors of personality, researchers can examine individual differences from a variety of theoretical standpoints. While personality studies use five traits to study children and adolescents, temperament researchers have consistently examined fewer. Specifically, in the case of neuroticism, there is evidence that this trait is often difficult to disentangle from disagreeableness in children.

Digman (1997) laid the foundation for this hierarchical approach to conceptualizing individual differences by proposing that personality has a hierarchical structure, and individual differences can be distilled down to two traits at the most basic level of analysis. These personality factors, called α and β, have been consistently replicated through studies of children and adults (Digman, 1997; Markon, Krueger, & Watson, 2005). While β reflects the extent to which the traits extraversion and openness hang together, α reflects covariation among conscientiousness, agreeableness, and neuroticism. This structure has been applied to both normal and abnormal personality traits, with α encompassing a large portion of the tendency toward psychopathology. As high neuroticism, low agreeableness, and low conscientiousness are associated with increased vulnerability to both internalizing and externalizing disorders, this has proven a useful framework for studying adjustment (De Pauw & Mervielde, 2010; Tackett, 2006). Lower levels of analysis are also important in the investigation of other research questions. At the three-factor level of analysis, α is decomposed into NA and disinhibition to form a three-factor structure, in total (Markon et al., 2005). This structure resembles that of temperament approaches, and it has been corroborated by bottom-up studies of personality, as well.

It seems that in childhood especially, neuroticism and agreeableness may be difficult to disentangle. When item-level descriptions of children are examined cross-culturally, the five factors of personality are not always conceptually identical to those of adults (Tackett et al., 2012). These descriptions often include a factor that combines neuroticism and antagonistic traits, while prosocial tendencies form a separate agreeableness domain. Across personality research, the same adults who are combative and uncooperative report experiencing more anxiety and misery than their more easygoing peers, but this relationship is especially strong in children and adolescents. Exactly when the association between neuroticism and disagreeableness attenuates in older individuals is as of yet unknown, though it has been suggested that the prefrontal maturation and increased self-regulatory abilities of early adulthood may play a prominent role in their divergence (DeYoung, Hirsh, Shane, & Papademetris, 2010).

Neuroticism/NA and psychopathology

Basic links to externalizing disorders

Externalizing disorders are most often associated with traits linked to undercontrolled behavior (e.g., low agreeableness and conscientiousness; Eisenberg et al., 2010; Henry, Caspi, Moffitt, & Silva, 1996; Kochanska, Barry, Jimenez, Hollatz, & Woodard, 2009; Tackett, Martel, & Kushner, 2012), they have also been associated with neuroticism, albeit less consistently than internalizing disorders (Ehrler, Evans, & McGhee, 1999; Kotov, Gamez, Schmidt, & Watson, 2010; Malouff, Thorsteinsson, & Schutte, 2005). Higher-order neuroticism is believed to account for correlations between internalizing and externalizing psychopathology (Krueger & Markon, 2006; Lahey et al., 2008, 2012; Tackett, Kushner, et al., 2013). At the facet-level, neuroticism is composed of traits that may differentially correlate with internalizing (e.g., depression and anxiety) versus externalizing (e.g., anger, frustration, hostility and irritability) psychopathology (Burke, 2012; Herzhoff & Tackett, 2016; Jeronimus et al., 2017; Ormel, Rosmalen, & Farmer, 2004). The contributions of facets may thus be obscured at the higher-order domain. Issues related to the measurement of childhood neuroticism (e.g., reliance on parent-reports; heavy weight given to observable aspects, such as anger and antagonism; measurement of different facets across different personality taxonomies) also impede any definite conclusions about facet-level correlations with externalizing psychopathology across the literature (Tackett et al., 2012).

Evidence that childhood neuroticism positively predicts later externalizing symptoms (e.g., Gilliom & Shaw, 2004; Gjone & Stevenson, 1997; Hayden, Klein, & Durbin, 2005; Schmitz et al., 1999) is consistent with the *vulnerability model*, which conceptualizes personality traits as antecedent factors that increase the probability of maladaptive outcomes, such as psychopathology (Nigg, 2006; Tackett, 2006). In contrast, longitudinal evidence showing that childhood antisocial behavior predicts increased neuroticism in young adulthood (Shiner, Masten, & Tellegen, 2002) is consistent with the *complication/scar model*, which proposes that the occurrence of psychological disorders can alter pre-existing traits. Like these models, the *pathoplasty/exacerbation model* assumes that personality and psychopathology are distinct constructs, but posits that traits can influence the course (e.g., chronicity) of a given disorder. In contrast, the *spectrum model* posits that personality traits and psychopathology exist along a single continuum and share common etiological factors.

One attempt to disentangle the effects of multiple models showed weaker evidence for the continuity of neuroticism and externalizing problems than for internalizing problems (De Bolle, Beyers, De Clercq, & De Fruyt, 2012). This study also showed evidence for reciprocal longitudinal associations whereby low neuroticism predicted subsequent increases in externalizing problems, which in turn predicted decreases in neuroticism. Support has also been found for the spectrum model. Specifically, Tackett, Kushner, et al. (2013) found that neuroticism shared substantial phenotypic variance with a specific externalizing psychopathology factor composed of conduct, oppositional defiant, inattentive, and hyperactive/impulsive symptoms, in addition to its phenotypic and genetic variance with a general psychopathology factor. These results were replicated across parents' and youth's reports of negative emotionality in a large representative twin sample. Together, these results suggest that models of personality-psychopathology associations are not mutually exclusive (Widiger, Verheul, & van den Brink, 1999), but rather may operate in tandem or even vary across types of psychopathology.

Neuroticism/NA, life stress, and externalizing disorders

Contextual nuances may be required to adequately explain the complexity of trait-psychopathology associations. For example, not all neurotic youth evince maladaptive outcomes (Rogosch & Cicchetti, 2004), suggesting that other etiological influences may contribute to the emergence of psychopathology. Several plausible processes whereby neuroticism increases vulnerability for psychopathology also feature the influence of stress, including heightened emotional reactivity and negative biases in the appraisal of stressful life events (Ormel et al., 2013). Indeed, youth who are prone to NA may construe events in negative ways (i.e., differential appraisal), thus inflating the correlations between stressors and neuroticism (Lengua & Long, 2002; Ormel et al., 2004; Suls & Martin, 2005; Watson & Pennebaker, 1989). The assumption that psychopathology results from the interactive influence of neuroticism and stressful life events is consistent with the diathesis-stress model (Ingram & Luxton, 2005; Monroe & Simons, 1991). Although considerable research has studied the role of stress in the development of youth psychopathology (Grant et al., 2006), relatively few studies have incorporated personality traits as potential moderators of this risk (Kushner, 2015). Moreover, most existing studies have focused exclusively on depression (Brown & Rosellini, 2011; Hankin, 2010; Kendler, Kuhn, & Prescott, 2004; Ormel, Oldehinkel, & Brilman, 2001; Wetter & Hankin, 2009), whereas few have examined neuroticism as a diathesis for stress-related externalizing problems.

Positive correlations between stressful life events and neuroticism have been attributed to heightened reactivity (e.g., physiological and emotional arousal) and negative biases in the cognitive appraisal of events (Bolger & Zuckerman, 1995; Compas, Connor-Smith, & Jaser, 2004; Ormel et al., 2013; Strelau, 2001). Interestingly, negative perceptions of life events may depend on the nature of the stressor. For example, adolescents who were prone to NA reported more youth-specific, nonindependent stressors (e.g., peer victimization)—but not independent family stressors (e.g., economic hardship)—than their parents did (Kushner & Tackett, 2017).

Similarly, high temperamental frustration has been associated with low perceptions of affection from parents and peers (Laceulle, Jeronimus, Van Aken, & Ormel, 2015). Negative appraisals of social events may subsequently trigger negative behavioral responses. For example, youth who are prone to irritability and frustration may interpret social interactions as threatening, and respond aggressively to these interactions (Dodge, 2006; Jeronimus et al., 2017; Laceulle et al., 2015). Youth who are prone to NA may also be exposed to stressors via environmental selection (Caspi et al., 2005; Laceulle et al., 2015; Shiner & Caspi, 2003). That is, neuroticism or its facets may drive individuals toward risky activities and situations where stressful events are more likely to arise. Alternatively, youth who are prone to NA may simply evoke negative reactions from others (i.e., environmental elicitation; Caspi et al., 2005; Shiner & Caspi, 2003). Indeed, evidence from cross-sectional and longitudinal studies have linked neuroticism and its temperamental correlates to negative social experiences, including low peer acceptance and bullying (Bollmer, Harris, & Milich, 2006; Buil et al., 2017; De Bolle & Tackett, 2013; Jensen-Campbell & Malcolm, 2007).

Exposure to stressful life experiences may also impede (i.e., "scar") the normative development of personality traits. Whereas the transition into adolescence is typically associated with decreases in frustration, fear, and shyness, these effects may be reduced or reversed by exposure to stressors (Laceulle, Nederhof, Karreman, Ormel, & Van Aken, 2012). Similar processes may be at play for youth exposed to severe adversity (e.g., maltreatment), who typically score higher on neuroticism than their peers (Rogosch & Cicchetti, 2004). Further, Neuroticism may uniquely contribute to the generation of negative interpersonal events among depressed youth with a history of physical, but not emotional or sexual, maltreatment (Kushner, Bagby, & Harkness, 2017). The contributions from personality and stressful events to externalizing psychopathology are further complicated by additional moderating variables, such as gender and age (Aldwin, 2011; Laceulle et al., 2012). Altogether, the available research provides a highly complex and dynamic sketch of the associations between neuroticism and stressful life events, and their contributions to externalizing psychopathology. Carefully designed longitudinal research is needed to disentangle the etiological mechanisms underlying these associations.

Neuroticism/NA and externalizing personality

Empirical studies of the structural organization of psychopathology have supported the inclusion of certain personality disorders in the externalizing spectrum, despite the historical separation of Axis I syndrome disorders and Axis II personality disorders (American Psychiatric Association [APA], 2000). The placement of antisocial personality disorder (ASPD) on this spectrum is intuitive, given that the current diagnostic criteria for ASPD require evidence of conduct disorder prior to age 15 (APA, 2013). Early empirical efforts to evaluate the externalizing spectrum showed that antisocial behavior fit well with conduct disorder and substance use problems (Krueger, 1999; Krueger et al., 2002). Further support for the inclusion of ASPD on the externalizing spectrum comes from research demonstrating common genetic factors underlying ASPD, substance use disorders, conduct disorder, novelty-seeking, and general externalizing behaviors (e.g., Dick et al., 2008); however, results from other studies have been mixed (Prom-Wormley et al., 2009; Young et al., 2006). The social deviance facet of psychopathy has also been associated with the externalizing dimension of psychopathology (Patrick, Hicks, Krueger, & Lang, 2005). In contrast to ASPD, borderline personality disorder (BPD) is best conceptualized as belonging to both the internalizing and externalizing spectra (Eaton et al., 2011). Whereas some features of BPD (e.g., emotional dysregulation) are consistent with symptoms of the distress disorders (e.g., major depressive disorder, dysthymic disorder, generalized anxiety disorder, and posttraumatic stress disorder), other features (e.g., aggression, impulsivity) are consistent with symptoms of the externalizing disorders (e.g., ASPD, substance use disorders).

Neuroticism is positively correlated with BPD, whereas correlations for ASPD are typically weak (Saulsman & Page, 2004). Neuroticism also accounts for unique variance in the social deviance facet of psychopathy, which encompasses impulsivity, instability, and antisocial behavior (Lynam et al., 2005). At the facet level, BDP is moderately correlated with high anxiety and low self-confidence, whereas ASPD is weakly correlated with self-confidence (De Clercq, De Fruyt, & Van Leeuwen, 2004). The available evidence supports both a vulnerability and spectrum account of the relationship between neuroticism and externalizing personality disorders (for a review on BPD, see Tackett & Kushner, 2014). Consistent with the spectrum hypothesis, the correlations between neuroticism and externalizing personality disorders may arise due to shared etiological features between normative personality development and features of personality disorders. For example, both normative variants of NA and pathological aggression and impulsivity have been linked to serotonin function (Crowell, Beauchaine, & Linehan, 2009; Greenberg et al., 2000; Hamer, Greenberg, Shabol, & Murphy, 1999; Lesch et al., 1996).

Covariation among externalizing disorders and neuroticism have also shown common genetic and nonshared environmental influences (Hink et al., 2013; Martel, Nikolas, Jernigan, Friderici, & Nigg, 2010; Singh & Waldman, 2010; Waldman et al., 2011). The development of normative personality traits and features of personality disorders also share common psychosocial risk factors, including early maltreatment, environmental instability, and negative interpersonal experiences (Ballard et al., 2015; Bandelow et al., 2005; Carlson, Egeland, & Sroufe, 2009; Gratz, Latzman, Tull, Reynolds, & Lejuez, 2011; Helgeland & Torgersen, 2004; Joyce et al., 2003; Shi, Bureau, Easterbrooks, Zhao, & Lyons-Ruth, 2012). Connections between childhood neuroticism and externalizing personality disorders may also be mediated by stressful life experiences. For example, children who were high on temperamental negative reactivity were rated less favorably by their peers in early adolescence, and engaged in antisocial behaviors in later adolescence (Buil et al., 2017). Although research on personality pathology in youth is growing, it has been impeded by a reluctance toward identifying personality disorders in childhood and adolescence (Crick, Murray-Close, & Woods, 2005; Miller, Muehlenkamp, & Jacobson, 2008). As a result, much remains unknown about their etiological roots and early manifestations. Building a fulsome understanding of the externalizing personality disorders will require careful measurement of normative and pathological personality traits throughout development.

Summary and future directions

Mechanisms underlying the development of neuroticism/NA and externalizing (and internalizing) disorders are dynamic and complex, consistent with vulnerability, spectrum, and scar models. High neuroticism/NA is associated with both internalizing and externalizing disorders, seemingly due to effects on and influences by life stress. Irritability, a potential subfacet of neuroticism/NA, seems particularly associated with externalizing disorders, although such conclusions are tentative due to trait measurement limitations and differences between childhood, adolescence, and adulthood, an area that needs further research attention. Disagreeableness, which clusters with neuroticism at higher levels of the trait hierarchy, is particularly associated with externalizing disorders and appears to be a specific risk marker for these problems. Early measurement and assessment of such traits as irritability as a subfacet of neuroticism/NA, and disagreeableness is an important future research direction with possible implications for predicting clinical course and outcomes.

References

Aldwin, C. (2011). Stress and coping across the lifespan. In S. Folkman (Ed.), *The Oxford handbook of stress, health, and coping* (pp. 15–34). New York, NY: Oxford University Press.

Allport, G. W., & Odbert, H. S. (1936). Trait-names: a psycho-lexical study. *Psychological Monographs*, *47*(211).

American Psychiatric Association. (2000). *Diagnostic and statistical manual of mental disorders* (4th ed). Washington, DC: Author, text revised.

American Psychiatric Association. (2013). *Diagnostic and statistical manual of mental disorders* (5th ed). Arlington, VA: American Psychiatric Publishing.

Ballard, E. D., Van Eck, K., Musci, R. J., Hart, S. R., Storr, C. L., Breslau, N., & Wilcox, H. C. (2015). Latent classes of childhood trauma exposure predict the development of behavioral health outcomes in adolescence and young adulthood. *Psychological Medicine*, *45*, 3305–3316.

Bandelow, B., Krause, J., Wedekind, D., Broocks, A., Hajak, G., & Rüther, E. (2005). Early traumatic life events, parental attitudes, family history, and birth risk factors in patients with borderline personality disorder and healthy controls. *Psychiatry Research*, *134*, 169–179.

Bolger, N., & Zuckerman, A. (1995). A framework for studying personality in the stress process. *Journal of Personality and Social Psychology*, *69*, 890–902.

Bollmer, J. M., Harris, M. J., & Milich, R. (2006). Reactions to bullying and peer victimization: Narratives, physiological arousal, and personality. *Journal of Research in Personality*, *40*(5), 803–828.

Brown, T. A., & Rosellini, A. J. (2011). The direct and interactive effects of neuroticism and life stress on the severity and longitudinal course of depressive symptoms. *Journal of Abnormal Psychology*, *120*, 844–856.

Buil, J. M., van Lier, P. C., Brendgen, M. R., Koot, H. M., & Vitaro, F. (2017). Developmental pathways linking childhood temperament with antisocial behavior and substance use in adolescence: Explanatory mechanisms in the peer environment. *Journal of Personality and Social Psychology*. Available from https://doi.org/10.1037/pspp0000132, Advance online article.

Burke, J. D. (2012). An affective dimension within oppositional defiant disorder symptoms among boys: Personality and psychopathology outcomes into early adulthood. *Journal of Child Psychology and Psychiatry*, *53*(11), 1176–1183. Available from https://doi.org/10.1111/j.1469-7610.2012.02598.x.

Carlson, E. A., Egeland, B., & Sroufe, L. A. (2009). A prospective investigation of the development of borderline personality symptoms. *Development and Psychopathology*, *21*, 1311–1334.

Caspi, A., Roberts, B. W., & Shiner, R. L. (2005). Personality development: stability and change. *Annual Review of Psychology*, *56*(1), 453–484. Available from https://doi.org/10.1146/annurev.psych.55.090902.141913.

Cattell, R. B. (1943). *The description of personality: basic traits resolved into clusters.* American Psychological Association.

Compas, B. E., Connor-Smith, J., & Jaser, S. S. (2004). Temperament, stress reactivity, and coping: Implications for depression in childhood and adolescence. *Journal of Clinical Child and Adolescent Psychology*, *33*, 21–31.

Costa, P. T., & McCrae, R. R. (1992). *Revised NEO personality inventory (NEO PI-R) and NEO five-factor inventory (NEO-FFI): professional manual.* Psychological Assessment Resources, Inc.

Crick, N. R., Murray-Close, D., & Woods, K. (2005). Borderline personality features in childhood: A short-term longitudinal study. *Development and Psychopathology*, *17*, 1051–1070.

Crowell, S. E., Beauchaine, T. P., & Linehan, M. M. (2009). A biosocial developmental model of borderline personality: Elaborating and extending Linehan's theory. *Psychological Bulletin*, *135*(3), 495–510.

De Bolle, M., & Tackett, J. L. (2013). Anchoring bullying and victimization in children within a five-factor model-based person-centred framework. *European Journal of Personality*, *27*, 280–289.

De Bolle, M., Beyers, W., De Clercq, B., & De Fruyt, F. (2012). General personality and psychopathology in referred and nonreferred children and adolescents: An investigation of continuity, pathoplasty, and complication models. *Journal of Abnormal Psychology*, *121*, 958–970.

De Clercq, B., De Fruyt, F., & Van Leeuwen, K. (2004). A" little five" lexically based perspective on personality disorder symptoms in adolescence. *Journal of Personality Disorders*, *18*, 479–499.

De Clercq, B., De Fruyt, F., & Widiger, T. A. (2009). Integrating a developmental perspective in dimensional models of personality disorders. *Clinical Psychology Review*, *29*, 154–162.

De Pauw, S. S. W. (2017). Childhood personality and temperament. In T. A. Widiger (Ed.), *The Oxford handbook of the Five Factor Model* (pp. 243–280). New York: Oxford University Press.

De Pauw, S. S. W., & Mervielde, I. (2010). Temperament, personality and developmental psychopathology: a review based on the conceptual dimensions underlying childhood traits. *Child Psychiatry and Human Development*, *41*(3), 313–329. Available from https://doi.org/10.1007/s10578-009-0171-8.

DeYoung, C. G., Hirsh, J. B., Shane, M. S., & Papademetris, X. (2010). Testing predictions from personality neuroscience: brain structure and the Big Five. *Psychological Science*, *21*(6), 820–828. Available from https://doi.org/10.1177/0956797610370159.Testing.

Dick, D. M., Aliev, F., Wang, J. C., Grucza, R. A., Schuckit, M., Kuperman, S., et al. (2008). Using dimensional models of externalizing psychopathology to aid in gene identification. *Archives of General Psychiatry*, *65*(3), 310–318.

Digman, J. M. (1997). Higher-order factors of the Big Five. *Journal of Personality and Social Psychology*, *73*(6), 1246–1256. Available from https://doi.org/10.1037/0022-3514.73.6.1246.

Dodge, K. A. (2006). Translational science in action: Hostile attributional style and the development of aggressive behavior problems. *Development and Psychopathology*, *18*(03), 791–814.

Eaton, N. R., Krueger, R. F., Keyes, K. M., Skodol, A. E., Markon, K. E., Grant, B. F., & Hasin, D. S. (2011). Borderline personality disorder co-morbidity: relationship to the internalizing–externalizing structure of common mental disorders. *Psychological Medicine*, *41*(05), 1041–1050.

Ehrler, D. J., Evans, J. G., & McGhee, R. L. (1999). Extending Big-Five theory into childhood: A preliminary investigation into the relationship between Big-Five personality traits and behavior problems in children. *Psychology in the Schools*, *36*(6), 451–458.

Eisenberg, N., Spinrad, T. L., & Eggum, N. D. (2010). Emotion-related self-regulation and its relation to children's maladjustment. *Annual Review of Clinical Psychology*, *6*, 495–525.

Eysenck, H. J. (1967). *The biological basis of personality*. Springfield, IL: Thomas, Charles C.

Farrell, A. H., Brook, C., Dane, A. V., Marini, Z. A., & Volk, A. A. (2015). Relations between adolescent ratings of Rothbart's temperament questionnaire and the HEXACO personality inventory. *Journal of Personality Assessment*, *97*, 163–171.

Gilliom, M., & Shaw, D. S. (2004). Codevelopment of externalizing and internalizing problems in early childhood. *Development and Psychopathology*, *16*, 313–333.

Gjone, H., & Stevenson, J. (1997). A longitudinal twin study of temperament and behavior problems: Common genetic or environmental influences? *Journal of the American Academy of Child and Adolescent Psychiatry*, *36*(10), 1448–1456.

Goldberg, L.R., John, O.P., Kaiser, H., Lanning, K., & Peabody, D. (1990). An alternative "description of personality": the Big-Five Factor Structure, *59*(6), 1216–1229. https://doi.org/10.1037/0022-3514.59.6.1216

Grant, K. E., Compas, B. E., Thurm, A. E., McMahon, S. D., Gipson, P. Y., Campbell, A. J., ... Westerholm, R. I. (2006). Stressors and child and adolescent psychopathology: Evidence of moderating and mediating effects. *Clinical Psychology Review*, *26*, 257–283.

Gratz, K. L., Latzman, R. D., Tull, M. T., Reynolds, E. K., & Lejuez, C. W. (2011). Exploring the association between emotional abuse and childhood borderline personality features: The moderating role of personality traits. *Behavior Therapy*, *42*, 493–508.

Greenberg, B. D., Li, Q., Lucas, F. R., Hu, S., Sirota, L. Q., Benjamin, J., ... Murphy, D. L. (2000). Association between the serotonin transporter promoter polymorphism and personality traits in a primarily female population sample. *American Journal of Medical Genetics*, *96*, 202–216.

Halverson, C. F., Havill, V. L., Deal, J. E., Baker, S. R., Victor, J. B., Pavlopoulos, V., ... Wen, L. (2003). Personality structure as derived from parental ratings of free descriptions of children: the inventory of child individual differences. *Journal of Personality*, *71*(6), 995–1026. Available from https://doi.org/10.1111/1467-6494.7106005.

Hamer, D. H., Greenberg, B. D., Shabol, S. Z., & Murphy, D. L. (1999). Role of the serotonin transporter gene in temperament and character. *Journal of Personality Disorder*, *13*(4), 312–328.

Hankin, B. L. (2010). Personality and depressive symptoms: Stress generation and cognitive vulnerabilities to depression in a prospective daily diary study. *Journal of Social and Clinical Psychology*, *29*, 369–401.

Hayden, E. P., Klein, D. N., & Durbin, C. E. (2005). Parent reports and laboratory assessments of child temperament: A comparison of their associations with risk for depression and externalizing disorders. *Journal of Psychopathology and Behavioral Assessment*, *27*, 89–100.

Helgeland, M. I., & Torgersen, S. (2004). Developmental antecedents of borderline personality disorder. *Comprehensive Psychiatry*, *45*, 138–147.

Henry, B., Caspi, A., Moffitt, T. E., & Silva, P. A. (1996). Temperamental and familial predictors of violent and nonviolent criminal convictions: Age 3 to age 18. *Developmental Psychology*, *32*, 614–623.

Herzhoff, K., & Tackett, J. L. (2016). Subfactors of oppositional defiant disorder: Converging evidence from structural and latent class analyses. *Journal of Child Psychology and Psychiatry*, *57*, 18–29.

Hink, L. K., Rhee, S. H., Corley, R. P., Cosgrove, V. E., Hewitt, J. K., Schulz-Heik, R. J., . . . Waldman, I. D. (2013). Personality dimensions as common and broadband-specific features for internalizing and externalizing disorders. *Journal of Abnormal Child Psychology*, *41*, 939–957.

Howland, M., Armeli, S., Feinn, R., & Tennen, H. (2017). Daily emotional stress reactivity in emerging adulthood: temporal stability and its predictors. *Anxiety, Stress, & Coping*, *30*, 121–132.

Ingram, R. E., & Luxton, D. D. (2005). Vulnerability-stress models. In B. L. Hankin, & J. R. Z. Abela (Eds.), *Development of psychopathology: A vulnerability-stress perspective* (pp. 32–46). Thousand Oaks, CA: Sage Publications, Inc.

Jensen-Campbell, L. A., & Malcolm, K. T. (2007). The importance of conscientiousness in adolescent interpersonal relationships. *Personality and Social Psychology Bulletin*, *33*(3), 368–383.

Jeronimus, B. F., Riese, H., Oldehinkel, A. J., & Ormel, J. (2017). Why Does Frustration Predict Psychopathology? Multiple Prospective Pathways Over Adolescence: A TRAILS Study. *European Journal of Personality*, *31*(1), 85–103.

John, O. P., Caspi, A., Robins, R. W., Moffitt, T. E., John, O. P., & Stouthamer-loeber, M. (1994). The "little five": Exploring the nomological network of the five-factor model of personality in adolescent boys. *Child Development*, *65*(1), 160–178.

John, O.P., & Srivastava, S. (1999). The big five trait taxonomy: History, measurement, and theoretical perspectives. In *Handbook of personality: theory and research* (pp. 102–138).

Joyce, P. R., McKenzie, J. M., Luty, S. E., Mulder, R. T., Carter, J. D., Sullivan, P. F., & Cloninger, C. R. (2003). Temperament, childhood environment and psychopathology as risk factors for avoidant and borderline personality disorders. *Australian and New Zealand Journal of Psychiatry*, *37*(6), 756–764.

Kendler, K. S., Kuhn, J., & Prescott, C. A. (2004). The interrelationship of neuroticism, sex, and stressful life events in the prediction of episodes of major depression. *American Journal of Psychiatry*, *161*, 631–636.

Kochanska, G., Barry, R. A., Jimenez, A. L., Hollatz, A. L., & Woodard, J. (2009). Guilt and effortful control: Two mechanisms that prevent disruptive developmental trajectories. *Journal of Personality and Social Psychology*, *97*(2), 322–333.

Kotov, R., Gamez, W., Schmidt, F., & Watson, D. (2010). Linking "big" personality traits to anxiety, depressive, and substance use disorders: A meta-analysis. *Psychological Bulletin*, *136*(5), 768–821.

Krueger, R. F. (1999). The structure of common mental disorders. *Archives of General Psychiatry*, *56*(10), 921–926.

Krueger, R. F., Hicks, B. M., Patrick, C. J., Carlson, S. R., Iacono, W. G., & McGue, M. (2002). Etiologic connections among substance dependence, antisocial behavior and personality: Modeling the externalizing spectrum. *Journal of Abnormal Psychology*, *111*(3), 411–424.

Krueger, R. F., & Markon, K. E. (2006). Reinterpreting comorbidity: A model-based approach to understanding and classifying psychopathology. *Annual Review of Clinical Psychology*, *2*, 111–133.

Kushner, S. C. (2015). A review of the direct and interactive effects of life stressors and dispositional traits on youth psychopathology. *Child Psychiatry and Human Development*, *46*, 810–819.

Kushner, S. C., Bagby, R. M., & Harkness, K. L. (2017). Childhood maltreatment, stress generation, and depression: The moderating effects of five-factor model (FFM) personality traits in adolescence. *Personality Disorders: Theory, Research, and Practice*, *8*(2), 150–161. Available from https://doi.org/10.1037/per0000194.

Kushner, S. C., & Tackett, J. L. (2017). Parent and adolescent agreement for reports of life stressors. *Assessment*, *24*(2), 143–156. Available from https://doi.org/10.1177/1073191115607972.

Laceulle, O. M., Jeronimus, B. F., Van Aken, M. G., & Ormel, J. (2015). Why not everyone gets their fair share of stress: Adolescent's perceived relationship affection mediates associations between temperament and subsequent stressful social events. *European Journal of Personality*, *29*(2), 125–137. Available from https://doi.org/10.1002/per.1989.

Laceulle, O. M., Nederhof, E., Karreman, A., Ormel, J., & Aken, M. A. G. (2012). Stressful events and temperament change during early and middle adolescence: The TRAILS study. *European Journal of Personality*, *26*(3), 276–284.

Lahey, B. B., Applegate, B., Chronis, A. M., Jones, H. A., Williams, S. H., Loney, J., et al. (2008). Psychometric characteristics of a measure of emotional dispositions developed to test a developmental propensity model of conduct disorder. *Journal of Clinical Child and Adolescent Psychology*, *37*, 794–807.

Lahey, B. B., Applegate, B., Hakes, J. K., Zald, D. H., Hariri, A. R., & Rathouz, P. J. (2012). Is there a general factor of prevalent psychopathology during adulthood? *Journal of Abnormal Psychology*, *121*, 971–977. Available from https://doi.org/10.1037/a0028355.

Lengua, L. J., & Long, A. C. (2002). The role of emotionality and self-regulation in the appraisal-coping process: Tests of direct and moderating effects. *Journal of Applied Developmental Psychology*, *23*, 471–493.

Lesch, K. P., Bengel, D., Heils, A., Sabol, S. Z., Greenberg, B. D., Petri, S., ... Murphy, D. L. (1996). Association of anxiety-related traits with a polymorphism in the serotonin transporter gene regulatory region. *Science*, *274*(5292), 1527–1531.

Lynam, D. R., Caspi, A., Moffitt, T. E., Raine, A., Loeber, R., & Stouthamer-Loeber, M. (2005). Adolescent psychopathy and the Big Five: Results from two samples. *Journal of Abnormal Child Psychology*, *33*, 431–443.

Malouff, J. M., Thorsteinsson, E. B., & Schutte, N. S. (2005). The relationship between the five-factor model of personality and symptoms of clinical disorders: A meta-analysis. *Journal of Psychopathology and Behavioral Assessment*, *27*, 101–114. Available from https://doi.org/10.1007/s10862-005-5384-y.

Markon, K. E., Krueger, R. F., & Watson, D. (2005). Delineating the structure of normal and abnormal personality traits: an integrative hierarchical approach. *Journal of Personality and Social Psychology*, *88*(1), 139–157. Available from https://doi.org/10.1037/0022-3514.88.1.139.

Martel, M. M., Nikolas, M., Jernigan, K., Friderici, K., & Nigg, J. T. (2010). Personality mediation of genetic effects on attention-deficit/hyperactivity disorder. *Journal of Abnormal Child Psychology*, *38*, 633–643.

McCrae, R. R., Costa, P. T., Jr, Ostendorf, F., Angleitner, A., Hřebíčková, M., Avia, M. D., & Saunders, P. R. (2000). Nature over nurture: Temperament, personality, and life span development. *Journal of Personality and Social Psychology*, *78*, 173–186.

McCrae, R. R., Costa, P. T., Jr, Terracciano, A., Parker, W. D., Mills, C. J., De Fruyt, F., & Mervielde, I. (2002). Personality trait development from age 12 to age 18: longitudinal, cross-sectional and cross-cultural analyses. *Journal of Personality and Social Psychology*, *83*(6), 1456–1468. Available from https://doi.org/10.1037/0022-3514.83.6.1456.

Mervielde, I., & De Fruyt, F. (1999). Construction of the Hierarchical Personality Inventory for Children (HiPIC). In I. Mervielde, I. Deary, F. De Fruyt, & F. Ostendorf (Eds.), *Personality psychology in Europe: Proceedings of the Eighth European Conference on personality psychology* (pp. 107–127). Tilburg, The Netherlands: Tilburg University Press.

Miller, A. L., Muehlenkamp, J. J., & Jacobson, C. M. (2008). Fact or fiction: Diagnosing borderline personality disorder in adolescents. *Clinical Psychology Review*, *28*, 969–981.

Monroe, S. M., & Simons, A. D. (1991). Diathesis-stress theories in the context of life stress research: Implications for the depressive disorders. *Psychological Bulletin*, *110*, 406–425.

Mroczek, D. K., Spiro, A., III, & Turiano, N. A. (2009). Do health behaviors explain the effect of neuroticism on mortality? Longitudinal findings from the VA Normative Aging Study. *Journal of Research in Personality*, *43*, 653–659.

Nigg, J. T. (2006). Temperament and developmental psychopathology. *Journal of Child Psychology and Psychiatry*, *47*, 395–422.

Oldehinkel, A. J., Hartman, C. A., De Winter, A. F., Veenstra, R., & Ormel, J. (2004). Temperament profiles associated with internalizing and externalizing problems in preadolescence. *Development and Psychopathology*, *16*(2), 421–440. Available from https://doi.org/10.1017/S0954579404044591.

Ormel, J., Jeronimus, B. F., Kotov, R., Riese, H., Bos, E. H., Hankin, B., . . . Oldehinkel, A. J. (2013). Neuroticism and common mental disorders: Meaning and utility of a complex relationship. *Clinical Psychology Review*, *33*(5), 686–697.

Ormel, J., Oldehinkel, A. J., & Brilman, E. I. (2001). The interplay and etiological continuity of neuroticism, difficulties, and life events in the etiology of major and subsyndromal, first and recurrent depressive episodes in later life. *American Journal of Psychiatry*, *158*, 885–891.

Ormel, J., Rosmalen, J., & Farmer, A. (2004). Neuroticism: A non-informative marker of vulnerability to psychopathology. *Social Psychiatry and Psychiatric Epidemiology*, *39*, 906–912.

Patrick, C. J., Hicks, B. M., Krueger, R. F., & Lang, A. R. (2005). Relations between psychopathy facets and externalizing in a criminal offender sample. *Journal of Personality Disorders*, *19*, 339–356.

Prom-Wormley, E. C., Eaves, L. J., Foley, D. L., Gardner, C. O., Archer, K. J., Wormley, B. K., et al. (2009). Monoamine oxidase A and childhood adversity as risk factors for conduct disorder in females. *Psychological Medicine*, *39*(4), 579–590.

Putnam, S. P., Rothbart, M. K., & Gartstein, M. A. (2008). Homotypic and heterotypic continuity of fine-grained temperament during infancy, toddlerhood, and early childhood. *Infant and Child Development*, *17*, 387–405.

Rogosch, F. A., & Cicchetti, D. (2004). Child maltreatment and emergent personality organization: Perspectives from the five-factor model. *Journal of Abnormal Child Psychology*, *32*, 123–145.

Rothbart, M. K., Ahadi, S. A., & Evans, D. E. (2000). Temperament and personality: origins and outcomes. *Journal of Personality and Social Psychology*, *78*(1), 122–135. Available from https://doi.org/10.1037/0022-3514.78.1.122.

Rothbart, M. K., & Bates, J. E. (2006). *Temperament*, . (6th ed., pp. 99–166). *Handbook of child psychology*, (Vol. 3, pp. 99–166). Wiley. https://doi.org/10.1073/pnas.0703993104.

Saulsman, L. M., & Page, A. C. (2004). The five-factor model and personality disorder empirical literature: A meta-analytic review. *Clinical Psychology Review*, *23*, 1055–1085. Available from https://doi.org/10.1016/j.cpr.2002.09.001.

Schmitz, S., Fulker, D. W., Plomin, R., Zahn-Waxler, C., Emde, R. N., & DeFreis, J. C. (1999). Temperament and problem behaviour during early childhood. *International Journal of Behavioral Development*, *23*, 333–355.

Shi, Z., Bureau, J. F., Easterbrooks, M., Zhao, X., & Lyons-Ruth, K. (2012). Childhood maltreatment and prospectively observed quality of early care as predictors of antisocial personality disorder features. *Infant Mental Health Journal*, *33*, 55–69.

Shiner, R., & Caspi, A. (2003). Personality differences in childhood and adolescence: Measurement, development, and consequences. *Journal of Child Psychology and Psychiatry*, *44*, 2–32.

Shiner, R. L., Masten, A. S., & Tellegen, A. (2002). A developmental perspective on personality in emerging adulthood: Childhood antecedents and concurrent adaptation. *Journal of Personality and Social Psychology*, *83*(5), 1165–1177.

Singh, A. L., & Waldman, I. D. (2010). The etiology of associations between negative emotionality and childhood externalizing disorders. *Journal of Abnormal Psychology*, *119*, 376–388.

Soto, C. J., John, O. P., Gosling, S. D., & Potter, J. (2008). The developmental psychometrics of big five self-reports: acquiescence, factor structure, coherence, and differentiation from ages 10 to 20. *Journal of Personality and Social Psychology*, *94*(4), 718–737. Available from https://doi.org/10.1037/0022-3514.94.4.718.

Soto, C. J., & Tackett, J. L. (2015). Personality traits in childhood and adolescence: structure, development, and outcomes. *Current Directions in Psychological Science*, *24*(5), 358–362. Available from https://doi.org/10.1177/0963721415589345.

Strelau, J. (2001). The role of temperament as a moderator of stress. In T. D. Wachs, & G. A. Kohnstamm (Eds.), *Temperament in context* (pp. 130–147). Mahwah, NJ: Lawrence Erlbaum Associates.

Suls, J., & Martin, R. (2005). The daily life of the garden-variety neurotic: Reactivity, stressor exposure, mood spillover, and maladaptive coping. *Journal of Personality*, *73*, 1485–1510.

Tackett, J. L. (2006). Evaluating models of the personality-psychopathology relationship in children and adolescents. *Clinical Psychology Review*, *26*(5), 584–599. Available from https://doi.org/10.1016/j.cpr.2006.04.003.

Tackett, J. L., Kushner, S. C., De Fruyt, F., & Mervielde, I. (2013). Delineating personality traits in childhood and adolescence: associations across measures, temperament, and behavioral problems. *Assessment*, *20*(6), 738–751. Available from https://doi.org/10.1177/1073191113509686.

Tackett, J. L., & Kushner, S. C. (2014). Conceptualizing youth borderline personality disorder within a normative personality framework. In C. Sharp, & J. L. Tackett (Eds.), *Handbook of borderline personality disorder in children and adolescents* (pp. 95–110). New York, NY: Springer.

Tackett, J. L., Lahey, B. B., Van Hulle, C., Waldman, I., Krueger, R. F., & Rathouz, P. J. (2013). Common genetic influences on negative emotionality and a general psychopathology factor in childhood and adolescence. *Journal of Abnormal Psychology, 122*, 1142–1153.

Tackett, J. L., Kushner, S. C., Herzhoff, K., Smack, A., & Reardon, K. (2014). Viewing relational aggression through multiple lenses: Temperament, personality, and personality pathology. *Development and Psychopathology, 26*, 863–877.

Tackett, J. L., Martel, M. M., & Kushner, S. C. (2012). Temperament, externalizing disorders, and attention deficit/hyperactivity disorder. In M. Zentner, & R. Shiner (Eds.), *Handbook of temperament* (pp. 562–580). New York, NY: Guilford.

Tackett, J. L., & Lahey, B. B. (2017). Neuroticism. In T. A. Widiger (Ed.), *The Oxford handbook of the five factor model* (pp. 39–56). New York, NY: Oxford University Press.

Tackett, J. L., Slobodskaya, H. R., Mar, R. A., Deal, J., Halverson, C. F., Baker, S. R., ... Besevegis, E. (2012). The hierarchical structure of childhood personality in five countries: continuity from early childhood to early adolescence. *Journal of Personality, 80* (4), 847–879. Available from https://doi.org/10.1111/j.1467-6494.2011.00748.x.

Waldman, I. D., Tackett, J. L., Van Hulle, C. A., Applegate, B., Pardini, D., Frick, P. J., & Lahey, B. B. (2011). Child and adolescent conduct disorder substantially shares genetic influences with three socioemotional dispositions. *Journal of Abnormal Psychology, 120*(1), 57.

Watson, D., & Pennebaker, J. W. (1989). Health complaints, stress, and distress: exploring the central role of negative affectivity. *Psychological Review, 96*, 234–254.

Wetter, E. K., & Hankin, B. L. (2009). Mediational pathways through which positive and negative emotionality contribute to anhedonic symptoms of depression: a prospective study of adolescents. *Journal of Abnormal Child Psychology, 37*, 507–520.

Widiger, T. A., Verheul, R., & van den Brink, W. (1999). Personality and psychopathology. In L. A. Pervin, & O. P. John (Eds.), *Handbook of personality: theory and research* (2nd ed., pp. 347–366). New York: Guilford.

Young, S. E., Smolen, A., Hewitt, J. K., Haberstick, B. C., Stallings, M. C., Corley, R. P., et al. (2006). Interaction between MAO-A genotype and maltreatment in the risk for conduct disorder: failure to confirm in adolescent patients. *The American Journal of Psychiatry, 163*(6), 1019–1025.

Callous–unemotional traits

6

Paul J. Frick[1,2], *Emily L. Robertson*[1], *and Julia E. Clark*[1]
[1]Department of Psychology, Louisiana State University, Baton Rouge, LA, United States, [2]Learning Sciences Institute Australia, Australian Catholic University, Banyo, QLD, Australia

Introduction

Serious antisocial behavior, which violates the rights of others (e.g., aggression, destruction of property) or violates major age appropriate norms and rules (e.g., deceitful behavior, truancy, running away from home), is a critical component of the externalizing spectrum of disorders. This is made explicit in the fifth edition of the *Diagnostic and Statistical Manual of Mental Disorders* (*DSM-5*; American Psychiatric Association, 2013) in which Conduct Disorder (CD) is placed under the broad heading, "Disruptive, Impulse Control, and Conduct Disorders." All disorders within this category are conditions involving problems in the self-control of emotions and/or behaviors (American Psychiatric Association, 2013). As also explicitly noted in the DSM-5, the underlying causes of problems in self-control can vary greatly across individuals within a given diagnostic category. Accordingly, there has been significant research focused on advancing our knowledge of the most common causes of the problems in self-control exhibited by children and adolescents with CD and on using this knowledge to design more effective treatments for this disorder (Frick, 2016).

In this chapter, we review research on one method for differentiating among the diverse causal processes that can lead to serious antisocial behavior and aggression. It has its roots in the construct of psychopathy that has been used to designate an important subgroup of antisocial adults for much of the past century (Cleckley, 1976; Hare, 1993). Specifically, the construct of psychopathy is defined by a constellation of affective (e.g., lack of guilt and empathy; poverty of emotion), interpersonal (e.g., grandiosity and manipulativeness), and behavioral (e.g., impulsivity and irresponsibility) features that are highly associated with antisocial behavior (Hare & Neumann, 2008). Importantly, research has shown that only a small proportion of antisocial adults show significant levels of psychopathic traits but these offenders exhibit a more severe, violent, and chronic pattern of antisocial behavior (Leistico, Salekin, DeCoster, & Rogers, 2008). Further, antisocial adults with and without psychopathic traits show a host of distinct neurological, cognitive, and emotional characteristics that could implicate different causal factors leading to their antisocial behavior across the two groups (Blair, Mitchell, & Blair, 2005). Thus, the construct of psychopathy has proven to have very important clinical (i.e., prediction of harmful behavior) and etiological (i.e., designating unique causal pathways to antisocial behavior) implications.

Developmental Pathways to Disruptive, Impulse-Control, and Conduct Disorders.
DOI: https://doi.org/10.1016/B978-0-12-811323-3.00006-7

Several findings from research on psychopathy led to a desire to study precursors to this serious mental health concern prior to adulthood. First, adults with psychopathic traits typically have long histories of antisocial behavior that begin early in childhood (Forth, 1995). Thus, it was quite possible that this construct could designate a subgroup of antisocial youth that also might show a particularly severe and stable pattern of conduct problems. Second, developmental psychologists had a long history of studying how guilt, empathy, and other moral emotions develop in children (Hoffman, 1970). These affective components to conscience were very similar to the affective components of psychopathy and, as a result, integrating these two bodies of work could potentially expand causal theories for how psychopathy might develop (Frick, 2009). Third, adults with psychopathy tend to be very difficult to treat and often do not respond to many interventions that are successful in reducing antisocial behavior in those without these traits (Salekin, 2002). Further, research has consistently indicated that treatment for antisocial behavior is more successful when it is implemented earlier in development (Frick, 2012). Thus, it is possible that treatments for psychopathic traits would be more successful prior to adulthood as well.

For these reasons, there have been a number of attempts to extend the construct of psychopathy to youth and some of the early approaches were quite promising. That is, children and adolescents with serious conduct problems who also showed significant psychopathic traits tended to have poorer adjustment in juvenile institutions and were more likely to continue to show antisocial behavior into adulthood compared to other adolescents with serious conduct problems (Quay, 1987). Further, the group with psychopathic traits was also more likely to show several neurophysiological correlates to their antisocial behavior, such as low serotonin levels and autonomic irregularities, supporting the possibility that these traits may be important for capturing the heterogeneity in causes of antisocial behavior, similar to the findings in adults (Lahey, Hart, Pliszka, Applegate, & McBurnett, 1993; Quay, 1993).

However, in an attempt to avoid the potential stigma associated with the term "psychopath," the name that was given to this group of youth was "undersocialized aggressive" (Quay, 1987). Unfortunately, this name resulted in considerable confusion as to the core features for defining this construct and the best way to operationalize these features when assessing children and adolescents (Lahey, Loeber, Quay, Frick, & Grimm, 1992). Some definitions focused on the child's ability to form and maintain social relationships, whereas others focused primarily on the context (alone or as a group) in which the antisocial acts were typically committed. Very few definitions focused directly on the interpersonal and affective characteristics that were central to the clinical descriptions of psychopathic individuals (Quay, 1987). As a result of this definitional confusion, the use of psychopathy to guide subtyping approaches in children and adolescents was abandoned in order to focus on other aspects of the child's behavior, such as whether the antisocial acts were committed alone and whether the pattern of antisocial behavior included aggressive symptoms (e.g., solitary aggressive subtype of CD; Lahey et al., 1992). Unfortunately, these definitions led to methods of subtyping children with serious conduct problems that were quite different from either the adult construct of psychopathy (Hare & Neumann, 2008) or developmental definitions of the affective components of conscience (Thompson & Newton, 2010). As a result, the findings from research did not show much convergence to research on adults with psychopathy or with research on the normal processes that lead to the development of prosocial emotions in children (Frick & Viding, 2009).

Developing the construct of callous–unemotional traits

As a result of these limitations, a second generation of attempts to extend the construct of psychopathy to youths were initiated and these attempts tried to be more closely tied to the conceptualization of psychopathy that emerged from research with the Psychopathy Checklist-Revised (PCL-R; Hare, 2003), one of the most widely used methods for assessing psychopathic traits in incarcerated adults. Direct attempts to downward extend items from the PCL-R for use with children and adolescents tended to find three dimensions that were very similar to those found in adult samples that included affective (e.g., lack of guilt and empathy; poverty of emotion), interpersonal (e.g., grandiosity and manipulativeness), and behavioral (e.g., impulsivity and irresponsibility) facets (Hare & Neumann, 2008). This three-factor structure was replicated across boys and girls, across diverse settings (e.g., community, clinic-referred, and forensic samples), and across different assessment formats (see Frick & Ray, 2015 for a review).

The results of these factor analyses and their consistency across development led to great debate as to whether psychopathy is best considered as (1) the shared variance of these multiple facets, (2) a multidimensional composite of these facets, or (3) whether there are certain facets that are "core" to the construct, with others being secondary or less important to defining psychopathy (Skeem, Polaschek, Patrick, & Lilienfeld, 2011). However, Frick and Ray (2015) argued that even without a conclusive answer to this debate, the affective dimension appeared to be most critical for designating a distinct group of youth with serious conduct problems. That is, these authors argue that this dimension captured traits that were not currently used in the assessment of youth with serious conduct problems, as opposed to traits like impulsivity that are included in the definition of Attention-deficit Hyperactivity Disorder (ADHD). Thus, if the goal is to provide better representation of dimensions of psychopathy that are not currently included in most classification systems, the affective and interpersonal dimensions would be most important. Further, all three dimensions of psychopathy are correlated with antisocial behavior and, in fact, the interpersonal and behavioral dimensions tend to be more highly correlated with antisocial behavior than the affective dimension (Edens, Campbell, & Weir, 2007; Leistico et al., 2008) and the combination of all three seems to lead to the strongest prediction of antisocial behavior (Salekin, 2016). However, the strength of the correlation with antisocial behavior for the behavioral and interpersonal dimensions likely contributes to their more limited utility for differentiating distinct subgroups *within* antisocial youth (Frick & Ray, 2015). That is, it appears that the affective traits seem to have the most utility for distinguishing a distinct subgroup of antisocial youth who show more severe behavior problems (Caputo, Frick, & Brodsky, 1999; Christian, Frick, Hill, Tyler, & Frazer, 1997) and distinct risk factors (Kimonis, Frick, Fazekas, & Loney, 2006) when compared to other subgroups.

As a result, measures were developed to expand the assessment of the affective traits in order to overcome the limitations involved in using scales that only included a limited number of items (Poythress, Dembo, Wareham, & Greenbaum, 2006) and the term callous–unemotional (CU) traits began to be used to provide a more specific description of the types of affective characteristics that were of interest (Frick, 2009). One of the most widely used of these measures of CU traits was the Inventory of Callous–Unemotional Traits (ICU; Kimonis et al., 2008). The content of the ICU provided comprehensive coverage of CU traits by including 24 items that can be rated by parents, teachers, and the child him or herself and includes an equal number of items worded in the positive or callous direction (e.g., "I do not care who I hurt to get what I want") and in the negative or prosocial direction (e.g., "I am concerned about the feelings of others") in an attempt to avoid response sets. A large number of studies have tested the factor structure of the ICU and across different ages, sex, and language translations, the best fitting model tends to be one specifying a general CU factor and three subfactors: callousness, uncaring, and unemotional (see Frick & Ray, 2015 for a review). However, most studies largely use the total scores from the scale because (1) subscales based on the factors often have modest internal consistency, whereas the total scale often shows strong reliability across samples; (2) the three factors were not based on any strong theoretical model for explaining the nature of CU traits nor has research consistently reported differential correlations with important external criteria for the subscales; and (3) there is evidence that these subscales may load on separate factors due largely to method variance (Frick & Ray, 2015). As to this last finding, Ray, Frick, Thornton, Steinberg, and Cauffman (2016a) evaluated the item functioning of the ICU in an ethnically diverse sample of 1190 adolescents and found that the positively worded items (i.e., items for which higher ratings were indicative of higher levels of CU traits) were more likely than the negatively worded items (i.e., items in which higher ratings were indicative or more prosocial emotions) to be rated in the lower response categories. That is, youth were less likely to rate themselves as being highly callous than they were to rate themselves as being very low on prosocial emotions. Thus, the positively worded items showed higher difficulty in item response theory analyses and, as a result, the factor structure may be partly an artifact of this differential item difficulty, rather than providing important information about the multidimensional nature of CU traits.

A final important issue for the construct of CU traits is its level of stability. Concerns have been raised about calling them "traits," especially in early childhood, because it implies a substantial level of stability that is not found for most constructs early in development (Waller & Hyde, 2017). Further, a critical goal for extending the construct of psychopathy prior to adulthood is that the traits are hopefully less stable at this point in development and, as a result, are more amenable to treatment. However, it also possible that CU traits are so unstable at certain points early in development that they are not useful as a psychopathological construct because children are likely to outgrow them and, as a result, do not require any intervention (Frick & Ray, 2015). Frick, Ray, Thornton, and Kahn (2014a) provided a comprehensive review of studies summarizing the stability of CU traits across various stages of development and reported that they show modest stability that at least is comparable to other psychopathological constructs, even before age 5. For example, Willoughby, Waschbusch, Moore, and Propper (2011) reported a stability of $r = 0.84$ ($P < 0.0001$) for a latent construct of CU traits from 3 to 5 years of age, which was comparable to the stability of symptoms of ADHD ($r = 0.79$, $P < 0.0001$) assessed in the same way. Similarly, Loeber, Pardini, Stouthamer-Loeber, Hipwell, and Sembower (2009) reported that, in a large ($n = 2451$) community sample of girls ages 5–12, the year-to-year stability for CU traits (mean Intra-Class Coefficient of 0.74) was comparable to that found for relational aggression (0.76), for symptoms of CD/oppositional defiant disorder (0.81), for the inattention symptoms of ADHD (0.75), and for the hyperactivity–impulsivity symptoms of ADHD (0.79; all $P < 0.001$).

In summary, CU traits have emerged from being one component to the larger construct of psychopathy to being studied as a construct worthy of study on its own. As noted above, this was primarily motivated by their utility in differentiating a distinct group *within* antisocial youth. That is, all three dimensions of psychopathy tend to be highly associated with antisocial behavior but it appears to be the affective dimension (i.e., CU traits) that is most useful for designating subgroups within antisocial youth who show more severe and aggressive patterns of antisocial behavior and who show a number of distinct correlates to their antisocial behavior that would seem to suggest that there are distinct causal processes leading to their behavior problems. The evidence evaluating in more detail both of these claims is provided in the following sections.

CU traits and severity of antisocial behavior

It appears that elevated CU traits are found in only a small percentage (i.e., 25%–30%) of children and adolescents with severe conduct problems (Kahn, Frick, Youngstrom, Findling, & Youngstrom, 2012). However, research also suggests that it is a clinically important minority of youth with conduct problems. For example, children and adolescents with conduct problems and elevated CU traits show more severe (Ray, Frick, Thornton, Steinberg, & Cauffman, 2016b) and more stable (McMahon, Witkiewitz, Kotler, & The Conduct Problems Prevention Research Group, 2010) conduct problems. Similarly, children and adolescents with conduct problems are more aggressive, show severe aggression that results in more harm to their victims, and show more instrumental (i.e., for personal gain or dominance) and premeditated aggression when they also show elevated CU traits (Fanti,

Frick, & Georgiou, 2009; Frick, Cornell, Barry, Bodin, & Dane, 2003; Kruh, Frick, & Clements, 2005; Lawing, Frick, & Cruise, 2010).

In short, CU traits clearly seem to designate a group of youth with conduct problems who are in need of treatment. However, research on youth with elevated CU traits in treatment also suggests that they present quite a treatment challenge. Specifically, research has found that children and adolescents high on CU traits are more likely to be aggressive and violent during treatment (White, Frick, Lawing, & Bauer, 2013) and are more likely to show poorer treatment outcomes (Frick, Ray, Thornton, & Kahn, 2014b) than other antisocial youth. Specifically, Frick et al. (2014b) reviewed 20 studies that compared the treatment outcome for youth with conduct problems with and without elevated levels of CU traits and found that 18 (90%) of these studies reported results suggesting that the group high on CU traits showed poorer treatment outcomes to traditional mental health interventions compared to other children and adolescents with serious conduct problems. Importantly, there are some comprehensive and intensive interventions that have led to reductions in the antisocial behavior of children and adolescents with elevated CU traits, which are discussed later in this chapter (see also Hawes, Price, & Dadds, 2014; Wilkinson, Waller, & Viding, 2016). However, even when positive changes are found after treatment, youth with CU traits often start treatment with poorer levels of adjustment and still leave treatment with higher levels of antisocial behavior, despite any positive changes (White et al., 2013).

In summary, there is a rather substantial body of research suggesting that, like the construct of psychopathy in adults, the presence of elevated CU traits designates a clinically important group of youth with serious conduct problems. Further, like research on psychopathic traits in adults, there is also evident that youth with CU traits present quite a treatment challenge. Frick et al. (2014b) reviewed a substantial body of research to suggest that antisocial youth with CU traits also show a number of distinct risk factors compared to other antisocial youth, again similar to research on psychopathic traits in adults. Further, these different risk factors need to be considered in both causal theories proposed to explain serious conduct problems in children and adolescents and in attempts to improve existing treatments for this clinically important group of youths. In the next section, we summarize the main conclusions from this review and evaluate whether research published after this review support them.

CU traits and distinct causal pathways to antisocial behavior

Distinct correlates

Genetic and biological correlates

Frick et al. (2014b) reviewed a number of studies suggesting that CU traits show moderate to large heritable influences, with estimates of genetic influence generally ranging from $h^2 = 0.42$ to $h^2 = 0.68$, which is consistent with more recent studies (Henry, Pingault, Boivin, Rijsdijk, & Viding, 2016). More importantly for documenting distinct causal factors influencing conduct problems in those with and without elevated CU traits, the heritable influences on conduct problems appear to be stronger in those with elevated CU traits and this appears to be independent of conduct problem severity (Viding, Blair, Moffit, & Plomin, 2005) and co-occurring problems of impulsivity (Viding, Frick, & Plomin, 2007). Based on this research, a number of studies have begun investigating potential polymorphisms that may play a role in the genetic risk for CU traits, with studies finding variations of a polymorphism of the oxytocin receptor gene (Beitchman et al., 2012; Dadds et al., 2014) and lower levels of serotonin *1B receptor* gene methylation (Moul, Dobson-Stone, Brennan, Hawes, & Dadds, 2015) as differentiating children with conduct problems who do and do not show elevated CU traits.

Frick et al. (2014b) also reviewed a number of brain imaging studies suggesting that elevated CU traits are consistently associated with significant hypoactivation in the amygdala when viewing emotional stimuli, especially those involving fearful facial expressions. Since this review, a number of other studies have been published supporting functional abnormalities involving the amygdala and its connections to other parts of the brain as being associated with CU traits. For example, children with elevated CU traits showed decreased functional connectivity between the anterior cingulate and amygdala while viewing images of people being harmed (Yoder, Lahey, & Decety, 2016). Cardinale et al. (2017) reported that adolescents with conduct problems and elevated CU traits showed left amygdala hypoactivation when asked to judge the acceptability of statements that might cause fear in others (i.e., You better watch your back). In addition to these functional brain abnormalities, studies have also found structural brain abnormalities in the amygdala and related regions that are associated with CU traits as well. For example, in a mixed gender sample of 134 adolescents and young adults (ages 12–20), CU traits were associated with reduced gray matter concentration in the amygdala and insula, while conduct problems themselves were associated with *increased* gray matter concentration in the amygdala (Cohn et al., 2016).

These findings of amygdala abnormalities could have important causal implications, given that this area of the brain is involved in emotional learning and attention to emotional cues (Marsh et al., 2008). Further, the amygdala and its connections to other areas of the brain (e.g., prefrontal cortex and ventral anterior cingulate cortex) are important for a person's ability to infer the affective state of another and make decisions based on that information, a critical skill for normal empathic responding (Marsh et al., 2013; Sakai et al., 2017; Szabó et al., 2017). Finally, there is evidence that the functional and structural abnormalities in the amygdala may play a role in the aggressive behavior displayed by youth with elevated CU traits. For example, Lozier, Cardinale, VanMeter, and Marsh (2014) reported that amygdala hypoactivation mediated the relationship between CU traits and proactive aggression in a sample of children and adolescents.

Importantly, there is also evidence that there are functional and structural abnormalities in brain regions other than the amygdala that are also related to CU traits. For example, children with conduct problems and elevated CU traits exhibited blunted activity in the medial prefrontal cortex during reward anticipation (Veroude et al., 2016) and in the ventromedial prefrontal cortex during punishment reversal (Finger et al., 2008). These findings support research reviewed below suggesting that, in addition to problems in recognizing and responding to others' emotional states, children and adolescents with CU traits show altered processing of reward and punishment cues.

It is also important to note that the underactivity of the amygdala in response to certain emotional cues is not the only sign of deficient emotional responding that has been consistently associated with CU traits. Frick et al. (2014b) also found evidence for other types of reduced emotional responding across a number of psychophysiological modalities. For example, compared to children with conduct problems and normative levels of CU traits, children with elevated CU traits show reduced attentional orienting to pictures depicting distress, reduced magnitude of heart rate change when watching emotionally arousing films, reduced skin conductance reactivity during the anticipation of aversive stimuli or in response to provocation, abnormal event-related potential activity when presented with images of individuals in pain, and reduced cortical reactivity to experimentally induced stress. Studies published since this review have supported these findings, by suggesting that children with elevated CU traits show reduced startle potentiation when presented with aversive stimuli or imagining a fearful event (Kimonis, Fanti, Goulter, & Hall, 2017), reduced attentional capture (i.e., distraction) to emotional faces (Hodsoll, Lavie, & Viding, 2014), and reduced attentional engagement by images of people in distress (Kimonis et al., 2017).

Of note, across all of these studies and across the diverse indices of emotional responsivity, the reduced reactivity found for youth with elevated CU traits tended to be limited to various types of negative emotional stimuli; most notably, faces or images depicting fear, distress, or pain in others or in response to or in anticipation of some aversive event, such as peer provocation. Few studies have found emotional responses to positive emotional stimuli to be associated with CU traits in children and adolescents. Another important issue across these studies that was noted by Frick et al. (2014b) is that children and adolescents with conduct problems who show normative levels of CU traits often show an opposite pattern of reactivity to the various forms of negative emotional stimuli. That is, relative to normal controls, children and adolescents with conduct problems who are not elevated on CU traits often show an enhanced level of reactivity across the various methods studied, such as amygdala responses to fear faces (Viding et al., 2012), startle reflex during fear imagery (Fanti, Panayiotou, Lazarou, Michael, and Georgiou, 2016), attentional orienting to pictures depicting distress (Kimonis et al., 2006), and self-report ratings of fear and sensitivity to punishment (Fanti et al., 2016). These findings illustrate the importance of considering the presence of elevated CU traits when studying potential causal processes that might lead to conduct problems. Ignoring these opposing patterns of emotional responding between the two groups high on conduct problems would have obscured important associations between the child's emotional responses and their problem behavior, and this would have led to erroneous conclusions on the potential importance of emotional responding for understanding the development of conduct problems.

Cognitive correlates

Given the interrelationships between the cognitive and biological responses to emotions, it is not surprising that research has also reported on a number of cognitive differences between children and adolescents with conduct problems depending on their level of CU traits. As reviewed by Frick et al. (2014b), youth with CU traits show a number of abnormalities in how they process punishment cues, such as showing insensitivity to punishment, especially around peers, which has been supported in studies published since this review (Gluckman, Hawes, & Russell, 2016). Youth with CU traits also have been found to view aggression as an acceptable method to use for instrumental gain or dominance and they are more likely than other youth to focus on the positive outcomes of their antisocial behavior and blame others for their poor behavior, again supported by studies published since the review (Guelker, Barry, Barry, & Malkin, 2014).

A number of studies have investigated the moral reasoning of children and adolescents with elevated CU traits and reported that they are more likely to engage in increased behavior that benefits themselves while harming others (Sakai, Dalwani, Gelhorn, Mikulich-Gilbertson, & Crowley, 2012; Sakai et al., 2016) and exhibit more moral disengagement (i.e., justifying their antisocial behavior; Dhingra, Debowska, Sharratt, Hyland, & Kola-Palmer, 2015) compared to those with normative levels of CU traits. Further, adolescents with elevated CU traits are less likely to interpret positive emotion in peers as an indication of impending collaboration, although they do not differ from other adolescents in using negative emotion in peers to predict less collaboration (Fawcett, Wesevich, Truedsson, Wåhlstedt, & Gredebäck, 2016).

As noted previously, youth with conduct problems and CU traits show reduced physiological responses to others' fear, pain, other signs of distress. Therefore, it is not surprising that research has also shown a negative association between CU traits and ratings of affective empathy in which the child rates their affective discomfort toward others' distress (Frick et al., 2014b). What is less consistent is whether CU traits are also negatively related to measures of cognitive empathy, which focuses on accurately recognizing the feelings of others and taking their perspective. Some studies report that youth with elevated CU traits show problems with emotional recognition and cognitive perspective taking and others do not find such deficits (see Kahn, Frick, Golmaryami, & Marsee, 2017 for an updated review of these findings). Dadds et al. (2009) provided data to suggest that these inconsistent findings may be related to age, in that affective empathy deficits were associated with CU traits across childhood, whereas cognitive perspective-taking deficits were only present in early childhood. These authors suggest that the emotional deficits to others' distress in children with elevated CU traits may make it difficult for a child to learn perspective-taking skills but that over time, he or she can eventually compensate for this emotional deficit and learn to accurately interpret others' emotions.

Family correlates

The correlates to CU traits that have been reviewed in the preceding sections focused largely on dispositional factors within the child. Research has also investigated a number of social–contextual correlates to CU traits and to the behavior problems in children with elevated CU traits. As noted in the review by Frick et al. (2014b), negative parenting practices, especially those associated with a hostile and coercive parenting style (e.g., inconsistent and harsh parenting practices), are often more strongly associated with conduct problems in children and adolescents without elevated CU traits. In contrast, warm and responsive parenting that relies on positive reinforcement is typically found to be more strongly associated with conduct problems in youth that are elevated on CU traits. The importance of warm parenting for children high on CU traits has been supported in a number of studies published after this review. Again, across these studies positive parenting has been consistently related to both the conduct problems in children with elevated CU traits (Elizur, Somech, & Vinokur, 2017; Fanti, Colins, Andershed, & Sikki, 2017; Hyde et al., 2016; Mills-Koonce, Willoughby, Garrett-Peters, Wagner, & Vernon-Feagans, 2016; Pasalich, Witkiewitz, McMahon, Pinderhughes, & Conduct Problems Prevention Research Group, 2015; Wagner et al., 2015; Waller et al., 2015) and to the CU traits themselves (Fanti et al., 2017; Graziano et al., 2017; Hyde et al., 2016; Kjøbli, Zachrisson, & Bjørnebekk, 2016; Mills-Koonce et al., 2016; Pasalich et al., 2015; Robinson, Azores-Gococo, Brennan, & Lilienfeld, 2016; Wagner et al., 2015; Waller, Hyde, Baskin-Sommers, & Olson, 2017).

A critical issue in this research is that the measures of positive parenting have varied greatly across studies and have typically included composite measures that combine various aspects of a warm and supportive parent–child relationship, such as use of positive reinforcement, display of positive affect to the child, degree of parental involvement in the child's activities, degree and quality of parent–child cooperation, and positive communication between parent and child. Clark and Frick (2016) reported data from an ethnically diverse sample of kindergarten students to suggest that distinguishing among these various dimensions of positive parenting may be important. Specifically, they reported that parental use of positive reinforcement was more strongly related (negatively) to teacher-rated conduct problems in children with CU traits, whereas measures of parental warmth were more strongly related (again negatively) to CU traits themselves.

The majority of this research linking parenting to CU traits has been cross-sectional. Thus, most studies have been unable to test potential bidirectional effects between parenting and either CU traits or the conduct problem displayed by youth with elevated CU traits. In the few studies that have tested these effects, the findings suggest that children with CU traits often evoke more harsh and uninvolved parenting, leading to less warmth in the parent–child relationship over time (Fanti & Centifanti, 2014; Fanti et al., 2017; Hawes Dadds, Frost, & Hasking, 2011; Muñoz, Pakalniskiene, & Frick, 2011; Waller et al., 2014). Thus, it is not surprising that CU traits are also associated with several deficits in the emotional relationships between parents and children, including disorganized attachment styles (Bohlin,

Eninger, Brocki, & Thorell, 2012; Fite, Greening, & Stoppelbein, 2008; Pasalich, Dadds, Hawes, & Brennan, 2012). Further, boys with elevated CU traits make less eye contact with their parents in social interactions (Dadds et al., 2012; Dadds, Jambrak, Pasalich, Hawes, & Brennan, 2011) and show less verbal and physical affection with mothers during a task where the mother says she loves her child and shows affection to him or her (Dadds et al., 2012). Although these deficits could be a result of the child's CU interpersonal style, the reduced eye contact appears to be present from a very early age and, as a result, they may also reflect very early deficits in innate reflexes involved in social bonding. For example, Bedford, Pickles, Sharp, Wright, and Hill (2015) reported that preferential face tracking of mothers at 5 weeks of age was negatively related to CU traits at 2.5 years of age.

Peer correlates

The review by Frick et al. (2014b) included studies suggesting that children and adolescents with elevated CU traits show a number of problems in their peer relationships, including that they often bully their peers and they tend to associate with other antisocial peers. These findings have been supported by more recent work (Centifanti, Fanti, Thomson, Demetriou, & Anastassiou-Hadjicharalambous, 2015; Ciucci & Baroncelli, 2014; Golmaryami et al., 2016; Thornberg & Jungert, 2017). Since Frick et al.'s (2014b) review, research has also documented that children with elevated CU traits tend to be disliked by their peers and to have more transient peer relationships than children and adolescents with normative levels of CU traits (Andrade, Sorge, Djordjevic, & Naber, 2015; Graziano et al., 2017; Waller et al., 2017). Research also suggests that youth with elevated CU traits often form relationships with peers with low self-esteem and they exert a great deal of influence on their peers antisocial behavior (Allen, Morris, & Chhoa, 2016; Eisenbarth, Demetriou, Kyranides, & Fanti, 2016; Fanti, Demetriou, & Kimonis, 2013; Van Zalk & Van Zalk, 2015). Further, antisocial adolescents high on CU traits are more likely to commit crimes in groups, to be members of a gang, and to report taking a leadership role in the crimes committed with other adolescents (Thornton et al., 2015). Taken together, the emerging picture of the peer relationships of youth with elevated CU traits suggests that they often have conflictual and unstable peer relationships with other antisocial peers but that they also tend to have a great deal of influence on the behavior of these antisocial peers, especially in terms of encouraging their deviant behavior.

Theoretical models

This research on the various correlates to CU traits has resulted in a number of causal theories for how CU traits develop. For example, Frick et al. (2014a) proposed that children with serious conduct problems and elevated CU traits have a temperament (i.e., fearless, insensitive to punishment, low responsiveness to cues of distress in others) that interferes with the normal development of conscience and places the child at risk for a particularly severe and aggressive pattern of antisocial behavior. That is, these emotional deficits can make it difficult for the child to learn to take perspective of others because the child may not experience the same level of aversive arousal to other's distress. Additionally, the child may not show the emotional responses to parental sanctions that help children learn to internalize societal standards for conduct. However, it is possible that if parents are able to provide a warm and responsive environment, the child may be able to overcome the temperamental risk and learn to regulate their behavior and develop perspective-taking skills. This potential interaction between temperamental risk and parenting is illustrated by the findings from a large ($n = 561$) sample of children who were adopted within a few days of birth (Hyde et al., 2016). Despite having no contact with their biological parents, the child's biological mother's self-report of fearlessness was related to the child's CU behavior at 27 months of age through the child's observed fearless and affiliative behavior at 18 months of age. Further, this link was modified by the child's adoptive parent's parenting, such that the adoptive parents' use of positive reinforcement reduced the association between the child's early fearlessness and later CU traits.

Thus, there appears to be a heritable risk to CU traits that can be modified by certain corrective environments. There is also evidence, however, that CU traits may also develop through exposure to environments in which the child experiences a great deal of abuse and trauma. That is, there appears to be a group of youth with elevated CU traits who show elevated levels of anxiety, who do not show deficits in emotional responding to others' distress, and who are more likely to have experienced abuse and trauma (Kahn et al., 2013; Kimonis, Frick, Cauffman, Goldweber, & Skeem, 2012). It is possible that this group of youth develop their CU traits as a consequence of their experience of trauma, rather than a heritable deficit in their emotional responsiveness to others' distress or to punishment. As a result of their trauma, it is possible that children can become hyper-vigilant toward threatening stimuli at the expense of being able to adequately detect other important aspects of the environment, such as accurately identifying nonthreatening emotional facial expressions (i.e., signs of distress) in others (Kahn et al., 2017).

These theoretical models all attempt to account for the characteristics that have been linked to CU traits in past research by suggesting ways that they could play a role in their development. This research also has important implications for advancing theories for the development of conduct problems in children and adolescents without elevated CU traits by showing how these youth may differ from those with elevated CU traits (Frick et al., 2014b; Frick & Viding, 2009). That is, children and adolescents with serious conduct problems but who show normative levels of CU traits by definition do not show problems in empathy and guilt and, in fact, appear to be more highly reactive to emotional cues in others compared to normal control children (Frick et al., 2014b). Further, this group seems to show high levels of reactivity to provocation from others and often show higher rates of reactive aggression in response to this provocation. However, unlike those with elevated CU traits, they are not more likely to show more premeditated and instrumental violence than other children (Frick et al., 2003). Finally, as noted above, the conduct problems in this group are more strongly associated with hostile and coercive parenting techniques when compared to children with elevated CU traits. Thus, it appears that children in this group show a temperament characterized by strong emotional reactivity combined with inadequate socializing experiences that lead to a failure to develop the skills needed to adequately regulate their emotional reactivity (Frick et al., 2014b). The resulting problems in emotional regulation can result in the child committing impulsive and unplanned aggressive and antisocial acts, for which he or she may feel remorseful afterward, but for which he or she may still have difficulty controlling in the future.

Summary and implications for diagnosis and treatment

In summary, the presence of elevated CU traits appears to designate a clinically and etiologically important subgroup of children and adolescents with conduct problems, just as the construct of psychopathy has proven to be important for designating an important subgroup of antisocial adults. As a result of this research, the DSM-5 (American Psychiatric Association, 2013) included for the first time a specifier for the diagnosis of CD to designate those youth who meet criteria for CD but who also show elevated rates of CU traits. The specifier was called "With Limited Prosocial Emotions" to use a label that would encourage use in clinical practice by avoiding potentially more pejorative terms, such as "callous" or "traits" (Frick et al., 2014b; Waller & Hyde, 2017). This specifier can be given to an individual if he or she meets criteria for CD and shows two or more of the following CU traits persistently over 12 months in more than one relationship or setting: (1) lack of remorse or guilt; (2) callous–lack of empathy; (3) unconcern about performance at school, work, or in other important activities; and (4) shallow or deficient affect. These four criteria were chosen because they are the dimensions of CU traits that form the affective features of psychopathy in adults (Hare & Neumann, 2008), and they proved to be the most consistent in capturing the overall construct of CU traits across different types of samples from various countries (Kimonis et al., 2015). Further, the two-symptom cutoff was selected to designate elevated CU traits for the specifier because it captured children with CD who were more severely impaired in ethnically diverse community (Kahn et al., 2012; Rowe et al., 2010), clinical (Kahn et al., 2012), and forensic (Kimonis et al., 2014) samples. Further, this two-symptom cutoff predicted greater risk for future impairment for both boys (McMahon et al., 2010) and girls (Pardini, Stepp, Hipwell, Stouthamer-Loeber, & Loeber, 2012).

As noted previously, one goal for extending research on psychopathy to children and adolescents was to capture precursors to this construct at a time when it would be more amenable to treatment. However, as also noted previously, children and adolescents who show elevated CU traits often do not respond as well as other youth with CD to typical mental health treatments (Frick et al., 2014b). However, a number of treatment studies have shown some success in reducing the level of antisocial behavior in youth with CU traits when they are (1) intensive and (2) tailored to the unique cognitive, emotional, and contextual risk factors that have been associated with CU traits (Hawes et al., 2014; Wilkinson et al, 2016). As one example, Hawes and Dadds (2005) reported that clinic-referred boys (ages 4–9) with conduct problems and CU traits were less responsive to a parenting intervention than other boys with conduct problems but they did respond with reduced conduct problems to the part of the intervention that focused on teaching parents methods of using positive reinforcement to encourage prosocial behavior. As another example, Caldwell, Skeem, Salekin, and Van Rybroek (2006) demonstrated that adolescent offenders with CU traits improved when treated using an intensive treatment program that utilized reward-oriented approaches, targeted the self-interests of the adolescent, and taught empathy skills (see also White et al., 2013).

Thus, there are some promising results to suggest that interventions developed and tailored to the unique causes of the problems in self-control exhibited by children and adolescents with elevated CU traits could be effective for reducing the level and severity of their conduct problems (Dadds et al., 2013; Kimonis & Armstrong, 2012; Miller et al., 2014). Furthermore, there is even evidence that intensive interventions implemented early in development and that help parents learn methods for teaching children the skills needed for perspective taking can reduce the level of the child's CU traits themselves (Somech & Elizur, 2012). In summary, it appears that children and adolescents with serious conduct problems and elevated CU traits present as a treatment challenge, but research also clearly suggests that they are by no means untreatable nor that the CU traits themselves are unchangeable. The most successful treatments are intensive, and they intervene early during development. Most importantly, they are also evidence-based approaches that consider the characteristics of children with CU traits and tailor treatment to address the unique emotional, cognitive, and social processes that lead to their problems in conscience development and behavior problems (Frick, 2012). As a result, these interventions are likely to continue to improve in their effectiveness as research expands on these causal models.

References

Allen, J. L., Morris, A., & Chhoa, C. Y. (2016). Callous–unemotional (CU) traits in adolescent boys and response to teacher reward and discipline strategies. *Emotional and Behavioural Difficulties*, *21*, 329–342.

American Psychiatric Association. (2013). *Diagnostic and statistical manual of mental disorders* (5th ed.). Washington, DC: Author.

Andrade, B. F., Sorge, G. B., Djordjevic, D., & Naber, A. R. (2015). Callous–unemotional traits influence the severity of peer problems in children with impulsive/overactive and oppositional/defiant behaviors. *Journal of Child and Family Studies*, *24*, 2183–2190.

Bedford, R., Pickles, A., Sharp, H., Wright, N., & Hill, J. (2015). Reduced face preference in infancy: A developmental precursor to callous-unemotional traits? *Biological Psychiatry*, *78*, 144–150.

Beitchman, J. H., Zai, C. C., Muir, K., Berall, L., Nowrouzi, B., Choi, E., & Kennedy, J. L. (2012). Childhood aggression, callous-unemotional traits and oxytocin genes. *European Child and Adolescent Psychiatry*, *21*, 125–132.

Blair, R. J. R., Mitchell, D., & Blair, K. (2005). *The psychopath: Emotion and the brain*. Malden, MA: Blackwell Publishing.

Bohlin, G., Eninger, L., Brocki, K. C., & Thorell, L. B. (2012). Disorganized attachment and inhibitory capacity: Predicting externalizing problem behaviors. *Journal of Abnormal Child Psychology*, *40*, 449–458.

Caldwell, M., Skeem, J., Salekin, R., & Van Rybroek, G. (2006). Treatment response of adolescent offenders with psychopathy features: A 2-year follow-up. *Criminal Justice and Behavior*, *33*, 571–596.

Caputo, A. A., Frick, P. J., & Brodsky, S. L. (1999). Family violence and juvenile sex offending: Potential mediating roles of psychopathic traits and negative attitudes toward women. *Criminal Justice and Behavior*, *26*, 338–356.

Cardinale, E.M., Breeden, A.L., Robertson, E.L., Lozier, L.M., VanMeter, J.W., & Marsh, A. A. (2017). Externalizing behavior severity in youths with callous-unemotional traits corresponds to patterns of amygdala activity and connectivity during judgments of causing fear. *Development and Psychopathology, published online*.

Centifanti, L., Fanti, K. A., Thomson, N. D., Demetriou, V., & Anastassiou-Hadjicharalambous, X. (2015). Types of relational aggression in girls are differentiated by callous-unemotional traits, peers and parental overcontrol. *Behavioral Sciences*, *5*, 518–536.

Christian, R., Frick, P. J., Hill, N., Tyler, L. A., & Frazer, D. (1997). Psychopathy and conduct problems in children: II. Subtyping children with conduct problems based on their interpersonal and affective style. *Journal of the American Academy of Child and Adolescent Psychiatry*, *36*, 233–241.

Ciucci, E., & Baroncelli, A. (2014). The emotional core of bullying: Further evidences of the role of callous–unemotional traits and empathy. *Personality and Individual Differences*, *67*, 69–74.

Clark, J. E., & Frick, P. J. (2016). Positive parenting and callous-unemotional traits: Their association with school behavior problems in young children. *Journal of Clinical Child and Adolescent Psychology*, 1–13.

Cleckley, H. (1976). *The mask of sanity* (*5th ed.*). St. Louis, MO: Mosby.

Cohn, M. D., Viding, E., McCrory, E., Pape, L., van den Brink, W., Doreleijers, T. A., ... Popma, A. (2016). Regional grey matter volume and concentration in at-risk adolescents: Untangling associations with callous-unemotional traits and conduct disorder symptoms. *Psychiatry Research: Neuroimaging*, *254*, 180–187.

Dadds, M. R., Allen, J. L., McGregor, K., Woolgar, M., Viding, E., & Scott, S. (2013). Callous-unemotional traits in children and mechanisms of impaired eye contact during expressions of love: A treatment target? *Journal of Child Psychology and Psychiatry*, *55*, 771–780.

Dadds, M. R., Allen, J. L., Oliver, B. R., Faulkner, N., Legge, K., Moul, C., ... Scott, S. (2012). Love, eye contact and the developmental origins of empathy v. psychopathy. *The British Journal of Psychiatry*, *200*, 191–196.

Dadds, M. R., Hawes, D. J., Frost, A. D. J., Vassallo, S., Bunn, P. B., Hunter, K., & Merz, S. (2009). Learning to 'talk the talk': The relationship of psychopathic traits to deficits in empathy across childhood. *Journal of Child Psychology and Psychiatry*, *50*, 599–606.

Dadds, M. R., Jambrak, J., Pasalich, D., Hawes, D. J., & Brennan, J. (2011). Impaired attention to the eyes of attachment figures and the developmental origins of psychopathy. *Journal of Child Psychology and Psychiatry*, *52*, 238–245.

Dadds, M. R., Moul, C., Cauchi, A., Dobson-Stone, C., Hawes, D. J., Brennan, J., ... Ebstein, R. E. (2014). Polymorphisms in the oxytocin receptor gene are associated with the development of psychopathy. *Development and Psychopathology*, *26*, 21–31.

Dhingra, K., Debowska, A., Sharratt, K., Hyland, P., & Kola-Palmer, S. (2015). Psychopathy, gang membership, and moral disengagement among juvenile offenders. *Journal of Criminal Psychology*, *5*, 13–24.

Edens, J. F., Campbell, J. S., & Weir, J. M. (2007). Youth psychopathy and criminal recidivism: A meta-analysis of the psychopathy checklist measures. *Law and Human Behavior*, *31*, 53–75.

Eisenbarth, H., Demetriou, C. A., Kyranides, M. N., & Fanti, K. A. (2016). Stability subtypes of callous–unemotional traits and conduct disorder symptoms and their correlates. *Journal of Youth and Adolescence*, *45*, 1889–1901.

Elizur, Y., Somech, L. Y., & Vinokur, A. D. (2017). Effects of parent training on callous-unemotional traits, effortful control, and conduct problems: Mediation by parenting. *Journal of Abnormal Child Psychology*, *45*, 15–26.

Fanti, K. A., & Centifanti, L. C. M. (2014). Childhood callous-unemotional traits moderate the relation between parenting distress and conduct problems over time. *Child Psychiatry and Human Development*, *45*, 173–184.

Fanti, K. A., Colins, O. F., Andershed, H., & Sikki, M. (2017). Stability and change in callous-unemotional traits: Longitudinal associations with potential individual and contextual risk and protective factors. *American Journal of Orthopsychiatry*, *87*, 62–75.

Fanti, K. A., Demetriou, C. A., & Kimonis, E. R. (2013). Variants of callous-unemotional conduct problems in a community sample of adolescents. *Journal of Youth and Adolescence*, *42*, 964–979.

Fanti, K. A., Frick, P. J., & Georgiou, S. (2009). Linking callous-unemotional traits to instrumental and non-instrumental forms of aggression. *Journal of Psychopathology and Behavioral Assessment*, *31*, 285–298.

Fanti, K. A., Panayiotou, G., Lazarou, C., Michael, R., & Georgiou, G. (2016). The better of two evils? Evidence that children exhibiting continuous problems high or low on callous-unemotional traits score on opposite directions on physiological and behavioral measures of fear. *Development and Psychopathology*, *28*, 185–198.

Fawcett, C., Wesevich, V., Truedsson, E., Wåhlstedt, C., & Gredebäck, G. (2016). Callous–unemotional traits affect adolescents' perception of collaboration. *Journal of Child Psychology and Psychiatry*, *57*, 1400–1406.

Finger, E. C., Marsh, A. A., Mitchell, D. G., Reid, M. E., Sims, C., Budhani, S., ... Blair, R. J. R. (2008). Abnormal ventromedial prefrontal cortex function in children with psychopathic traits during reversal learning. *Archives of General Psychiatry*, *65*, 586–594.

Fite, P. J., Greening, L., & Stoppelbein, L. (2008). Relation between parenting stress and psychopathic traits among children. *Behavioral Sciences and the Law*, *26*, 239–248.

Forth, A. E. (1995). Psychopathy in adolescent offenders: Assessment, family background, and violence. *Issues in Criminological and Legal Psychology*, *24*, 42–44.

Frick, P. J. (2009). Extending the construct of psychopathy to youths: Implications for understanding, diagnosing, and treating antisocial children and adolescents. *Canadian Journal of Psychiatry*, *12*, 803–812.

Frick, P. J. (2012). Developmental pathways to conduct disorder: Implications for future directions in research, assessment, and treatment. *Journal of Clinical Child and Adolescent Psychology*, *41*, 378–389.

Frick, P. J. (2016). Current research on conduct disorder in children and adolescents. *South African Journal of Psychology*, *46*, 160–174.

Frick, P. J., Cornell, A. H., Barry, C. T., Bodin, S. D., & Dane, H. A. (2003). Callous-unemotional traits and conduct problems in the prediction of conduct problem severity, aggression, and self-report of delinquency. *Journal of Abnormal Child Psychology, 31*, 457–470.

Frick, P. J., Cornell, A. H., Bodin, S. D., Dane, H. A., Barry, C. T., & Loney, B. R. (2003). Callous-unemotional traits and developmental pathways to severe aggressive and antisocial behavior. *Developmental Psychology, 39*, 246–260.

Frick, P. J., & Ray, J. V. (2015). Evaluating callous-unemotional traits as a personality construct. *Journal of Personality, 83*, 710–722.

Frick, P. J., Ray, J. V., Thornton, L. C., & Kahn, R. E. (2014a). Annual research review: A developmental psychopathology approach to understanding callous-unemotional traits in children and adolescents with serious conduct problems. *Journal of Child Psychology and Psychiatry, 55*, 532–548.

Frick, P. J., Ray, J. V., Thornton, L. C., & Kahn, R. E. (2014b). Can callous-unemotional traits enhance the understanding, diagnosis, and treatment of serious conduct problems in children and adolescents? A comprehensive review. *Psychological Bulletin, 140*, 1–57.

Frick, P. J., & Viding, E. M. (2009). Antisocial behavior from a developmental psychopathology perspective. *Development and Psychopathology, 21*, 1111–1131.

Gluckman, N. S., Hawes, D. J., & Russell, A. M. (2016). Are callous-unemotional traits associated with conflict adaptation in childhood? *Child Psychiatry and Human Development, 47*, 583–592.

Golmaryami, F. N., Frick, P. J., Hemphill, S. A., Kahn, R. E., Crapanzano, A. M., & Terranova, A. M. (2016). The social, behavioral, and emotional correlates of bullying and victimization in a school-based sample. *Journal of Abnormal Child Psychology, 44*, 381–391.

Graziano, P. A., Fabiano, G., Willoughby, M. T., Waschbusch, D., Morris, K., Schatz, N., & Vujnovic, R. (2017). Callous-unemotional traits among adolescents with attention-deficit/hyperactivity disorder (ADHD): Associations with parenting. *Child Psychiatry and Human Development, 48*, 1–14.

Guelker, M. D., Barry, C. T., Barry, T. D., & Malkin, M. L. (2014). Perceived positive outcomes as a mediator between adolescent callous-unemotional traits and antisocial behavior. *Personality and Individual Differences, 69*, 129–134.

Hare, R. D. (1993). *Without a conscience: The disturbing world of the psychopaths among us*. New York, NY: Pocket.

Hare, R. D. (2003). *The Psychopathy Checklist—Revised manual* (2nd ed.). Toronto, ON: Multi-Health Systems.

Hare, R. D., & Neumann, C. S. (2008). Psychopathy as a clinical and empirical construct. *Annual Review of Clinical Psychology, 4*, 217–246.

Hawes, D. J., & Dadds, M. R. (2005). The treatment of conduct problems in children with callous-unemotional traits. *Journal of Consulting and Clinical Psychology, 73*, 737–741.

Hawes, D. J., Dadds, M. R., Frost, A. D., & Hasking, P. A. (2011). Do childhood callous-unemotional traits drive change in parenting practices? *Journal of Clinical Child and Adolescent Psychology, 40*, 507–518.

Hawes, D. J., Price, M. J., & Dadds, M. R. (2014). Callous-unemotional traits and the treatment of conduct problems in childhood and adolescence: A comprehensive review. *Clinical Child and Family Psychology Review, 17*, 248–267.

Hodsoll, S., Nilli, L., & Viding, E. (2014). Emotional attentional capture in children with conduct problems: The role of callous-unemotional traits. *Frontiers in Human Neuroscience*, *8*, 570.

Henry, J., Pingault, P. B., Boivin, M., Rijsdijk, F., & Viding, E. (2016). Genetic and environmental aetiology of the dimensions of callous-unemotional traits. *Psychological Medicine*, *46*, 405–414.

Hoffman, M. L. (1970). Moral development. In P. Mussen (Ed.), *Carmichael's handbook of child psychology* (Vol. 2, pp. 261–361). New York, NY: Wiley.

Hyde, L. W., Waller, R., Trentacosta, C. J., Shaw, D. S., Neiderhiser, J. M., Ganiban, J. M., ... Leve, L. D. (2016). Heritable and nonheritable pathways to early callous-unemotional behaviors. *American Journal of Psychiatry*, *173*, 903–910.

Kahn, R. E., Frick, P. J., Golmaryami, F. N., & Marsee, M. A. (2017). The moderating role of anxiety in the associations of callous-unemotional traits with self-report and laboratory measures of affective and cognitive empathy. *Journal of Abnormal Child Psychology*, *45*, 1–14.

Kahn, R. E., Frick, P. J., Youngstrom, E., Findling, R. L., & Youngstrom, J. K. (2012). The effects of including a callous-unemotional specifier for the diagnosis of conduct disorder. *Journal of Child Psychology and Psychiatry*, *53*, 271–282.

Kahn, R. E., Frick, P. J., Youngstrom, E. A., Kogos Youngstrom, J., Feeny, N. C., & Findling, R. L. (2013). Distinguishing primary and secondary variants of callous-unemotional traits among adolescents in a clinic-referred sample. *Psychological Assessment*, *25*, 966–978.

Kimonis, E. R., & Armstrong, K. (2012). Adapting parent-child interaction therapy to treat severe conduct problems with callous-unemotional traits: A case study. *Clinical Case Studies*, *11*, 234–252.

Kimonis, E. R., Fanti, K. A., Frick, P. J., Moffitt, T. E., Essau, C., Bijjtebier, P., & Marsee, M. A. (2015). Using self-reported callous-unemotional traits to cross-nationally assess the DSM-5 "With Limited Prosocial Emotions" specifier. *Journal of Child Psychology and Psychiatry*, *56*, 1249–1261.

Kimonis, E. R., Fanti, K., Goldweber, A., Marsee, M. A., Frick, P. J., & Cauffman, E. (2014). Callous-unemotional traits in incarcerated adolescents. *Psychological Assessment*, *26*, 227–237.

Kimonis, E. R., Fanti, K. A., Anastassiou-Hadjicharalambous, X., Mertan, B., Goulter, N., & Katsimicha, E. (2016). Can callous-unemotional traits be reliably measured in preschoolers? *Journal of Abnormal Child Psychology*, *44*, 625–638.

Kimonis, E. R., Fanti, K. A., Goulter, N., & Hall, J. (2017). Affective startle potentiation differentiates primary and secondary variants of juvenile psychopathy. *Development and Psychopathology*, *29*, 1149–1160.

Kimonis, E. R., Frick, P. J., Cauffman, E., Goldweber, A., & Skeem, J. (2012). Primary and secondary variants of juvenile psychopathy differ in emotional processing. *Development and Psychopathology*, *24*, 1091–1103.

Kimonis, E. R., Frick, P. J., Fazekas, H., & Loney, B. R. (2006). Psychopathy, aggression, and the emotional processing of emotional stimuli in non-referred girls and boys. *Behavioral Sciences and the Law*, *24*, 21–37.

Kimonis, E. R., Frick, P. J., Skeem, J., Marsee, M. A., Cruise, K., Muñoz, L. C., ... Morris, A. S. (2008). Assessing callous-unemotional traits in adolescent offenders: Validation of the Inventory of Callous-Unemotional Traits. *Journal of the International Association of Psychiatry and Law*, *31*, 241–252.

Kjøbli, J., Zachrisson, H. D., & Bjørnebekk, G. (2016). Three randomized effectiveness trials —one question: Can callous-unemotional traits in children be altered? *Journal of Clinical Child and Adolescent Psychology*, 1–8.

Kruh, I. P., Frick, P. J., & Clements, C. B. (2005). Historical and personality correlates to the violence patterns of juveniles tried as adults. *Criminal Justice and Behavior*, *32*, 69–96.

Lahey, B. B., Hart, E. L., Pliszka, S., Applegate, B., & McBurnett, K. (1993). Neurophysiological correlates of conduct disorder: A rationale and a review of research. *Journal of Clinical Child Psychology*, *22*, 141–153.

Lahey, B. B., Loeber, R., Quay, H. C., Frick, P. J., & Grimm, J. (1992). Oppositional defiant disorder and conduct disorders: Issues to be resolved for DSM-IV. *Journal of the American Academy of Child and Adolescent Psychiatry*, *31*, 539–546.

Lawing, K., Frick, P. J., & Cruise, K. R. (2010). Differences in offending patterns between adolescent sex offenders high or low in callous-unemotional traits. *Psychological Assessment*, *22*, 298–305.

Leistico, A. R., Salekin, R. T., DeCoster, J., & Rogers, R. (2008). A large-scale meta-analysis relating the Hare measures of psychopathy to antisocial conduct. *Law and Human Behavior*, *32*, 28–45.

Loeber, R., Pardini, D., Stouthamer-Loeber, M., Hipwell, A. E., & Sembower, M. (2009). Are there stable factors in girls externalizing behaviors in middle childhood? *Journal of Abnormal Child Psychology*, *37*, 777–791.

Lozier, L. M., Cardinale, E. M., VanMeter, J. W., & Marsh, A. A. (2014). Mediation of the relationship between callous-unemotional traits and proactive aggression by amygdala response to fear among children with conduct problems. *JAMA Psychiatry*, *71*, 627–636.

Marsh, A. A., Finger, E. C., Fowler, K. A., Adalio, C. J., Jurkowitz, T. N., Schechter, J. C., ... Blair, R. J. R. (2013). Empathic responsiveness in amygdala and anterior cingulate cortex in youths with psychopathic traits. *Journal of Child Psychology and Psychiatry*, *54*(8), 900–910.

Marsh, A. A., Finger, E. C., Mitchell, D. G. V., Reid, M. E., Sims, C., Kosson, D. S., ... Blair, R. J. R. (2008). Reduced amygdala response to fearful expressions in children and adolescents with callous-unemotional traits and disruptive behavior disorders. *The American Journal of Psychiatry*, *165*, 712–720.

McMahon, R. J., Witkiewitz, K., Kotler, J. S., & The Conduct Problems Prevention Research Group. (2010). Predictive validity of callous-unemotional traits measures in early adolescence with respect to multiple antisocial outcomes. *Journal of Abnormal Psychology*, *119*, 752–763.

Miller, N. V., Haas, S. M., Waschbusch, D. A., Willoughby, M. T., Helseth, S. A., Crum, K. I., ... Pelham, W. E. (2014). Behavior therapy and callous-unemotional traits: Effects of a pilot study examining modified behavioral contingencies on child behavior. *Behavior Therapy*, *45*, 606–618.

Mills-Koonce, W. R., Willoughby, M. T., Garrett-Peters, P., Wagner, N., & Vernon-Feagans, L. (2016). The interplay among socioeconomic status, household chaos, and parenting in the prediction of child conduct problems and callous–unemotional behaviors. *Development and Psychopathology*, *28*, 757–771.

Moul, C., Dobson-Stone, C., Brennan, J., Hawes, D. J., & Dadds, M. R. (2015). Serotonin 1B receptor gene (HTR1B) methylation as a risk factor for callous-unemotional traits in antisocial boys. *PLoS One*, *10*(5), e0126903.

Muñoz, L. C., Pakalniskiene, V., & Frick, P. J. (2011). Parental monitoring and youth behavior problems: Moderation by callous-unemotional traits over time. *European Child and Adolescent Psychiatry*, *20*, 261–269.

Pardini, D. A., Stepp, S., Hipwell, A., Stouthamer-Loeber, M., & Loeber, R. (2012). The clinical utility of the propose DSM-5 callous-unemotional subtype of conduct disorder in young girls. *Journal of the American Academy of Child and Adolescent Psychiatry*, *51*, 62–73.

Pasalich, D. S., Dadds, M. R., Hawes, D. J., & Brennan, J. (2012). Do callous-unemotional traits moderate the relative importance of parental coercion versus warmth in child conduct problems? An observational study. *Journal of Child Psychology and Psychiatry*, *52*, 1308–1315.

Pasalich, D. S., Witkiewitz, K., McMahon, R. J., Pinderhughes, E. E., & Conduct Problems Prevention Research Group. (2015). Indirect effects of the fast track intervention on conduct disorder symptoms and callous-unemotional traits: Distinct pathways involving discipline and warmth. *Journal of Abnormal Child Psychology*, *44*, 587–597.

Poythress, N. G., Dembo, R., Wareham, J., & Greenbaum, P. E. (2006). Construct validity of the youth psychopathic traits inventory (YPI) and the antisocial process screening devices (APSD) with justice-involved adolescents. *Criminal Justice and Behavior*, *33*, 26–55.

Quay, H. C. (1987). Patterns of delinquent behavior. In H. C. Quay (Ed.), *Handbook of juvenile delinquency* (pp. 118–138). New York, NY: Wiley.

Quay, H. C. (1993). The psychobiology of undersocilaized aggressive conduct disorder. *Development and Psychopathology*, *5*, 165–180.

Ray, J. V., Frick, P. J., Thornton, L. C., Steinberg, L., & Cauffman, E. (2016a). Positive and negative item wording and its influence on the assessment of callous-unemotional traits. *Psychological Assessment*, *28*, 394–404.

Ray, J. V., Frick, P. J., Thornton, L. C., Steinberg, L., & Cauffman, E. (2016b). Impulse control and callous-unemotional traits distinguish patterns of delinquency and substance use in justice involved adolescents: Examining the moderating role of neighborhood context. *Journal of Abnormal Child Psychology*, *44*, 599–611.

Robinson, B. A., Azores-Gococo, N., Brennan, P. A., & Lilienfeld, S. O. (2016). The roles of maternal psychopathic traits, maternal antisocial personality traits, and parenting in the development of child psychopathic traits. *Parenting*, *16*, 36–55.

Rowe, R., Maughan, B., Moran, P., Ford, T., Briskman, J., & Goodman, R. (2010). The role of callous unemotional traits in the diagnosis of conduct disorder. *Journal of Child Psychology and Psychiatry*, *51*, 688–695.

Sakai, J. T., Dalwani, M. S., Gelhorn, H. L., Mikulich-Gilbertson, S. K., & Crowley, T. J. (2012). A behavioral test of accepting benefits that cost others: Associations with conduct problems and callous-unemotionality. *PLoS One*, *7*(4), e36158.

Sakai, J. T., Dalwani, M. S., Mikulich-Gilbertson, S. K., McWilliams, S. K., Raymond, K. M., & Crowley, T. J. (2016). A behavioral measure of costly helping: Replicating and extending the association with callous unemotional traits in male adolescents. *PLoS One*, *11*(3), e0151678.

Sakai, J. T., Dalwani, M. S., Mikulich-Gilbertson, S. K., Raymond, K. M., Tanabe, J., McWilliams, S. K., . . . Crowley, T. J. (2017). Imaging decision about whether to benefit self by harming others: Adolescent with conduct and substance problems, with or without callous-unemotionality, or developing typically. *Psychiatry Research: Neuroimaging*, *263*, 103–112.

Salekin, R. T. (2002). Psychopathy and therapeutic pessimism: Clinical lore or clinical reality. *Clinical Psychology Review*, *22*, 79–112.

Salekin, R. T. (2016). Psychopathy in childhood: Toward better informing the DSM-5 and ICD-11 conduct disorder specifiers. *Personality Disorders: Theory, Research, and Treatment*, *7*, 180–191.

Skeem, J. L., Polaschek, D. L. L., Patrick, C. J., & Lilienfeld, S. O. (2011). Psychopathic personality: Bridging the gap between scientific evidence and public policy. *Psychological Science in the Public Interest*, *12*, 95–162.

Somech, L. Y., & Elizur, Y. (2012). Promoting self-regulation and cooperation in prekindergarten children with conduct problems: A randomized controlled trial. *Journal of the American Academy of Child and Adolescent Psychiatry*, *51*, 412–422.

Szabó, E., Kocsel, N., Édes, A., Pap, D., Galambos, A., Zsombók, T., ... Kökönyei, G. (2017). Callous-unemotional traits and neural responses to emotional faces in a community sample of young adults. *Personality and Individual Differences*, *111*, 312–317.

Thompson, R. A., & Newton, E. K. (2010). Emotion in early conscience. In W. F. Arsenio, & E. A. Lemerise (Eds.), *Emotions, aggression, and morality in children: Bridging development and psychopathology* (pp. 13–31). Washington, DC: American Psychological Association.

Thornberg, R., & Jungert, T. (2017). Callous-unemotional traits, harm-effect moral reasoning, and bullying among Swedish children. *Child and Youth Care Forum*, *46*, 559–575.

Thornton, L. C., Frick, P. J., Shulman, E. P., Ray, J. V., Steinberg, L., & Cauffman, E. (2015). Callous-unemotional traits and adolescents' role in group crime. *Law and Human Behavior*, *39*, 368–377.

Van Zalk, M. H. W., & Van Zalk, N. (2015). Violent peer influence: The roles of self-esteem and psychopathic traits. *Development and Psychopathology*, *27*, 1077–1088.

Veroude, K., von Rhein, D., Chauvin, R. J., van Dongen, E. V., Mennes, M. J., Franke, B., ... Glennon, J. C. (2016). The link between callous-unemotional traits and neural mechanisms of reward processing: An fMRI study. *Psychiatry Research: Neuroimaging*, *255*, 75–80.

Viding, E., Frick, P. J., & Plomin, R. (2007). Aetiology of the relationship between callous-unemotional traits and conduct problems in childhood. *The British Journal of Psychiatry*, *190*, s33–s38.

Viding, E., Blair, R. J., Moffit, T. E., & Plomin, R. (2005). Evidence for substantial genetic risk for psychopathy in 7-year-olds. *Journal of Child Psychology and Psychiatry*, *46*, 592–597.

Viding, E., Sebastian, C. L., Dadds, M. R., Lockwood, P. L., Cecil, C. A., De Brito, S. A., & McCrory, E. J. (2012). Amygdala response to preattentive masked fear in children with conduct problems: The role of callous-unemotional traits. *American Journal of Psychiatry*, *169*, 1109–1116.

Wagner, N. J., Mills-Koonce, W. R., Willoughby, M. T., Zvara, B., Cox, M. J., & The Family Life Project Key Investigators. (2015). Parenting and children's representations of family predict disruptive and callous-unemotional behaviors. *Developmental Psychology*, *51*, 935–948.

Waller, R., Gardner, F., Shaw, D. S., Dishion, T. J., Wilson, M. N., & Hyde, L. W. (2015). Callous-unemotional behavior and early-childhood onset of behavior problems: The role of parental harshness and warmth. *Journal of Clinical Child and Adolescent Psychology*, *44*, 655–667.

Waller, R., Gardner, F., Viding, E., Shaw, D. S., Dishion, T. J., Wilson, M. N., & Hyde, L. W. (2014). Bidirectional associations between parental warmth, callous unemotional behavior, and behavior problems in high-risk preschoolers. *Journal of Abnormal Child Psychology*, *42*, 1275–1285.

Waller, R., & Hyde, L. W. (2017). Callous-unemotional behaviors in early childhood: Measurement, meaning, and the influence of parenting. *Child Development Perspectives*, *11*, 120–126.

Waller, R., Hyde, L. W., Baskin-Sommers, A. R., & Olson, S. L. (2017). Interactions between callous unemotional behaviors and executive function in early childhood predict later aggression and lower peer-liking in late-childhood. *Journal of Abnormal Child Psychology*, *45*, 597–609.

White, S. F., Frick, P. J., Lawing, S. K., & Bauer, D. (2013). Callous-unemotional traits and response to functional family therapy in adolescent offenders. *Behavioral Science and the Law*, *31*, 271–285.

Wilkinson, S., Waller, R., & Viding, E. (2016). Practitioner review: Involving young people with callous unemotional traits in treatment—does it work? A systematic review. *Journal of Child Psychology and Psychiatry*, *57*, 552–565.

Willoughby, M. T., Waschbusch, D. A., Moore, G. A., & Propper, C. B. (2011). Using the ASEBA to screen for callous unemotional traits in early childhood: Factor structure, temporal, stability, and utility. *Journal of Psychopathology and Behavioral Assessment*, *33*, 19–30.

Yoder, K. J., Lahey, B. B., & Decety, J. (2016). Callous traits in children with and without conduct problems predict reduced connectivity when viewing harm to others. *Scientific Reports*, *6*, Article number: 20216.

Cognitive attribution bias

7

Holly E. Poore, and Irwin D. Waldman
Emory University, Atlanta, GA, United States

Social information processing model of children's social adjustment

Childhood social cognition—which can include emotional understanding, social cue interpretation, perspective-taking, attitudes toward behaviors, and empathy—is associated with a variety of important social behaviors including antisocial behaviors such as aggression and prosocial behaviors like sharing and helping (Barnes, Howell, Thurston, & Cohen, 2017; Bussey, Quinn, & Dobson, 2015; Denham et al., 2002; Kuhnert, Begeer, Fink, & de Rosnay, 2017; Li et al., 2015; Meece & Mize, 2010). Social cognitive abilities also predict social standing and social interactions with both peers and parents (Comparini, Douglas, & Perez, 2014; Meece & Mize, 2010; Rah & Parke, 2008).

The Social Information Processing (SIP) Model is an important model of social cognition that seeks to characterize the processes by which children encode, interpret, and react to social information (Crick & Dodge, 1994). Research has shown that deficits and biases in these processing steps predict various aspects of social behavior and adjustment (Dodge et al., 2003; Dodge & Price, 1994; Guy, Lee, & Wolke, 2017; Lansford, Malone, Dodge, Pettit, & Bates, 2010). Children can be classified into groups based on with which steps in SIP they struggle, and group status, without intervention, is stable across development (Lansford et al., 2006). Children with deficits in SIP exhibited more externalizing behaviors at many stages of development compared with children without SIP deficits. In addition, children with deficits in multiple steps of SIP exhibited more externalizing behavior compared to children without SIP deficits and children with deficits in only one step. These results suggest that children have distinct patterns of processing that correlate with severity of externalizing behavior. As such, the SIP Model is a promising method of describing children's cognitive processing during social situations that can explain the development and maintenance of maladaptive behavior and social interactions.

In this chapter, we first describe the stages in the SIP Model, followed by methods for assessing SIP and related Social Cognitive Processes. We then review studies that have examined the relations of SIP deficits and biases to social behavior and interactions with parents and peers, the relations between basic cognitive abilities and SIP, and the etiology of SIP deficits and biases. We then describe studies of the effects of interventions aimed at ameliorating SIP deficits and biases and

Developmental Pathways to Disruptive, Impulse-Control, and Conduct Disorders.
DOI: https://doi.org/10.1016/B978-0-12-811323-3.00007-9

conclude by discussing limitations of the extant literature and future directions in research on SIP and its links to social behavior and other important outcomes.

Stages in the SIP model

The SIP Model comprises six steps: encoding of cues, interpretation of cues, clarification of goals, response access or construction, response decision, and behavioral enactment. The first two steps of this model are the encoding and interpretation of any social informational cues perceived. During this time, individuals attend to and encode particular social cues which they then interpret and use to construct a mental representation of the social situation, including inferring motives for others' actions. Interpretation of cues may involve processes such as the analysis of events in the situation and making causal attributions, the assessment of whether the goals for a social exchange have been achieved, accessing long-term memory to evaluate situational cues and past performance, and self and peer evaluations of previous and current exchanges. The interpretation process may also result in changes made to social information (e.g., schemas, scripts) stored in memory.

After encoding and interpreting cues, individuals engage in selecting a goal for the social interaction. Goals refer to states that serve to orient the actor toward producing a particular outcome. These goals can be predetermined prior to the start of the social exchange or can be revised in response to immediate social stimuli. Based on their interpretation of the situation, individuals conduct a mental search of possible responses to the situation. Then, they choose a response to enact. This process involves taking the possible responses retrieved from memory and evaluating their appropriateness and consequences, and then selecting a response to enact.

The first version of this model was proposed in 1986 (Dodge, 1986) and included the aforementioned five steps that occur independently and in sequential order. The clarification of goals step, which is laid out explicitly in subsequent revisions of the model (Crick & Dodge, 1994), was not present in the initial model. Additionally, in this model, the steps occur in sequential order such that the results of one process influence the results of the process next in the sequence, but not a process a few steps away. For example, the individual's preexisting cognitive capabilities, database of available social knowledge, and the immediate social cue influenced the first encoding process. Results from the encoding process directly influence interpretation of cues and representation of the social situation. The results of this process influence the process of searching for a response, which in turn influences the response decision process. These processes were proposed to occur independently such that the individual was engaging in only one process at a time. The model does not allow for the possibility that results from the encoding process would directly influence the response search process, such that the mental representation step was temporarily skipped. It also does not allow the processes to take place in reverse order, such that results from the response search process, for instance, influence the representation process. Each of these five steps eventually leads to a behavioral response.

An updated model of SIP (Crick & Dodge, 1994; see Fig. 7.1) addressed several of the limitations of the first version. First, with respect to the flow of information processing, the updated model posited that individuals are engaged in multiple cognitive processes at once. For example, they engage in the interpretation of social cues while in the process of encoding this information. Despite the possibility for parallel information processing to occur, the authors maintained that the steps of processing a particular stimulus occur in sequential order, but that there are two exceptions to this. First, results of the representation process can influence the encoding process such that the mental representation may influence which social cues the individual attends to and how he or she interprets that information. Second, the response decision process can influence the response search process in a similar fashion. In this model, information processing steps occur simultaneously and influence each other in both directions, but the processing of a single stimulus still follows the sequential order.

Second, the authors consider the potential impact social adjustment has on SIP. The impact of SIP on social adjustment was studied previously (Dodge, 1980; Harter, 1983), but little attention was paid to the reciprocal relationship. This allowed for the examination of how previous social experiences and peer

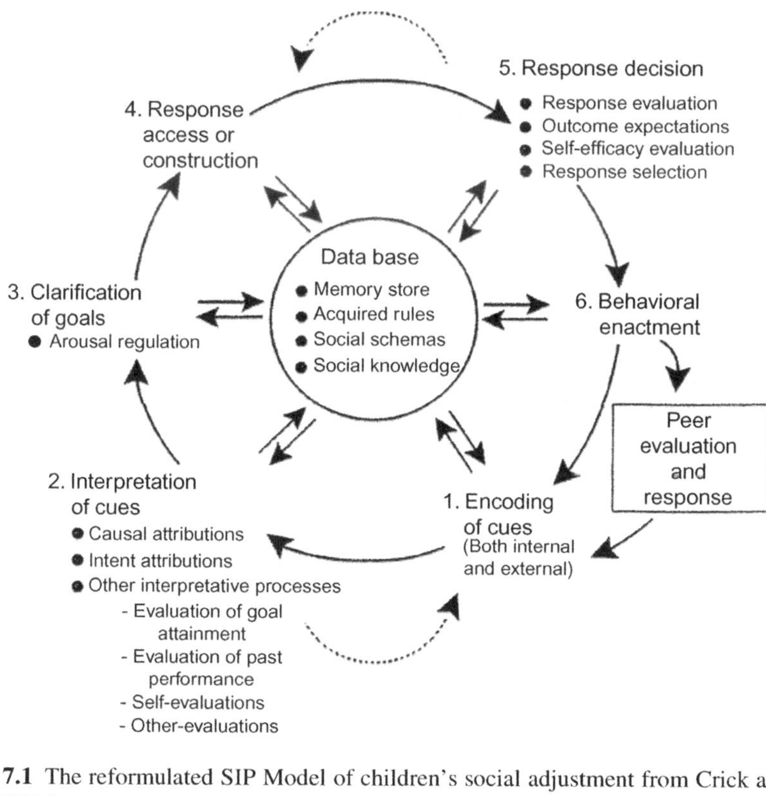

Figure 7.1 The reformulated SIP Model of children's social adjustment from Crick and Dodge (1994).

evaluations impact processing and decision making in social situations. For instance, the authors hypothesized that previous peer evaluations of behaviors would influence the process by which children evaluate and select a behavior.

Third, the authors reconceptualized how previous social knowledge may influence processing. Instead of exerting influence only on the encoding step of processing, the database of a child's social information was proposed to influence each level of processing. Additionally, the relationship between this database and each step was modeled bidirectionally to allow for the possibility that online social processing could influence broader conceptualizations of social rules, schemas, and knowledge.

Finally, the authors included hypotheses about the role of emotion in SIP, which had previously been excluded from the model. Emotion was hypothesized to influence processing at each step. For example, the authors hypothesized that emotional arousal may influence encoding (e.g., Steinberg & Dodge, 1983) such that the experience of arousal itself was encoded as a relevant cue. The authors made several additional revisions to the model that reflected the most updated information about social interactions and cognitive processing, but a full discussion of these changes is outside the scope of this review.

This model has subsequently been used to study how social cognition influences behavior, social interactions, and long-term outcomes. The following is a review of the ways in which SIP is measured, how it influences or is influenced by behavior and social experiences, the role of basic cognitive abilities in SIP, and how interventions have targeted specific steps in SIP to change behavior.

Assessing SIP and related social cognitive processes

Measurement of an online process like SIP can take many forms. Most studies include stories of some kind, either in video, audio, written, or picture form. The stories include information about a social interaction between at least two peers, one of whom is the "target" character and one of whom is the "provocateur." The nature of the interactions between the two actors is meant to be neutral or ambiguous to allow children to infer the motives and feelings of the actors. Of note, SIP patterns appear to be situation-specific, and recommendations have been made to include scenarios that involve situations of direct interest (Dodge et al., 2003). As such, studies that aim to examine the effects of SIP on peer interactions typically include stories of two same-aged peers in a school or other familiar social situation (e.g., De Castro, Merk, Koops, Veerman, & Bosch, 2005; Dodge et al., 2003). Studies of SIP in parent interactions include stories that involve a social situation with a parent and child (e.g., Haskett & Willoughby, 2007; Rah & Parke, 2008).

After hearing the stories, children are then asked several questions about the important social information conveyed in the story, to interpret the motives of actors in the story, and to generate and evaluate responses to the situation. In most studies, interviewers ask questions about the situation that was presented, although some use a questionnaire measure (Calvete & Orue, 2012) in which children select one of multiple options for each question. Most studies assess SIP using similar questions adopted from early work by Dodge and colleagues (Crick & Dodge, 1996). Examination of the methodology in a study by Dodge et al. (2003) provides an illustrative example of measurement of SIP. In this study, children watched 12 filmed, scripted scenarios that involved a child being rebuffed by peers (the provocateurs). The intent of the peer in rejecting the child varied between studies and was either hostile, benign, or ambiguous. The encoding step was assessed by asking children to describe what happened in the story. Responses were coded based on how much relevant information the child recalled. Attributions were coded based on whether the child thought the provocateur was being mean. Assessment of hostile attribution bias was based on the number of times the child interpreted ambiguous or nonhostile cues as hostile. Then, children were told the provocateur's true intention and asked to generate possible responses. Responses were coded as competent, aggressive, or inept. Children were then presented with varying response strategies and asked to evaluate how each possible response would impact how much other children liked them and how successful the response would be. Finally, children were given possible competent responses and asked to show the interviewer how they would enact those responses. Demonstrations were coded as incompetent or competent. Many studies have incorporated similar methodologies to access functioning at varying steps of SIP (e.g., Arsenio, Adams, & Gold, 2009; Crick & Dodge, 1996; Gully, 2000).

Fig. 7.2 provides a brief example of a scenario that is described to participants and the questions they are subsequently asked to answer (Crick & Dodge, 1996). These questions are meant to measure the response decision and evaluation process children engage in when presented with a common scenario that involves a social interaction with same-aged peers. In the first question, children are presented with an aggressive response option and asked how this response might influence both their instrumental goal (playing with the ball) and relational goal (how the other children in the scenario would feel toward the child after enacting a certain response). The second question assesses how easy the children believe it would be to enact an aggressive response. Finally, the third question gives children a choice between an instrumental goal and a relational goal and asks them to select a goal based on what they would like to happen in the scenario.

Studies of SIP in children have focused primarily on school-aged children and adolescents (De Castro, Veerman, Koops, Bosch, & Monshouwer, 2002) and, as such, the aforementioned methodologies have been validated primarily using children of those age groups. Schultz et al. (2010) sought to develop a measure that could be used with preschool children to reliably assess their social cognition and test the association between SIP and behavior in early childhood. The Schultz Test of Emotion Processing—Preliminary Version includes videos that depict preschool and elementary school-aged children in a variety of common social situations. Each video displays a situation related to emotions, provocation, or goal acquisition. To assess cue interpretation, children are either asked to choose which emotion (happy, sad, angry, or scared) the actor in the video was likely feeling or to predict what the

Things That Happen to Me

Ball Situation
On the playground one day, you have nothing to do. You see some kids in your class playing a game with a ball. You walk over to where they are playing.

1. What would happen if you grabbed the ball away from one of the kids?

a. The kids would *not* like you.
This would happen most of the time.
This would happen sometimes.

OR

The kids would like you.
This would happen most of the time.
This would happen sometimes.

b. The kids would let you have the ball.
This would happen most of the time.
This would happen sometimes.

OR

The kids would *not* let you have the ball.
This would happen most of the time.
This would happen sometimes.

2. How hard or easy would it be for you to grab the ball away from one of the kids?
very hard
hard
easy
very easy

3. Which of these two things would you most like to have happen in this situation?
The kids like you.
The kids let you have the ball.

Figure 7.2 An example of a brief vignette of peer interaction and questions related to the story that participants would be asked. These questions measure response decision and evaluation processes.

children in the video would do next, depending on the category of the video. This is in contrast to other measures that ask children to describe how *they* would feel or act in a particular scenario, because young children may not yet have developed perspective-taking skills (Newcombe & Huttenlocher, 1992). The child is then asked to generate other possible responses that children in the video could have, which is a measure of response access. Finally, response decision making was measured using the goal acquisition videos, which portray scenarios in which children attempt to attain a goal in either a cooperative or an aggressive manner. Children are then asked if they believe the actor will be successful. Children with higher levels of disruptive behavior problems were more likely to generate aggressive solutions and less likely to interpret ambiguous social provocations as accidental.

These results are consistent with findings from studies with older children and suggest that this measure adequately assesses SIP in preschool children.

A meta-analysis of the influence of hostile attribution bias on aggression (De Castro et al., 2002) found that the largest effect sizes were observed in studies that staged an actual interaction. The next largest effect sizes were observed in studies in which participants listened to stories or were required to read stories themselves, followed by studies that presented the stimuli on video. The smallest effect sizes were observed in studies in which social information cues were presented using only pictures. Studies that scored the number of hostile intent responses to calculate hostile attribution bias had larger effects than studies that used a combination of hostile and benign responses. However, effect sizes were not related to context, response format, setting, or reliability.

In summary, SIP can be measured using a variety of mediums including audio stories, pictures, videos, or live stage interactions. These stories typically show scenarios in which a hostile, neutral, or ambiguous interaction occurs between peers. Children are asked direct questions about the story they observed or heard to assess how they interpreted the stimuli and how they believed the actors in the story could or should act next. These questions can be tailored such that they are appropriate for preschool as well as school-aged and adolescent populations. A meta-analysis suggests that the method used to deliver the stories is associated with the observed effect size of the association between hostile attribution bias and aggression.

Relation of processing biases to behavior and interactions with parents and peers

Biases and deficits in SIP have been linked to various behavior problems and social adjustment. When studying how SIP influences behavior, some researchers examine how variation in each step of the model influences behavior, while others focus on only one or two steps in the model. Some studies also include the role of a child's database of social information to predict SIP and behavior. There are also large variations in how SIP is measured in these studies, as described previously, and the following review includes studies that used a variety of these paradigms.

Externalizing behaviors

Externalizing behaviors include a wide variety of disruptive behaviors, including rule breaking, hyperactivity, aggression, and antisocial behaviors (Krueger, Markon, Patrick, & Iacono, 2005). Antisocial behaviors include recurrent actions that lead to injury to others or arrest, such as violent crime, verbal assault, vandalism, delinquency, and damage to another's social standing (Dodge & Pettit, 2003). Aggression in humans is usually defined as any behavior that is directed toward another individual that is intended to cause harm (Bushman & Anderson, 2001).

There is a large existing literature linking steps in the SIP Model to these kinds of externalizing behaviors, which is reviewed below.

Aggression and antisocial behavior

Antisocial behaviors and aggression are key symptoms in a variety of prevalent and debilitating psychiatric disorders. These include the diagnoses of Oppositional Defiant Disorder and Conduct Disorder (CD) in children and Antisocial Personality Disorder in adults (American Psychiatric Association, 2013). Deficits in SIP such as hostile attribution biases, response generation, cue detection, and selection of goals have been associated with increased aggressive behavior (De Castro et al., 2002; Helseth, Waschbusch, King, & Willoughby, 2015; Quiggle, Garber, Panak, & Dodge, 1992; Schultz & Shaw, 2003; Waldman, 1996). Many researchers have examined the differential relations of these deficits with subtypes of aggression such as reactive and proactive aggression (Arsenio et al., 2009; Crick & Dodge, 1996; Dodge & Coie, 1987; Oostermeijer, Nieuwenhuijzen, van de Ven, Popma, & Jansen, 2016).

Studies of the relation between SIP and aggression have focused extensively on the early steps, encoding and interpretation of cues. These steps guide interpretation and understanding of ongoing social stimuli. Aggressive children are less likely to use the correct or relevant social cues compared with nonaggressive children (Dodge & Tomlin, 1987). Hostile attribution bias, which is a deficit in interpretation of social information such that individuals interpret neutral or ambiguous stimuli as hostile, has been extensively studied in relation to aggression. Hostile attribution bias has been shown to predict aggressive behavior and unsuccessful social interactions (Burks, Laird, Dodge, Pettit, & Bates, 1999; Dodge & Pettit, 2003; Waldman, 1996). Waldman (1996) found that aggressive boys showed hostile biases, but not general deficits, in their perceptions of children's intentions in video stimuli. Aggressive boys also were more likely than nonaggressive boys to suggest aggressive behavioral responses, even when the intentions were perceived as nonhostile. A meta-analysis of the association between hostile attribution bias and aggression found that this bias significantly predicts aggression ($r = 0.17$; De Castro et al., 2002). Larger effect sizes were associated with studies that included participants with more severe aggressive behavior and studies that used experience of peer rejection as an inclusion criterion. Age moderated the effect size such that studies that included 8- to 12-year olds had larger effect sizes than those that included children ages 4–6, 6–12, and over 12.

Other studies have found that severity of aggressive and antisocial behavior is related to differences in SIP. Helseth et al. (2015) conducted a study contrasting SIP patterns in three groups: control children, children with conduct problems (CP only), and children with conduct problems as well as callous–unemotional traits (CPCU). Callous–unemotional (CU) traits include lack of guilt, lack of empathy, and use of others for one's own gain. CU traits have been shown to predict the severity of future antisocial behavior over and above previous assessments of antisocial behavior and have distinct developmental pathways compared to other forms of antisocial behavior (Frick & White, 2008). Helseth et al. (2015) measured response generation and hostile attribution bias and compared the profiles of these variables among the three groups. Although both groups generated significantly more aggressive responses than controls, there were no significant differences in response generation between the CP only and CPCU groups. This provides some supporting evidence that severity of aggressive and antisocial behavior predicts differences in SIP. Of note, this study may have been underpowered as each clinical group included only 14 participants.

A study of 650 adolescents examined the relationships between social schemas, steps in SIP, and aggression (Calvete & Orue, 2012). The participants' social schemas related to aggression were measured by assessing to what extent they justified violent behavior. Three aspects of SIP were measured: hostile attribution bias, aggressive response access, and angry reactions, which were measured using a five-question scale to assess how angry the participant would feel in the described scenario. Aggressive response access was defined here as the participant's report of the degree to which they would use aggressive behavior against another person. Hostile attribution bias, a commonly studied error in SIP, is the extent to which participants interpret neutral or other nonhostile stimuli as hostile. In this study, adolescents were presented with ambiguous scenarios and asked if they believed the person in the story acted with ill-intentions and was glad about the outcome later. Results indicated that the extent to which participants justified violent behavior predicted aggressive response access, which in turn predicted reactive aggression.

Deficits in SIP may also explain the stability of aggressive behavior (Burks et al., 1999; Dodge, Laird, Lochman, & Zelli, 2002; Lansford et al., 2006). Extensive evidence indicates that aggression is stable over time such that, without intervention, aggressive children are more likely than other children to become aggressive adults (Kokko & Pulkkinen, 2005; Moffitt, 1993; Tuvblad, Narusyte, Grann, Sarnecki, & Lichtenstein, 2011). In a longitudinal study of 585 children, Burks et al. (1999) found that hostile attributional biases in kindergarten predicted externalizing behaviors, including rule breaking and aggression, in eighth grade. Furthermore, they found that externalizing behaviors in kindergarten predicted externalizing behaviors in eighth grade and that this association was mediated by hostile attribution bias.

Although aggression can be construed as a global construct, some have partitioned it into subdimensions that have separable underlying motives (Dodge & Coie, 1987), including reactive and proactive aggression (e.g., Card & Little, 2006; Jung, Krahé, & Busching, 2017; Poulin & Boivin, 2000). Indeed, investigations of the relationship between SIP and aggression frequently examine reactive and proactive aggression separately (Arsenio et al., 2009; Crick & Dodge, 1996; Dodge & Coie, 1987). Reactive aggression includes retaliatory behavior that is a defensive reaction in response to a perceived threat, whereas proactive aggression includes behaviors that occur without apparent provocation such as dominance, coercion, bullying, and instrumental aggression. These forms of aggression overlap substantially, however, and as such, others have argued that such a distinction is artificial (Bushman & Anderson, 2001).

Across studies, researchers have found differential associations between SIP steps and the two subtypes of aggression. In general, reactive aggression is more highly related to perceived ease of enacting aggressive responses and hostile attribution bias (Arsenio et al., 2009; Crick & Dodge, 1996; De Castro et al., 2005; Dodge & Coie, 1987), whereas proactive aggression is more related to expectation of positive outcomes from aggressive responses and positive evaluations of aggressive behavior (Crick & Dodge, 1996; De Castro et al., 2005)

In a study of 624 children, Crick and Dodge (1996) examined the associations of response biases, evaluative biases, and biases in selection of goals with reactive and proactive aggression. Results indicated that older children in the reactive aggression group were more likely to make hostile attributions compared to the proactive aggression and control groups. Consistent with moderation results in a meta-analysis of hostile attribution bias (De Castro et al., 2002), this association was not significant when they collapsed across age groups. Children in the proactive aggression group reported more positive expectations of aggressive behaviors and efficacy for enacting aggression. There were also group differences in selection of goals such that children in the proactive aggression group selected instrumental rather than relational goals significantly more often than did children in the other two groups.

The updated model of SIP includes emotion as a particular influencer of each processing step. To that end, De Castro et al. (2005) examined how emotions in SIP are associated with general aggression as well as reactive and proactive aggression in boys. Compared with controls, aggressive boys were more likely to attribute hostile intent to ambiguous stimuli and happiness to peers. Item-level analysis revealed that aggressive boys were less likely to believe the provocateur in the scenario would feel guilty or ashamed. With respect to their own emotions, aggressive boys reported more anger than controls. Additionally, aggressive boys were more likely to generate aggressive responses to the situation and rate aggressive responses as more positive options. Differential associations of these variables with reactive and proactive aggression were found. When controlling for proactive aggression, reactive aggression was uniquely associated with increased hostile attribution bias and decreased attributions of sadness, aggressive response generation, and reports of their own anger. When controlling for reactive aggression, proactive aggression was uniquely associated with increased approval of aggressive responses. Both reactive and proactive aggression were negatively related to emotion regulation.

Other externalizing behaviors

In addition to aggression and antisocial behavior, SIP has been examined in relation to Attention-Deficit Hyperactivity Disorder (ADHD). Although children with ADHD are more likely to engage in aggressive behaviors (Biederman, Newcorn, & Sprich, 1991), aggression is not a key symptom of ADHD. As such, one might expect associations between ADHD and deficits in SIP to differ compared with those between SIP and aggression. Indeed, some important differences in social cognitive deficits between children with ADHD and aggressive children have been found. For instance, one study found that participants with ADHD were more likely to encode fewer positive, negative, and neutral social cues as opposed to exhibiting deficits in processing a particular type of social cue (Andrade et al., 2012).

There are some similarities between the profiles of SIP in children with ADHD and aggressive children. Both groups have shown a bias in response generation such that they generate more negative or aggressive responses compared to peers (Andrade et al., 2012; King et al., 2009; Thurber, Heller, & Hinshaw, 2002). Some studies have also found that children with ADHD display similar attribution biases (Andrade et al., 2012; Milich & Dodge, 1984), although this finding is not consistent across studies (Mikami, Lee, Hinshaw, & Mullin, 2008).

In summary, deficits and biases in SIP are associated with aggression, which is a key symptom in several childhood externalizing disorders, including externalizing disorders like ADHD that are not primarily defined by aggression. Increased aggression is associated with the interpretation of neutral or ambiguous stimuli as hostile, increased aggressive response access, positive evaluation of aggressive responses, and the belief that aggressive responses in a social situation will lead to the desired outcome. Aggression can be partitioned into subdimensions, which are differentially associated with SIP. Reactive aggression tends to be associated with perceived ease of enacting aggressive responses and hostile attribution bias, whereas proactive aggression is associated with positive evaluation of aggressive behaviors and expectations of positive outcomes from aggressive behavior. ADHD is also associated with aggressive response access and hostile attribution biases in a pattern similar to aggressive behavior but is uniquely related to encoding fewer social cues overall.

Peer and parental interactions

SIP patterns also have important implications for social interactions with both peers and parents. Deficits in SIP in the areas of encoding, attributions, and processing related to generating and enacting responses have been associated with peer victimization and aggression, which predict increases in aggression and maladaptive outcomes later in life (Dodge et al., 2003; Dodge & Price, 1994; Guy et al., 2017; Lansford et al., 2010).

Dodge et al. (2003) tested the mediating effects of SIP on early rejection and later aggressive behaviors. Results indicated that early peer rejection predicted later aggression and that this effect was mediated by patterns of social cue encoding, attributions, and response generation, evaluation, and enactment. Results from this study also indicated that early aggression moderated the effects of rejection such that rejection exacerbated antisocial behavior only in children who already displayed early aggressive behaviors.

In a similar developmental cascade model of peer rejection, Lansford et al. (2010) found that peer rejection, deficits in encoding, attributions, and response generation, and aggressive behavior each predicted the other factor over time, such that increases in any of the factors predicted increases in each of the other factors.

The authors concluded that the progression of deficits in SIP and aggression cascaded through peer rejection and that both better processing skills and lower aggression predicted later improvement in social status.

Although the influence of SIP on parental interactions has been less studied, some evidence indicates that these two variables are linked. Specifically, hostile attribution biases in children have been shown to predict increases in child-to-parent aggression, and levels of child-to-parent aggression in turn predicted later decreases in processing skills (Calvete, Gamez-Guadix, & Garcia-Salvador, 2015). In addition, several studies have suggested that parental interactions predicted SIP skills, which in turn predicted peer interactions (Haskett & Willoughby, 2007; Rah & Parke, 2008). In one study, harsh and insensitive parenting was associated with hostile intent attributions and response access, which predicted social maladjustment at a later time point, as measured by teacher report and observed play (Haskett & Willoughby, 2007). Similarly, positive parental interactions have been associated with children's goal selection and attributions regarding both parent and peer interaction, which in turn predict social standing with peers (Rah & Parke, 2008). In this way, SIP mediates the relationship between parenting and social acceptance.

The relationship between basic cognitive abilities and SIP

In addition to aggression and other externalizing behaviors, deficits in SIP have been related to basic cognitive abilities. These include attention, impulsivity, inhibition, broad executive functioning, and intelligence (Dodge, Price, Bachorowski, & Newman, 1990; Mikami et al., 2008; Nas, Orobio De Castro, & Koops, 2005; Van Nieuwenhuijzen et al., 2017; Waldman, 1996).

In a study of adolescents with severe behavior disorders, Nieuwenhuijzen et al. (2015) assessed the relationship of SIP with attention, inhibition, and working memory. They hypothesized that focused attention would predict better encoding and interpretation of social cues, inhibition would predict more accurate interpretation and response generation, evaluation, and selection, and, finally, working memory would predict response generation and selection. They found that attention and inhibition were associated with response evaluation and selection, such that attentional errors were associated with higher aggressive response selection and greater inhibition was associated with less aggressive response selection and positive evaluation of aggressive responses. These associations held even when accounting for intelligence and age.

Given that basic cognitive abilities are associated with SIP, many researchers control for intelligence when testing the association between SIP and behavior. Intelligence is related to SIP, but results indicate that this association does not explain the relationship between SIP and behavior (Dodge et al., 1990; Nas et al., 2005; Waldman, 1996). Nas et al. (2005) tested the relations among SIP, intelligence, and delinquency. Adaptive emotion regulation strategies, aggressive response generation, and problem-solving response generation were related to intelligence, but SIP did not mediate the relationship between intelligence and delinquency. Similarly, Waldman (1996) found that measures of attention and impulsivity were significantly related to hostile attribution biases and general social perceptual deficits, even after controlling for intelligence, and that hostile attribution biases mediated the relations of attention and impulsivity with aggression.

The exception to this trend is found in a study of SIP in children with ADHD (Mikami et al., 2008). Results from this study indicated that the relation between ADHD status and SIP was not significant when controlling for verbal intelligence. This may suggest that basic cognitive abilities interact with SIP differently in hyperactive and inattentive children as compared to aggressive children.

Etiology

Direct investigation of potential genetic influences on SIP is limited, although some evidence suggests that social cognition and both prosocial and antisocial behavior broadly defined are heritable (Cesarini et al., 2008; Knafo & Plomin, 2006; Knafo, Zahn-Waxler, Van Hulle, Robinson, & Rhee, 2008; Rhee & Waldman, 2002; Rushton, Fulker, Neale, Blizard, & Eysenck, 1984; Scourfield, Martin, Lewis, & McGuffin, 1999). Nonetheless, most behavior genetic studies of social cognition have limited their focus to empathy.

Twin studies allow researchers to estimate the variance in a trait accounted for by genetic, shared environmental, and nonshared environmental influences. Monozygotic twins share 100% of their DNA while dizygotic twins share, on average, 50%. Assuming that the twins share the same common environment, differences in the degree of similarity of a trait between monozygotic and dizygotic twins are due in part to genetic influences (Neale & Cardon, 1992). Twin studies have demonstrated that social cognitive abilities are influenced by genetic factors. Genetic influences account for a moderate portion of the variance in empathy (Knafo et al., 2008), prosocial behavior (Knafo & Plomin, 2006; Rushton et al., 1984), parent-reported social cognition (Scourfield et al., 1999), and trust (Cesarini et al., 2008).

Investigations of specific genes that influence social cognition and behavior have implicated several genes. For instance, research on the Oxytocin Receptor Gene (*OXTR*) variation in humans implicates the gene in a variety of social cognitive and behavioral processes, including parental attachment, romantic relationships, friendship, empathy, and psychopathology including Autism Spectrum Disorders, depression, and schizophrenia (reviewed in the work of Feldman, Monakhov, Pratt, & Ebstein, 2016). Specific Single Nucleotide Polymorphisms (SNPs) in *OXTR* have been associated with facial recognition memory (Skuse et al., 2014) and pair bonding traits and social interaction deficits (Walum et al., 2012).

There is also a large body of literature demonstrating the moderate to large heritability of aggression. A meta-analysis of the genetic and environmental influences on antisocial behavior estimated that the proportion of variance due to additive genetic influences was 0.32, 0.09 for nonadditive genetic influences, 0.16 for shared environmental influences, and 0.43 for nonshared environmental influences (Rhee & Waldman, 2002). In addition, a relatively recent review of the literature on aggression found heritability estimates ranging from 20% to 64% (Rhee & Waldman, 2011).

In summary, research investigating the heritability of SIP and specific genes that influence SIP is limited. There is preliminary evidence, however, suggesting that elements of social cognition, including empathy, trust, and prosocial behavior, are heritable. Studies suggest that variation in the *OXTR* may be associated with social cognition and social behavior as well. Additional research is needed to examine the etiology of SIP specifically.

Interventions

Several treatment programs have aimed to address aggression and disruptive behavior by targeting deficits in SIP. The Fast Track Program (Conduct Problems Prevention Research Group, 1999; Dodge & Conduct Problems Prevention Research Group, 2007; Dodge, Godwin, & Conduct Problems Prevention Research Group, 2013) is a school-based intervention that incorporates a curriculum delivered in a group setting, parenting groups, child social skills training groups, and academic tutoring, some of which are offered to all participants and some of which are offered only to children in families identified as "high risk." For the universal component of the intervention, teachers implemented classroom-based lessons twice or three times a week. Lessons covered four domains of social skills, including skills for emotion understanding and communication such as recognizing and labeling emotions; friendship skills such as cooperation, fair play, and negotiation; self-control skills such as behavioral inhibition; and social problem-solving skills including problem identification, response generation, evaluation, and planning. Selective interventions included parenting groups, child social skills training groups, and academic tutoring. In social skills groups, children engaged in discussions, as well as modeling social interactions through stories and role-playing to demonstrate and promote social skills concepts. Parenting group curricula included helping parents establish positive relationships with school personnel, building parental self-control, teaching developmentally appropriate expectations for their child's behavior, and developing skills to improve parent and child interactions and reduce disruptive behaviors.

Results from this intervention indicated that the intervention group showed improvement in emotion recognition, emotion coping, aggressive retaliation, and social problem-solving. With respect to peer interactions, the intervention groups spent more time in positive peer interaction and received higher peer social preference scores than the control group. Parents in the intervention group also reported improvements in parenting behavior and attitudes about parenting. Finally, children in the intervention group engaged in fewer aggressive behaviors compared to the control group. This study provided evidence for early success of an intervention targeting SIP in aggressive youth. Further investigation of the mechanisms of behavioral change indicated that the intervention's impact on antisocial behavior was mediated by its effect on hostile attribution bias, response generation, and evaluation (Dodge et al., 2013).

As a follow-up to this study, Dodge and Conduct Problems Prevention Research Group (2007) tested the efficacy of the Fast Track Program in preventing the development of antisocial behavior in children considered at-risk. At-risk children in the intervention group had fewer symptoms and diagnoses of CD and ADHD and displayed fewer antisocial behaviors than did at-risk children assigned to the control group. This indicates that early intervention for youth at risk for developing externalizing behavior problems may decrease the likelihood of severe antisocial behaviors later in childhood.

Another similarly designed intervention, the Making Choices program, has been shown to improve SIP and behaviors (Terzian, Li, Fraser, Day, & Rose, 2015). The Making Choices program is delivered in school settings and includes lessons related to cue encoding, emotion processing skills, emotion regulation, goal formulation, response access, evaluation, and enactment. The Making Choices Plus program includes additional opportunities for parent and teacher involvement, including didactic training programs for parents. Participation in both programs was associated with reduced levels of aggression and improvement in SIP skills, although this effect was only significant for boys.

Taken together, the evidence from the above studies suggests that school-based interventions that target deficits in SIP and emotion regulation can be effective in reducing aggression and externalizing behaviors and improving peer and parental interactions.

Limitations and future directions

The SIP Model has been used to explain the sequential and parallel processes that occur when children encounter social information. Deficits in processing during each of the steps in this model are associated with aggressive behavior, peer relations, and parental interactions. In addition, targeting interventions toward improving SIP lead to improvements in prosocial behavior and peer and parental relations.

There are several limitations of the research presented above that should be considered when interpreting this body of literature. First, many studies, particularly earlier studies, grouped children into categories based on their behavioral characteristics (e.g., aggressive, popularity). For example, some studies examined SIP in aggressive cases versus normal controls, or in children who are primarily reactively aggressive compared with children who are primarily proactively aggressive. Dichotomizing variables in this manner decreases statistical power to detect associations and makes it more difficult to understand the specific nature of the association between levels of aggression, or symptoms of a disorder, and SIP. Future studies should endeavor to measure aggression, or other externalizing behavior, continuously to best characterize these associations.

Second, many studies only include male participants. Aggression, and other externalizing behavior problems, tends to be more common in males, which may explain why studies were designed in this way. Nonetheless, this limits the generalizability of results to girls. A few studies also include only female participants, which provides some information about SIP in girls, but still prohibits the direct comparison of SIP and its relations to behavior problems between genders. For gender differences to be effectively examined, both boys and girls must be included in the same study.

Future research in this area should focus on several areas of study. First, quantitative and molecular genetic studies should examine the genetic influences on SIP steps specifically, thus better elucidating their etiology. Extant studies suggest that some social cognitive abilities and social behavior, including aggression, show substantial genetic influences. Nonetheless, this area of research is only in its infancy, and many further studies are needed to fully understand the pattern and magnitude of genetic and environmental influences on SIP and its relation to various aspects of social behavior and peer and parent–child relations. In addition, studies examining the effects of specific genes and gene pathways are warranted. Existing research in this area, including *OXTR*, is still in the early stages and replications and meta-analyses are needed to better characterize the extant literature. Although it can be difficult to achieve the large sample sizes required for twin and molecular genetic studies in laboratory-based studies, the use of questionnaire or online measures of SIP may mitigate this difficulty.

Second, intervention efforts can be expanded in a variety of ways. Most interventions are delivered in schools and require the participation of many families and teachers (Conduct Problems Prevention Research Group, 1999; Terzian et al., 2015). Efforts to integrate these practices into behavior family therapy and parent training would increase the number of individuals to whom the intervention could be delivered. School-based interventions already include group parent training components, so it may be feasible to adapt these to use with individual families in private practice or community mental health settings. Efforts to expand the target behaviors and emotions of intervention for SIP may also be warranted. Evidence suggests that children with a variety of psychiatric conditions, including depression and anxiety, have deficits in SIP (Luebbe, Bell, Allwood, Swenson, & Early, 2010; Pössel, Seemann, Ahrens, & Hautzinger, 2006), and changes in their processing patterns may improve some areas of function for these children.

Finally, although there is substantial research linking various SIP stages to externalizing behaviors, impaired social adjustment, and peer and parent interactions, less is known about the interrelations between SIP steps that occur while processing a single event. For instance, the model allows for some reverse sequencing, such that response evaluations can influence the previous step of response access, whereby evaluation of a given response can lead a child to disregard that response and return to search long-term memory for another potential response (Crick & Dodge, 1994). Similarly, the interpretation of cues can influence the previous encoding response. Less is known about how this reverse processing might take place, in what context it is most likely to occur, and how this influences behavioral outcomes. Researchers should endeavor to create measures that more accurately assess the online processes of SIP as children process a single social event in real time.

Conclusions

The SIP Model describes the sequence of events by which children encode, interpret, construct responses, evaluate responses, and enact behaviors in social settings. Deficits and biases in SIP are associated with externalizing disorders and predict aggressive behavior, which in turn leads to social maladjustment and problems in peer and parent interactions. Interventions designed to improve SIP have been shown to improve both externalizing behaviors and peer and parent interactions. Future research should seek to better understand the genetic and environmental underpinnings of SIP, expand interventions to include behavioral problems other than aggression, and measure SIP in a more online manner.

References

American Psychiatric Association. (2013). *Diagnostic and statistical manual of mental disorders (DSM-5)*. American Psychiatric Publishing.

American Psychiatric Association. (2013). *Diagnostic and statistical manual of mental disorders* (5th ed.). Arlington, VA: American Psychiatric Publishing.

Andrade, B. F., Waschbusch, D. A., Doucet, A., King, S., MacKinnon, M., McGrath, P. J., ... Corkum, P. (2012). Social information processing of positive and negative hypothetical events in children with ADHD and conduct problems and controls. *Journal of Attention Disorders*, *16*(6), 491–504.

Arsenio, W. F., Adams, E., & Gold, J. (2009). Social information processing, moral reasoning, and emotion attributions: Relations with adolescents' reactive and proactive aggression. *Child Development*, *80*(6), 1739–1755.

Barnes, S. E., Howell, K. H., Thurston, I. B., & Cohen, R. (2017). Children's attitudes toward aggression: Associations with depression, aggression, and perceived maternal/peer responses to anger. *Journal of Child and Family Studies*, *26*(3), 748–758.

Biederman, J., Newcorn, J., & Sprich, S. (1991). Comorbidity of attention deficit hyperactivity disorder. *American Journal of Psychiatry*, *148*(5), 564–577.

Burks, V. S., Laird, R. D., Dodge, K. A., Pettit, G. S., & Bates, J. E. (1999). Knowledge structures, social information processing, and children's aggressive behavior. *Social Development*, *8*(2), 220–236.

Bushman, B. J., & Anderson, C. A. (2001). Is it time to pull the plug on hostile versus instrumental aggression dichotomy? *Psychological Review*, *108*(1), 273–279.

Bussey, K., Quinn, C., & Dobson, J. (2015). The moderating role of empathic concern and perspective taking on the relationship between moral disengagement and aggression. *Merrill-Palmer Quarterly*, *61*(1), 10–29.

Calvete, E., Gamez-Guadix, M., & Garcia-Salvador, S. (2015). Social information processing in child-to-parent aggression: Bidirectional associations in a 1-year prospective study. *Journal of Child and Family Studies*, *24*(8), 2204–2216.

Calvete, E., & Orue, I. (2012). Social information processing as a mediator between cognitive schemas and aggressive behavior in adolescents. *Journal of Abnormal Child Psychology*, *40*(1), 105–117.

Card, N. A., & Little, T. D. (2006). Proactive and reactive aggression in childhood and adolescence: A meta-analysis of differential relations with psychosocial adjustment. *International Journal of Behavioral Development*, *30*(5), 466–480.

Cesarini, D., Dawes, C. T., Fowler, J. H., Johannesson, M., Lichtenstein, P., & Wallace, B. (2008). Heritability of cooperative behavior in the trust game. *Proceedings of the National Academy of Sciences*, *105*(10), 3721–3726.

Conduct Problems Prevention Research Group. (1999). Initial impact of the Fast Track Prevention Trial for Conduct Problems: I. The high-risk sample. *Journal of Consulting and Clinical Psychology*, 67, 631–647.

Comparini, L., Douglas, E. M., & Perez, S. N. (2014). The development of social cognition: Preschoolers' use of mental state talk in peer conflicts. *Early Education and Development*, *25*(7), 1083–1101.

Crick, N. R., & Dodge, K. A. (1994). A review and reformulation of social information-processing mechanisms in children's social adjustment. *Psychological Bulletin*, *115*(1), 74.

Crick, N. R., & Dodge, K. A. (1996). Social information-processing mechanisms in reactive and proactive aggression. *Child Development*, *67*(3), 993–1002.

De Castro, B. O., Merk, W., Koops, W., Veerman, J. W., & Bosch, J. D. (2005). Emotions in social information processing and their relations with reactive and proactive aggression in referred aggressive boys. *Journal of Clinical Child and Adolescent Psychology*, *34* (1), 105–116.

De Castro, B. O., Veerman, J. W., Koops, W., Bosch, J. D., & Monshouwer, H. J. (2002). Hostile attribution of intent and aggressive behavior: A meta-analysis. *Child development*, *73*(3), 916–934.

Denham, S. A., Caverly, S., Schmidt, M., Blair, K., DeMulder, E., Caal, S., ... Mason, T. (2002). Preschool understanding of emotions: Contributions to classroom anger and aggression. *Journal of Child Psychology and Psychiatry*, *43*(7), 901–916.

Dodge, K. A., & Price, J. M. (1994). On the relation between social information processing and socially competent behavior in early school-aged children. Child development, 65 (5), 1385–1397.

Dodge, K. A. (1980). Social cognition and children's aggressive behavior. *Child Development*, *51*(1), 162–170.

Dodge, K. A. (1986). *A social information processing model of social competence in children, . Minnesota symposium on child psychology* (Vol. 18, pp. 77–125). Erlbaum.

Dodge, K. A., & Coie, J. D. (1987). Social-information-processing factors in reactive and proactive aggression in children's peer groups. *Journal of Personality and Social Psychology*, *53*(6), 1146.

Dodge, K. A., & Conduct Problems Prevention Research Group. (2007). Fast track randomized controlled trial to prevent externalizing psychiatric disorders: Findings from grades 3 to 9. *Journal of the American Academy of Child and Adolescent Psychiatry*, *46*(10), 1250–1262.

Dodge, K. A., Godwin, J., & Conduct Problems Prevention Research Group. (2013). Social-information-processing patterns mediate the impact of preventive intervention on adolescent antisocial behavior. *Psychological Science, 24*(4), 456–465.

Dodge, K. A., Laird, R., Lochman, J. E., & Zelli, A. (2002). Multidimensional latent-construct analysis of children's social information processing patterns: Correlations with aggressive behavior problems. *Psychological Assessment, 14*(1), 60.

Dodge, K. A., Lansford, J. E., Burks, V. S., Bates, J. E., Pettit, G. S., Fontaine, R., & Price, J. M. (2003). Peer rejection and social information-processing factors in the development of aggressive behavior problems in children. *Child Development, 74*(2), 374–393.

Dodge, K. A., & Pettit, G. S. (2003). A biopsychosocial model of the development of chronic conduct problems in adolescence. *Developmental Psychology, 39*(2), 349.

Dodge, K. A., Price, J. M., Bachorowski, J. A., & Newman, J. P. (1990). Hostile attributional biases in severely aggressive adolescents. *Journal of Abnormal Psychology, 99*(4), 385.

Dodge, K. A., & Tomlin, A. M. (1987). Utilization of self-schemas as a mechanism of interpretational bias in aggressive children. *Social Cognition, 5*(3), 280–300.

Feldman, R., Monakhov, M., Pratt, M., & Ebstein, R. P. (2016). Oxytocin pathway genes: Evolutionary ancient system impacting on human affiliation, sociality, and psychopathology. *Biological Psychiatry, 79*(3), 174–184.

Frick, P. J., & White, S. F. (2008). Research review: The importance of callous-unemotional traits for developmental models of aggressive and antisocial behavior. *Journal of Child Psychology and Psychiatry, 49*(4), 359–375.

Gully, K. J. (2000). Initial development of the Expectations Test for children: A tool to investigate social information processing. *Journal of Clinical Psychology, 56*(12), 1551–1563.

Guy, A., Lee, K., & Wolke, D. (2017). Differences in the early stages of social information processing for adolescents involved in bullying. *Aggressive Behavior, 43*, 578–587.

Harter, S. (1983). Developmental perspectives on the self-system. In P. H. Mussen (Series Ed.) & E. M. Hetherington (Vol. Ed.), *Handbook of child psychology: Vol. 4. Socialization, personality, and social development* (pp. 275–386). New York, NY: Wiley.

Haskett, M. E., & Willoughby, M. (2007). Paths to child social adjustment: Parenting quality and children's processing of social information. *Child: Care, Health and Development, 33*(1), 67–77.

Helseth, S. A., Waschbusch, D. A., King, S., & Willoughby, M. T. (2015). Aggression in children with conduct problems and callous-unemotional traits: Social information processing and response to peer provocation. *Journal of Abnormal Child Psychology, 43*(8), 1503–1514.

Jung, J., Krahé, B., & Busching, R. (2017). Differential risk profiles for reactive and proactive aggression. *Social Psychology, 48*(2), 71–84.

King, S., Waschbusch, D. A., Pelham, W. E., Jr, Frankland, B. W., Andrade, B. F., Jacques, S., & Corkum, P. V. (2009). Social information processing in elementary-school aged children with ADHD: Medication effects and comparisons with typical children. *Journal of Abnormal Child Psychology, 37*(4), 579–589.

Knafo, A., & Plomin, R. (2006). Prosocial behavior from early to middle childhood: Genetic and environmental influences on stability and change. *Developmental Psychology, 42*(5), 771.

Knafo, A., Zahn-Waxler, C., Van Hulle, C., Robinson, J. L., & Rhee, S. H. (2008). The developmental origins of a disposition toward empathy: Genetic and environmental contributions. *Emotion, 8*(6), 737.

Kokko, K., & Pulkkinen, L. (2005). Stability of aggressive behavior from childhood to middle age in women and men. *Aggressive Behavior, 31*(5), 485–497.

Krueger, R. F., Markon, K. E., Patrick, C. J., & Iacono, W. G. (2005). Externalizing psychopathology in adulthood: A dimensional-spectrum conceptualization and its implications for DSM-V. *Journal of Abnormal Psychology, 114*(4), 537.

Kuhnert, R., Begeer, S., Fink, E., & de Rosnay, M. (2017). Gender-differentiated effects of theory of mind, emotion understanding, and social preference on prosocial behavior development: A longitudinal study. *Journal of Experimental Child Psychology, 154*, 13–27.

Lansford, J. E., Malone, P. S., Dodge, K. A., Crozier, J. C., Pettit, G. S., & Bates, J. E. (2006). A 12-year prospective study of patterns of social information processing problems and externalizing behaviors. *Journal of Abnormal Child Psychology, 34*(5), 709–718.

Lansford, J. E., Malone, P. S., Dodge, K. A., Pettit, G. S., & Bates, J. E. (2010). Developmental cascades of peer rejection, social information processing biases, and aggression during middle childhood. *Development and Psychopathology, 22*(3), 593–602.

Li, X., Bian, C., Chen, Y., Huang, J., Ma, Y., Tang, L., ... Yu, Y. (2015). Indirect aggression and parental attachment in early adolescence: Examining the role of perspective taking and empathetic concern. *Personality and Individual Differences, 86*, 499–503.

Luebbe, A. M., Bell, D. J., Allwood, M. A., Swenson, L. P., & Early, M. C. (2010). Social information processing in children: Specific relations to anxiety, depression, and affect. *Journal of Clinical Child and Adolescent Psychology, 39*(3), 386–399.

Meece, D., & Mize, J. (2010). Multiple aspects of preschool children's social cognition: Relations with peer acceptance and peer interaction style. *Early Child Development and Care, 180*(5), 585–604.

Mikami, A. Y., Lee, S. S., Hinshaw, S. P., & Mullin, B. C. (2008). Relationships between social information processing and aggression among adolescent girls with and without ADHD. *Journal of Youth and Adolescence, 37*(7), 761–771.

Milich, R., & Dodge, K. A. (1984). Social information processing in child psychiatric populations. *Journal of Abnormal Child Psychology, 12*(3), 471–489.

Moffitt, T. E. (1993). Adolescence-limited and life-course-persistent antisocial behavior: A developmental taxonomy. *Psychological Review, 100*(4), 674.

Nas, C. N., Orobio De Castro, B., & Koops, W. (2005). Social information processing in delinquent adolescents. *Psychology, Crime and Law, 11*(4), 363–375.

Neale, M. C., & Cardon, L. R. (1992). *Methodology for genetic studies of twins and families* (pp. 35–53). The Netherlands: Springer.

Newcombe, N., & Huttenlocher, J. (1992). Children's early ability to solve perspective-taking problems. *Developmental Psychology, 28*(4), 635.

Oostermeijer, S., Nieuwenhuijzen, M., Van de Ven, P. M., Popma, A., & Jansen, L. M. C. (2016). Social information processing problems related to reactive and proactive aggression of adolescents in residential treatment. *Personality and Individual Differences, 90*, 54–60.

Pössel, P., Seemann, S., Ahrens, S., & Hautzinger, M. (2006). Testing the causal mediation component of Dodge's social information processing model of social competence and depression. *Journal of Youth and Adolescence, 35*(5), 842–851.

Poulin, F., & Boivin, M. (2000). Reactive and proactive aggression: evidence of a two-factor model. *Psychological Assessment, 12*(2), 115.

Quiggle, N. L., Garber, J., Panak, W. F., & Dodge, K. A. (1992). Social information processing in aggressive and depressed children. *Child Development*, *63*(6), 1305–1320.

Rah, Y., & Parke, R. D. (2008). Pathways between parent–child interactions and peer acceptance: The role of children's social information processing. *Social Development*, *17*(2), 341–357.

Rhee, S. H., & Waldman, I. D. (2002). Genetic and environmental influences on antisocial behavior: A meta-analysis of twin and adoption studies. *Psychological Bulletin*, *128*(3), 490.

Rhee, S. H., & Waldman, I. D. (2011). Genetic and environmental influences on aggression. In P. R. Shaver, & M. Mikulincer (Eds.), *Human aggression and violence. Causes, manifestations, and consequences* (pp. 143–163). Washington, DC: American Psychological Association.

Rushton, J. P., Fulker, D. W., Neale, M. C., Blizard, R. A., & Eysenck, H. J. (1984). Altruism and genetics. *AMG Acta Geneticae Medicae et Gemellologiae: Twin Research*, *33*(2), 265–271.

Schultz, D., Ambike, A., Logie, S. K., Bohner, K. E., Stapleton, L. M., VanderWalde, H., ... Betkowski, J. A. (2010). Assessment of social information processing in early childhood: Development and initial validation of the Schultz test of emotion processing—Preliminary version. *Journal of Abnormal Child Psychology*, *38*(5), 601–613.

Schultz, D., & Shaw, D. S. (2003). Boys' maladaptive social information processing, family emotional climate, and pathways to early conduct problems. *Social Development*, *12*(3), 440–460.

Scourfield, J., Martin, N., Lewis, G., & McGuffin, P. (1999). Heritability of social cognitive skills in children and adolescents. *The British Journal of Psychiatry*, *175*(6), 559–564.

Skuse, D. H., Lori, A., Cubells, J. F., Lee, I., Conneely, K. N., Puura, K., ... Young, L. J. (2014). Common polymorphism in the oxytocin receptor gene (*OXTR*) is associated with human social recognition skills. *Proceedings of the National Academy of Sciences*, *111*(5), 1987–1992.

Steinberg, M. S., & Dodge, K. A. (1983). Attributional bias in aggressive adolescent boys and girls. *Journal of Social and Clinical Psychology*, *1*(4), 312–321.

Terzian, M. A., Li, J., Fraser, M. W., Day, S. H., & Rose, R. A. (2015). Social information-processing skills and aggression: A quasi-experimental trial of the making choices and making choices plus programs. *Research on Social Work Practice*, 25(3), 358–369.

Thurber, J. R., Heller, T. L., & Hinshaw, S. P. (2002). The social behaviors and peer expectation of girls with attention deficit hyperactivity disorder and comparison girls. *Journal of Clinical Child and Adolescent Psychology*, *31*(4), 443–452.

Tuvblad, C., Narusyte, J., Grann, M., Sarnecki, J., & Lichtenstein, P. (2011). The genetic and environmental etiology of antisocial behavior from childhood to emerging adulthood. *Behavior Genetics*, *41*(5), 629–640.

Van Nieuwenhuijzen, M., Van Rest, M. M., Embregts, P. J. C. M., Vriens, A., Oostermeijer, S., Van Bokhoven, I., & Matthys, W. (2017). Executive functions and social information processing in adolescents with severe behavior problems. *Child Neuropsychology*, *23*(2), 228–241.

Waldman, I. D. (1996). Aggressive boys' hostile perceptual and response biases: The role of attention and impulsivity. *Child Development*, *67*(3), 1015–1033.

Walum, H., Lichtenstein, P., Neiderhiser, J. M., Reiss, D., Ganiban, J. M., Spotts, E. L., ... Westberg, L. (2012). Variation in the oxytocin receptor gene is associated with pair-bonding and social behavior. *Biological Psychiatry*, *71*(5), 419–426.

Sensation seeking and risk-taking

8

Joseph Glicksohn, Revital Naor-Ziv, and Rotem Leshem
Bar-Ilan University, Ramat Gan, Israel

Sensation seeking

Sensation seeking is "defined by the seeking of varied, novel, complex, and intense sensations and experiences, and the willingness to take physical, social, legal, and financial risks for the sake of such experience," as measured by Zuckerman's Sensation Seeking Scale (Appendix A in Zuckerman, 1994, p. 27; Zuckerman, 2007, p. 49). We stress the fact that sensation seeking and impulsivity, while being related, are nevertheless separate traits (Zuckerman & Glicksohn, 2016). As Glicksohn and Naor-Ziv (2016) have recently suggested, "Impulsivity implicates impulsive decision-making, hence possibly incurring risk, but not necessarily involving risk-seeking *per se*. Sensation Seeking, in contrast, refers to the active seeking of novel experiences, some of which involve risk, hence implicating risk-seeking." Nevertheless, following Zuckerman (2005, p. 255), one can distinguish between an impulsive form of sensation seeking, and a nonimpulsive form of sensation seeking. The impulsive form of sensation seeking is specifically related to disinhibited behaviors, criminality, sexuality, and substance abuse (Zuckerman, 1994, 2007). Indeed, impulsive sensation seeking is clearly predictive of future antisocial behavior, and especially of the progression from conduct disorder (CD) to antisocial personality disorder (ASPD), as indicated by Zuckerman (2002).

Risk-taking

Not only is risk-taking behavior not to be equated with sensation seeking (Zuckerman, 2007, pp. 58–59), it is also not to be equated with impulsivity. As Zuckerman (2007, p. 53) writes: "Decisions about whether to accept risks in any activity depend on the benefits, or anticipated positive outcomes, as well as the risks." Such risks include potential losses, which might be minor (losing some money), but which could also be major (losing an arm). Thus, risk-taking occurs whenever the benefits of some activity outweigh the potential hazards (Zuckerman, 2007). Arnett's (1996) catalog of reckless behavior leaves little room for doubt that adolescents in general, and those having a history of CD, in particular, are intrepid risk-takers, engaging in: Reckless driving, risky sexual activity, alcohol and drug use, vandalism, and theft. To this list, one can add gambling (Nower, Derevensky, & Gupta, 2004) and smoking (Kopstein, Crum, Celentano, & Martin, 2001). We stress, however, that risk-taking is not necessarily negative; risk-taking can be

Developmental Pathways to Disruptive, Impulse-Control, and Conduct Disorders.
DOI: https://doi.org/10.1016/B978-0-12-811323-3.00008-0

channeled into prosocial activities, such as volunteering or working in high-risk prosocial professions, as well as into skillful engagement in risky sports (Glicksohn & Naor-Ziv, 2016).

Reyna, Chaudhry, Brust-Renck, Wilhelms, and Royer (2013) conclude from their overview of the risk-taking literature that impulsivity can often lead to risk-taking. Of present relevance is the fact that, for an age range between 11 and 23, sensation seeking and impulsivity "were both more likely to influence the behavioral expression of risk-taking in escalating risk tasks during middle–late adolescence and young adulthood than during early adolescence or preadolescence" (Lauriola, Panno, Levin, & Lejuez, 2014, p. 31). This is a natural consequence of the diverging developmental trajectories for sensation seeking and impulsivity.

Developmental trajectories of sensation seeking, impulsivity, and risk-taking

Sensation seeking and impulsivity have different trajectories during adolescence and young adulthood. Steinberg et al. (2008, p. 1764) summarize their data by noting that between the ages of 10 and 30 "age differences in sensation seeking, which are linked to pubertal maturation, follow a curvilinear pattern, with sensation seeking increasing between 10 and 15 and declining or remaining stable thereafter." In contrast, "age differences in impulsivity, which are unrelated to puberty, follow a linear pattern, with impulsivity declining steadily from age 10 on" (p. 1764). We shall be returning to these different trajectories in due course.

Further, individuals can follow several different trajectories of sensation seeking development. Lynne-Landsman, Graber, Nichols, and Botvin (2011) delineate three trends: (1) stable-low sensation seekers; (2) moderately-increasing sensation seekers; (3) stable-high sensation seekers. As one might expect, the stable-low sensation seekers reported considerably low levels of risky behavior during adolescence with risky behavior being indexed by substance use, aggression, and delinquency. In contrast, the stable-high sensation seekers reported consistently high levels of such activities.

Risk-taking also exhibits normative increases at adolescence (Maslowsky, Buvinger, Keating, Steinberg, & Cauffman, 2011). Furthermore, it is important to acknowledge that adolescent risk-taking is subject to considerable individual variation. High proportions of adolescents do not use drugs, drive unsafely, or engage in delinquent behavior (Dahl, 2004; Romer et al., 2011). In fact, most adolescents do not have significant problems. They succeed in school and have good relationships with adults (i.e., teachers, parents) and peers. However, there is also evidence that a significant proportion of adolescents do experience social problems with peers, report stress, experience emotional turmoil, and have difficulty in controlling and regulating strong feelings. These adolescents may be especially vulnerable to the negative consequences of certain risks (Dahl, 2004).

It can be difficult to determine when risk-taking behaviors move from normal experimentation to problem behavior (Adams, 2005). Many risky behaviors that are closely related to behavioral and emotional problems in adolescence, such as drunk driving, substance use, and criminal arrests, remain limited to adolescence, with few adolescents developing into persistent criminals or exhibiting other maladaptive behaviors (Moffitt et al., 2011). Further, trajectories beginning in adolescence can culminate in difficulties in adulthood. Specifically, criminal and maladaptive behaviors that arise later in life often have their roots and warning signs in adolescence (Adams, 2005; Dahl, 2004).

Thus, even within normal development, risk-taking is implicated in both the benefits and the drawbacks of being a teenager. On the one hand, risk-taking does not always lead to adverse outcomes. Some level of risk-taking underlies many positive aspects of growing up, such as shaping identity and acquiring new skills. On the other hand, this can go far beyond normal experimentation into a wide range of externalizing behavioral problems, such as violence, substance use, gambling, and criminal activity, as well as internalizing behavioral problems, such as eating disorders, depression, and anxiety (Leshem, 2016a; Naor-Ziv & Glicksohn, 2016).

Sensation seeking does not always lead to risk-taking

How should one view this significant increase in risk-taking behavior during adolescence when there is also a normative increase in sensation seeking during adolescence? From an intra-individual perspective, it is tantalizing to conclude that risk-taking is developmentally tied to sensation seeking, such that an increase in the latter necessitates an increase in the former. Yet, there are a number of factors that can influence the likelihood that sensation seeking will manifest in risk-taking behavior, described later.

Factors that may influence the impact of sensation seeking on risk-taking behaviors

Reinforcement and reward

Adolescents are capable of appreciating the consequences of their actions, and they do have the capacity to engage in behavioral control (Luna, Paulsen, Padmanabhan, & Geier, 2013; Steinberg et al., 2008). Nevertheless, they are less able to do so when the context is arousing, or emotionally stimulating, such as when in the presence of peers (Chein, Albert, O'Brien, Uckert, & Steinberg, 2011; Figner, Mackinlay, Wilkening, & Weber, 2009). Given that adolescents appear to have a heightened sensitivity to rewards (Casey, 2015; Cauffman et al., 2010; Shulman et al., 2016; Steinberg, Graham et al., 2009), their behaviors are often reinforced by incentives. When adolescents are rewarded for better performance, or when the potential outcomes of their choices are made known, incentives enhance their performance to adult levels (Teslovich et al., 2014) and can be beneficial for the establishment of adaptive and goal-directed behaviors (Geier, Terwilliger, Teslovich, Velanova, & Luna, 2010; Teslovich et al., 2014).

In contrast, suboptimal decisions and impulsive responses typically occur in tasks with immediate reward conditions (Cauffman et al., 2010; Figner et al., 2009; Shulman et al., 2016; Steinberg, et al., 2009), or in tasks requiring the suppression of an action toward cues previously associated with positive outcomes (Somerville, Hare, & Casey, 2011). Somerville et al. (2011) showed that relative to both children and adults, adolescents demonstrated a unique pattern of errors characterized by a reduction in impulse control, in response to salient appetitive cues (i.e., happy faces). The authors proposed that adolescents' greater emotional response to the (rewarding) happy face made it harder for them to restrain the impulse to "approach" it. This behavioral profile is consistent with theoretical accounts that associate adolescence with a bias for engaging in risky behavior in the service of approaching potential rewards (Steinberg, 2008). Another study, by Cohen et al. (2016), examined cognitive control under sustained states of negative and positive arousal among adolescents and adults (ages 13–25 years). They found diminished cognitive control of adolescents and young adults in response to negative cues.

Adolescence-specific changes in the ability to suppress inappropriate emotions, desires, and actions in favor of alternative appropriate ones are thus diminished in the presence of salient environmental cues. An apparent sensitivity to social and environmental cues—positive and negative—leads to heightened reactivity and decreased regulation in adolescents relative to both children and adults (Casey, 2015; Shulman et al., 2016). Thus, high sensation seekers are more likely to engage in risk-taking behaviors in the presence of rewards. Furthermore, the ability to withhold impulsive responses is also highly dependent on other contextual factors, such as social setting (Casey, 2015; Chein et al., 2011; Dreyfuss et al., 2014; Geier et al., 2010; Luna et al., 2013; Teslovich et al., 2014).

Peer influences

Peers have a substantial impact on risk-taking in adolescence. Gardner and Steinberg (2005) examined risk-taking in adolescents, college undergraduates, and adults who were engaged in a simulated driving task, either alone or in the presence of two friends. They found that adolescents, compared to college undergraduates and adults, took a substantially greater number of risks when observed by peers. They are more responsive to and more easily influenced by their peers and thus more likely to change their decisions and alter their behavior in response to social pressure (Chein et al., 2011; Somerville, 2013). This can result in a greater likelihood of engagement in risky behaviors, alone and/or in groups, in an attempt to elevate social status.

Another study, by Peake, Dishion, Stormshak, Moore, and Pfeifer (2013), examined the influence of peers on adolescents' behavior by exploring effects of social exclusion on behavioral risk-taking. They used a modified version of the driving task (Stoplight task, adopted from Chein et al., 2011; Gardner & Steinberg, 2005) with a manipulation producing an experience of social exclusion. In their study, the Stoplight task features a series of intersections at which participants must decide whether to stop at a yellow traffic light (safe option) or try to make it through the intersection (risk option). While the risk option often results in a shorter travel time, it is accompanied by the possibility of crashing and losing time if another car crosses the intersection. The social aspect of the study came from the presence and actions of two hypothetical peers implied to be watching the participant via an internet connection. First, the participants completed the Stoplight task while the peers were watching, then the Stoplight task was completed a second time after an experience of being excluded from a different game by these peers. During this second Stoplight task, the participants were supposedly being watched by the same peers who had just recently excluded them. This manipulation created an additional layer of risky decision factors, whereby the participants expected social evaluation of their performance by these peers, above and beyond the risky decisions entailed in the task. The researchers found that exclusion was associated with greater behavioral risk-taking among adolescents having low self-reported resistance to peer influence.

Peer influence works on a number of levels. Consider, for example, the evidence indicating assortative matching, or clustering, based on sensation seeking (Donohew et al., 1999, p. 629). When one's unsocialized, impulsive, sensation seeking peers use alcohol, smoke, and experiment with drugs, then their substance use impacts on all members of this homogeneous group. As Donohew et al. (1999, p. 622) suggest, "high levels of sensation seeking are positively related to prodrug attitudes and susceptibility to peer influence to use alcohol or drugs which, in turn, predict use." Trait and social environment interact here to predict adolescent risk-taking. Higher-order interactions are also evident, such as that involving parental monitoring (Mann, Kretsch, Tackett, Harden, & Tucker-Drob, 2015).

The path of influence from sensation seeking to risk-taking can, of course, be a direct one: High sensation seekers are willing to engage in certain risk-taking activities (Zuckerman, 2007), but this is not necessarily a preferred life style. Indeed, Horvath and Zuckerman (1993, p. 50) concluded that impaired risk perception is not necessarily a consequence of sensation seeking, even if sensation seekers tend to depreciate the degree of riskiness of risky activities (Glicksohn, Ben-Shalom, & Lazar, 2004). Impaired risk perception (and specifically, impaired risk appraisal) might well be "a consequence rather than a cause of risky behaviour... after one has had any experience with the activity (the experience may be observational as well as personal) one's level of sensation seeking may determine how that experience is interpreted" (Horvath & Zuckerman, 1993, p. 50). And if that experience is a joint activity with one's sensation-seeking peers, then the indirect path of influence linking sensation seeking and risk-taking takes center stage: Adolescents tend to pick "persons of similar sensation seeking levels and the sensation seeking level of these peers [tend] to influence peer alcohol and marijuana use" (Donohew et al., 1999, p. 629). Support for this comes, in part, from the criminology literature. There is a small but compelling body of evidence suggesting that when adolescents commit crimes—acts that are inherently risky—they generally do so with their peers (Erickson & Jensen, 1977; Zimring, 1998). Adolescents' generally greater inclination toward risky behavior, in combination with their greater susceptibility to peer influence should, in theory, result in a larger effect of peer presence on their risky behavior than among adults (Gardner & Steinberg, 2005; Steinberg, 2004).

In turn, the repertoire of risky activities engaged in by the group itself undergoes a developmental trajectory. As Newcomb and McGee (1991, p. 615) write, this entails "decreasing cohesiveness among deviant attitudes and behavior as [the] adolescent population grew into young adulthood . . . [differentiating] into at least two sets of deviant behavior over time, one set of behaviors including problems related to drug use and another set including other forms of deviance." In short, high sensation seekers who affiliate with each other may well engage in risky behavior that is maladaptive and that itself evolves over time.

Self-regulation

Adolescent risk-taking is a function of an increased level of sensation seeking coupled with relatively insufficient self-regulation (Casey, Jones, & Somerville, 2011; Steinberg, 2008). While sensation seeking increases substantially around the time of puberty, and remains high well into the early 20s, when it begins to decline, impulse control is low during childhood and improves gradually over the course of adolescence and early adulthood. Mid-adolescence, therefore, is a time of high sensation seeking but still developing impulse control, which may predispose individuals toward risky behavior (Steinberg, 2013). Thus, high sensation seeking, particularly in the context of low cognitive control, may predispose individuals to risk-taking behaviors.

Progressive cognitive changes that strengthen the ability to learn and to act rationally, alongside increasing rates of reckless and risky behavior, reflect the duality of the adolescent period. This duality provides a framework for important research on the neuropsychological underpinnings of adolescent development (Leshem, 2016a, b) and for understanding individual differences in the affinity for externalizing and risk-taking behaviors, discussed later.

Neurobiological development of sensation seeking and risk-taking

The pathway of escalating risk-taking, just like these developmental trajectories for both sensation seeking and impulsivity, seem likely to be working in tandem. In their review of the impulse-control literature, Hammond, Potenza, and Mayes (2011, p. 232) reflect on this:

> *. . . impulse control, self-regulation, and other impulsivity-related phenomena may follow different temporal trajectories, with impulsivity decreasing linearly over*

time and sensation seeking and reward responsiveness following an inverted U-shaped trajectory across the lifespan. These different trajectories coincide with developmental brain changes, including early maturation of subcortical regions in relation to the later maturation of the frontal lobes, and may underlie the frequent risk-taking behavior often observed during adolescence.

Let us begin to unpack just what these developmental brain changes are.

There tends to be widespread agreement that adolescents' relatively greater propensity toward risky behavior reflects the joint contribution of two brain systems. One is the socioemotional system (or *incentive processing system*), involving the limbic and paralimbic areas of the brain, including the amygdala, ventral striatum, medial prefrontal cortex (PFC), orbitofrontal cortex (OFC), and superior temporal sulcus—which is known to have an important role in the processing of emotional and social information, and in the valuation and prediction of reward and punishment. The other is the cognitive control system, which is mainly composed of the lateral prefrontal and parietal cortices and parts of the anterior cingulated cortex (ACC) to which they are connected, which supports impulse control, planning, reasoning, and other aspects of executive functioning (Steinberg, 2013).

Neuroimaging studies (as well as lesion data), conducted in both adult and adolescent populations, show that different forms of externalizing behaviors (e.g., sensation seeking, impulsivity, lack of forethought, disinhibition, lack of self-control, and risk-taking) are all products of the reciprocal interactions between, and within, these two brain systems (Bechara, 2005; Bechara, Damasio, Tranel, & Damasio, 1997; Bechara, Tranel, & Damasio, 2000; Berlin, Rolls, & Kischka, 2004; Bunge, Dudukovic, Thomason, Vaidya, & Gabrieli, 2002; Castellanos, Sonuga-Barke, Milham, & Tannock, 2006; Chambers & Potenza, 2003; Chein et al., 2011; Gansler et al., 2011; Horn, Dolan, Elliott, Deakin, & Woodruff, 2003; McHugh & Wood, 2008; Romer et al., 2009; Torregrossa, Quinn, & Taylor, 2008).

These two brain systems undergo considerable modification during adolescence, but with different timetables, involving the rapid development of subcortical functioning in conjunction with the slow development of prefrontal functioning (Casey, Getz, & Galván, 2008). These differences in the developmental trajectories of PFC versus subcortical structures (e.g., ventral striatum and amygdala), along with the connections between them, may account for adolescent behavioral propensities. Recent work has focused on elucidating the contributions of such a maturational imbalance between these brain systems that lead to sensation seeking and risk-taking behavior (Somerville, Jones, & Casey, 2010; Steinberg, 2008). The cognitive control system undergoes comparatively gradual and protracted maturation, involving reductions in gray matter density and increases in myelination, from preadolescence through at least the mid-20s (Crews & Boettiger, 2009; Eshel, Nelson, Blair, Pine, & Ernst, 2007; Spear, 2000). Over the course of adolescence, the connections between higher-order association areas in the prefrontal lobes become stronger and these strengthen the ability to exert cognitive control. This maturation is thought to support improvements in executive abilities such as response inhibition (Luna, Padmanabhan, & O'Hearn, 2010), strategic planning (Luciana, Collins, Olson, &

Schissel, 2009), impulse regulation (Steinberg et al., 2008), and flexible rule use (Crone, Donohue, Honomichl, Wendelken, & Bunge, 2006).

In contrast to the cognitive control system that develops gradually over a longer period of time, the socioemotional system undergoes extensive remodeling in early adolescence, particularly with respect to subcortical structures (e.g., ventral striatum and amygdala). During adolescence, the amygdala grows in volume and changes in response to socially relevant stimuli and contexts. A key node for affective and motivational processes, it responds more strongly to social and emotional stimuli during adolescence due to the influx of pubertal hormones (Steinberg, 2008). Consequently, as reported in a number of studies, there is hyperactivation in the amygdala during adolescence in response to all emotional expressions and rewards, as compared to both childhood and adulthood (Hare et al., 2008; Scherf, Smyth, & Delgado, 2013). Over-activation of the limbic system (i.e., amygdala, ventral striatum) may lead to an inability to regulate subcortical activity. When limbic regions have a greater influence on behavior than do prefrontal regions, the tendency to succumb to impulses becomes more likely. Furthermore, puberty enhances signaling in the limbic system, which, in turn, is believed to take over from the more rational prefrontal control system (Steinberg, 2008).

Potentially important contributors to adolescent-typical, risk-taking behaviors (e.g., substance abuse and criminal activity) are those changes that take place around the time of puberty (Spear, 2013). One of the important developmental changes, thought to be critical for the processing of rewarding stimuli, occurs in the dopaminergic system (DA), within regions critical to incentive processing and to the valuation and prediction of potential reward (Spear, 2009, 2013). There is evidence that changes in the density and the distribution of dopamine receptors D1 and D2 in the striatum occur early in adolescence, followed by a loss of these receptors by young adulthood. In contrast, the PFC does not show peaks in D1 and D2 receptor density until late adolescence and young adulthood (Casey & Jones, 2010). Because dopamine plays a critical role in the brain's reward circuitry, the increase, reduction, and redistribution of dopamine receptor concentration around puberty, especially in projections from the limbic system to the prefrontal area, may have important implications for sensation seeking (Steinberg, 2008). Similar developmental changes have been shown in gamma-aminobutyric acid (GABA) neurotransmission.

Neurochemical evidence suggests that both GABAergic and dopaminergic neurotransmission, particularly in the PFC, remain under construction during adolescence. As such, delayed development of GABAergic neurotransmission is believed to be responsible for risk-taking behavior, whereas dopaminergic neurotransmission, which is developmentally regulated by sex hormones, is implicated in drug-seeking behavior during adolescence (Arain et al., 2013).

Beyond these significant neurochemical changes, there are also extensive hormonal changes that occur during adolescence (Arain et al., 2013; Spear, 2000, 2009). For example, sex hormones (i.e., estrogen, progesterone, and testosterone) act in the limbic system and in the raphe nucleus, source of the neurotransmitter serotonin which is important for the regulation of impulse control, arousal, and mood (Arain et al., 2013; Spear, 2000; Steinberg, 2008). Another important change is linked to oxytocin, which plays an important role in social bonding and in regulating the recognition and memory of social stimuli (Steinberg, 2008). During puberty, there is an increase in oxytocin receptors within various limbic structures (including the amygdala and nucleus accumbens), which in turn make adolescents more prone to take risks in order to gain rewards, especially in the presence of peers (Steinberg, 2008).

Consider the familiar biomarker for sensation seeking, namely testosterone (Zuckerman, 2005, p. 198): High sensation seekers tend to have very high levels of testosterone; low sensation seekers tend to have normal levels. And yet, as Raine (2013, p. 252) has written, "... if you have high testosterone levels and a deviant peer group you may become conduct disordered—yet if you have the same high testosterone and circulate in a non-deviant peer group you are instead led to become a leader." This predisposition (high sensation seeking, high testosterone, and high risky behavior) is clearly moderated by the nature of one's peer group. Indeed, Johnson, Leedom, and Muhtadie (2012, p. 706) have concluded from their review of the literature that testosterone "may relate more strongly to externalizing symptoms in the context of high-risk social environments."

So how might sensation seeking relate to risk-taking in Conduct Disorder?

The trait of sensation seeking (Zuckerman, 1994, 2007), particularly that variant identified as impulsive sensation seeking, is a primary candidate underlying the progression from CD to ASPD in some individuals from adolescence into emerging adulthood. (Zuckerman, 2002). As Zuckerman (1994, p. 260) has suggested, one would expect to find some degree of commonality among sensation seeking, hyperactivity, and CD. Yet, the behaviors indicative of CD, such as stealing, truancy, vandalism, starting fights, lying, cruelty, and forcing sexual relations on others (Zuckerman, 1994, p. 260), are not the same as those characterizing sensation seeking. Studies involving participants drawn from juvenile/late adolescence/emerging adulthood samples indicate that risk-taking associated with both negative and positive outcomes is highly correlated with sensation seeking (Fischer & Smith, 2004; Hansen & Breivik, 2001). What might differentiate between these two types of risk-taking, or risk takers, is impulsivity (Fischer & Smith, 2004, p. 529). Indeed, we note the emphasis on impulsive aggression that seems to be clearly related to CD (Fanti, 2016). Hence, it might well be that it is a particular combination of sensation seeking and impulsivity that underlies the whole spectrum of features exhibited in CD.

Further, sensation seeking and impulsivity emerge early in childhood and prospectively predict CD behaviors in longitudinal studies (Mann et al., 2017). With respect to individual differences in sensation seeking, Waldman et al. (2011) found that genetic influences on children's preference for novelty, intensity, and danger (i.e., "daring" dispositions) were shared with genetic influences on CD symptoms, even after accounting for common variance attributable to genetic and environmental associations with prosociality and negative emotionality. As Lahey and Waldman (2003) suggest, there is heterogeneity in the etiology of CD, which is related to different subgroups of adolescents with CD; they hypothesize that this heterogeneity in both the etiology and characteristics of CD can best be understood by considering variation in three continuous socioemotional dispositions. First, children with a tendency to exhibit negative emotions (negative emotionality) are hypothesized to be at increased risk for engaging in antisocial behavior. Second, children who are less likely to respond sympathetically to distress in others, to experience guilt, to respect rules, or to care about doing well in school and related settings (low prosociality), are at increased risk for CD because they find the adverse social consequences of their transgressions to be less punishing, they are less upset when they violate rules, and they are less rewarded by positive responses of adults and peers to their prosocial behavior. Third, children who respond positively to novelty, intensity, and danger (daring) are more likely to develop CD because they find fighting, destroying property, and engaging in misdeeds for which they could be apprehended, to be attractive and reinforcing.

Waldman et al. (2011) examined this theoretical model and found that CD symptoms were related uniquely to lower prosociality (21% of the variance), higher negative emotionality (8%), and higher daring or sensation seeking (2%), while controlling for each of the other dispositions. Furthermore, a nationally representative study of American adolescents found that a substantial portion (> 80%) of genetic influence on longitudinal change in delinquency was mediated by genes influencing longitudinal change in sensation seeking (Harden, Quinn, & Tucker-Drob, 2012).

For the present, in the absence of empirical data on this issue, let us speculate: Could it be that CD children suffer from "double jeopardy" (high impulsivity and high sensation seeking), leading to a pathway resulting in maladaptive behavior and maladaptive risk-taking? If preadolescent CD children already score high on both sensation seeking and impulsivity, they might well already be on this pathway of escalating risk-taking from an early age. Risk-taking in the presence of normative peers should be exacerbated for youth with CD, and especially so when in the presence of peers with CD, given that risk factors noted by Bassarath (2001) include both antisocial peers and impoverished social ties.

From an inter-individual perspective, one might consider the paramount importance of antisocial peers in defining an antisocial trajectory of risk-taking activities in adolescence. One of the defining features of adolescence is a newfound importance of peer relationships (Somerville, 2013). During this period, adolescents become less dependent on adults, and are more influenced by their peers (Casey, 2015). It appears that one of the main motives underlying adolescent behavior is the wish to gain acceptance and confirmation from peers and significant others, often as a means of gaining self-acceptance (Leshem, 2016a; Somerville, 2013). This wish for acceptance can make adolescents socially sensitive and, in some cases, socially dependent (Scott & Steinberg, 2008; Steinberg, 2008). They are more responsive to and more easily influenced by their peers, and thus are more likely to change their decisions and alter their behavior in response to social pressure (Chein et al., 2011; Somerville, 2013). This can result in a greater likelihood of engagement in risky behaviors, alone and/or in groups, in an attempt to elevate social status. Such affiliation with deviant peers may increase the likelihood that high sensation seeking will manifest behaviorally in CD.

Within the context of brain development, the neurobiological changes during adolescence are likely to play an integral role in the relationship between sensation seeking and adolescent risk-taking exhibited in CD. Furthermore, it is on the backdrop of these neurobiological changes that occur contemporaneously within the adolescent peer group that risk-taking takes on either an antisocial or maladaptive form, or a prosocial or adaptive form. Importantly, CD and other related crime behaviors are not a matter of cognitive maturity *per se*. Rather, these behaviors result from this developmental imbalance between the socioemotional and cognitive control systems of the brain, together with the immaturity of the neural connections between them that are still taking place during adolescence (Casey, 2015; Steinberg, 2008).

When the socioemotional network is not highly activated (for example, when individuals are not emotionally excited, or are alone), the cognitive-control system is strong enough to impose regulatory control over impulsive and risky behavior, even in early adolescence. However, in the presence of peers, or under conditions of emotional arousal, the socioemotional system becomes sufficiently activated, such as to diminish the regulatory effectiveness of the cognitive-control system (Balocchini, Chiamenti, & Lamborghini, 2013; Hammond et al., 2011; Luna et al., 2013; Spear, 2000). Indeed, the impulsive sensation seeker will probably be attracted to other adolescents exhibiting impulsive sensation seeking. Thus, it would seem that high impulsive sensation seeking, coupled with low neurobiologically-mediated cognitive control, increases the risk for CD, particularly given a context of affiliation with deviant peers. We now address the resultant important future directions and possible implications for interventions that such a model would advocate.

Important future directions

The social-neuroscience model for understanding risk-taking and sensation seeking during adolescence posits that risky behaviors are shaped by differences in the developmental trajectories of networks that subserve emotional processing and cognitive control, along with reinforcement and reward, peer influence, and self-regulation factors. Particularly important future directions for this comprehensive model that emerge are potential biomarkers and the possibility of a differential gender influence.

Biomarkers

A possible biomarker of both sensation seeking and CD is heart rate. Low resting heart rate is indicative (or predictive) of high sensation seeking (Zuckerman, 1994, p. 324)—though this is not clear-cut, and it might well be heart rate responsivity, and not tonic heart rate, which is the biomarker. It is also a biomarker of CD (Fanti, 2016; Raine, 2013, p. 107). In fact, impulsive sensation seeking mediates the relationship between low heart rate and CD (Portnoy et al., 2014). If, as Zuckerman and Glicksohn (2016) have recently suggested, sensation seeking might be more related to arousability than to baseline (resting, tonic) arousal, then heart-rate responsivity should be further investigated with respect to both sensation seeking and CD.

Gender differences

Sensation seeking has a pronounced gender difference, with males scoring higher than females (Zuckerman, 2007, p. 14), in line with the higher incidence of CD among young males (Baron-Cohen, 2011, p. 67; MacDonald, 2012, p. 261), in the region of 5% (± 2%), this being three times higher than the prevalence rate among young females. This fact might be relatively simple to explain, given the familiar gender difference in sensation seeking (Zuckerman, 2007, p. 14) and impulsivity, as well as in risk-taking (Cross, Copping, & Campbell, 2011); in fact, one might conclude that there might well be a hormonal factor involved, such as testosterone (Zuckerman, 2007, p. 21). The combination of this biological predisposition with greater social acceptability of male aggression (Baillargeon et al., 2007) marks CD as being predominantly a male disposition.

One can further look at the relationship between antisocial behavior and/or maladaptive risk-taking and impulsive sensation seeking, exploring possible moderating and mediating factors, such as gender. In line with this idea, gender moderates the relationship between impulsive sensation seeking and maladaptive behaviors, such as alcohol use (Baker & Yardley, 2002; Magid, MacLean, & Colder, 2007); impulsive sensation seeking, in turn, mediates observed gender differences in risk-taking (Zuckerman & Kuhlman, 2000, p. 1009). These types of study have taken center stage in the literature. More complex models, taking into consideration the influence of peers, the direction of this influence, the possibility of reciprocal or bidirectional relationships, and so forth (Donohew et al., 1999; Mann et al., 2015, 2016; Quinn, Stappenbeck, & Fromme, 2011), are gaining in prominence and merit further consideration.

Gender differences in sensation seeking (or impulsive sensation seeking) may have complicated influences on the developmental trajectory from CD to ASPD. As Berkout, Young, and Gross (2011, p. 509) conclude, "Early physical maturation has been found to influence female, but not male development of externalizing behaviors, suggesting a unique gender relevant interaction with the social environment...." As they indicate, "Development of CD is not as well understood among girls; behavioral trajectories which fit male data have been found to be unable to adequately describe findings among females, suggesting factors influencing disorder development differ across gender…" (p. 508).

There are several reasons for expecting gender differences in both sensation seeking and impulse control, as well as in the development of the neurobiological systems that underlie their expression. As mentioned before, the psychological traits of sensation seeking and impulse control are thought to reflect the functional status of the socioemotional (incentive) processing and cognitive control systems, respectively. Thus, high sensation seeking and low impulse control appear to contribute to risk-taking behavior spanning the transition from adolescence to adulthood because of the temporary imbalance during this period between the brain's responsiveness to reward and its ability to restrain impulses. To date, little attention has been paid to gender differences in the mechanisms (e.g., different pubertal timing, neurobiological changes) that contribute to adolescent risky behavior. One of the studies that examined whether and how the development of sensation seeking and impulse control differs for males and females was conducted by Shulman, Harden, Chein, and Steinberg (2014). In their study, they investigated gender differences in the developmental trajectories of impulse control and sensation seeking between the ages of 10 and 25 using longitudinal data from the National Longitudinal Study of Youth 1979 Child and Young Adult Survey. Consistent with previous work on gender differences in the levels of these traits (e.g., Cross et al., 2011; Zuckerman & Kuhlman, 2000), they found that for both females and males, sensation seeking rises and falls across adolescence, whereas impulse control increases into the 20s. Importantly, they found key gender differences. First, males exhibited higher levels of sensation seeking and lower levels of impulse control than females. Second, females reach peak levels of sensation seeking earlier than males and decline in sensation seeking more rapidly thereafter. Third, males exhibit an increase in impulse control more gradually than do females.

These findings correspond to the development of the socioemotional and the cognitive systems along different timetables from childhood through late adulthood. The earlier peak in sensation seeking for females relative to males is consistent with the notion that the development of the socioemotional system (which is thought to heighten sensation seeking) is tied to pubertal maturation, with girls beginning puberty earlier than boys (Steinberg, 2008). Indeed, individual variation in the age of puberty onset creates individual variation in the point at which the brain is influenced by hormones, which in turn create individual variation in both developmental trajectory and behavioral maturation (Sisk & Zehr, 2005).

There is growing evidence to suggest that puberty onset may signal the onset of risky behaviors and conduct problems (Mendle, Turkheimer, & Emery, 2007; Weissman et al., 2015). In general, early maturers are more likely than other adolescents to report delinquency and risky behavior; however, early maturing girls have higher rates of CD and greater involvement in risky behavior when compared to boys (Graber, Seeley, Brooks-Gunn, & Lewinsohn, 2004). Risky behaviors and conduct problems increase during adolescence, especially among adolescents having less cognitive capacity, who are more likely to be exposed to situations that can lead to risky behaviors (de Azevedo et al., 2017; Weissman et al., 2015).

Specifically, the dramatic hormonal shifts associated with puberty may result in arousal, excitability, or excessive emotionality that may be complicated by neurological changes that spark an increased affinity for risk-taking and sensation seeking early in adolescence, whereas the development of judgment and self-regulatory skills to master these impulses only evolve toward the end of maturation (Dahl, 2004). Thus, adolescents are not believed to be at increased risk because of biological or hormonal changes associated with puberty, but rather due to a complex interaction among biological, environmental, and social factors. There is now an appreciation for the complex reciprocal relationships and interaction between biological and social environments, and the interaction between these environments and adolescent behavior (Graber, Lewinsohn, Seeley, & Brooks-Gunn, 1997).

Environmental influences become increasingly important for understanding female antisocial behavior, as girls transition into adolescence and adulthood (Javdani, Sadeh, & Verona, 2011). Consider, for example, the fact that these girls might appear to be older than they are to their peers, and/or might be presumed to be "more developed" (both physically and mentally) than the boys in their age group. This might "exert a powerful press towards antisocial behavior, perhaps by signalling to older peers or to the girl herself that she looks old enough to join in prohibited activities" (Moffitt, Caspi, Rutter, & Silva, 2001, pp. 240–241). Girls who experience early physical maturity appear to experience additional risk, potentially due to the social reinforcement of age-inappropriate behavior, and the greater likelihood of association with a deviant peer group (Burt, McGue, DeMarte, Krueger, & Iacono, 2006; Graber et al., 1997).

Moreover, research has found that affiliation with delinquent peers, especially with opposite-sex romantic partners and peers, is one of the strongest predictors of antisocial behavior for girls (Haynie, Steffensmeier, & Bell, 2007; Hubbard & Pratt, 2002; Moffitt et al., 2001; Rebellon & Manasse, 2004; Seffrin, Giordano, Manning, & Longmore, 2009; Simons, Stewart, Gordon, Conger, & Elder, 2002). In line with this, longitudinal research of twins has found that male externalizing problems are increasingly attributable to genetic variation and heritability, from adolescence to adulthood, whereas the trend is toward the decreasing effects of genes and the increasing effects of the environment on women (Hicks et al., 2007). Hicks et al. (2007) interpreted this as signifying greater environmental influence for females than for males as they leave the home and are increasingly influenced by both partners and peers.

This unique gender-relevant interaction with the social environment, including also the effect of familial factors, is important given that females may be more sensitive to family factors (Cutrín, Gómez-Fraguela, & Sobral, 2017). Both gender and behavior may evoke and elicit different responses from the social environment (Berkout et al., 2011). Some studies have found that the protective role of parenting with respect to delinquent development is stronger in female than in male adolescents (Javdani et al., 2011; Racz & McMahon, 2011). Perhaps these gender differences are based on the general tendency of parents to establish more responsive relationships with their daughters, as well as the apparent tendency of females to respond positively to proactive and supportive parenting (Anderson, 2012; Kerr &

Stattin, 2000; Zahn-Waxler & Polanichka, 2004). In fact, Tiet, Wasserman, Loeber, McReynolds, and Miller (2001) have argued that the distribution of conduct problems among females supports the gender paradox: CD is more severe among females, where it is less prevalent; and those girls who present with CD are thought to manifest greater pathology (Viding, Simmonds, Petrides, & Frederickson, 2009).

However, many social factors, such as negative parenting and an impoverished environment, appear to serve as risk factors for both males and females. The parental modeling of negative social interactions and an inappropriate provision of consequences, and/or a disadvantaged environmental background, which may provide poorer availability of resources and greater reinforcement of antisocial behavior, both appear to be related to CD development, among both males and females (Hipwell et al., 2008; Keenan et al., 2010; Pajer et al., 2008). Javdani et al. (2011) argue that the factors thought to confer risk for antisocial behavior in boys are more likely to exert influence at earlier stages in development, whereas female-specific risk factors are more likely to exert influence at later stages in development. This is in keeping with late-onset trajectories of antisocial behavior, but also extends these by suggesting that the emerging salience of gender as an organizer of girls' social worlds may instigate risk later in development, particularly because of the interpersonal context and greater environmental press.

It is important to note that, although gender differences exist in personality traits, making the combination of antisocial-related traits less predictive of antisocial behaviors in girls relative to boys, the majority of personality traits is similarly predictive of antisocial behavior in both males and females (Caspi, Henry, McGee, Moffitt, & Silva, 1995; Guerin, Gottfried, & Thomas, 1997; Javdani et al., 2011; Miller & Lynam, 2001). Similar personality characteristics increase risk for female antisocial behavior (Javdani et al., 2011). But, there are some gender differences in personality trait associations with CD: Unlike boys, girls typically display unhelpfulness toward others, in addition to general sensitivity to reinforcement, in relation to CD (Côté, Tremblay, Nagin, Zoccolillo, & Vitaro, 2002). Additionally, females with CD differ from males in a stronger association of internalizing disorders with these same personality traits (Berkout et al., 2011), suggesting the presence of a general tendency toward greater behavioral inhibition.

In contrast to what is found for males, autonomic hypoarousal and decreased reactivity do not appear to be related to female social deviance and externalizing (Isen et al., 2010; Loeber & Keenan, 1994; Marsman et al., 2008). Females who develop CD and exhibit risky behavior appear to develop this in spite of, rather than because of, a greater tendency toward behavioral disinhibition. Hence, for them a larger constellation of CD risk factors may be needed in order to develop the disorder (Berkout et al., 2011). Furthermore, the combination of a biological predisposition, such as high testosterone, that is related to sensation seeking (Zuckerman, 2007, p. 21), together with greater social acceptability of male aggression (Baillargeon et al., 2007) suggests that CD behaviors may be more normative for males. Females exhibiting CD are therefore an intriguing population for future research.

Intervention implications

In order to channel the risk-taking behavior of such impulsive sensation seekers, as described earlier, our review suggests that an intervention must somehow temper the impulsivity of these adolescents. This will not be an easy matter for two major reasons. First, as noted earlier, the impulsive sensation seeker will probably be attracted to other adolescents exhibiting such impulsive sensation seeking, and such a distinct peer group has all the markings of a deviant, delinquent peer group associated with CD. Second, this impulsivity can only be brought under control once their cognitive control system becomes dominant. This will take time because of the protracted developmental course of the PFC and its associated degree of cognitive control. Yet, protective factors against future delinquency among CD adolescents include the existence of positive relationships with adults. Conceivably, the adults might expose these adolescents to "effective decision-making skills [which] would deter involvement in antisocial behavior" (Jenson, 2010, p. 703).

The possibility of channeling impulsive sensation seeking into a less impulsive form of sensation seeking with subsequent, or concomitant, less impulsive (or, maladaptive) risk-taking—especially one in which such "effective decision-making skills" can be bolstered by adult guides—must also be on the agenda. Consider Zuckerman's (2007, pp. 58–59) thoughts regarding adolescents:

> *I have said previously that although sensation seeking is defined by a tolerance for risk, risk is not the point of it (Zuckerman, 1994). But this may not be true for adolescents looking for thrills through sports. The higher sensation seekers may find the riskiness of the activity part of the attraction to extreme sports. Parachuting may be preferred to volleyball not only for the novel sensations it provides but also because the risk makes it more exciting.*

As Romer et al. (2011) insightfully induce, such an approach provides an outlet for deriving an effective intervention strategy for handling these risky activities of sensation-seeking adolescents, which would be different from the intervention strategy that is required for those adolescents "whose impulsivity is characterized by early signs of acting without thinking" (p. 1119). Impulsivity suggests impulsive decision-making; hence, a relevant intervention strategy should try to present a more reflective form of decision-making for the adolescent. Sensation seeking, in contrast, suggests the possibility for maladaptive risk-taking; hence, a relevant intervention strategy here should try to present a more socially-accepted form of risk-taking to the adolescent. Indeed, as Newcomb and McGee (1991, p. 615) note, sensation seeking is a "displaceable motive that can be satisfied by a variety of activities. This characteristic of Sensation Seeking suggests one way to change behavior through substitution of stimulating activities."

This has implications for intervention (Glicksohn & Naor-Ziv, 2016) both with respect to ASPD, but perhaps more importantly for CD. Readers of this chapter who work with children and adolescents with CD who are high in sensation seeking might well want to consider an intervention that focuses on extreme sport and perhaps one that depends on group participation with suitable instructors. For, as Hansen and Breivik (2001, p. 639) speculate, based on their correlational study, "... high risk sports and challenging activities probably could prevent problem behavior and criminality among adolescents." To this we add that participation in extreme sport, or action sport (Thorpe, 2016), especially one in which adolescents come into contact with others who are also interested in channeling their sensation-seeking motivation into daring activities that require skill and self-efficacy, would help to keep them affiliated with peers who are not interested in maladaptive sensation-seeking behavior. Furthermore, contact with instructors who devote their time to developing the skills required by these adolescents to become confident and proficient in their performance in these action sports has the fringe benefit of providing role models for the successful channeling of sensation seeking into risky, but not maladaptive, activity. As Thorpe (2016, p. 100) recommends, "When appropriately supported, action sports offer ample opportunities for individual empowerment through skills mastery ... as well as valuable social skills (e.g., communication, sharing of social space, understanding difference)." Therefore, extreme sport activities with responsible adults may be an effective adjunct intervention for adolescents with CD characterized by high sensation seeking.

Since impulsive and risky behaviours are elevated in the presence of peers, or under conditions of emotional arousal, and since studies have shown familial influences on psychosocial maturity in adolescence, we can further suggest an intervention strategy based on social or family support, entailing interpersonal emotion regulation (Aldao & Nolen-Hoeksema, 2012; Gross, 2014). Interpersonal emotion regulation refers to the interactive regulation of one person's feelings by another. The goal here is to facilitate effective strategies of cognitive control (Zaki & Williams, 2013). Such an intervention, when employed in conjunction with strategies that change the context in which risky behavior occurs, might very well be more effective than those educational interventions, whose goal it is to change knowledge, beliefs, or attitudes about risk. Further research is needed to see whether it is possible to influence self-regulatory competence with impulsive sensation seeking adolescents and to examine the effectiveness of interpersonal emotion-regulation strategies.

Conclusions

Thus, overall, typical developmental considerations, and the relationships among sensation seeking, risk-taking behaviors, and brain development during adolescence, are all crucial for understanding externalizing behaviors and dysfunctional behavior later in life, such as CD and ASPD. Our literature review suggests that it is the particular combination of sensation seeking and impulsivity that underlies the whole spectrum of features exhibited in CD. Risk-taking, which is correlated with sensation seeking, has negative outcomes, but also positive outcomes, and what might differentiate between the two types of outcome is impulsivity (Fischer & Smith,

2004, p. 529), and limited capacity for executive functioning during these years (Glicksohn & Naor-Ziv, 2016). Hence, adolescents with CD who suffer from "double jeopardy," that is, high impulsivity and high sensation seeking, together with immature executive functioning, are particularly likely to move down a pathway resulting in maladaptive behavior and maladaptive risk-taking consistent with CD.

Heightened risk-taking during adolescence is normative, biologically-driven, and, to some extent, inevitable. As described earlier, vulnerability for risky behaviors during adolescence results from a temporal gap in puberty between the development of two neuropsychological systems, one depending on the rapid development of the socioemotional system, impelling adolescents toward sensation seeking behavior (including risky sensation seeking), and the other depending on a slow development of the cognitive-control system, which regulates these impulses (Steinberg, 2007). Nevertheless, the combination of high impulsive sensation seeking and poor/immature executive functioning resulting in risky behaviors is clearly moderated by the nature of one's peer group, other environmental influences, and gender.

Maintaining a distinction between cognitive and psychosocial maturity has important implications for lawmakers and public policy in the discussion of legal status and legal regulation of juvenile crime (Scott & Steinberg, 2008). Our review suggests that in the heat of the moment, under potential incentives and in the presence of peers, the socioemotional system of the adolescent brain may take over less mature prefrontal control circuits, leading to reckless behaviors. Immature brain functioning in adolescence influences adolescents' judgment, decision-making, risk-taking, and criminal behavior. Adolescents can be overwhelmed by the urge for new experiences, by sensation seeking, and by sexual and aggressive impulses (Steinberg, Cauffman, Woolard, Graham & Banich, 2009). One should consider an effective intervention strategy for these risky activities of impulsive sensation-seeking adolescents that include more positive stimulating activities (such as action sport) in order to redirect maladaptive behaviors.

References

Adams, G. R. (2005). Adolescent development. In T. P. Gullotta, & G. R. Adams (Eds.), *Handbook of adolescent behavioral problems: evidence-based approaches to prevention and treatment* (pp. 3–16). New York, NY: Springer.

Aldao, A., & Nolen-Hoeksema, S. (2012). When are adaptive strategies most predictive of psychopathology? *Journal of Abnormal Psychology*, *121*, 276–281.

Anderson, S. H. (2012). Girls in the juvenile justice system: the causes and correlates of girls' involvement. In S. Miller, L. Leve, & P. K. Kerig (Eds.), Delinquent girls: contexts, relationships, and adaptation (pp. 41–54). New York: Springer Science.

Arain, M., Haque, M., Johal, L., Mathur, P., Nel, W., Rais, A., ... Sharma, S. (2013). Maturation of the adolescent brain. *Neuropsychiatric Disease and Treatment*, *9*, 449–461.

Arnett, J. J. (1996). Sensation seeking, aggressiveness, and adolescent reckless behavior. *Personality and Individual Differences, 20*, 693–702.

Baillargeon, R. H., Zoccolillo, M., Keenan, K., Côté, S., Pérusse, D., Wu, H. X., ... Tremblay, R. E. (2007). Gender differences in physical aggression: a prospective population-based survey of children before and after 2 years of age. *Developmental Psychology, 43*, 13–26.

Baker, J. R., & Yardley, J. K. (2002). Moderating effect of gender on the relationship between sensation seeking-impulsivity and substance use in adolescents. *Journal of Child & Adolescent Substance Abuse, 12*, 27–43.

Balocchini, E., Chiamenti, G., & Lamborghini, A. (2013). Adolescents: which risks for their life and health? *Journal of Preventive Medicine and Hygiene, 54*, 191–194.

Baron-Cohen, S. (2011). *The science of evil: on empathy and the origins of cruelty*. New York: Basic Books.

Bassarath, L. (2001). Conduct disorder: a biopsychosocial review. *Canadian Journal of Psychiatry, 46*, 609–616.

Bechara, A. (2005). Decision making, impulse control and loss of willpower to resist drugs: a neurocognitive perspective. *Nature Neuroscience, 8*, 1458–1463.

Bechara, A., Damasio, H., Tranel, D., & Damasio, A. R. (1997). Deciding advantageously before knowing the advantageous strategy. *Science, 275*, 1293–1295.

Bechara, A., Tranel, D., & Damasio, H. (2000). Characterization of the decision-making deficit of patients with ventromedial prefrontal cortex lesions. *Brain, 123*, 2189–2202.

Berkout, O. V., Young, J. N., & Gross, A. M. (2011). Mean girls and bad boys: recent research on gender differences in conduct disorder. *Aggression and Violent Behavior, 16*, 503–511.

Berlin, H. A., Rolls, E. T., & Kischka, U. (2004). Impulsivity, time perception, emotion and reinforcement sensitivity in patients with orbitofrontal cortex lesions. *Brain, 127*, 1108–1126.

Bunge, S. A., Dudukovic, N. M., Thomason, M. E., Vaidya, C. J., & Gabrieli, J. D. (2002). Immature frontal lobe contributions to cognitive control in children: evidence from fMRI. *Neuron, 33*, 301–311.

Burt, S. A., McGue, M., DeMarte, J. A., Krueger, R. F., & Iacono, W. G. (2006). Timing of menarche and origins of conduct disorder. *Archives of General Psychiatry, 63*, 890–896.

Casey, B. J. (2015). Beyond simple models of self-control to circuit-based accounts of adolescent behavior. *Annual Review of Psychology, 66*, 295–319.

Casey, B. J., Getz, S., & Galván, A. (2008). The adolescent brain. *Developmental Review, 28*, 62–77.

Casey, B. J., & Jones, R. M. (2010). Neurobiology of the adolescent brain and behavior: implications for substance use disorders. *Journal of the American Academy of Child & Adolescent Psychiatry, 49*, 1189–1201.

Casey, B. J., Jones, R. M., & Somerville, L. H. (2011). Braking and accelerating of the adolescent brain. *Journal of Research on Adolescence, 21*, 21–33.

Caspi, A., Henry, B., McGee, R. O., Moffitt, T. E., & Silva, P. A. (1995). Temperamental origins of child and adolescent behavior problems: from age three to fifteen. *Child Development, 66*, 55–68.

Castellanos, F. X., Sonuga-Barke, E. J., Milham, M. P., & Tannock, R. (2006). Characterizing cognition in ADHD: beyond executive dysfunction. *Trends in Cognitive Sciences, 10*, 117–123.

Cauffman, E., Shulman, E. P., Steinberg, L., Claus, E., Banich, M. T., Graham, S., & Woolard, J. (2010). Age differences in affective decision making as indexed by performance on the Iowa Gambling Task. *Developmental Psychology*, *46*, 193–207.

Chambers, A., & Potenza, M. N. (2003). Neurodevelopment, impulsivity and adolescent gambling. *Journal of Gambling Studies*, *19*, 53–84.

Chein, J., Albert, D., O'Brien, L., Uckert, K., & Steinberg, L. (2011). Peers increase adolescent risk-taking by enhancing activity in the brain's reward circuitry. *Developmental Science*, *14*, F1–F10.

Cohen, A. O., Breiner, K., Steinberg, L., Bonnie, R. J., Scott, E. S., Taylor-Thompson, K. A., & Casey, B. J. (2016). When is an adolescent an adult? Assessing cognitive control in emotional and nonemotional contexts. *Psychological Science*, *27*, 549–562.

Côté, S., Tremblay, R. E., Nagin, D. S., Zoccolillo, M., & Vitaro, F. (2002). Childhood behavioral profiles leading to adolescent conduct disorder: risk trajectories for boys and girls. *Journal of the American Academy of Child & Adolescent Psychiatry*, *41*, 1086–1094.

Crews, E. T., & Boettiger, C. A. (2009). Impulsivity, frontal lobes and risk for addiction. *Pharmacology, Biochemistry and Behavior*, *93*, 237–247.

Crone, E. A., Donohue, S. E., Honomichl, R., Wendelken, C., & Bunge, S. A. (2006). Brain regions mediating flexible rule use during development. *Journal of Neuroscience*, *26*, 11239–11247.

Cross, C. P., Copping, L. T., & Campbell, A. (2011). Sex differences in impulsivity: a meta-analysis. *Psychological Bulletin*, *137*, 97–130.

Cutrín, O., Gómez-Fraguela, J. A., & Sobral, J. (2017). Two faces of parental support: risk and protection for antisocial youth depending on parental knowledge. *Journal of Child and Family Studies*, *26*, 296–305.

Dahl, R. E. (2004). Adolescent brain development: a period of vulnerabilities and opportunities. Keynote address. *Annals of the New York Academy of Sciences*, *1021*, 1–22.

de Azevedo, K. P. M., dos Santos, I. K., Dantas, P. M. S., Knackfuss, M. I., Bento, T., de Leitão, J. C., & de Medeiros, H. J. (2017). Pubertal maturation and health risk behaviors in adolescents: a systematic review. *Epidemiology, Biostatistics and Public Health*, *14*, e12156-1 - e12156-7.

Donohew, R. L., Hoyle, R. H., Clayton, R. R., Skinner, W. F., Colon, S. E., & Rice, R. E. (1999). Sensation seeking and drug use by adolescents and their friends: models for marijuana and alcohol. *Journal of Studies on Alcohol*, *60*, 622–631.

Dreyfuss, M., Caudle, K., Drysdale, A. T., Johnston, N. E., Cohen, A. O., Somerville, L. H., ... Casey, B. J. (2014). Teens impulsively react rather than retreat from threat. *Developmental Neuroscience*, *36*, 220–227.

Erickson, M., & Jensen, G. F. (1977). Delinquency is still a group behavior! Toward revitalizing the group premise of the sociology of deviance. *Journal of Criminal Law and Criminology*, *68*, 262–273.

Eshel, N., Nelson, E. E., Blair, R. J., Pine, D. S., & Ernst, M. (2007). Neural substrates of choice selection in adults and adolescents: development of the ventrolateral prefrontal and anterior cingulate cortices. *Neuropsychologia*, *45*, 1270–1279.

Fanti, K. A. (2016). Understanding heterogeneity in conduct disorder: a review of psychophysiological studies. *Neuroscience and Biobehavioral Reviews*.

Figner, B., Mackinlay, R. J., Wilkening, F., & Weber, E. U. (2009). Affective and deliberative processes in risky choice: age differences in risk-taking in the Columbia Card Task. *Journal of Experimental Psychology: Learning, Memory, and Cognition*, *35*, 709–730.

Fischer, S., & Smith, G. T. (2004). Deliberation affects risk-taking beyond sensation seeking. *Personality and Individual Differences*, *36*, 527–537.

Gansler, D. A., Lee, A. K., Emerton, B. C., D'Amato, C., Bhadelia, R., Jerram, M., & Fulwiler, C. (2011). Prefrontal regional correlates of self-control in male psychiatric patients: Impulsivity facets and aggression. *Psychiatry Research*, *191*, 16–23.

Gardner, M., & Steinberg, L. (2005). Peer influence on risk-taking, risk preference, and risky decision making in adolescence and adulthood: an experimental study. *Developmental Psychology*, *41*, 625–635.

Geier, C. F., Terwilliger, R., Teslovich, T., Velanova, K., & Luna, B. (2010). Immaturities in reward processing and its influence on inhibitory control in adolescence. *Cerebral Cortex*, *20*, 1613–1629.

Glicksohn, J., Ben-Shalom, U., & Lazar, M. (2004). Elements of unacceptable risk taking in combat units: an exercise in offender profiling. *Journal of Research in Personality*, *38*, 203–215.

Glicksohn, J., & Naor-Ziv, R. (2016). Personality and risk-seeking. In B. J. Carducci (Ed.), *The Wiley-Blackwell encyclopedia of personality and individual differences*. London: Wiley.

Graber, J. A., Lewinsohn, P. M., Seeley, J. R., & Brooks-Gunn, J. (1997). Is psychopathology associated with the timing of pubertal development? *Journal of the American Academy of Child & Adolescent Psychiatry*, *36*, 1768–1776.

Graber, J. A., Seeley, J. R., Brooks-Gunn, J., & Lewinsohn, P. M. (2004). Is pubertal timing associated with psychopathology in young adulthood? *Journal of the American Academy of Child & Adolescent Psychiatry*, *43*, 718–726.

Gross, J. J. (Ed.), (2014). *Handbook of emotion regulation*. New York: Guilford Press.

Guerin, D. W., Gottfried, A. W., & Thomas, C. W. (1997). Difficult temperament and behaviour problems: a longitudinal study from 1.5 to 12 years. *International Journal of Behavioral Development*, *21*, 71–90.

Hammond, C. J., Potenza, M. N., & Mayes, L. C. (2011). Development of impulse control, inhibition, and self-regulatory behaviors in normative populations across the lifespan. In J. E. Grant, & M. N. Potenza (Eds.), *The Oxford handbook of impulse control disorders* (pp. 232–244). Oxford: Oxford University Press.

Hansen, E. B., & Breivik, G. (2001). Sensation seeking as a predictor of positive and negative risk behaviour among adolescents. *Personality and Individual Differences*, *30*, 627–640.

Harden, K. P., Quinn, P. D., & Tucker-Drob, E. M. (2012). Genetically influenced change in sensation seeking drives the rise of delinquent behavior during adolescence. *Developmental Science*, *15*, 150–163.

Hare, T. A., Tottenham, N., Galvan, A., Voss, H. U., Glover, G. H., & Casey, B. J. (2008). Biological substrates of emotional reactivity and regulation in adolescence during an emotional go-nogo task. *Biological Psychiatry*, *63*, 927–934.

Haynie, D. L., Steffensmeier, D., & Bell, K. E. (2007). Gender and serious violence: untangling the role of friendship sex composition and peer violence. *Youth Violence and Juvenile Justice*, *5*, 235–253.

Hicks, B. M., Blonigen, D. M., Kramer, M. D., Krueger, R. F., Patrick, C. J., Iacono, W. G., & McGue, M. (2007). Gender differences and developmental change in externalizing disorders from late adolescence to early adulthood: a longitudinal twin study. *Journal of Abnormal Psychology*, *116*, 433–447.

Hipwell, A., Keenan, K., Kasza, K., Loeber, R., Stoethamer-Loeber, M., & Bean, T. (2008). Reciprocal influences between girls' conduct problems and depression, and parental punishment and warmth: a six year prospective analysis. *Journal of Abnormal Child Psychology*, *36*, 663–677.

Horn, N. R., Dolan, M., Elliott, R., Deakin, J. F., & Woodruff, P. W. (2003). Response inhibition and impulsivity: an fMRI study. *Neuropsychologia*, *41*, 1959–1966.

Horvath, P., & Zuckerman, M. (1993). Sensation seeking, risk appraisal, and risky behavior. *Personality and Individual Differences*, *14*, 41–52.

Hubbard, D., & Pratt, T. C. (2002). A meta-analysis of the predictors of delinquency among girls. *Journal of Offender Rehabilitation*, *34*, 1–13.

Isen, J., Raine, A., Baker, L., Dawson, M., Bezdjian, S., & Lozano, D. (2010). Sex-specific association between psychopathic traits and electrodermal reactivity in children. *Journal of Abnormal Psychology*, *119*, 216–225.

Javdani, S., Sadeh, N., & Verona, E. (2011). Expanding our lens: Female pathways to antisocial behavior in adolescence and adulthood. *Clinical Psychology Review*, *31*, 1324–1348.

Jenson, J. M. (2010). Advances in preventing childhood and adolescent problem behavior. *Research on Social Work Practice*, *20*, 701–713.

Johnson, S. L., Leedom, L. J., & Muhtadie, L. (2012). The dominance behavioral system and psychopathology: evidence from self-report, observational, and biological studies. *Psychological Bulletin*, *138*, 692–743.

Keenan, K., Hipwell, A., Chung, T., Stepp, S., Stouthamer-Loeber, M., Loeber, R., & McTigue, K. (2010). The Pittsburgh Girls Study: overview and initial findings. *Journal of Clinical Child & Adolescent Psychology*, *39*, 506–521.

Kerr, M., & Stattin, H. (2000). What parents know, how they know it, and several forms of adolescent adjustment: further support for a reinterpretation of monitoring. *Developmental Psychology*, *36*, 366–380.

Kopstein, A. N., Crum, R. M., Celentano, D. D., & Martin, S. S. (2001). Sensation seeking needs among 8th and 11th graders: characteristics associated with cigarette and marijuana use. *Drug and Alcohol Dependence*, *62*, 195–203.

Lahey, B. B., & Waldman, I. D. (2003). A developmental propensity model of the origins of conduct problems during childhood and adolescence. In B. B. Lahey, T. E. Moffitt, & A. Caspi (Eds.), *The causes of conduct disorder and serious juvenile delinquency* (pp. 76–117). New York: Guilford Press.

Lauriola, M., Panno, A., Levin, I. P., & Lejuez, C. W. (2014). Individual differences in risky decision making: a meta-analysis of sensation seeking and impulsivity with the Balloon Analogue Risk Task. *Journal of Behavioral Decision Making*, *27*, 20–36.

Leshem, R. (2016a). Brain development, impulsivity, risky decision making, and cognitive control: integrating cognitive and socioemotional processes during adolescence—an introduction to the special issue. *Developmental Neuropsychology*, *41*, 1–5.

Leshem, R. (2016b). Using dual process models to examine impulsivity throughout neural maturation. *Developmental Neuropsychology*, *41*, 125–143.

Loeber, R., & Keenan, K. (1994). Interaction between conduct disorder and its comorbid conditions: effects of age and gender. *Clinical Psychology Review*, *14*, 497–523.

Luciana, M., Collins, P. F., Olson, E. A., & Schissel, A. M. (2009). Tower of London performance in healthy adolescents: the development of planning skills and associations with self-reported inattention and impulsivity. *Developmental Neuropsychology*, *34*, 461–475.

Luna, B., Padmanabhan, A., & O'Hearn, K. (2010). What has fMRI told us about the development of cognitive control through adolescence? *Brain and Cognition*, *72*, 101–113.

Luna, B., Paulsen, D. J., Padmanabhan, A., & Geier, C. (2013). The teenage brain: cognitive control and motivation. *Current Directions in Psychological Science*, *22*, 94–100.

Lynne-Landsman, S. D., Graber, J. A., Nichols, T. R., & Botvin, G. J. (2011). Is sensation seeking a stable trait or does it change over time? *Journal of Youth and Adolescence*, *40*, 48–58.

MacDonald, K. (2012). Cutting nature at its joints: toward an evolutionarily informed theory of natural types of conduct disorder. *Journal of Social, Evolutionary, and Cultural Psychology*, *6*, 260–291.

Magid, V., MacLean, M. G., & Colder, C. R. (2007). Differentiating between sensation seeking and impulsivity through their mediated relations with alcohol use and problems. *Addictive Behaviors*, *32*, 2046–2061.

Mann, F. D., Engelhardt, L., Briley, D. A., Grotzinger, A. D., Patterson, M. W., Tackett, J. L., ... Harden, K. P. (2017). Sensation seeking and impulsive traits as personality endophenotypes for antisocial behavior: evidence from two independent samples. *Personality and Individual Differences*, *105*, 30–39.

Mann, F. D., Kretsch, N., Tackett, J. L., Harden, K. P., & Tucker-Drob, E. M. (2015). Person × environment interactions on adolescent delinquency: sensation seeking, peer deviance and parental monitoring. *Personality and Individual Differences*, *76*, 129–134.

Mann, F. D., Patterson, M. W., Grotzinger, A. D., Kretsch, N., Tackett, J. L., Tucker-Drob, E. M., & Harden, K. P. (2016). Sensation seeking, peer deviance, and genetic influences on adolescent delinquency: evidence for person-environment correlation and interaction. *Journal of Abnormal Psychology*, *125*, 679–691.

Marsman, R., Swinkels, S. H., Rosmalen, J. G., Oldehinkel, A. J., Ormel, J., & Buitelaar, J. K. (2008). HPA-axis activity and externalizing behavior problems in early adolescents from the general population: the role of comorbidity and gender: the TRAILS study. *Psychoneuroendocrinology*, *33*, 789–798.

Maslowsky, J., Buvinger, E., Keating, D. P., Steinberg, L., & Cauffman, E. (2011). Cost-benefit analysis mediation of the relationship between sensation seeking and risk behavior among adolescents. *Personality and Individual Differences*, *51*, 802–806.

McHugh, L., & Wood, R. L. (2008). Using a temporal discounting paradigm to measure decision-making and impulsivity following traumatic brain injury: a pilot study. *Brain Injury*, *22*, 715–721.

Mendle, J., Turkheimer, E., & Emery, R. E. (2007). Detrimental psychological outcomes associated with early pubertal timing in adolescent girls. *Developmental Review*, *27*, 151–171.

Miller, J. D., & Lynam, D. (2001). Structural models of personality and their relation to antisocial behavior: a meta-analytic review. *Criminology*, *39*, 765–798.

Moffitt, T. E., Caspi, A., Rutter, M., & Silva, P. A. (2001). *Sex differences in antisocial behaviour: conduct disorder, delinquency, and violence in the Dunedin longitudinal study*. Cambridge: Cambridge University Press.

Moffitt, T. E., Arseneault, L., Belsky, D., Dickson, N., Hancox, R. J., Harrington, H., ... Sears, M. R. (2011). A gradient of childhood self-control predicts health, wealth, and public safety. *Proceedings of the National Academy of Sciences of the United States of America*, *108*, 2693–2698.

Naor-Ziv, R., & Glicksohn, J. (2016). Investigating cognitive deficits as risk factors for developing eating disorders during adolescence. *Developmental Neuropsychology*, *41*, 107–124.

Newcomb, M. D., & McGee, L. (1991). Influence of sensation seeking on general deviance and specific problem behaviors from adolescence to young adulthood. *Journal of Personality and Social Psychology*, *61*, 614–628.

Nower, L., Derevensky, J. L., & Gupta, R. (2004). The relationship of impulsivity, sensation seeking, coping, and substance use in youth gamblers. *Psychology of Addictive Behaviors*, *18*, 49–55.

Pajer, K., Stein, S., Tritt, K., Chang, C., Wang, W., & Gardener, W. (2008). Conduct disorder in girls: neighborhoods, family characteristics, and parenting behaviors. *Child and Adolescent Psychiatry and Mental Health*, *2*, 1–11.

Peake, S. J., Dishion, T. J., Stormshak, E. A., Moore, W. E., & Pfeifer, J. H. (2013). Risk-taking and social exclusion in adolescence: neural mechanisms underlying peer influences on decision-making. *NeuroImage*, *82*, 23–34.

Portnoy, J., Raine, A., Chen, F. R., Pardini, D., Loeber, R., & Jennings, J. R. (2014). Heart rate and antisocial behavior: the mediating role of impulsive sensation seeking. *Criminology*, *52*, 292–311.

Quinn, P. D., Stappenbeck, C. A., & Fromme, K. (2011). Collegiate heavy drinking prospectively predicts change in sensation seeking and impulsivity. *Journal of Abnormal Psychology*, *120*, 543–556.

Racz, S. J., & McMahon, R. J. (2011). The relationship between parental knowledge and monitoring and child and adolescent conduct problems: a 10-year update. *Clinical Child and Family Psychology Review*, *14*, 377–398.

Raine, A. (2013). *The anatomy of violence: the biological roots of crime*. London: Penguin Books.

Rebellon, C., & Manasse, M. (2004). Do "bad boys" really get the girls? Delinquency as a cause and consequence of dating behavior among adolescents. *Justice Quarterly*, *21*, 355–389.

Reyna, V. F., Chaudhry, S. A., Brust-Renck, P. G., Wilhelms, E. A., & Royer, C. E. (2013). Risk taking. In D. S. Dunn (Ed.), *Oxford bibliographies in psychology*. New York: Oxford University Press.

Romer, D., Betancourt, L. M., Brodsky, N. L., Giannetta, J. M., Yang, W., & Hurt, H. (2011). Does adolescent risk taking imply weak executive function? A prospective study of relations between working memory performance, impulsivity, and risk taking in early adolescence. *Developmental Science*, *14*, 1119–1133.

Romer, D., Betancourt, L., Giannetta, J. M., Brodsky, N. L., Farah, M., & Hurt, H. (2009). Executive cognitive functions and impulsivity as correlates of risk taking and problem behavior in preadolescents. *Neuropsychologia*, *47*, 2916–2926.

Scherf, K. S., Smyth, J. M., & Delgado, M. R. (2013). The amygdala: an agent of change in adolescent neural networks. *Hormones and Behavior*, *64*, 298–313.

Scott, E. S., & Steinberg, L. (2008). Adolescent development and the regulation of youth crime. *The Future of Children*, *18*, 15–33.

Seffrin, P., Giordano, P., Manning, W., & Longmore, M. (2009). The influence of dating relationships on friendship networks, identity development, and delinquency. *Justice Quarterly*, *26*, 238–267.

Shulman, E. P., Harden, K. P., Chein, J. M., & Steinberg, L. (2014). Sex differences in the developmental trajectories of impulse control and sensation-seeking from early adolescence to early adulthood. *Journal of Youth and Adolescence*, *44*, 1–17.

Shulman, E. P., Smith, A. R., Silva, K., Icenogle, G., Duell, N., Chein, J., & Steinberg, L. (2016). The dual systems model: review, reappraisal, and reaffirmation. *Developmental Cognitive Neuroscience*, *17*, 103–117.

Simons, R. L., Stewart, E., Gordon, L. C., Conger, R. D., & Elder, G. H. (2002). A test of life-course explanations for stability and change in antisocial behavior from adolescence to young adulthood. *Criminology*, *40*, 401–434.

Sisk, C. L., & Zehr, J. L. (2005). Pubertal hormones organize the adolescent brain and behavior. *Frontiers in Neuroendocrinology*, *26*, 163–174.

Somerville, L. H. (2013). The teenage brain: sensitivity to social evaluation. *Current Directions in Psychological Science*, *22*, 121–127.

Somerville, L. H., Hare, T., & Casey, B. J. (2011). Frontostriatal maturation predicts cognitive control failure to appetitive cues in adolescents. *Journal of Cognitive Neuroscience*, *23*, 2123–2134.

Somerville, L. H., Jones, R. M., & Casey, B. J. (2010). A time of change: behavioral and neural correlates of adolescent sensitivity to appetitive and aversive environmental cues. *Brain and Cognition*, *72*, 124–133.

Spear, L. (2000). Modeling adolescent development and alcohol use in animals. *Alcohol Research & Health*, *24*, 115–123.

Spear, L. P. (2009). Heightened stress responsivity and emotional reactivity during pubertal maturation: implications for psychopathology. *Development and Psychopathology*, *21*, 87–97.

Spear, L. (2013). The teenage brain: adolescents and alcohol. *Current Directions in Psychological Science*, *22*, 152–157.

Steinberg, L. (2004). Risk taking in adolescence: what changes and why? *Annals of the New York Academy of Science*, *1021*, 1051–1058.

Steinberg, L. (2007). Risk taking in adolescence: new perspectives from brain and behavioral science. *Current Directions in Psychological Science*, *16*, 55–59.

Steinberg, L. (2008). A social neuroscience perspective on adolescent risk-taking. *Developmental Review*, *28*, 78–106.

Steinberg, L. (2013). The influence of neuroscience on US Supreme Court decisions about adolescents' criminal culpability. *Nature Reviews Neuroscience*, *14*, 513–518.

Steinberg, L., Albert, D., Cauffman, E., Banich, M., Graham, S., & Woolard, J. (2008). Age differences in sensation seeking and impulsivity as indexed by behavior and self-report: evidence for a dual systems model. *Developmental Psychology*, *44*, 1764–1778.

Steinberg, L., Cauffman, E., Woolard, J., Graham, S., & Banich, M. (2009). Are adolescents less mature than adults? Minors'access to abortion, the juvenile death penalty, and the alleged APA "flip-flop". *American Psychologist*, *64*, 583–594.

Steinberg, L., Graham, S., O'Brien, L., Woolard, J., Cauffman, E., & Banich, M. (2009). Age differences in future orientation and delay discounting. *Child Development*, *80*, 28–44.

Teslovich, T., Mulder, M., Franklin, N. T., Ruberry, E. J., Millner, A., Somerville, L. H., ... Casey, B. J. (2014). Adolescents let sufficient evidence accumulate before making a decision when large incentives are at stake. *Developmental Science*, *17*, 59–70.

Thorpe, H. (2016). Action sports for youth development: critical insights for the SDP community. *International Journal of Sport Policy and Politics*, *8*, 91–116.

Tiet, Q. Q., Wasserman, G. A., Loeber, R., McReynolds, L. S., & Miller, L. S. (2001). Developmental and sex differences in types of conduct problems. *Journal of Child and Family Studies*, *10*, 181–197.

Torregrossa, M. M., Quinn, J. J., & Taylor, J. R. (2008). Impulsivity, compulsivity, and habit: the role of orbitofrontal cortex revisited. *Biological Psychiatry*, *63*, 253–255.

Viding, E., Simmonds, E., Petrides, K. V., & Frederickson, N. (2009). The contribution of callous-unemotional traits and conduct problems to bullying in early adolescence. *Journal of Child Psychology and Psychiatry*, *50*, 471–481.

Waldman, I. D., Tackett, J. L., Van Hulle, C. A., Applegate, B., Pardini, D., Frick, P. J., & Lahey, B. B. (2011). Child and adolescent conduct disorder substantially shares genetic influences with three socioemotional dispositions. *Journal of Abnormal Psychology, 120*, 57–61.

Weissman, D. G., Schriber, R. A., Fassbender, C., Atherton, O., Krafft, C., Robins, R. W., ... Guyer, A. E. (2015). Earlier adolescent substance use onset predicts stronger connectivity between reward and cognitive control brain networks. *Developmental Cognitive Neuroscience, 16*, 121–129.

Zahn-Waxler, C., & Polanichka, N. (2004). All things interpersonal: socialization and female aggression. In M. Putallaz, & K. L. Bierman (Eds.), *Aggression, antisocial behavior, and violence among girls:a developmental perspective* (pp. 48–68). New York: The Guilford Press.

Zaki, J., & Williams, W. C. (2013). Interpersonal emotion regulation. *Emotion, 13*, 803–810.

Zimring, F. E. (1998). *American youth violence*. Oxford: Oxford University Press.

Zuckerman, M. (1994). *Behavioral expressions and biosocial bases of sensation seeking*. Cambridge: Cambridge University Press.

Zuckerman, M. (2002). Personality and psychopathy: shared behavioral and biological traits. In J. Glicksohn (Ed.), *The neurobiology of criminal behavior* (pp. 27–49). Boston: Kluwer Academic.

Zuckerman, M. (2005). *Psychobiology of personality* (2nd ed., revised and updated). Cambridge: Cambridge University Press.

Zuckerman, M. (2007). *Sensation seeking and risky behavior*. Washington: American Psychological Association.

Zuckerman, M., & Glicksohn, J. (2016). Hans Eysenck's personality model and the constructs of sensation seeking and impulsivity. *Personality and Individual Differences, 103*, 48–52.

Zuckerman, M., & Kuhlman, D. M. (2000). Personality and risk-taking: common biosocial factors. *Journal of Personality, 68*, 999–1029.

Further Reading

Galvan, A., Hare, T., Voss, H., Glover, G., & Casey, B. J. (2007). Risk-taking and the adolescent brain: who is at risk? *Developmental Science, 10*, F8–F14.

Grimshaw, G. M., & Carmel, D. (2014). An asymmetric inhibition model of hemispheric differences in emotional processing. *Frontiers in Psychology, 5*, article 489.

Gruber, S. A., Silveri, M. M., Dahlgren, M. K., & Yurgelun-Todd, D. (2011). Why so impulsive? White matter alterations are associated with impulsivity in chronic marijuana smokers. *Experimental and Clinical Psychopharmacology, 19*, 231–242.

Hampson, S. E., Severson, H. H., Burns, W. J., Slovic, P., & Fisher, K. J. (2001). Risk perception, personality factors and alcohol use among adolescents. *Personality and Individual Differences, 30*, 167–181.

Leshem, R., & Glicksohn, J. (2007). The construct of impulsivity revisited. *Personality and Individual Differences, 43*, 681–691.

Romer, D. (2010). Adolescent risk taking, impulsivity, and brain development: implications for prevention. *Developmental Psychobiology, 52*, 263–276.

Part III

Evidence-Based Treatment Components of Disruptive Behavior Disorders

Behavioral treatments

9

Corey Lieneman, Desireé N. Williford, Lauren B. Quetsch, Benjamin Thomas, and Cheryl B. McNeil
West Virginia University, Morgantown, WV, United States

In this chapter, we provide an overview of evidence-based behavioral treatments for disruptive behavior disorders (DBDs) in young children. To begin, DBDs and theories behind their behavioral treatment in this age range are described. Next, a foundational definition of evidence-based practice in psychology is laid, followed by a basic description of behavioral parent training with emphasis on its efficacious components. Later, the inclusion criteria for behavioral approaches in this chapter are explicated, and major models of therapy in this domain are summarized. Then, Parent-Child Interaction Therapy (PCIT) is used as an exemplar to offer an in-depth look at the similarities and differences among behavioral treatments for DBDs in young children. Finally, future directions are discussed.

Disruptive behavior disorders (DBDs)

Individuals diagnosed with DBDs often experience difficulties with emotions, behaviors, and self-control which violate others' rights, bringing about conflict with authority figures and opposing social norms (American Psychiatric Association, 2013). Examples of DBDs in the *Diagnostic and Statistical Manual of Mental Disorders (DSM−5)* are oppositional defiant disorder, conduct disorder, and intermittent explosive disorder. DBDs are some of the most common reasons for child referrals to mental health treatment. Childhood DBDs are often comorbid with other disorders (e.g., mood, anxiety, and other impulse-control disorders) and are correlated with increased risk of developing secondary disorders, such as conduct disorder and substance use disorders (Nock, Kazdin, Hiripi, & Kessler, 2007). For a more in-depth discussion of disruptive, impulse-control, and conduct disorders, see Chapter 1, "Disruptive, Impulse-Control, and Conduct Disorders."

Behavioral theory for treatment of DBDs in young children

Behavioral approaches are the most common, evidence-based methods for the treatment of DBDs. Behavioral approaches toward the treatment of DBDs are based on principles of operant conditioning and social learning theory. The theory of operant

Developmental Pathways to Disruptive, Impulse-Control, and Conduct Disorders.
DOI: https://doi.org/10.1016/B978-0-12-811323-3.00009-2

conditioning holds that the probability of a behavior (broken down into a stimulus-response pattern) changes based on the actions of neutral operants, reinforcers, or punishers (Skinner, 1938). An environmental response that makes a stimulus-response pattern more likely is a reinforcer. An action that makes a stimulus-response pattern less likely is a punisher, and a response that does not change the probability of a stimulus-response pattern is a neutral operant. For example, if a child is told "no" (stimulus), tantrums (response), and is provided with caregiver attention (reinforcer), the likelihood of tantrums in response to being told "no" will increase. Behavioral treatments for DBDs focus on appropriately implementing reinforcers for positive behavior, neutral operants for minor misbehavior, and punishers for severe misbehavior. Using the previous example, caregivers being taught to implement a behavioral treatment may learn to decrease the pattern of their child's tantrums by replacing the reinforcer of caregiver attention to tantrums with the neutral operant of ignoring minor outbursts or the punisher of using time-out for destructive outbursts. In line with behavioral therapy, these environmental or caregiver responses are most effective when they are consistent, immediate, and dependent on child behavior (Kazdin, 2005).

Social learning theory, which evolved from earlier behavioral theories including operant conditioning, recognizes the importance of social variables (e.g., observation and imitation) on learning and behavior (Bandura & Walters, 1963). Guided by social learning theory, our example of a child's tantrum demonstrates the impact of caregiver attention on reinforcing the disruptive behavior and removal of caregiver attention as a neutral operant or punisher. Caregivers also learn to increase the use of positive social skills such as imitation and praise in order to model these skills and create a rewarding social experience with their children.

Evidence-based practice in psychology

Behavioral treatments in this overview meet criteria for evidence-based practices in psychology (EBPP). The EBPP designation reflects the integration of practice and science, most notably defined by attention to clinical expertise and research approaches focused on patient characteristics, perceptions, and experiences (American Psychological Association, 2005). Clinical expertise encompasses a series of therapeutic competencies around (1) assessment, diagnosis, and case conceptualization, (2) clinical decision making, intervention delivery, and monitoring client progress, (3) interpersonal skills and the therapeutic relationship, (4) ongoing self-reflection and incorporation of new knowledge and skills, (5) utilization of consultation, supervision, or other resources as needed, and (6) providing rationale for treatment (APA, 2005).

To be considered best research evidence, scientific findings must be relevant to intervention techniques or strategies, assessment methods, clinical concerns, and patient populations as well as applied across multiple sources and in a manner that addresses both internal (e.g., laboratory studies) and external validity (e.g., field studies; APA, 2005). This can be accomplished using a variety of methodologies and research types, including efficacy and effectiveness trials, meta-analyses, systematic case studies, and cost-benefit or cost-effectiveness studies, to name a few (APA, 2005). Further, psychological interventions are deemed most effective when they are responsive to the needs of specific client concerns, sociocultural needs, environmental factors, and other contextual considerations. These characteristics can include variations in clinical presentation, diagnosis, behavior, chronological age, developmental level, historical factors, sociocultural and familial factors, current and prior environmental context, and personal preferences, values, and beliefs about treatment (APA, 2005).

Though EBPPs are interventions with empirical evidence, it is also important to note that there are varying levels of this support, driven by five methodological factors and the amount of scientific evidence (Chambless & Hollon, 1998; Southam-Gerow & Prinstein, 2014). Methodological criteria include: (1) group design [i.e., randomized controlled trial (RCT)], (2) a defined treatment and the use of a manual or its equivalent, (3) a population target with delineated inclusion criteria, (4) reliable and valid measurement of treatment outcomes, and (5) appropriate data analyses, adequate sample size, and power to detect effects (Chambless & Hollon, 1998; Southam-Gerow & Prinstein, 2014). The five levels of empirical support are: (1) well-established treatments, (2) probably efficacious treatments, (3) possibly efficacious treatments, (4) experimental treatments, and (5) treatments of questionable efficacy (Chambless & Hollon, 1998; Southam-Gerow & Prinstein, 2014). Levels of empirical support are described in more detail in Fig. 9.1. All interventions described in the current chapter have substantial research evidence and fall within the three highest levels of empirical support; for example, PCIT meets criteria for a well-established treatment (Society of Clinical Child and Adolescent Psychology, 2015).

Behavioral parent training (BPT)

As young children interact largely within the context of caregiver relationships, caregivers play major roles in these treatment models. Overall, BPT approaches aim to help caregivers learn how to effectively reinforce positive child behaviors to increase their frequencies and deter acute problem behavior with noncoercive punishment techniques (MacKenzie, 2007). The five most effective, well-researched BPT programs (PCIT; McNeil & Hembree-Kigin, 2010, Triple P Positive Parenting Program; Sanders, 1999, Helping the Noncompliant Child; McMahon & Forehand, 2003, The Incredible Years; Webster-Stratton & Reid, 2010, and Parent Management Training-Oregon; Dishion, Forgatch, Chamberlain, & Pelham, 2016) covered in this chapter target disruptive behaviors by intervening in the coercive family process (Patterson, 1982).

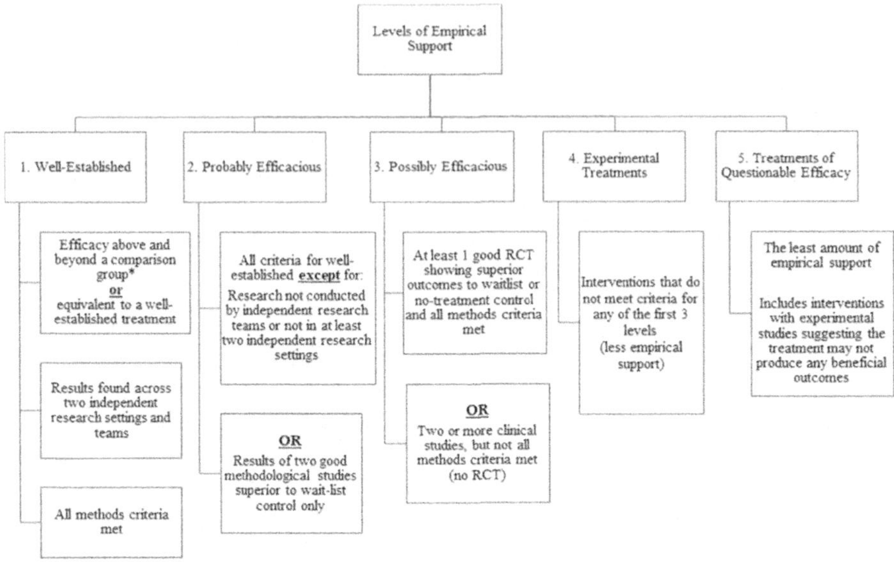

Figure 9.1 Levels of empirical support.
Note: This figure was created from information detailed in Chambless and Hollon (1998) and Southam-Gerow and Prinstein (2014).
*Comparison groups may include placebos, pharmaceutical drugs/medications, or other interventions, such as behavioral or cognitive therapies.

Patterson's coercive family process (1982)

Informed by his research with children and families, Dr. Gerald Patterson conceptualized the coercive family process, also referred to as coercion theory, to explain the development of aggression in young children (Patterson, Dishion, & Bank, 1984). Patterson proposed that reciprocal caregiver-child dynamics, especially those related to disciplinary practices, contribute to the development of childhood disruptive behaviors. This highly influential theory on BPT includes two components: (1) the caregiver models aggressive behavior, and (2) the caregiver and child become entrenched in a cycle of reinforcing the others' negative or aggressive behavior. In this cycle, the caregiver makes a demand, and the child defies it. The caregiver, in turn, makes the demand more aggressively, to which the child more aggressively contests. The cycle escalates until either the child or caregiver gives in, reinforcing the other's aggressive behavior. In the end, either the child complies with the caregiver's request, reinforcing the caregiver's aggressive approach, or the child avoids or escapes the command, reinforcing the child's aggressive approach. In the future, the caregiver and child will be more likely to engage in these negative behaviors to get their needs met. Here, too, caregiver and child inadvertently begin to pay less attention to the others' positive behaviors and more attention to the negative ones. This coercive family process is associated with a higher risk of conduct problems for children later in life (Dishion & Patterson, 2006), but interventions guided by coercion theory have been shown to improve outcomes (e.g., emotional and behavioral problems; Dishion, Patterson, & Kavanagh, 1992).

Historical overview of Hanf-model programs

Many of the major approaches to BPT in practice today were patterned after the two-stage Hanf-model, developed by Dr. Constance Hanf in the late 1960s at the University of Oregon Medical School (Reitman & McMahon, 2013). Stage I of Hanf's model, the Child's Game, focuses on enhancing the caregiver–child relationship. During caregiver-child play sessions, caregivers practice skills describing child behavior, praising, following the child's lead, and using differential attention for desirable and undesirable behaviors. Stage II of Hanf's model, the Parent's Game, emphasizes caregiver direction of child task completion and follow-through with a time-out sequence for noncompliance. The Hanf-model employs social reinforcement and performance criteria to advance through treatment. Hanf's influence extended to the creators of several well-known parent training programs including Forehand and McMahon's Helping the Noncompliant Child (McMahon & Forehand, 2003), Eyberg's PCIT (Eyberg, 1988), Barkley's Defiant Children (DC; Barkley, 2013), Webster-Stratton's The Incredible Years (Webster-Stratton & Reid, 2010), and Cunningham's Community Parent Education (COPE; Cunningham, Bremner, & Boyle, 1995). The most well-studied and empirically supported of this list are described subsequently in more detail.

Components of BPT programs for DBDs

A meta-analysis examining effectiveness of components of parenting programs aimed at reducing externalizing behavior problems in children 0–7 years found several unique components that predict larger effect sizes for changes in caregiver and child behavior (Kaminski, Valle, Filene, & Boyle, 2008). Overall, in support of extant literature, parenting programs demonstrated significant effects on improving parenting skills and reducing child behavior problems. Specifically, programs emphasizing positive parenting practices (e.g., building positive relationships between child and caregiver) and in vivo practice (e.g., being coached through skills practice) predicted larger effect sizes for changes in parenting and child behavior, regardless of other component parts. Programs that emphasized teaching caregivers emotional communication (e.g., reflecting child statements) demonstrated larger effect sizes on changing caregiver behavior and skill acquisition. Programs emphasizing training caregivers in using time-out and being consistent with discipline demonstrated larger effect sizes on reducing externalizing behaviors in children with behavior disorders. Using a more conservative assessment of components of parenting programs, Kaminski et al. (2008) found only four components that continued to predict larger effect sizes in improving both caregiver and child behaviors: (1) requiring in vivo practice of skills learned, (2) teaching caregivers emotional communication techniques, (3) increasing positive caregiver-child interactions, and (4) requiring consistency in implementing disciplinary techniques.

Major treatment models for DBDs in young children

Inclusion criteria

In addition to having strong scientific evidence, as described in the section on EBPP earlier, the five EBPPs included in this chapter are predominantly behavioral in nature and focus primarily on young children rather than older children and adolescents. Given the limited scope of this chapter, only treatments most often studied in the DBD literature for this population will be discussed. A detailed list of each of the included interventions can be found in Table 9.1 along with a list of sources from which information was obtained. The sources utilized are varied, including a review publication (Eyberg, Nelson, & Boggs, 2008), an edited textbook (Weisz & Kazdin, 2010), and credible, nationally-recognized websites (e.g., Society of Clinical Child and Adolescent Psychology, 2015). Only treatments cited by two or more of our sources are included. The five treatments discussed are (1) The Incredible Years, (2) Parent Management Training – Oregon Model, (3) Triple P Positive Parenting Program, (4) Helping the Noncompliant Child, and (5) PCIT.

The Incredible Years Series (IY)

The IY series is a set of evidence-based programs developed for caregivers, teachers, and children. The program was developed by Dr. Carolyn Wester-Stratton with foci on strengthening and promoting skills in parent/teacher behavior management, improving the quality of caregiver-child or teacher-child interactions and relations, and promoting positive child outcomes, such as social and emotional competence, appropriate play, school readiness, self-control, self-regulation, problem-solving, self-esteem, and self-confidence (The Incredible Years, 2013; Webster-Stratton & Reid, 2010).

The IY parent interventions for parents of youth aged 0–12 years include the BASIC, ADVANCE, and SCHOOL parent programs. Each of these programs include discussion of video vignettes, brainstorming and values-based activities, homework assignments and handouts, psychoeducation, and role play activities (The Incredible Years, 2013). In the BASIC program, initial content focuses on methods for improving the caregiver–child relationship via child-directed interaction (CDI) and play, the use of praise and incentives, and the coaching of academic skills, persistence, socialization, and emotionality (The Incredible Years, 2013; Webster-Stratton & Reid, 2010). Following progress in these areas, caregivers learn behavior management techniques (routines and rules, selective ignoring and parental monitoring, effective commands, logical consequences, and time-out procedures) and how to encourage problem solving (The Incredible Years, 2013; Webster-Stratton & Reid, 2010). The subsequent ADVANCE programming attends to conflict management, maintenance, and generalizability of effects (The Incredible Years, 2013; Webster-Stratton & Reid, 2010). SCHOOL programing focuses on academic success and skills training over four to six sessions, including teacher-parent collaboration and rapport, school readiness and academic success, effective

Table 9.1 **Evidence-based behavioral treatments for DBDs in young children by source**

		Source				
		Eyberg et al. (2008) Review	**Weisz and Kazdin (2010)**	**Blueprints for Healthy Young Development (2012–2017)**	**SAMHSA, National Registry of Evidence- Based Programs and Practices (2016)**	**Society of Clinical Child and Adolescent Psychology – Div. 53 of APA, Effective Child Therapy.org (2015)**
Evidence-Based Treatments	PCIT	X	X	X	X	X
	The Incredible Years	X	X	X	X	X
	Parent Management Training-Oregon Model	X	X	X	X	
	Triple P: Positive Parenting program	X			X	X
	Helping the Noncompliant Child	X				X

after-school and peer monitoring, homework completion, and promoting reading competency (Webster-Stratton & Reid, 2010).

The IY programing for teachers and other school-based providers includes the Teacher Classroom Management Program and Incredible Beginnings. The former focuses on effective classroom management and strengthening positive relations among teachers and students over a 6-day group training format. Topics such as effective transition plans, parent-teacher interactions, the importance of positive communication and collaboration with parents, and generalization of skills across classroom, bus, lunchroom, and playground are discussed (The Incredible Years, 2013; Webster-Stratton & Reid, 2010). Conducted similarly, the Incredible Beginnings program focuses on social and emotional coaching, child-directed play interactions, and consistent behavior management strategies (The Incredible Years, 2013).

The IY Child Training Programs (ages 3–8 years) focuses on deficits in attention, social-cognitive skills, emotion regulation, early aggressive behavior, difficulties with peers and cooperative play, and negative attributions using a video-modeling approach (The Incredible Years, 2013; Webster-Stratton & Reid, 2010). Two programs have been developed including Small Group Dinosaur and Classroom Dinosaur School, each focusing on seven major components: (1) introduction to approach and rules, (2) promoting empathy and emotion understanding, (3) problem solving, (4) anger control, (5) peer interactions and social skills, (6) communication skills, and (7) school success/academic skills (The Incredible Years, 2013; Webster-Stratton & Reid, 2010). Small Group Dinosaur is intended for small group sessions (about six children) over 18–22 weeks. The Classroom Dinosaur School Program is a 22-week program delivered by a teacher twice weekly over consecutive years (The Incredible Years, 2013; Webster-Stratton & Reid, 2010).

The IY series of training programs were the first interventions to be recognized as EBPPs for children with conduct problems based on criteria set forth by Chambless and Hollon (1998). Since 1998, these programs have been given many similar designations in reviews conducted by the Substance Abuse and Mental Health Services Administration (SAMHSA), Blueprints for Health Youth Development, and Promising Practices Network, among others (The Incredible Years, 2013). The IY series has demonstrated efficacy across many RCTs by their developer and other researchers since 1988 (Webster-Stratton & Reid, 2010). For example, outcome research on IY has shown reductions in youth aggression, disruptive and destructive behaviors, increased prosocial behaviors, and increased social competence as compared to youth in waitlist or untreated controls (e.g., Beauchaine, Webster-Stratton, & Reid, 2005; Webster-Stratton, 1994; Webster-Stratton & Hammond, 1997; Webster-Stratton, Reid, & Hammond, 2004; Webster-Stratton, Reid, & Stoolmiller, 2008). Improvements in caregiver and teacher outcomes have also been shown, for example, reduced use of corporal punishment and other negative discipline strategies, decreased use of critical statements, and increased use of positive discipline strategies and praise (e.g., Beauchaine et al., 2005; Gross, Fogg, Webster-Stratton, & Grady, 1999; Reid, Webster-Stratton, & Hammond, 2003; Webster-Stratton et al., 2004, 2008).

Parent Management Training-Oregon (PMT-O)

The Oregon Model of family behavior therapy was developed through extensive research on family interaction and behavior change theory. Researchers recognized that parents were the key agents for change in children and developed strategies to reduce child behavior problems (Patterson, Chamberlain, & Reid, 1982) including antisocial problems, academic issues, delinquency, and depression (Dishion et al., 2016). These strategies were developed to address family formation and adaptation (Family Check-Up Model), family disruption and maladaptation (PMT-O), and family attenuation and dissolution (Treatment Foster Care—Oregon Model; Formerly Multidimensional Treatment Fostercare).

PMT-O was proposed by Patterson and Reid (1975) and then tested to become one of the leading treatments for children with severe problem behaviors from preschool (3 years) to adolescence (16 years). Core components of PMT-O include contingent positive reinforcement, discipline, positive involvement, interpersonal problem solving, and supervision (Dishion et al., 2016). Secondary skills are used to strengthen the core skills including clear directions, emotion identification and regulation, and communication. PMT-O is delivered to individual families in outpatient and in-home settings (averaging 25 sessions), as well as via parent groups or telehealth (averaging 6–14 sessions). Typical delivery includes weekly parent sessions, weekly homework practice, and a mid-week check-in call. One unique component of PMT-O is the use of a teaching/learning approach (via role-play and interactive problem solving) with families (compared to teaching or confronting clients) which is more consistent with motivational interviewing and reduces familial resistance to treatment (Dishion et al., 2016).

PMT-O yields positive outcomes for both caregivers and their children. Findings indicate reductions in levels of noncompliance, self-reported depression, aggressive behavior, arrests and time incarcerated, and drug use (for a review, see Forgatch & Patterson, 2010). For caregivers in PMT-O, increases in positive parenting skills, marital satisfaction, and socioeconomic status and decreases in negative parenting skills and depression have been found (Forgatch & DeGarmo, 2007; Forgatch & Patterson, 2010; Patterson, Forgatch, & DeGarmo, 2010). PMT-O is an effective treatment for youth with significant reductions in negative life outcomes. The treatment model continues to expand across the United States and the world. New sites around the globe include Mexico, the Netherlands, Denmark, Iceland, and Uganda (Dishion et al., 2016).

Triple P: Positive Parenting Program

Developed at the University of Queensland by Sanders and Markie-Dadds (1996), Triple P is a multitier treatment focused on addressing the unique needs of families based on the intensity of a child's behavior problems. Triple P aims to prevent behavioral, emotional, and developmental problems in children by advancing parenting knowledge and skills (Sanders, 1999). Categorized by five levels of intervention with increasing strength, Triple P addresses a range of needs from universal prevention to severe behavioral problems. The five levels are as follows: (1) Universal Triple P is a prevention-based program which disseminates content through public sources, such as the media; (2) Selected Triple P is a one- to two-session developmental guidance-based approach delivered by primary care personnel to address mild child behavior problems; (3) Primary Care Triple P is a four-session parenting skills training intervention administered by primary care workers to improve children's mildly to moderately disruptive behavior; (4) Standard Triple P is an individual, group, or self-directed parent training intervention delivered by mental health practitioners focused on treating child DBDs; (5) Enhanced Triple P is the most involved form of treatment which aims to reduce disruptive child behaviors complicated by other family stressors. The unique structure of Triple P is intended to maximize efficiency and scope of risk reduction and protective factor enhancement (Sanders, 1999).

Intervention and treatment components in Triple P train caregivers to impart language, social, problem-solving, and developmental skills to their children in daily interactions (de Graaf, Speetjens, Smit, de Wolff, & Tavecchio, 2008). Caregivers also learn child management skills, for example, using clear, succinct instructions, providing positive attention as a reinforcer for positive behavior, employing redirection, allowing logical consequences for misbehavior, and implementing effective disciplinary strategies (e.g., ignoring, time-out, and quiet time; Sanders, Markie-Dadds, & Turner, 2003).

Both Standard Triple P and Enhanced Triple P are recognized as established evidence-based treatments for childhood disruptive behavior (Eyberg et al., 2008). One meta-analysis revealed that families participating in Triple P experienced significant improvements in child behavior problems, positive parenting, and parental well-being (Nowak & Heinrichs, 2008). Another meta-analysis conducted during the same period demonstrated that Triple P successfully reduced dysfunctional parenting and increased parental competence in dealing with clinical and nonclinical child behavior problems (de Graaf et al., 2008). Triple P also shows lasting treatment outcomes in long-term follow-up studies (de Graaf et al., 2008; Heinrichs, Kliem, & Hahlweg, 2014) and is effective for families from diverse cultures (Au et al., 2014; Matsumoto, Sofronoff, & Sanders, 2010; Sumargi, Sofronoff, & Morawska, 2015).

Helping the Noncompliant Child (HNC)

Drs. Robert McMahon and Rex Forehand's HNC is a unique BPT program in that it involves the child in all teaching, modeling, and role-playing components (McMahon & Forehand, 2003). HNC consists of three primary objectives: (1) breaking the coercive parenting cycle and replacing it with more positive, productive caregiver-child interactions, (2) improving parenting skills in such areas as praising appropriate behavior, ignoring minor inappropriate behavior, and provision of clear instructions and consequences, and (3) increasing prosocial behavior and reducing noncompliance in children. HNC was designed for families of children ages 3–8 years demonstrating noncompliance or conduct problems and has also been successfully adapted to diverse populations, such as children hospitalized in psychiatric facilities, children of caregivers with substance abuse problems, families at-risk for child abuse and neglect, and children with developmental disabilities, attention-deficit/hyperactivity disorder (ADHD), enuresis, and encopresis (McMahon & Forehand, 2003; McMahon, Long, & Forehand, 2010). However, HNC may be contraindicated for families in which caregivers demonstrate severe, untreated psychopathology that interferes with skill acquisition (McMahon et al., 2010).

The HNC protocol involves two phases. In the first phase, differential attention (Phase I), therapists encourage caregivers to increase positive interactions with their children to break the coercive cycle of long-term child noncompliance maintenance. Specifically, caregivers are taught to attend to and reward appropriate child behaviors while ignoring minor misbehaviors. Attending to appropriate behaviors involves providing a running commentary of these appropriate, overt behaviors (e.g., Child stacks block. Parent: "You put the red block on the green block.") and rewarding prosocial behaviors (e.g., Parent: "You're playing nicely with the toys."). In addition, caregivers are instructed to reduce the use of questions, commands, and criticisms, as these frequently result in negative caregiver-child interactions. Rewarding appropriate behaviors can take three forms in the HNC protocol: physical rewards (e.g., hugging), unlabeled verbal rewards (e.g., "Great job!"), and labeled verbal rewards (e.g., "Thank you for handing me the block."). Finally, ignoring inappropriate behaviors involves avoiding eye contact, nonverbal attention, verbal responses, and physical contact. Ignoring is employed for minor misbehaviors (e.g., whining or interrupting) but is not recommended for serious misbehavior (e.g., hitting, kicking, or biting).

The second phase of the HNC protocol involves compliance training. In Phase II, parents learn how to give clear, appropriate instructions. Specifically, caregivers are trained to get the child's attention (e.g., make eye contact), give a simply stated instruction (i.e., phrased positively, one at a time), and wait 5 seconds for the child to comply. If the child complies, the caregiver provides the child with verbal praise. If the child fails to comply within 5 seconds, caregivers are instructed to give a warning (i.e., "If you do not do. . ., then you will go to time out."). At this point, if the child complies, the caregiver verbally praises the child. If the child again fails to comply, the child is placed in a chair for a 3 minute time-out. If the child resists time-out, back-up procedures are implemented (e.g., additional time-out, response cost, or removal to a different room). Phase II begins in the therapy setting but is gradually generalized to other settings (e.g., the grocery store; McMahon & Forehand, 2003).

The HNC protocol was originally designed to be implemented with one therapist working with one family in a clinic setting. When possible, therapists use a bug-in-the-ear device from behind a one-way mirror to unobtrusively provide caregivers with feedback during sessions. The HNC program also uses modeling and role-play to teach both the caregiver and the child the components of the treatment.

HNC has a wide evidence base supporting the efficacy of its component parts in laboratory settings, clinical outcomes in noncompliant children, and generalization of HNC to various settings, times, and behaviors. Laboratory studies have demonstrated that the HNC program is useful in improving caregiver-child interactions and reducing child noncompliance. In addition, these studies have demonstrated that including children in the didactic process improves outcomes (McMahon & Forehand, 2003). Multiple clinical outcome studies have demonstrated that caregivers of noncompliant children rate their children as equally or better adjusted upon completion of the HNC program when compared to caregivers of nonreferred children (McMahon & Forehand, 2003). Treatment effects generalize to the home setting, to siblings, and to long-term maintenance (McMahon & Forehand, 2003).

Efforts have been made to implement an extension of the HNC, the Fast Track program, in school settings (Slough & McMahon, 2008). The Fast Track program is a multisite research collaboration examining a multipronged intervention for at-risk youth, following the participants annually from kindergarten through high school. The Fast Track program utilizes core components from the HNC program and is based on the early starter conceptualization of conduct problems. The Fast Track intervention has demonstrated effectiveness in reducing child problem behaviors, improving child social, emotional, and academic skills, reducing negative parenting practices (e.g., use of physical discipline), and improving caregiver involvement in the school system (Conduct Problems Prevention Research Group, 2002). These changes have been shown to persist past third grade, especially in children with high levels of problem behaviors (Conduct Problems Prevention Research Group, 2007, 2010).

In addition to the Fast Track program, the HNC program has been adapted for use as a parent education group. Parenting the Strong-Willed Child is designed for parents of 2–6 year old children demonstrating problem behaviors (Forehand & Long, 2002). Parents attend 5, 2-hour sessions, during each of which 1 of the main skills from HNC is taught. A study of the Parenting the Strong-Willed Child program with children ages 2–8 years has demonstrated sustained reductions in child problem behaviors and improved parenting practices at least 6 months after conclusion of the course (Conners, Edwards, & Grant, 2007).

Parent-Child Interaction Therapy (PCIT)

PCIT is an evidence-based parent training program for children ages 2–7 years with severe behavior problems (Eyberg & Funderburk, 2011; McNeil & Hembree-Kigin, 2010). Developed at the Oregon Health Sciences University by Dr Sheila Eyberg, PCIT focuses on reducing child behavior problems through two phases: (1) contingent positive attention and (2) effective discipline strategies.

The first stage of PCIT is called child-direct interaction (CDI). In this stage, caregivers work on strengthening their relationship with their child through play. Caregivers are instructed to foster positive interactions with their child by following the child's lead during the play and using positive parenting skills. The key skills caregivers employ during play sessions include the PRIDE skills (Praise, Reflection, Imitation, Description, and Enjoyment) as well ignoring and redirecting inappropriate or annoying behaviors. Moreover, caregivers are not to use the avoid skills which include commands, questions, or negative talk (sarcasm, criticism, words including "no," "don't," "stop," "quit," and "not"). Mastery of CDI is reached when caregivers are able to use 10 labeled praises, 10 behavioral descriptions, and 10 reflections as well as 3 or fewer avoid skills in a 5 minute coded interaction period at the start of the therapy session. The second phase of PCIT can only be started once caregivers have reached mastery criteria of CDI.

The second stage of PCIT is called parent-directed interaction (PDI). PDI is focused on increasing child compliance through the implementation of an effective and consistent discipline procedure. Caregivers continue to use the skills learned in CDI but also learn how to give effective commands with appropriate follow-through. Caregivers are taught a scripted time-out procedure where child compliance to a command is given a labeled praise, child noncompliance is given a warning statement, and further noncompliance is followed by time-out. To master PDI, caregivers must be able to deliver at least four commands with 75% effective commands given and 75% effective follow-through during a 5 minute coded period at the start of a therapy session. Although not required for mastery of PDI, families typically complete the PDI ladder where they gradually increase the use of commands with their children from play situations, to house rules, to public behavior.

To graduate from PCIT, families must have mastered both CDI and PDI, have child behavior problems reduced to within normal limits (caregiver-report via the Eyberg Child Behavior Inventory; Eyberg & Pincus, 1999), and feel confident to handle their child's behavior problems independently (McNeil & Hembree-Kigin, 2010).

For more than 40 years, researchers have continued to develop the strong evidence base supporting PCIT. PCIT boasts large effect sizes (e.g., $d = 1.88-1.99$; Abrahamse et al., 2012 and $d = 2.30$; Danko, Garbacz, & Budd, 2015) for pre- to post-treatment child problem behavior change scores on the Eyberg Child Behavior Inventory. In addition to impressive improvements in childhood disruptive behaviors, caregivers involved with PCIT experience dramatic increases in positive parenting skills and decreases in negative parenting practices (Thomas & Zimmer-Gembeck, 2007). These positive outcomes have been demonstrated across laboratory-based efficacy trials and community-based effectiveness trials (Eyberg et al., 2008; Lanier, Kohl, Benz, Swinger, & Drake, 2014; Leung, Tsang, Heung, & Yiu, 2009; Self-Brown et al., 2012; Ward, Theule, & Cheung, 2016).

In more recent years, many treatment developers and researchers have begun to recognize the clinical utility of PCIT and its potential to extend to a larger range of ages, symptoms, and family circumstances (e.g., Carpenter, Puliafico, Kurtz, Pincus, & Comer, 2014). This is particularly relevant given the recent research suggesting that PCIT components can be beneficial to a variety of populations and can be used in combination with other therapeutic approaches (e.g., Carpenter et al., 2014). Though more evidence is needed on the effectiveness of PCIT adaptations, these directions show the potential of additional clinical benefits, generalizability beyond the typical age range, use with unique child and caregiver populations, and use in more varied and applied circumstances (McNeil & Hembree-Kigin, 2010).

The focus of the current section, therefore, will be to discuss the generalizability of PCIT across ages of children, comorbid conditions, and parental psychopathology.

Given growth in popularity of PCIT over the years, many clinicians and researchers have become interested in adapting PCIT for populations outside of the typical age range of 2–7 years. Efforts have focused on adapting PCIT to a younger population, including infants and toddlers, as well as to older children, aged 7–10 years (McNeil & Hembree-Kigin, 2010; Stokes, Scudder, Costello, & McNeil, 2017). Some success has been noted with these adaptations, such as focusing on the CDI portion of PCIT to improve attachment and communication between caregivers and infants/toddlers (Kohlhoff & Morgan, 2014). PDI skills may also be helpful as a preemptive strategy for maximizing compliance skills during toddlerhood (McNeil & Hembree-Kigin, 2010). Research on older child protocols has found PCIT to be successful when reducing the use of certain CDI skills, using more developmentally appropriate activities/toys, and relying on hands-off discipline strategies like restriction of privilege instead of time-out (Chaffin et al., 2004; McNeil & Hembree-Kigin, 2010; Stokes et al., 2017).

In addition to being a well-established treatment for families of children with primary externalizing behaviors, recent research shows that PCIT has the potential to be effective at reducing behavioral problems in more specialized child and family populations. For example, an RCT conducted by Bagner and Eyberg (2007) found PCIT to be effective at reducing disruptive behaviors among children with intellectual disability as compared to a waitlist control, and Chengappa, McNeil, Norman, Quetsch, and Travers (in press) demonstrated the use of the intervention with caregivers with intellectual disability. Similarly, PCIT has been applied to families of children with autism spectrum disorder (ASD) with some initial support for improving child compliance and positive parenting behaviors (e.g., Zlomke, Jeter, & Murphy, 2017). PCIT adaptations for ASD often include an adjunctive component focused on communication and social skill development (Ginn, Clionsky, Eyberg, Warner-Metzger, & Abner, 2017; Masse, 2010; Masse, McNeil, Wagner, & Chorney, 2007; Masse, McNeil, Wagner, & Quetsch, 2016). Finally, recent evidence supports the generalizability of PCIT to young children with comorbid ADHD, as well as an early intervention approach for young children with only a diagnosis of ADHD (Chronis-Tuscano et al., 2016; Matos, Bauermeister, & Bernal, 2009; McNeil & Hembree-Kigin, 2010; Wagner & McNeil, 2008).

In addition to these developmental disorders, PCIT has also been adapted to address children who have experienced physical abuse and have comorbid externalizing symptoms (e.g., Chaffin et al., 2004; Thomas & Zimmer-Gembeck, 2011, 2012; Ware & Herschell, 2010). These findings suggest that PCIT may serve the function of a parent-treatment for prior abusive behavior by improving caregiver–child relations, such as reducing negative and coercive patterns, and implementing effective and appropriate discipline strategies (e.g., Batzer, Berg, Godinet, & Stotzer, 2015; Chaffin et al., 2004; Ware & Herschell, 2010). Similar outcomes have been found for maltreated children and those who have experienced sexual abuse or neglect (e.g., Timmer, Urquiza, & Zebell, 2006; Urquiza & Blacker, 2011). Further, PCIT has also been successfully adapted to treat children with comorbid internalizing symptoms, particularly anxiety, trauma symptoms, and depression (e.g., Carpenter et al., 2014; McNeil & Hembree-Kigin, 2010). With regard to caregiver improvements, studies have suggested that PCIT coaching may serve as an opportunity to provide emotion regulation skills to parents and address symptoms of psychopathology directly (e.g., Luby, Lenze, & Tillman, 2012; Maliken & Katz, 2013). Some studies suggest that PCIT may be effective for parents with histories of maltreatment, substance abuse, and domestic violence (e.g., Chaffin et al., 2004; Maliken & Katz, 2013).

Several defining features of PCIT set it apart from some other BPT programs. First, PCIT employs the bug-in-the-ear approach in which a caregiver wears a bluetooth device that connects to the therapist's microphone. Live coaching during the session allows caregivers to practice in the moment and seamlessly improve upon new skills at a rapid pace. Second, as its name implies, PCIT strongly emphasizes the caregiver–child relationship, teaching caregivers to employ principles of play therapy and attachment theory (Eyberg, 1988; Reitman & McMahon, 2013). Play therapy taps into the natural setting of play, allowing children to experience growth and express themselves in a positive, self-directed environment (Axline, 1947). This relational focus draws from attachment theories with the goal of creating a balance of warmth and consistent control in the caregiver–child relationship (Ainsworth, 1963; Baumrind, 1978; Bowlby, 1969). Third, PCIT models a parallel process between therapist and caregiver as is desired between caregiver and child. For example, therapists model the use of positive reinforcement, PRIDE skills, and selective attention while coaching caregivers. This modeling encourages a positive relationship between therapist and caregiver and demonstrates the effectiveness of specific behavioral principles. Fourth, PCIT uses a data-based, mastery-focused progression of treatment, ensuring that caregivers demonstrate adequate skill acquisition in the relationship-building phase of CDI before embarking on the discipline phase of PDI and meet mastery criteria for all skills before treatment graduation. In fact, PCIT requires a high rate of caregiver skill demonstration, capitalizing on the idea of "over-practice," that intense frequency of skill use in practice will translate into spontaneous, habitual use of positive skills in everyday life (McNeil & Hembree-Kigin, 2010). In addition to skill-based mastery criteria, PCIT protocol requires that caregiver report of child behavior intensity be within normal limits (i.e., within one-half of one standard deviation from the mean) on the Eyberg Child Behavior Inventory (Eyberg & Funderburk, 2011). These data-based requirements provide clear decision-making criteria for therapists, create measurable goals for families, and allow both families and therapists to understand change in skills and behavior over time.

As previously mentioned, PCIT has a core behavioral emphasis, which lends itself well to treating children with DBDs effectively and improving relations between youth and their caregivers. In fact, a meta-analysis of early interventions supports the idea that behaviorally-focused, short-term treatments most effectively improve sensitive caregiving and secure caregiver–child relationships (Bakermans-Kranenburg, van IJzendoorn, & Juffer, 2003). Additional comparisons among PCIT and other BPT approaches are highlighted in Table 9.2.

Table 9.2 **Component comparison of BPT models**

	Behavioral parent training model				
	PCIT	**HNC**	**IY**	**PPP**	**PMT-O**
Components associated with large effect sizes (Kaminski et al., 2008)					
Time-out	X	X	X	X	X
Increasing positive interactions	X	X	X	X	X
Emotional communication	X	X	X	X	X
In-session practice with child	X	X		X[a]	
Common components (Garland et al., 2008)					
Therapeutic content					
Principles of positive reinforcement	X	X	X	X	X
Principles of effective limit-setting/ punishment	X	X	X	X	X
Parent–child relationship building	X	X	X	X	X
Problem-solving skills			X	X	X
Anger management methods					
Affect education			X	X	X
Anticipating/training for setbacks	X		X	X	X
Treatment techniques					
Delivering positive reinforcement	X	X	X	X	X
Delivering punishment/limit-setting	X	X	X	X	X
Psychoeducation/didactics	X	X	X	X	X
Assigning and reviewing homework	X	X	X	X	X
Role-playing/behavioral rehearsal	X	X	X	X	X
Modeling	X	X	X	X	X
Providing materials	X	X	X	X	X
Reviewing goals and progress	X	X	X	X	X
Working alliance					
Consensual goal setting				X	X
Building rapport/affective bond	X	X	X	X	X
Treatment parameters					
At least 12 sessions	X	X	X	X[b]	
Approximately 1hour sessions	X	X		X[b]	X
Meet at least once weekly	X	X	X	X[b]	X
Both child and parent participate	X	X	X	X[a]	X
Other defining features					
Live coaching	X	X			
Feedback	X	X	X	X	X
Group format option		X		X	X
Mastery criteria	X	X	X		

[a]In Level 5.
[b]In Levels 4 and 5.

The component comparison among BPT models in Table 9.2 is informed largely by two major reviews. In the first review, Kaminski et al. (2008) conducted a meta-analysis to investigate effective components of BPT programs. PCIT involves three of the four treatment components identified by this meta-analysis as being associated with large treatment effect sizes (Kaminski et al., 2008). In the second review, Garland, Hawley, Brookman-Frazee, and Hurlburt (2008) reviewed eight evidence-based treatments for childhood DBDs, including three of the BPT programs highlighted in this chapter (IY, PMT-O, and PCIT) to identify common treatment elements. PCIT includes 20 of the 25 common elements identified in this study (Garland et al., 2008). This table illustrates the range of effective therapeutic components of evidence-based treatments for DBDs in children and demonstrates the utility of PCIT and other BPT programs in addressing these domains.

Future directions

Based on the discussion presented in this chapter, one can gather that there are overlapping common elements of the evidence-based treatments for DBDs in children. To capitalize on these elements, researchers have proposed a distillation and matching model as a feasible way to derive profiles of common elements of EBPPs (Chorpita, Daleiden, & Weisz, 2005). Based on the model, these profiles could then be used to match treatment facets and approaches to individual clients based on demographic and other contextual factors (Chorpita et al., 2005). In the future, it would be helpful for BPT programs to incorporate their evidence-based components on a more individualized basis to maximize effectiveness.

Garland et al. (2008) also advocated for attention to, discussion of, and teaching of EBPP common elements in both research and clinical contexts. In the research context, these elements may directly impact quality improvement studies and other types of research designed to describe and/or improve clinical practice. Additionally, this focus would influence EBPP implementation research (Garland et al., 2008). In the context of clinical practice, acknowledgment, discussion, and training around these core elements could improve preparedness of clinicians and implementation efforts at the clinician and administrative levels (Garland et al., 2008). More specifically, training in these elements could advance individual clinicians' competencies and make evidence-based treatments more accessible to clients (Garland et al., 2008). Despite these benefits, Garland et al. (2008) point out challenges in implementing a common elements approach which are similar to challenges faced in other implementation efforts (e.g., obtaining buy-in from all agency levels). Additional potential problems include diluted treatment effects through combining multiple approaches, the possibility of training aspects of treatments that are not as clinically important or essential to treatment outcomes, and the idea that small-scale implementation alone of this common elements approach may result in little-to-no improvements (Garland et al., 2008). Nevertheless, recent preliminary evidence from Hawaii appears positive, suggesting that implementation of this type of common elements approach may result in improved care (Daleiden et al., 2006; Garland et al., 2008).

Finally, an additional concern of the distillation and matching model is the large amount of clinical data required to improve accuracy (Chorpita et al., 2005). To be as precise as possible in matching individual clients with profiles of evidence-based interventions, comprehensive evaluation of each treatment method (e.g., behavioral parent training, cognitive behavioral therapy), patient characteristic (e.g., age, race/ethnicity, gender), and treatment component (e.g., reward/reinforcement system, behavioral contingencies) included in the model is needed. In other words, each variable would not only need to be thoroughly investigated on its own, as a predictor of treatment outcome, but would also need to be studied for mediating, moderating, and interaction effects with all other variables included in the model (e.g., a Spanish-speaking family × 10-year old male × ADHD × behavioral parent training). As such, the model is reliant on the state of the current literature and information known about each of the variables or treatment factors included in the model. Despite this overreliance, the distillation and matching model approach has potential to grow and improve over time in the domains of training, research, and clinical practice.

Limitations

PCIT and the other behavioral treatments described in this chapter are constrained by several factors. First, although a strong evidence base supports these therapies, their dissemination and implementation in community settings have proven challenging (Lieneman, Brabson, Highlander, Wallace, & McNeil, 2017). Several research groups have targeted these issues to delineate effective strategies for improvement (Beveridge et al., 2015; Herschell et al., 2015; Timmer et al., 2016). Collaboration among researchers, community stakeholders, and consumers is key to these efforts (Herschell et al., 2015). Barriers to successful implementation efforts often include trainee attrition, clinician turnover, lack of consumer engagement, and low administrative commitment (Beveridge et al., 2015; Timmer et al., 2016). As described earlier in the chapter, Triple P avoids many of these challenges through its population-based approaches, employing agents such as the media and primary healthcare workers. It is hoped that researchers and community stakeholders will continue to work to improve dissemination and implementation of all efficacious treatments described in this chapter.

Another major limitation of the effective behavioral treatment of DBDs in young children is the rate of client attrition, which has been estimated to fall between 18% and 35% in a meta-analysis of PCIT and Triple P (Thomas & Zimmer-Gembeck, 2007). A host of demographic and environmental variables are associated with increased risk for attrition in PCIT, such as low socioeconomic status, younger caregiver age, and high levels of parental stress (Lanier et al., 2011; Werba, Eyberg, Boggs, & Algina, 2006). These risk factors may represent what have been conceptualized as barriers to treatment participation, including limited transportation, childcare resources, and scheduling flexibility (Kazdin, Holland, Crowley, &

Breton, 1997). To reduce attrition in PCIT, researchers have incorporated such strategies as home-based treatment (Beveridge et al., 2015; Ware, McNeil, Masse, & Stevens, 2008), motivational enhancement (Chaffin et al., 2009; Webb, Thomas, McGregor, Avdagic, & Zimmer-Gembeck, 2017), internet-based services (Comer et al., 2017), and incentives (Quetsch, Girard, McNeil, & Herschell, 2015). In summary, the effectiveness of PCIT and other BPT programs hinges upon the ability of the behavioral healthcare system to reach families in need, and more work in this area is needed.

Conclusion

Drawing upon theories of operant conditioning and social learning, behavioral approaches to the treatment of DBDs in young children have demonstrated great success (Dretzke et al., 2009). Evidence-based BPT programs in particular are dominant in this arena, with many weaving together early influences of Hanf's two-stage model and Patterson's coercive process. The five well-supported BPT models described in this chapter, PCIT, HNC, Triple P, IY, and PMT-O, harness the power of the family environment to create change in the caregiver–child relationship. PCIT, in particular, employs an innovative use of technology, principles of play therapy and attachment theory, parallel therapeutic processes, the idea of over-practice, and a data-focused, mastery-based treatment progression to achieve its impressive effects at reducing disruptive behavior and improving the caregiver–child relationship. Continued study, particularly in the areas of dissemination and implementation, a common elements approach, and client attrition is needed to ensure that these effective treatments are available to the children and families who need them most.

References

Abrahamse, M. E., Junger, M., Chavannes, E. L., Coelman, F. G., Boer, F., & Lindauer, R. L. (2012). Parent–child interaction therapy for preschool children with disruptive behaviour problems in the Netherlands. *Child and Adolescent Psychiatry and Mental Health*, 6. Available from https://doi.org/10.1186/1753-2000-6-24.

Ainsworth, M. D. S. (1963). The development of infant-mother interaction among the Ganda. In B. M. Foss (Ed.), *Determinants of infant behavior* (pp. 67–104). New York: Wiley.

American Psychiatric Association. (2013). *Diagnostic and statistical manual of mental disorders* (5th ed). Arlington, VA: American Psychiatric Publishing.

American Psychological Association, Presidential Task Force on Evidence-Based Practice. (2005). *Report of the 2005 presidential task force on evidence-based practice*. Washington, DC. Retrieved from https://www.apa.org/practice/resources/evidence/evidence-based-report.pdf

Au, A., Lau, K., Wong, A. H., Lam, C., Leung, C., Lau, J., & Lee, Y. K. (2014). The efficacy of a group Triple P (positive parenting program) for Chinese parents with a child diagnosed with ADHD in Hong Kong: a pilot randomised controlled study. *Australian Psychologist, 49*(3), 151–162. Available from https://doi.org/10.1111/ap.12053.

Axline, V. M. (1947). *Play therapy; the inner dynamics of childhood.* Oxford, England: Houghton Mifflin.

Bagner, D. M., & Eyberg, S. M. (2007). Parent–child interaction therapy for disruptive behavior in children with mental retardation: a randomized controlled trial. *Journal of Clinical Child and Adolescent Psychology, 36*(3), 418–429. Available from https://doi.org/10.1080/15374410701448448.

Bakermans-Kranenburg, M. J., van IJzendoorn, M. H., & Juffer, F. (2003). Less is more: meta-analyses of sensitivity and attachment interventions in early childhood. *Psychological Bulletin, 129*(2), 195–215. Available from https://doi.org/10.1037/0033-2909.129.2.195.

Bandura, A., & Walters, R. (1963). *Social learning and personality development.* New York: Holt Rinehart and Winston.

Barkley, R. A. (2013). *Defiant children: a clinician's manual for assessment and parent training* (3rd ed.). New York, NY, US: Guilford Press.

Batzer, S., Berg, T., Godinet, M. T., & Stotzer, R. L. (2015). Efficacy or chaos? Parent–child interaction therapy in maltreating populations: a review of research. *Trauma, Violence, & Abuse.* Available from https://doi.org/10.1177/1524838015620819.

Baumrind, D. (1978). Parental disciplinary patterns and social competence in children. *Youth and Society, 9,* 238–276.

Beauchaine, T. P., Webster-Stratton, C., & Reid, M. J. (2005). Mediators, moderators, and predictors of 1-year outcomes among children treated for early-onset conduct problems: a latent growth curve analysis. *Journal of Consulting and Clinical Psychology, 73*(3), 371. Available from https://doi.org/10.1037/0022-006X.73.3.371.

Beveridge, R. M., Fowles, T. R., Masse, J. J., McGoron, L., Smith, M. A., Parrish, B. P., ... Widdoes, N. (2015). State-wide dissemination and implementation of parent–child interaction therapy (PCIT): Application of theory. *Children and Youth Services Review, 48,* 38–48. Available from https://doi.org/10.1016/j.childyouth.2014.11.013.

Blueprints for Healthy Youth Development (2012-2017). *Blueprints programs.* Retrieved from http://www.blueprintsprograms.com

Bowlby, J. (1969). *Attachment and loss: Vol. 1. Attachment.* New York, NY: Basic Books.

Carpenter, A. L., Puliafico, A. C., Kurtz, S. M., Pincus, D. B., & Comer, J. S. (2014). Extending parent–child interaction therapy for early childhood internalizing problems: new advances for an overlooked population. *Clinical Child and Family Psychology Review, 17*(4), 340–356. Available from https://doi.org/10.1007/s10567-014-0172-4.

Chaffin, M., Silovsky, J. F., Funderburk, B., Valle, L. A., Brestan, E. V., Balachova, T., ... Bonner, B. L. (2004). Parent-child interaction therapy with physically abusive parents: efficacy for reducing future abuse reports. *Journal of Consulting and Clinical Psychology, 72*(3), 500–510. Available from https://doi.org/10.1037/0022-006X.72.3.500.

Chaffin, M., Valle, L. A., Funderburk, B., Gurwitch, R., Silovsky, J., Bard, D., ... Kees, M. (2009). A motivational intervention can improve retention in PCIT for low-motivation child welfare clients. *Child Maltreatment, 14*(4), 356–368. Available from https://doi.org/10.1177/1077559509332263.

Chambless, D. L., & Hollon, S. D. (1998). Defining empirically supported therapies. *Journal of Consulting and Clinical Psychology, 66*(1), 7–18. Available from https://doi.org/10.1037/0022-006X.66.1.7.

Chengappa, K., McNeil, C.B., Norman, M., Quetsch, L.B., & Travers, R. (in press). Efficacy of parent-child interaction therapy with parents with intellectual disability. *Child and Family Behavior Therapy*.

Chorpita, B. F., Daleiden, E. L., & Weisz, J. R. (2005). Identifying and selecting the common elements of evidence based interventions: a distillation and matching model. *Mental Health Services Research*, *7*(1), 5–20. Available from https://doi.org/10.1007/s11020-005-1962-6.

Chronis-Tuscano, A., Lewis-Morrarty, E., Woods, K. E., O'Brien, K. A., Mazursky-Horowitz, H., & Thomas, S. R. (2016). Parent–child interaction therapy with emotion coaching for preschoolers with attention-deficit/hyperactivity disorder. *Cognitive and Behavioral Practice*, *23*(1), 62–78. Available from https://doi.org/10.1016/j.cbpra.2014.11.001.

Comer, J. S., Furr, J. M., Miguel, E. M., Cooper-Vince, C. E., Carpenter, A. L., Elkins, R. M., . . . Chase, R. (2017). Remotely delivering real-time parent training to the home: an initial randomized trial of internet-delivered parent–child interaction therapy (I-PCIT). *Journal of Consulting and Clinical Psychology*. Available from https://doi.org/10.1037/ccp0000230.

Conduct Problems Prevention Research Group. (2002). Evaluation of the first three years of the fast track prevention trail with children at high risk for adolescent conduct problems. *Journal of Abnormal Child Psychology*, *30*, 19–35.

Conduct Problems Prevention Research Group. (2007). Fast Track randomized controlled trial to prevent externalizing psychiatric disorders: findings from grades 3 to 9. *Journal of the American Academy of Child and Adolescent Psychiatry*, *46*(10), 1250–1262.

Conduct Problems Prevention Research Group. (2010). The effects of a multiyear universal social-emotional learning program: the role of student and school characteristics. *Journal of Consulting and Clinical Psychology*, *78*(2), 156–168. Available from https://doi.org/10.1037/a0018607.

Conners, N. A., Edwards, M. C., & Grant, A. S. (2007). An evaluation of a parenting class curriculum for parents of young children: parenting the strong-willed child. *Journal of Child and Family Studies*, *16*, 321–330. Available from https://doi.org/10.1007/s10826-006-9088-z.

Cunningham, C. E., Bremner, R., & Boyle, M. (1995). Large group community-based parenting programs for families of preschoolers at risk for disruptive behaviour disorders: utilization, cost effectiveness, and outcome. *Journal of Child Psychology & Psychiatry*, *36*, 1141–1159. Available from https://doi.org/10.1111/j.1469-7610.1995.tb01362.x.

Daleiden, E. L., Chorpita, B. F., Donkervoet, C., Arensdorf, A. M., Brogan, M., & Hamilton, J. D. (2006). Getting better at getting them better: health outcomes and evidence-based practice within a system of care. *Journal of the American Academy of Child & Adolescent Psychiatry*, *45*(6), 749–756. Available from https://doi.org/10.1097/01.chi.0000215154.07142.63.

Danko, C. M., Garbacz, L. L., & Budd, K. S. (2015). Outcomes of parent-child interaction therapy in an urban community clinic: a comparison of treatment completers and dropouts. *Children and Youth Services Review*, *60*, 42–51. Available from https://doi.org/10.1016/j.childyouth.2015.11.007.

de Graaf, I., Speetjens, P., Smit, F., de Wolff, M., & Tavecchio, L. (2008). Effectiveness of the Triple P Positive Parenting Program on parenting: a meta-analysis. Family relations: an interdisciplinary. *Journal of Applied Family Studies*, *57*(5), 553–566. Available from https://doi.org/10.1111/j.1741-3729.2008.00522.x.

Dishion, T., Forgatch, M., Chamberlain, P., & Pelham, W. E., III (2016). The Oregon model of behavior family therapy: from intervention design to promoting large-scale system change. *Behavior Therapy*, *47*, 812–837.

Dishion, T. J., & Patterson, G. R. (2006). The development and ecology of antisocial behavior. In D. Cicchetti, & D. J. Cohen (Eds.), *Developmental psychopathology: Vol 3 Risk, disorder, and adaptation* (pp. 503–541). New York, NY: Wiley.

Dishion, T. J., Patterson, G. R., & Kavanagh, K. (1992). An experimental test of the coercion model: linking theory, measurement, and intervention. In J. McCord, & R. Tremblay (Eds.), *Preventing antisocial behavior: interventions from birth through adolescence* (pp. 253–282). New York, NY: Guilford.

Dretzke, J., Davenport, C., Frew, E., Barlow, J., Stewart-Brown, S., Bayliss, S., . . . Hyde, C. (2009). The clinical effectiveness of different parenting programmes for children with conduct problems: a systematic review of randomised controlled trials. *Child and Adolescent Psychiatry and Mental Health*, *3*, 7. Available from https://doi.org/10.1186/1753-2000-3-7.

Eyberg, S. (1988). Parent-child interaction therapy: integration of traditional and behavioral concerns. *Child & Family Behavior Therapy*, *10*(1), 33–46. Available from https://doi.org/10.1300/J019v10n01_04.

Eyberg, S. M., & Funderburk, B. (2011). *Parent–child interaction therapy protocol.* Gainesville, FL: PCIT International.

Eyberg, S. M., Nelson, M. M., & Boggs, S. R. (2008). Evidence-based psychosocial treatments for children and adolescents with disruptive behavior. *Journal of Clinical Child & Adolescent Psychology*, *37*(1), 215–237. Available from https://doi.org/10.1080/15374410701820117.

Eyberg, S. M., & Pincus, D. (1999). *Eyberg child behavior inventory and sutter-eyberg student behavior inventory-revised: professional manual.* Odessa, FL: Psychological Assessment Resources.

Forehand, R., & Long, N. (2002). *Parenting the strong-willed child: the clinically-proven five-week program for parents of two- to six-year olds* (2nd ed.). New York: McGraw-Hill.

Forgatch, M. S., & DeGarmo, D. S. (2007). Accelerating recovery from poverty: prevention effects for recently separated mothers. *Journal of Early and Intensive Behavior Intervention*, *4*(4), 681–702. Available from https://doi.org/10.1037/h0100400.

Forgatch, M. S., & Patterson, G. R. (2010). Parent management training - oregon model: an intervention for antisocial behavior in children and adolescents. In J. R. Weisz, & A. E. Kazdin (Eds.), *Evidence-based psychotherapies for children and adolescents* (pp. 159–178). New York, NY: Guilford Press.

Garland, A. F., Hawley, K. M., Brookman-Frazee, L., & Hurlburt, M. S. (2008). Identifying common elements of evidence-based psychosocial treatments for children's disruptive behavior problems. *Journal of the American Academy of Child & Adolescent Psychiatry*, *47*(5), 505–514. Available from https://doi.org/10.1097/CHI.0b013e31816765c2.

Ginn, N. C., Clionsky, L. N., Eyberg, S. M., Warner-Metzger, C., & Abner, J. P. (2017). Child-directed interaction training for young children with autism spectrum disorders: parent and child outcomes. *Journal of Clinical Child & Adolescent Psychology*, *46*(1), 101–109. Available from https://doi.org/10.1080/15374416.2015.1015135.

Gross, D., Fogg, L., Webster-Stratton, C., & Grady, J. (1999). *Parent training with low-income multiethnic parents of toddlers.* Paper presented at the Society for Research in Child Development, Albuquerque, New Mexico.

Heinrichs, N., Kliem, S., & Hahlweg, K. (2014). Four-year follow-up of a randomized controlled trial of Triple P group for parent and child outcomes. *Prevention Science, 15*(2), 233–245. Available from https://doi.org/10.1007/s11121-012-0358-2.

Herschell, A., Kolko, D., Scudder, A., Taber-Thomas, S., Schaffner, K., Hiegel, S., ... Mrozowski, S. (2015). Protocol for a statewide randomized controlled trial to compare three training models for implementing an evidence-based treatment. *Implementation Science, 10*(1), 133.

Kaminski, J. W., Valle, L. A., Filene, J. H., & Boyle, C. L. (2008). A meta-analytic review of components associated with parent training program effectiveness. *Journal of Abnormal Child Psychology, 36*(4), 567–589. Available from https://doi.org/10.1007/s10802-007-9201-9.

Kazdin, A. E., Holland, L., Crowley, M., & Breton, S. (1997). Barriers to treatment participation scale: evaluation and validation in the context of child outpatient treatment. *Child Psychology & Psychiatry & Allied Disciplines, 38*(8), 1051–1062. Available from https://doi.org/10.1111/j.1469-7610.1997.tb01621.x.

Kohlhoff, J., & Morgan, S. (2014). Parent-child interaction therapy for toddlers: a pilot study. *Child & Family Behavior Therapy, 36*(2), 121–139. Available from https://doi.org/10.1080/07317107.2014.910733.

Kazdin, A. E. (2005). *Parent management training: treatment for oppositional, aggressive, and antisocial behavior in children and adolescents.* New York, NY, US: Oxford University Press.

Lanier, P., Kohl, P. L., Benz, J., Swinger, D., & Drake, B. (2014). Preventing maltreatment with a community-based implementation of parent–child interaction therapy. *Journal of Child and Family Studies, 23*(2), 449–460. Available from https://doi.org/10.1007/s10826-012-9708-8.

Lanier, P., Kohl, P. L., Benz, J., Swinger, D., Moussette, P., & Drake, B. (2011). Parent–child interaction therapy in a community setting: examining outcomes, attrition, and treatment setting. *Research on Social Work Practice, 21*(6), 689–698. Available from https://doi.org/10.1177/1049731511406551.

Leung, C., Tsang, S., Heung, K., & Yiu, I. (2009). Effectiveness of parent—child interaction therapy (PCIT) among Chinese families. *Research On Social Work Practice, 19*(3), 304–313. Available from https://doi.org/10.1177/1049731508321713.

Lieneman, C., Brabson, L., Highlander, A., Wallace, N., & McNeil, C. (2017). Parent-child interaction therapy: current perspectives. *Psychology Research and Behavior Management, 10*, 1–18.

Luby, J., Lenze, S., & Tillman, R. (2012). A novel early intervention for preschool depression: findings from a pilot randomized controlled trial. *Journal of Child Psychology and Psychiatry, 53*(3), 313–322. Available from https://doi.org/10.1111/j.1469-7610.2011.02483.x.

MacKenzie, E. P. (2007). Improving treatment outcome for oppositional defiant disorder in young children. *Journal of Early and Intensive Behavior Intervention, 4*(2), 500–510. Available from https://doi.org/10.1037/h0100387.

Maliken, A. C., & Katz, L. F. (2013). Exploring the impact of parental psychopathology and emotion regulation on evidence-based parenting interventions: a transdiagnostic approach to improving treatment effectiveness. *Clinical Child and Family Psychology Review, 16*(2), 173–186. Available from https://doi.org/10.1007/s10567-013-0132-4.

Masse, J. (2010). Autism spectrum disorders. In C. B. McNeil, & T. L. Hembree-Kigin (Eds.), *Parent-child interaction therapy* (2nd ed.). New York: Springer.

Masse, J. J., McNeil, C. B., Wagner, S., & Quetsch, L. B. (2016). Examining the efficacy of parent–child interaction therapy with children on the autism spectrum. *Journal of Child and Family Studies*, *25*(8), 2508–2525.

Masse, J. J., McNeil, C. B., Wagner, S. M., & Chorney, D. B. (2007). Parent-child interaction therapy and high functioning autism: a conceptual overview. *Journal of Early and Intensive Behavior Intervention*, *4*(4), 714–735. Available from https://doi.org/10.1037/h0100402.

Matos, M., Bauermeister, J. J., & Bernal, G. (2009). Parent-child interaction therapy for Puerto Rican preschool children with ADHD and behavior problems: a pilot efficacy study. *Family Process*, *48*(2), 232–252. Available from https://doi.org/10.1111/j.1545-5300.2009.01279.x.

Matsumoto, Y., Sofronoff, K., & Sanders, M. R. (2010). Investigation of the effectiveness and social validity of the Triple P Positive Parenting Program in Japanese society. *Journal of Family Psychology*, *24*(1), 87–91. Available from https://doi.org/10.1037/a0018181.

McMahon, R. J., & Forehand, R. L. (2003). *Helping the noncompliant child: family-based treatment for oppositional behavior* (2nd ed.). New York: Guilford Press.

McMahon, R. J., Long, N., & Forehand, R. L. (2010). Parent training for the treatment of oppositional behavior in young children: helping the noncompliant child. In R. C. Murrihy, A. D. Kidman, & T. H. Ollendick (Eds.), *Clinical handbook of assessing and treating conduct problems in youth* (pp. 163–191). New York: Springer.

McNeil, C. B., & Hembree-Kigin, T. L. (2010). *Parent-child interaction therapy*. New York, NY: Springer.

Nock, M. K., Kazdin, A. E., Hiripi, E., & Kessler, R. C. (2007). Lifetime prevalence, correlates, and persistence of oppositional defiant disorder: results from the National Comorbidity Survey Replication. *Journal of Child Psychology And Psychiatry*, *48*(7), 703–713. Available from https://doi.org/10.1111/j.1469-7610.2007.01733.x.

Nowak, C., & Heinrichs, N. (2008). A comprehensive meta-analysis of Triple P-Positive Parenting Program using hierarchical linear modeling: effectiveness and moderating variables. *Clinical Child And Family Psychology Review*, *11*(3), 114–144. Available from https://doi.org/10.1007/s10567-008-0033-0.

Patterson, G. R. (1982). *A social learning approach: Vol. 3: coercive family process*. Eugene, OR: Castalia.

Patterson, G. R., Chamberlain, P., & Reid, J. B. (1982). A comparative evaluation of a parent-training program. *Behavior Therapy*, *13*, 638–650. Available from https://doi.org/10.1016/s0005-7894(82)80021-x.

Patterson, G. R., Dishion, T. J., & Bank, L. (1984). Family interaction: a process model of deviancy training. *Aggressive Behavior*, *10*(3), 253–267. https://doi.org/10.1002/1098-2337(1984)10:3 < 253::AID-AB2480100309 > 3.0.CO;2-2.

Patterson, G. R., Forgatch, M. S., & DeGarmo, D. S. (2010). Cascading effects following intervention. *Development & Psychopathology*, 22, 949–970. Available from https://doi.org/10.1017/S0954579410000568.

Patterson, G. R., & Reid, J. B. (1975). *Families with aggressive children*. Eugene, OR: Castalia Pub.

Quetsch, L.B., Girard, E., McNeil, C.B., & Herschell, A.D. (2015, October). *Treatment incentives for parent-child interaction therapy*. Poster presented at the 2015 Parent-Child Interaction Therapy Convention, Pittsburgh, PA.

Reid, M. J., Webster-Stratton, C., & Hammond, M. (2003). Follow-up of children who received the incredible years intervention for oppositional-defiant disorder: maintenance and prediction of 2-year outcome. *Behavior Therapy*, *34*, 471–491.

Reitman, D., & McMahon, R. J. (2013). Constance 'Connie' Hanf (1917–2002): The mentor and the model. *Cognitive and Behavioral Practice*, *20*(1), 106–116. Available from https://doi.org/10.1016/j.cbpra.2012.02.005.

Sanders, M. R. (1999). Triple P-Positive Parenting Program: towards an empirically validated multilevel parenting and family support strategy for the prevention of behavior and emotional problems in children. *Clinical Child and Family Psychology Review*, *2*(2), 71–90. Available from https://doi.org/10.1023/A:1021843613840.

Sanders, M. R., & Markie-Dadds, C. (1996). Triple P: a multilevel family intervention program for children with disruptive behaviour disorders. In P. Cotton, H. Jackson, P. Cotton, & H. Jackson (Eds.), *Early intervention & prevention in mental health* (pp. 59–85). Carlton South VIC, Australia: Australian Psychological Society.

Sanders, M. R., Markie-Dadds, C., & Turner, K. M. T. (2003). Theoretical, scientific and clinical foundations of the Triple P-Positive Parenting Program: a population approach to the promotion of parenting competence. *Parenting Research and Practice Monograph*, *1*, 1–21.

Self-Brown, S., Valente, J. R., Wild, R. C., Whitaker, D. J., Galanter, R., Dorsey, S., & Stanley, J. (2012). Utilizing benchmarking to study the effectiveness of parent-child interaction therapy implemented in a community setting. *Journal of Child And Family Studies*, *21*(6), 1041–1049. Available from https://doi.org/10.1007/s10826-012-9566-4.

Skinner, B. F. (1938). *The behavior of organisms: an experimental analysis*. Oxford, England: Appleton-Century.

Slough, N. M., & McMahon, R. J. (2008). Preventing serious conduct problems in school-age youth: the Fast Track program. *Cognitive and Behavioral Practice*, *15*, 3–17.

Society of Clinical Child and Adolescent Psychology. (2015). *Effective child therapy: evidence-based mental health treatment for children and adolescents*. Retrieved from http://effectivechildtherapy.org/

Southam-Gerow, M. A., & Prinstein, M. J. (2014). Evidence base updates: the evolution of the evaluation of psychological treatments for children and adolescents. *Journal of Clinical Child & Adolescent Psychology*, *43*(1), 1–6. Available from https://doi.org/10.1080/15374416.2013.855128.

Stokes, J. O., Scudder, A., Costello, A. H., & McNeil, C. B. (2017). Parent-child interaction therapy with an eight-year-old child: a case study. *Evidence-based practice in child and adolescent mental health*, *2*(1), 1–11.

Substance Abuse and Mental Health Services Administration (SAMHSA) (2016, January 7). *National registry of evidence-based programs and practices (NREPP)*. Retrieved from https://www.samhsa.gov/nrepp.

Sumargi, A., Sofronoff, K., & Morawska, A. (2015). A randomized-controlled trial of the Triple P-Positive Parenting Program seminar series with Indonesian parents. *Child Psychiatry and Human Development*, *46*(5), 749–761. Available from https://doi.org/10.1007/s10578-014-0517-8.

The Incredible Years. (2013). *The incredible years: parents, teachers, and children training series*. Retrieved from http://www.incredibleyears.com/

Thomas, R., & Zimmer-Gembeck, M. J. (2007). Behavioral outcomes of parent-child interaction therapy and Triple P-Positive Parenting Program: a review and meta-analysis. *Journal of Abnormal Child Psychology*, *35*(3), 475–495. Available from https://doi.org/10.1007/s10802-007-9104-9.

Thomas, R., & Zimmer-Gembeck, M. J. (2011). Accumulating evidence for parent–child interaction therapy in the prevention of child maltreatment. *Child Development*, *82*(1), 177–192. Available from https://doi.org/10.1111/j.1467-8624.2010.01548.x.

Thomas, R., & Zimmer-Gembeck, M. J. (2012). Parent–child interaction therapy: an evidence-based treatment for child maltreatment. *Child Maltreatment*, *17*(3), 253–266. Available from https://doi.org/10.1177/1077559512459555.

Timmer, S. G., Urquiza, A. J., Boys, D. K., Forte, L. A., Quick-Abdullah, D., Chan, S., & Gould, W. (2016). Filling potholes on the implementation highway: evaluating the implementation of parent–child interaction therapy in Los Angeles County. *Child Abuse & Neglect*, *53*, 40–50. Available from https://doi.org/10.1016/j.chiabu.2015.11.011.

Timmer, S. G., Urquiza, A. J., & Zebell, N. (2006). Challenging foster caregiver–maltreated child relationships: the effectiveness of parent–child interaction therapy. *Children and Youth Services Review*, *28*(1), 1–19. Available from https://doi.org/10.1016/j.childyouth.2005.01.006.

Urquiza, A. J., & Blacker, D. (2011). Parent-child interaction therapy for sexually abused children. In P. Goodyear-Brown (Ed.), *Handbook of child sexual abuse: identification, assessment, and treatment*. Hoboken, NJ: John Wiley & Sons, Inc.

Wagner, S. M., & McNeil, C. B. (2008). Parent-child interaction therapy for ADHD: a conceptual overview and critical literature review. *Child & Family Behavior Therapy*, *30* (3), 231–256. Available from https://doi.org/10.1080/07317100802275546.

Ward, M. A., Theule, J., & Cheung, K. (2016). Parent–child interaction therapy for child disruptive behaviour disorders: a meta-analysis. *Child & Youth Care Forum*, *45*(5), 675–690. Available from https://doi.org/10.1007/s10566-016-9350-5.

Ware, L. M., McNeil, C. B., Masse, J., & Stevens, S. (2008). Efficacy of in-home Parent-Child Interaction Therapy. *Child & Family Behavior Therapy*, *30*(2), 99–126. http://doi.org/10.1080/07317100802060302.

Ware, L. M., & Herschell, A. D. (2010). Child physical abuse. In C. B. McNeil, & T. L. Hembree-Kigin (Eds.), *Parent-child interaction therapy* (2nd ed.). New York: Springer.

Webb, H. J., Thomas, R., McGregor, L., Avdagic, E., & Zimmer-Gembeck, M. J. (2017). An evaluation of parent-child interaction therapy with and without motivational enhancement to reduce attrition. *Journal of Clinical Child & Adolescent Psychology*, *46*(4), 537–550.

Webster-Stratton, C. (1994). Advancing videotape parent training: a comparison study. *Journal of Consulting and Clinical Psychology*, *62*, 583 593. Available from https://doi.org/10.1037/0022-006X.62.3.583.

Webster-Stratton, C., & Hammond, M. (1997). Treating children with early-onset conduct problems: a comparison of child and parent training interventions. *Journal of Consulting and Clinical Psychology*, *65*(1), 93–109. Available from https://doi.org/10.1037/0022-006X.65.1.93.

Webster-Stratton, C., & Reid, M. J. (2010). In J. R. Weisz, & A. E. Kazdin (Eds.), *Evidence-based psychotherapies for children and adolescents*. New York: Guilford Press.

Webster-Stratton, C., Reid, M. J., & Hammond, M. (2004). Treating children with early-onset conduct problems: intervention outcomes for parent, child, and teacher training. *Journal of Clinical Child and Adolescent Psychology*, *33*(1), 105–124. Available from https://doi.org/10.1207/S15374424JCCP3301_11.

Webster-Stratton, C., Reid, M. J., & Stoolmiller, M. (2008). Preventing conduct problems and improving school readiness: evaluation of the incredible years teacher and child training programs in high-risk schools. *Journal of Child Psychology and Psychiatry*, *49*(5), 471–488. Available from https://doi.org/10.1111/j.1469-7610.2007.01861.x.

Weisz, J. R., & Kazdin, A. E. (Eds.), (2010). *Evidence-based psychotherapies for children and adolescents*. New York: Guilford Press.

Werba, B. E., Eyberg, S. M., Boggs, S. R., & Algina, J. (2006). Predicting outcome in parent-child interaction therapy: success and attrition. *Behavior Modification*, *30*(5), 618–646. Available from https://doi.org/10.1177/0145445504272977.

Zlomke, K. R., Jeter, K., & Murphy, J. (2017). Open-trial pilot of parent-child interaction therapy for children with autism spectrum disorder. *Child & Family Behavior Therapy*, *39*(1), 1–18.

Further reading

Sanders, M. R., & Calam, R. (2012). Enhancing dissemination outcomes through a population-based approach to parenting intervention. In R. K. McHugh, D. H. Barlow, R. K. McHugh, & D. H. Barlow (Eds.), *Dissemination and implementation of evidence-based psychological interventions* (pp. 209–226). New York, NY, US: Oxford University Press.

Cognitive therapies: anger management

10

Caroline L. Boxmeyer, John E. Lochman, Francesca Kassing, Qshequilla P. Mitchell, and Devon Romero
The University of Alabama, Tuscaloosa, AL, United States

Introduction

Disruptive behavior disorders can be highly impairing to children and families and costly to society. They increase risk for a host of negative outcomes across the developmental cascade, including incarceration, unemployment, relationship problems, substance use, and the intergenerational transmission of violence (e.g., Broidy et al., 2003; Dodge, Greenberg, Malone, & Conduct Problems Prevention Research Group, 2008). Thus, the availability of effective prevention, early identification, and treatment strategies for disruptive behavior disorders is critically important.

This chapter describes cognitive therapy approaches to improve anger management in children with, or at risk for, disruptive behavior disorders. Empirically based components of cognitive therapies for correcting interpersonal perceptions and planning effective responses are explicated, using the Coping Power program as an exemplar treatment approach. Applied examples are provided to illustrate how to use treatments like Coping Power in practice. Other efficacious prevention and treatment programs that include cognitive components are also described and contrasted. Outcomes of these programs are summarized, as well as the generalizability of their effects. Finally, future directions in the development, testing, and dissemination of cognitive therapies to improve anger management in children with, or at risk for, disruptive behavior disorders are summarized.

Coping Power program for anger and aggression

Positive effects have been found for group interventions for youth with disruptive behavior problems in meta-analytic studies (e.g., Lipsey, 2006). Group formats have several advantages over individual formats, including the opportunity to use modeling, role-playing, group problem-solving, and reinforcement of children's behavior with peers to address children's difficulties with social competence. One group-based preventive intervention that has been shown to successfully reduce disruptive behavior and aggression among at-risk youth is the Coping Power program. Coping Power is a multicomponent program for preadolescent youth who are at

Developmental Pathways to Disruptive, Impulse-Control, and Conduct Disorders.
DOI: https://doi.org/10.1016/B978-0-12-811323-3.00010-9

risk for disruptive behavior disorders due to exhibiting elevated levels of aggressive behavior. A contextual social-cognitive model provides the framework for Coping Power's intervention objectives (Lochman, Wells, & Lenhart, 2008; Wells, Lochman, & Lenhart, 2008).

Coping Power consists of separate, complementary child and parent intervention components that are implemented concurrently over 16 to 18 months in a small group format. The child component (Lochman et al., 2008) consists of 34 sessions, is typically delivered to groups of five to seven children in 4th through 6th grade, and is an extension of the Anger Coping Program (Larson & Lochman, 2010). Early sessions focus on helping children identify meaningful long-term goals and to break up these goals into short-term, daily goals. Once identified, children's behavior goals are monitored throughout the program, and children receive feedback on their goals daily from teachers. The program then moves to focus on organizational and study skills, identifying cognitive, behavioral, and physiological signs of anger, and using different cognitive techniques to cope with anger and arousal. During the second half of the program, children work on perspective-taking, problem-solving, and consequence identification, as well as coping with peer pressure, entering pro-social peer groups, and cooperating with peers.

Child sessions are led by two leaders and typically last about 45 minutes. Coping Power was developed for school-based implementation, but can be delivered in a variety of settings (e.g., mental health clinics, residential programs). The program may also be modified to be delivered in an individual format and to children who are slightly older or younger than the intended age group. All sessions of the program are very structured and include a consistent format of opening activities, active teaching methods (e.g., discussions, games, role-plays), and closing activities. To supplement the group sessions, each child is seen individually every month.

The Coping Power parent component (Wells et al., 2008) consists of 16 group sessions that take place during the same time period as the child groups, but are conducted separately. Sessions are typically 60–90 minutes and are used to introduce strategies to foster positive family relationships and manage children's behavior. The parent component covers topics including: Developing and maintaining a positive parent-child relationship, managing the stress of parenting, rewarding appropriate child behaviors, ignoring minor disruptions, establishing age-appropriate rules and expectations, giving effective instructions, and applying effective consequences for negative child behaviors. Parents also learn about the skills taught in the child component and are encouraged to reinforce their children for using these new skills at home. Because school performance and behavior can be a particular source of conflict, parents also learn strategies for supporting their child's learning and collaborating with their child's teacher.

The Coping Power program has been chosen as an exemplar treatment approach for this chapter given its strong research support as an evidence-based preventive intervention for youth with aggressive behavior. Efficacy and effectiveness studies have demonstrated that group-administered Coping Power maintains youth's lower preadolescent rates of substance abuse and delinquency 1-year post-intervention compared to control group participants (Lochman & Wells, 2003, 2004). The intervention has also been shown to help prevent declines in language arts grades seen in control group participants 2-year post-intervention (Lochman et al., 2012). Long-term effects (i.e., 3-year post-intervention) have also been found on externalizing behaviors (e.g., Lochman et al., 2014; Lochman, Wells, Qu, & Chen, 2013).

Research has shown that including a brief universal prevention component (Lochman & Wells, 2003), involving a set of meetings on social-emotional learning issues related to Coping Power aims and offered to teachers and to all parents in a school, results in lower rates of self-reported substance use, lower teacher-rated aggression, higher perceived social competence, and greater teacher-rated behavioral improvement, compared to a control group (Lochman & Wells, 2002b). When examining 3-year outcomes, the universal intervention no longer had effects, but Coping Power maintained positive effects on youths' behavior 3 years after the intervention had been completed (Lochman et al., 2013).

Two randomized controlled trials (RCTs) have also examined outcomes associated with an abbreviated version of Coping Power that can be implemented in one school year (reduced to 24 child sessions and 10 parent sessions). This abbreviated version addresses all of the core objectives of the full Coping Power program, but has fewer activities addressing each objective. The abbreviated program has been shown to produce significant reductions in externalizing behavior for children who had a caregiver attend at least one parent session compared to control children (Lochman, Boxmeyer, Powell, Roth, & Windle, 2006). At a 3-year follow-up, Coping Power had more generalized long-term effects on reducing children's externalizing behavior problems in comparison to the control condition, regardless of parental attendance (Lochman et al., 2014). Research by an independent investigative team found that the abbreviated child component alone produced significant teacher-rated behavioral improvements in learning, study skills, school problems, behavioral symptoms, and social withdrawal compared to control children (Peterson, Hamilton, & Russell, 2009).

Research has also examined the Coping Power program in other, nonschool settings. For example, it has been adapted for use in juvenile correctional settings for girls (Goldstein et al., 2013, in press) and as part of a universal preventive intervention to reduce relational aggression in classrooms (Leff et al., 2010). Coping Power has also been adapted for use with clinical populations in international settings. For example, a version of Coping Power delivered to children with disruptive behavior disorders in a child outpatient unit in the Netherlands has been found to produce significant improvements in disruptiveness, reductions in overt aggression, and long-term reductions in marijuana and tobacco use (Van De Wiel et al., 2007; Zonnevylle-Bender, Matthys, van de Wiel, & Lochman, 2007). In addition to the clinic sample in the Netherlands described earlier, variants of Coping Power have been tested for children diagnosed with disruptive behavior disorders in Canada (Lochman et al., 2012), Italy (Muratori et al., 2017), and Puerto Rico (Cabiya et al., 2008) and as a preventive intervention for children in Pakistan (Mushtaq, Lochman, Tariq, & Sabih, 2016) and Italy (Muratori et al., 2015). In most cases, these international adaptations primarily involved translating the program to the relevant language, but the Pakistan adaptation required deeper cultural changes to the introductions to topics, typically by framing them within Islamic practices and stories.

Social information processing in aggressive youth

Coping Power and other cognitive therapies for anger management are based upon social information processing (SIP) models. Crick and Dodge (1994) proposed a framework for competent SIP in children, which was a modification of an earlier model (Dodge, 1986). According to this model, children approach social situations with biologically limited abilities, memories of their past social experiences, and a database of social schemas, rules, and knowledge (Crick & Dodge, 1994; Dodge, 1986). As social cue inputs are received, the child's behavioral response is a function of the way he or she processes this social information.

Children's social behavior is suggested to be a function of specific sequential mental steps of processing. Although Crick and Dodge (1994) propose six processing steps, it is noted that SIP is not posited to be a linear process, but rather each step may influence the others through a series of feedback loops (Crick & Dodge, 1994; Dodge, 1986).

The six processing steps include: (1) encoding of external and internal cues, (2) interpretation and mental representation of those cues, (3) selection of goals, (4) response access or construction, (5) response decision, and (6) behavioral enactment (Crick & Dodge, 1994). It is hypothesized that skillful processing at each step leads to competent performance within a social situation. In contrast, deficient or biased processing is assumed to lead to deviant social behavior (e.g., aggression; Dodge, 1986).

Step 1: encoding of external and internal cues

The first step of SIP is the encoding of specific external and internal cues. Encoding occurs when social cues in the environment are received from the child's sensory systems and are then perceived. Due to the vast amount of information present in the social environment at any given moment, it is hypothesized that children selectively attend to particular cues (Crick & Dodge, 1994). For competent performance, the child must not only perform the encoding process in real time, but the child must also perform skillfully, accurately, and free of bias. Examples of difficulties at this step in children with aggressive behavior include either hypervigilance to hostile cues or neglecting relevant nonhostile cues (Dodge, Bates, & Pettit, 1990).

Step 2: interpretation of social cues

Once social cues have been encoded, the child then needs to give meaning to these cues through mental representation and interpretation (Crick & Dodge, 1994). In this process, the child must integrate the cue with his or her memory, looking for an understanding of the meaning of the cue. In the instance, when a child is unable to assign meaning to a particular cue (i.e., lack of information), a feedback loop to step one may be enacted for additional information gathering (Dodge, 1986). Children with aggressive behavior have been found to process social information in distinctive ways, such as by exhibiting hostile attribution biases in response to ambiguous provocation situations (Crick & Dodge, 1996). For example, a child who has a history of being victimized by peers is likely to attribute an act such as being bumped by a peer in the hallway to the peer's hostile intentions rather than to accidental circumstances.

Step 3: selection of goals

After the child has encoded and interpreted a stimulus situation, the child engages in a goal selection process. This process reveals the child's desired affective or behavioral outcomes for the social situation (Crick & Dodge, 1994). Difficulties at this step in children with aggressive behavior include a tendency to select instrumental (e.g., winning a game or being socially dominant) rather than interpersonal (e.g., developing or maintaining a friendship) goals.

Step 4: response access or construction

Once the child has encoded and interpreted information in a meaningful way, he or she searches long-term memory for possible behavioral responses for the situation that align with the selected goal (Crick & Dodge, 1994; Dodge, 1986). Difficulties at this step in children with aggressive behavior include generating fewer behavioral responses overall, as well as generating a higher proportion of aggressive responses to problems rather than other responses such as bargaining, compromise, verbal assertion, direct action, or help seeking.

Step 5: response decision

In this step, the child selects from the possible behavioral responses identified in step four and selects a specific response to implement. Competent processing at this stage would include an evaluation of the potential consequences of each possible response identified, while also estimating the probability of favorable outcomes (Dodge, 1986). Difficulties at this step in children with aggressive behavior include selecting a behavioral response without taking time to evaluate the likelihood of a positive outcome, as well as over-estimating the positive interpersonal and instrumental outcomes of selecting an aggressive response (such as in children whose goal in Step 3 is to be dominant, rather than to maintain a friendship).

Step 6: behavioral enactment

Once the child has selected an optimal response in the step earlier, the child proceeds to enact the response selected (Crick & Dodge, 1994; Dodge, 1986). The manner in which the response is enacted can affect the likelihood of a favorable outcome. Not only do children with aggressive behavior have difficulty generating and selecting effective responses, they also have difficulty in the enactment stage. For example, if a child with aggressive behavior decides to try to talk to a peer about a problem, he or she may use a loud or blaming tone of voice or exhibit off-putting nonverbal behaviors, which reduce the likelihood of the interaction leading to a favorable outcome.

Emotional processing of social information

In a further modification of Crick and Dodge's (1994) model, Lemerise and Arsenio (2000) advocated for the inclusion of an emotion component in this process. They proposed an integrated model of emotion processes and cognition in SIP. They posited that emotion also plays a critical role in each step of the model and the interactive feedback loops that occur across steps. For example, the angrier a child feels during a social situation (e.g., being bumped in the hallway), the more difficult it might be for that child to take time to think of more than one response option, the likely outcomes of each response option, or to enact the response selected effectively.

Research on social information processing in aggressive youth

The ways in which children typically present aggressive behavior and conduct problems can vary from relatively minor oppositional behaviors, such as yelling or temper tantrums, to more serious antisocial behaviors such as violent aggression, physical destructiveness, and stealing (McMahon & Frick, 2007). Based on children's temperament and biological dispositions, and on children's contextual experiences from their family, peers, and community, they begin to form stable patterns of processing social information and of regulating their emotions. Consistent with early Anger Control models (Lochman, Nelson, & Sims, 1981), the contextual social-cognitive model (Lochman & Wells, 2002a) stresses the reciprocal interactive relationships between children's cognitions about events and their physiological arousal (Williams, Lochman, Phillips, & Barry, 2003).

Aggressive children can have cognitive distortions at the appraisal phases of social-cognitive processing because of difficulties in encoding incoming social information, partially due to neurocognitive difficulties in their executive functions (Ellis, Weiss, & Lochman, 2009), and in accurately interpreting social events and others' intentions. Reactively aggressive children have been found to recall fewer relevant cues about events (Dodge, Lochman, Harnish, Bates, & Pettit, 1997; Lochman & Dodge, 1994) and to misperceive the levels of aggression that they and peers emit in dyadic interactions (Lochman & Dodge, 1998). These misperceptions are due in part to strongly held schemas about self and other behavior, developed through children's experience within their family and peer environment. Based on their hypersensitivity to hostile cues, reactively aggressive children develop a hostile attributional bias, as they excessively infer that others are acting toward them in an intentionally provocative and hostile manner (Dodge et al., 1997; Lochman & Dodge, 1994), and these distorted attributions typically operate in an automatic manner (Yaros, Lochman, Rosenbaum, & Jimenez-Camargo, 2014).

How Coping Power addresses deficits in early SIP steps for aggressive youth

Intervention strategies from the Coping Power program (Lochman et al., 2008; Wells et al., 2008) will be described to illustrate how SIP deficits in children with aggressive behavior can be addressed with cognitive therapy. Table 10.1 provides an overview of treatment strategies from the Coping Power program that help to address the SIP deficits observed in children with aggressive and disruptive behavior. In addition to the strategies depicted in Table 10.1, it is important for the clinician to understand as much as possible about the child's past experiences, including the acquired social knowledge, schemas and goals that are likely driving the child's current social interactions. Additionally, as advocated by Lemerise and Arsenio (2000), it is important for clinicians to help children learn to recognize and manage anger arousal, as emotional and SIP co-occur to affect children's social interactions. Specific intervention strategies that can be used to accomplish these aims are summarized in Table 10.1 and described in greater detail later.

The following section will describe intervention strategies to address deficits in early SIP steps, including: Encoding of social cues, interpretation of social cues, and selecting goals.

Understanding children's prior experiences and acquired social knowledge, schemas and goals

Prior to initiating the Coping Power intervention, comprehensive psychosocial assessments are conducted with each child and family. The information gleaned from these assessments is used to better understand each child's upbringing, temperament and past social experiences and to conceptualize how these factors might affect the child's current SIP and emotion regulation and contribute to the child's aggressive behavior. Input about target social and behavioral goals is also obtained from parents, teachers and children, which provides further insight into the child's treatment needs as well as how the child currently prioritizes social goals.

Table 10.1 Strategies for addressing deficits in social information processing in aggressive youth

Social information processing model (Crick & Dodge, 1994)	Deficits in youth with aggressive and disruptive behavior	Sample treatment strategies to address processing deficits
Step 1: Encoding of cues	• Hypervigilance to cues that might indicate a threat • Neglecting relevant nonhostile cues	• Teach children about verbal and nonverbal cues, and the potential for ambiguity • Practice cue encoding, including noticing nonhostile cues that might be initially missed
Step 2: Interpretation of cues	• Hostile attribution bias, which is a tendency to over-interpret others' intentions as hostile or threatening and often accompanied by excessive anger arousal	• Practice seeing situations from others' perspectives • Practice questioning one's initial assumptions and generating alternative explanations • Practice coping with anger arousal in difficult social situation, using anger management tools
Step 3: Selection of goals	• Prioritize instrumental over interpersonal goals • Often have "muddy" goal structures, wishing to dominate others as well as to maintain positive affiliations with them	• Teach a range of social goals and which goals tend to lead to desired social outcomes
Step 4: Response access or construction	• Generate fewer behavioral response options overall • Generate more aggressive response options and fewer alternative responses (e.g., verbal assertion, bargaining, compromise, non-aggressive action, help-seeking, ignoring)	• Teach a range of response options, including non-aggressive solutions • Practice taking time to brainstorm multiple ways to handle a situation, rather than selecting the first option that comes to mind
Step 5: Response decision	• Selecting a behavioral response when highly anger-aroused, without taking time to evaluate the likely outcomes first • Over-estimating the positive outcomes of aggressive response	• Practice taking time to calm down and think ahead about the likely outcomes of various responses first • Notice which responses tend to lead to desirable vs. undesirable outcomes (in the short- vs long-term)

(*Continued*)

Table 10.1 **(Continued)**

Social information processing model (Crick & Dodge, 1994)	Deficits in youth with aggressive and disruptive behavior	Sample treatment strategies to address processing deficits
Step 6: Behavioral enactment	• Lack of skillful implementation of chosen behavioral response • For example, child stands too close, talks too loudly or angrily, uses blaming rather than problem-solving words, or has difficulty adapting his or her response during the interaction in light of new social cues	• Practice effective verbal and nonverbal communication and negotiation skills • Identify good times and bad times to approach another person about a problem • Practice resilient problem-solving, not giving up if first response does not work out

Emotion awareness and emotional regulation

Before children can begin to successfully use social problem-solving skills to handle perceived difficulties, it is necessary for them to regulate the arousal they often experience in problem situations. Emotion awareness strategies typically allow children to learn to recognize the situations and emotions that tend to lead them to engage in aggressive and disruptive behaviors. Recognition of negative emotions, and the degree to which they are experienced, enables children to determine the conditions, or triggers, under which they are most prone to act out.

In Coping Power, child participants first learn to describe their emotions in terms of physiological sensations (e.g., heart racing, tight muscles, face becomes flushed), behaviors (e.g., raising your voice, making a threatening gesture, pushing or shoving), and cognitions (e.g., I hate my mom; my teacher always picks on me; I am going to show that kid he can't mess with me). Children practice noticing and describing their experience of many types of emotions. Then, the discussion eventually focuses on anger. Using a thermometer analogy, children are taught to identify varying intensities of particular emotions. Situational triggers and thought patterns associated with varying levels of anger are then identified (e.g., I felt a little bit upset when my teacher gave us an extra homework assignment, I felt medium angry when my brother took something from my room, I felt enraged when someone made fun of my family). Through in-session activities and self-monitoring homework assignments, children are taught to identify the physiological cues of varying levels of anger arousal and common situational triggers for anger arousal.

To address the cue encoding step, children practice identifying verbal and nonverbal behaviors that are displayed by themselves and others, particularly in emotionally arousing situations. Through discussion and practice activities, they learn to identify social cues more accurately and to pay attention to cues that they may have initially minimized or overlooked (e.g., I noticed that he looked right at me with a scowl on his face and thought he hated me. Then, I noticed that he was holding his script for the school play. His character is mean, so he may have been rehearsing and not thinking about me at all). Emphasis is also placed on learning to make room for ambiguity and potential discrepancies (e.g., sometimes I smile or laugh when I am feeling nervous; sometimes I get a mean look on my face when I am lost in my thoughts and not even upset about anything; sometimes I yell or lash out at when I am feeling tired or worried about something). By recognizing such discrepancies in their own feelings and behavior, children learn to attend to a greater range of cues in others' behavior and to be more flexible in their interpretation of these cues in later processing stages.

Emotion regulation, specifically anger coping, is key to the successful decrease of associated hostile attributions of intent and to associated reactive aggression. As previously noted, deficits in emotion regulation are thought to contribute to externalizing behaviors; thus it is essential to incorporate anger management in any Cognitive Behavioral Therapy (CBT)-based intervention. With a working awareness of their experience of anger and its triggers, children are more likely to successfully implement anger management techniques before becoming inundated by an unmanageable level of anger arousal. A number of strategies can be taught to children to help them manage their anger arousal, including: Distraction, relaxation, and coping self-statements. With regard to relaxation, the children are taught guided imagery, deep breathing and progressive muscle relaxation techniques, to help them prevent escalation beyond low levels of anger in real life anger arousal situations. In terms of distraction, exercises are conducted through which the child is taught to divert his or her attention away from the anger-provoking stimulus. For example, in a group setting, a child may be given a set of letters or numbers to memorize while the rest of the group is instructed to taunt and disturb the child as much as possible. By focusing on the task at hand (memorizing the letters or numbers rather than responding to the peer teasing), the child learns that he or she can prevent his or her anger from escalating by ignoring, or focusing attention away from, the anger-evoking stimulus.

The use of coping self-statements is also taught, through a series of graded exposure role-plays. After children learn to identity the types of thoughts that they have when they are feeling angry ("angry thoughts," e.g., I hate my mom; my teacher always picks on me; I am going to show that kid he can't mess with me), they learn to "talk back" to these thoughts by saying coping self-statements to themselves. Coping self-statements are short prompt(s) or situation-specific statements that children can say to themselves to feel calmer and to prepare to handle trigger situations better than if their mind stayed stuck on their "angry thoughts," which is likely to cause further anger escalation.

Initially, children are provided with a list of sample coping self-statements that they may find helpful to lower their anger (e.g., "It's not worth it to get angry"; "he is trying to make me mad, but I am not going to let it get to me"; "I'm going to stay cool, not be a fool"; "I believe in the Golden Rule and am going to try to be an example of that to others"). Children are encouraged to generate their own coping statements, which may have a greater impact on their anger management, especially if the child is able to access the coping statement more readily when anger-aroused and if the child finds the coping statement very believable and relevant to the specific trigger situation. Children are given time to become familiar with a range of coping statements and to choose several coping statements that they find the most helpful.

After selecting two to three preferred coping statements (or demonstrating the ability to generate coping statements spontaneously during anger-arousing situations), children are exposed to a situation in which they practice using coping statements in a relatively benign and impersonal anger-arousing scenario. For example, in a group setting, children can use puppets to tease a specific child's puppet. The child holding the puppet being teased can state aloud the coping statements his puppet is using to avoid anger escalation. This activity can also be completed by having students take turns shooting basketball free throws while the other group members pretend to be rowdy fans hollering at the free throw shooter, or by having the group members take turns wearing a silly hat, shirt, or bag and being teased while wearing it. With increasing proficiency in the use of coping statements, children can be progressively challenged with more direct anger arousal scenarios until they can utilize coping statements effectively and spontaneously in direct verbal taunting (role-play) scenarios. With this type of technique, it is very important to establish ground rules and monitor children closely to avoid situations in which the teasing gets out of hand.

Perspective-taking

This component is designed to teach children the difficulty involved in accurately determining others' intentions. Along with improved anger regulation skills, this component is expected to reduce children's high rates of hostile attributions of others. Children who exhibit aggressive and disruptive behavior tend to overly interpret others' intentions as hostile; thus, it is necessary to teach children about other more benign alternate explanations for others' behaviors (Dodge et al., 1997; Lochman & Dodge, 1994). The clinician can have children role-play different characters in an ambiguous situation. Upon completion of the role-play, children are encouraged to discuss the different viewpoints of each of the characters portrayed. This helps the children recognize that there are many different sides to a situation and that it is sometimes hard to quickly tell what another person's motives are. Children are also asked to recall real life incidents in which they later realized they had misinterpreted the reason for another person's actions in an overly hostile light. In school settings, clinicians may also wish to have children interview their teachers to allow children the opportunity to obtain a firsthand account of common student misconceptions regarding disciplinary procedures and classroom management.

Short versus long-term social goals

Early in Coping Power, children learn to differentiate between short- and long-term behavior goals. They then work on weekly personal goals throughout the program. As the intervention advances to focus on solving social problems, children are taught to think about their short versus long-term goals for resolving specific problem situations. They are taught that their short- and long-term goals can be at odds with each other at times. For example, if a peer teases you in front of your class, you might like to punch them or tease them back even worse. While it might feel good in the moment to get revenge or show your strength, responding in these ways could also lead to problems for you in the long run (e.g., you might get suspended, you might get kicked off the basketball team for poor sportsmanship, you parents might take away a privilege at home, or much farther in the future, you might get arrested or fired from your job, if you don't learn how to work out problems calmly and effectively).

Discussion and practice activities are employed to alter children's perceptions about which social goals are most likely to lead to desired long-term outcomes (e.g., reducing the perceived benefits of dominance and revenge goals and increasing the perceived benefits of affiliative goals). Children are also taught to employ coping strategies to reduce anger arousal before identifying their social goals and response options.

How Coping Power addresses deficits in later SIP steps for aggressive youth

This section will focus on intervention strategies to address deficits in later SIP steps, including: Response access or construction, response decision, and behavioral enactment.

Brainstorming solutions to social problems

After children in Coping Power learn to manage their anger arousal and take time to view problem situations from others' perspectives, they are taught additional steps for solving social problems. The acronym PICC is used to summarize these problem-solving steps, which include: (1) Problem Identification, which entails noticing that there is a problem and describing it as specifically as possible, (2) brainstorming a variety of Choices to solve the problem, and (3) identifying the likely Consequences of each choice and using this information to determine which choice to try first. After being oriented to the PICC model, children spend several Coping Power sessions learning and practicing each step. Parents are also taught the PICC model and are encouraged to reinforce the use of this approach at home, to solve individual and family-level problems.

To improve their ability to generate a variety of solutions to a problem, children are taught about the practice of brainstorming. They are shown hypothetical problem situations and practice generating as many different choices for solving the problem as possible. For example, Coping Power participants watch a video that shows a child shoving and cutting in front of another child in line. The Coping Power participants are then given a time limit to think of as many different choices for solving this problem as possible, without evaluating whether each choice is likely to lead to a good or bad outcome (e.g., push him back, ignore him, yell at him, politely ask him to go to the end of the line, tell the teacher, recruit a friend to help make him move to the end of the line). Comparative analyses help Coping Power participants recognize that this brainstorming process tends to yield more choices/better choices than are generated otherwise. Group members are also taught to categorize different types of responses to problems (e.g., verbal assertion, aggressive assertion, direct action, aggressive action, avoidance, help-seeking, bargaining, or compromise), which become helpful in the response appraisal step.

Thinking ahead about consequences

The next series of activities teaches Coping Power participants to anticipate and evaluate the likely consequences of each solution. For example, in the line-cutting situation above, if the child pushes the instigator back, he might get his place back in line but he could also get in trouble if he is caught by the teacher. If he tells on the instigator, the instigator might get in trouble and the child might get his place back in line; however, the teacher could also tell both boys to stop fighting and work it out themselves. If the child politely asks the instigator to move, the instigator might move or he might not. If the child ignores what happened, the situation is likely to de-escalate; however, the instigator might try to mistreat him again in the future. After hypothesizing the likely short- and long-term consequences of each choice, the Coping Power participants evaluate which choices are likely to work out best. This can lead to an iterative process in which they generate entirely new choice(s) that have even better expected outcomes.

Over several sessions, Coping Power participants practice brainstorming choices and evaluating their expected consequences for hypothetical and real life problem situations. This occurs both in and out of group sessions. In one session, group members practice automatic versus thoughtful responding. In the automatic responding activity, the group members list all of the problem solutions they can think of, without anticipating the consequences of each one. In the thoughtful responding activity, the group members are asked to anticipate the likely consequences of each choice and to record only the choices that are expected to yield positive outcomes. The group members compare the choices generated in the two conditions and observe that taking even a short time to stop and think ahead about consequences can lead to making better choices. They also discuss how taking time to calm down before engaging in this brainstorming process can lead to better decisions as well.

In another activity, the Coping Power participants are taught to be resilient problem solvers. The group members break into two groups ("blockers" and "solvers") and take turns in each role. The role of the "blockers" is to come up with barriers or reasons why a problem solution will not work out as planned. The role of the "solvers" is to come up with a creative new solution that will bypass the barrier presented by the "blockers." This back and forth action continues until one of the groups is unable to come up with a new idea in the allotted time. This activity is intended to increase children's ability to generate multiple solutions and different types of solutions (rather than resorting to a narrow skill-set, such as fighting), even when they encounter unexpected barriers.

Social skills training and behavioral rehearsal

Later Coping Power sessions focus on teaching children social and communication skills (e.g., body position, voice tone, eye contact, assertive communication, turn-taking, sportsmanship, good and bad times to approach another person about a problem). These skills are then utilized during role-play activities enacting different problem solutions using the PICC model. For example, Coping Power participants would return to the line-cutting problem described earlier and act out each of the potential solutions generated (e.g., push him back, ignore him, yell at him, politely ask him to go to the end of the line, tell the teacher, recruit a friend to help make him move to the end of the line) to observe how each choice might play out in practice. They discuss how specific behaviors such as where you stand, how your voice sounds, the words you use, and whether you react in anger or take time to calm yourself down first, make a difference in how well the choice works out. They will then re-enact some of the choices, making adjustments to the timing and manner of their delivery, until they settle upon a choice that is likely to lead to a desirable outcome.

Group leaders provide modeling and coaching throughout this process, to ensure that the children gain an accurate understanding of effective versus noneffective social behaviors and communication styles. Group leaders and participants bring in real life problem situations to practice solving using PICC and also record their experiences using PICC between sessions. The participants practice using PICC in a wide range of social situations, including to solve problems with peers, siblings, teachers, parents, family members, and neighbors. Through discussion and reflection, the leaders seek to highlight the specific types of responses (e.g., verbal assertion, bargaining, direct action, help seeking, ignoring minor problems) and social behaviors (talking calmly and respectfully, describing your own needs and feelings rather than criticizing or blaming others, suggesting a solution or making a polite request, showing willingness to compromise) that tend to lead to desired outcomes. Through behavioral rehearsal, they seek to prepare each child to generate and enact more effective responses as readily as possible. To solidify their expertise, the children make a video teaching others about the PICC model.

Other evidence-based cognitive treatment strategies

There are several empirically supported cognitive treatments and interventions for anger management in children. Many of these efficacious programs address parent and familial factors, as well as maladaptive social-cognitive processes and deficits in problem-solving in children. In this section, we will highlight several child, parent, and family-directed prevention and treatment programs that include a focus on cognitive strategies for managing anger. Brief summaries of each prevention and treatment program, demonstrated outcome effects, and the generalizability of these outcomes are provided later.

Universal prevention programs

Promoting Alternative Thinking Strategies (PATHS) is a comprehensive classroom-based program designed to promote social-emotional competencies and cognitive skill-building in elementary school children (Greenberg & Kusche, 2006). Grounded in the affective-behavioral-cognitive dynamic model of development (Greenberg & Kusche, 1993), PATHS is designed for use by classroom teachers who receive training to instruct children in emotional awareness, self-regulation and social problem-solving skills. Currently, the PATHS program is available in preschool through 5th grade and classroom lessons address the following five conceptual domains: (1) self-control; (2) emotional understanding; (3) positive self-esteem; (4) relationships; and (5) interpersonal problem-solving skills. Cognitive aspects of the program include teaching children to identify and name different feeling states, to remember to use a self-control strategy when experiencing anger arousal, and to apply thinking skills to manage conflicts and resolve problem situations.

A number of rigorous evaluations of the PATHS program have demonstrated the effectiveness of the curriculum on the emotional development of elementary-aged children and results have been replicated in different populations of children that include deaf/hearing impaired and a variety of special education-classified children (Mihalic & Irwin, 2003). Specifically, two independent RCTs found PATHS to produce significant reductions in teacher reported conduct problems and significant linear effects on student-reported normative beliefs about aggression, aggressive problem-solving, and hostile attribution bias (Crean & Johnson, 2013; Schonfeld et al., 2015). Additionally, children who received multiyear versions of PATHS program, across first through 3rd grades, when compared to control children, exhibited reduced aggression, increased prosocial behavior, and increased academic functioning (Dodge & Godwin, 2013).

Across multiple studies, PATHS has shown increased social competence, emotion knowledge and improvements in children's ability to resolve peer conflicts relative to a control group (e.g., Boxmeyer et al., 2015; Domitrovich et al., 2016). PATHS effects have been found to be strongest in less disadvantaged schools and among more at-risk children (Domitrovich, Cortes, & Greenberg, 2007). Moreover, effects of the PATHS program on aggression seem to be stronger for boys.

Linking the Interests of Families and Teachers

Similar to the PATHS program, the Linking Interests of Families and Teachers (LIFT) program is aimed at reducing conduct problems and aggression. The specific goal of the LIFT program is to prevent the development of youth antisocial behaviors by positively influencing interactions between youth and parents in the home and between youth and peers in the classroom (DeGarmo, Eddy, Reid, & Fetrow, 2009). LIFT targets elementary-aged children and their families by addressing parental limit-setting and effective discipline practices, and active involvement in school and social activities (Reid & Eddy, 2002). Based on a developmental model grounded in moment-to-moment social interaction processes, the LIFT program includes classroom-based lessons designed to increase children's social skills and problem-solving skills, with an emphasis on resisting negative peer groups (Patterson, Reid, & Dishion, 1992). Children are taught to stop and think about the best way to solve social problems and how to affiliate with positive peers. They then actively practice these behaviors during free play periods and are reinforced for positive behavior (thus it is an integrated cognitive-behavioral program).

Also like PATHS, LIFT addresses child self-regulation and emotion-knowledge and has been effective in reducing playground aggression, increasing systematic communication between teachers, and improving classroom behavior (Embry & Straatemeier, 2001). In a randomized trial with 671 families, Reid, Patterson, and Snyder (2002) found significant improvements in family problem-solving and child social competence following LIFT. Additionally, LIFT significantly reduced youths' self-reported substance use (DeGarmo et al., 2009).

Life skills training

The Botvin life skills training (LST) program is designed to prevent substance abuse in early adolescent and adolescent children. Similar to both PATHS and LIFT, LST is a prevention program that seeks to improve children's anger management, interpersonal assertiveness and conflict resolution skills (Botvin, Griffin, & Nichols, 2006). Primarily developed for use with middle school students, LST prevention lessons are taught over 15 class periods during the child's 6th grade year and supplemental boosters are administered during the 7th and 8th grade years. Cognitive behavioral techniques are the core components of LST, and three major program components include: (1) personal self-management skills; (2) social skills; and (3) information and resistance training specifically associated with drug use (Botvin et al., 2006). In addition to employing cognitive strategies similar to the programs described earlier, LST includes unique cognitive elements designed to provide students with information regarding specific drugs (e.g., tobacco) as well as strategies advertisers use to entice consumers to use their products. Students also complete writing tasks to identify effective social behaviors, enhance self-esteem and self-awareness, solidify knowledge regarding drugs and advertising, and practice effective communication skills.

Two randomized controlled studies have demonstrated LST's short-term and long-term effectiveness. Specifically, at 3-month follow-up the intervention group showed reductions of 32% in delinquency and 26% in fighting (Botvin et al., 2006). Furthermore, across several studies, the LST intervention group has shown significantly greater improvements when compared to the control group in life skills knowledge and substance use knowledge (MacKillop, Ryabchenko, & Lisman, 2006). LST is found to be generalizable to a variety of ethnic groups and have been proven effective with White, middle-class, suburban, and rural youth as well as low-income, high-poverty populations (Botvin et al., 2006; MacKillop et al., 2006). The LST program has been adapted for use in international replication and dissemination studies. A German replication study found positive program effects on school bonding and alcohol use (Wenzel, Weichold, & Silbereisen, 2009). Stronger prevention effects on verbal and physical aggression, fighting and delinquency have been found in students who receive at least half of the intervention (Botvin et al., 2006).

Second Step

The Second Step program is a classroom-based program that focuses on building children's skills in empathy, impulse control, problem-solving, and anger management. Like PATHS, LIFT, and LST, the Second Step program is designed to promote social-emotional competence and self-regulation. Second Step lessons address children's emotional responses, patterns of thought, and behavioral skills, and the ways these aspects interact with each other and impact children's social and emotional development. Specific cognitive elements include children's attributions about social situations, social goals, and their ability to generate, evaluate and enact solutions to social problems.

Delivered among children aged 4-14 in the classroom setting, sequential lessons are provided by counselors or classroom teachers and there are separate kits available for both elementary and middle school delivery. Longitudinal efficacy evaluation studies have found the Second Step program to reduce impulsive and aggressive behavior and increase prosocial behavior across many school districts in the United States (Edwards, Hunt, Meyers, Grogg, & Jarrett, 2005; Frey, Nolen, Edstrom, & Hirschstein, 2005). In another evaluation study, students in the intervention group were rated higher on social competence 1 year following the Second Step program when compared to students in the control group (Taub, 2002). The Second Step program has been primarily examined in rural settings with a high proportion of low Socioeconomic Status (SES) students in a fairly homogenous population (Reid, Eddy, Bank, & Fetrow, 1994; Taub, 2002).

Targeted prevention and treatment programs

Fast Track

The Fast Track program is a comprehensive targeted prevention program for children who display early onset disruptive behaviors in kindergarten (Conduct

Problems Prevention Research Group, 1992). It has been tested across multiple sites in the United States. Well-established and grounded in developmentally guided intervention, the Fast Track program provides multimodal programing during 1st through 5th grades, including the PATHS social emotional curriculum, behavioral parent training, home visiting, child social skills training groups, child friendship enhancement, and child tutoring. The PATHS program, child social skills training groups, and child friendship enhancement elements all include cognitive treatment strategies similar to those described in other programs earlier.

Research findings reveal significant intervention effects on peer ratings of aggression, disruptive behavior and ratings on classroom behavior (Conduct Problems Prevention Research Group, 1999). In a large-scale randomized trial including 891 kindergarteners, significant reductions in child aggressive and disruptive behavior were reported by both teachers and parents by the end of the 3rd grade (Conduct Problems Prevention Research Group, 1999). Many of these effects on children's behavior and social-cognitive processes were maintained through 4th and 5th grades (Conduct Problems Prevention Research Group, 2004). Long-term studies following the children through 12th grade have found that the Fast Track program prevented externalizing behaviors among the highest risk group (Conduct Problems Prevention Research Group, 1999).

Incredible Years

Incredible Years (IY) is a series of programs that address multiple risk factors for conduct disorders and includes training programs for parents, teachers, and children (Webster-Stratton, 2011). The child component consists of 18 weeks of training on social skills, conflict resolution, empathy-building, problem-solving, and cooperation; while teachers and parents receive weekly letters explaining these concepts and strategies to reinforce skill development. Specific cognitive elements of the classroom program include: Teaching children to use positive self-statements (e.g., "I will get this eventually if I keep working," vs "I am stupid and will never get it"), to see situations in less hostile terms, to generate prosocial ways of solving interpersonal problems, and to think ahead about the consequences of their actions before they act.

The IY series has been shown to have positive effects on child disruptive behaviors and has been utilized for universal or indicated prevention as well as a treatment program for youth with conduct disorder (Webster-Stratton & Herman, 2010). There have been significant reductions in conduct problems shown for the child training alone, combined child and teacher training, and the child, teacher and parent training combined (Webster-Stratton, Reid, & Hammond, 2004). Specifically, there have been reductions in conduct problems at school and home (Webster-Stratton et al., 2004), fewer observed negative behaviors and more prosocial skills (Webster-Stratton & Hammond, 1997), and increased conflict management skills (Webster-Stratton & Hammond, 2004) following IY delivery.

Problem solving skills training

This approach focuses on interpersonal cognitive processes with the aim of decreasing oppositional, aggressive, and antisocial behaviors in children. The program primarily targets children aged 7 to 14 with diagnoses of Oppositional Defiant Disorder (ODD) and Conduct Disorder (CD). Depending on the age of the child, a parent component offering parent management training (PMT) may be used as a standalone treatment program or in combination with PSST. PSST consists of 12-25 individual sessions, though parents may be brought in to observe and support their child in implementing PSST (Kazdin, 2010; Kazdin, Esveldt-Dawson, French, & Unis, 1987; Kazdin, Siegel, & Bass, 1992). Sessions last 40–50 minutes and are typically conducted in hospital and outpatient settings.

Through modeling, shaping, practice and repeated rehearsal, corrective feedback, positive reinforcement, and mild punishment (e.g., time out or loss of reinforcement), children learn effective problem-solving skills. Over the course of the program, children learn how to use problem-solving skills (e.g., generating alternative solutions, consequential thinking, perspective taking) to manage simple and eventually more challenging interpersonal situations. Further, a homework component, referred to as supersolvers (in vivo practice assignments), is used as an extension of sessions where the skills learned are applied to everyday situations (Kazdin, 2010).

Research suggests that PSST significantly reduces antisocial behavior and increases prosocial behaviors immediately after treatment and during 1-year follow-up periods. Although PSST has resulted in increased children's social competence and reduced problem behaviors, a combination of PSST and PMT has also been found to result in effective and long-lasting outcome effects (Kazdin, 2010; Kazdin et al., 1987, 1992)

Conclusions and future directions

This chapter has summarized the skill deficits in SIP and emotion regulation that are commonly observed in children with aggressive and disruptive behavior. Examples from the Coping Power program have been provided to illustrate cognitive treatment strategies that have proven useful in addressing these deficits. Other evidence-based prevention and treatment programs for children with aggressive and disruptive behavior have also been described.

The work in this area is ongoing. In the future, more tailored, precision medicine approaches may be applied to this work, by identifying each child's specific areas of strength and difficulty in terms of SIP and emotion regulation, as well as the broader family context in which the child is being raised, and providing skills training that directly targets the areas of greatest need. Ongoing research is also examining how clinician style impacts outcomes of interventions for children with aggressive and disruptive behavior, as it is important to strike the optimal balance between maintaining a positive therapeutic alliance and enforcing limits on problem behavior. It can be challenging to understand cognitive processes, especially for children. Thus, clinician skill may be especially important for effective delivery of cognitive treatment with children. The utility of technology to deliver or augment existing interventions and to teach SIP is also an important area of future research.

References

Botvin, G. J., Griffin, K. W., & Nichols, T. D. (2006). Preventing youth violence and delinquency through a universal school-based prevention approach. *Prevention Science*, *7*(4), 403–408.

Boxmeyer, C., Gilpin, A., DeCaro, J., Lochman, J., Qu, L., Mitchell, Q., & Snead, S. (2015). Power PATH: Integrated two-generation social emotional intervention for Head Start preschoolers and their parents. Online paper collection of the *Association for Public Policy Analysis and Management's 37th Annual Fall Research Conference: The Golden Age of Evidence-Based Policy*. Retrieved from the World Wide Web at: https://appam.confex.com/appam/2015/webprogram/Paper12784.html

Broidy, L. M., Tremblay, R. E., Brame, B., Fergusson, D., Horwood, J. L., Laird, R., . . . Vitaro, F. (2003). Developmental trajectories of childhood disruptive behaviors and adolescent delinquency: a six site cross-national study. *Developmental Psychology*, *39*, 222–245.

Cabiya, J. J., Padilla-Cotto, L., González, K., Sanchez-Cestero, J., Martínez-Taboas, A., & Sayers, S. (2008). Effectiveness of a cognitive-behavioral intervention for Puerto Rican children. *Interamerican Journal of Psychology*, *42*, 195–202.

Conduct Problems Prevention Research Group. (1992). A developmental and clinical model for the prevention of conduct disorder: the FAST Track Program. *Development and Psychopathology*, *4*, 509–527.

Conduct Problems Prevention Research Group. (1999). Initial impact of the Fast Track prevention trial for conduct problems: I. The high-risk sample. *Journal of Consulting and Clinical Psychology*, *67*, 631–647.

Conduct Problems Prevention Research Group. (2004). The Fast Track experiment: translating the developmental model into a prevention design. In J. B. Kupersmidt, & K. A. Dodge (Eds.), *Children's peer relations: from development to intervention* (pp. 181–208). Washington DC: American Psychological Association.

Crean, H. F., & Johnson, D. B. (2013). Promoting alternative thinking strategies (PATHS) and elementary school aged children's aggression: results from a cluster randomized trial. *American Journal of Community Psychology*, *52*(1-2), 56–72.

Crick, N. R., & Dodge, K. A. (1994). A review and reformulation of social information-processing mechanisms in children's social adjustment. *Psychological Bulletin*, *115*, 74–101.

Crick, N. R., & Dodge, K. A. (1996). Social information-processing mechanisms in reactive and proactive aggression. *Child Development*, *67*, 993–1002. Available from https://doi.org/10.1111/j.1467-8624.1996.tb01778.x.

DeGarmo, D. S., Eddy, J. M., Reid, J. B., & Fetrow, R. A. (2009). Evaluating mediators of the impact of the linking the onterests of families and teachers (LIFT) multimodal preventive intervention on substance use initiation and growth across adolescence. *Prevention Science*, *10*(3), 208–220.

Dodge, K. A. (1986). A social information processing model of social competence in children. In M. Perlmutter (Ed.), *Minnesota symposium on child psychology* (Vol. 18, pp. 77–125). Hillsdale, NJ: Erlbaum.

Dodge, K. A., Bates, J. E., & Pettit, G. S. (1990). Mechanisms in the cycle of violence. *Science, 250*, 1678–1683.

Dodge, K. A., & Godwin, J. (2013). Social-information-processing patterns mediate the impact of preventive intervention on adolescent antisocial behavior. *Psychological Science, 24*(4), 456–465.

Dodge, K. A., Greenberg, M. T., Malone, P. S., & Conduct Problems Prevention Research Group. (2008). Testing an idealized dynamic cascade model of the development of serious violence in adolescence. *Child Development, 79*, 1907–1927.

Dodge, K. A., Lochman, J. E., Harnish, J. D., Bates, J. E., & Pettit, G. S. (1997). Reactive and proactive aggression in school children and psychiatrically impaired chronically assaultive youth. *Journal of Abnormal Psychology, 106*, 37–51.

Domitrovich, C. E., Bradshaw, C. P., Berg, J. K., Pas, E. T., Becker, K. D., Musci, R., & Ialongo, N. (2016). How do school-based prevention programs impact teachers? Findings from a randomized trial of an integrated classroom management and social-emotional program. *Prevention Science, 17*(3), 325.

Domitrovich, C. E., Cortes, R. C., & Greenberg, M. T. (2007). Improving young children's social and emotional competence: a randomized trial of the preschool "PATHS" curriculum. *The Journal of Primary Prevention, 28*, 67–91.

Edwards, D., Hunt, M. H., Meyers, J., Grogg, K. R., & Jarrett, O. (2005). Acceptability and student outcomes of a violence prevention curriculum. *The Journal of Primary Prevention, 26*(5), 401–418.

Ellis, M. L., Weiss, B., & Lochman, J. E. (2009). Executive functions in children: associations with aggressive behavior and social appraisal processing. *Journal of Abnormal Child Psychology, 37*, 945–956.

Embry, D. D., & Straatemeier, G. (2001). *The PAX acts game manual: how to apply the good behavior game. Tucson, AZ: PAXIS Institute.*

Frey, K. S., Nolen, S. B., Edstrom, L. V. S., & Hirschstein, M. K. (2005). Effects of a school-based social–emotional competence program: linking children's goals, attributions, and behavior. *Journal of Applied Developmental Psychology, 26*(2), 171–200.

Goldstein, N.E.S., Giallella, C.L. Peterson, L., Serico, J., Kemp, K., Romaine, C.R., ... Lochman, J. (in press). Juvenile Justice Anger Management (JJAM) Treatment for Girls: Results of a randomized controlled trial. *Psychological Services* https://doi.org/10.1037/ser0000184

Goldstein, N. E. S., Serico, J. M., Riggs Romaine, C. L., Zelechoski, A. D., Kalbeitzer, R., Kemp, K., & Lane, C. (2013). Development of the juvenile justice anger management treatment for girls. *Cognitive and Behavioral Practice, 20*, 171–188. Available from https://doi.org/10.1016/j.cbpra.2012.06.003.

Greenberg, M. T., & Kusche, C. A. (1993). *Promoting social and emotional development in deaf children: the PATHS project*. Seattle: University of Washington Press.

Greenberg, M. T., & Kusche, C. A. (2006). Building social and emotional competence: the PATHS curriculum. In S. R. Jimerson, & M. J. Furlong (Eds.), *Handbook of school violence and school safety: from research to practice* (pp. 395–412). Mahwah, NJ: Erlbaum.

Kazdin, A. E. (2010). Problem-solving skills training and parent management training for oppositional defiant disorder and conduct disorder. In J. R. Weisz, & A. E. Kazdin (Eds.), *Evidence based psychotherapies for children and adolescents* (2nd. ed., pp. 159–178). New York, NY: Guilford.

Kazdin, A. E., Esveldt-Dawson, K., French, N. H., & Unis, A. S. (1987). Problem-solving skills training and relationship therapy in the treatment of antisocial child behavior. *Journal of Consulting and Clinical Psychology*, *55*, 76–85.

Kazdin, A. E., Siegel, T. C., & Bass, D. (1992). Cognitive problem-solving skills training and parent management training in the treatment of antisocial behavior in children. *Journal of Consulting and Clinical Psychology*, *60*(5), 733–747.

Larson, J., & Lochman, J. E. (2010). *Helping schoolchildren cope with anger: a cognitive-behavioral intervention*. Guilford Press.

Leff, S. S., Waasdorp, T. E., Paskewich, B., Gullan, R. L., Jawad, A. F., MacEvoy, J. P., ... Power, T. J. (2010). The preventing relational aggression in schools everyday program: a preliminary evaluation of acceptability and impact. *School Psychology Review*, *39*, 569–587.

Lemerise, E. A., & Arsenio, W. F. (2000). An integrated model of emotion processes and cognition in social information processing. *Child Development*, *71*, 107–118.

Lipsey, M. W. (2006). The effects of community-based group treatment for delinquency: a meta-analytic search for cross-study generalizations. In K. A. Dodge, T. J. Dishion, & J. E. Lansford (Eds.), *Deviant peer influences in programs for youth: problems and solutions* (pp. 162–184). New York, NY, US: Guilford Press.

Lochman, J. E., Baden, R. E., Boxmeyer, C. L., Powell, N. P., Qu, L., Salekin, K. L., & Windle, M. (2014). Does a booster intervention augment the preventive effects of an abbreviated version of the coping power program for aggressive children? *Journal of Abnormal Child Psychology*, *42*, 367–381. Available from https://doi.org/10.1007/s10802-013-9727-y.

Lochman, J. E., Boxmeyer, C., Powell, N., Roth, D. L., & Windle, M. (2006). Masked intervention effects: analytic methods for addressing low dosage of intervention. *New Directions for Evaluation*(110), , 19–32.

Lochman, J. E., Boxmeyer, C. L., Powell, N. P., Qu, L., Wells, K., & Windle, M. (2012). Coping Power dissemination study: intervention and special education effects on academic outcomes. *Behavioral Disorders*, *37*, 192–205.

Lochman, J. E., & Dodge, K. A. (1994). Social-cognitive processes of severely violent, moderately aggressive and nonaggressive boys. *Journal of Consulting and Clinical Psychology*, *62*, 366–374.

Lochman, J. E., & Dodge, K. A. (1998). Distorted perceptions in dyadic interactions of aggressive and nonaggressive boys: effects of prior expectations, context, and boys' age. *Development and Psychopathology*, *10*, 495–512.

Lochman, J. E., Nelson, W. M., III, & Sims, J. P. (1981). A cognitive behavioral program for use with aggressive children. *Journal of Clinical Child Psychology*, *10*, 146–148.

Lochman, J. E., Powell, N., Boxmeyer, C., Andrade, B., Stromeyer, S. L., & Jimenez-Camargo, L. A. (2012). Adaptations to the coping power program's structure, delivery settings, and clinician training. *Psychotherapy*, *49*, 135–142. Available from https://doi.org/10.1037/a0027165.

Lochman, J. E., & Wells, K. C. (2002a). Contextual social-cognitive mediators and child outcome: a test of the theoretical model in the Coping Power Program. *Development and Psychopathology*, *14*, 971–993.

Lochman, J. E., & Wells, K. C. (2002b). The Coping Power program at the middle-school transition: universal and indicated prevention effects. *Psychology of Addictive Behaviors*, *16*, S40–S54. Available from https://doi.org/10.1037/0893-164X.16.4S.S40.

Lochman, J. E., & Wells, K. C. (2003). Effectiveness of the Coping Power program and of classroom intervention with aggressive children: outcomes at a 1-year follow-up. *Behavior Therapy*, 493–515.

Lochman, J. E., & Wells, K. C. (2004). The Coping Power program for preadolescent aggressive boys and their parents: outcome effects at the 1-year follow-up. *Journal of Consulting and Clinical Psychology*, *72*, 571–578. Available from https://doi.org/10.1037/0022-006X.72.4.571.

Lochman, J. E., Wells, K. C., & Lenhart, L. A. (2008). *Coping Power child group program: facilitator guide*. New York, NY: Oxford.

Lochman, J. E., Wells, K. C., Qu, L., & Chen, L. (2013). Three year follow-up of Coping Power intervention effects: evidence of neighborhood moderation?. *Prevention Science*, *14*, 364–376. Available from https://doi.org/10.1007/s11121-012-0295-0.

MacKillop, J., Ryabchenko, K. A., & Lisman, S. A. (2006). Life skills training outcomes and potential mechanisms in a community implementation: a preliminary investigation. *Substance Use & Misuse*, *41*(14), 1921–1935.

McMahon, R., & Frick, P. (2007). *Conduct and oppositional disorders. Assessment of childhood disorders* (*4th Ed.*, pp. 132–183). New York, NY US: Guilford Press.

Mihalic, S. F., & Irwin, K. (2003). Blueprints for violence prevention: from research to real-world settings—factors influencing the successful replication of model programs. *Youth Violence and Juvenile Justice*, *1*(4), 307–329.

Muratori, P., Bertacchi, I., Giuli, C., Lombardi, L., Bonetti, S., Nocentini, A., ... Lochman, J. (2015). First adaptation of Coping Power program as a classroom-based prevention intervention on aggressive behaviors among elementary school children. *Prevention Science*, *16*, 432–439. Available from https://doi.org/10.1007/s11121-014-0501-3.

Muratori, P., Milone, A., Manfredi, A., Polidori, L., Ruglioni, L., Lambruschi, F., ... Lochman, J. E. (2017). Evaluation of improvement in externalizing behaviors and callous-unemotional traits in children with disruptive behavior disorder: a 1-year follow up clinic-based study. *Administration and Policy in Mental Health and Mental Health Services Research*, *44*, 452–462. Available from https://doi.org/10.1007/s10488-015-0660-y.

Mushtaq, A., Lochman, J. E., Tariq, P. N., & Sabih, F. (2016). Preliminary effectiveness study of Coping Power program for aggressive children in Pakistan. *Prevention Science*, 1–10. Available from https://doi.org/10.1007/s11121-016-0721-9.

Patterson, G. R., Reid, J. B., & Dishion, T. J. (1992). *Antisocial boys: a social interactional approach*. Eugene, OR: Castalia.

Peterson, M. A., Hamilton, E. B., & Russell, A. D. (2009). Starting well: facilitating the middle school transition. *Journal of Applied School Psychology*, *25*, 286–304. Available from https://doi.org/10.1080/15377900802487219.

Reid, J.B., Eddy, J.M., Bank, L., & Fetrow, R. (1994). Some preliminary findings from a universal prevention program for Conduct Disorder. In *Fourth National Institute of Mental Health National Conference on Prevention Research, Washington, DC.*

Reid, J. B., & Eddy, J. M. (2002). Preventive efforts during the elementary school years: The linking the interests of families and teachers project. In J. B. Reid, G. R. Patterson, & J. Snyder (Eds.), *Antisocial behavior in children and adolescents: A developmental analysis and model for intervention* (pp. 219–233). Washington DC: American Psychological Association.

Reid, J. B., Patterson, G. R., & Snyder, J. (2002). *Antisocial behavior in children and adolescents: a developmental analysis and model for intervention* (pp. 219–233). Washington, DC, US: American Psychological Association.

Schonfeld, D. J., Adams, R. E., Fredstrom, B. K., Weissberg, R. P., Gilman, R., Voyce, C., & Speese-Linehan, D. (2015). Cluster-randomized trial demonstrating impact on academic achievement of elementary social-emotional learning. *School Psychology Quarterly*, *30*(3), 406–420. Available from https://doi.org/10.1037/spq0000099.

Taub, J. (2002). Evaluation of the Second Step violence prevention program at a rural elementary school. *School Psychology Review*, *31*, 186–200.

Van De Wiel, N. M. H., Matthys, W., Cohen-Kettenis, P. T., Maassen, G. H., Lochman, J. E., & Van Engeland, H. (2007). The effectiveness of an experimental treatment when compared to care as usual depends on the type of care as usual. *Behavior Modification*, *31*, 298–312.

Webster-Stratton, C. (2011). *The incredible years: parents, teachers, and children's training series*. Seattle, WA: The Incredible Years.

Webster-Stratton, C., & Hammond, M. (1997). Treating children with early-onset conduct problems: a comparison of child and parent training interventions. *Journal of Consulting and Clinical Psychology*, *65*(1), 93–99.

Webster-Stratton, C., & Herman, K. C. (2010). Disseminating Incredible Years series early-intervention programs: integrating and sustaining services between school and home. *Psychology in the Schools*, *47*(1), 36–54.

Webster-Stratton, C., Reid, M. J., & Hammond, M. (2004). Treating children with early-onset conduct problems: intervention outcomes for parent, child, and teacher training. *Journal of Clinical Child and Adolescent Psychology*, *33*(1), 105–124.

Wells, K. C., Lochman, J. E., & Lenhart, L. A. (2008). *Coping power parent group program: facilitator guide*. New York, NY: Oxford.

Wenzel, V., Weichold, K., & Silbereisen, R. K. (2009). The life skills program IPSY: positive influences on school bonding and prevention of substance misuse. *Journal of Adolescence*, *32*(6), 1391–1401.

Williams, S. C., Lochman, J. E., Phillips, N. C., & Barry, T. (2003). Aggressive and nonaggressive boys' physiological and cognitive processes in response to peer provocations. *Journal of Clinical Child and Adolescent Psychology*, *32*, 568–576.

Yaros, A., Lochman, J. E., Rosenbaum, J., & Jimenez-Camargo, L. A. (2014). Real-time hostile attribution measurement and aggression in children. *Aggressive Behavior*, *40*, 409–420.

Zonnevylle-Bender, M., Matthys, W., van de Wiel, N., & Lochman, J. (2007). Preventive effects of treatment of disruptive behavior disorder in middle childhood on substance use and delinquent behavior. *Journal of the American Academy of Child and Adolescent Psychiatry*, *46*, 33–39.

Family- and community-based treatments

11

Alex R. Dopp, Allison B. Smith, Ilana S. Berman, and Morgan A. Hill
University of Arkansas, Fayetteville, AR, United States

Youth who develop disruptive behavior disorders (DBDs), such as oppositional defiant disorder and conduct disorder, often have complex developmental histories that involve a variety of risk and protective factors (Boden, Fergusson, & Horwood, 2010; Dodge & Pettit, 2003; Frick, 2012; Loeber, Burke, & Pardini, 2009). In addition to individual characteristics (e.g., male gender, problems with executive functioning, limited prosocial personality traits), the onset of DBDs is strongly associated with characteristics of the youths' familial and social backgrounds such as poor parent–child relationships, ineffective monitoring and discipline, association with antisocial peers, exposure to maltreatment, and community violence. As a result, families that present for treatment of a youth DBD frequently evidence multiple problems that impact treatment participation and success (Weisz, Ugueto, Cheron, & Herren, 2013). Indeed, these families may be the recipients of interventions from multiple youth service systems (e.g., mental health, juvenile justice, education), whose efforts are difficult to coordinate and often fail to fully conceptualize families' strengths and challenges (Greenberg & Lippold, 2014). Thus, a small proportion of youth with severe behavior problems receive the majority of resources and services from those systems (Shufelt & Cocozza, 2006). Taken together, these observations indicate a clear need for comprehensive, family- and community-based treatments that can address the complex needs of youth with serious DBDs and their families.

Unfortunately, even youth with severe, chronic behavior problems rarely receive such comprehensive treatments in the United States. Instead, typical interventions focus on individual youth characteristics associated with behavior problems, rather than familial and social characteristics, and are delivered in restrictive or difficult-to-access settings (e.g., outpatient clinic, group home, juvenile detention) that may impede generalization to the youth's daily life and relationships (see McCart & Sheidow, 2016). In fact, only 5% of youth who engage in serious and violent criminal behavior receive a treatment that targets factors in the familial and social background (Greenwood, 2008; Henggeler & Schoenwald, 2011). On the other hand, individually-focused interventions with demonstrated null or even negative effects continue to be widely used, including Scared Straight and wilderness challenge programs (Lipsey, 2009) and antipsychotic medications (Correll et al., 2009; Maayan & Correll, 2011). Without effective treatment, persistent patterns of antisocial

Developmental Pathways to Disruptive, Impulse-Control, and Conduct Disorders.
DOI: https://doi.org/10.1016/B978-0-12-811323-3.00011-0

behavior are associated with poor educational, occupational, and health outcomes (Moore, Silberg, Roberson-Nay, & Mezuk, 2017; Odgers et al., 2008) and result in serious personal (e.g., victimization) and economic effects (Kilpatrick & Acierno, 2003; McCollister, French, & Fang, 2010; Robinson & Keithley, 2000). Thus, an increased emphasis on family- and community-based treatments is necessary to address the needs of youth with DBDs and their families, with the resultant reductions in antisocial behavior in turn benefitting taxpayers, victims, and society at large (see Greenwood & Welsh, 2012).

Despite the need for additional large-scale progress, several family- and community-based treatments of DBDs have demonstrated considerable promise over the past several decades both in controlled research studies and in widespread dissemination to community settings. This chapter provides an overview of the family- and community-based models with the strongest empirical support for treatment of DBDs. We begin by introducing the five models, including their respective clinical characteristics and associated research evidence. We then discuss the common theoretical, empirical, and clinical foundations that underlie all family- and community-based treatment models and likely account for their effectiveness with serious and complex DBD cases. A case example involving one such model, multisystemic therapy (MST), is used to illustrate all of these foundational characteristics. Finally, we conclude by discussing several areas that will require additional attention in the continued development of family- and community-based treatments for youth DBDs.

Family and community-based treatment models

Inclusion criteria

We reviewed treatment models in the present chapter that met the following three inclusion criteria: (1) Used a family- or community-based mode of intervention, defined as interventions that addressed DBD symptoms by making positive changes in the youth's family and broader social ecology through direct interventions (e.g., home-based service delivery involving multiple family members). (2) Targeted youth (i.e., less than 18 years of age at the beginning of treatment) with a history of behavior problems requiring treatment due to associated distress, impairment, or risk of harm. We did not require specific DBD diagnoses because youth were often referred by service systems, such as juvenile justice, and were not necessarily assigned a formal diagnosis. (3) In at least two published, prospective research studies, showed positive effects on a measure of behavior problems or related outcomes (e.g., arrests) relative to a comparison condition (e.g., alternative treatment, treatment as usual, no-intervention control). Inclusion criteria were met by five treatments: multisystemic therapy (MST; Henggeler & Borduin, 1990; Henggeler, Schoenwald, Borduin, Rowland, & Cunningham, 2009; see www.mstservices.com), treatment foster care Oregon (TFCO; Chamberlain, 2003; see www.tfcoregon.com), functional family therapy (FFT; Alexander & Parsons, 1982; Sexton, 2011; see www.fftllc.com); brief strategic family therapy (BSFT; Szapocznik, Hervis, & Schwartz, 2003; Szapocznik & Kurtines, 1989; see www.bsft.org), and multidimensional family therapy (MDFT; Liddle, 2002, 2009; see www.mdft.org).

MST

MST (Henggeler & Borduin, 1990; Henggeler et al., 2009) is a family- and community-based treatment for serious conduct problems in youth. MST interventions target risk factors that have a demonstrated association with illegal and/or violent behaviors, such as individual mental health problems, caregiver parenting skills, family functioning, association with antisocial peers, and poor academic performance. Therapists use clinical techniques from evidence-based behavioral, cognitive-behavioral, and structural/strategic family therapies to achieve short-term therapeutic goals, which are designed to address the needs and strengths of the social–ecological systems in which the youth is embedded (i.e., family, peers, school, community). Treatment proceeds through an iterative process of assessment, case conceptualization, and intervention that follows nine core treatment principles. To facilitate engagement and minimize barriers to treatment, MST therapists deliver services in the home and other community settings (e.g., school, recreation center) at times convenient to the youths and caregivers (including evenings, weekends, and 24-7 crisis management). MST teams consist of two to four therapists and a supervisor, with each therapist carrying a caseload of four to six families. The average course of treatment lasts 3 to 5 months, with frequent initial contacts (i.e., 3+ per week) that are reduced commensurate with clinical progress.

The developers of MST have prioritized rigorous evaluation of the model over the past 40 years (see Henggeler, 2011), with more than a dozen clinical trials demonstrating that MST can produce reductions in youth behavior problems and related negative outcomes (e.g., incarceration and probation). Early quasi-experimental (Henggeler et al., 1986) and randomized (Borduin et al., 1995; Henggeler, Melton, & Smith, 1992) trials by the MST developers indicated that the model produced significant reductions, relative to usual mental health (i.e., individual or group) treatment or probation services, in youth behavior problems, rearrests, weeks incarceration, association with deviant peers, and youth and family psychiatric symptoms, as well as increases in family functioning and peer relations. Long-term follow-ups of those randomized trials demonstrated that reductions in arrest rates were robust for as long as 2.4 years (Henggeler, Melton, Smith, Schoenwald, & Hanley, 1993) to 21.9 years (Sawyer & Borduin, 2011) post-treatment. Furthermore, for families in the Borduin et al. study, MST also produced reductions in arrests and incarceration for closest-in-age siblings (Wagner, Borduin, Sawyer, & Dopp, 2014) and primary caregivers (Johnides, Borduin, Wagner, & Dopp, 2017) over 20 years post-treatment. In addition to research conducted by treatment developers, several randomized trials conducted by independent investigators have replicated the effectiveness of MST for severe conduct problems in the United States (Timmons-Mitchell, Bender, Kishna, & Mitchell, 2006), Norway (Ogden & Hagen,

2006; Ogden & Halliday-Boykins, 2004), the United Kingdom (Butler, Baruch, Hickey, & Fonagy, 2011), and the Netherlands (Asscher et al., 2013).

Adaptations of MST

The MST model has been flexibly adapted for the treatment of a number of complex clinical problems. Two of those adaptations, MST for problem sexual behaviors (MST-PSB; Borduin & Munschy, 2014; see www.mstpsb.com) and MST for substance abuse (MST-SA; see www.mstservices.com), are relevant to the present chapter. Both models consider the targeted problem behaviors to be specific manifestations of a general underlying tendency for antisocial behavior, rather than representing unique populations each requiring a different treatment approach, as in adult populations.

MST-PSB is an adaptation of MST for youth who engage in serious (e.g., repeated, violent) problematic sexual behaviors. The MST-PSB model uses the same social–ecological framework and model of service delivery as in standard MST, but focuses on aspects of the youth's ecology that are functionally related to PSB (e.g., caregiver and youth denial about sexual offenses, barriers to effective parental monitoring of sexual development, developmentally inappropriate peer relations) as well as relapse prevention and victim safety. To date, three clinical trials of MST-PSB are the only randomized trials that have been conducted with juvenile sexual offenders (see Dopp, Borduin, Rothman, & Letourneau, 2017) and include (1) a small initial trial (Borduin, Henggeler, Blaske, & Stein, 1990) of MST-PSB vs individual therapy, as well as (2) a hybrid efficacy–effectiveness trial (Borduin, Schaeffer, & Heiblum, 2009) and (3) an effectiveness trial (Letourneau et al., 2009, 2013) that each compared MST-PSB to cognitive-behavioral therapy. Across studies, MST-PSB has been found to produce greater improvements in behavior problems (sexual and nonsexual) than the comparison treatments; the efficacy trials found lower rearrest rates (for sexual and nonsexual offenses) and fewer days incarcerated up to 8.9 years post-treatment in the MST-PSB conditions.

MST-SA focuses on youth who engage in serious antisocial behavior in the context of a substance use disorder. As in MST-PSB, MST-SA applies the standard MST framework and service delivery model to address social–ecological factors that increase the risk of substance use (e.g., physiological addiction, parental modeling of substance use behavior, association with substance-using peers). The therapist also helps caregivers to regularly monitor youth substance use (e.g., with urine drug screens) and enforce consequences associated with use and abstinence. Two randomized trials of MST-SA have demonstrated decreases in substance use relative to usual community treatment (Henggeler, Clingempeel, Brondino, & Pickrel, 2002; Henggeler, Pickrel, & Brondino, 1999) and when delivered to participants in a juvenile drug court (vs. drug court alone; Henggeler et al., 2006). In the former study, MST-SA was also associated with decreased violent crime (Henggeler et al., 2002). A follow-up of the latter study revealed decreased substance use among siblings in the MST-SA group (Rowland, Chapman, & Henggeler, 2008).

TFCO

TFCO (Chamberlain, 2003), previously known as multidimensional treatment foster care, is an intensive community-based foster care intervention used as an alternative to residential settings, group care, and juvenile detention centers. The TFCO model primarily targets youth with severe emotional and behavior disturbances whose difficulties have not been well-managed by intensive outpatient treatment. Youth receiving TFCO are placed in highly trained therapeutic foster homes for periods of 6 to 9 months, during which time a multidisciplinary TFCO team supports the youth and families through daily monitoring, weekly individual and family therapy focused on behavioral (e.g., behavior management), and cognitive-behavioral (e.g., problem-solving skills training) interventions, medication management, and on-call crisis management. Each team carries a caseload of approximately 10 families at a time. Interventions focus on close supervision, consistency and stability of placement, supportive relationships with adults and peers, and diversions from association with deviant peers. Involvement of caregivers from the youth's aftercare placement is emphasized to maximize the maintenance and generalization of gains made during the TFCO placement. Separate adaptations of TFCO target the developmental needs of preschool-age children (TFCO-P), school-age children (TFCO-C), and adolescents (TFCO-A); TFCO-C and TFCO-A are most relevant to this chapter, whereas TFCO-P is primarily used to address child maltreatment rather than DBDs.

Controlled evaluations have provided support for the clinical effectiveness of TFCO over the past several decades. Previous studies have demonstrated the benefits of TFCO versus group care-as-usual in terms of decreases in DBD-related outcomes such as arrest rates, number days in detention centers, disruption of placement, and self-reported delinquency in samples of male (Chamberlain & Moore, 1998; Chamberlain & Reid, 1998) and female (Leve, Chamberlain, & Reid, 2005) adolescents. Other studies have found evidence of additional positive outcomes for the samples in the aforementioned clinical trials, such as reduced teen pregnancy rates (Kerr, Leve, & Chamberlain, 2009), depressive symptoms (Harold et al., 2013), substance use (Rhoades, Leve, Harold, Kim & Chamberlain,2014), and psychotic symptoms (Poulton et al., 2014), as well as increased school attendance and homework completion (Leve & Chamberlain, 2007). In addition, follow-up studies of these TFCO clinical trials have demonstrated the persistence of gains over periods as long as 24 months post-treatment (Chamberlain, Leve, & DeGarmo, 2007; Eddy, Whaley, & Chamberlain, 2004). Moreover, the positive effects of TFCO on youth behavior problems were replicated in randomized clinical trials conducted by independent researchers in the United Kingdom (Westermark, Hansson, & Olsson, 2011) and Sweden (Bergström & Höjman, 2016).

FFT

FFT (Alexander & Parsons, 1982; Sexton, 2011) is a family-based treatment designed to work with families of adolescents who engage in a range of problematic externalizing behaviors such as status offenses (e.g., breaking curfew, skipping school), delinquency, and substance use. FFT therapists seek to address dysfunctional youth behavior by changing family interactions and improving intrafamilial relationship functioning. Given the lower acuity of its target population, FFT teams can support up to eight therapists (per supervisor) each with caseloads of 15–20 families; furthermore, the treatment can be delivered as a home-based model or in traditional outpatient settings. FFT is comprised of five major phases delivered over 3 to 4 months of weekly sessions: (1) engagement, (2) motivation, and (3) relational assessment, which together comprise assessment and treatment planning; (4) behavior change, in which problem behaviors are targeted for change using behavioral (e.g., communication training) and cognitive-behavioral (e.g., assertiveness training, anger management) interventions; and (5) generalization, during which the therapist helps the family extend gains into multiple behavioral domains and systems (e.g., increasing endogenous support from family or school personnel) while planning for future challenges.

Several controlled trials support the efficacy and effectiveness of FFT. Compared to alternative treatment conditions (e.g., family group treatment, group homes), FFT has demonstrated greater reductions in status offenses in randomized (Alexander & Parsons, 1973) and quasie-xperimental (Barton, Alexander, Waldron, Turner, & Warburton, 1985) studies. More recently, a large ($N = 917$) quasi-experimental effectiveness study demonstrated that FFT produced lower rates of felony and violent crimes compared to usual probation services, but only when therapists had high supervisor ratings of adherence to the FFT model (Sexton & Turner, 2010). In addition, siblings of participants in the Alexander and Parsons (1973) trial had less court involvement in the FFT group vs comparison groups at 40-month follow-up (Klein, Alexander,& Parsons, 1977). Regarding replication by independent investigators, quasi-experimental trials have found favorable recidivism rates for FFT participants with a predominantly rural sample (Gordon, Arbuthnot, Gustafson, & McGreen,1988; Gordon, Graves, & Arbuthnot, 1995) in follow-ups from 2.5 to 5.0 years. Other studies have found benefits of FFT in terms of reduced emotional and behavioral problems (Celinska, Furrer, & Cheng, 2013; Hartnett, Carr, & Sexton, 2016). FFT has also shown some promise, albeit with inconsistent results, in the treatment of youth substance use problems (Waldron, Brody, & Hops, 2017). However, a recent study found no difference between FFT and probation as usual with a racially diverse sample (Darnell & Schuler, 2015) and it has not shown effectiveness with juvenile sexual offenders (Erickson, 2008). Overall, the evidence for effectiveness of FFT is promising but is generally limited to youth with less serious or complex DBD presentations.

BSFT

BSFT (Szapocznik et al., 2003; Szapocznik & Kurtines, 1989) is a family-based treatment that primarily targets substance use in youth (ages 8–17) but has also demonstrated significant effects on associated behavior problems (e.g., vandalism, truancy). BSFT focuses on the role of the family as a foundation for socilization and development and uses a variety of behavioral (e.g., contingency management), cognitive-behavioral (e.g., communication skills training), and structural–strategic interventions, over approximately 12 to 16 weekly sessions, to target individual, family, school, and peer factors that contribute to problem behaviors. Early BSFT research focused primarily on intervention with black and Hispanic youth in southern Florida and, as such, the model provides more explicit guidance for consideration of cultural factors than other family- and community-based treatments (see Robbins et al., 2003). BSFT can be delivered in home-based or outpatient mental health formats; in either case, the therapist incorporates a number of engagement strategies that maximize family participation in treatment (Coatsworth, Santisteban, McBride, & Szapocznik, 2001; Santisteban et al., 1996). BSFT teams typically consist of four therapists and a supervisor, with each therapist carrying a caseload of approximately 12 families at a time.

In addition to evidence for its effectiveness in reducing adolescent substance use (see Hogue, Henderson, Ozechowski,& Robbins, 2014; Robbins et al., 2011), the results of several controlled trials suggest that BSFT can reduce youth DBD symptoms as well as improve family functioning and socialized aggression (Santisteban et al., 2003; Szapoczniket al., 1989). In fact, a recent effectiveness study found lower incidences of incarceration and decreased externalizing behaviors 3–7 years following treatment for the BSFT group versus treatment as usual (Horigian et al., 2015). The generalizability of the aforementioned study findings is limited by the involvement of BSFT developers, but an independent effectiveness trial recently demonstrated the promise of BSFT (vs. phone contact and referrals) in reducing conduct problems and substance use with gang-affiliated Mexican–American adolescents (Valdez, Cepeda, Parrish, Horowitz, & Kaplan, 2013).

MDFT

MDFT (Liddle, 2002, 2009) is a family-based treatment for substance use and associated behavior problems in youth and young adults (ages 9–26). It is similar to other family- and community-based treatments in that problem behaviors are conceptualized in terms of risk and protective factors associated with the individual, parent, family, and community (e.g., school, juvenile court). These risk and protective factors are targeted through weekly sessions across three stages of treatment: (1) engagement ("build the foundation"); (2) behavior change ("prompt action and change") through behavioral, cognitive, and structural–strategic interventions; and (3) generalization and sustainment ("seal the changes and exit"). A course of MDFT typically lasts 3 months, with 2–3 sessions per week in the first two phases and less frequent (weekly or biweekly) contact in the third phase. MDFT teams primarily operate in outpatient office settings but therapists sometimes deliver in-home services.

As with BSFT, controlled studies of MDFT have indicated considerable effectiveness in the treatment of substance use disorders (see Hogue et al., 2014; Van der pol et al., 2017). Moreover, several of those studies (e.g., Liddle et al., 2001; Liddle, Rowe, Dakof, Henderson, & Greenbaum, 2009) revealed that MDFT resulted in greater reductions in DBD symptoms, as well as associated risk factors in family, peer, and school domains, than did comparison group therapy conditions up to 12 months post-treatment. The positive impact of MDFT has also been replicated with youth participating in juvenile drug court (Dakof et al., 2015) and at sites in five European nations (Schaub et al., 2014). It is important to note that a core group of researchers, often including the treatment developer, has generated all of the aforementioned data. Thus, independent replications of the effects of MDFT on DBD symptoms is warranted to assess the generalizability of findings to date.

Theoretical foundations

Family- and community-based treatments for DBDs are rooted in several theoretical traditions that emphasize contextual factors in the development, maintenance, and amelioration of mental disorders and symptoms. These theories inform the emphasis in each of these models on intervention capacity to address a comprehensive and individualized (i.e., specific to a particular youth and family) set of risk factors while concomitantly building protective factors. Moreover, the importance of parents and other caregivers is highlighted across theoretical schools, given that those individuals are the most proximal (i.e., direct) influence on youth behavior. Nevertheless, as we discuss next, there are key differences between various theories and the relative emphasis on each theory differs between treatment models.

Family systems theory (Bateson, 1972; Hoffman, 1981; P. P. Minuchin, 1985) underlies all of the family- and community-based treatments for DBDs to some extent. This theory views the family as a rule-based system in which all behaviors, including problematic ones such as DBD symptoms, "fit" within the context of reciprocal and circular relations between family members (Pinsof & Lebow, 2005). Thus, a family systems therapist might consider how caregiver discipline strategies influence youth aggressive behaviors, how the aggressive behaviors of the youth shape and guide the responses of the caregivers, and what function each of these behaviors serves in the family's daily functioning when planning interventions. Therapeutic approaches that are based on family systems theory include structural therapy, which emphasizes the organization of relationships within the family and seeks to reorganize dysfunctional structures into functional ones (S. Minuchin, 1974); strategic therapy, in which problem behaviors are understood in the context of modifiable behavioral sequences that serve functions within the family (Haley, 1987); and family communications therapy, which attempts to modify the ways in which family members communicate about and jointly understand problems (Watzlawick, Bavelas, & Jackson, 1967). MST, BSFT, and MDFT tend to emphasize structural and strategic interventions in particular, through processes such as "joining" the family system and targeting sequences of family interaction for modification. On the other hand, FFT is most strongly associated with communication-focused interventions, given the strong emphasis on developing a shared understanding (e.g., through reframing and communication skills training) in FFT (see Alexander & Parsons, 1982; Sexton, 2011).

Social learning theory (Bandura, 1977) is an extension of classic behavioral theories that complements family systems theory in several ways. Most importantly, this theory emphasizes the influence of social context on learning (e.g., through modeling and vicarious reinforcement) as well as the reciprocal nature of those learning experiences. Of particular relevance to DBDs is coercion theory, an extension of social learning theory that describes a cyclical pattern of behavioral contingencies in which parent and youth engage in aggressive behavior (e.g., yelling, threatening, physical force) to control one another's actions, increasingly eroding both family members' abilities to engage in alternative, noncoercive behaviors over time due to differential reinforcement (Granic & Patterson, 2006). For example, if a parent and teenager disagree about household rules, either could escalate coercion until the family reaches a crisis (e.g., parent hits the teenager as punishment, after which the teenager complies; teenager threatens to run away from home, after which the parent acquiesces their demands). Social learning theory is relevant to all family- and community-based treatments for DBD, but it was most influential to the development of TFCO (see Chamberlain, 2003) as indicated by a heavy emphasis on learning-based (e.g., behavioral, cognitive-behavioral) interventions in that model.

The aforementioned theories are most readily applied to interactions between immediate family members, yet all of the treatment models presented in this chapter include interventions involving external systems with which families interact. The theory of social ecology (Bronfenbrenner, 1979) extends the basic tenets of family systems and social learning theories to characterize broader and more numerous contextual influences on psychosocial functioning: The individual is viewed as nested within a network of interconnected systems that include the family, peers, school, neighborhood, and community. In terms of youth behavior problems, the theory of social ecology suggests that such behaviors can be maintained by problematic transactions between the youth and any given system (e.g., a youth is truant from school due to a history of negative experiences in academic settings) as well as among the pertinent systems (e.g., disagreement between parents and school personnel undermines enforcement of consistent consequences for youth truancy). This theory also emphasizes the importance of ecological validity in understanding human behavior; i.e., the assumption that behavior should be understood within its naturally occurring contexts. Thus, all family- and community-based treatments for DBDs are consistent with the theory of social ecology to the extent to which assessment and treatment take place in the same contexts in which problem behaviors occur. In particular, MST (see Henggeler, Schoenwald, et al., 2009) most explicitly incorporates principles of the theory of social ecology into its model of clinical services (i.e., service delivery in home, school, and community settings) and interventions (i.e., extrafamilial drivers of behavior targeted from the outset of therapy).

Empirical foundations

As would be predicted by the previously reviewed theories, empirical research has identified a number of risk factors for DBDs across family, peer, school, and neighborhood domains (see Farrington & Loeber, 2000; Frick, 2012; Henry, Tolan, & Gorman-Smith, 2001; Herrenkohl et al., 2001; Liberman, 2008; Loeber et al., 2009; Monahan, Steinberg, & Cauffman, 2009). Individual youth characteristics, such as impulsivity, hostile attribution biases, and limited prosocial traits are also associated with DBDs and may serve as important clinical targets or moderators of treatment effectiveness in family- and community-based treatments. Nevertheless, those individual-level variables also have been well-characterized in previous reviews, as well as in other chapters in this book, and thus are not discussed in detail here. Moreover, it should be noted that many social–ecological risk factors for DBDs are also associated with youth problem sexual behaviors (Ronis & Borduin, 2013; van Wijk et al., 2005) and substance abuse (American Academy of Child and Adolescent Psychiatry, 2005; Hawkins, Catalano, & Miller, 1992).

Family context is a key influence on the development of DBDs in youth. Parents of youth with DBDs have been found to use frequent, yet unpredictable, punitive behaviors (e.g., yelling, nagging, threatening, spanking) and infrequent reinforcement, including highly aggressive forms of punishment (e.g., hitting, slapping) meant to gain control over the youth's behavior (Salzinger, Feldman, Hammer, & Rosario, 1993; Stormshak, Bierman, McMahon, & Lengua, 2000). Furthermore, parental relationships of youths with DBDs are often characterized by low warmth, high rigidity, and ineffective communication (Burke, Loeber, Lahey, & Rathouz, 2005; Caspi et al., 2004; McCarty & McMahon, 2003) that exceed the effects of passive genotype–environment correlations (Bornovalova et al., 2014). However, it is important to note that parenting behaviors may be influenced by various social–ecological factors, such as youth temperament and behavior (Pardini, 2008) or cumulative socioeconomic disadvantage across generations (Scaramella, Neppl, Ontai, & Conger, 2008), in addition to individual characteristics of the parent such as learning history, intelligence, or psychopathology. Moreover, the behavior of other members of the family can indirectly influence the development of youth DBDs through modeling of conflict and antisocial behavior. For example, discord in caregiver relationships is linked to delinquency and externalizing behaviors in youth (Amato, 2001; Burt, Barnes, McGue, & Iacono, 2009; Bornovalova et al., 2014), and children of parents who engage in antisocial behavior are more likely to engage in similar behaviors (Herndon & Iacono, 2005).

Outside of family functioning, association with deviant peers is the other correlate with the strongest relationship to behavior problems in youth (Gifford-Smith, Dodge, Dishion, & McCord, 2005; Keenan, Loeber, Zhang, Stouthamer-Loeber, & van Kammen, 1995; Monahan et al., 2009). Youth with behavior problems are often rejected by their typically developing peers, leading to delays in social development and increased affiliation with peers who also exhibit behavior problems (Cillessen & Mayeux, 2004; Dishion, Spracklen, Andrews, & Patterson, 1996). This is concerning because many of the typical interventions (e.g., group treatment, residential settings) for youth behavior problems group together peers with similar disruptive behaviors and isolate them from prosocial peers (Gifford-Smith et al., 2005). Furthermore, school underachievement is associated with DBDs, although the causal pathways of this relation are highly complex. Indeed, DBD symptoms may interfere with school performance, especially in the context of attention-deficit/hyperactivity symptoms (Frick et al., 1991; Metcalfe, Harvey, & Laws, 2013), yet, academic difficulties may also lead to poor self-image and social bonding that increases problematic behaviors (Hinshaw, 1992) or affiliation with deviant peers (Herrenkohl et al., 2001). Moreover, neighborhood and community factors may provide an important context for the development of DBDs. Youth from economically disadvantaged neighborhoods are exposed to significantly more stress, which may heighten aggressive behavior (Attar, Guerra, & Tolan,1994). Youth who reside in neighborhoods with high levels of community violence are at greater risk of engaging in violent behavior themselves (Margolin & Gordis, 2000; Schwartz & Proctor, 2000) and families in such neighborhoods experience less cohesion and social support among community members (Sampson, Raudenbush, & Earls, 1997).

Finally, it is important to note that the relative importance of various risk factors may depend on other youth characteristics. For example, youth gender appears to differentiate both the strength and relevance of certain risk factors, yet the findings presented in this section are based on samples largely or entirely comprised of male youth (see Keenan, Loeber, & Green, 1999). Female youth seem to be more strongly affected by conflictual or disengaged relationships with caregivers (Kroneman, Loeber, Hipwell, & Koot, 2009; Pittman & Chase-Lansdale, 2001) and also engage in higher rates of relational aggression in family interactions (Taylor & Borduin, 2014). Furthermore, compared to male peers with DBDs, they show greater susceptibility to peer influence (e.g., from deviant peers; Rose & Rudolph, 2006) and can be more strongly ostracized due to their aggressive behavior conflicting with stereotypical gender roles (Kroneman et al., 2009). In sum, treatment providers need to consider risk and protective factors for DBDs from all levels of a youth's social ecology as well as interactions between those factors and the youth's characteristics.

Clinical foundations

Consistent with their theoretical and empirical foundations, family- and community-based treatments for DBDs are designed to provide intensive interventions that target the social–ecological risk factors that influence serious antisocial behaviors. As a result, the five treatment models described in this chapter share a number of common features in terms of clinical service delivery strategies. For example, parents and other family members are directly involved in therapy, as these individuals are viewed as valuable resources even if they are characterized by serious and multiple needs. The models also place a high degree of responsibility on the therapist to select (and continuously refine) intervention strategies that will achieve targeted changes in youth behaviors and associated risk factors. Nevertheless, there is some variability between models depending on their theoretical underpinnings and specific target population.

Family- and community-based treatments use different strategies to address the challenge of engaging families and other relevant stakeholders. Such efforts are critical, given the inconsistent attendance and high drop-out rates in more traditional services (e.g., office-based treatment; Kazdin, 2015). MST and TFCO therapists deliver all services in home, school, and community settings as a way to decrease barriers to service access. FFT, BSFT, and MDFT providers sometimes deliver services in this way, but may also deliver office-based services depending on the needs of each case or the administrative structure of their service organization. Regardless of delivery method, therapists who provide these models seek to engage and increase motivation of family members through processes such as "joining" with the family (i.e., establishing and balancing a complex network of therapeutic alliances with all members), identifying benefits to all family members for making desired changes, and problem-solving practical barriers to treatment attendance.

An added benefit to the delivery of interventions in natural settings is the increased ecological validity of services. By assessing and intervening with problem behaviors within the relevant social contexts, family- and community-based treatments maximize the likelihood that changes will generalize across time, settings, and family members. In FFT, BSFT, and MDFT programs, the family is viewed as the primary social ecology for the youth's behavior problems and thus even office-based services can be ecologically valid to the extent that they involve the entire family. For the more severe forms of DBD treated by MST and TFCO programs, delivery of services in home, school, and community settings is essential to allow participation of all relevant family members (e.g., siblings, godparents, grandparents) as well as promote participation of other important adults in the youth's life (e.g., teachers, probation officers) across all phases of treatment. Due to the high risk of harm (e.g., by assault, runaway, self-harm) in more clinically complex families, MST and TFCO provide on-call crisis services 24 hours a day, 7 days a week, to ensure that an interventionist can coach the family through clinical crises at the moment they occur. Overall, by providing intensive, accessible, and ecologically valid services for brief periods, family- and community-based treatments can produce large reductions in DBD symptoms that are sustained many years after completion of treatment.

The organizational structure of service provision should be matched to support differences in clinical procedures between the various models of family- and community-based treatments. For instance, organizations must support the ability of MST or TFCO therapists to travel to community settings for service delivery, flex schedules to hold appointments at times convenient to the family (e.g., evenings and weekends), and provide multiple services to a family in a given week. Moreover, these family- and community-based treatments are all delivered by licensed teams who together attend training, participate in group supervision and expert consultation, and (when relevant) provide on-call crisis coverage while exclusively delivering the selected treatment model. MST and FFT providers are generalists who provide all clinical services to a limited caseload of families, whereas clinical roles in TFCO are highly specialized such that an individual therapist, family therapist, and skills coach each provide services to all families on the entire team's caseload. These role differences reflect the relatively higher emphasis on skills training versus family interventions in TFCO. In contrast to those three models, BSFT and MDFT (as well as MST-SA) require extensive specialized knowledge of youth substance use disorders and treatment, as does MST-PSB for problem sexual behaviors.

It is notable that all of these treatment models allow for considerable flexibility in delivery, with fidelity to the model guided by general principles rather than specification of session-by-session content. Such an approach facilitates use with complex cases that present a variety of clinical needs and strengths. The specific guiding principles differ from model to model but typically emphasize factors such as consideration of the social–ecological context of behaviors; present-focused and action-oriented solutions to problems that require effort from all individuals involved; matching of interventions to the developmental needs of the youth; and empowerment of parents and other caregivers to effect long-term change. FFT, BSFT, and MDFT further organize the tasks of treatment into phases that guide engagement, behavior change, and generalization of gains. To promote therapist fidelity to the specified model and principles, each family- and community-based treatment requires quality assurance activities such as training, expert consultation, and monitoring of outcomes. The nature and duration of these strategies differ between treatment developers; e.g., all require a period of expert consultation, with MDFT permitting full certification after the shortest period (6 months) and MST requiring ongoing quality assurance for the duration of program certification.

Case example: MST with Carlos

The following case example illustrates the theoretical, empirical, and clinical foundations of MST. The individuals described in the case example are composites of various families whom we have seen benefit—or suspect would have benefitted — from MST over the years. All identifying information has been modified to protect confidentiality.

Carlos was a 14-year-old Hispanic male who lived with his mother, maternal uncle, and three younger siblings (ages 12, 8, and 5) in Springdale, AR. He was referred to MST following an incident in which he stole his uncle's car and ran away from home overnight following an argument. That incident was the culmination of an escalating pattern of interpersonal conflicts between Carlos and various family members, coupled with occasional property offenses (e.g., shoplifting), over the past 2 years. Based on a psychosocial evaluation conducted in juvenile detention, the family court judge assigned Carlos and his family to participate in MST as a term of his probation. However, she warned them that she could execute an order of incarceration for any future offense (e.g., minor probation violation). The case was referred to Mary, a clinical social worker, who provided the family with a 4-month course of MST.

Initial sessions focused on engaging with the family and other relevant systems, developing overarching treatment goals, and identifying proximal intervention targets to achieve those goals. At the first session, Mary met with Carlos and his mother in their home and was also introduced to each of the younger siblings. All parties agreed to family goals of spending quality time together, solving problems through words, and respecting others' property. Carlos agreed to pass on what he learned in treatment to his younger siblings, and they agreed to listen. However, it quickly became clear that Mary had failed to identify a key driver of conflict in the family—Carlos's uncle—which resulted in failure of this initial plan. The uncle had moved in and become the primary disciplinarian in the home after Carlos's father left his mother 4 years ago; when Carlos entered puberty, he began insisting that his uncle no longer had authority over him and that he should be the "man of the house." After a particularly heated argument in which Carlos punched a wall, his mother privately admitted to Mary that she would prefer to be in charge of disciplining her own children, but doubted her ability to manage Carlos's "out of control" behavior on her own. Mary and the mother invited the uncle to participate in future sessions, which required a change to evening appointments to accommodate his work schedule.

Over the course of several weeks, Mary—in consultation with the supervisor and other therapists on her MST team—designed a series of tailored interventions to address the individual and familial factors that influenced the Carlos–mother–uncle triad. Ongoing assessment was a critical component to ensuring that the case conceptualization was accurate and for determining when each family member was prepared for the next step in the sequence. For example, Mary conducted several individual meetings with Carlos to teach him anger management skills such as relaxation and cognitive reappraisal (e.g., "I am becoming a man, and that means learning to be in touch with my emotions"), so that he could exert better self-regulation during heated family discussions. On the other hand, Mary quickly discontinued parent management training with Carlos's mother; it became clear that the mother had adequate skills in this area, but did not want to disrespect her brother by asking him to provide less support. Using a structural family therapy approach recently covered in a booster training by her MST Expert Consultant, Mary placed the mother back at the head of the family by assigning her the role of mediator between Carlos and his uncle; mother monitored the appropriateness of their discussions and was tasked with determining when an issue had been adequately resolved. As she gained confidence, she suggested that her brother teach her son about "the ways of being a man" —topics such as shaving, sexual education, and respecting women. These "man-to-man" talks were uncomfortable at first but brought Carlos and his uncle closer together over time.

Everyone agreed that family life was better with mom in charge. An increasingly warm, cohesive, and structured family life freed up additional resources to address factors outside the home that had impacted Carlos's behavior. For example, approximately 2 months into treatment, Carlos was caught with a pack of cigarettes by one of his teachers. Initially, his mother was furious and called his probation officer to complain about the behavior, but she regretted that decision when the probation officer informed her that Carlos would have to go back to court because he had committed a probation violation. Noting a chance for the mother to develop better advocacy skills, Mary arranged a meeting with her and the probation officer and conducted extensive preparation with the mother ahead of time. In contrast to her previous passive approaches, mother was able to convince the probation officer to forego another court hearing by stating "I'm gonna come down on him with much tougher consequences than anything the court can throw at him." Indeed, Carlos was grounded for a month and his mother arranged for him to volunteer at the local Ronald McDonald House, so that he could learn more about the effects of smoking and cancer. She also worked with Mary to identify prosocial peers with whom he could spend time on a "trial basis" before his grounding officially ended. Carlos attempted to defy the terms of his consequences—e.g., by sneaking out of the house after curfew—several times, but mother had "learned her lesson" about crises and always consulted with the on-call MST therapist rather than the probation officer. Through coaching from Mary, mother was able to maintain control of the family dynamic for that critical month. During one session, Carlos told his siblings, "Mom is different now—she really means business. We better do what she says." The siblings listened attentively to his advice.

Three years after the end of treatment, Mary received a phone call from Carlos's mother informing her that Carlos was getting ready to graduate from high school and that she could not be more proud. His uncle had eventually moved out of the home, but Carlos still looked up to him—in fact, his plan was to attend trade school and get a job at his uncle's company. The mother started to thank Mary for getting their family "back on track," but Mary quickly pointed out—as she had many times during their 4 months of working together—that every good thing in Carlos's life could be traced back to his mother's influence. They agreed to disagree.

Future research directions

Despite the promise of family- and community-based treatments to reduce the individual, familial, and societal impacts of youth problem behaviors, none is effective with every youth and even the most well-researched models still have limited availability in community settings. Thus, continued development and refinement of family- and community-based treatments for youth DBDs should be a priority for scientists and policymakers alike who are interested in maximizing the public health impact of these treatments. In this section, we offer several recommendations for key research that would expand the existing literature in this area.

Moderators and mediators of change

Most studies evaluating family- and community-based treatments for youth DBDs have focused on comparison of group means (vs. comparison conditions) on key post treatment outcome measures. It would also useful be for researchers to identify the mechanisms by which the treatments achieve their effects (i.e., mediators) as well as the conditions under which they are most effective (i.e., moderators), yet far less research has rigorously evaluated these aspects of effectiveness.

Regarding mediators of clinical effects, identification of such variables is key to validating the theories of change that underlie family- and community-based treatment models and might ultimately help to improve their efficiency in achieving clinically significant changes. All of the treatment models reviewed in this chapter propose that changes in family functioning (e.g., adaptability and cohesion, parenting skills) are a primary mechanism for reductions in youth problem behaviors. In the most comprehensive mediation study in this area, Deković, Asscher, Manders, Prins, & van der Laan (2012) demonstrated that reduced DBD symptoms in MST (vs. treatment-as-usual) were mediated by month-to-month improvements in parental self-efficacy and positive discipline skills, with change in self-efficacy preceding change in discipline skills. Other, simpler mediation studies have also found changes in parenting practices to mediate the effects of MST (Henggeler, Letourneau, et al., 2009; Huey, Henggeler, Brondino, & Pickrel, 2000) and TFCO (Eddy & Chamberlain, 2000) on youth antisocial behavior (including problem sexual behaviors). Findings regarding BSFT (Horigian et al., 2015; Santistebanet al., 2003) and MDFT (Henderson, Rowe, Dakof, Hawes, & Liddle, 2009) are consistent but have focused primarily on mechanisms for reduced substance use, and the proposed mechanisms of FFT have not been formally evaluated. Moreover, reduced association with deviant peers has been found to mediate effectiveness of TFCO (Eddy & Chamberlain, 2000; Van Ryzin & Leve, 2012) and MST-PSB (Henggeler, Letourneau, et al., 2009), although it remains unclear whether changes in peer relations are themselves mediated by changes in parenting. Given the heterogeneous risk factors for youth DBDs, studies that match specific clinical techniques (e.g., interventions targeting peer relations) to youths' clinical presentations (i.e., risk profiles) may be necessary to conduct adequately powered tests of all possible mediating pathways (see Dopp, Borduin, White, & Kuppens, 2017).

In terms of moderating variables, identification of factors that influence the effectiveness of a treatment can help to define the appropriate scope of its delivery or suggest refinements to address subpopulations of interest. For example, several studies have indicated that MST does not show differential effectiveness with youth from a variety of racial and ethnic backgrounds (Letourneau et al., 2009; Sawyer & Borduin, 2011), but outcomes may be enhanced by ethnic match between the therapist and caregiver (S. L. Foster et al., 2009; Halliday-Boykins, Schoenwald, & Letourneau, 2005). In contrast, other studies have found reduced effects of FFT with black and Hispanic youth (Darnell & Schuler, 2015), of MDFT with Hispanic youth (Greenbaum et al., 2015), and of BSFT for some subpopulations of Hispanic youth (Santisteban et al., 1996). Thus, attention to cultural sensitivity will likely be of critical importance to the continued refinement of these treatment models, given their high levels of family involvement and emphasis on contextual variables. Similarly, it would be useful to consider treatment modifications that enhance appropriateness for female youth (as has been done for TFCO).

More controversial is the role of limited prosocial (i.e., callous–unemotional; see Frick, 2012) traits in responsiveness of youth DBDs to treatment; some studies found that youth with such traits demonstrated smaller reductions in symptoms (Manders, Dekovic, Asscher, van der Laan, & Prins, 2013), whereas others showed the opposite relation (Sinclair et al., 2016; White, Frick, Lawing, & Bauer, 2013). Additional research is needed to disentangle these processes of clinical change, perhaps by specifying and testing candidate mediators that are specific to youth with limited prosocial traits. Finally, systems-level characteristics beyond the youth and family may also serve as important moderators. For instance, Woolfenden, Williams, & Peet (2001) noted that involvement in the juvenile justice system should be explored as a moderator of family- and community-based treatment effects, given the emphasis on justice-involved youth in most clinical trials in this area. As one such example, Letourneau et al. (2009) did not find differential effectiveness of MST-PSB for youth who were diverted from legal intervention versus referred as a term of probation (i.e., pre- vs. post-adjudication).

Economic impact

Crime and other problematic behaviors of youth with DBDs are associated with high societal costs (E. M. Foster, Jones, & the Conduct Problems Prevention Research Group, 2006; McCollister et al., 2010); yet the comprehensive family- and community-based treatments that are best suited to the treatment of those behaviors are also quite expensive. Therefore, administrators, policymakers, and researchers have been increasingly interested in documenting the economic costs and benefits of clinically effective treatments for this population (see Greenwood & Welsh, 2012). In one of the most comprehensive economic research efforts in this area, researchers at the Washington State Institute for Public Policy developed a cost-benefit model (i.e., WSIPP model; see WSIPP, 2017b) to estimate the economic costs and benefits of various social services, including family- and community-based treatments for DBDs. Their most recent estimates (WSIPP, 2017a) indicated returns per dollar spent (i.e., across taxpayers and crime victims) of $1.14–$2.42 for MST (including MST-PSB and MST-SA), $2.08 for TFCO, $8.87 for FFT, $0.65 for BSFT, and $0.28 for MDFT. These findings indicate that family- and community-based treatments are sometimes capable of producing economic as well as clinical benefits, with the treatments that focus on youth at high risk for particularly expensive outcomes (e.g., incarceration) being the most likely to recoup the cost of treatment. Nevertheless, the WSIPP analytic strategy is limited by reliance on general information to estimate treatment costs, such as market rates for labor and services, and benefits, such as pooled treatment effect sizes for dichotomous outcomes (e.g., presence or absence of arrest, substance use disorder, etc.).

In response to the aforementioned limitations, researchers have modified the WSIPP model to incorporate more precise data (e.g., real-world program costs, continuous measures of post-treatment outcomes) from clinical trials of MST. For example, Dopp, Borduin, Wagner, & Sawyer (2014) adapted the WSIPP model to analyze rearrest data for serious juvenile offenders (Sawyer & Borduin, 2011) and their siblings (Wagner et al., 2014) who had participated in the Borduin et al. (1995) clinical trial of MST. The results showed that every dollar spent on MST recovered $5.04 in savings to taxpayers and crime victims over the 25 years following treatment. Similarly, Borduin and Dopp (2015) applied the adapted WSIPP model to rearrest data from the Borduin et al. (2009) clinical trial to estimate the economic benefit of MST-PSB. That cost-benefit study found that every dollar spent on MST-PSB recovered $48.81 in savings to taxpayers and crime victims. Moreover, the economic savings from the Dopp et al. (2014) and Borduin and Dopp (2015) analyses were even greater when estimated on a year-by-year basis rather than averaged across a lengthy follow-up period, although the analytic procedures for such computations are highly complex (see Dopp, Borduin, Willroth, & Sorg, 2017). Taken together, these three studies suggest that economic analyses that incorporate detailed data from clinical trials are useful to consider alongside population-level estimation methods (e.g., WSIPP, 2017b). It is unfortunate that no such studies of TFCO, FFT, BSFT, and MDFT have yet been published.

Overall, it is important for administrators and policymakers to consider the economic impact of family- and community-based treatment models, given that treatments of no or unknown effectiveness are often cheaper to implement in the short-term (see Schoenwald & Henggeler, 2004). Moreover, future economic studies of all of family- and community-based treatment models should expand the scope of monetized outcomes beyond the prevailing focus on crime rates and incorporate service utilization in other sectors (e.g., social welfare, mental health, primary care) to explore the possibility of cost-shifting during treatment or follow-up.

Dissemination and implementation

As noted previously, the developers of family- and community-based treatments for youth DBDs use a variety of training and quality assurance strategies to maintain treatment integrity in community settings. These strategies are executed by purveyor organizations (i.e., MST Services [MST Associates for MST-PSB]; TFC Consultants; FFT, LLC; BSFT Institute; and MDFT International), who oversee the dissemination and implementation process for a given treatment model. In addition to training in clinical intervention techniques, purveyor organizations often provide technical assistance in the substantial changes in the organizational structure (e.g., a shift to community-based services) and culture (e.g., a continuous quality assurance and improvement system) required by these models.

Despite the associated costs and burden, intensive support for the dissemination and implementation of family- and community-based treatment models are critical. Indeed, there is a well-established positive association between fidelity to the model and reductions in targeted problem behaviors in MST (Henggeler, Melton, Brondino, Scherer, & Hanley, 1997; Schoenwald, Chapman, Sheidow, & Carter, 2009), FFT (Sexton & Turner, 2010), BSFT (Rohrbaugh, 2014), and MDFT (Hogue et al., 2008). To use MST as an example, a randomized clinical trial in Sweden (Sundell et al., 2008) had low fidelity to the MST model and failed to find a significant treatment effect relative to community services. In the time since that trial, Sweden has sustained MST and demonstrated associated improvements in both treatment fidelity and outcomes (Löfholm, Eichas, & Sundell, 2014). In contrast, discontinuation of quality assurance from MST services has been associated with decreases in fidelity and treatment effectiveness within three years of discontinuation (Smith-Boydston, Holtzman, & Roberts, 2014). In sum, research has consistently supported the importance of treatment fidelity in maximizing the clinical benefits of family- and community-based treatments, which are exceptionally complex and would be challenging to implement in isolation. However, it is important to note that statistics on fidelity are rarely reported in journal articles unless implementation problems occurred during the study. Systematic assessment and reporting of implementation variables in clinical trials would allow for more rigorous examination of their moderating effects.

Numerous additional areas of research have the potential to inform efforts by treatment developers and purveyor organizations in their efforts to promote treatment fidelity. For instance, measurement of fidelity is challenging and must balance scientific validity with feasibility and usefulness in routine care (Schoenwald et al., 2011). This task is complicated by the multiply-determined nature of fidelity in family- and community-based treatment models for youth DBDs, which captures various aspects of provider behavior (e.g., frequency of behaviors, competence in service delivery) among therapists, supervisors, and consultants (see e.g., MST Services, n.d.). The "gold-standard" of observational coding is rarely used in this area, even in clinical trials (cf. Robbins et al., 2011; Hogue et al., 2008), as it is time- and cost-prohibitive. One example of innovation in fidelity measurement is a multimedia web-based system for monitoring TFCO fidelity that permits video observation for supervision and consultation (Feil, Sprengelmeyer, Davis, & Chamberlain, 2012). It will be important for future research to evaluate the validity, feasibility, and usefulness of these and other fidelity measurement strategies, especially in light of recent indications that existing measures may not demonstrate measurement equivalence in novel contexts (e.g., Lange et al., 2016). Moreover, little research has examined organizational factors that predict the adoption, implementation, and sustainment of family- and community-based treatment models for youth DBDs. To date, examples of organizational variables such as therapist job satisfaction, participatory decision-making, and opportunities for growth and advancement have predicted fidelity and outcomes in MST (Schoenwald, Chapman,

Henry, & Sheidow, 2012). Additional research in this area is indicated, given the implications of such variables for maintaining high-quality service delivery with complex treatment models and challenging clinical populations.

Conclusions

The present review demonstrated that family- and community-based treatments (in particular, MST, TFCO, FFT, BSFT, and MDFT) for youth with complex or severe DBDs have the potential to produce greater reductions in behavior problems and more improvements in a variety of secondary outcomes than usual community services. When considered along with endorsements from numerous national organizations (e.g., Blueprints for Healthy Youth Development, http://www.blueprintsprograms.com/; National Registry of Evidence-based Programs and Practices, http://nrepp.samhsa.gov/landing.aspx; Office of Juvenile Justice and Delinquency Prevention Model Programs Guide, https://www.ojjdp.gov/mpg/), our review suggests that increased implementation of family- and community-based treatments are likely to result in greater reductions in youth problem behaviors, financial savings for taxpayers, and decreases in criminal victimization (see e.g., Dopp et al., 2014).

Our conclusions must be considered in the context of three key limitations. First, continued validation and replication are needed for even the most well-established treatment models and especially for those, such as BSFT and MDFT, for which the bulk of existing research has directly involved the treatment model developer(s). As the evidence base for family- and community-based treatments expands over time, it should be subjected to regular review through a combination of narrative and meta-analytic (see e.g., Dopp et al.,2017) reviews. Second, we focused on published research regarding family- and community-based treatments for DBDs, but it may be useful for other reviews with different purposes to more thoroughly explore unpublished research as well (e.g., to mitigate effects of publication bias). Finally, it is notable that all of the reviewed treatment models were developed in the United States, which may limit how well the present results generalize to family- and community-based treatments that have been developed in other countries, cultural contexts, and languages. Nevertheless, it is encouraging that research on these models in international settings has demonstrated their ability to achieve comparable effects as in the United States.

In sum, given the importance of reducing the personal, social, and financial consequences of DBDs in youth, we believe that priority should be placed on the evaluation and dissemination of promising family- and community-based treatment models. However, we also wish to emphasize effective large-scale strategies to address youth DBDs will require strong partnerships between provider organizations, treatment developers, and policymakers. These stakeholders should consider the research described in this chapter as they select treatment options to meet the needs of youth with DBDs, their families, and the communities in which they live.

References

Alexander, J. F., & Parsons, B. V. (1973). Short-term behavioral intervention with delinquent families: Impact on family process and recidivism. *Journal of Abnormal Psychology, 81*, 219–225.

Alexander, J. F., & Parsons, B. V. (1982). *Functional family therapy*. Pacific Grove, CA: Brooks/Cole. Available from https://doi.org/10.1037/11621-000.

Amato, P. R. (2001). Children of divorce in the 1990s: An update of the Amato and Keith (1991) meta-analysis. *Journal of Family Psychology, 15*(3), 355–370. Available from https://doi.org/10.1037/0893-3200.15.3.355.

American Academy of Child and Adolescent Psychiatry. (2005). Practice parameter for the assessment and treatment of children and adolescents with substance use disorders. *Journal of the American Academy of Child & Adolescent Psychiatry, 44*(6), 609–621. Available from https://doi.org/10.1097/01.chi.0000159135.33706.37.

Asscher, J. J., Deković, M., Manders, W. A., van der Laan, P. H., Prins, P. J. M., ... the Cost-Effectiveness Study Group. (2013). A randomized controlled trial of the effectiveness of multisystemic therapy in the Netherlands: Post-treatment changes and moderator effects. *Journal of Experimental Criminology, 9*, 169–187. Available from https://doi.org/10.1007/s11292-012-9165-9.

Attar, B. K., Guerra, N. G., & Tolan, P. H. (1994). Neighborhood disadvantage, stressful life events and adjustments in urban elementary-school children. *Journal of Clinical Child Psychology, 23*(4), 391–400.

Bandura, A. (1977). *Social learning theory*. Englewood Cliffs, NJ: Prentice-Hall.

Barton, C., Alexander, J. F., Waldron, H., Turner, C. W., & Warburton, J. (1985). Generalizing treatment effect of functional family therapy: Three replications. *American Journal of Family Therapy, 13*, 16–26.

Bateson, G. (1972). *Steps to an ecology of the mind*. New York: Ballentine.

Bergström, M., & Höjman, L. (2016). Is multidimensional treatment foster care (MTFC) more effective than treatment as usual in a three-year follow-up? Results from MTFC in a Swedish setting. *European Journal of Social Work, 19*, 219–235. Available from https://doi.org/10.1080/13691457.2015.1030361.

Boden, J. M., Fergusson, D. M., & Horwood, L. J. (2010). Risk factors for conduct disorder and oppositional/defiant disorder: Evidence from a New Zealand birth cohort. *Journal of the American Academy of Child & Adolescent Psychiatry, 49*(11), 1125–1133. Available from https://doi.org/10.1016/j.jaac.2010.08.005.

Borduin, C. M., & Dopp, A. R. (2015). Economic impact of multisystemic therapy with juvenile sexual offenders. *Journal of Family Psychology, 29*, 687–696. Available from https://doi.org/10.1037/fam0000113.

Borduin, C. M., Henggeler, S. W., Blaske, D. M., & Stein, R. J. (1990). Multisystemic treatment of adolescent sexual offenders. *International Journal of Offender Therapy and Comparative Criminology, 34*, 105–113. Available from https://doi.org/10.1177/0306624X9003400204.

Borduin, C. M., Mann, B. J., Cone, L. T., Henggeler, S. W., Fucci, B. R., Blaske, D. M., & Williams, R. A. (1995). Multisystemic treatment of serious juvenile offenders: Long-term prevention of criminality and violence. *Journal of Consulting and Clinical Psychology, 63*, 569–578. Available from https://doi.org/10.1037/0022-006X.63.4.569.

Borduin, C.M., & Munschy, R.M. (2014). *Multisystemic therapy for youths with problem sexual behaviors*. Unpublished manuscript, Department of Psychological Sciences, University of Missouri.

Borduin, C. M., Schaeffer, C. M., & Heiblum, N. (2009). A randomized clinical trial of multisystemic therapy with juvenile sexual offenders: Effects on youth social ecology and criminal activity. *Journal of Consulting and Clinical Psychology*, *77*(1), 26–37. Available from https://doi.org/10.1037/a0013035.

Bornovalova, M. A., Cummings, J. R., Hunt, E., Blazei, R., Malone, S., & Iacono, W. G. (2014). Understanding the relative contributions of direct environmental effects and passive genotype-environment correlations in the association between familial risk factors and child disruptive behavior disorders. *Psychological Medicine*, *44*(4), 831–844. Available from https://doi.org/10.1017/S0033291713001086.

Bronfenbrenner, U. (1979). *The ecology of human development: Experiments by nature and design*. Cambridge, MA: Harvard University Press.

Burke, J. D., Loeber, R., Lahey, B. B., & Rathouz, P. J. (2005). Developmental transitions among affective and behavioral disorders in adolescent boys. *Journal of Child Psychology and Psychiatry*, *46*(11), 1200–1210. Available from https://doi.org/10.1111/j.1469-7610.2005.00422.x.

Burt, S. A., Barnes, A. R., McGue, M., & Iacono, W. G. (2009). Parental divorce and adolescent delinquency: Ruling out the impact of common genes. *Developmental Psychology*, *44*(6), 1668–1677. Available from https://doi.org/10.1037/a0013477.

Butler, S., Baruch, G., Hickey, N., & Fonagy, P. (2011). A randomized controlled trial of multisystemic therapy and a statutory therapeutic intervention for young offenders. *Journal of the American Academy of Child & Adolescent Psychiatry*, *50*, 1220–1235. e2. Available from https://doi.org/10.1016/j.jaac.2011.09.017.

Caspi, A., Moffitt, T. E., Morgan, J., Rutter, M., Taylor, A., & Polo-Tomas, M. (2004). Maternal expressed emotion predicts children's antisocial behavior problems: Using monozygotic-twin differences to identify environmental effects on behavioral development. *Developmental Psychology*, *40*(2), 149–161. Available from https://doi.org/10.1037/0012-1649.40.2.149.

Celinska, K., Furrer, S., & Cheng, C. (2013). An outcome-based evaluation of functional family therapy for youth with behavioral problems. *Journal of Juvenile Justice*, *2*(2), 23–36.

Chamberlain, P. (2003). *Treating chronic juvenile offenders: Advances made through the Oregon multidimensional treatment foster care model*. Washington, DC: American Psychological Association. Available from https://doi.org/10.1037/10596-000.

Chamberlain, P., Leve, L. D., & DeGarmo, D. S. (2007). Multidimensional treatment foster care for girls in the juvenile justice system: 2-year follow-up of a randomized clinical trial. *Journal of Consulting and Clinical Psychology*, *75*, 187–193.

Chamberlain, P., & Moore, K. (1998). A clinical model for parenting juvenile offenders: A comparison of group care versus family care. *Clinical Child Psychology and Psychiatry*, *3*, 375–386.

Chamberlain, P., & Reid, J. B. (1998). Comparison of two community alternatives to incarceration for chronic juvenile offenders. *Journal of Consulting and Clinical Psychology*, *66*, 624–633. Available from https://doi.org/10.1037/0022-006X.66.4.624.

Cillessen, A. H. N., & Mayeux, L. (2004). From censure to reinforcement: Developmental changes in the association between aggression and social status. *Child Development*, *75* (1), 147–163.

Coatsworth, J. D., Santisteban, D. A., McBride, C. K., & Szapocznik, J. (2001). Brief strategic family therapy versus community control: Engagement, retention, and an exploration of the moderating role of adolescent symptom severity. *Family Process*, *40*, 313–332. Available from https://doi.org/10.1111/j.1545-5300.2001.4030100313.x.

Correll, C. U., Manu, P., Olshanskiy, V., Napolitano, B., Kane, J. M., & Malhotra, A. K. (2009). Cardiometabolic risk of second-generation antipsychotic medications during first-time use in children and adolescents. *Journal of the American Medical Association, 302*, 1765–1773. Available from https://doi.org/10.1001/jama.2009.1549.

Dakof, G. A., Henderson, C., Rowe, C. L., Boustani, M., Greenbaum, P. E., Wang, W., ... Liddle, H. A. (2015). A randomized clinical trial of family therapy in juvenile drug court. *Journal of Family Psychology, 29*(2), 232–241. Available from https://doi.org/10.1037/fam0000053.

Darnell, A. J., & Schuler, M. S. (2015). Quasi-experimental study of Functional Family Therapy effectiveness for juvenile justice aftercare in a racially and ethnically diverse community sample. *Children and Youth Services Review, 50*, 75–82. Available from https://doi.org/10.1016/j.childyouth.2015.01.013.

Deković, M., Asscher, J. J., Manders, W. A., Prins, P. J. M., & van der Laan, P. (2012). Within-intervention change: Mediators of intervention effects during multisystemic therapy. *Journal of Consulting and Clinical Psychology, 80*(4), 574–587. Available from https://doi.org/10.1037/a0028482.

Dishion, T. J., Spracklen, K. M., Andrews, D. W., & Patterson, G. R. (1996). Deviancy training in male adolescent friendships. *Behavior Therapy, 27*(3), 373–390.

Dodge, K. A., & Pettit, G. S. (2003). A biopsychosocial model of the development of chronic conduct problems in adolescence. *Developmental Psychology, 39*, 349–371.

Dopp, A. R., Borduin, C. M., Rothman, D., & Letourneau, E. J. (2017). Evidence-based treatments for youths who engage in illegal sexual behaviors. *Journal of Clinical Child and Adolescent Psychology, 46*(5), 631–645. Available from https://doi.org/10.1080/15374416.2016.1261714.

Dopp, A. R., Borduin, C. M., Wagner, D. V., & Sawyer, A. M. (2014). Economic impact of multisystemic therapy through midlife: A cost-benefit analysis with serious juvenile offenders and their siblings. *Journal of Consulting and Clinical Psychology, 82*, 694–705. Available from https://doi.org/10.1037/a0036415.

Dopp, A. R., Borduin, C. M., White, M. H., & Kuppens, S. (2017). Family-based treatments for serious juvenile offenders: A multilevel meta-analysis. *Journal of Consulting and Clinical Psychology, 85*(4), 335–354. Available from https://doi.org/10.1037/ccp0000183.

Dopp, A. R., Borduin, C. M., Willroth, E. C., & Sorg, A. A. (2017). Long-term economic benefits of psychological interventions for criminality: Comparing and integrating estimation methods. *Psychology, Public Policy, and Law, 23*(3), 312–323. Available from https://doi.org/10.1037/law0000134.

Eddy, J. M., & Chamberlain, P. (2000). Family management and deviant peer association as mediators of the impact of treatment condition on youth antisocial behavior. *Journal of Consulting and Clinical Psychology, 68*, 857–863.

Eddy, M. J., Whaley, R. B., & Chamberlain, P. (2004). The prevention of violent behavior by chronic and serious male juvenile offenders: A 2-year follow-up of a randomized clinical trial. *Journal of Emotional and Behavioral Disorders, 12*, 2–8. Available from https://doi.org/10.1177/10634266040120010101.

Erickson, C.J. (2008). *The effectiveness of functional family therapy in the treatment of juvenile sexual offenders* (Unpublished doctoral dissertation). Indiana University, Bloomington, IN.

Farrington, D. P., & Loeber, R. (2000). Epidemiology of juvenile violence. *Child and Adolescent Psychiatric Clinics of North America, 9*, 733–748.

Feil, E. G., Sprengelmeyer, P. G., Davis, B., & Chamberlain, P. (2012). Development and testing of a multimedia internet-based system for fidelity and monitoring of multidimensional treatment foster care. *Journal of Medical Internet Research*, *14*(5), e139. Available from https://doi.org/10.2196/jmir.2034.

Foster, S. L., Cunningham, P. B., Warner, S. E., McCoy, D. M., Barr, T. S., & Henggeler, S. W. (2009). Therapist behavior as a predictor of Black and White caregiver responsiveness in multisystemic therapy. *Journal of Family Psychology*, *23*(5), 626–635. Available from https://doi.org/10.1037/a0016228.

Foster, E. M., Jones, D., & the Conduct Problems Prevention Research Group. (2006). Can a costly intervention be cost-effective? An analysis of violence prevention. *Archives of General Psychiatry*, *63*, 1284–1291. Available from https://doi.org/10.1001/archpsyc.63.11.1284.

Frick, P. J. (2012). Developmental pathways to conduct disorder: Implications for future directions in research, assessment, and treatment. *Journal of Clinical Child & Adolescent Psychology*, *41*(3), 378–389. Available from https://doi.org/10.1080/15374416.2012.664815.

Frick, P. J., Kamphaus, R. W., Lahey, B. B., Loeber, R., Christ, M. A. G., Hart, E. L., & Tannenbaum, L. E. (1991). Academic underachievement and the disruptive behavior disorders. *Journal of Consulting and Clinical Psychology*, *59*(2), 289–294. Available from https://doi.org/10.1037/0022-006X.59.2.289.

Gifford-Smith, M., Dodge, K. A., Dishion, T. J., & McCord, J. (2005). Peer influence in children and adolescents: Crossing the bridge from developmental to intervention science. *Journal of Abnormal Child Psychology*, *33*(3), 255–265. Available from https://doi.org/10.1007/s10802-005-3563-7.

Gordon, D. A., Arbuthnot, J., Gustafson, K. E., & McGreen, P. (1988). Home-based behavioral-systems family therapy with disadvantaged juvenile delinquents. *American Journal of Family Therapy*, *16*, 243–255.

Gordon, D. A., Graves, K., & Arbuthnot, J. (1995). The effect of functional family therapy for delinquents on adult criminal behavior. *Criminal Justice and Behavior*, *22*, 60–73.

Granic, I., & Patterson, G. R. (2006). Toward a comprehensive model of antisocial development: A dynamic systems approach. *Psychological Review*, *113*, 101–131. Available from https://doi.org/10.1037/0033-295X.113.1.101.

Greenberg, M. T., & Lippold, M. A. (2014). Promoting healthy outcomes among youth with multiple risks: Innovative approaches. *Annual Review of Public Health*, *34*, 253–270. Available from https://doi.org/10.1146/annurev-publhealth-031811-124619.

Greenbaum, P. E., Wang, W., Henderson, C. E., Kan, L., Hall, K., Dakof, G. A., & Liddle, H. A. (2015). Gender and ethnicity as moderators: Integrative data analysis of multidimensional family therapy randomized clinical trials. *Journal of Family Psychology*, *29* (6), 919–930. Available from https://doi.org/10.1037/fam0000127.

Greenwood, P. (2008). Prevention and intervention programs for juvenile offenders: The benefits of evidence-based practice. *Future of Children*, *18*, 11–36.

Greenwood, P. W., & Welsh, B. C. (2012). Promoting evidence-based practice in delinquency prevention at the state level: Principles, progress, and policy directions. *Criminology & Public Policy*, *11*, 493–513. Available from https://doi.org/10.1111/j.1745-9133.2012.00826.x.

Haley, J. (1987). *Problem-solving therapy* (2nd ed.). San Francisco, CA: Jossey-Boss, Inc.

Halliday-Boykins, C. A., Schoenwald, S. K., & Letourneau, E. J. (2005). Caregiver-therapist ethnic similarity predicts youth outcomes from an empirically based treatment. *Journal of Consulting and Clinical Psychology*, *73*, 808–818.

Harold, G. T., Kerr, D. C. R., Van Ryzin, M., DeGarmo, D. S., Rhoades, K. A., & Leve, L. D. (2013). Depressive symptom trajectories among girls in the juvenile justice system: 24-month outcomes of an RCT of multidimensional treatment foster care. *Prevention Science*, *14*(5), 437–446. Available from https://doi.org/10.1007/s11121-012-0317-y.

Hartnett, D., Carr, C., & Sexton, T. (2016). The effectiveness of functional family therapy in reducing adolescent mental health risk and family adjustment difficulties in an Irish context. *Family Process*, *55*(2), 287–304. Available from https://doi.org/10.1111/famp.12195.

Hawkins, J. D., Catalano, R. F., & Miller, J. Y. (1992). Risk and protective factors for alcohol and other drug problems in adolescence and early adulthood: Implications for substance abuse prevention. *Psychological Bulletin*, *112*(1), 64–105. Available from https://doi.org/10.1037/0033-2909.112.1.64.

Henderson, C. E., Rowe, C. L., Dakof, G. A., Hawes, S. W., & Liddle, H. A. (2009). Parenting practices as mediators of treatment effects in an early-intervention trial of multidimensional family therapy. *The American Journal of Drug and Alcohol Abuse*, *35*, 220–226. Available from https://doi.org/10.1080/00952990903005890.

Henggeler, S. W. (2011). Efficacy studies to large-scale transport: The development and validation of MST programs. *Annual Review of Clinical Psychology*, *7*, 351–381. Available from https://doi.org/10.1146/annurev-clinpsy-032210-104615.

Henggeler, S. W., & Borduin, C. M. (1990). Family therapy and beyond: A multisystemic approach to treating the behavior problems of children and adolescents. Pacific Grove, CA: Brooks/Cole.

Henggeler, S. W., Clingempeel, W. G., Brondino, M. J., & Pickrel, S. G. (2002). Four-year follow-up of multisystemic therapy with substance-abusing and substance-dependent juvenile offenders. *Journal of the American Academy of Child & Adolescent Psychiatry*, *41*, 868–874. Available from https://doi.org/10.1097/00004583-200207000-00021.

Henggeler, S. W., Halliday-Boykins, C. A., Cunningham, P. B., Randall, J., Shapiro, S. B., & Chapman, J. E. (2006). Juvenile drug court: Enhancing outcomes by integrating evidence-based treatments. *Journal of Consulting and Clinical Psychology*, *74*, 42–54. Available from https://doi.org/10.1037/0022-006X.74.1.42.

Henggeler, S. W., Letourneau, E. J., Chapman, J. E., Borduin, C. M., Schewe, P. A., & McCart, M. R. (2009). Mediators of change for multisystemic therapy with juvenile sexual offenders. *Journal of Consulting and Clinical Psychology*, *77*, 451–462. Available from https://doi.org/10.1037/a0013971.

Henggeler, S. W., Melton, G. B., Brondino, M. J., Scherer, D. G., & Hanley, J. H. (1997). Multisystemic therapy with violent and chronic juvenile offenders and their families: The role of treatment fidelity in successful dissemination. *Journal of Consulting and Clinical Psychology*, *65*, 821–833. Available from https://doi.org/10.1037/0022-006X.65.5.821.

Henggeler, S. W., Melton, G. B., & Smith, L. A. (1992). Family preservation using multisystemic therapy: An effective alternative to incarcerating serious juvenile offenders. *Journal of Consulting and Clinical Psychology*, *60*, 953–961. Available from https://doi.org/10.1037/0022-006X.60.6.953.

Henggeler, S. W., Melton, G. B., Smith, L. A., Schoenwald, S. K., & Hanley, J. H. (1993). Family preservation using multisystemic treatment: Long-term follow-up to a clinical trial with serious juvenile offenders. *Journal of Child and Family Studies*, *2*, 283–293. Available from https://doi.org/10.1007/BF01321226.

Henggeler, S. W., Pickrel, S. G., & Brondino, M. J. (1999). Multisystemic treatment of substance-abusing and dependent delinquents: Outcomes, treatment fidelity, and transportability. *Mental Health Services Research, 1*, 171–184. Available from https://doi.org/10.1023/A:1022373813261.

Henggeler, S. W., Rodick, J. D., Borduin, C. M., Hanson, C. L., Watson, S. M., & Urey, J. R. (1986). Multisystemic treatment of juvenile offenders: Effects on adolescent behavior and family interaction. *Developmental Psychology, 22*, 132–141. Available from https://doi.org/10.1037/0012-1649.22.1.132.

Henggeler, S. W., & Schoenwald, S. K. (2011). Evidence-based interventions for juvenile offenders and juvenile justice policies that support them. *Society for Research in Child Development: Social Policy Report, 25*, 1–20.

Henggeler, S. W., Schoenwald, S. K., Borduin, C. M., Rowland, M. D., & Cunningham, P. B. (2009). *Multisystemic therapy for antisocial behavior in children and adolescents.* New York, NY: Guilford Press.

Henry, D. B., Tolan, P. H., & Gorman-Smith, D. (2001). Longitudinal family and peer group effects on violence and nonviolent delinquency. *Journal of Clinical Child Psychology, 30*, 172–186.

Herndon, R. W., & Iacono, W. G. (2005). Psychiatric disorder in the children of antisocial parents. *Psychological Medicine, 35*, 1815–1824. Available from https://doi.org/10.1017/S0033291705005635.

Herrenkohl, T. I., Huang, B., Kosterman, R., Hawkins, J. D., Catalano, R. F., & Smith, B. H. (2001). A comparison of social development processes leading to violent behavior in late adolescence for childhood initiators and adolescent initiators of violence. *Journal of Research in Crime and Delinquency, 38*, 45–63.

Hoffman, L. (1981). *Foundations of family therapy*. New York: Basic Books.

Hinshaw, S. P. (1992). Externalizing behavior problems and academic underachievement in childhood and adolescence: Causal relationships and underlying mechanisms. *Psychological Bulletin, 111*(1), 127–155.

Hogue, A., Henderson, C. E., Dauber, S., Barajas, P. C., Fried, A., & Liddle, H. A. (2008). Treatment adherence, competence, and outcome in individual and family therapy for adolescent behavior problems. *Journal of Consulting and Clinical Psychology, 76*, 544–555. Available from https://doi.org/10.1037/0022-006X.76.4.544.

Hogue, A., Henderson, C. E., Ozechowski, T. J., & Robbins, M. S. (2014). Evidence base on outpatient behavioral treatments for adolescent substance use: Updates and recommendations 2007–2013. *Journal of Clinical Child & Adolescent Psychology, 43*(5), 695–720. Available from https://doi.org/10.1080/15374416.2014.915550.

Horigian, V. E., Feaster, D. J., Robbins, M. S., Brincks, A. M., Ucha, J., & Szapocznik, J. (2015). A cross-sectional assessment of the long term effects of brief strategic family therapy for adolescent substance use. *The American Journal on Addictions, 24*(7), 637–645. Available from https://doi.org/10.1111/ajad.12278.

Huey, S. J., Henggeler, S. W., Brondino, M. J., & Pickrel, S. G. (2000). Mechanisms of change in multisystemic therapy: Reducing delinquent behavior through therapist adherence and improved family and peer functioning. *Journal of Consulting and Clinical Psychology, 68*, 451–467.

Johnides, B. D., Borduin, C. M., Wagner, D. V., & Dopp, A. R. (2017). Effects of multisystemic therapy on caregivers of serious juvenile offenders: A 20-year follow-up to a randomized clinical trial. *Journal of Consulting and Clinical Psychology, 85*(4), 323–334. Available from https://doi.org/10.1037/ccp0000199.

Kazdin, A. E. (2015). Clinical dysfunction and psychosocial interventions: The interplay of research, methods, and conceptualization of challenges. *Annual Review of Clinical Psychology*, *11*, 25–52. Available from https://doi.org/10.1146/annurev-clinpsy-032814-112720.

Keenan, K., Loeber, R., & Green, S. (1999). Conduct disorder in girls: A review of the literature. *Clinical Child and Family Psychology Review*, *2*(1), 3–19. Available from https://doi.org/10.1023/A:1021811307364.

Keenan, K., Loeber, R., Zhang, Q., Stouthamer-Loeber, M., & van Kammen, W. B. (1995). The influence of deviant peers on the development of boys' disruptive and delinquent behavior: A temporal analysis. *Developmental Processes in Peer Relations and Psychopathology*, *7*(4), 715–726. Available from https://doi.org/10.1017/S0954579400006805.

Kerr, D. C. R., Leve, L. D., & Chamberlain, P. (2009). Pregnancy rates among juvenile justice girls in two randomized controlled trials of multidimensional treatment foster care. *Journal of Consulting and Clinical Psychology*, *77*, 588–593. Available from https://doi.org/10.1037/a0015289.

Kilpatrick, D. G., Ruggiero, K. J., Acierno, R., Saunders, B. E., Resnick, H. S., & Best, C. L. (2003). Violence and risk of PTSD, major depression, substance abuse/dependence, and comorbidity: Results from the National Survey of Adolescents. *Journal of Consulting and Clinical Psychology*, *71*(4), 692–700. Available from https://doi.org/10.1037/0022-006X.71.4.692.

Klein, N. C., Alexander, J. F., & Parsons, B. V. (1977). Impact of family systems intervention on recidivism and sibling delinquency: A model of primary prevention and programme evaluation. *Journal of Consulting and Clinical Psychology*, *45*, 469–474.

Kroneman, L. M., Loeber, R., Hipwell, A. E., & Koot, H. M. (2009). Girls' disruptive behavior and its relationship to family functioning: A review. *Journal of Child and Family Studies*, *18*(3), 259–273.

Lange, A., Scholte, R. H., van Geffen, W., Timman, R., Busschbach, J. J., & van der Rijken, R. E. (2016). The lack of cross-national equivalence of a Therapist Adherence Measure (TAM-R) in multisystemic therapy (MST). *European Journal of Psychological Assessment*, *32*(4), 312–325. Available from https://doi.org/10.1027/1015-5759/a000262.

Letourneau, E. J., Henggeler, S. W., Borduin, C. M., Schewe, P. A., McCart, M. R., Chapman, J. E., & Saldana, L. (2009). Multisystemic therapy for juvenile sexual offenders: 1-year results from a randomized effectiveness trial. *Journal of Family Psychology*, *23*, 89–102. Available from https://doi.org/10.1037/a0014352.

Letourneau, E. J., Henggeler, S., McCart, M., Borduin, C., Schewe, P., & Armstrong, K. (2013). Two-year follow-up of a randomized effectiveness trial evaluating MST for juveniles who sexually offend. *Journal of Family Psychology*, *27*, 978–985. Available from https://doi.org/10.1037/a0034710.

Leve, L. D., & Chamberlain, P. (2007). A randomized evaluation of multidimensional treatment foster care: Effects on school attendance and homework completion in juvenile justice girls. *Research on Social Work Practice*, *17*, 657–663. Available from https://doi.org/10.1177/1049731506293971.

Leve, L. D., Chamberlain, P., & Reid, J. B. (2005). Intervention outcomes for girls referred from juvenile justice: Effects on delinquency. *Journal of Consulting and Clinical Psychology*, *73*, 1181–1185. Available from https://doi.org/10.1037/0022-006X.73.6.1181.

Liberman, A. M. (Ed.), (2008). *The long view of crime: A synthesis of longitudinal research.* New York, NY: Springer.

Liddle, H. A. (2002). *Multidimensional family therapy treatment (MDFT) for adolescent cannabis users: Vol. 5. Cannabis Youth Treatment (CYT) manual series.* Rockville, MD: Center for Substance Abuse Treatment, Substance Abuse Mental Health Services Administration.

Liddle, H. A. (2009). *Multidimensional Family Therapy for adolescent drug abuse: Clinician's manual.* Center City, MN: Hazelden Publishing Co.

Liddle, H. A., Dakof, G. A., Parker, K., Diamond, G. S., Barrett, K., & Tejeda, M. (2001). Multidimensional amily Therapy for adolescent drug abuse: Results of a randomized clinical trial. *American Journal of Drug and Alcohol Abuse*, *27*(4), 651–688.

Liddle, H. A., Rowe, C. L., Dakof, G. A., Henderson, C., & Greenbaum, P. (2009). Multidimensional Family Therapy for young adolescent substance abuse: Twelve month outcomes of a randomized controlled trial. *Journal of Consulting and Clinical Psychology*, *77*(1), 12–25. Available from https://doi.org/10.1037/a0014160.

Lipsey, M. W. (2009). The primary factors that characterize effective interventions for juvenile offenders: A meta-analytic overview. *Victims and Offenders*, *4*, 124–147. Available from https://doi.org/10.1080/15564880802612573.

Loeber, R., Burke, J. D., & Pardini, D. A. (2009). Development and etiology of disruptive and delinquent behavior. *Annual Review of Clinical Psychology*, *5*, 291–310. Available from https://doi.org/10.1146/annurev.clinpsy.032408.153631.

Löfholm, C. A., Eichas, K., & Sundell, K. (2014). The Swedish implementation of multisystemic therapy for adolescents: Does treatment experience predict treatment adherence. *Journal of Clinical Child & Adolescent Psychology*, *43*, 643–655. Available from https://doi.org/10.1080/15374416.2014.883926.

Maayan, L., & Correll, C. U. (2011). Weight gain and metabolic risks associated with antipsychotic medications in children and adolescents. *Journal of Child and Adolescent Psychopharmacology*, *21*, 517–535. Available from https://doi.org/10.1089/cap.2011.0015.

Manders, W. A., Dekovic, M., Asscher, J. J., van der Laan, P. H., & Prins, P. J. M. (2013). Psychopathy as predictor and moderator of Multisystemic Therapy outcomes among adolescents treated for antisocial behavior. *Journal of Abnormal Child Psychology*, *41*, 1121–1132. Available from https://doi.org/10.1007/s10802-013-9749-5.

Margolin, G., & Gordis, E. B. (2000). The effects of family and community violence on children. *Annual Review of Psychology*, *51*(1), 445–479.

McCarty, C. A., & McMahon, R. J. (2003). Mediators of the relation between maternal depressive symptoms and child internalizing and disruptive behavior disorders. *Journal of Family Psychology*, *17*(4), 545–556. Available from https://doi.org/10.1037/0893-3200.17.4.545.

McCart, M. R., & Sheidow, A. J. (2016). Evidence-based psychosocial treatments for adolescents with disruptive behavior. *Journal of Clinical Child and Adolescent Psychology*, *45* (5), 529–563. Available from https://doi.org/10.1080/15374416.2016.1146990.

McCollister, K. E., French, M. T., & Fang, H. (2010). The cost of crime to society: New crime-specific estimates for policy and program evaluation. *Drug & Alcohol Dependence*, *108*(1), 98–109. Available from https://doi.org/10.1016/j.drugalcdep.2009.12.002.

Metcalfe, L. A., Harvey, E. A., & Laws, H. B. (2013). The longitudinal relation between academic/cognitive skills and externalizing behavior problems in preschool children. *Journal of Educational Psychology*, *105*(3), 881–894. Available from https://doi.org/10.1037/a0032624.

Minuchin, S. (1974). *Families and family therapy*. Cambridge, MA: Harvard University Press.

Minuchin, P. P. (1985). Families and individual development: Provocations from the field of family therapy. *Child Development*, *56*, 289–302.

Monahan, K., Steinberg, L., & Cauffman, E. (2009). Affiliation with antisocial peers, susceptibility to peer influence, and antisocial behavior during the transition to adulthood. *Developmental Psychology*, *45*(6), 1520–1530.

Moore, A. A., Silberg, J. L., Roberson-Nay, R., & Mezuk, B. (2017). Life course persistent and adolescence limited conduct disorder in a nationally representative US sample: Prevalence, predictors, and outcomes. *Social Psychiatry and Psychiatric Epidemiology*, *52*, 435–443. Available from https://doi.org/10.1007/s00127-017-1337-5.

MST Services (n.d.). *Multisystemic Therapy: Continuous quality improvement*. Retrieved June 18, 2017 from http://mstservices.com/files/QA_system.pdf.

Odgers, C. L., Moffitt, T. E., Broadbent, J. M., Dickson, N., Hancox, R. J., Harrington, H., . . . Caspi, A. (2008). Female and male antisocial trajectories: From childhood origins to adult outcomes. *Development and Psychopathology*, *20*, 673–716. Available from https://doi.org/10.1017/s0954579408000333.

Ogden, T., & Hagen, K. A. (2006). Multisystemic therapy of serious behaviour problems in youth: Sustainability of therapy effectiveness two years after intake. *Journal of Child and Adolescent Mental Health*, *11*, 142–149. Available from https://doi.org/10.1111/j.1475-3588.2006.00396.x.

Ogden, T., & Halliday-Boykins, C. A. (2004). Multisystemic treatment of antisocial adolescents in Norway: Replication of clinical outcomes outside of the US. *Child and Adolescent Mental Health*, *9*, 77–83. Available from https://doi.org/10.1111/j.1475-3588.2004.00085.x.

Pardini, D. A. (2008). Novel insights into longstanding theories of bidirectional parent-child influences: Introduction to the special section. *Journal of Abnormal Child Psychology*, *36*, 627–631.

Pinsof, W. M., & Lebow, J. L. (2005). *Family psychology: The art of the science*. New York, NY: Oxford University Press.

Pittman, L. D., & Chase-Lansdale, P. L. (2001). African American adolescent girls in impoverished communities: Parenting style and adolescent outcomes. *Journal of Research on Adolescence*, *11*(2), 199–224. Available from https://doi.org/10.1111/1532-7795.00010.

Poulton, R., Van Ryzin, M. J., Harold, G. T., Chamberlain, P., Fowler, D., & Leve, L. D. (2014). Effects of multidimensional treatment foster care on psychotic symptoms in girls. *Journal of the American Academy of Child & Adolescent Psychiatry*, *53*(12), 1279–1287. Available from https://doi.org/10.1016/j.jaac.2014.08.014.

Rhoades, K. A., Leve, L. D., Harold, G. T., Kim, H., & Chamberlain, P. (2014). Drug use trajectories after a randomized controlled trial of MTFC: Associations with partner drug use. *Journal of Research on Adolescence*, *24*, 40–54. Available from https://doi.org/10.1111/jora.12077.

Robbins, M. S., Feaster, D. J., Horigian, V. E., Rohrbaugh, M., Shoham, V., & Szapocznik, J. (2011). Brief strategic family therapy versus treatment as usual: Results of a multisite randomized trial for substance using adolescents. *Journal of Consulting and Clinical Psychology*, *79*(6), 713–727. Available from https://doi.org/10.1037/a0025477.

Robbins, M. S., Szapocznik, J., Santisteban, D. A., Hervis, O. E., Mitrani, V. B., & Schwartz, S. J. (2003). Brief strategic family therapy for Hispanic youth. In A. E. Kazdin, & J. R. Weisz (Eds.), *Evidence-based psychotherapies for children and adolescents* (pp. 407–424). New York, NY, US: Guilford Press.

Robinson, F., & Keithley, J. (2000). The impacts of crime on health and health services: A literature review. *Health, Risk & Society*, *2*(3), 253–266.

Rohrbaugh, M. J. (2014). Old wine in new bottles: Decanting systemic family process research in the era of evidence-based practice. *Family Process*, *53*(3), 434–444. Available from https://doi.org/10.1111/famp.12079.

Ronis, S. T., & Borduin, C. M. (2013). Antisocial behavior trajectories of adolescents and emerging adults with histories of sexual aggression. *Psychology of Violence*, *3*, 367–380. Available from https://doi.org/10.1037/a0033597.

Rose, A. J., & Rudolph, K. D. (2006). A review of sex differences in peer relationship processes: Potential trade-offs for the emotional and behavioral development of girls and boys. *Psychological Bulletin*, *132*(1), 98–131. Available from https://doi.org/10.1037/0033-2909.132.1.98.

Rowland, M. R., Chapman, J. E., & Henggeler, S. W. (2008). Sibling outcomes from a randomized trial of evidence-based treatments with substance abusing juvenile offenders. *Journal of Child & Adolescent Substance Abuse*, *17*, 11–26.

Salzinger, S., Feldman, R. S., Hammer, M., & Rosario, M. (1993). The effects of physical abuse on children's social relationships. *Child Development*, *64*(1), 169–187. Available from https://doi.org/10.2307/1131444.

Sampson, R. J., Raudenbush, S. W., & Earls, F. (1997). Neighborhoods and violent crime: A multilevel study of collective efficacy. *Science*, *277*(5328), 918–924. Available from https://doi.org/10.1126/science.277.5328.918.

Santisteban, D. A., Coatsworth, J. D., Perez-Vidal, A., Kurtines, W. M., Schwartz, S. J., LaPerriere, A., & Szapocznik, J. (2003). The efficacy of brief strategic family therapy in modifying Hispanic adolescent behavior problems and substance use. *Journal of Family Psychology*, *17*, 121–133. Available from https://doi.org/10.1037/0893-3200.17.1.121.

Santisteban, D. A., Szapocznik, J., Perez-Vidal, A., Kurtines, W. M., Murray, E. J., & LaPerriere, A. (1996). Efficacy of intervention for engaging youth and families into treatment and some variables that may contribute to differential effectiveness. *Journal of Family Psychology*, *10*(1), 35–44. Available from https://doi.org/10.1037/0893-3200.10.1.35.

Sawyer, A. M., & Borduin, C. M. (2011). Effects of multisystemic therapy through midlife: A 21.9-year follow-up to a randomized clinical trial with serious and violent juvenile offenders. *Journal of Consulting and Clinical Psychology*, *79*, 643–652. Available from https://doi.org/10.1037/a0024862.

Scaramella, L. V., Neppl, T. K., Ontai, L. L., & Conger, R. D. (2008). Consequences of socioeconomic disadvantage across three generations: Parenting behavior and child externalizing problems. *Journal of Family Psychology*, *22*(5), 725–733. Available from https://doi.org/10.1037/a0013190.

Schaub, M. P., Henderson, C. E., Pelc, I., Tossmann, P., Phan, O., Hendriks, V., … Rigter, H. (2014). Multidimensional Family Therapy decreases the rate of externalising behavioural disorder symptoms in cannabis abusing adolescents: Outcomes of the INCANT trial. *BMC Psychiatry*, *14*(1), 26–34. Available from https://doi.org/10.1186/1471-244X-14-26.

Schoenwald, S. K., Chapman, J. E., Henry, D. B., & Sheidow, A. J. (2012). Taking effective treatments to scale: Organizational effects on outcomes of multisystemic therapy for youths with co-occurring substance use. *Journal of Child & Adolescent Substance Abuse*, *21*(1), 1–31. Available from https://doi.org/10.1080/1067828X.2012.636684.

Schoenwald, S. K., Chapman, J. E., Sheidow, A. J., & Carter, R. E. (2009). Long-term youth criminal outcomes in MST transport: The impact of therapist adherence and organizational climate and structure. *Journal of Clinical Child & Adolescent Psychology, 38*(1), 91–105. Available from https://doi.org/10.1080/15374410802575388.

Schoenwald, S. K., Garland, A. F., Chapman, J. E., Frazier, S. L., Sheidow, A. J., & Southam-Gerow, M. A. (2011). Toward the effective and efficient measurement of implementation fidelity. *Administration and Policy in Mental Health and Mental Health Services Research, 38*(1), 32–43. Available from https://doi.org/10.1007/s10488-010-0321-0.

Schoenwald, S. K., & Henggeler, S. W. (2004). A public health perspective on the transport of evidence-based practices. *Clinical Psychology: Science and Practice, 11*, 360–363. Available from https://doi.org/10.1093/clipsy.bph092.

Schwartz, D., & Proctor, L. J. (2000). Community violence exposure and children's social adjustment in the school peer group: The mediating roles of emotion regulation and social cognition. *Journal of Consulting and Clinical Psychology, 68*(4), 670–683. Available from https://doi.org/10.1037/0022-006X.68.4.670.

Sexton, T. L. (2011). *Functional family therapy in clinical practice: An evidence-based treatment model for working with troubled adolescents*. New York, NY: Taylor & Francis.

Sexton, T., & Turner, C. W. (2010). The effectiveness of functional family therapy for youth with behavioral problems in a community practice setting. *Journal of Family Psychology, 24*, 339–348. Available from https://doi.org/10.1037/a0019406.

Shufelt, J. S., & Cocozza, J. C. (2006). *Youth with mental health disorders in the juvenile justice system: Results from a multi-state, multi-system prevalence study*. Delmar, NY: National Center for Mental Health and Juvenile Justice.

Sinclair, I., Parry, E., Biehal, N., Freesen, J., Kay, C., Scott, S., & Green, J. (2016). Multidimensional Treatment Foster Care in England: Differential effects by level of initial antisocial behavior. *European Child and Adolescent Psychiatry, 25*, 843–852. Available from https://doi.org/10.1007/s00787-015-0799-9.

Smith-Boydston, J. M., Holtzman, R. J., & Roberts, M. C. (2014). Transportability of multisystemic therapy to community settings: Can a program sustain outcomes without MST Services oversight? *Child & Youth Care Forum, 43*, 593–605. Available from https://doi.org/10.1007/s10566-014-9255-0.

Stormshak, E. A., Bierman, K. L., McMahon, R. J., & Lengua, L. J. (2000). Parenting practices and child disruptive behavior problems in early elementary school. *Journal of Clinical Child Psychology, 29*(1), 17–29. Available from https://doi.org/10.1207/S15374424jccp2901_3.

Sundell, K., Hansson, K., Löfholm, C. A., Olsson, T., Gustle, L. H., & Kadesjo, C. (2008). The transportability of MST to Sweden: Short-term results from a randomized trial of conduct disordered youth. *Journal of Family Psychology, 22*, 550–560. Available from https://doi.org/10.1037/a0012790.

Szapocznik, J., Hervis, O., & Schwartz, S. (2003). *Brief strategic family therapy for adolescent drug abuse*. Bethesda, MD: National Institute on Drug Abuse. (NIH Pub. No. 03–4751).

Szapocznik, J., & Kurtines, W. M. (1989). *Breakthroughs in family therapy with drug abusing and problem youth*. New York, NY: Springer.

Szapocznik, J., Rio, A., Murray, E., Cohen, R., Scopetta, M., & Kurtines, W. (1989). Structural family versus psychodynamic child therapy for problematic Hispanic boys.

Journal of Consulting and Clinical Psychology, *57*(5), 571–578. Available from https://doi.org/10.1037/0022-006X.57.5.571.

Taylor, E. K., & Borduin, C. M. (2014). The family context of relational aggression in "difficult to treat" female juvenile offenders. *Journal of Marital and Family Therapy*, *40*(3), 357–366. Available from https://doi.org/10.1111/jmft.12038.

Timmons-Mitchell, J., Bender, M. B., Kishna, M. A., & Mitchell, C. C. (2006). An independent effectiveness trial of multisystemic therapy with juvenile justice youth. *Journal of Clinical Child and Adolescent Psychology*, *35*, 227–236. Available from https://doi.org/10.1207/s15374424jccp3502_6.

Valdez, A., Cepeda, C., Parrish, D., Horowitz, R., & Kaplan, C. (2013). An adapted brief strategic family therapy for gang-affiliated Mexican American adolescents. *Research on Social Work Practice*, *23*, 383–396. Available from https://doi.org/10.1177/1049731513481389.

Van der pol, T. M., Machteld, H., Noom, M. J., Stams, G. J. M., Doreleijers, T. A. H., van Domburgh, L., & Vermeiren, R. R. J. M. (2017). Research review: The effectiveness of multidimensional family therapy in treating adolescents with multiple behavior problems–a meta-analysis. *Journal of Child Psychology and Psychiatry*. Available from https://doi.org/10.1111/jcpp.12685, Advanced online publication.

Van Ryzin, M. J., & Leve, L. D. (2012). Affiliation with delinquent peers as a mediator of the effects of multidimensional treatment foster care for delinquent girls. *Journal of Consulting and Clinical Psychology*, *80*(4), 588–596. Available from https://doi.org/10.1037/a0027336.

van Wijk, A., Loeber, R., Vermeiren, R., Pardini, D., Bullens, R., & Doreleijers, T. (2005). Violent juvenile sex offenders compared with violent juvenile nonsex offenders: Explorative findings from the Pittsburgh youth study. *Sexual Abuse*, *17*, 333–352. Available from https://doi.org/10.1177/107906320501700306.

Wagner, D. V., Borduin, C. M., Sawyer, A. M., & Dopp, A. R. (2014). Long-term prevention of criminality in siblings of serious and violent juvenile offenders: A 25-year follow-up to a randomized clinical trial of multisystemic therapy. *Journal of Consulting and Clinical Psychology*, *82*, 492–499. Available from https://doi.org/10.1037/a0035624.

Waldron, H. B., Brody, J. L., & Hops, H. (2017). Functional family therapy for adolescent substance use disorders. In J. R. Weisz, & A. E. Kazdin (Eds.), *Evidence-based psychotherapies for children and adolescents* (3rd ed, pp. 342–360). New York, NY, US: Guilford Press.

Washington State Institute for Public Policy. (2017a). *Benefit-cost results*. Olympia, WA: Author. Retrieved June 18, 2017 from http://www.wsipp.wa.gov/BenefitCost.

Washington State Institute for Public Policy. (2017b). *Benefit-cost technical documentation*. Olympia, WA: Author. Retrieved June 18, 2017 from http://www.wsipp.wa.gov/TechnicalDocumentation/WsippBenefitCostTechnicalDocumentation.pdf.

Watzlawick, P., Bavelas, J. B., & Jackson, D. D. (1967). *Pragmatics of human communication: A study of interactional patterns, pathologies and paradoxes*. New York, NY: W. W. Norton & Company, Inc.

Weisz, J. R., Ugueto, A. M., Cheron, D. M., & Herren, J. (2013). Evidence-based youth psychotherapy in the mental health ecosystem. *Journal of Clinical Child and Adolescent Psychology*, *42*, 274–286. Available from https://doi.org/10.1080/15374416.2013.764824.

Westermark, P. K., Hansson, K., & Olsson, M. (2011). Multidimensional Treatment Foster Care (MTFC): Results from an independent replication. *Journal of Family Therapy*, *33*, 20–41.

White, S. F., Frick, P. J., Lawing, K., & Bauer, D. (2013). Callous-unemotional traits and response to Functional Family Therapy in adolescent offenders. *Behavioral Sciences and the Law*, *31*, 271–285. Available from https://doi.org/10.1002/bsl.204.

Woolfenden, S., Williams, K. J., & Peat, J. (2001). Family and parenting interventions in children and adolescents with conduct disorder and delinquency aged 10-17. *Cochrane Database of Systematic Reviews*(Issue 2). Available from https://doi.org/10.1002/14651858.CD003015, Article No. CD003015.

Part IV

New Directions for Disruptive, Impulse-Control, and Conduct Disorders

Developmental pathways

12

Michelle M. Martel, Patrick Goh, Tess Smith, and Christine A. Lee
University of Kentucky, Lexington, KY, United States

Oppositional defiant disorder (ODD), conduct disorder (CD), and antisocial personality disorder (ASPD) are prime examples of substantial intra- and interindividual heterogeneity and heterotypic continuity and discontinuity, or longitudinal change, in externalizing psychopathology across the lifespan. ODD symptoms often first appear in preschool and precede the development of CD, whereas CD develops in a subset of children with ODD during middle childhood through middle adolescence. CD can further be distinguished into subtypes depending on whether symptoms arise in childhood (i.e., prior to 10 years of age) or, more commonly, in adolescence (APA, 2013; Moffitt, 1993). Age of onset is associated with different patterns of symptoms, with childhood-onset being associated with more aggressive behaviors and adolescent-onset being associated with more delinquent, rule-breaking behaviors (Lahey et al., 1999). Furthermore, CD includes a specifier of limited prosocial emotions, which includes lack of remorse or guilt, callousness (i.e., lack of empathy), unconcerned about performance, and shallow or deficient affect. These limited prosocial emotions are seen as a precursor to adult psychopathy (Frick & Nigg, 2012).

Only some individuals with CD go on to develop ASPD. ASPD, long considered an adulthood disorder given that the Diagnostic and Statistical Manual of Mental Disorders-Fifth Edition (DSM-5) requires the presence of problem behaviors since the age of 15 years, is defined as a pattern of disregard for and violation of the rights of others, including a failure to conform to social norms, deceitfulness, impulsivity, irritability and aggressiveness, disregard for safety, irresponsibility, and a lack of remorse (APA, 2013). These symptoms are related to, but are broader than, the limited prosocial emotions or callous–unemotional traits described above, the latter being termed psychopathy in adulthood (Cleckley, 1976). Individuals with externalizing disorders during childhood are at greater risk of developing adult-onset externalizing disorders, and those with childhood-onset problems exhibit worse trajectories and outcomes (Moffitt, 1993). Further, these problems are highly comorbid with substance-related and addictive disorders and, for that reason, are believed to fall on a common externalizing spectrum (Krueger et al., 2002; Krueger, Markon, Patrick, Benning, & Kramer, 2007).

Longitudinal work examining trait relations with ODD suggests differential trait associations with ODD and concurrent comorbidity, as well as differential trait prediction of other disorders over time. Negative emotionality and activity, which is related to surgency, both predict later development of ODD (Stringaris, Maughan, & Goodman,2010). Further, these traits show differential associations with comorbidity, as individuals with high emotionality at age 3 may be more likely to exhibit comorbid ODD and internalizing problems 4 years later, while individuals with

Developmental Pathways to Disruptive, Impulse-Control, and Conduct Disorders.
DOI: https://doi.org/10.1016/B978-0-12-811323-3.00012-2

high activity levels may be more prone to later comorbid ODD and attention-deficit/hyperactivity disorder (ADHD; Stringaris et al., 2010). Therefore, high negative affect and high surgency both appear to predict ODD and differentially relate to common comorbidities of internalizing problems and ADHD, respectively.

Longitudinal work examining trait pathways to CD suggests two distinct pathways. The first pathway involves low withdrawal, more specifically low fear response, predicting later development of CD (reviewed by Nigg, 2006) through low guilt and empathy (Blair, 2001). The second pathway emphasizes high levels of negative affect and low reactive or effortful control (reviewed by Nigg, 2006) through high anger reactivity, irritability, and high sensation-seeking which lead to the development of behaviors and symptoms consistent with CD (Frick & Morris, 2004). Thus, it appears children may develop CD through either low fear or high negative affect.

Longitudinal research examining trait pathways in relation to antisocial behaviors has found that early impulsivity and negative affect predict later antisocial behavior (reviewed by Tackett, 2006). Specifically, impulsivity at age 3 and later is predictive of antisocial behaviors (Caspi, 2000), and this predictive pattern of impulsivity continues throughout middle childhood and adolescence (White, Bates, & Buyske, 2001). Additionally, high negative affect in childhood followed by low disinhibition during adolescence is predictive of antisocial behaviors continuing into later adulthood (Moffit et al., 1996). Therefore, high negative affect and disinhibition appear to predict the development of ASPD.

Callous–unemotional traits refer to a lack of guilt, absence of empathy, and shallow or constricted emotions and are a downward extension of adult psychopathy (Cleckley, 1976; Frick, 1995; Frick & White, 2008). Frick and Morris (2004) suggest the presence of callous–unemotional traits may damage a child's interpersonal style and conscience development, thus leading to later proactive aggression (Frick, Ray, Thornton, & Kahn, 2014a, 2014b; Frick & Viding, 2009). Such traits are hypothesized to make it easier for one to engage in future conduct problems, such as law-breaking or deceit. Accordingly, high callous–unemotional traits have been linked to conduct problems and higher rates of delinquency (Frick, Cornell, Barry, Bodin, & Dane, 2003; Frick, Stickle, Dandreaux, Farrell, & Kimonis, 2005; Stadler et al., 2011).

Therefore, high negative affect, high approach, low fear, disinhibition, and callous–unemotional traits seem to contribute to developmental pathways to disruptive behavior disorders such as ODD, CD, and ASPD.

Implications of pathway information for early assessment and personalized intervention advances

Given this information about trait markers of developmental pathways to ODD, CD, and ASPD, there are several implications for early assessment and personalized intervention advances. One key assessment implication would involve early assessment of traits. Although ODD can be diagnosed as early as preschool, CD is not diagnosed until middle childhood, and more commonly adolescence, while ASPD cannot be diagnosed until age 18 (APA, 2013; Moffitt, 1993). However, temperament traits that have been shown to be predictive of the development of these disorders can be assessed as early as infancy (Gartstein & Rothbart, 2003). Therefore, early assessment of these traits could allow for targeted personalized interventions prior to the development of the disorder.

A particular focus of personalized intervention approaches would likely be callous–unemotional traits as they have proven more resistant to treatment. For example, Hawes and Dadds (2005, 2007) found that after parent training, children with higher levels of callous–unemotional traits did not show improvement, even when trained parents used effective discipline techniques and time-out procedures. In these studies, there were no differences between how parents implemented treatment based on children's callous–unemotional traits (Hawes & Dadds, 2005,2007). However, research using tailored approaches has shown that children with callous–unemotional traits are not completely resistant to treatment. A multisystemic approach combining aspects of behavior training, cognitive-behavior therapy, problem-solving behaviors, and crisis management produced a moderate effect size for the reduction of callous–unemotional traits between pre- and post-treatment in a sample of elementary age children (Kolko et al., 2009). In this study, callous–unemotional traits did not predict poorer treatment outcome in a sample of elementary age children (Kolko & Pardini, 2010). Furthermore, parent–child interaction therapy approaches have led to reductions in conduct problems for those with high callous–unemotional traits (Kimonis, Bagner, Linares, Blake, & Rodriguez, 2014). Therefore, although individuals with high callous–unemotional traits seem more resistant to treatment, particularly those regarding parental discipline techniques, recent recommendations suggest those with callous–unemotional traits may respond better to parenting strategies emphasizing positive rewards for good behavior rather than negative consequences for misbehavior. Thus, assessing for the presence of callous–unemotional traits and personalizing intervention for those high in such traits appears to be a potentially promising avenue for reducing the risk and severity of conduct problems.

Finally, future work should examine the utility of trait profiles, including traits such as negative affect, surgency, disinhibition, and effortful control, for prospectively predicting the development of ODD, CD, and ASPD and mitigating their course through targeted intervention. Research has yet to examine the efficacy of such an approach in early childhood related to the development of ODD, CD, and ASPD. However, research using this approach has targeted substance use in adolescents and adults, which, as discussed within this chapter, is often comorbid with ODD, CD, and ASPD. In these studies, participants completed personality profiles (i.e., anxiety, sensitivity, hopelessness, sensation-seeking, impulsivity) and were matched to a brief intervention focused on elevations in a particular trait (e.g., high sensation-seeking). Each unique intervention took place over two sessions and included psychoeducation about that trait and differential behavioral and cognitive coping skills specific to the particular trait that was the focus (Conrod, Stewart,

Comeau, & Maclean, 2006). Such individualized treatment has been found to reduce chances of marijuana, cocaine, and other drug use in youth over a 2-year period compared to a placebo condition (Conrod, Castellanos-Ryan, & Strang, 2010). Similar success for personality trait-targeted interventions was found for reducing the onset and severity of problematic and risky alcohol use in youth, when compared to no treatment or treatment as usual (i.e., drug education in class; Conrod, Castellanos, & Mackie, 2008; Conrod, Castellanos-Ryan, & Mackie, 2011; Conrod et al., 2013), with these effects persisting over time. Moreover, these results replicated in an adult substance-using sample, with success apparent only when given the personality-matched intervention, but not when given a mismatched intervention (Conrod et al., 2000). Thus, the targeting of personality traits in brief substance use interventions appears to be efficacious and possibly time-efficient in adolescents. An important future direction is examining whether such an approach could be extended to personalized trait interventions for the development of ODD, CD, and ASPD.

Although research has suggested somewhat clear developmental pathways to ODD, CD, and ASPD, assessment and treatment have yet to be tailored to better intervene in the development of these disorders. Two potential avenues involve (1) early identification of callous–unemotional traits and negative affect, surgency, and effortful control and (2) implementing tailored personalized interventions. Future research should examine the efficacy of such interventions and treatments. Perhaps, early interventions or even preventive strategies targeting traits as a developmental pathway to ODD, CD, and ASPD could offset the later development of these disorders.

Important gaps in knowledge

Developmental pathways of comorbidity

Evidence suggests individuals with ODD, CD, and ASPD are likely to meet criteria for additional disorders, including ADHD, substance abuse, mania, schizophrenia, mood disorders, and other social dysfunction, at rates far exceeding what would be predicted from base rates alone (Angold, Costello, & Erkanli, 1999). While some of these comorbidities may result from definitional ambiguities or artifacts (reviewed in Drabick & Kendall, 2010), comorbidity tends to be the rule, rather than the exception. Therefore some studies have utilized a developmental psychopathology perspective to develop several conceptual models that link disruptive behavior disorders to other psychiatric conditions, described next.

Transdiagnostic processes

Transdiagnostic or cross-cutting processes, which contribute to the development of multiple disorders, have aided in clarifying developmental pathways underlying disruptive behavior disorder comorbidity (Ehring & Watkins, 2008; Krueger & Eaton,

2015; McLaughlin, Aldao, Wisco, & Hilt, 2014). Models including these processes have become prominent in the research literature, particularly in response to the Research Domain Criteria initiative by the National Institute of Mental Health (Insel et al., 2010). These models have helped clarify the nature of seemingly heterogeneous disorders and the potential underlying factors that contribute to them, including environmental experiences, inter- and intrapersonal factors, cognitive processes, personality, emotion regulation, and psychobiological factors (Cannon & Keller, 2006; Krueger & Markon, 2006; Nolen-Hoeksema & Watkins, 2011).

One hypothesis based on a developmental psychopathology approach proposes that multiple diagnoses within the context of comorbidity are associated with common genetic or psychosocial transdiagnostic processes (Multiformity Model; Angold et al., 1999; Caron & Rutter, 1991; Klein & Riso, 1993; Wolff & Ollendick, 2006). In line with such an idea, poor behavior control has been found to contribute to both health risk behaviors and aggression, and thus may underlie comorbidity between the two conditions (Donohew et al., 1999; Luengo, Carrillo-de-la-Pena, Otero, & Romero, 1994; Tarter et al., 2003). One study by Krueger and colleagues (2002) discovered that an externalizing transdiagnostic factor largely driven by disinhibitory personality traits accounted for comorbidity among CD, ASPD, marijuana dependence, and alcohol dependence in adults. Similarly, behavioral genetic studies have indicated that comorbidity among childhood externalizing disorders (ADHD, ODD, CD, and related disorders) may result from a core predisposing vulnerability, which studies have identified as trait impulsivity (Beauchaine, Klein, Crowell, Derbidge, & Gatzke-Kopp, 2009; Beauchaine, Zisner, & Sauder, 2017).

Thus, impulsivity and disinhibition may serve as transdiagnostic factors for externalizing psychopathology. Moreover, these vulnerability factors have been found to contribute to disorders across the externalizing spectrum, including ODD, CD, ASPD, ADHD, and drug and alcohol dependency, and thus may serve as core risk factors for comorbidity as well (Kendler, Prescott, Myers, & Neale, 2003; Krueger & Markon, 2006). Other proposed mechanisms that may predispose an individual to comorbidity involving disruptive behavior disorders include rumination, emotion dysregulation, social rejection, social-information-processing deficits, and biological vulnerabilities, including dopaminergic and to a lesser extent serotonergic vulnerabilities (Beauchaine et al., 2009; Burke, Loeber, & Birmaher, 2002; Dodge, 1993). Yet, such ideas require additional testing, with different transdiagnostic factors pitted against one another to further elucidate their explanatory power.

Multifinality vs equifinality

The developmental psychopathology framework suggests complex causal processes related to developmental psychopathology, namely multi- and equifinality (Cicchetti & Rogosch, 1996). Multifinality is defined as a single risk factor contributing to multiple outcomes based on other contextual or environmental factors (Cicchetti & Rogosch, 1996). The origin of these contextual factors ranges from the family environment to peer influences and neighborhood effects, all of which contribute to the development and continuance of disruptive behavior disorders (reviewed in Beauchaine et al., 2009). For example, during adolescence, exposure to neighborhood violence and criminality increases delinquency and other maladaptive outcomes among impulsive boys (Lynam et al., 2000; Meier, Slutske, Arndt, & Cadoret, 2008).

Equifinality, in contrast to multifinality, suggests that multiple, different risk factors can lead to the same outcomes (Cicchetti & Rogosch, 1996). For example, aggressive behavior may result from a variety of factors, including impaired verbal ability and heightened arousal, maternal depression and distress, greater use of harsh disciplinary practices, poor parenting, and negative peer experiences (Deater-Deckard et al., 2009; Gatzke-Kopp, Greenberg, Fortunato, & Coccia, 2012). Thus, the shared outcome of aggression likely results from a specific combination of factors that may differ across individuals. Yet, little work has examined multi- and equifinality in relation to the specific diagnostic categories of disruptive behavior disorders (vs more general forms of aggression and delinquency).

One disorder confers risk for another: acting out vs failure models

Several models also support a causal unidirectional association between disruptive behavior disorders and comorbid psychopathology. According to this model, one disorder may present as a proximal risk factor that predisposes an individual to a wide range of comorbidity based on other transdiagnostic factors. However, research on whether disruptive behavior disorders precede (Acting Out Model; Capaldi, 1992; Overbeek, Wilma, Meeus, Engels, & Luijpers, 2001) or succeed (Failure Model; Capaldi, 1992; Kiesner, Cadinu, Poulin, & Bucci, 2002) comorbid psychopathology remains divided, with some work supporting both hypotheses. For instance, disruptive behavior disorders typically precede comorbid psychopathology, particularly depression and anxiety, supporting the Acting Out Model (Lahey et al., 2000; Nock, Kazdin, Hiripi, & Kessler, 2006). In line with this model, strongly heritable and difficult emotional and behavioral patterns associated with disruptive behavior disorders may elicit negative reactions from the environment (increased peer rejection, etc.), with comorbid psychopathology likely to develop from the resultant coercion and stress (Capaldi, 1991; Lahey, Waldman, & McBurnett, 1999; Patterson, DeGarmo, & Knutson, 2000). Additional support comes from prevalence studies, where CD was found to be a powerful predictor of later substance abuse (Robins & McEvoy, 1990). Further, children with CD showed markedly increased rates of unemployment and marital breakdown in adult life, both of which are well-established risk factors for depressive disorders (Robins, 1986).

Alternatively, impulsive and aggressive behavior may result from negative experiences associated with disorders other than those related to disruptive behavior. In line with the failure model, children exhibiting anxiety or depression may develop maladaptive patterns of responding to stressful situations that typically elicit negative emotions (Bubier & Drabick, 2009; Polman, Orobio de Castro, Koops, van Boxtel, & Merk, 2007). According to this model, reactive aggression may result from frustration that originates when one's goals are blocked, and this association may be stronger in those exhibiting high levels of anxiety or depression. Specifically, anxious children may be more likely to respond impulsively and aggressively in contexts that elicit negative emotions. These patterns might become more consistent and automatic over time, culminating in the development of disruptive behavior disorders. For example, an anxious child who is provoked by another child and unable to withdraw from the situation may experience heightened levels of negative emotions that are difficult to regulate and thus respond with reactive aggression. Thus, overall, there seems to be some support for both directional models, and further study is required comparing both models' utility in representing disruptive behavior disorder comorbidity.

Mutual influence/concurrent comorbidity/indirect comorbidity

It is also possible that disruptive behavior disorders and comorbid psychopathology may occur concurrently and reciprocally reinforce each other over time (Overbeek et al., 2001; Wiesner, 2003), as has been found in certain cases involving disruptive behavior disorders and substance abuse (Hovens, Cantwell, & Kiriakos, 1994; Lahey, Loeber, Burke, & Rathouz, 2002; White, Loeber, Stouthamer-Loeber, & Farrington, 1999). Thus, two or more disorders may develop at the same time or at least during the same period, rather than a secondary disorder being influenced by a pre-existing primary disease (Angold et al., 1999). High levels of concurrent comorbidity between adolescent antisocial behavior and depression have been well-established in both clinical and population-based samples and have been replicated throughout the lifespan (Beyers & Loeber, 2003; Biederman, Faraone, Mick, & Lelon, 1995; Boylan, Vaillancourt, Boyle, & Szatmari, 2007; Capaldi, 1991). Finally, comorbidity may also result from indirect comorbidity patterns. In a hypothetical scenario where three disorders are comorbid with one another, one of the three associations between disorders may be a product of the other two associations (Angold et al., 1999). For example, while anxiety, CD, and depression are all related, it is possible the association between CD and anxiety may be a product of the other two associations. CD may be correlated with anxiety disorders primarily because both CD and anxiety disorders are correlated with depression. Thus, the apparent comorbidity between CD and anxiety is "indirect," or secondary to both disorders' association with depression. Indirect comorbidity may aid in simplifying the causes of comorbidity, since the number of combinations of interest (direct comorbidity) may be smaller than the total number of possible combinations. Such ideas remain difficult to test, given current statistical and methodological approaches, but merit further attention.

Important future directions in comorbidity models

While several prominent models have been proposed to underlie comorbidity between disorders, empirical research comparing the accuracy and generalizability of these models is lacking, especially with respect to disruptive behavior disorders.

Other notable limitations of extant work are that the utility of different models can be difficult to distinguish in small samples, especially when they are inherently similar (i.e., directional vs reciprocal causation). Further, it has proven difficult to compare directional vs concurrent models without longitudinal data, which is difficult and costly to obtain. Despite these limitations, elucidation of the most accurate and parsimonious models is an essential future direction for comorbidity research, as findings in this area could improve the accuracy of developmental pathways underlying comorbidity between disorders and potentially provide more parsimonious models as well. For example, preliminary support for a bifactor model of disruptive behavior disorders, which includes a general "g" factor along with distinct specific "s" ODD and ADHD factors (Martel, von Eye, & Nigg, 2010) could provide an important future direction for tests of underlying mechanisms such as impulsivity or disinhibition, which in turn could be useful assessment or treatment targets.

Additionally, little work has been conducted examining the utility of comorbidity models across development, and it is possible that the best models of comorbidity may change across development. For example, while anxiety disorders have been found to decrease the likelihood of substance use problems comorbid with disruptive behavior disorders, this effect has only been found in childhood and adulthood, but not adolescence (Lansford et al., 2008). There is also work to suggest that genetic and environmental effects on psychopathology and comorbidity may change over development (Burt, McGue, Carter, & Iacono, 2007; Burt, McGue, Krueger, & Iacono, 2005). Another gap in the literature concerns gender effects on prevalence rates of comorbidity (Klostermann, Connell, & Stormshak, 2016; Kofler et al., 2011; Wiesner, 2003). For example, it is possible that comorbidity may increase in girls, particularly during adolescence, but this idea has not yet been empirically tested. Finally, additional research exploring understudied moderators and mediators that contribute to disruptive behavior disorder comorbidity (culture, parenting style, etc.) may inform the specificity of developmental pathways, clarify developmental trajectories, and inform interventions aimed at disruptive behavior disorders and their comorbidity (Munkvold, Lundervold, & Manger, 2011).

Intermittent explosive disorder, pyromania, and kleptomania

While research investigating developmental pathways underlying disruptive behavior disorder pathways is needed, there are also several specific disorders related to the disruptive behavior disorder category whose development is still not fully understood. For example, little is known about developmental pathways to intermittent explosive disorder (IED), with current conclusions limited by retrospective self-report data examined cross-sectionally. Demographically, IED diagnoses are correlated with being male, younger than 50 years old, non-white, and having a lower level of education (Kessler et al., 2006). Those with IED report more urgency, or impulsivity, when experiencing high levels of positive and negative emotion, compared to psychiatric and healthy controls (Puhalla, Ammerman, Uyeji,

Berman, & McCloskey, 2016), and this may differentiate those with IED who demonstrate impulsive aggression from those with IED who demonstrate premediated aggression. Due to its earlier age of onset (13 – 21 years, Coccaro, 2010) compared to CD or ASPD, IED is thought to precede other comorbid disorders, but there is little empirical investigation of this idea.

There is evidence for a genetic component for IED, particularly for impulsive aggression, one of the cardinal features of IED. About one-third of first degree relatives of those with IED are diagnosed with IED (Coccaro, 2010). Biologically, those with IED may exhibit altered serotonin functioning (i.e., fewer binding sites) and functional differences in the amygdala and orbitofrontal cortex compared to psychiatric and healthy controls (Coccaro, 2010; Coccaro, Lee, & Kavoussi, 2010). For instance, those with IED had a higher amygdala response to angry faces compared to healthy controls, suggesting that those with IED may be overly responsive to perceiving others' anger (McCloskey et al., 2016). Those with IED also had more plasma markers of oxidative stress, which may relate to inflammation and neuronal membrane damage (Coccaro, Lee, & Gozal, 2016). These findings suggest biological differences may help explain the development of IED.

Lastly, it has been hypothesized that those with a history of abuse or maltreatment may be more likely to develop IED. Based on retrospective self-reports, those with IED experience more childhood maltreatment compared to psychiatric or healthy controls, with physical abuse independently associated with IED (Fanning, Meyerhoff, Lee, & Coccaro, 2014). Moreover, those with IED have greater trauma exposure, particularly interpersonal traumatic events (Nickerson, Aderka, Bryant, & Hofmann, 2012) and report less parental care and higher levels of parental control (Lee, Meyerhoff, & Coccaro, 2014). A history of trauma or abuse may contribute to later development of IED in multiple ways. For example, trauma history may impact the development of emotion regulation skills,as well as serve as a model of violent behavior (Nickerson et al., 2012). Abuse history or trauma may also influence social information processing, such as an increased hostile attribution bias. Though angry or aggressive responses may have been adaptive in previously dangerous situations, such responses are not appropriate in day-to-day life (Fanning et al., 2014). However, these results remain limited due to their reliance on one reporter at one time point. Longitudinal research is needed, particularly during the age of onset of IED, in order to better understand the mechanisms underlying IED.

While many hypotheses have been suggested for what may contribute to the etiology of both pyromania and kleptomania, no empirical study has been conducted to our knowledge. Rather, existing literature has relied on anecdotal case studies or small sample sizes of convenience. Similar to IED, future directions for pyromania and kleptomania should focus on empirical investigations and longitudinal samples. Though some correlates have been suggested for IED, pyromania, and kleptomania, the lack of empirical, longitudinal research limits the conclusions that can be made about the development of these disorders. Further research is needed in order to better understand the onset, course, and possible treatment for these disorders.

Summary

Extant research suggests that high negative affect, high approach, low fear, disinhibition, and callous–unemotional traits seem to be part of developmental pathways to disruptive behavior disorders such as ODD, CD, and ASPD. Such work suggests potential clinical applications of early assessment identification of callous–unemotional traits, negative affect, surgency, and effortful control, as well as the speculative possible utility of implementation of tailored personalized interventions. Future research should examine the efficacy of such interventions. In addition, more comprehensive tests of models of comorbidity are needed in order to elucidate potentially complex pathways of risk for such outcomes. Finally, more empirical work is needed examining IED, pyromania, and kleptomania.

References

American Psychiatric Association. (2013). *Diagnostic and statistical manual of mental disorders* (5th ed.). Washington, DC: Author.

Angold, A., Costello, E. J., & Erkanli, A. (1999). Comorbidity. *Journal of Child Psychology and Psychiatry and Allied Disciplines*, *40*, 57–87.

Beauchaine, T. P., Klein, D. N., Crowell, S. E., Derbidge, C., & Gatzke-Kopp, L. (2009). Multifinality in the development of personality disorders: A biology x sex x environment interaction model of antisocial and borderline traits. *Development and Psychopathology*, *21*, 735–770.

Beauchaine, T. P., Zisner, A. R., & Sauder, C. L. (2017). Trait impulsivity and the externalizing spectrum. *Annual Review of Clinical Psychology*, *13*, 343–368.

Beyers, J. M., & Loeber, R. (2003). Untangling developmental relations between depressed mood and delinquency in male adolescents. *Journal of Abnormal Child Psychology*, *31*, 247–266.

Biederman, J., Faraone, S., Mick, E., & Lelon, E. (1995). Psychiatric comorbidity among referred juveniles with major depression: Fact or artifact? *Journal of the American Academy of Child and Adolescent Psychiatry*, *34*, 579–590.

Blair, R. J. R. (2001). Neurocognitive models of aggression, the antisocial personality disorders, and psychopathy. *Journal of Neurology, Neurosurgery, and Psychiatry*, *71*, 727–731.

Boylan, K., Vaillancourt, T., Boyle, M., & Szatmari, P. (2007). Comorbidity of internalizing disorders in children with Oppositional Defiant Disorder. *European Child and Adolescent Psychiatry*, *16*, 484–494.

Bubier, J. L., & Drabick, D. A. (2009). Co-occurring anxiety and Disruptive Behavior Disorders: The roles of anxious symptoms, reactive aggression, and shared risk processes. *Clinical Psychology Review*, *29*, 658–669.

Burke, J. D., Loeber, R., & Birmaher, B. (2002). Oppositional Defiant Disorder and Conduct Cisorder: A review of the past 10 years, part II. *Journal of the American Academy of Child and Adolescent Psychiatry*, *41*, 1275–1293.

Burt, S. A., McGue, M., Carter, L. A., & Iacono, W. G. (2007). The different origins of stability and change in Antisocial Personality Disorder symptoms. *Psychological Medicine*, *37*, 27–38.

Burt, S. A., McGue, M., Krueger, R. F., & Iacono, W. G. (2005). How are parent-child conflict and childhood externalizing symptoms related over time? Results from a genetically informative cross-lagged study. *Development and Psychopathology*, *17*, 145–165.

Cannon, T. D., & Keller, M. C. (2006). Endophenotypes in the genetic analyses of mental disorders. *Annual Review of Clinical Psychology*, *2*, 267–290.

Capaldi, D. M. (1991). Co-occurrence of conduct problems and depressive symptoms in early adolescent boys: I. Familial factors and general adjustment at grade 6. *Development and Psychopathology*, *3*, 277–300.

Capaldi, E. J. (1992). The organization of behavior. *Journal of Applied Behavior Analysis*, *25*, 575–577.

Caron, C., & Rutter, M. (1991). Comorbidity in child psychopathology: Concepts, issues and research strategies. *Journal of Child Psychology and Psychiatry and Allied Disciplines*, *32*, 1063–1080.

Caspi, A. (2000). The child is father of the man: Personality continuities from childhood to adulthood. *Journal of Personality and Social Psychology*, *78*, 158–172.

Cicchetti, D., & Rogosch, F. A. (1996). Equifinality and multifinality in developmental psychopathology. *Development and Psychopathology*, *8*, 597–600.

Cleckley, H. (1976). *The mask of sanity* (5th ed.). St. Louis: Mosby.

Coccaro, E. F. (2010). A family history study of intermittent explosive disorder. *Journal of Psychiatric Research*, *44*(15), 1101–1105.

Coccaro, E. F., Lee, R., & Kavoussi, R. J. (2010). Aggression, suicidality, and intermittent explosive disorder: serotonergic correlates in personality disorder and healthy control subjects. *Neuropsychopharmacology*, *35*(2), 435.

Coccaro, E. F., Lee, R., & Gozal, D. (2016). Elevated plasma oxidative stress markers in individuals with intermittent explosive disorder and correlation with aggression in humans. *Biological Psychiatry*, *79*(2), 127–135.

Conrod, P. J., Castellanos, N., & Mackie, C. (2008). Personality-targeted interventions delay the growth of adolescent drinking and binge drinking. *Journal of Child Psychology and Psychiatry*, *49*, 181–190.

Conrod, P. J., Castellanos-Ryan, N., & Mackie, C. (2011). Long-term effects of a personality-targeted intervention to reduce alcohol use in adolescents. *Journal of Consulting and Clinical Psychology*, *79*, 296–306.

Conrod, P. J., Castellanos-Ryan, N., & Strang, J. (2010). Brief, personality-targeted coping skills interventions and survival as a non-drug user over a 2-year period during adolescence. *JAMA Psychiatry*, *67*, 85–93.

Conrod, P. J., O'Leary-Barrett, M., Newton, N., Topper, L., Castellanos-Ryan, N., Mackie, C., & Girard, A. (2013). Effectiveness of a selective, personality-targeted prevention program for adolescent alcohol use and misuse: A cluster randomized controlled trial. *JAMA Psychiatry*, *70*, 334–342.

Conrod, P. J., Stewart, S. H., Comeau, N., & Maclean, A. M. (2006). Efficacy of cognitive-behavioral interventions targeting personality risk factors for youth alcohol misuse. *Journal of Clinical Child and Adolescent Psychology*, *35*, 550–563.

Conrod, P. J., Stewart, S. H., Pihl, R. O., Côté, S., Fontaine, V., & Dongier, M. (2000). Efficacy of a brief coping skills interventions that match personality profiles of female substance abusers. *Psychology of Addictive Behaviors*, *14*, 231–242.

Deater-Deckard, K., Mullineaux, P. Y., Beekman, C., Petrill, S. A., Schatschneider, C., & Thompson, L. A. (2009). Conduct problems, IQ, and household chaos: A longitudinal multi-informant study. *Journal of Child Psychology and Psychiatry and Allied Disciplines*, *50*, 1301–1308.

Dodge, K. A. (1993). Social-cognitive mechanisms in the development of Conduct Disorder and depression. *Annual Review of Psychology*, *44*, 559–584.

Donohew, R. L., Hoyle, R. H., Clayton, R. R., Skinner, W. F., Colon, S. E., & Rice, R. E. (1999). Sensation seeking and drug use by adolescents and their friends: Models for marijuana and alcohol. *Journal of Studies on Alcohol*, *60*, 622–631.

Drabick, D. A., & Kendall, P. C. (2010). Developmental psychopathology and the diagnosis of mental health problems among youth. *Clinical Psychology*, *17*, 272–280.

Ehring, T., & Watkins, E. R. (2008). Repetitive negative thinking as a transdiagnostic process. *International Journal of Cognitive Therapy*, *1*, 192–205.

Fanning, J. R., Meyerhoff, J. J., Lee, R., & Coccaro, E. F. (2014). History of childhood maltreatment in intermittent explosive disorder and suicidal behavior. *Journal of Psychiatric Research*, *56*, 10–17.

Frick, P. J. (1995). Callous-unemotional traits and conduct problems: A two-factor model of psychopathy in children. *Issues in Criminological & Legal Psychology*, 47–51.

Frick, P. J., Cornell, A. H., Barry, C. T., Bodin, S. D., & Dane, H. E. (2003). Callous-unemotional traits and conduct problems in the prediction of conduct problem severity, aggression, and self-report of delinquency. *Journal of Abnormal Child Psychology*, *31*, 457–470.

Frick, P. J., & Morris, A. S. (2004). Temperament and developmental pathways to conduct problems. *Journal of Clinical Child & Adolescent Psychology*, *33*, 54–68.

Frick, P. J., & Nigg, J. T. (2012). Current issues in the diagnosis of Attention Deficit Hyperactivity Disorder, Oppositional Defiant Disorder, and Conduct Disorder. *Annual Review of Clinical Psychology*, *8*, 77–107.

Frick, P. J., Ray, J. V., Thornton, L. C., & Kahn, R. E. (2014a). Annual research review: A developmental psychopathology approach to understanding callous-unemotional traits in children and adolescents with serious conduct problems. *Journal of Child Psychology and Psychiatry*, *55*, 532–548.

Frick, P. J., Ray, J. V., Thornton, L. C., & Kahn, R. E. (2014b). Can callous-unemotional traits enhance the understanding, diagnosis, and treatment of serious conduct problems in children and adolescents? A comprehensive review. *Psychological Bulletin*, *140*, 1–57.

Frick, P. J., Stickle, T. R., Dandreaux, D. M., Farrell, J. M., & Kimonis, E. R. (2005). Callous–unemotional traits in predicting the severity and stability of conduct problems and delinquency. *Journal of Abnormal Child Psychology*, *33*, 471–487.

Frick, P. J., & Viding, E. (2009). Antisocial behavior from a developmental psychopathology perspective. *Development and Psychopathology*, *21*, 1111–1131.

Frick, P. J., & White, S. F. (2008). The importance of callous-unemotional traits for the development of aggressive and antisocial behavior. *Journal of Child Psychology & Psychiatry*, *49*, 359–375.

Gartstein, M. A., & Rothbart, M. K. (2003). Studying infant temperament via the revised infant behavior questionnaire. *Infant Behavior and Development*, *26*, 64–86.

Gatzke-Kopp, L. M., Greenberg, M. T., Fortunato, C. K., & Coccia, M. A. (2012). Aggression as an equifinal outcome of distinct neurocognitive and neuroaffective processes. *Development and Psychopathology*, *24*, 985–1002.

Hawes, D. J., & Dadds, M. R. (2005). The treatment of conduct problems in children with callous-unemotional traits. *Journal of Consulting and Clinical Psychology*, *73*, 737–741.

Hawes, D. J., & Dadds, M. R. (2007). Stability and malleability of callous-unemotional traits during treatment for childhood conduct problems. *Journal of Clinical Child and Adolescent Psychology*, *36*, 347–355.

Hovens, J. G., Cantwell, D. P., & Kiriakos, R. (1994). Psychiatric comorbidity in hospitalized adolescent substance abusers. *Journal of the American Academy of Child and Adolescent Psychiatry*, *33*, 476–483.

Insel, T., Cuthbert, B., Garvey, M., Heinssen, R., Pine, D. S., Quinn, K., ... Wang, P. (2010). Research domain criteria (RDoC): Toward a new classification framework for research on mental disorders. *American Journal of Psychiatry*, *167*, 748–751.

Kendler, K. S., Prescott, C. A., Myers, J., & Neale, M. C. (2003). The structure of genetic and environmental risk factors for common psychiatric and substance use disorders in men and women. *Archives of General Psychiatry*, *60*, 929–937.

Kiesner, J., Cadinu, M., Poulin, F., & Bucci, M. (2002). Group identification in early adolescence: Its relation with peer adjustment and its moderator effect on peer influence. *Child Development*, *73*, 196–208.

Kimonis, E. R., Bagner, D. M., Linares, D., Blake, C. A., & Rodriguez, G. (2014). Parent training outcomes among young children with callous-unemotional conduct problems with or at-risk for developmental delay. *Journal of Child and Family Studies*, *23*, 437–448.

Klein, D. N., & Riso, L. P. (1993). Psychiatric disorders: Problems of boundaries and comorbidity. In C. G. Costello (Ed.), *Basic issues in psychopathology* (pp. 19–66). New York: Guilford.

Klostermann, S., Connell, A., & Stormshak, B. (2016). Gender differences in the developmental links between conduct problems and depression across early adolescence. *Journal of Research on Adolescence*, *26*, 76–89.

Kofler, M. J., McCart, M. R., Zajac, K., Ruggiero, K. J., Saunders, B. E., & Kilpatrick, D. G. (2011). Depression and delinquency covariation in an accelerated longitudinal sample of adolescents. *Journal of Consulting and Clinical Psychology*, *79*, 458–469.

Kolko, D. J., Dorn, L. D., Bukstein, O. G., Pardini, D., Holden, E. A., & Hart, J. (2009). Community vs. clinic-based modular treatment of children with early-onset ODD or CD: A clinical trial with 3-year follow-up. *Journal of Abnormal Child Psychology*, *37*, 591–609.

Kolko, D. J., & Pardini, D. A. (2010). ODD dimensions, ADHD, and callous-unemotional traits as predictors of treatment response in children with Disruptive Behavior Disorders. *Journal of Abnormal Psychology*, *119*, 713–725.

Krueger, R. F., & Eaton, N. R. (2015). Transdiagnostic factors of mental disorders. *World Psychiatry*, *14*, 27–29.

Krueger, R. F., Hicks, B. M., Patrick, C. J., Carlson, S. R., Iacono, W. G., & McGue, M. (2002). Etiologic connections among substance dependence, antisocial behavior, and personality: Modeling the externalizing spectrum. *Journal of Abnormal Psychology*, *111*, 411–424.

Krueger, R. F., & Markon, K. E. (2006). Reinterpreting comorbidity: A model-based approach to understanding and classifying psychopathology. *Annual Review of Clinical Psychology*, *2*, 111–133.

Krueger, R. F., Markon, K. E., Patrick, C. J., Benning, S. D., & Kramer, M. D. (2007). Linking antisocial behavior, substance use, and personality: An integrative quantitative model of the adult externalizing spectrum. *Journal of Abnormal Psychology*, *116*, 645.

Lahey, B. B., Goodman, S. H., Walkman, I. D., Bird, H., Canino, G., Jensen, P., ... Applegate, B. (1999). Relation of age of onset to the type and severity of child and adolescent conduct problems. *Journal of Abnormal Child Psychology*, *27*, 247–260.

Lahey, B. B., Loeber, R., Burke, J., & Rathouz, P. J. (2002). Adolescent outcomes of childhood Conduct Disorder among clinic-referred boys: Predictors of improvement. *Journal of Abnormal Child Psychology*, *30*, 333–348.

Lahey, B. B., Schwab-Stone, M., Goodman, S. H., Waldman, I. D., Canino, G., Rathouz, P. J., ... Jensen, P. S. (2000). Age and gender differences in oppositional behavior and conduct problems: A cross-sectional household study of middle childhood and adolescence. *Journal of Abnormal Psychology*, *109*, 488–503.

Lahey, B. B., Waldman, I. D., & McBurnett, K. (1999). Annotation: The development of antisocial behavior: An integrative causal model. *Journal of Child Psychology and Psychiatry and Allied Disciplines*, *40*, 669–682.

Lansford, J. E., Erath, S., Yu, T., Pettit, G. S., Dodge, K. A., & Bates, J. E. (2008). The developmental course of illicit substance use from age 12 to 22: Links with depressive, anxiety, and behavior disorders at age 18. *Journal of Child Psychology and Psychiatry and Allied Disciplines*, *49*, 877–885.

Lee, R., Meyerhoff, J., & Coccaro, E. F. (2014). Intermittent explosive disorder and aversive parental care. *Psychiatry Research*, *220*(1), 477–482.

Luengo, M. A., Carrillo-de-la-Pena, M. T., Otero, J. M., & Romero, E. (1994). A short-term longitudinal study of impulsivity and antisocial behavior. *Journal of Personality and Social Psychology*, *66*, 542–548.

Lynam, D. R., Caspi, A., Moffitt, T. E., Wikstrom, P. O., Loeber, R., & Novak, S. (2000). The interaction between impulsivity and neighborhood context on offending: The effects of impulsivity are stronger in poorer neighborhoods. *Journal of Abnormal Psychology*, *109*, 563–574.

Martel, M. M., von Eye, A., & Nigg, J. T. (2010). Revisiting the latent structure of ADHD: Is there a 'g' factor? *Journal of Child Psychology and Psychiatry and Allied Disciplines*, *51*, 905–914.

McCloskey, M. S., Phan, K. L., Angstadt, M., Fettich, K. C., Keedy, S., & Coccaro, E. F. (2016). Amygdala hyperactivation to angry faces in intermittent explosive disorder. *Journal of Psychiatric Research*, *79*, 34–41.

McLaughlin, K. A., Aldao, A., Wisco, B. E., & Hilt, L. M. (2014). Rumination as a transdiagnostic factor underlying transitions between internalizing symptoms and aggressive behavior in early adolescents. *Journal of Abnormal Psychology*, *123*, 13–23.

Meier, M. H., Slutske, W. S., Arndt, S., & Cadoret, R. J. (2008). Impulsive and callous traits are more strongly associated with delinquent behavior in higher risk neighborhoods among boys and girls. *Journal of Abnormal Psychology*, *117*, 377–385.

Moffitt, T. E. (1993). Adolescence-limited and life-course-persistent antisocial behavior: A developmental taxonomy. *Psychological Review*, *100*, 674–701.

Munkvold, L. H., Lundervold, A. J., & Manger, T. (2011). Oppositional Defiant Disorder-gender differences in co-occurring symptoms of mental health problems in a general population of children. *Journal of Abnormal Child Psychology*, *39*, 577–587.

Nickerson, A., Aderka, I. M., Bryant, R. A., & Hofmann, S. G. (2012). The relationship between childhood exposure to trauma and intermittent explosive disorder. *Psychiatry Research*, *197*(1), 128–134.

Nigg, J. T. (2006). Temperament and developmental psychopathology. *Journal of Child Psychology and Psychiatry*, *47*, 395–422.

Nock, M. K., Kazdin, A. E., Hiripi, E., & Kessler, R. C. (2006). Prevalence, subtypes, and correlates of DSM-IV Conduct Disorder in the National Comorbidity Survey Replication. *Psychological Medicine*, *36*, 699–710.

Nolen-Hoeksema, S., & Watkins, E. R. (2011). A heuristic for developing transdiagnostic models of psychopathology: Explaining multifinality and divergent trajectories. *Perspectives on Psychological Science*, *6*, 589–609.

Overbeek, G., Wilma, V., Meeus, W., Engels, R., & Luijpers, E. (2001). Course, co-occurrence, and longitudinal associations of emotional disturbance and delinquency from adolescence to young adulthood: A six-year three-wave study. *Journal of Youth and Adolescence*, *30*, 401–426.

Patterson, G. R., DeGarmo, D. S., & Knutson, N. (2000). Hyperactive and antisocial behaviors: Comorbid or two points in the same process? *Development and Psychopathology*, *12*, 91–106.

Polman, H., Orobio de Castro, B., Koops, W., van Boxtel, H. W., & Merk, W. W. (2007). A meta-analysis of the distinction between reactive and proactive aggression in children and adolescents. *Journal of Abnormal Child Psychology*, *35*, 522–535.

Puhalla, A. A., Ammerman, B. A., Uyeji, L. L., Berman, M. E., & McCloskey, M. S. (2016). Negative urgency and reward/punishment sensitivity in intermittent explosive disorder. *Journal of Affective Disorders*, *201*, 8–14.

Robins, L. N. (1986). The consequences of Conduct Disorder in girls. In D. Olweus, J. Block, & M. Radke-Yarrow (Eds.), *The development of antisocial and prosocial behavior: Research, theories, and issues* (pp. 385–414). Orlando, FL: Academic Press.

Robins, L. N., & McEvoy, L. (1990). Conduct problems as predictors of substance abuse. In L. N. Robins, & M. Rutter (Eds.), *Straight and devious pathways from childhood to adulthood*. Cambridge, England: Cambridge University Press.

Stadler, C., Kroeger, A., Weyers, P., Grasmann, D., Horschinek, M., Freitag, C., & Clement, H. (2011). Cortisol reactivity in boys with Attention-Deficit/Hyperactivity Disorder and disruptive behavior problems: The impact of callous unemotional traits. *Psychiatry Research*, *187*, 204–209.

Stringaris, A., Maughan, B., & Goodman, R. (2010). What's in a disruptive disorder? Temperamental antecedents of Oppositional Defiant Disorder: Findings from the Avon Longitudinal Study. *Journal of the American Academy of Child & Adolescent Psychiatry*, *49*, 474–483.

Tackett, J. L. (2006). Evaluating models of the personality–psychopathology relationship in children and adolescents. *Clinical Psychology Review*, *26*, 584–599.

Tarter, R. E., Kirisci, L., Mezzich, A., Cornelius, J. R., Pajer, K., Vanyukov, M., ... Clark, D. (2003). Neurobehavioral disinhibition in childhood predicts early age at onset of substance use disorder. *American Journal of Psychiatry*, *160*, 1078–1085.

White, H. R., Bates, M. E., & Buyske, S. (2001). Adolescence-limited versus persistent delinquency: Extending Moffitt's hypothesis into adulthood. *Journal of Abnormal Psychology*, *110*, 600–609.

White, H. R., Loeber, R., Stouthamer-Loeber, M., & Farrington, D. P. (1999). Developmental associations between substance use and violence. *Development and Psychopathology*, *11*, 785–803.

Wiesner, M. (2003). A longitudinal latent variable analysis of reciprocal relations between depressive symptoms and delinquency during adolescence. *Journal of Abnormal Psychology*, *112*, 633–645.

Wolff, J. C., & Ollendick, T. H. (2006). The comorbidity of conduct problems and depression in childhood and adolescence. *Clinical Child and Family Psychology Review*, *9*(3-4), 201–220.

Further reading

Caspi, A., Houts, R. M., Belsky, D. W., Goldman-Mellor, S. J., Harrington, H., Israel, S., ... Moffitt, T. E. (2014). The p factor: One general psychopathology factor in the structure of psychiatric disorders? *Clinical Psychological Science*, *2*, 119–137.

Caspi, A., Moffitt, T. E., Newman, D. L., & Silva, P. A. (1996). Behavioral observations at age 3 years predict adult psychiatric disorders: Longitudinal evidence from a birth cohort. *Archives of General Psychiatry*, *53*, 1033–1039.

Frick, P. J. (2012). Developmental pathways to Conduct Disorder: Implications for future directions in research, assessment, and treatment. *Journal of Clinical Child & Adolescent Psychology*, *41*, 378–389.

Hankin, B. L., Davis, E. P., Snyder, H., Young, J. F., Glynn, L. M., & Sandman, C. A. (2017). Temperament factors and dimensional, latent bifactor models of child psychopathology: Transdiagnostic and specific associations in two youth samples. *Psychiatry Research*, *252*, 139–146.

Kotov, R., Chang, S. W., Fochtmann, L. J., Mojtabai, R., Carlson, G. A., Sedler, M. J., & Bromet, E. J. (2011). Schizophrenia in the internalizing-externalizing framework: A third dimension?. *Schizophrenia Bulletin*, *37*, 1168–1178.

Kotov, R., Ruggero, C. J., Krueger, R. F., Watson, D., Yuan, Q., & Zimmerman, M. (2011). New dimensions in the quantitative classification of mental illness. *Archives of General Psychiatry*, *68*, 1003–1011.

Ormel, J., Oldehinkel, A. J., Ferdinand, R. F., Hartman, C. A., De Winter, A. F., Veenstra, R., ... Verhulst, F. C. (2005). Internalizing and externalizing problems in adolescence: General and dimension-specific effects of familial loadings and preadolescent temperament traits. *Psychological Medicine*, *35*, 1825–1835.

Snyder, H. R., Gulley, L. D., Bijttebier, P., Hartman, C. A., Oldehinkel, A. J., Mezulis, A., ... Hankin, B. L. (2015). Adolescent emotionality and effortful control: Core latent constructs and links to psychopathology and functioning. *Journal of Personality and Social Psychology*, *109*, 1132–1149.

Snyder, H. R., Young, J. F., & Hankin, B. L. (2017). Chronic stress exposure and generation are related to the p-factor and externalizing specific psychopathology in youth. *Journal of Clinical Child and Adolescent Psychology*, Advance online publication.

Wright, A. G., Krueger, R. F., Hobbs, M. J., Markon, K. E., Eaton, N. R., & Slade, T. (2013). The structure of psychopathology: Toward an expanded quantitative empirical model. *Journal of Abnormal Psychology*, *122*, 281–294.

Integrative theory and treatment

13

David J. Hawes
The University of Sydney, Sydney, NSW, Australia

The evidence-based interventions now available for conduct problems (i.e., oppositional defiant disorder and conduct disorder) owe much to the emphasis on theory building that drove early advances in the family-based treatment of these problems. Guided by the dictum "if you want to understand something, try to change it," a new wave of behavioral scientists used experimental treatment outcome research as a tool for building causal models of these disorders across the 1960s and 1970s. This research demonstrated that this theory could be successfully translated into parenting interventions for these problems that were superior to existing forms of child and family therapy (see Patterson, Reid, & Eddy, 2002). This emphasis on testing and refining theories of conduct problems in order to improve their treatment has endured, and in recent years innovations in the conceptualization of conduct problems have been concerned increasingly with the heterogeneous risk pathways through which such problems are thought to emerge in distinct subgroups of children. Such innovations have provided a promising basis for investigating the personalization of treatments based on specific child risk factors and markers, with neuroscientific research increasingly informing comprehensive accounts of the multilevel risk mechanisms that contribute to these pathways. At the same time, progress in research aiming to shift the success rates of treatment beyond those of existing interventions has often been painstaking. This chapter provides a background to the role that theories of psychopathology have played in the development of treatments for child conduct problems and addresses some of the major issues and challenges associated with current translational research in this area. Based on evidence that the most high-risk trajectories of these problems are initiated in early in childhood (Frick & Viding, 2009), and the established importance of early intervention, the periods of early and middle childhood are a predominant focus.

It is proposed that three bodies of theory and evidence are particularly key to informing the development of personalized treatments for children with conduct problems, or indeed any mental health problem. The first is that which provides a basis for characterizing a phenotype, or profile of child symptoms and markers, that identifies children whose needs are not sufficiently met by existing best-practice treatments. For the purpose of this chapter, a focus is placed on the example of callous and unemotional (CU) traits (e.g., a lack of guilt and empathy), which in recent years have been subject to considerable investigation in research aiming to identify and overcome poor treatment outcomes among children with conduct problems. Second, the potential to design novel treatment components to target the unique needs of a specific subgroup of children relies on basic research into the risk mechanisms implicated in those needs. As presented later in this chapter, such

Developmental Pathways to Disruptive, Impulse-Control, and Conduct Disorders.
DOI: https://doi.org/10.1016/B978-0-12-811323-3.00013-4

research into CU traits has identified a range of neurobiological and neurocognitive correlates, leading to predictions about a range of potential biological and behavioral directions for intervention. Third, the successful development of such an intervention is likely to rely on the availability of theory to inform the integration of novel treatment components with those of existing interventions. With regard to the treatment of conduct problems in children with CU traits, the questions that have arisen regarding such integration present potentially important clinical implications and warrant careful consideration. Two novel interventions based on theory-driven strategies arising from such research are presented, which have been evaluated in randomized controlled trials in Australia.

Child conduct problems: a brief history of evidence-based theory and practice

Current evidence-based interventions for conduct problems are among the most effective and established for any problem in child mental health. Indeed, the empirical support for these interventions has been so compelling that in recent decades the field has shifted somewhat from a focus on refining the clinical strategies within treatment programs to a focus on scaling up these programs to meet the needs of communities at large (e.g., Dishion, Forgatch, Chamberlain, & Pelham, 2016; McWilliam, Brown, Sanders, & Jones, 2016), as well as exploring the potential for innovative eHealth technologies to enhance their delivery and reach (e.g., Kirkman, Hawes, & Dadds, 2016; Sanders, Baker, & Turner, 2012). Well before this, the emergence of these interventions was marked not only by controversy regarding the theoretical predictions on which they are based, but a need to develop new research methods that were suited to testing these predictions where none had existed.

As concluded by major reviews of the literature in recent years, the interventions that currently have the strongest support in the treatment of conduct problems are parenting interventions based on social learning theory (e.g., Comer, Chow, Chan, Cooper-Vince, & Wilson, 2013; Eyberg, Nelson, & Boggs, 2008; Kaminski & Claussen, 2017; Michelson, Davenport, Dretzke, Barlow, & Day, 2013). Historically, these interventions were attempts to formulate and test predictions of behavior change through the careful collection and analysis of observational data on the moment-to-moment behavior of children with conduct problems in their natural environments. Beginning in the 1960s these data were subject to behavior analysis in landmark stimulus control studies. Aggressive children were observed in family interactions to identify antecedents and consequences of target behaviors, which researchers systematically modified in order to observe the effects this produced on behavioral responses. This approach to theory building in the service of clinical intervention represented a radical departure from the psychoanalytic perspective that had dominated accounts of child mental health previously. What came to be known as coercion theory was formulated from the application of operant conditioning principles to such data, often through much trial and error according to historical accounts (Patterson et al., 2002). Such accounts have also highlighted the role that advances in research methods have played in shaping coercion theory, with the advent of new tools for data collection and statistical analysis allowing researchers to answer a growing range of questions regarding the mechanisms by which conduct problems emerge and persist across development. Importantly, some of the most challenging questions for coercion theory have emerged—and re-emerged—from recent theories of individual differences in risk pathways to antisocial behavior, as addressed later in this chapter.

Fundamental to coercion theory is the assumption that the frequency with which children engage in oppositional and aggressive behavior, and the amplification of this behavior over time, are linked to its functional value in the child's daily social environment (Patterson, 2016). As such, it is concerned primarily with micro-social mechanisms in the moment-to-moment dynamics of relationships. Coercive dynamics based in the parent–child relationship are understood to function as particularly proximal influences on child conduct problems, particularly across early and middle childhood when the most chronic trajectories of antisocial behavior are often initiated. The core dynamic of coercion is that conflict is solved by emotional manipulation rather than by negotiation, with children and parents engaging in behaviors that may span low level aversive behaviors (e.g., whining, complaining, nagging, scolding, threatening) through to acts of physical aggression, intimidation, and hostile rejection. Not only does such coercive behavior occur more often in the family contexts of children with conduct problems than those without, but once initiated, such behavior is more likely to be reciprocated by family members and escalate. Such escalation often comprises responses that are enacted largely outside of conscious awareness, with all the automaticity of highly overlearned behaviors such as driving a car.

According to coercion theory the central reinforcement of children's problem behaviors provided by families occurs during family-conflict episodes, with the critical factor being the relative rate at which a child's coercive behavior is reinforced (Snyder & Stoolmiller, 2002). That is, among the broad array of behaviors that a child performs in response to the aversive behavior of another person, are coercive behaviors reinforced more frequently than adaptive behaviors? In theoretical terms, this reflects matching law (Herrnstein, 1974), whereby the frequency with which a specific response (e.g., aggression) will be performed is determined by the frequency with which that response is reinforced relative to the frequency of reinforcement for other responses (e.g., cooperation). A child's coercive behavior may be highly functional in gaining social attention, desired outcomes, and preferred activities (positive reinforcement). However, the data suggest that negative reinforcement or escape conditioning may be the lynchpin of such dynamics, with these behaviors performed in so far as they are functional in escaping or avoiding punishment (e.g., deflecting a parents' command), or in terminating conflicts with others (e.g., hitting a sibling to stop them teasing). In line with this assumption, early treatment outcome research showed that interventions were largely ineffective when based only on ignoring or extinction of aggressive behavior and positive reinforcement of desirable behavior. It was only when consequences for setting limits on child coercion such as time-out or point loss were added that improvements in child behavior were seen according to objective indices (Patterson et al., 2002).

Importantly, the very same operant mechanisms identified in the family-based studies of Patterson and colleagues (Snyder & Stoolmiller, 2002) not only accounted for parent-driven effects on child conduct problems, but child-driven effects on parental coercion. In families of children with conduct problems, the contingencies supplied by parent–child interactions were found to reinforce the harsh and inconsistent discipline that, in turn, was found to reinforce child coercion. As such, these parent–child interactions were conceptualized as escalating cycles of parent–child coercion that function as interlocking "reinforcement traps." This reinforcement is bilateral, with children and parents continually shaping each other's behavior, and as children become increasingly skilled in the use of coercion, they become increasingly difficult to discipline. For families trapped in such cycles, it is predicted that over time, the coercion in which both parent and child engage during conflict will escalate more and more rapidly and will reach higher and higher amplitudes. At the same time, the more frustrating and exhausting parent–child interactions become for a parent, the more a parent is likely to avoid engaging with a child unless necessary. Given that healthy, age-appropriate child behaviors are less likely to require parental attention, these behaviors are likely to receive decreasing rates of positive reinforcement in day-to-day life, with such engagement becoming increasingly contingent on the child's misbehavior. In other words, conflict and discipline become the ways that parent and child spend time together, and the quality of their relationship suffers accordingly.

Current interventions for conduct problems in young children

The advent of coercion theory had a profound influence on the treatment of these problems, shifting the focus of intervention from the individual child to the contexts and relationships in which child behavior is embedded. Parenting interventions based on this theory assume that reductions in child conduct problems are achieved by shutting down and replacing escalating cycles of parent–child coercion with family-based contingencies and relationship dynamics that promote healthy and effective behavior across the family as a system. Although specific versions of these social learning based programs vary in terms of scope and format, an emphasis is generally placed on two core components. The first of these comprises strategies to increase rates of positive reinforcement for appropriate child behaviors, through the provision of immediate and rewarding responses (e.g., contingent praise). The second component comprises strategies to promote effective limit-setting on child behaviors that generally escalate, and to avoid the "reinforcement traps" through which ineffective discipline commonly provides pay-offs for children's escalation. These strategies often take the form of a behavior correction routine, in which an age-appropriate consequence will be applied if a child does not respond after first being presented with clear parental instructions and an opportunity to cooperate. The most widely used consequence for children below 8 or so years of age is brief time-out, while for older children, some form of response cost, such as the loss of a privilege, is considered more appropriate. The aim here is create consistent, predictable, and nonaggressive consequences for misbehavior, by providing parents with a routine that can be generalized broadly across negative child behaviors. The demands placed on parents during potentially stressful discipline encounters are thereby reduced, which is critical given that the emotional arousal provoked by child misbehavior can overwhelm rationale decision making and lead parents to revert to previously overlearned harsh reactions (Mence et al., 2014). As such, one of the key functions of consequences such as time-out is that they provide something of a circuit breaker for escalating cycles of parent–child coercion.

Prominent examples of widely evaluated and disseminated treatment programs based primarily on social learning theory include the Parent Management Training Oregon Model (PMTO; Forgatch & Patterson, 2010); the Triple P—Positive Parenting Program (Sanders, 2012); Helping the Noncompliant Child (McMahon & Forehand, 2003) Incredible Years (IY; Webster-Stratton & Reid, 2003), and Parent–Child Interaction Therapy (PCIT; Brinkmeyer & Eyberg, 2003; McNeil & Hembree-Kigin, 2010). Some are generally delivered individually with families (e.g., HNC), while others are more commonly delivered in groups (e.g., Triple-P). Likewise, some utilize distinct skills-training methods such video recorded demonstrations (e.g., IY) and the coaching of parents via an earpiece—usually from behind a one-way mirror— as they interact with their child during treatment sessions (e.g., PCIT). Differences are also seen in the various skills and components that supplement those focused primarily on parenting practices to reverse cycles of coercion, such as strategies for parents to teach problem-solving skills to their children (e.g., IY) and to target other stressors in the family such as conflict in the parents' own relationship (e.g., Dadds & Hawes, 2006).

Notwithstanding these differences, such programs share much in common with regard to conceptualizations of risk mechanisms. In line with this, they often perform comparably according to treatment outcome data, while showing superiors results to treatments based primarily on alternative mechanisms such as systemic family therapy (Wells & Egan, 1988). From a theoretical perspective, a further strength is apparent on the grounds of parsimony. That is, the components of coercion theory are more amenable to observation and measurement than those of competing theories, and able to account for causal influence in fewer mechanisms. For example, accounts of child adjustment based on social learning theory and attachment theory both agree on the centrality of caregiver contingencies (or responsiveness) in bringing about self-regulated behavior. However, in predicting how it changes child behavior, attachment theory relies on constructs that refer to internal states and representations that are not easily operationalized without the use of proxy measures (see Patterson & Fisher, 2002). At the same time, this perspective does not preclude the integration of other theoretical principles into a clinical model based on coercion theory primarily. One example of a model integrating social learning and attachment theory is Integrated Family Intervention for Child Conduct

Problems (IFI: Dadds & Hawes, 2006). This model, which has its origins in work by Sanders and Dadds (1993), has in recent years formed the basis for much of the research on treatment innovations conducted at the Child Behavior Research Clinic (CBRC) at the University of Sydney.

IFI is a parenting intervention comprising social learning based components at its core, the delivery of which is guided by theory concerning attachment, cognition, and family structure. A key assumption is that the unique dynamics that characterize the attachment system can explain some child behaviors that operant principles cannot, such as why some children seem driven to elicit potentially harmful attention from parents and why parent attention is so powerful a reinforce at particular ages (Greenberg, Speltz, & DeKlyen, 1993). Attachment theory may likewise help to explain some of the major impediments to behavior change commonly faced by families attempting to implement social learning based strategies, particularly among children who may have an insecure attachment. For example, it is common for parents in these strategies to prioritize or rely on tangible or token forms of positive reinforcement (e.g., treats, stickers) that lack potency in comparison to those more embedded in the parent–child relationship. Furthermore, given that conduct problems often elicit parent responses that are not only harsh but also rejecting, parents may engage in a range of subtle behaviors that inadvertently communicate attachment-threat when implementing strategies to set limits on misbehavior (e.g., expressed emotion when implementing time-out). This can, in turn, lead to escalations in the child's maladaptive attempts to establish physical and emotional proximity during discipline, analogous to that demonstrated in the experimental studies of attachment by Harlow and colleagues using animal paradigms (e.g., Harlow & Harlow, 1971). IFI is not designed to target attachment variables, nor does it assume that improvement in conduct problems usually necessitates change in attachment security. Rather, parents are trained to implement social learning based strategies in ways that are sensitive to, and capitalize on, parent–child attachment processes. This includes maximizing parents' use of contingent reinforcement strategies that emphasize caregiver proximity (e.g., periods of joint activity) and targeting coercive escalation by training parents to implement limit-setting strategies (e.g., brief time-out) in ways that do not inadvertently threaten attachment security. Research has provided growing support for the notion that interplay between operant and attachment dynamics may for some children play a key role in risk and behavior change, as assumed in our model. For example, Kochanska, Barry, Stellern, and O'Bleness (2009) found that early attachment insecurity did not predict latter conduct problems directly, but that such outcomes were predicted by an interaction between coercive parenting and attachment insecurity.

For children with conduct problems referred to the CBRC at the University of Sydney, IFI is generally delivered individually with families over a period of approximately 8 weeks following a comprehensive assessment. In addition to this intensive format, IFI has also been adapted for eHealth delivery, in one form that incorporates therapist assistance (Kirkman et al., 2016), and another that is entirely self-guided (Tully et al., 2017). Given that children are often referred to our clinic due to the relative complexity of their presentation and that referrals often follow from unsuccessful attempts at similar forms of treatment elsewhere, our treatment outcome data are highly favorable. At the same time, a significant proportion of the children we treat show limited gains, consistent with international data on current best-practice interventions. Although the majority of children with conduct problems appear to respond to social learning based parent training, effect sizes for clinical change are often not large (e.g., McCart, Priester, Davies, & Azen, 2006). Treatment outcome data from trials in which such interventions, including IFI, are delivered under optimal conditions often fail to produce clinically significant change in as many as a third of such children (e.g., Beauchaine, Webster-Stratton, & Reid, 2005; Hawes & Dadds, 2005a). Accordingly, a major focus of the research conducted in the CBRC has been the development of novel interventions, and a key method has been the use of IFI as an active control condition in clinical trials.

Recent shifts in the conceptualizations of conduct problems

The history of evidence-based treatment in the field of child conduct problems has taught us, among other things, that a theory of a disorder can be translated into an effective treatment for that disorder. A question we now face is how to best apply this lesson to the theoretical shifts that have occurred in accounts of conduct problems in recent years, which have placed a growing emphasis on individual differences in risk pathways to these problems. As outlined in the following sections, these shifts have not only influenced revisions to diagnostic criteria for the disruptive behavior disorders, but have challenged the field to re-examine existing models of intervention. Much like early scientific research into novel treatments for conduct problems, recent translational research informed by emerging theory has at times involved controversy, as well as the need for innovation in the measurement of child and family variables.

Attempts to explain the poor treatment outcomes shown by nonresponders have focused primarily on aspects of social adversity that may interfere with families' implementation of treatment strategies and engagement with clinical services. Factors including socioeconomic disadvantage, marital discord, parental psychopathology, and substance abuse have all been linked—albeit somewhat inconsistently—to poor treatment outcomes (e.g., Beauchaine et al., 2005; Gardner, Hutchings, Bywater, & Whitaker, 2010). Such a focus is consistent with the focus on social contexts that is core to social learning based interventions, and the notion that nonresponders would otherwise show good outcomes if not for contextual impediments to treatment delivery and engagement. In other words, children with comparable presentations of the same disruptive behavior disorder all have the potential to derive the same gains from such treatment if they could be treated "on a level playing field" with regard to the barriers that can interfere with attempts to target the parent–child mechanisms emphasized in coercion theory. Although there is no doubt that many of the barriers to successful treatment outcomes can be found in the ecologies of such children, growing evidence suggests that individual differences in developmental risk processes among children with conduct problems may also explain variation in treatment response.

Theories of conduct problems have evolved significantly in recent years, alongside broader shifts in conceptualizations of psychopathology across the lifespan. There has been growing interest in new ways of classifying and treating psychopathology that move away from traditional diagnoses of specific disorders and toward approaches that may better account for the high comorbidity often seen between disorders, and the marked heterogeneity often seen within the same diagnostic categories (Levy, Hawes, & Johns, 2015; Marchette & Weisz, 2017). Such a move has been promoted by the National Institute for Mental Health (NIMH) through their Research Domain Criteria (RDoC) initiative, which has not only emphasized the importance of basic dimensions of functioning that cut across disorders, but also the potential for neurobiological indices to characterize pathways to psychopathology (Insel et al., 2010). Researchers have hypothesized that genetic and environmental influences on a range of disorders operate through a relatively small set of psychobiological mechanisms (e.g., responsiveness to reward), and that distinct dimensions of psychopathology can be differentiated partly by their associations with various transdiagnostic dispositions. These dispositions refer to individual differences that span typical through to abnormal functioning and include characteristics such as negative emotionality (i.e., individual differences in the labile expression of negative emotions), callousness (i.e., lack of guilt, empathy, and prosocial behavior), and daring (i.e., adventurousness and risk-taking). According to the taxonomic model published by Lahey, Krueger, Rathouz, Waldman, and Zald (2017), the extent to which children are high or low on these dispositional dimensions may in part explain overlap between externalizing and internalizing disorders, as well as overlap and differentiation among externalizing dimensions of oppositional defiant disorder (ODD), conduct disorder (CD), hyperactivity–impulsivity, and inattention.

The potential for transdiagnostic theory to inform the development of novel treatments for externalizing problems has been suggested by research into patterns of comorbidity that predict outcomes in the treatment of conduct problems (ODD/CD), and in the treatment of attention-deficit/hyperactivity disorder (ADHD). This includes research that has examined the effects of comorbid internalizing problems on treatment of externalizing problems in childhood. Rather than indicating that comorbidity is always a risk factor for poor treatment outcomes, children and adolescents with conduct problems and comorbid internalizing symptoms may benefit more from such interventions than those with conduct problems alone. Beauchaine et al. (2005) examined treatment outcome data collected via multiinformant report, in a large sample of children aged 3–8 years ($N = 514$) with conduct problems. Latent growth curve modeling of symptoms revealed that higher levels of anxiety/depression were associated with a better treatment response, independent of baseline symptoms. Likewise, Connell et al. (2008) used latent transition analysis to examine symptom trajectories among children aged 2–4 years in disadvantaged families. Cooccurrence of externalizing and internalizing symptoms was associated positively with transitions to problem-free levels following family-based intervention. Similarly, in a study investigating psychophysiological markers for treatment response in inpatient adolescents with conduct disorder and ADHD, comorbid depression conferred improved short-term prognosis among participants with high levels of heart rate variability (Beauchaine, Gartner, & Hagen, 2000).

Comorbid internalizing problems have also been associated with responses to psychosocial and pharmacological treatments for ADHD. Since Tannock, Ichowitcz, and Schachar (1995) demonstrated that methylphenidate improved working memory among nonanxious ADHD children but not among comorbid children, there has been considerable interest in implications of comorbid anxiety for the treatment of ADHD. However, findings associating comorbid anxiety with differential response to pharmacological treatments for ADHD have often been inconsistent (Abikoff et al., 2005; Garcia et al., 2009; Jensen et al., 2001). There is also evidence that youth with ADHD and comorbid anxiety/depression may benefit more from cognitive behavior therapy (CBT) for ADHD than those with ADHD alone (Antshel, Faraone, & Gordon, 2014). Following speculation that CBT interventions for childhood anxiety may target regulatory mechanisms implicated in hyperactivity/impulsivity (e.g., Kendall, Brady, & Verduin, 2001), research aimed at maximizing the treatment gains of children with comorbid externalizing and internalizing disorders has begun to investigate theory-driven integration of evidence-based components from the ADHD and anxiety literatures. Some support for such approaches has been reported, with data emphasizing more limited gains in relation to ADHD than anxiety symptoms (Jarrett & Ollendick, 2012).

Research into transdiagnostic approaches to psychopathology has also highlighted that emotion-related dispositions may be more core to conduct problems than has often been assumed. This has been accompanied by growing interest in the role that parental socialization of children's emotional development may play in pathways to conduct problems. With regard to theoretical mechanisms, it has been proposed that emotion socialization shapes conduct problems in part via children's emotion regulation, as operationalized in terms of the temperament dimension of effortful control (see Eisenberg, Spinrad, & Eggum, 2010). Consistent with this, effortful control has been found to partially mediate associations between maternal emotion socialization and prospective change in conduct problems across early childhood (Spinrad et al., 2007). A recent metaanalysis by Johnson, Hawes, Eisenberg, Kohlhoff, and Dudeney (2017) offered further support for this account, finding that nonsupportive emotion socialization (e.g., dismissive and punitive reactions to child emotion) was associated with severity of concurrent and longitudinal conduct problems. The authors argued that although the effect size for this association appears to be somewhat smaller than that seen for parenting variables implicated in coercion theory, such evidence supports the integration of emotion socialization processes into family-based theories of conduct problems.

Emotion-related dispositions have also been a focus of recent accounts of heterogeneity among children with early onset conduct problems, as reflected in changes to diagnostic criteria related to ODD and CD in DSM-5. For ODD, the same symptoms that defined the disorder in DSM-IV were retained in DSM-5, but the DSM-5 conceptualization of ODD groups these symptoms into three dimensions based on the idea that distinct symptom patterns may provide clinically meaningful information with regard to prognosis and treatment planning. Based on factor analytic research, these dimensions are (1) angry/irritable mood (e.g., Often loses temper), (2) argumentative/defiant behavior (e.g., Often actively defies or refuses to comply with requests from authority figures or with rules), and (3) vindictiveness (Has been spiteful or vindictive at least twice within the past 6 months). The notion that variation in type of ODD symptoms reflects meaningful heterogeneity among children with ODD was based on the evidence of divergent associations between these dimensions and other forms of dysfunction. For example, the angry/irritable dimension is closely associated with anxiety/mood disorders, while the defiant/headstrong dimension is more related to attention deficit hyperactivity disorder. Alternatively, the spiteful/vindictive dimension has been related to callousness (Frick & Nigg, 2012).

There is also some evidence that distinct presentations of ODD based on these dimensions may be associated with distinct treatment outcomes. Kolko and Pardini (2010) examined predictors of treatment outcomes among children (6–11 years) diagnosed with ODD or CD, who were randomized to a modular intervention (parent and child skills training, medication, school consultation), or treatment as usual in community health settings. The most robust predictor of persistent disruptive behavior problems following treatment was the spiteful/vindictive dimension of ODD, which accounted for poor response independent of ODD severity and the presence of comorbid ADHD. Evidence reported by Scott and O'Connor (2012) subsequently indicated that these ODD symptom dimensions may be used to characterize children who are particularly responsive to treatment. In a randomized controlled trial (RCT) for young children with ODD (aged 5–6 years), the authors found that participants characterized by symptoms on the angry/irritable dimension were those most likely to benefit from a social learning based parenting intervention. Interestingly, these children were also found to be particularly vulnerable to the effects of negative parenting, leading the authors to propose that angry/irritable symptoms may be a marker for differential susceptibility to parenting among children with ODD (Scott & O'Connor, 2012).

Like ODD, the most significant change to criteria for CD in DSM-5 reflected recent theory regarding heterogeneity among children with the disorder. The most significant change here was the introduction of a diagnostic specifier for children and adolescents who meet full criteria for the disorder but also present with limited prosocial emotions (e.g., lack of remorse or guilt, callousness–lack of empathy, shallow or deficient affect). The term "limited prosocial emotions" was a re-branding of the construct most often referred to as CU traits in the research literature. In theoretical terms, CU traits correspond to the affective component of psychopathy. The application of the psychopathy construct to children has drawn understandable scrutiny, but at the same time recognition that effective prevention and early intervention is most likely to arise from a truly developmental perspective on antisocial behavior that encompasses the earliest stages of life (Rutter, 2012). Among children and adolescents with disruptive behavior problems, those with high levels of CU traits exhibit a particularly severe and chronic trajectory of antisocial behavior that often features high levels of proactive or instrumental aggression (Frick, Ray, Thornton, & Kahn, 2013). Such individuals are also characterized by a range of unique social-cognitive and neurobiological correlates related to the processing of emotional stimuli and reinforcement learning (Moul, Hawes, & Dadds, in press), as examined in further detail in the following sections. Research into childhood CU traits has been far more extensive than that which has investigated the symptom dimensions introduced for ODD, yet it is important to note that this research has not focused exclusively on samples with CD. Rather, much of the support for the unique correlates associated with CU traits has come from research with samples characterized by ODD, and there is considerable evidence that the correlates of CU traits among children with clinically severe conduct problems are relatively consistent with those of CU traits among nonclinical samples (Salekin, 2017; Viding & McCrory, 2012).

CU traits as markers for investigating treatment response

It was proposed at the outset of this chapter that among the key theory and evidence necessary for the development of personalized treatments for children with conduct problems, that which provide a basis for characterizing children whose needs are not met sufficiently by current best-practice treatments is of primary importance. As outlined already, research into comorbid forms of psychopathology and specific patterns of emotion-related dispositions has provided a growing basis for conceptualizing heterogeneity among children with conduct problems in recent years, both in terms of risk as well as treatment response. Among the various approaches to conceptualizing this heterogeneity that have emerged, that based on CU traits has been subject to more translational research than most others. This includes programmatic research conducted at the CBRC spanning measurement research and basic science through to experimental treatment outcome studies. Key to such work has been an emphasis on understanding the interplay between environmental mechanisms and psychological markers that shapes risk pathways to conduct problems, and examining these markers in relation to treatment outcomes.

The definition and measurement of CU traits in children and adolescents has been subject to considerable research and controversy in its' own right. Although CU traits have long been thought to covary with the severity of conduct problems, they are nonetheless assumed to be distinct from the general features of conduct problems. It was noteworthy then when one of the earliest and most widely used questionnaire measures of CU traits, the antisocial process screening device (APSD; Frick & Hare, 2002), was criticized for containing multiple items that are similar to traditional features of disruptive behavior problems (Burns, 2000). In response to this, Dadds, Fraser, Frost, and Hawes (2005) factor analyzed the pooled items from the APSD and a measure of broader features of child psychopathology, the strengths and difficulties questionnaire (SDQ; Goodman, 1997), in a representative sample of community children. Consistent with the theoretical assumptions underlying CU traits, this measure identified two distinct factors corresponding to CU traits and conduct problems, and prospective research based on these factor scales found that CU traits scores predicted increased levels of conduct problems over a 12-month period independent of baseline conduct problems. Interestingly, concurrent research in the United Kingdom produced a remarkably similar CU scale through a similar joint factor analysis of the APSD−SDQ measures, which was supported in twin research showing substantial genetic risk for CU traits in 7-year-old children (Viding, Blair, Moffitt, & Plomin, 2004). This measurement research was key to characterizing the construct of CU traits as operationalized in the various studies since conducted in the CBRC. At the same time, other researchers have also adapted measures of CU traits in various ways (e.g., Elizur, Somech, & Vinokur, 2017), which may account in part for some mixed findings in the literature. For example, in contrast to numerous other approaches to operationalizing CU traits, the scale developed by Dadds et al. (2005) omits the feature "does not show feelings" from the construct that is indexed.

The emergence of research into the treatment outcomes of children with high CU traits following interventions for conduct problems was based in large part on the rationale that the family environment factors typically targeted in these interventions may play less of a role in maintaining conduct problems among these children compared to those with low CU traits. The notion that child dispositions, or temperament factors, moderate the effects of parenting on child outcomes features in various models, including those in which temperament is predicted to enhance a child's vulnerability to specific forms of parental dysfunction, or to determine a child's sensitivity to environmental influences more generally (Belsky & Van IJzendoorn, 2017; Kiff, Lengua, & Zalewski, 2011). CU traits have attracted considerable interest as a potential disposition of this kind. Not only do childhood CU traits show moderate-to-high levels of heritability (Viding & McCrory, 2012), but behavioral genetics research has found the conduct problems of children with high levels of CU traits to be under less environmental influence than those of low CU children (Viding et al., 2004). There is also considerable evidence that CU traits moderate associations between parenting processes and child conduct problems. Compared to the conduct problems of children with normative levels of these traits, those of children with high CU traits appear to be less proximally associated with negative parenting practices such as harsh/inconsistent discipline (Oxford, Cavell, & Hughes, 2003; Wootton, Frick, Shelton, & Silverthorn, 1997). Additionally, there is evidence to suggest that parental warmth may be more robustly associated with the conduct problems of children with high CU traits than children with low CU traits (e.g., Kochanska, Kim, Boldt, & Yoon, 2013; Pasalich, Dadds, Hawes, & Brennan, 2011; cf. O'Connor, Humayun, Briskman, & Scott, 2016). This evidence is consistent with that of analogous research into interactions between child temperament (e.g., fearlessness) and conscience development in early childhood (e.g., Fowles & Kochanska, 2000).

Although the findings of this research have at times been inconsistent (see Waller, Gardner, & Hyde, 2013), this evidence has called to question the extent to which the clinical mechanisms through existing parent training interventions for conduct problems operate map onto those that account for the problems of children with high CU traits. Interestingly, evidence regarding mechanisms of change in these interventions is perhaps also less consistent than might be expected given the long history of clinical research into these interventions. That is, findings have been somewhat mixed regarding the extent to which increases in positive parenting (e.g., praise, positive affect) versus reductions in negative parenting (e.g., criticism, harsh commands) account for child behavior change. Gardner et al. (2010) found that improvements in conduct problems among at-risk preschoolers following parent training were mediated by improvements in positive parenting, but not negative parenting. Yet in a similar sample treated with a similar program, Hanisch et al. (2014) found the opposite, with child behavior change mediated by reductions in negative parenting only. As noted by the authors, although seemingly divergent, such results cannot discount the likelihood that change in one domain of parenting may facilitate change in another, with these programs often targeting parent behaviors within broader parenting processes that are embedded within one another (Hanisch et al., 2014). Indeed, in a metaanalysis of mediators of parent training programs delivered for the purposes of prevention and intervention, Forehand, Lafko, Parent, and Burt (2014) found that change in child and adolescent conduct problems were better explained by a composite index of parenting and discipline rather than positive or negative parenting practices in isolation. Support for the putative mechanisms of behavioral parent training has also come from research involving the collection of intensive time-series data on moment-to-moment change, with such data suggesting that change in child behavior patterns are attributable in part to parents' differential attention to specific behaviors (Pemberton, Borrego, & Sherman, 2013). It can be assumed that these mixed findings reflect in part the range and complexity of the methods used to study treatment mechanisms, but it is possible that they also reflect heterogeneity among participants whose behavior changes through somewhat distinct mechanisms.

Based on evidence that the contributions of various parenting processes to conduct problems may vary across children as a function of CU traits, there has been considerable interest in whether these traits predict or moderate response to family-based interventions for conduct problems. The first study of this kind was reported by Hawes and Dadds (2005b), who examined the treatment outcomes of boys with ODD (aged 4–8 years) following a 10-week parenting intervention (IFI). Mother-reported CU traits were found to uniquely predict diagnostic status at 6-month follow-up, independent of pretreatment symptom severity and observational measures of parents' implementation of the skills in which they were trained. A review of such research conducted over the subsequent decade identified 11 studies in which CU traits were tested as predictors or moderators of clinical outcomes following family-based interventions for conduct problems, 9 of which reported such effects in some form or other (Hawes, Price, & Dadds, 2014).

Findings suggest that the measures of CU traits used in this research are not simply a proxy for ecological risk factors, or for features of psychopathology that may covary or overlap with CU traits. For example, in a mixed-gender sample of children

(3–9 years) with primary presentations of ODD and high levels of comorbid symptoms (anxiety disorders, ADHD, and autism spectrum disorder), Hawes, Dadds, Brennan, Rhodes, and Cauchi (2013) found that ODD symptoms at 6-month follow-up were independently predicted by pretreatment data on child CU traits collected from mothers, fathers, and teachers, when examined as a multi-informant latent variable. This is consistent with previous findings that poor treatment outcomes are associated with CU traits when controlling for parental stress, depression, and socioeconomic disadvantage (e.g., Hawes & Dadds, 2007). Likewise, recent research has replicated the finding that this reduced response is independent of individual differences in parents' acquisition and implementation of established child management strategies (e.g., Hogstrom, Enebrink, & Ghaderi, 2013). As such, there has been growing interest in novel clinical approaches that may better meet the needs of this subgroup.

Theories of CU traits as a basis for specifying therapeutic targets

The finding that established forms of intervention for conduct problems show reduced effectiveness for children with high levels of CU traits can be seen as consistent with the evidence that conduct problems among such children are less proximally associated with the forms of negative parenting targeted in these interventions. This evidence is part of the broader evidence base that has been used to formulate theory regarding the distinct risk processes that have been proposed to shape the conduct problems of children with high versus low levels of CU traits. Such theory has also drawn on neurobiological evidence that CU traits are associated with functional abnormalities in brain regions involved in the processing of basic emotional salience, reinforcement learning, and emotion regulation (e.g., amygdala, ventromedial, prefrontal, orbitofrontal cortex, and caudate; Jones, Laurens, Herba, Barker, & Viding, 2009). In addition, structural MRI data from children with CU traits has indicated increased gray matter concentration in several brain regions implicated in decision making, moral processing, and self-reflection (e.g., De Brito et al., 2009). Furthermore, emerging research into the molecular genetics of CU traits has implicated the serotinergic (Moul, Dadds, Dobson-Stone, Hawes, & Brennan, 2015) and oxytocin systems (Dadds et al., 2014a,b).

These neurobiological underpinnings are thought to account for the specific neurocognitive correlates exhibited by children with CU trait. One of the most replicated such correlates is poor recognition of emotional states in others, which appears to be particularly pronounced for, though is not limited to, expressions of fear and distress (see Dawel, O'Kearney, McKone, & Palermo, 2012; Marsh & Blair, 2008). Some evidence suggests that this "fear blindness" may occur also when processing cues in vocal tones (Blair et al., 2005; Stevens, Charman, & Blair, 2001) and bodily poses (Muñoz, 2009). Although some forms of atypical emotion processing have been documented in children exposed to maltreatment, current research indicates that maltreatment cannot account for the poor emotion recognition exhibited by children with CU traits (Dadds, Kimonis, Schollar-Root, Moul, & Hawes, 2018). Consistent with the evidence of amygdala dysfunction among children with high levels of CU traits (e.g., Deeley et al., 2006; Jones et al., 2009), it has been proposed that the poor recognition of fear and distress cues that characterizes these children may be attributable to impairments in the allocation of attention to emotionally salient cues—in particular the eyes of faces. Eye-tracking research has found support for this among children with CU traits viewing images of emotional faces (Dadds, El Masry, Wimalaweera, & Guastella, 2008), and research conducted in social contexts has indicated that such an impairment is evident among these children during family interactions. Specifically, observational studies of families have found that boys with high levels of CU traits demonstrate impairments in eye contact toward their parents and suggest that this lack of eye contact is primarily child driven. This reduced eye contact does not appear to be a function of reduced eye contact from mothers. However, it does appear that fathers of boys with high levels of CU traits may show a similar deficit (Dadds, Allen, McGregor, Woolgar, Viding, & Scott, 2014; Dadds, Jambrak, Pasalich, Hawes, & Brennan, 2011). Similarly, longitudinal infant research has found that preferential tracking of a face with direct gaze at 5 weeks of age predicts CU traits later in childhood, suggesting that for children at risk for high CU traits, this deficit may characterize a risk pathway that is initiated very early in life (Bedford, Pickles, Sharp, Wright, & Hill, 2015). Dadds et al. (2011) proposed that for children with high CU traits, a lack of eye contact with attachment figures early in life may not only reduce the influence of parenting and socialization processes, but prevent them from participating in the critical parent–child exchanges that establish the foundations for emotion understanding, conscience, and empathy. This is likely to set in train a developmental cascade involving ongoing failures of adaptation across these domains over time.

Frick and Viding (2009) outlined a number of theoretical mechanisms thought to shape two common pathways to severe conduct problems characterized by high versus low/normative levels of CU traits, respectively. The first and most common of these, followed by children with low/normative levels of CU traits, is proposed to be driven largely by coercive parenting practices, in conjunction with cognitive-emotional deficits related to verbal abilities and hyperreactivity to negative stimuli and provocation (e.g., hostile attribution biases). It is assumed that interplay between these risk processes may contribute to problems in the executive control of behavior, including poor emotion regulation, an inability to anticipate the negative consequence of behavior, and difficulty delaying gratification. The second pathway, followed by children high in CU traits, emphasizes the potential for a very different set of dispositions (i.e., fearlessness, insensitivity to punishment, low responsiveness to distress cues in others) to interfere with the typical development of conscience and empathy and contribute to a particularly severe and aggressive pattern of antisocial behavior.

Among the key assumptions of this high CU pathway are that fearlessness and underarousal interfere with emotional responses to punishment among these children, thereby preventing them experiencing the anxiety and discomforting arousal that typically follows wrong doing. As a result they may fail to develop the "deviation anxiety" that, in healthy children, is key to the internal system that functions to inhibit misbehavior in the absence of a punishing agent (see Kochanska, 1993). Although evidence regarding CU traits and punishment specifically has been limited, a recent review by Byrd, Loeber, and Pardini (2014) concluded that children and adolescents with high levels of CU traits appear to be characterized by punishment insensitivity and difficulties suspending reward-seeking behaviors when faced with a high probability of punishment. Elsewhere, Blair (1995), Blair, Monson, and Frederickson (2001) have theorized that a failure to experience negative arousal in response to distress cues may interfere with the conditioning necessary for the development of empathic concern. It is assumed that humans are biologically prepared to respond to distress cues in others with increased autonomic activity that serves to inhibit ongoing aggression when faced with such cues (termed the Violence Inhibition Mechanism). Based on the experience of this negative arousal, a child learns (i.e., is conditioned) to inhibit the behaviors that lead to distress in others (e.g., aggression) in order to avoid this arousal. However, for a child with CU traits, the lack of such arousal may prevent this conditioning from occurring and thereby disrupt the development of healthy empathic responses.

Novel interventions for children with CU traits: design and integration

The theories that have emerged to account for the risk pathway followed by children with CU traits have the potential to specify therapeutic targets of potential importance to this subgroup and have therefore provided a basis for the design of novel interventions. At the same time, these theories can be seen to raise questions regarding the appropriateness of established interventions for the treatment of conduct problems in these children. These questions warrant attention also, given that the successful design of novel interventions in this area and others is likely to rely on the theory-driven integration of both novel and existing components. In the example of CU traits, evidence from a range of sources can be brought to bear on this integration, as reflected in the broader design and structure of the novel interventions that follow.

First and foremost is the question of whether such intervention should target quality of parenting, as per established interventions for conduct problems. This may seem a reasonable question given that these interventions have been found to show reduced effectiveness for these problems among children with high CU traits. The potential role for biological therapies that instead target the neurobiological systems that have been implicated in CU traits, such as intranasal oxytocin, has been subject to growing interest accordingly (Cecil et al., 2014; Moul et al., in press). On the whole, however, current evidence suggests that optimal outcomes among children with high CU traits are likely to come from models that enhance the effects of social learning based parent training for conduct problems with adjunctive components designed to target the risk processes associated with these traits, rather than designing novel components as alternatives to this form of intervention. Specifically, although the effectiveness of these interventions appears to be reduced for children with CU traits, clinically significant gains may nonetheless result. For example, Hawes et al. (2013) found that although children with high levels of CU traits were twice as likely as low-CU children to retain diagnosable levels of ODD 6 months following parent training, the majority of children with high levels of CU traits shifted out of a diagnosable range nonetheless (Hawes et al., 2013). Furthermore, it is this form of treatment that currently has the best evidence base for producing change in CU traits themselves. The strongest support for such effects has been reported in early childhood studies, where RCTs have reported that mean levels of CU traits among children with conduct problems decrease as a result of this parent training (e.g., McDonald, Dodson, Rosenfield, & Jouriles, 2011; Somech & Elizur, 2012). Tests of mediation have indicated that such intervention may serve to reduce CU traits through its proximal effects on parental psychological aggression (McDonald et al., 2011), negative/inconsistent practices, and perceived parenting inefficacy (Elizur et al., 2017).

A related question is whether specific components of social learning based parent training, such as that addressing discipline strategies including time-out, should be omitted due to the evidence regarding punishment insensitivity in children with CU traits. Indeed, multiple studies examining time-out specifically have found some evidence that it may be less effective in reducing conduct problems among these children than those without CU traits (Haas et al., 2011; Hawes & Dadds, 2005a). There are nonetheless theoretical reasons for including this established strategy for reducing negative parenting, as opposed to strategies for increasing sensitivity and positive parenting only. Most notably, research has suggested that parents of children with high levels of CU traits are at particular risk for engaging in increasingly negative parenting practices over time, which has been theorized to occur because parents are likely to find typical forms of punishment to be somewhat ineffective for these children (Hawes, Dadds, Frost, & Hasking, 2011; Salihovic, Kerr, Özdemir, & Pakalniskiene, 2012). This is important given that negative parenting has, in turn, been found to amplify child CU traits over time (Hawes et al., 2011; Pardini, Lochman, Powell, 2007; Waller et al., 2012). When these parents are not equipped with nonforceful strategies for setting limits on problem behaviors (e.g., time-out), the child-driven effects of CU traits on parents may therefore be more likely to elicit reactions that feed back into the CU traits of predisposed children.

Two novel interventions for children with conduct problems and high levels of CU traits have been developed and evaluated through the CBRC to date, both of which are based on the integration of IFI (Dadds & Hawes, 2006), the parenting intervention previously described, with novel components based on theories of CU traits. The first of these incorporated components designed to target the emotion recognition deficits exhibited by these children (Dadds et al., 2012). Children ($n = 195$; aged 6–16 years) with clinic-referred conduct problems and various levels of CU traits were randomized to IFI versus IFI plus a child-focused emotion recognition training (ERT) component. The ERT component was based on the Mind Reading program originally developed to train children with autism to accurately identify and interpret emotional expressions in interpersonal contexts (Baron-Cohen, Golan, Wheelwright, & Hill, 2004). This component was delivered to families through a combination of four (90 min) child and parent–child sessions involving interactive computerized modules and homework in the form of parent–child emotion-focused games that were manualized for the purposes of the study (see Datyner, Kimonis, & Hunt, 2016 for a related intervention elsewhere in the literature). During this time, the therapist guided the child through the computer-based component, which involved a range of multimedia demonstrations of common emotional cues. The child then performed a range of related tasks, such as describing and enacting specific features of these cues, playing games based on aims such as matching emotional faces and words, drawing emotional cues, and recalling relevant autobiographical events and experiences. Parents were present for the last 5 min of the first three of these ERT sessions and trained in the homework activities that they were to engage the child in between sessions. The final ERT session involved the parent more extensively, for the purpose of setting up ongoing home-based activities for parents and children to complete together. The parent–child activities mirrored the computer-based component, and were detailed in a workbook provided to families.

Results indicated that among the children randomized to standard parent training for child conduct problems (IFI), those with high levels of levels of CU traits exhibited increased levels of conduct problems at 6-month follow-up, even after controlling for greater baseline severity (Dadds et al., 2012). However, those high in CU traits showed significantly more improvement when randomized to IFI plus ERT, in the order of a small effect size. This adjunctive intervention offered added benefit to these children only, and not those with normative levels of CU traits, suggesting that the emotion-focused component acted on mechanisms that differentiated these subgroups. However, tests of mediation to formally identify mechanisms of change showed surprising results. ERT produced improvements in parent ratings of children's affective empathy (e.g., arousal to emotional cues), but had no effect on independent measures of emotion recognition, which had been the explicit target of the intervention. Furthermore, neither mechanism was found to account for the added improvement in conduct problems that ERT produced. These findings drove speculation regarding the alternative mechanisms underlying the enhanced outcomes associated with ERT. Given that the computer-based child training had been supplemented with extensive parent–child homework activities focused on emotion, parent–child mechanisms were chief suspects. It was proposed that ERT may have inadvertently enhanced warmth and emotional engagement (EE) in the parent–child relationship, which research has previously found to be of unique importance to children with CU traits (Pasalich et al., 2011). The question was soon raised as to whether critical parent–child processes could be targeted more precisely and potently by translating neurocognitive theories of CU traits into a novel parenting intervention, as was investigated in our next trial.

A key basis for the design of this parenting intervention was the theory that children with CU traits show deficits in the allocation of attention to critically salient aspects of the environment, but that like patients with amygdala damage (see Adolphs et al., 2005), they seem to be able to overcome their "fear blindness" when they are directed to "look at the eyes" of faces (Dadds et al., 2008, 2006). Given the apparent importance of warmth and EE suggested by our prior intervention work, and our findings that children with CU traits show reduced eye contact during interactions with caregivers, it was proposed that behaviors such as reciprocal eye contact between children and parents may be key to operationalizing and targeting the specific aspects of EE of most potential benefit to these children. Hawes et al. (2014) proposed at least three mechanisms by which the remediation of deficits in reciprocated eye contact may improve the effectiveness of parent training interventions for conduct problems among young children with CU traits. First, in the short term, increased eye contact between the parent and child was predicted to increase the quality of the relationship and allow for parental responses to function as motivating rewards for prosocial behavior (Wahler & Meginnis, 1997). Second, such remediation may potentially increase the child's attention to the emotional content of parental instructions and in turn improve child responses to parental limit-setting. Third, increases in healthy eye contact early in life may initiate cascading neuropeptide (e.g., oxytocin: Ross & Young, 2009) and connectionist changes (e.g., amygdala to higher processing circuitry; Blair, 2003; Viding, Sebastion, Dadds et al., 2012) that increase the salience of emotional stimuli to these children and facilitate a normalization of dysfunctional neural systems over time (Shaw et al., 2004; Skuse, Morris, & Lawrence, 2003).

Accordingly, the major aim of the "emotional engagement" (EE) intervention developed and evaluated by Dadds, English, Wimalaweera, Schollar-Root, and Hawes (submitted) is to increase children's eye contact with their parents, through parent-focused skills-training and structured *in vivo* parent–child interactions designed to be used in conjunction with IFI. The EE intervention was designed to be delivered using video interactive guidance (VIG: Fukkink, 2008), in which parents are provided with positive and negative feedback and specific goals set for future interactions. These interactions are implemented during "compliance" situations, wherein EE and eye contact is used to promote the child's attention to parental communication, as well as during reading, storytelling, and casual conversation (e.g., in the bedtime routine), for the purpose of promoting reciprocated EE and positive relationship growth. The initial trial of this intervention involved intensive, multi-method data collection, consisting of parent report and independent coding of observational data on parent–child interactions during an EE task, collected at six time points across treatment. Observational coding was used to measure parental warmth and indices of eye contact including that initiated and reciprocated by the mother/father/child, based on who it was directed toward. Various aspects of the participant sample are also noteworthy, with the inclusion criteria permitting only participants meeting diagnostic criteria for ODD and high levels of CU traits. The protocol that was used to establish eligibility further involved requiring high CU traits at multiple assessment points (initial intake, pre-treatment), meaning that the sample was characterized by particularly high and stable levels of CU traits. The participation of both mothers and fathers in treatment was also required, in order to examine the family-based processes of each in relation to child CU traits, which previous research has suggested may be somewhat distinct (e.g., Dadds et al., 2011). Families were randomized to receive either 10 weekly sessions of IFI plus EE or IFI plus child centered play—a component that focuses on parents' ability to attend to, and support the child during free-play in a nondirective manner, as found in various parent training programs.

One of the chief questions of this study was whether clinical strategies delivered in a parenting intervention are capable of producing change in reciprocated eye contact among children with CU traits. Given the novel nature of this therapeutic target in families of any children, this outcome was of key interest in its own right. Results indicated that EE significantly increased children's reciprocated eye gaze across the intervention. However, this change was not maintained at 3-month follow-up. This rebound suggests that the effects may have relied on the intensive nature of the EE intervention during the time families were seen and raises questions regarding the methods that may be needed to enhance treatment durability. In other populations characterized by deficits in eye contact, in particular children with autism, bio-behavioral intervention involving the administration of nasal oxytocin during parent–child interactions has been investigated in emerging translational research. Yet, effects on eye contact have been elusive to date (e.g., Dadds et al., 2014).

In terms of effects on conduct problems, participants randomized to EE showed reductions in the order of a large effect size; yet, such change did not differ from that in the control condition. Perhaps most surprisingly, however, neither condition was associated with reductions in CU traits. Given that parenting interventions not designed to target deficits associated with CU traits, including IFI, have previously been associated with medium-to-large reductions in CU traits (e.g., Hawes & Dadds, 2007; McDonald et al., 2011; Somech & Elizur, 2012), the lack of any such change from IFI plus EE was highly unexpected. Explanations for this are open to speculation, but it seems likely that by sampling only children with high-stable levels of CU traits, the CU traits of these children may have been particularly treatment resistant. Assuming this were true, it is possible that EE may produce somewhat different effects among the broader population of children with high levels of CU traits, for whom such traits may be more malleable. Our findings further suggest that any intervention shown to be effective in reducing general levels of CU traits in a sample of children with conduct problems will not necessarily reduce high-stable CU traits, which may indeed be most reflective of "real" CU traits. In any case, the ERT intervention developed by Dadds, Cauchi, Wimalaweera, Hawes, and Brennan (2012) remains at present the only novel approach shown to enhance the conduct problem outcomes of children with CU traits beyond the effects produced by standard parent training alone.

Recommendations for future research

As evident from the scope of this chapter, the research that is necessary to inform the development of personalized treatments for heterogeneous subgroups of children with conduct problems spans basic research on individual differences and associated risk mechanisms through to controlled tests of novel, theory-driven treatment components. Future research into transdiagnostic accounts of early risk pathways to externalizing problems, including overlap with neurodevelopmental disorders such as autism (e.g., Johnson, Gliga, Jones, & Charman, 2014; Schwenck et al., 2012), is likely to inform the identification of additional subgroups of children who may benefit from targeted intervention. At the same time, it is important to build on the noteworthy progress that has already been made in work of this kind focused on children with high CU traits. Importantly, despite this progress, basic questions regarding phenotypic aspects of CU traits remain a priority. For example, there is growing evidence for further heterogeneity within children with high CU traits based on comorbid anxiety and maltreatment histories (Kimonis et al., 2016). In contrast to the CU traits of children without anxiety, it has been proposed that those of children with cooccurring anxiety may develop as a consequence of exposure to adverse environmental influences, who exhibit not hypoarousal, but hyperarousal (Fanti, in press). Given that this distinction has been largely absent from the intervention literature to date, research is needed to examine the treatment response characteristics of children with these two variants of CU traits, particularly the lesser-known subgroup whose CU traits have arisen from maltreatment.

Other recommendations can be made regarding methodological issues related to study design and measurement. As demonstrated by recent RCTs of novel interventions for children with high CU traits, there is much to be gained by measuring not only treatment outcomes, but putative mechanisms of change, such as emotion recognition (Dadds et al., 2012) and eye contact during parent–child interactions (Dadds et al., submitted). However, the investigation of such mechanisms is not always best served by RCT designs. Indeed, small-scale designs that allow for the intensive examination of change processes may at times be more likely to inform the early stages of intervention development. Just as early stimulus control studies used repeated observational measurement to translate operant theory into behavioral interventions for child conduct problems in single-case experimental designs (e.g., Patterson, 1974), such designs now stand to inform translational research based on emerging models of heterogeneity within these problems. A final recommendation concerns the sampling of participants for the purpose of examining intervention effects on child characteristics that are thought to reflect stable, individual differences, such as CU traits. Although parenting interventions have been shown to reduce mean levels of CU traits in samples that comprises low through to high levels of these traits indexed at one pretreatment time-point only (e.g., Elizur et al, 2017; McDonald et al., 2011), evidence suggests that such effects may not necessarily generalize to children sampled due to a stable baseline of high CU traits (Dadds et al., submitted). The baseline screening of CU traits for both high and stable levels is therefore a key recommendation for future trials of novel interventions in this area.

Conclusions

In recent years, key progress has been made in characterizing phenotypic markers that may serve to identify children with conduct problems whose needs are beyond those addressed by existing interventions. The example of CU traits is particularly noteworthy in terms of the wealth of evidence that has accumulated with regard to developmentally sensitive measurement, patterns of response to existing interventions, and neuroscientific accounts of corresponding risk mechanisms. Such evidence has not only provided a basis for specifying novel therapeutic targets, but for guiding the integration of such targets into existing evidence-based interventions. However, much like the trial and error that characterized the early development of these existing interventions, research into the development of novel interventions for children with CU traits has at times raised more questions than it has answered. These include questions regarding the child and family-level mechanisms through which clinical change in conduct problems may occur among children with CU traits, as well as questions regarding CU traits as treatment outcome variables in their own right. Compared to basic research into causal models of conduct problems, treatment outcome research concerned with high-risk subgroups of this kind will most likely continue on a slow path, yet one that is of the utmost importance.

References

Abikoff, H., McGough, J., Vitiello, B., McCracken, J., Davies, M., Walkup, J., et al. (2005). Sequential pharmacotherapy for children with comorbid attention deficit/hyperactivity and anxiety disorders. *Journal of the American Academy of Child and Adolescent Psychiatry*, *44*, 418–427. Available from: https://doi.org/10.1097/01.chi.0000155320.52322.37.

Adolphs, R., Gosselin, F., Buchanan, T. W., Tranel, D., Schyns, P., & Damasio, A. R. (2005). A mechanism for impaired fear recognition after amygdala damage. *Nature*, *433* (7021), 68–72. Available from: https://doi.org/10.1038/nature03086.

Antshel, K. M., Faraone, S. V., & Gordon, M. (2014). Cognitive behavioral treatment outcomes in adolescent ADHD. *Journal of Attention Disorders*, *18*(6), 483–495. Available from: https://doi.org/10.1177/1087054712443155.

Baron-Cohen, S., Golan, O., Wheelwright, S., & Hill, J. J. (2004). *Mind reading: The interactive guide to emotions*. London: Jessica Kingsley Limited.

Beauchaine, T. P., Gartner, J., & Hagen, B. (2000). Comorbid depression and heart rate variability as predictors of aggressive and hyperactive symptom responsiveness during inpatient treatment of conduct-disordered, ADHD boys. *Aggressive Behavior*, *26*, 425–441.

Beauchaine, T. P., Webster-Stratton, C., & Reid, M. J. (2005). Mediators, moderators, and predictors of 1-year outcomes among children treated for early-onset conduct problems: A latent growth curve analysis. *Journal of Consulting and Clinical Psychology*, *73*, 371–388.

Bedford, R., Pickles, A., Sharp, H., Wright, N., & Hill, J. (2015). Reduced face preference in infancy: A developmental precursor to callous–unemotional traits? *Biological Psychiatry*, *78*(2), 144–150.

Belsky, J., & Van IJzendoorn, M. H. (2017). Genetic differential susceptibility to the effects of parenting. *Current Opinion in Psychology*, *15*, 125–130.

Blair, R. J. R. (1995). A cognitive developmental approach to morality: Investigating the psychopath. *Cognition*, *57*, 1–29. Available from: https://doi.org/10.1016/0010-0277(95)00676-P.

Blair, R. J. R. (2003). Facial expressions, their communicatory functions and neuro-cognitive substrates. *Philosophical Transactions of the Royal Society of London. Series B: Biological Sciences*, *358*(1431), 561–572. Available from: https://doi.org/10.1098/rstb.2002.1220.

Blair, R. J. R., Monson, J., & Frederickson, N. (2001). Moral reasoning and conduct problems in children with emotional and behavioural difficulties. *Personality and Individual Differences*, *31*, 799–811. Available from: https://doi.org/10.1016/S0191-8869(00)00181-1.

Blair, R. J., Budhani, S., Colledge, E., & Scott, S. (2005). Deafness to fear in boys with psychopathic tendencies. *Journal of Child Psychology and Psychiatry*, *46*, 327–336. Available from https://doi.org/10.1111/j.1469-7610.2004.00356.x.

Brinkmeyer, M. Y., & Eyberg, S. M. (2003). Parent–child interaction therapy for oppositional children. In A. E. Kazdin, & J. R. Weisz (Eds.), *Evidenced-based psychotherapies for children and adolescents* (pp. 204–223). New York: Guilford.

Burns, G. L. (2000). Problem of item overlap between the psychopathy screening device and attention-deficit/hyperactivity disorder, oppositional defiant disorder, and conduct disorder rating scales. *Psychological Assessment*, *12*, 447–450.

Byrd, A. L., Loeber, R., & Pardini, D. A. (2014). Antisocial behavior, psychopathic features and abnormalities in reward and punishment processing in youth. *Clinical Child and Family Psychology Review*, *17*(2), 125–156. Available from: https://doi.org/10.1007/s10567-013-0159-6.

Cecil, C. A., Lysenko, L. J., Jaffee, S. R., Pingault, J. B., Smith, R. G., Relton, C. L., … Barker, E. D. (2014). Environmental risk, oxytocin receptor gene (OXTR) methylation and youth callous–unemotional traits: A 13-year longitudinal study. *Molecular Psychiatry*, *19*(10), 1071–1077. Available from: https://doi.org/10.1038/mp.2014.95.

Comer, J. S., Chow, C., Chan, P. T., Cooper-Vince, C., & Wilson, L. A. S. (2013). Psychosocial treatment efficacy for disruptive behavior problems in very young children: A meta-analytic examination. *Journal of the American Academy of Child and Adolescent Psychiatry*, *52*(1), 26–36. Available from: https://doi.org/10.1016/j.jaac.2012.10.001.

Connell, A., Bullock, B. M., Dishion, T. J., Shaw, D., Wilson, M., & Gardner, F. (2008). Family intervention effects on co-occurring early childhood behavioral and emotional problems: A latent transition analysis approach. *Journal of Abnormal Child Psychology*, *36*, 1211–1225.

Dadds, M. R., Cauchi, A. J., Wimalaweera, S., Hawes, D. J., & Brennan, J. (2012). Outcomes, moderators, and mediators of empathic-emotion recognition training for complex conduct problems in childhood. *Psychiatry Research*, *199*(3), 201–207. Available from: https://doi.org/10.1016/j.psychres.2012.04.033.

Dadds, M. R., Allen, J. L., McGregor, K., Woolgar, M., Viding, E., & Scott, S. (2014). Callous-unemotional traits in children and mechanisms of impaired eye contact during expressions of love: A treatment target? *Journal of Child Psychology and Psychiatry*, *55*(7), 771–780. Available from https://doi.org/10.1111/jcpp.12155.

Dadds, M. R., El Masry, Y., Wimalaweera, S., & Guastella, A. J. (2008). Reduced eye gaze explains "fear blindness" in childhood psychopathic traits. *Journal of the American Academy of Child and Adolescent Psychiatry*, *47*(4), 455–463.

Dadds, M.R., English, T., Wimalaweera, S., Schollar-Root, O., Hawes, D.J. (submitted). Mechanisms and outcomes of an intensive theory-driven parenting intervention for children with conduct problems and high levels of callous-unemotional traits.

Dadds, M. R., Fraser, J., Frost, A., & Hawes, D. J. (2005). Disentangling the underlying dimensions of psychopathy and conduct problems in childhood: A community study. *Journal of Consulting and Clinical Psychology*, *73*, 400–410.

Dadds, M. R., & Hawes, D. J. (2006). *Integrated family Intervention for child conduct problems: A behaviour-attachment-systems intervention for parents*. Brisbane, Queensland: Australian Academic Press.

Dadds, M. R., Jambrak, J., Pasalich, D., Hawes, D. J., & Brennan, J. (2011). Impaired attention to the eyes of attachment figures and the developmental origins of psychopathy. *Journal of Child Psychology and Psychiatry*, *52*(3), 238–245.

Dadds, M. R., Kimonis, E. R. K., Schollar-Root, O., Moul, C., & Hawes, D. J. (2018). Are impairments in emotion recognition a core feature of callous-unemotional traits? Testing the primary versus secondary variants model in children. Development & Psychopathology, 30(1), 67–77.

Dadds, M. R., MacDonald, E., Cauchi, A., Williams, K., Levy, F., & Brennan, J. (2014). Nasal oxytocin for social deficits in childhood autism: A randomized controlled trial. *Journal of Autism and Developmental Disorders*, *44*, 521–531. Available from: https://doi.org/10.1007/s10803-013-1899-3.

Dadds, M. R., Moul, C., Cauchi, A., Dobson-Stone, C., Hawes, D. J., Brennan, J., Urwin, R., & Ebstein, R. (2014a). Polymorphisms in the oxytocin receptor gene are associated with the development of psychopathy. *Development and Psychopathology*, *26*(1), 21–31.

Dadds, M. R., Moul, C., Cauchi, A., Dobson-Stone, C., Hawes, D. J., Brennan, J., & Ebstein, R. (2014b). Methylation of the oxytocin receptor gene and oxytocin blood levels in the development of psychopathy. *Development and Psychopathology*, *26*(1), 33–40.

Dadds, M. R., Perry, Y., Hawes, D. J., Merz, S., Riddell, A., Haines, D., . . . Abey, A. (2006). Attention to the eyes and fear-recognition deficits in child psychopathy. *British Journal of Psychiatry*, *189*(3), 280–281.

Datyner, A., Kimonis, E. R., Hunt, E., & Armstrong, K. (2016). Using a novel emotional skills module to enhance empathic responding for a child with conduct disorder with limited prosocial emotions. *Clinical Case Studies*, *15*, 35–52. Available from https://doi.org/10.1177/1534650115588978.

Dawel, A., O'Kearney, R., McKone, E., & Palermo, R. (2012). Not just fear and sadness: Meta-analytic evidence of pervasive emotion recognition deficits for facial and vocal expressions in psychopathy. *Neuroscience and Biobehavioral Reviews*, *36*, 2288–2304.

De Brito, S. A., Mechelli, A., Wilke, M., Laurens, K. R., Jones, A. P., Barker, G. J., . . . Viding, E. (2009). Size matters: Increased grey matter in boys with conduct problems and callous-unemotional traits. *Brain: A Journal of Neurology*, *132*(Pt 4), 843–852. Available from: https://doi.org/10.1093/brain/awp011.

Deeley, Q., Daly, E., Surguladze, S., Tunstall, N., Mezey, G., Beer, D., . . . Brammer, M. J. (2006). Facial emotion processing in criminal psychopathy preliminary functional magnetic resonance imaging study. *British Journal of Psychiatry*, *189*(6), 533–539.

Dishion, T., Forgatch, M., Chamberlain, P., & Pelham, W. E. (2016). The Oregon model of behavior family therapy: From intervention design to promoting large-scale system change. *Behavior Therapy*, *47*, 812–837.

Eisenberg, N., Spinrad, T. L., & Eggum, N. D. (2010). Emotion-related self-regulation and its relation to children's maladjustment. *Annual Review of Clinical Psychology, 6*, 495–525.

Elizur, Y., Somech, L. Y., & Vinokur, A. D. (2017). Effects of parent training on callous-unemotional traits, effortful control, and conduct problems: Mediation by parenting. *Journal of Abnormal Child Psychology, 45*(1), 15–26.

Eyberg, S. M., Nelson, M. M., & Boggs, S. R. (2008). Evidence-based psychosocial treatments for children and adolescents with disruptive behavior. *Journal of Clinical Child and Adolescent Psychology, 37*(1), 215–237. Available from: https://doi.org/10.1080/15374410701820117.

Fanti, K.A. (in press). Understanding heterogeneity in conduct disorder: A review of psychophysiological studies. *Neuroscience and Biobehavioral Reviews*. https://doi.org/10.1016/j.neubiorev.2016.09.022.

Forehand, R., Lafko, N., Parent, J., & Burt, K. B. (2014). Is parenting the mediator of change in behavioral parent training for externalizing problems of youth? *Clinical Psychology Review, 34*, 608–619.

Forgatch, M. S., & Patterson, G. R. (2010). Parent management training—Oregon model: An intervention for antisocial behavior in children and adolescents. In J. R. Weisz, & A. E. Kazdin (Eds.), *Evidence-based psychotherapies for children and adolescents* (pp. 159–178). NewYork, NY: Guilford Press.

Fowles, D. C., & Kochanska, G. (2000). Temperament as a moderator of pathways to conscience in children: The contribution of electrodermal activity. *Psychophysiology, 37*, 788–795.

Frick, P. J., & Hare, R. D. (2002). *The psychopathy screening device*. Toronto, ON, Canada: Multi-Health Systems.

Frick, P. J., & Nigg, J. T. (2012). Current issues in the diagnosis of attention deficit hyperactivity disorder, oppositional defiant disorder, and conduct disorder. *Annual Review of Clinical Psychology, 8*, 77–107.

Frick, P. J., Ray, J. V., Thornton, L. C., & Kahn, R. E. (2013). Can callous-unemotional traits enhance the understanding, diagnosis, and treatment of serious conduct problems in children and adolescents? A comprehensive review. *Psychological Bulletin, 140*, 1–57.

Frick, P. J., & Viding, E. M. (2009). Antisocial behavior from a developmental psychopathology perspective. *Development and Psychopathology, 21*, 1111–1131. Available from: https://doi.org/10.1017/S0954579409990071.

Fukkink, R. G. (2008). Video feedback in widescreen: A meta-analysis of family programs. *Clinical Psychology Review, 28*(6), 904–916.

Garcia, S. P., Guimarães, J., Zampuri, J. F., Martinez, A. L., Polanczyk, G., & Rohde, L. A. (2009). Response to methylphenidate in children and adolescents with ADHD: Do comorbid anxiety disorders matter? *Biological Child and Adolescent Psychiatry, 116*, 631–636.

Gardner, F., Hutchings, J., Bywater, T., & Whitaker, C. (2010). Who benefits and how does it work? Moderators and mediators of outcome in an effectiveness trial of a parenting intervention. *Journal of Clinical Child and Adolescent Psychology, 39*(4), 568–580.

Goodman, R. (1997). The strengths and difficulties questionnaire: A research note. *Journal of Child Psychology and Psychiatry, 38*, 581–586.

Greenberg, M. T., Speltz, M. L., & DeKlyen, M. (1993). The role of attachment in the early development of disruptive behavior problems. *Development and Psychopathology, 5*, 191–213.

Haas, S. M., Waschbusch, D. A., Pelham, W. E., King, S., Andrade, B. F., & Carrey, N. J. (2011). Treatment response in CP/ADHD children with callous/unemotional traits. *Journal of Abnormal Child Psychology*, *39*, 541–552. Available from: https://doi.org/10.1007/s10802-010-9480-4.

Hanisch, C., Hautmann, C., Plück, J., Eichelberger, I., & Döpfner, M. (2014). The prevention program for externalizing problem behavior (PEP) improves child behavior by reducing negative parenting: Analysis of mediating processes in a randomized controlled trial. *Journal of Child Psychology and Psychiatry*, *55*, 473–484. Available from https://doi.org/10.1111/jcpp.12177.

Harlow, H. H., & Harlow, M. K. (1971). Psychopathology in monkeys. In H. D. Kimmel (Ed.), *Experimental psychopathology: Recent research and theory* (pp. 203–229). New York: Academic Press.

Hawes, D. J., & Dadds, M. R. (2005a). Oppositional and conduct problems. In J. Hudson, & R. Rapee (Eds.), *Current thinking on psychopathology and the family* (pp. 73–91). New York: Elsevier.

Hawes, D. J., & Dadds, M. R. (2005b). Treatment of conduct problems in children with callous-unemotional traits. *Journal of Consulting and Clinical Psychology*, *73*, 737–741.

Hawes, D. J., & Dadds, M. R. (2007). Stability and malleability of callous-unemotional traits during treatment for childhood conduct problems. *Journal of Clinical Child and Adolescent Psychology*, *35*(3), 347–355.

Hawes, D. J., Dadds, M. R., Brennan, J., Rhodes, T., & Cauchi, A. (2013). Re-visiting treatment of conduct problems in children with callous-unemotional traits. *Australian & New Zealand Journal of Psychiatry*, *47*, 646–653.

Hawes, D. J., Dadds, M. R., Frost, A. D. J., & Hasking, P. A. (2011). Do childhood callous-unemotional traits drive change in parenting practices? *Journal of Clinical Child and Adolescent Psychology*, *40*(4), 507–518. Available from: https://doi.org/10.1080/15374416.2011.581624.

Hawes, D. J., Price, M. J., & Dadds, M. R. (2014). Callous-unemotional traits and the treatment of conduct problems in childhood and adolescence: A comprehensive review. *Clinical Child and Family Psychology Review*, *17*(3), 248–267.

Herrnstein, R. J. (1974). Formal properties of the matching law. *Journal of the Experimental Analysis of Behavior*, *21*, 159–164.

Hogstrom, J., Enebrink, P., & Ghaderi, A. (2013). The moderating role of child callous-unemotional traits in an internet-based parent-management training program. *Journal of Family Psychology*, *27*(2), 314–323. Available from: https://doi.org/10.1037/a0031883.

Insel, T., Cuthbert, B., Garvey, M., Heinssen, R., Pine, D. S., Quinn, K., ... Wang, P. (2010). Research domain criteria: Toward a new classification framework for research on mental disorders. *American Journal of Psychiatry*, *167*, 748–751.

Jarrett, M. A., & Ollendick, T. H. (2012). Treatment of comorbid attention-deficit/hyperactivity disorder and anxiety in children: A multiple baseline design analysis. *Journal of Consulting and Clinical Psychology*, *80*, 239–244.

Jensen, P., Hinshaw, S. P., Kraemer, H. C., Lenora, N., Newcorn, J. H., Abikoff, H. B., ... Vitiello, B. (2001). ADHD comorbidity findings from the MTA study: Comparing comorbid subgroups. *Journal of the American Academy of Child and Adolescent Psychiatry*, *40*, 147–158.

Johnson, A. M., Hawes, D. J., Eisenberg, N., Kohlhoff, J., & Dudeney, J. (2017). Emotion socialization and child conduct problems: A comprehensive review and meta-analysis. *Clinical Psychology Review*, *54*, 65–80.

Johnson, M. H., Gliga, T., Jones, E., & Charman, T. (2014). Annual research review: Infant development, autism, and ADHD—early pathways to emerging disorders. *Journal of Child Psychology and Psychiatry*, *56*(3), 228–247.

Jones, A., Laurens, K., Herba, C., Barker, G., & Viding, E. (2009). Amygdala hypoactivity to fearful faces in boys with conduct problems and callous-unemotional traits. *American Journal of Psychiatry*, *166*(1), 95–102.

Kaminski, J. W., & Claussen, A. H. (2017). Evidence base update for psychosocial treatments for disruptive behaviors in children. *Journal of Clinical Child and Adolescent Psychology*, *46*(4), 477–499. Available from: https://doi.org/10.1080/15374416.2017.1310044.

Kendall, P. C., Brady, E. U., & Verduin, T. L. (2001). Comorbidity in childhood anxiety disorders and treatment outcome. *Journal of the American Academy of Child and Adolescent Psychiatry*, *40*, 787–794.

Kiff, C. J., Lengua, L. J., & Zalewski, M. (2011). Nature and nurturing: Parenting in the context of child temperament. *Clinical Child and Family Psychology Review*, *14*, 251–301. Available from: https://doi.org/10.1007/s10567-011-0093-4.

Kimonis, E. R., Goulter, N., Hawes, D. J., Wilbur, R. R., & Groer, M. W. (2016). Neuroendocrine factors distinguish juvenile psychopathy variants. *Developmental Psychobiology*, *59*(2), 161–173.

Kirkman, J. J. L., Hawes, D. J., & Dadds, M. R. (2016). An open trial for an e-health treatment for child behavior disorders II: Outcomes and clinical implications. *Evidence-Based Practice in Child and Adolescent Mental Health*, *1*(4), 213–229.

Kochanska, G. (1993). Toward a synthesis of parental socialization and child temperament in early development of conscience. *Child Development*, *64*, 325–347. Available from: https://doi.org/10.2307/1131254.

Kochanska, G., Barry, R. A., Stellern, S. A., & O'Bleness, J. J. (2009). Early attachment organization moderates the parent-child mutually coercive pathway to children's antisocial conduct. *Child Development*, *80*, 1288–1300. Available from: https://doi.org/10.1111/j.1467-8624.2009.01332.x.

Kochanska, G., Kim, S., Boldt, L. J., & Yoon, J. E. (2013). Children's callous-unemotional traits moderate links between their positive relationships with parents at preschool age and externalizing behavior problems at early school age. *Journal of Child Psychology and Psychiatry*, *54*(11), 1251–1260.

Kolko, D. J., & Pardini, D. A. (2010). ODD dimensions, ADHD, and callous–unemotional traits as predictors of treatment response in children with disruptive behavior disorders. *Journal of Abnormal Psychology*, *119*(4), 713–725. Available from: https://doi.org/10.1037/a0020910.

Lahey, B. B., Krueger, R. F., Rathouz, P. J., Waldman, I. D., & Zald, D. H. (2017). A hierarchical causal taxonomy of psychopathology across the life span. *Psychological Bulletin*, *143*(2), 142–186. Available from: https://doi.org/10.1037/bul0000069.

Levy, F., Hawes, D. J., & Johns, A. (2015). Externalizing and internalizing comorbidity. In T. P. Beauchaine, & S. P. Hinshaw (Eds.), *The Oxford handbook of externalizing spectrum disorders* (pp. 443–460). New York: Oxford: University Press.

Marchette, L. K., & Weisz, J. R. (2017). Practitioner review: Empirical evolution of youth psychotherapy toward transdiagnostic approaches. *Journal of Child Psychology and Psychiatry*, *58*, 970–984.

Marsh, A. A., & Blair, R. J. (2008). Deficits in facial affect recognition among antisocial populations: A meta-analysis. *Neuroscience and Biobehavioral Reviews*, *32*, 454–465.

McCart, M. R., Priester, P. E., Davies, W. H., & Azen, R. (2006). Differential effectiveness of behavioral parent-training and cognitive-behavioral therapy for antisocial youth: a meta-analysis. *Journal of Abnormal Child Psychology*, *34*(4), 527–543. Available from: https://doi.org/10.1007/s10802-006-9031-1.

McDonald, R., Dodson, M. C., Rosenfield, D., & Jouriles, E. N. (2011). Effects of a parenting intervention on features of psychopathy in children. *Journal of Abnormal Child Psychology*, *39*(7), 1013–1023. Available from: https://doi.org/10.1007/s10802-011-9512-8.

McMahon, R. J., & Forehand, R. L. (2003). *Helping the noncompliant child: Family-based treatment for oppositional behavior* (2nd ed). New York: Guilford Press.

McNeil, C. B., & Hembree-Kigin, T. (2010). *Parent-child interaction therapy* (2nd ed.). New York: Springer.

McWilliam, J., Brown, J., Sanders, M. R., & Jones, L. (2016). The Triple P implementation framework: The role of purveyors in the implementation and sustainability of evidence-based programs. *Prevention Science*, *17*(5), 636–645.

Mence, M., Hawes, D. J., Wedgwood, L., Morgan, S., Barnett, B., Kohlhoff, J., & Hunt, C. (2014). Emotional flooding and hostile discipline in the families of toddlers with disruptive behavior problems. *Journal of Family Psychology*, *28*(1), 12–21.

Michelson, D., Davenport, C., Dretzke, J., Barlow, J., & Day, C. (2013). Do evidence-based interventions work when tested in the "real world?" A systematic review and meta-analysis of parent management training for the treatment of child disruptive behavior. *Clinical Child & Family Psychology Review*, *16*, 18–34. Available from: https://doi.org/10.1007/s10567-013-0128-0.

Moul, C., Dadds, M. R., Dobson-Stone, C., Hawes, D. J., & Brennan, J. (2015). Serotonin 1B receptor gene (HTR1B) methylation as a risk factor for callous-unemotional traits in antisocial boys. *PLoS ONE*, *10*(5).

Moul, C., Hawes, D.J., Dadds, M.R. (in press). Mapping the developmental pathways of child conduct problems through the neurobiology of empathy. *Neuroscience and Biobehavioral Reviews,* Available from: https://doi.org/10.1016/j.neubiorev.2017.03.016.

Muñoz, L. C. (2009). Callous-unemotional traits are related to combined deficits in recognizing afraid faces and body poses. *Journal of the American Academy of Child and Adolescent Psychiatry*, *48*, 554–562.

O'Connor, T. G., Humayun, S., Briskman, J. A., & Scott, S. (2016). Sensitivity to parenting in adolescents with callous/unemotional traits: observational and experimental findings. *Journal of Abnormal Psychology*, *125*(4), 502–513. Available from: https://doi.org/10.1037/abn0000155.

Oxford, M., Cavell, T. A., & Hughes, J. N. (2003). Callous–unemotional traits moderate the relation between ineffective parenting and child externalizing problems: A partial replication and extension. *Journal of Clinical Child and Adolescent Psychology*, *32*, 577–585.

Pardini, D. A., Lochman, J. E., & Powell, N. (2007). The development of callous-unemotional traits and antisocial behavior in children: are there shared and/or unique predictors? *Journal of Clinical Child and Adolescent Psychology*, *36*(3), 319–333. Available from: https://doi.org/10.1080/15374410701444215.

Pasalich, D. S., Dadds, M. R., Hawes, D. J., & Brennan, J. (2011). Do callous-unemotional traits moderate the relative importance of parental coercion versus warmth in child conduct problems? An observational study. *Journal of Child Psychology and Psychiatry, and Allied Disciplines*, *52*(12), 1308–1315. Available from: https://doi.org/10.1111/j.1469-7610.2011.02435.x.

Patterson, G. F. (1974). A basis for identifying stimuli which control behaviors in natural settings. *Child Development*, *45*, 900–911.

Patterson, G. R. (2016). Coercion theory: The study of change. In T. J. Dishion, & J. J. Snyder (Eds.), *The Oxford handbook of coercive relationship dynamics* (pp. 7–22). New York, NY: Oxford University Press.

Patterson, G. R., & Fisher, P. A. (2002). Recent developments in our understanding of parenting: Bidirectional effects, causal models, and the search for parsimony. In M. H. Bornstein (Ed.), *Handbook of parenting: Vol. 5. Practical issues in parenting* (pp. 59–88). Mahwah, NJ: Erlbaum.

Patterson, G. R., Reid, J. B., & Eddy, J. M. (2002). A brief history of the Oregon model. In J. B. Reid, G. R. Patterson, & J. J. Snyder (Eds.), *Antisocial behavior in children and adolescents: A developmental analysis and model for intervention* (pp. 3–21). Washington, DC: American Psychological Association.

Pemberton, J. R., Borrego, J., & Sherman, S. (2013). Differential attention as a mechanism of change in parent child interaction therapy: Support from time-series analysis. *Journal of Psychopathology and Behavioral Assessment*, *35*(1), 35–44.

Ross, H. E., & Young, L. J. (2009). Oxytocin and the neural mechanisms regulating social cognition and affiliative behavior. *Frontiers in Neuroendocrinology*, *30*(4), 534–547. Available from https://doi.org/10.1016/j.yfrne.2009.05.004.

Rutter, M. (2012). Psychopathy in childhood: is it a meaningful diagnosis? *British Journal of Psychiatry*, *200*(3), 175–176. Available from: https://doi.org/10.1192/bjp.bp.111.092072.

Salekin, R. T. (2017). Research review: What do we know about psychopathic traits in children? *Journal of Child Psychology and Psychiatry*. Available from: https://doi.org/10.1111/jcpp.12738, Advance online publication.

Salihovic, S., Kerr, M., Özdemir, M., & Pakalniskiene, V. (2012). Directions of effects between adolescent psychopathic traits and parental behavior. *Journal of Abnormal Child Psychology*, *40*(6), 957–969.

Sanders, M. R. (2012). Development, evaluation, and multinational dissemination of the Triple P-positive parenting program. *Annual Review of Clinical Psychology*, *8*(2012), 1–35. Available from: https://doi.org/10.1146/annurev-clinpsy-032511-143104.

Sanders, M. R., Baker, S., & Turner, K. M. T. (2012). A randomized controlled trial evaluating the efficacy of Triple P Online with parents of children with early-onset conduct problems. *Behavior Research and Therapy*, *50*, 675–684.

Sanders, M. R., & Dadds, M. R. (1993). *Behavioral family intervention*. Needham Heights, MA: Allyn & Bacon.

Schwenck, C., Mergenthaler, J., Keller, K., Zech, J., Salehi, S., Taurines, R., et al. (2012). Empathy in children with autism and conduct disorder: Group-specific profiles and developmental aspects. *Journal of Child Psychology and Psychiatry*, *53*, 651–659.

Scott, S., & O'Connor, T. G. (2012). An experimental test of differential susceptibility to parenting among emotionally-dysregulated children in a randomized controlled trial for oppositional behavior. *Journal of Child Psychology & Psychiatry*, *53*, 1184–1193.

Shaw, P., Lawrence, E. J., Radbourne, C., Bramham, J., Polkey, C. E., & David, A. S. (2004). The impact of early and late damage to the human amygdala on "theory of mind" reasoning. *Brain*, *127*(7), 1535–1548.

Skuse, D., Morris, J., & Lawrence, K. (2003). The amygdala and development of the social brain. *Annals of the New York Academy of Sciences*, *1008*, 91–101.

Snyder, J. J., & Stoolmiller, M. (2002). Reinforcement and coercion mechanism in the development of antisocial behavior: The family. In J. B. Reid, G. R. Patterson, & J. Snyder (Eds.), *Antisocial behavior in children and adolescents: A developmental analysis and model for intervention* (pp. 65–100). Washington, DC: American Psychological Association.

Somech, L. Y., & Elizur, Y. (2012). Promoting self-regulation and cooperation in pre-kindergarten children with conduct problems: A randomized controlled trial. *Journal of the American Academy of Child and Adolescent Psychiatry*, *51*(4), 412–422.

Spinrad, T. L., Eisenberg, N., Gaertner, B., Popp, T., Smith, C. L., Kupfer, A., ... Hofer, C. (2007). Relations of maternal socialization and toddlers' effortful control to children's adjustment and social competence. *Developmental Psychology*, *43*, 1170–1186.

Stevens, D., Charman, T., & Blair, R. J. (2001). Recognition of emotion in facial expressions and vocal tones in children with psychopathic tendencies. *Journal of Genetic Psychology*, *162*, 201–211. Available from: https://doi.org/10.1080/00221320109597961.

Tannock, R., Ichowitcz, A., & Schachar, R. (1995). Differential effects of methylphenidate on working memory in children with and without comorbid anxiety. *Journal of the American Academy of Child and Adolescent Psychiatry*, *34*, 886–896.

Tully, L.A., Piotrowska, P.J., Collins, D.A., Mairet, K.S., Hawes, D.J., Kimonis, E.R., ... Dadds, M.R. (2017). Study protocol: Evaluation of an online, father-inclusive, universal parenting intervention to reduce child externalising behaviours and improve parenting practices. *BMC Psychology*, *5*(1), 21. Available from: https://doi.org/10.1186/s40359-017-0188-x.

Viding, E., Blair, J. R., Moffitt, T. E., & Plomin, R. (2004). Evidence for substantial genetic risk for psychopathy in 7-year-olds. *Journal of Child Psychology and Psychiatry*, *45*, 1–6.

Viding, E., & McCrory, E. J. (2012). Genetic and neurocognitive contributions to the development of psychopathy. *Development and Psychopathology*, *24*(3), 969–983. Available from: https://doi.org/10.1017/S095457941200048X.

Viding, E., Sebastian, C. L., Dadds, M. R., Lockwood, P. L., Cecil, C. A., De Brito, S. A., & McCrory, E. J. (2012). Amygdala response to preattentive masked fear in children with conduct problems: The role of callous-unemotional traits. *American Journal of Psychiatry*, *169*(10), 1109–1116.

Wahler, R. G., & Meginnis, K. L. (1997). Strengthening child compliance through positive parenting practices: What works? *Journal of Clinical Child Psychology*, *26*(4), 433–440.

Waller, R., Gardner, F., & Hyde, L. W. (2013). What are the associations between parenting, callous-unemotional traits, and antisocial behavior in youth? A systematic review of evidence. *Clinical Psychology Review*, *33*(4), 593–608. Available from: https://doi.org/10.1016/j.cpr.2013.03.001.

Waller, R., Gardner, F., Hyde, L. W., Shaw, D. S., Dishion, T. J., & Wilson, M. N. (2012). Do harsh and positive parenting predict parent reports of deceitful-callous behavior in early childhood? *Journal of Child Psychology and Psychiatry*, *53*(9), 946–953.

Webster-Stratton, C., & Reid, M. (2003). The incredible years parents, teachers, and children training series: A multifaceted treatment approach for young children with conduct problems. In A. E. Kazdin, & J. R. Weisz (Eds.), *Evidenced-based psychotherapies for children and adolescents* (pp. 224–240). New York: Guilford.

Wells, K. C., & Egan, J. (1988). Social learning and systems family therapy for childhood oppositional disorder: Comparative treatment outcome. *Comprehensive Psychiatry*, *29*, 138–146.

Wootton, J. M., Frick, P. J., Shelton, K. K., & Silverthorn, P. (1997). Ineffective parenting and childhood conduct problems: The moderating role of callous–unemotional traits. *Journal of Consulting and Clinical Psychology*, *65*, 301–308.

Further Reading

Cavell, T. A. (2000). *Working with parents of aggressive children: A practitioner's guide.* Washington, DC: American Psychological Association.

Dadds, M. R., Allen, J. L., Oliver, B. R., Faulkner, N., Legge, K., Moul, C., ... Scott, S. (2012). Love, eye contact, and the developmental origins of empathy versus psychopathy. *British Journal of Psychiatry*, *200*, 191–196.

Fossum, S., Handegård, B. H., Adolfsen, F., Vis, S. A., & Wynn, R. (2016). A meta-analysis of long-term outpatient treatment effects for children and adolescents with conduct problems. *Journal of Child & Family Studies*, *25*, 15–29.

Granic, I., & Patterson, G. R. (2006). Toward a comprehensive model of antisocial development: A systems dynamic systems approach. *Psychological Review*, *113*, 101–131. Available from: https://doi.org/10.1037/0033-295X.113.1.101.

Hanisch, C., Freund-Braier, I., Hautmann, C., Jänen, N., Plück, J., Brix, G., ... Döpfner, M. (2010). Detecting effects of the indicated prevention programme for externalizing problem behaviour (PEP) on child symptoms, parenting, and parental quality of life in a randomized controlled trial. *Behavioural and Cognitive Psychotherapy*, *38*, 95–112.

Hawes, D. J., & Allen, J. (2016). Evidence-based parenting interventions: Current perspectives and clinical strategies. In M. Hodes, & S. Gau (Eds.), *Positive mental health, fighting stigma, and promoting resiliency for children and adolescents* (pp. 185–204). Academic Press, Elsevier, Chap 10.

Hawes, D. J., & Dadds, M. R. (2013). Parent and family assessment strategies. In B. D. McLeod, A. Jensen-Doss, & T. Ollendick (Eds.), *Handbook of child and adolescent diagnostic and behavioral assessment* (pp. 316–347). New York: Guilford Press.

Hubble, K., Bowen, K. L., Moore, S. C., & van Goozen, S. H. M. (2015). Improving negative emotion recognition in young offenders reduces subsequent crime. *PloS One*, *10*(6), e0132035. Available from: https://doi.org/10.1371/journal.pone.0132035.

Kaminski, J. W., Valle, L. A., Filene, J. H., & Boyle, C. L. (2008). A meta-analytic review of components associated with parent training program effectiveness. *Journal of Abnormal Child Psychology*, *36*(4), 567–589. Available from: https://doi.org/10.1007/s10802-007-9201-9.

Liber, J. M., van Widenfelt, B. M., Leeden, A. J., Goedhart, A. W., Utens, E. M., & Treffers, P. D. (2010). The relation of severity and comorbidity to treatment outcome with cognitive behavioral therapy for childhood anxiety disorders. *Journal of Abnormal Child Psychology*, *38*, 683–694.

Lunkenheimer, E. S., Olson, S. L., Hollenstein, T., Sameroff, A. J., & Winter, C. (2011). Dyadic flexibility and positive affect in parent-child coregulation and the development of child behavior problems. *Development and Psychopathology*, *23*, 577–591. Available from: https://doi.org/10.1017/S095457941100006X.

MacKinnon, D. P., Lockhart, G., Baraldi, A., & Gelfand, L. (2013). Evaluating treatment mediators and moderators. In J. S. Comer, & P. C. Kendall (Eds.), *The Oxford handbook of research strategies for clinical psychology* (pp. 262–286). New York: Oxford University Press.

Sawyer, A. M., Borduin, C. M., & Dopp, A. R. (2015). Long-term effects of prevention and treatment on youth antisocial behavior: A meta-analysis. *Clinical Psychology Review*, *42*, 130–144. Available from: https://doi.org/10.1016/j.cpr.2015.06.009.

Storch, E. A., Larson, M. J., Merlo, L. J., Keeley, M. L., Jacob, M. L., Geffken, G. R., ... Goodman, W. K. (2008). Comorbidity of pediatric obsessive-compulsive disorder and anxiety disorders: Impact on symptom severity and impairment. *Journal of Psychopathology and Behavioral Assessment*, *30*, 111–120.

Vance, A., Harris, K., Boots, M., Talbot, J., & Karamitsios, M. (2003). Which anxiety disorders may differentiate ADHD, combined type with dysthymic disorder from ADHD combined type alone? *Australian and New Zealand Journal of Psychiatry*, *37*, 563–569.

Viding, E. (2013). Commentary: Study of gene–environment interplay–a lesson in how to keep oneself busy for the foreseeable future. *Journal of Child Psychology and Psychiatry*, *54*(10), 1144–1146.

Prevention of disruptive behavior problems in children

14

Anil Chacko, Megan Granski, E. Parham Horn, Michael D. Levy, Victoria Dahl, Rachel S. Lacks, and Amrita Ramakrishnan
New York University, New York, NY, United States

Introduction

The prevention of disruptive behavior problems in children is a significant, long-standing issue given the substantial personal, familial, and societal costs associated with these problems, particularly when left un/undertreated (Loeber & Ahonen, 2014). Prevention efforts are inherently complex, given the often multiple pathways to development (see chapters in this book) and the various dynamic micro- and macrolevel factors/social determinants that interact over time to heighten/mitigate risk for development of disruptive behavior problems in youth. Prior to discussion of these determinants, we believe it is useful to utilize a theoretical framework that acknowledges the interrelated nature of these microlevel factors and macrolevel/social determinants. Dynamic systems theory (DST) provides this type of lens and recognizes the layers of dynamic complexity that underlie these developmental processes, which offers guidance into prevention efforts. Following this, we discuss macrolevel/social determinants that have broad effects on mental health functioning and are often the target of prevention efforts. We then briefly discuss early developmental signs of disruptive behavior problems which are cause for concern and often the targets of early intervention efforts. Using toxic stress as a model, we link social determinants to these more microlevel factors and overall health. We conclude the chapter with a discussion of the public/population health (PPH) model as well as policy targeting broad social determinants and multi-tier prevention interventions.

Dynamic systems theory

DST asserts that human development must be conceptualized as the "multiple, mutual, and continuous interaction of all the levels of the developing system, from the molecular to the cultural" (Thelen & Smith, 2006, p. 258). Furthermore, the DST perspective holds that the process of human development is a continually self-organized one and the dynamic nuanced product of patterned interactions between multiple parts of an interconnected micro- and macrolevel system (Thelen & Smith, 2006). Thelen and Smith employ the use of the mountain stream as a metaphor to illustrate the variety of proximal and distal variables that synergistically interact to

Developmental Pathways to Disruptive, Impulse-Control, and Conduct Disorders.
DOI: https://doi.org/10.1016/B978-0-12-811323-3.00014-6

determine human development. This metaphor is useful in understanding the "dynamic cascade" of development (Thelen & Smith, 2006, p. 263). Rather than following a linear approach that identifies isolated, seemingly static, developmental ingredients, this model highlights the continuously evolving and interdependent nature of contributing developmental processes. Furthermore, dynamic system theorists recognize that the developmental outcomes being seen in the here-and-now are the product of pervasive current and historical patterns which continuously influence and co-construct the present. The mountain stream metaphor is useful in conceptualizing these ideas: current weather patterns that influence how quickly (or slowly) the mountain snow melts to create the stream, the molecular composition of the water and how this impacts the pace and flow of the current, and the mountain's vegetation and its impact on evaporative processes. Historical geological factors that act over periods of time also help to shape present-day patterns. Thelen and Smith (2006) provide but one illustration of this interdependent process: "the long-range climate of the region led to particular vegetation on the mountain and the consequent patterns of water absorption and runoff" (p. 263).

Applying this metaphor to developmental psychopathology research, a more simplistic linear causality approach to disruptive behavior problems is insufficient to capture the complexity and dynamism of the human developmental process. As illustrated in previous chapters, it is evident that no one factor or process is necessary and sufficient for the development of disruptive behavior problems in youth nor does any particular model account for the entire proportion of the variance in the manifestation of disruptive behavior problems. The complexity inherent to these problems calls for a lens of examination that considers inextricable, active components. DST provides a framework through which to consider the multiple pathways of effective intervention at both macro- and microlevels.

With this theoretical perspective in mind, the purpose of this chapter is to present the macro (often referred to as social determinants) that have been examined as potential attractors that either push children towards or pull them away from developmental trajectories that perpetuate problematic and disruptive behaviors. A number of microlevel factors/mediating mechanisms such as temperament, callous/unemotional traits, and attributional bias have been identified as factors that potentially impact the development and maintenance of disruptive behavior problems; we refer readers to chapters in this book for a comprehensive review of these microlevel factors (see Chapters 5–8: Negative affect, Callous–unemotional traits, Cognitive attribution bias, and Sensation seeking and risk-taking, respectively). Relatedly, broad-based contextual and systematic considerations such as social determinants of health have also been studied to inform how elements of broad factors (e.g., housing) impact and how disruptive behavior problems develop, and these macro factors/social determinants are the focus of the remainder of the chapter. The authors aim to present the various leverage points in the complex developmental system from which researchers have approached intervention work. Thus, we encourage the reader to digest the following research with the preface that each intervention is but one way of approaching a complex problem

Macro factors/social determinants

It is essential to recognize that a set of macro factors/social determinants sets the stage for the development of problematic health, including mental health, outcomes for youth. Importantly, these macro factors/social determinants are not uniquely predictive of, nor necessary and sufficient to explain the development of disruptive behavior problems in children. Rather, these broad set of factors increase children's risk for maladaptive outcomes across a wide set of key functional domains. As such, it is critical that we appreciate these macro factors/social determinants and, in the context of preventions efforts (situated within a population/public health model as discussed later in this chapter), focus policy and large-scale primary and secondary promotion, and prevention efforts at these levels given the potential wider spread benefit for reducing overall risk for development of various poor outcomes for youth and enhancing mental health wellness.

The National Institute of Health defines health disparities as variation in rates of disease occurrence and disabilities between different levels of socioeconomic status (SES) and/or geographically defined population groups (National Information Center on Health Services Research and Health Care Technology NICHSR, 2009). Health disparities are closely linked to social and economic disadvantage. Health disparities disproportionately affect racial and ethnic minorities who live in disenfranchised, low SES communities (Blane, 1995), making it imperative to locate an understanding of health disparities within a sociopolitical and historical context. Within the arena of mental health, racial and ethnic disparities in access to, utilization of, and quality of mental health care predominate over disparities in mental health itself (McGuire & Miranda, 2008).

Disparities in mental health exhibit a noticeably different pattern from disparities in general health, in that, in general, minorities have poorer health outcomes than do whites, while numerous studies suggest that minorities have either lower or equivalent rates of mental disorders as compared with whites (McGuire & Miranda, 2008). However, despite rates of mental disorders not being higher among minorities, psychological symptoms do tend to be higher among minorities and, to some degree interrelatedly, among the poor. This discrepancy between rate of psychological symptoms and rate of diagnosed disorders may very well result from inequality in access to high-quality mental health services. This inference is supported by the mental health disparity literature as a whole, and, in particular, by the literature on racial and ethnic disparities in pediatric mental health, which shows that racial/ethnic minority children are more likely to receive fewer and inferior health services than their non-Latino white peers (Alegria, Vallas, & Pumariega, 2010). Additionally, some studies have suggested higher population prevalence rates of sad mood, suicidal ideation, and suicidal attempts among Latino and African American youth than non-Latino whites, and a greater prevalence rate for the symptoms of eating disorders among Latino youth (Eaton et al., 2008) Simultaneously, significant diagnostic ethnic/racial disparities have been demonstrated within children's mental health, with African American and Latino children receiving appropriate diagnoses less often than white children (Alegria et al., 2010).

There are several possible explanations for why racial/ethnic minority children and adolescents are underserved with respect to mental health services. One explanation is that, rather than being referred for mental health treatment, minority youth experience higher rates of entry into the juvenile justice system, especially if they display aggressive or disruptive behaviors (Alegria et al., 2010). Another possible explanation is minority youth experience higher rates of child welfare and poverty, and there has been increasing recognition that impoverished children and children in the child welfare system have extremely high mental health needs, but less access to services due to lack of local providers and/or due to a lack of insurance to cover the costs of treatment (Garland et al., 2001). Additionally, clinicians and researchers have postulated that there are several sociocultural issues that play a role in not only the initiation but also the continuation of mental health treatment for minority youth. In particular, minority children and adolescents face several barriers to effective mental health care that have been outlined in the literature; including population barriers (e.g., socioeconomic disparities, stigma, poor health education), provider factors (e.g., deficits in cross-cultural competence, skills, patient orientation), and systemic factors (e.g., convenience, services organization, training, culturally competent services) (Pumariega, Rogers, & Rothe, 2005).

In the following section, we examine the relationship between four social determinants of health, including community violence, access to childcare, stability of housing, and access to high quality food/nutrition, and children's mental health functioning. Importantly, these macro factors/social determinants are not uniquely predictive of, nor necessary and sufficient to explain the development of disruptive behavior problems in children. Rather, these broad set of factors increase children's risk for maladaptive outcomes across a wide set of key functional domains. As such, it is critical that we appreciate these macro factors/social determinants. In particular, these social determinants of mental health in children translate into clear opportunities for targeted health promotion and prevention efforts.

Community violence

Community violence encompasses children's direct experiences of violence as well as indirect experiences, such as witnessing or hearing about family members and friends being victimized (Margolin & Gordis, 2000). Racial and ethnic minority children, who are more likely to live in divested, urban neighborhoods, experience community violence at disproportionate rates (Cooley-Quille et al., 2001). Indeed, it has been posited that community violence mediates the relationship between living in a disenfranchised neighborhood and poor mental health outcomes (Chauhan, Burnette & Repucci, 2009; Javdani et al., 2014). Age has an effect on exposure to community violence, with older children being more likely to experience community violence than younger children (Buka et al., 2001). Findings on the role of gender are somewhat mixed, although a number of studies have found that both boys and girls who experience direct violence are at risk for externalizing and internalizing mental health outcomes (Fowler et al., 2009; Javdani et al., 2014). Meanwhile, girls, but not boys, who experience indirect violence, are at risk for mental health outcomes (Foster et al., 2004; Javdani et al., 2014).

Cross-sectional and longitudinal studies have consistently demonstrated that exposure to community violence is associated with mental health issues in children, including disruptive behavior problems (Fowler et al., 2009; Gorman-Smith, Henry, & Tolan, 2004; Youngstrom, Weist, & Albus, 2003). Young children in contexts characterized by high rates of violence have been shown to have higher rates of depression, anxiety, irritability, impulsivity, anger, sleep disturbances, somatic distress, low self-esteem, and fear of being alone (Lynch & Cicchetti, 1998; Margolin & Gordis, 2000; Osofsky, 1997).

Importantly, children's responses to chronic stressors, such as hypervigilance, may be adaptive in their context but maladaptive with regard to their developmental trajectory. For instance, a hypervigilant child in a nonviolent situation, such as in a classroom setting, might have a tendency to exhibit aggressive and impulsive behaviors, which is demonstrative of reduced capacity to regulate emotion (Lynch & Cicchetti, 1998; Margolin & Gordis, 2000). Since youth learn to operate from a self-protective stance in the world, what appears to be antisocial behavior is often in fact adaptive behavior aimed at prioritizing survival over being cooperative and kind (Ford, Chapman, MACK, & Pearson, 2006). Children who have experienced community violence may be less inclined to explore their environment, which hinders their development (Lynch & Cicchetti, 1998; Osofsky, 1995). Exposure to community violence has also been linked to difficulty sustaining attention and declines in cognitive performance (Lorion & Saltzman, 1993).

Community violence is related to a number of relevant ecological risk factors. For instance, chronic community violence is associated with lower levels of parental monitoring, which is related to children's exposure to violence and mental health problems (Javdani et al., 2011). In Lynch & Cichetti's (1998) longitudinal study of 322 children, they found that rates of maltreatment were higher among children who experienced higher rates of community violence. Parents' abilities and capacities to effectively parent and protect their children may be impeded by the various stressors and traumas associated with community violence (Aisenberg & Herrenkohl, 2008). Likewise, there are a number of mediating ecological factors associated with the prevention of detrimental child outcomes. Studies have shown that youth living in violent neighborhoods whose families are characterized by high levels of cohesion and support are less likely to develop disruptive behavior problems (Gorman-Smith & Tolan, 1998; Plybon & Kliewer, 2001). Moreover, research has found that school support, such as teacher support and perceived school safety, plays a protective role in the relationship between exposure to community violence and deleterious mental health outcomes (O'Donnell, Schwab-Stone, & Muyeed, 2002; Ozer & Weinstein, 2004).

Access to childcare/early education

The majority of children attend nonparental child care before the age of 3 years (NICHD Early Child Care Research Network [ECCRN], 2001; Peisner-Feinberg et al., 2001; Phillips & Adams, 2001). The quality of early care that children received has been linked to important long-term social–emotional and academic outcomes, regardless of later care (Duncan & Brooks-Gunn, 2000; Heckman, 2006;

NICHD ECCRN, 2001). High-quality early child care is characterized by sensitivity, warmth, and responsiveness on the part of the caregiver, as well as exposure to language (Phillips & Adams, 2001). The ratio of child-to-caregiver and caregiver qualifications is also associated with the quality of care (Phillips & Adams, 2001; Whitebook, 2003).

High-quality care is linked to lower disruptive behavior problems, including decreased impulsivity and greater compliance as well as increased persistence, as reported by caregivers and teachers through toddlerhood and early elementary school (Anderson, 2003; Belsky, Vandell, Burchinal, Clarke-Stewart, McCartney, & Owen, 2007; Duncan & Brooks-Gunn, 2000; NICHD ECCRN, 2001; Peisner-Feinberg et al., 2001). These findings are especially important for low-income children, as children from low-income backgrounds are 1.3 times more likely to have emotional or behavioral problems than their non-poor peers (Duncan & Brooks-Gunn, 2000). Furthermore, high-quality child care has stronger positive effects for low-SES families (Peisner-Feinberg et al., 2001). For example, high-quality out-of-home care can buffer against the influences of high-risk home environments by promoting positive parent–child interactions, greater parental engagement, and reduction of maternal mental health problems (Duncan & Brooks-Gunn, 2000; Phillips & Adams, 2001).

However, in the United States, the quality of programs for young children greatly varies. In general, children from low-SES families are less likely to receive high-quality child care or early education (Blair & Raver, 2012; NICHD ECCRN, 2001). Outside of subsidized child care programs, which meet the standards for high-quality care, child care options for low-income families are of poor quality when compared with families who have more resources (Phillips & Adams, 2001). Furthermore, although subsidized programs are targeted toward low-income working families, the majority of eligible families do not have access to the programs (Phillips & Adams, 2001). Thus, the children most at risk for the development of disruptive behavior problems do not have access to the care necessary to prevent such problems.

Stability of housing

Housing can be conceptualized as a social determinant of health. Housing can refer to the quality of housing, its affordability, and its long-term stability determined by variables such as cost and urban development. Much current research indicates clearly the associations between poor housing quality and various health conditions including mental health diagnosis (Hernandez & Suglla, 2016). Hernández (2016) found that families would even forego optimal health, such as development of physical conditions (such as asthma), poor sanitation, pest infestation, and poor mental health for the sake of affordable housing.

Quality of housing and housing stability not only affects adults but can have serious impact on children's well-being. While there have been various research studies that have examined the link between housing and mental health, we focus our attention on findings from the MacArthur Foundation funded initiative—"How Housing

Matters to Families and Communities"—that supports multiple studies within this area. Within this initiative, affordable housing, neighborhood cohesiveness, and poor housing are some of the factors examined to determine their impact on children's mental health. One study found that poor housing conditions and overcrowding were associated with more depressive symptomatology in adults (Chambers, Fuster, Suglia, & Rosenbaum, 2015), which has been shown to affect children's mental health (Coley, Leventhal, Lynch & Kull, 2013; Olfson, Marcus, Druss, Pincus, & Weissman, 2003). The study by Coley et al. (2013) found that poor quality housing was consistently predictive of a child's well-being throughout the duration of childhood. Their study also found that children who lived in lower quality homes had more emotional and disruptive behavioral problems compared to their peers who lived in higher quality homes (Coley et al., 2013). Solari and Mare (2012) found that crowded housing was negatively associated with various characteristics of child well-being, including disruptive behavior problems. The accumulating literature and research seek to emphasize the impact of housing on physical and mental health, a connection that citizens and policy makers cannot overlook.

Access to high-quality food/nutrition

It has been widely recognized that individuals living in low-SES neighborhoods disproportionately suffer from increased rates of morbidity, mortality, and adverse health outcomes (Cubbin, Hadden, & Winkleby, 2001; Deaton & Lubotsky, 2003); these disparities are believed to be associated with factors, including residential segregation (based on race/ethnicity) and neighborhood deprivation (Gee & Payne-Sturges, 2004), which can lead to adverse health outcomes. Neighborhood deprivation in particular contributes to the presence of health—both physical and mental—disparities in children living in low-SES neighborhoods, in that one component of neighborhood deprivation is the presence of fewer supermarkets, which offer a larger variety of affordable and healthy foods, especially when compared to smaller convenience stores typically found in low income neighborhoods (Morland, Wing, Diez Roux, & Poole, 2002). This phenomenon has become so prevalent that many impoverished and low-SES communities have come to be referred to as "food deserts," a term defined by the USDA (Gallagher, 2010) as "parts of the country vapid of fresh fruit, vegetables, and other healthful whole foods, usually found in impoverished areas. This is largely due to a lack of grocery stores, farmers' markets, and healthy food providers." Walker, Keane, & Burke (2010) reviewed the food desert literature and found that the lowest income neighborhoods had nearly 30% less supermarkets than the highest income neighborhoods; one of the included studies investigated the food environment in Philadelphia and found that the highest income neighborhoods had 156% more supermarkets than the lowest income neighborhoods. Another study conducted by Powell, Slater, Mirtcheva, Bao, and Chaloupka (2007) examined the associations between the availability of food stores in the United States and race, ethnicity, and SES, and found that the availability of chain supermarkets in black neighborhoods was only 52% that of their white counterpart, even after controlling for relevant covariates, like neighborhood income.

Lack of access to high-quality, nutritious food can lead to numerous adverse health effects, particularly in developing children, affecting both a child's physical health (e.g., diabetes and obesity) and mental health, including the promotion of the symptoms of disruptive behavior problems. The strongest link that has been drawn between disruptive behavior problems and food quality is seen in the research around the presence of polychlorinated biphenyls (PCBs) in food and their impact on child neurodevelopment, particularly pre- or postnatally (via the placenta or breast milk) given the vulnerability of the developing brain (Caspersen et al., 2016). PCBs are highly persistent, organic pollutants that accumulate in foods of animal origin (i.e., meat and dairy products) and in human tissue; one of the best ways to avoid them is to eat fruit and vegetables, which, as just discussed, lower SES families tend to lack access to (or are unable to afford) due to factors like neighborhood deprivation and the emergence of food deserts in low SES neighborhoods. Boucher et al. (2009) conducted a review of studies examining the effects of prenatal PCB exposure on neuropsychological test performance, finding that the evidence suggests a particular vulnerability of executive functions to impairment due to PCB exposure. Stewart et al. (2008) have repeatedly demonstrated a behaviorally specific effect of PCB exposure on impulsive responding: Their research shows that children (approximately 4.5 years old) who have been more highly exposed to PCBs respond excessively and inappropriately when asked to discriminate target from nontarget stimuli on a continuous performance task, due specifically to impaired response inhibition. Their research has also provided evidence to suggest that the association between PCB exposure and impulsive responding persists as children age, at least through 9.5 years of age.

In summary, macrolevel/social determinants are broad based and both facilitate wellness but also can yield illness in a population. The social determinants are often intertwined and occur prominently in communities. As such, broad-based policy and interventions are often necessary to address these issues. Yet, in order to maximize the utility of efforts targeting such social determinants, it is necessary to identify early manifestations or precursors of disruptive behavior, a topic to which we now turn.

Early developmentally sensitive manifestations and warning signs of disruptive behavior

Targeted prevention relies on early and accurate identification of children exhibiting disruptive behavior. While disruptive behavior disorders are identifiable in young children (Chacko, Wakschlag, Hill, Danis, & Espy, 2009), due to the natural variation in cognitive, social, emotional, and behavioral development within and between young children, there has been emerging consensus in the field about criteria for defining and distinguishing between adaptive and maladaptive behaviors (Egger & Angold, 2006). It is important to identify meaningful disruptive behavior problems early in childhood because early identification and intervention have long been known to be associated with better outcomes (Sroufe, 1997), and early manifestations of disruptive behavior tend to predict later manifestations (Patterson, DeBaryshe, & Ramsey, 1989). For instance, although most children with oppositional defiant disorder (ODD) will not develop conduct disorder, they are at greater risk for developing conduct disorder (CD), and particularly at risk for childhood-onset CD (Thomas, 2017). Unfortunately, the majority of prevention efforts target older children and adolescents (Tremblay, 2010), which is problematic because pre- and early school years are a critical developmental window for intervention. As the child's social and learning contexts expand, the child's capacity to regulate behavior becomes important to their ability to engage in and sustain social relationships and develop competencies necessary for future academic success (Hart et al., 2016). Accurate identification of children who are likely to develop persistent behavioral problems is crucial so that prevention efforts and resources can be maximized (Chacko et al., 2009).

A number of scholars have promoted a dimensional approach that defines disruptive behavior on a continuum from normative to nonnormative as an alternative to categorical classification systems (i.e., Chacko et al., 2009; Frick & Nigg, 2012; Wakschlag, Tolan & Leventhal, 2010). Dimensional patterns can identify children who exhibit symptoms at subclinical levels, and thus may be at risk for more severe impairment over time (Wakschlag et al., 2015). Given the developmentally normative nature of many disruptive and impulsive behaviors during early childhood (Keenan & Wakschlag, 2002), it is critical to distinguish developmentally normative manifestations of disruptive behavior from clinically significant disruptive behavior. Likewise, it is also important to differentiate antisocial, maladaptive disruptive behaviors from adaptive, prosocial displays of disruptive behaviors (Newcorn et al., 2015). Within a "bottom-up" approach to classification of disruptive behavior problems, clinical significance is based on the frequency and quality of disruptive behaviors (Chacko et al., 2009). Quality includes intensity, expectability in context, flexibility, and organization of behavior (Chacko, Anderson, & Rajwan, 2012).

A dimensional approach to classification of disruptive behavior problems needs to be developmentally sensitive (Frick & Nigg, 2012). Indeed, it has been suggested that categorical differentiation between CD and ODD is not psychometrically appropriate in preschool children, but rather there is a single disorder in preschool children (Sterba, Egger, & Angold, 2007). While some disruptive behaviors are likely to be overpathologized due to their overlap with developmentally normative behavior, others are developmentally impossible for young children to exhibit, such as truancy (Chacko et al., 2009). Moreover, some behaviors are more accurately assessed in school-age children as opposed to preschool children, such as "makes careless mistakes in schoolwork, work, or other activities" (Chacko et al., 2009). This lack of developmentally appropriate criteria for young children likely leads to underidentification of some preschoolers who may have clinically concerning behavioral difficulties (Chacko et al., 2009). Given the importance of key behaviors along a dimension, rather than counts of categorically defined behaviors, we focus the next section on select early manifestations and signs of behavioral difficulties.

In particular, we focus on aggression, emotion dysregulation/temper tantrums, and noncompliance/oppositionality which give the ubiquitous nature of these problems, developmental manifestations of these behaviors, and the relation between these behaviors and clinically disorders (Chacko et al., 2009; Curchack-Lichtin, Chacko, & Halperin, 2014).

Aggression

Aggression is behavior that intentionally intends to harm people (Parke & Slaby, 1983). Children typically develop aggression in the first year of life as a reaction to anger and frustration (Chacko et al., 2012). Wakschlag et al. (2010) note that, while aggression in early childhood is common, it is not normative for aggression to be frequent. For instance, less than 10% of parents to children ages 2–3 years indicate that their children hit others often (Baillargeon et al., 2007). Physical aggression tends to normatively increase throughout the second year (Wakschlag et al., 2010) and then starts to decrease in the third year with the emergence of verbal and problem-solving abilities (Chacko et al., 2009). Physical aggression is replaced by relational aggression (i.e., rumor spreading, peer group exclusion, threatening to withdraw friendship) (Chacko et al., 2012; Matthys & Lochman, 2017). Thus, aggression that is frequent and continues to escalate beyond the normative developmental trajectory is considered atypical.

Moreover, reactive aggression is much more common in young children as opposed to proactive aggression (Hay, 2005). Reactive aggression is a response to frustration or a perceived threat, whereas proactive aggression is a controlled behavior that aims to hurt another person (Matthys & Lochman, 2017; Wakschlag et al., 2010). Nonnormative aggression tends to be stable over time and is linked to a pathway associated with maladaptive outcomes in adolescence, such as drug and alcohol use, violence, and truancy (Lochman et al., 2006).

Emotion dysregulation/temper tantrums

Emotion regulation plays a central role in mood and disruptive disorders. It has received increasing attention for its role in disruptive behavior disorders, particularly in ODD (Cavanagh et al., 2017). Emotion regulation refers to the ability to amplify and reduce the intensity and duration of emotions as needed (Cole, Michel, & Teti, 1994). Emotion regulation capacities have important implications for the child's ability to effectively engage with the environment in a way that supports development. For instance, a child who is not able to tolerate emotional arousal may isolate himself from peers at school, which further distances the child from a context that is important to social development and the ability to effectively regulate arousing emotion (Sroufe, 1997).

Temper loss is defined by Wakshlag et al. (2012) as "the pattern and modulation of expressions of overt anger, including both temper tantrums and regulation of angry mood" (p. 1100). Temper loss has been identified as a key marker of behavioral disorders. Qualities indicative of clinically concerning disruptive behaviors tend to differ from qualities of developmentally normative temper with regard to the intensity of the tantrum, destructiveness of the tantrum, and difficulty recovering from the tantrum (Chacko et al., 2009; Wakschlag et al., 2014). Temper loss frequency tends to peak at 18 months (Chacko et al., 2012), although frequency of temper tantrums is not as salient for identifying clinically significant behavior, given their developmentally normative nature. Chacko et al. (2009) suggest that temper loss be considered in light of both frequency and quality to best determine clinical significance. This is supported by Belden, Thomson, and Luby (2008) finding that developmentally normative tantrums in preschool age children differed from those that were characteristics of those that are clinically concerning in frequency, severity, and behavioral characteristics (Belden et al., 2008).

Noncompliance/oppositionality

Children's failure to follow directives, rules, or norms is referred to as noncompliance (Wakschlag et al., 2010). The ability to modify behavior to comply to external demands is present by the age of 2 years (Kochanska, Coy, & Murray, 2001). Adaptive noncompliance also emerges at age 2 and tends to grow through the preschool years (Chacko et al., 2012). Common noncompliant behaviors in children include arguing and failure to follow directives, rules, and social norms (Wakschlag et al., 2007). Rates of noncompliance in children are high, making quality, such as the form of noncompliance, rather than quantity, important in identifying clinically significant disruptive behaviors (Wakschlag et al., 2007). Normative noncompliance is characterized by negotiation that aims to divert a parent's demands with the goal of self-assertion or autonomy. The child may use bargaining and negotiating but is responsive to alternative directions (Wakschlag et al., 2007). In contrast, behavior that is defiant, stubborn, inflexible, associated with negative affect, and is not amenable to redirection may be clinically significant (Chacko et al., 2009). Children are expected to comply with adult requests the majority of the time by the time they reach school age (Matthys & Lochman, 2017).

In summary, aggression, emotion dysregulation/temper tantrums, and noncompliance/oppositionality are normative misbehaviors of early childhood but, given the function and form of these behaviors, these behaviors may be clinically concerning, and efforts to address and prevent further exacerbation of difficulties and development of clinical disorders are critical. Intervention scientists (in both prevention and early intervention) as well as mental health professionals should focus concerted efforts on identifying and addressing disruptive behavior problems in young children given the developmental trajectory of these children if left untreated.

Toxic stress—linking social determinants to microlevel factors and health

As DST suggests, connecting social determinants to microlevel factors and ultimately disruptive behavior problems can be conceptualized through multiple pathways. One such pathway is through the lens of toxic stress. The literature on stress responses can be utilized to examine the mediating influence that stress has in the relationship between social determinants of health and disruptive behavior problems during childhood and beyond (Shonkoff et al., 2012). According to the National Scientific Council on the Developing Child, toxic stress occurs when a child experiences frequent or prolonged adversity linked to social determinants, which results in extended activation of stress systems within the body (Shonkoff et al., 2012). Many different factors contribute to the development of toxic stress, often (but not necessarily) concurrent with low-SES and race/ethnicity, such as prenatal factors, abuse, witnessing violence, and unsupportive home environments (Shonkoff et al., 2012). For instance, prenatal maternal stress is associated with early delivery and smaller size at birth, which place children at risk for developing cognitive and social impairments (Talge, Neal, & Glover, 2007). In terms of the development of behavior problems, the most consistent adverse outcome as a result of prenatal stress is attention-deficit hyperactivity disorder (Talge et al., 2007). Furthermore, home environments that are characterized by overt family conflict and a lack of nurturing, in which relationships are "cold, unsupportive, and neglectful" are linked to mental and physical disorders in children (Repetti, Taylor, & Seeman, 2002, p. 330). Finally, adverse events in the home and social environments, specifically witnessing violence or child victimization, have been related to aggression, anger, depression, and anxiety in children (Johnson et al., 2002). Thus, social, biological, and environmental factors influence the development of toxic stress in early childhood, which in turn, can influence the behavioral and mental health trajectories of children.

In addition, toxic stress can alter immune functioning and increase inflammatory markers, which may result in poor health outcomes, such as cardiovascular disease, asthma, and depression (Shonkoff et al., 2012). These changes modify the biological systems that are involved in maintaining physiological stability throughout environmental changes, e.g., allostasis (Danese & McEwen, 2012). Allostasis relies on the ability to detect environmental and physiological changes and activate adaptive responses, and the nervous, endocrine, and immune systems mediate allostatic processes (Danese & McEwen, 2012). Repeated and chronic exposure to psychosocial stressors has been linked to prolonged activation of the allostatic system, which has been correlated with lasting physiological consequences, as well as changes to the nervous, endocrine, and immune systems (Danese & McEwen, 2012). The alterations of these systems can be observed in childhood and adulthood and have lasting impacts on all areas of mental and physical development.

Prevention and intervention from the lens of DST

From a DST perspective, macro- and microlevel factors influence the development of disruptive behavior problems in youth. As we have discussed, macrolevel, broad factors such as housing and community violence, as well as microlevel, specific factors, including the emergence of select early manifestation of clinically significant behaviors and behavioral patterns, must all be considered for prevention efforts. The prevention of disruptive behavior problems should translate science into efforts at critical leverage points to develop nuanced approaches to intervention. Importantly, however, from a DST perspective, the development of disruptive behavior problems will likely occur through multiple pathways, whereas macro- and microlevel risk and protective factors interact, augment, and attenuate the development of disruptive behavior problems. Given the number of potential pathways and the general risk posed by many social determinants on the development of poor health and mental health outcomes, including disruptive behavior problems, many have called upon a broad public health approach to prevention. This public health approach recognizes the key role of policy, as well as primary and secondary prevention efforts.

PPH model

The PPH model, a multipronged, comprehensive, concerted, connected, and consistent approach to addressing PPH issues, includes prevention as just one aspect. The interested reader is directed to several substantial publications, of which we herein heavily draw upon (e.g., DHHS, 1998, 2002; Miles, Espiritu, Horen, Sebian, & Waetzig, 2010). We focus our attention in this section of four aspects of this model (promotion, prevention, treatment, and re/claiming) which, collectively, maximize the potential to reduce and improve outcomes for children with disruptive behavioral difficulties. Moreover, we briefly discuss key issues related to implementation of a PPH model.

"The absence of illness is not health" is a key statement often used to focus attention on the goals of a PPH model—which is to identify and address determinants of health and illness in efforts to optimize functioning in population. Importantly, determinants must focus on both broad and specific factors related to both health and illness. Determinants for positive aspects of health and those for illness may likely be unique and orthogonal and as such, efforts must be made to identifying determinants of wellness and illness if a PPH model is to be employed. Moreover, there is recognition that many of these determinants are at the broadest level—communities (e.g., built environments, social networks) that place children at risk for or promote mental health. As such, attention to both broad and specific determinants (as reviewed in previous chapters) is necessary to translate into approaches targeting various outcomes in the population.

Given the identification of broad and specific determinants of both health and illness, a PPH model translates determinants into four approaches which, when connected seamlessly, implemented comprehensively, in a concerted and consistent manner, offer great benefits for children's mental health, including improving the lives of children with or at risk for disruptive behavior problems. As described in Miles et al. (2010), Promotion approaches focus on optimizing health by addressing determinants of positive mental health before a problem has been identified for the entire population. Prevention approaches focus on reducing mental health problems by addressing determinants of problems before a specific problem has been identified in an individual, group, or population with the goal of reducing future mental health problems in the population. The third approach in a PPH model is Treatment which focuses on diminishing the effects of an identified mental health problem after the problem has been identified with goal of approaching as close to a problem-free state of possible in the population. Finally, according to Miles et al. (2010), the Re/Claim approach focuses on optimizing positive mental health while taking into consideration an identified mental health problem after a specific mental health problem has been identified with the goal of improving the positive mental health of the population of focus.

The PPH model embraces these four approaches as necessary to shift the population toward health while addressing, ameliorating, and enhancing outcomes for those who are ill. As an example, tacking childhood obesity by focusing on treatment of children who are obese through psychosocial treatment approaches (e.g., exercise) will not have maximal impact unless determinants of health (i.e., body mass index within normal limits) are addressed through health promotion approaches (e.g., ensuring adequate access to high-quality food; ensuring knowledge about nutrition), prevention (e.g., improving food selection habits in high-risk children), and re/claiming approaches (e.g., addressing social cognition and self-esteem issues in children who are obese).

Implementation of effective, efficient, and sustainable PPH models requires addressing integrated efforts over multiple sectors over time, felt needs of the community, parsimonious efforts affecting common determinants across various health outcomes, and understanding of the complexity of intervening to change behavior in context. We briefly highlight these points. As evident in the example above, a PPH model approach requires involvement from multiple sectors (e.g., government, private sector), institutions (e.g., schools, businesses), and people (e.g., teachers, parents), coordination, and concerted efforts consistently applied over time. Inherent in the success of this comprehensive PPH model is that the target of these efforts indeed represents a significant and relatively high-priority felt need of the community. Decisions to leverage and utilize scarce resources are based on more than just data. The extent to which the community is aware of, perceives impairment associated with, and prioritizes a specific target relative to others is critical to ensuring the success of a PPH model, particularly the sustainability of a model. In the case of disruptive behavior disorders, it may be the case, as we have experienced in our own work that focusing on this addressing disruptive behavior problems in children is a relatively low priority, given the numerous issues faced by children and their families in particular communities. Families have often reported concerns about social issues (e.g., exposure to community violence, bullying) as well as health issues (e.g., asthma) that compete with attending to disruptive behavior problems in children.

Given the difficulties of addressing all challenges faced by a community or focusing on a set of challenges in lieu of others, an important approach within a PPH model is to develop PHH models affecting common determinants across various health outcomes—in other words, taking a common elements approach (e.g., Chorpita, Daleiden & Weisz, 2005) to focusing on determinants that maximally promote health and prevent illness. As an example, parenting has long been a key determinant to promoting health and preventing illness, particularly as it relates to various mental health and educational issues in children (Chacko, Allan et al., 2015; Chacko, Fabiano, Doctoroff, & Fortson, 2017). Ensuring that common, broad determinants of health and illness are identified and leveraged appears a useful approach to maximizing health promotion and reduction of illness.

In addition, there have been numerous efforts toward prevention of disruptive behavior problems (a select number which we highlight below), with many of these being conducted to determine effectiveness rather than sustainability of such approaches. While there are numerous examples of effective approaches, the staffing, resources, and costs may be prohibitive for scalable and sustainable models. In line with Weisz and colleagues (2013) critique of the clinical treatment literature, there is a need for preventive interventions, including those that focus on disruptive behavior disorders, to consider the complexity of the setting, resources, staff, and funding mechanisms to develop intervention models to begin with "the end in mind." An example of such an approach was Atkins and colleagues (Atkins et al., 2008, 2015; Atkins & Frazier, 2011; Frazier, Chacko, Van Gessel, O'Boyle, & Pelham, 2012; Frazier, Mehta, Atkins, Hur, & Rusch, 2013), whereby key settings in which children live and [illegible] are targets for intervention, and endogenous staff are supported to implement select interventions that align with their institution's goals. A central tenet of this work is that the goals of child-serving institutions often focus on improving social, emotional, behavioral, and academic competence, competencies which are related to one other and, therefore, improvement in one of these competencies can often improves others (Nadeem, Maslak, Chacko, & Hoagwood, 2010).

In this line of work, both school and after-school settings have been the focus of intervention efforts [illegible] helping these settings achieve their goals, rather than having [illegible] prioritize, ascribe, or adopt new intervention goals. Such an approach [illegible] supports existing priorities and therefore increases the likelihood of scalability and sustainability of the model. Atkins and colleagues have utilized existing endogenous staff (e.g., teachers and after-school program staff), supported though existing community-based mental health providers (often as consultants) to deliver select interventions (e.g., Good Behavior Game) that focus on helping the setting achieve their goals. The Good Behavior Game fosters group cooperation and behavior management in a classroom such that students maximize academic opportunities, thereby indirectly affecting social, emotional, and behavioral competence. In line with other efforts, traditional outpatient mental health services can be better linked to these settings to provide treatment for those youth with more significant mental health issues. Overall, supporting child-serving settings to achieve their goals (which often align with broad determinants of health and illness), utilizing and supporting endogenous staff to implement specific interventions with more intensive services provided through outpatient mental health agencies aligns with the PHH model.

[illegible]y, an important perspective in implementing a PPH model is an appreciation for complexity theory (Kannampallil, Schauer, Cohen, & Patel, 2011). The analogy of considering intervention as a machine with key inputs, processes, and outputs ignores that social approaches are much more complex given the nature of the targets and processes. Within social systems wherein interventions are embedded, there is unpredictability and change, which must be recognized and, as much as possible, planned for. Inherent in this is that the whole (i.e., PPH model) is different than its parts (i.e., promotion, prevention, treatment, re/claiming approaches). In complex systems, relationships are central to supporting an approach. As such, a successful PPH model utilizes empirically sound determinants to provide evidence-based approaches, but it is the relationship among all these that help fully support the PPH model. An often-used example to illustrate the differences between a machine analogy (a simple system) to a social intervention approach (complex system) is one comparing baking a cake (simple model), to building a rocket to the moon (complicated model), to raising a child (complex model). When baking a cake, one needs to have the correct ingredients and follow a good recipe, and a high-quality cake should consistently result. This process is likely improved through experience and fine tuning the recipe. A complicated system is akin to building a rocket to the moon. You need the right materials and directions in order to build the rocket, and a high level of knowledge and training. While certainly not easy, it is reasonable that rocket builders can build rockets quite well repeatedly, especially with increasing experience. A complex system is like raising a child. While there are generally agreed-upon broad parenting approaches that help when raising a child, there is no set of instructions or a how-to manual. Experience helps but does not guarantee success with parenting the next child. In many ways, each child is unique and therefore parenting must be somewhat unique to the child. In raising a child, the key is in the relationships between what to do and how to do it within the unique parent–child relationship. PPH models are akin to complex systems given that these models exist in social contexts and utilize and interact with various people, also which varies from community to community. An appreciation of the importance of relationships among and between these various components is an essential framework when considering a PPH model approach.

In summary, a PPH model, which includes prevention, is a comprehensive approach that connects various approaches to both enhance health and reduce illness in a population. The PPH model requires addressing integrated efforts over multiple sectors over time, starting with the felt needs of the community and may be best approached through focusing on parsimonious efforts affecting common determinants across various health outcomes, all while appreciating the complexity of intervening to change behavior in context. In the subsequent section, we highlight various efforts at addressing social determinants/macrolevel factors through policy, as well as more comprehensive prevention efforts to address disruptive behavior problems in youth. It is important to note that many comprehensive models utilize specific setting-, family-, and child-level interventions (e.g., Promoting Alternative Thinking Strategies (PATHS) program; Kusche & Greenberg, 1994; Behavioral Parent Training; Chacko, Allan et al., 2015), which are covered in other chapters (see Chapters 9–11: Behavioral treatments, Cognitive therapies: anger management, Family- and community-based treatments, respectively).

Efforts targeting macrolevel/social determinants

Stability of housing

Across the United States, low-income or public housing programs have been instituted in order to provide affordable and stable housing for low-income individuals and families. At the federal level, the US Department of Housing and Urban Development (HUD) implements rental assistance programs, such as privately owned subsidized housing, wherein apartment owners offer reduced rent, or the housing choice voucher program (Section 8) that allows individuals to find their own apartment and use a voucher to pay some or all of rent. Affordable apartments for low-income families can also be found through the public housing agency. In addition, the Office of Affordable Housing Programs (OAHP) has created grant programs, such as the HOME Investments Partnerships Program (HOME) and the National Housing Trust Fund (HTF) to support building, buying, constructing, and rehabilitating housing for rent or ownership at the state and local government level. Although states across the United States may have different housing programs, many states provide public housing or subsidized housing services, and accept Section 8 vouchers as rent. For example, in New York City, the New York City Housing Authority (NYCHA) provides quality and affordable housing in safe environments for low- to moderate-income renters. Without a safe and stable living environment, interventions for children with disruptive behaviors may not be as effective. Thus, practitioners should consider these programs when working with individuals without housing stability.

Community violence

Research has shown that experiencing the chronic stress that results from exposure to community and domestic violence can alter and harm prenatal, child, and adolescent brain development, which can negatively impact attention, impulsivity, decision-making, learning, emotional control, and response to stress later in life (CDC, 2016; Hamby & Grych, 2013; NSCDC, 2005). Given the significant impact exposure to violence can have on child development, numerous government- and private-funded programs and policies have been implemented in those communities which report the highest prevalence of violence, which have tended to be urban and impoverished communities. However, community violence is present in all types of communities, including urban, suburban, rural, and tribal, and as such, when practitioners engage with families and their children in prevention/intervention work, consideration should be given to whether and to what extent community and domestic violence is present in their environment (David-Ferdon et al., 2016). Practitioners should also be aware of whether there are any violence prevention programs in place within a particular family's community, and if the family currently does, or could potentially, benefit from involvement in the program. Within the United States, the Centers for Disease Control and Prevention's (CDC's) Division of Violence Prevention funds the development and implementation of a number of violence prevention programs, including Essentials for Childhood and National Centers for Excellence in Youth Violence Prevention.

Essentials for Childhood is a framework designed by the CDC's Division of Violence Prevention that proposes strategies communities can consider to promote relationships and environments that help children grow up to be healthy and productive citizens (NCIPC:DVP, 2014). The framework specifically targets the prevention of child abuse and neglect by promoting four specific program goals and suggesting the steps—based on the best available evidence—that will best help achieve those goals. The four goals include (1) Raise awareness and commitment to promote safe, stable, nurturing relationships and environments and prevent child maltreatment; (2) use data to inform actions; (3) create the context for healthy children and families through norms change and programs; and (4) create the context for healthy children and families through policies. Goal 3 is particularly relevant to practitioners in prevention and intervention work, as it calls for the promotion of the community norm that we all share responsibility for the well-being of children and of positive community norms about parenting programs and acceptable parenting behaviors, as well as for the implementation of evidence-based programs for parents and caregivers. Currently, the Division of Violence Prevention is funding five state health departments in California, Colorado, Massachusetts, North Carolina, and Washington to implement the four strategies/goals in the *Essentials for Childhood* framework using a collective impact process. Additionally, the CDC also offers technical assistance and training to many other states that do not receive CDC funding but are engaged at varying levels in implementing the *Essentials for Childhood* framework.

The CDC established the National Centers of Excellence in Youth Violence Prevention (YVPC) program in 2000, with the primary goals of linking research to practice and preventing youth violence by building infrastructure and enhancing academic and community partnerships (NCIPC:DVP, 2016). The CDC's Division of Violence Prevention funds several National Centers of Excellence in Youth Violence Prevention (formerly Academic Centers of Excellence) within the United States. One of these centers is the Denver National Center for Excellence in Youth Violence Prevention, whose Steps to Success initiative aims to reduce youth violence in Denver's Montbello neighborhood through working closely with residents and community partners to coordinate a community-wide effort focused on effectively implementing a package of evidence-based programs at the individual, family, and community levels (Brown, 2015; STS, 2014). Another center is the Michigan Youth Violence Prevention Center, which coordinates several programs in Flint, Michigan, that seek to reduce violence and create a supportive and healthy environment for youth, ages 10–24 years (Michigan Youth Violence Prevention Center, 2017). Their programs are designed to focus on the individual, on relationships, or on the community, and all of the programs are organized or led by a community organization. Interested state/local governments and agencies may utilize many of the resources on community, school, relationship, and individual-based interventions (https://www.cdc.gov/violenceprevention/ace/index.html).

Access to high-quality food

Given the lack of access to nutritious and affordable food that many low-income individuals and families experience, as well as the detrimental links between low-quality food and poorer health outcome, several programs have been implemented on the federal level by the US Department of Agriculture, Food and Nutrition Service. The Supplemental Nutrition Assistance Program (SNAP) was created to provide monthly assistance for groceries for low-income individuals and households (USDA, 2017a). The monthly allotment can be used to buy only nutritious foods, such as breads, fruits, vegetables, meats, and dairy products. In addition, the Special Supplemental Nutrition Program for Women, Infants, and Children (WIC) applies specifically to pregnant, breastfeeding, and non-breastfeeding postpartum women and infants and children through age 5 years who are at risk for poor nutrition (USDA, 2017b). For this program, federal grants are allotted to states in order to provide nutritional food, healthcare referrals, and education on nutrition to low-income mothers and children. For children specifically, families can apply for free and reduced price meals in the school. Children from low-income families who receive SNAP or Temporary Assistance for Needy Families (TANF) automatically qualify for free and reduced price meals (USDA, 2017c). In order to intervene with children with disruptive behavior problems, basic needs, such as access to food, need to be met. Furthermore, access to nutritious and affordable food can influence children's physical and mental health, perhaps aiding in the reduction of behavior problems.

Access to child care/early education

There is an intersection between public health policies and child achievement and overall healthy development (Fiscella & Kitzman, 2009). Policy efforts targeting broad social determinants both at federal and state or local levels are integral to shifting the landscape in terms of increasing access to quality child care, nutrition support, and housing stability. Policies that make an effort to combat barriers to healthy development, such as community and domestic violence, are also essential in working to promote healthy child development.

For example, federal policies that target access to childcare and early education are critical in the developmental trajectory of disruptive behavior disorders in childhood. Early Head Start provides a variety of services to pregnant women and families with infants and young children (Raikes & Love, 2002). Love et al. (2005) found that 3-year-old children in the program outperformed children in the control group in terms of cognitive and language development, displayed less aggressive behavior, and demonstrated enhanced sustained attention and emotional engagement of the parent during unstructured play. The reduction of aggressive behavior in particular is noteworthy in light of findings that evidence that early aggressive behaviors are predictive of later disruptive behaviors (Campbell, Shaw, & Gilliom, 2000). The Child Care and Development Fund (CCDF) provides federal funding to low-income families to increase access to childcare (Greenberg, Lombardi, &

Schumacher, 2000). However, these efforts have been met with mixed results; studies have indicated that parents who receive subsidies often have children who receive low-quality childcare, which has been associated with poor achievement in kindergarten and other negative outcomes (Herbst & Tekin, 2010). There have been conflicting viewpoints on whether the goal of child care subsidies is to support child development, in addition to parental work (Adams & Rohacek, 2002). It is therefore important to be mindful of the quality of childcare parents are accessing and have available in their neighborhoods when federal funds are allocated for this purpose, so results are not deleterious.

Head Start offers a number of services to low-income families to promote children's school readiness (Webster-Stratton, 1998). Children enrolled in Head Start who had experienced violence or crime demonstrated positive social–emotional outcomes, with gains being greater for those children who had experienced violence or crime compared to children who had not (Lee & Ludington, 2016). Additionally, intervention that more directly addresses child disruptive behaviors has also been heavily documented. Providing parents with interventions aimed at enhancing parental involvement and parenting practices can result in a reduction of later child behavior problems. Mothers of children in Head Start who received a parent training program (the Incredible Years program; Webster-Stratton & Reid, 2010) reported that their children had significantly fewer conduct problems at home (Webster-Stratton, Reid, & Hammond, 2001).

In summary, many broad social determinants undermine the overall health, including mental health, of children. Policymakers have advocated and initiated broad policies to improve housing stability (HOME; HTF), address community violence (via state/local initiatives through the CDC), increase access to nutritional food (SNAP; WIC), and support early social, emotional, behavioral, and academic competencies through access to child care/early education (Early Head Start; Head Start). Practitioners should be aware of and assess for difficulties families may have in these areas and support families in accessing local, state, and federal programs/assistance. In fact, the American Academy of Pediatrics suggests that pediatricians routinely screen for issues related to poverty and toxic stress—which include the above noted social determinants—in routine child health screenings.

Multi-tier prevention program

Policy and programs to effect change in social determinants largely fall under health promotion and prevention efforts with a PPH model. It is important to note that these policies and programs when offered together represent likely the most stable source of intervention with a PPH model, as long as federal and state funding continues to be available to support these initiatives. Importantly, however, there have been concerted efforts at developing and addressing more intensive prevention focused efforts which often include multi-tier interventions targeting various key processes and levels within the environment (schools, classroom, peers, and families; many of which are more fully reviewed in chapters within this book). These multi-tier prevention programs, when implemented within the context of existing federal, state, and local policies addressing social determinants, are exemplars of a comprehensive PPH model. We review several such multi-tier prevention models.

Metropolitan Area Child Study

The Metropolitan Area Child Study (MACS) evaluated the effectiveness of school-based, peer-based, and family-based interventions in preventing and addressing disruptive behavior problems in an ethnically and racially diverse sample of elementary school aged youth. The *general enhancement classroom program* was a universal intervention that provided teacher consultation and implementation of a social cognitive curriculum. The *general enhancement plus small-group peer-skills training* delivered the general enhancement program plus a 2-year, peer-group training to high-risk children. In addition to the general enhancement classroom and the small-group peer-skills training, the *general enhancement plus small-group peer-skills training plus family interventions* included a 1-year family intervention for high-risk children and their families. Results demonstrated that children in well-resourced schools who received the early, most comprehensive intervention had significant decreases in aggressive behavior, and this effect was doubled when followed by the additional 2-year intervention. However, when the early, comprehensive intervention was implemented in resource-poor schools, rates of aggression did not decrease for children but children evinced improved academic performance as function of the intervention. In sum, results support that a multi-tier family and peer comprehensive intervention in schools can improve aggression and academic outcomes, which is moderated by the baseline resources available at the school. As such, more or different types of support may be necessary for resource-poor schools to evince the same benefits.

Fast Track Prevention Program

Fast (Families and Children Together) track is a multi-tier intervention that provides social skills, lessons in behavior regulation, and academic tutoring to children and examines how these intervention components impact children's development across their lives (Conduct Problems Prevention Research Group [CPPRG], 1992). Fast Track continues from first grade into high school and is geared towards those children with early-onset disruptive behavior problems. The premise behind Fast Track was to integrate five intervention components to help build competence in home sphere, peer sphere, and school sphere, with the aim of reducing disruptive behavior problems and improving social relations and school failure.

The study found moderate positive effects on children's emotional, social, and academic skills at the end of Grade 1 as well as improvements in disruptive behavior (Conduct Problems Prevention Research Group, 1999). In a 2010 study released by the group, continued modest positive outcomes were reported in reduced aggressive behavior and increased academic engagement and prosocial behavior. The implications from the follow-up date demonstrate that a multi-tier longitudinal program can have an impact on "rates of aggression, social competence, and academic engagement in the elementary school years."

Multisite Violence Prevention Program

The Multisite Violence Prevention Program (MVPP), a program created in collaboration by the National Center for Injury Prevention and Control (NCIPC) as well as the CDC, utilized an ecological lens to assess student-, school-, teacher-, and environmental-level outcomes aimed at reducing various types of violence among sixth graders MVPP consisted of schools assigned to interventions at a broad universal level, a more specific targeted level, or a combined approach. Schools in the universal condition randomly selected 100 students, whereas schools in the targeted condition had core teachers identify 15–25 "high-risk" students that evidenced aggressive tendencies who were also perceived to be influential to their peers. Schools in the combined condition received both targeted and universal interventions, whereas control schools received neither. From a theoretical perspective, by implementing an ecological approach including outcomes at the individual, classroom, family, and institutional level, the MVPP attempted to identify key mechanisms of change that exist within these interdependent systems in an effort to inform how to best prevent disruptive behavior.

The foundational intervention adopted in the MVPP was the Guiding Responsibility and Expectations in Adolescents Today and Tomorrow (GREAT) Schools and Family Program (Greenberg, Kusche, Cook, & Quamma, 1995; Reid, Eddy, Fetrow & Stoolmiller, 1999). This program was designed to help sixth graders develop social–cognitive skills to navigate conflicts as well as to increase prosocial attitudes, with a particular focus paid to contextual and cultural impacts. Trained research staff ran 20 weekly 45-minute lessons with 100 randomly selected students. Teachers also received special training in solution-focused approaches designed to help them manage problem behaviors in their classrooms and better support students perpetrating and being victimized by violence. Teachers also attended a 12-hour workshop covering these topics in depth as well as participated in 10 subsequent support groups to help teachers troubleshoot and practice implementing their newly learned skills. All students in the combined and universal conditions received these arms of the prevention program. Children in the targeted condition received a variant of the GREAT Families program, wherein students and their families received a social–cognitive intervention designed to decrease acts of violence. In 15 sessions led by research staff members, behavioral parent training, problem solving, and information on the relationships between schools and families were covered weekly by a group of five families.

Data drawn from various sources were included in the outcome measures for each sixth grader as they received the intervention and again at additional follow-up points during seventh and eighth grade. Notably, the intervention was conducted with two consecutive sixth grade cohorts. Student-level data including disciplinary violations and teacher-reported student behaviors were gathered from each school, while "perpetration and victimization of violence, school climate. . .social problem solving skills, norms and beliefs among the students," were also collected (Miller-Johnson, Sullivan, & Simon, 2004, p. 49). Self-report information from teachers pertaining to perceived school climate, violence, and perceived self-efficacy in applying learned intervention skills is collected. Qualitative interviews were also conducted with school principals to explore issues related to fidelity of implementation and the potential for any confounding events or programs that overlapped with MVPP. Finally, independent research staff members conducted environmental assessments of each school which examined "the physical environment both within and outside the school walls. . .with regard to cleanliness, lighting, temperature, the presence of liquor or weapons stores nearby, and graffiti" (Miller-Johnson et al., 2004, p. 49).

Results from the MVPP were complex: two main effects of MVPP were found; students receiving the universal intervention indicated elevated levels of norms related to nonviolent behavior when compared to other schools involved in the program. However, these students, despite having more nonviolent norms, also reported higher levels of social–cognitive strategies that endorsed the use of aggression. MVPP also showed long-term positive effects with regard to lower school levels of violence for those schools in the targeted condition (with high-risk students) as compared to students in the control school. However, iatrogenic effects were observed at posttest when comparing girls in the universal program with those at control schools (Effect Size ($ES = 0.16$)). This finding potentially highlights the unique gender pathways involved in the development and maintenance of disruptive behavior, as well as demonstrating the benefits of engaging high-risk students rather than all students, regardless of risk level. Similarly, only those students in the targeted intervention demonstrated a significant positive intervention effect in domains measuring attitudes toward violence (Gavine, Donnelly, & Williams, 2016).

In a recent analysis of MVPP examining only school-level variables associated with middle-school aggression, no significant effects were observed for violence-related norms. A small interpersonal climate effect was also noted; however, this weakened significantly as students moved from sixth to eighth grade. In addition, evidence suggests that female students are more affected by school-level variables such as awareness and reporting of violent behaviors (Henry, Farrell, Schoeny, Tolan, & Dymnicki, 2011). Though nonsignificant program effects related to self-efficacy for nonviolent actions were also observed at the school level, significant positive effects for high-risk students at baseline were observed (Multisite Violence Prevention Project, 2008).

The data gathered during the MVPP provided the chance to examine different levels of change under contrasting intervention conditions at an age where disruptive behaviors begin to shift. The implications of these complex multilevel findings highlight that targeted interventions focusing on high-risk and influential youth may be a more cost-effective approach to prevention science within this population. Specifically, it has been argued that effect sizes may have suffered in the universal and combined conditions since "many of the participants would score near the lower limit on many of the outcome measures, suggesting the potential for a floor effect" (Gavine, Donnelly, & Williams, 2016, p. 395; Hessling, Schmidt, & Traxel, 2004). This hypothesis makes sense considering that program effects were observed to be greatest for those students characterized as high risk at baseline.

In summary, several multi-tier prevention programs have been developed that target various levels within a community, notably focused on implementing interventions within a school setting. Findings of these prevention approaches highlight the utility of combining sociocognitive and social network approaches (Neville, 2015). Capitalizing on both of these approaches has been shown to yield the most significant success in altering proviolent attitudes (Gavine, Donnelly, & Williams, 2016). It should be noted, however, that despite the ecological approach of these prevention programs, recent reviews paint a hazy picture wherein effect sizes for preventing disruptive behaviors and aggression, when positive, are often modest or insignificant (Gavine, Donnelly, & Williams, 2016). From a financial perspective, targeted interventions among high-risk students may be the prudent approach to future intervention programs. However, it is important to note that these prevention programs have mostly been conducted without consideration to other aspects of the PPH model (promotion, treatment, re/claiming interventions). As such, the benefits of a more holistic model are understudied. Additional knowledge should also be harnessed through conducting qualitative interviews aimed at finding out how and why certain interventions "fail" among key stake holders at various levels of the prevention program (Gavine, Donnelly, & Williams, 2016; Williams, Gavine, Ward & Donnelly, 2015).

Conclusions

The DST lays a foundation for the complexity of prevention efforts. Prevention efforts, from a PPH model perspective, is just one aspect of a comprehensive, multi-level approach that requires concerted and consistent implementation to affect macrolevel social determinants and microlevels factors that contribute to health and illness (e.g., disruptive behavior) in a population. As this chapter illustrated, these types of efforts require consideration of complex systems in which PPH models exist and must fit within the constraints of routine practice settings (e.g., priorities, staffing, funding). Given this complexity, a PPH model requires the active and ongoing involvement from the community, professionals across various disciples, public and private sectors, and key child serving settings (e.g., schools, sports organizations, after school programs, faith organizations).

There are numerous future directions in the development of the PPH model for addressing disruptive behavior in children. Given that treatment is a critical aspect of such a model, we refer the reader to prior chapters focused on treatment approaches. We focus herein on three important aspects/future directions in the development of PPH models. First, we believe there is great need for effective communication or communication framing around the issue of addressing disruptive behavior problems in children. Understanding how various stakeholders (e.g., policymakers, public, parents) view and understand the issue of disruptive behavior problems is essential to framing a communication strategy that will better advance this field. Frameworks Institute (www.frameworksinstitute.org) utilizes Strategic Frame Analysis to develop the "most effective ways of reframing social and scientific topics," including child mental health. As a field, we must begin to use more effective communication strategies to both build a case for the necessity of a PPH model for disruptive behavior and also leverage this evidence-based communication strategy when developing and employing PPH models to derive maximum benefits. This is an undervalued area in the field and requires further investigation.

A second future direction is incorporation of behavioral economics into PPH models, including prevention efforts. Behavioral economics studies the effects of psychological, social, cognitive, and emotional factors on decision-making, including those made by individuals. Behavioral economic principles translated into interventions, popularly termed as "nudges," may offer specific, low-cost, opportunities to support prevention interventions. As an example, Gennetian, Darling, and Aber (2016) offer insights into how behavioral economics can be translated into intervention supports to help improve engagement of parents in early education (e.g., offering small financial incentives for attendance, affirmation of parental behaviors in context of parental identity, linking education recommendations into routine situations at home). Behavioral economics may also offer opportunities to enhance prevention efforts in PPH models for addressing disruptive behavioral difficulties in children.

Finally, similar to the development of the evidence base in many areas, including those related to the development of evidence-based treatments for disruptive behavior problems in children (Chorpita, Daleiden & Weisz, 2005; Weisz et al., 2013), a key future area of investigation of prevention approaches with in a PPH model is scalability and sustainability. Early efforts of many prevention studies were to demonstrate efficacy that the intervention approach could affect change. As detailed in the previous section, prevention program can affect this change, at least for a subset of children. This may be enhanced by situating the prevention approaches as part of a larger PPH model. Given this, how do we move forward toward scalable and sustainable models? It appears that a deployment model (Weisz & Kazdin, 2010) which focuses on beginning with the end in mind and leveraging existing resources and appreciating existing constraints is necessary. As exemplified by Atkins and colleagues (e.g., Atkins et al., 2015), as well as in our own work (Chacko et al., 2017; Chacko, Gopalan et al., 2015; Chacko & Scavenius, 2017), we must begin to creatively balance various key factors (e.g., intensity of interventions models, training/supervision needs, costs), so that a prevention approach within a PPH model can be readily sustained and can be scalable within existing contexts.

References

Adams, G., & Rohacek, M. (2002). More than a work support? Issues around integrating child development goals into the child care subsidy system. *Early Childhood Research Quarterly*, *17*(4), 418–440.

Aisenberg, E., & Herrenkohl, T. (2008). Community violence in context: Risk and resilience in children and families. *Journal of Interpersonal Violence*, *23*(3), 296–315.

Alegria, M., Vallas, M., & Pumariega, A. J. (2010). Racial and ethnic disparities in pediatric mental health. *Child and Adolescent Psychiatric Clinics of North America*, *19*(4), 759–774.

Anderson, S. E. (2003). The school district role in educational change: A review of the literature. *International Centre for Educational Change*.

Atkins, M. S., & Frazier, S. L. (2011). Expanding the toolkit or changing the paradigm: Are we ready for a public health approach to mental health? *Perspectives on Psychological Science*, *6*, 483–487.

Atkins, M., Frazier, S., Leathers, S., Graczyk, P., Talbott, E., Adil, J., . . . Gibbons, R. (2008). Teacher key opinion leaders and mental health consultation in urban lowincome schools. *Journal of Consulting and Clinical Psychology*, *76*, 905–908.

Atkins, M. S., Shernoff, E. S., Frazier, S. L., Schoenwald, S. K., Cappella, E., Marinez-Lora, A., . . . Bhaumik, D. (2015). Redesigning community mental health services for urban children: Supporting schooling to promote mental health. *Journal of Consulting and Clinical Psychology*, *83*(5), 839–852. Available from: https://doi.org/10.1037/a0039661.

Baillargeon, R. H., Normand, C. L., Séguin, J. R., Zoccolillo, M., Japel, C., Pérusse, D., . . . Tremblay, R. E. (2007). The evolution of problem and social competence behaviors during toddlerhood: A prospective population-based cohort survey. *Infant Mental Health Journal*, *28*(1), 12–38.

Belden, A. C., Thomson, N. R., & Luby, J. L. (2008). Temper tantrums in healthy versus depressed and disruptive preschoolers: Defining tantrum behaviors associated with clinical problems. *The Journal of Pediatrics*, *152*(1), 117–122.

Belsky, J., Vandell, D. L., Burchinal, M., Clarke-Stewart, K. A., McCartney, K., & Owen, M. T. (2007). Are there long-term effects of early child care? *Child Development*, *78*(2), 681–701.

Blair, C., & Raver, C. C. (2012). Child development in the context of adversity: Experiential canalization of brain and behavior. *American Psychologist*, *67*(4), 309.

Blane, D. (1995). Social determinants of health-socioeconomic status, social class, and ethnicity. *American Journal of Public Health*, *85*(7), 903–905.

Boucher, O., Muckle, G., & Bastien, C. H. (2009). Prenatal exposure to polychlorinated biphenyls: a neuropsychologic analysis. *Environmental Health Perspectives*, *117*(1), 7.

Brown, S. L., Manning, W. D., & Stykes, J. B. (2015). Family structure and child well-being: Integrating family complexity. *Journal of Marriage and Family*, *77*(1), 177–190.

Buka, S. L., Stichick, T. L., Birdthistle, I., & Earls, F. J. (2001). Youth exposure to violence: prevalence, risks, and consequences. *American Journal of Orthopsychiatry*, *71*(3), 298.

Campbell, S. B., Shaw, D. S., & Gilliom, M. (2000). Early externalizing behavior problems: Toddlers and preschoolers at risk for later maladjustment. *Development and Psychopathology*, *12*(3), 467–488.

Caspersen, I. H., Kvalem, H. E., Haugen, M., Brantsæter, A. L., Meltzer, H. M., Alexander, J., ... Granum, B. (2016). Determinants of plasma PCB, brominated flame retardants, and organochlorine pesticides in pregnant women and 3 year old children in The Norwegian Mother and Child Cohort Study. *Environmental Research, 146*, 136–144.

Cavanagh, M., Quinn, D., Duncan, D., Graham, T., & Balbuena, L. (2017). Oppositional defiant disorder is better conceptualized as a disorder of emotional regulation. *Journal of Attention Disorders, 21*(5), 381–389.

Centers for Disease Control and Prevention (CDC). (2016). *Preventing multiple forms of violence: A strategic vision for connecting the dots*. Atlanta, GA: Division of Violence Prevention, National Center for Injury Prevention and Control, Centers for Disease Control and Prevention. Retrieved from http://www.cdc.gov/violenceprevention/pdf/strategic_vision.pdf.

Chacko, A., Alan, C., Uderman, J., Cornwell, M., Anderson, L., & Chimiklis, A. (2015). *Training parents of children with ADHD. Attention deficit hyperactivity disorder: A handbook for diagnosis and treatment*. Guilford Press.

Chacko, A., Anderson, L., & Rajwan, E. (2012). A developmental perspective on behavioral indicators of early onset disruptive behavior disorders. In C. Thomas, & K. Pope (Eds.), The origins of antisocial behavior. New York, NY: Oxford University Press.

Chacko, A., Fabiano, G. A., Doctoroff, G. L., & Fortson, B. (2017). *Engaging fathers in effective parenting for preschool children using shared book reading: A randomized controlled trial. Journal of Clinical Child & Adolescent Psychology* (pp. 1–14).

Chacko, A., Gopalan, G., Franco, L., Dean-Assael, K., Jackson, J., Marcus, S., ... McKay, M. (2015). Multiple family group service model for children with disruptive behavior disorders: Child outcomes at post-treatment. *Journal of Emotional and Behavioral Disorders, 23*(2), 67–77.

Chacko, A., & Scavenius, C. (2017). Bending the curve: A community-based behavioral parent training model to address ADHD-related concerns in the voluntary sector in Denmark. *Journal of Abnormal Child Psychology*, 1–13.

Chacko, A., Wakschlag, L., Hill, C., Danis, B., & Espy, K. A. (2009). Viewing preschool disruptive behavior disorders and attention-deficit/hyperactivity disorder through a developmental lens: What we know and what we need to know. *Child and Adolescent Psychiatric Clinics of North America, 18*(3), 627–643.

Chambers, E. C., Fuster, D., Suglia, S. F., & Rosenbaum, E. (2015). Depressive symptomology and hostile affect among Latinos using housing rental assistance: The AHOME study. *Journal of Urban Health, 92*(4), 611–621. Available from: https://doi.org/10.1007/s11524-015-9965-0.

Chauhan, P., Burnette, M. L., & Repucci, N. D. (2009). Racial disparities among female juvenile offenders: The contribution of neighborhood disadvantage and exposure to violence in antisocial behavior. *Court Review, 46*, 10.

Chorpita, B. F., Daleiden, E. L., & Weisz, J. R. (2005). Identifying and selecting the common elements of evidence based interventions: A distillation and matching model. *Mental health services research, 7*(1), 5–20.

Cole, P. M., Michel, M. K., & Teti, L. O. D. (1994). The development of emotion regulation and dysregulation: A clinical perspective. *Monographs of the Society for Research in Child Development, 59*(2-3), 73–102.

Coley, R. L., Leventhal, T., Lynch, A. D., & Kull, M. (2013). Relations between housing characteristics and the well-being of low-income children and adolescents.

Developmental Psychology, *49*(9), 1775–1789. Available from: https://doi.org/10.1037/a0031033.

Cooley-Quille, M., Boyd, R. C., Frantz, E., & Walsh, J. (2001). Emotional and behavioral impact of exposure to community violence in inner-city adolescents. *Journal of Clinical Child Psychology*, *30*(2), 199–206.

Conduct Problems Prevention Research Group. (1992). A developmental and clinical model for the prevention of conduct disorder: The FAST Track Program. *Development and Psychopathology*, *4*(4), 509–527. Available from: https://doi.org/10.1017/S0954579400004855.

Conduct Problems Prevention Research Group. (1999). Initial impact of the Fast Track prevention trial for conduct problems: I. The high-risk sample. *Journal of Consulting and Clinical Psychology*, *67*(5), 631–647.

Cubbin, C., Hadden, W. C., & Winkleby, M. A. (2001). Neighborhood context and cardiovascular disease risk factors: The contribution of material deprivation. *Ethnicity & Disease*, *11*, 687–700.

Curchack-Lichtin, J. T., Chacko, A., & Halperin, J. M. (2014). Changes in ADHD symptom endorsement: Preschool to school age. *Journal of Abnormal Child Psychology*, *42*(6), 993–1004.

Danese, A., & McEwen, B. S. (2012). Adverse childhood experiences, allostasis, allostatic load, and age-related disease. *Physiology & Behavior*, *106*(1), 29–39.

David-Ferdon, C., Vivolo-Kantor, A.M., Dahlberg, L.L., Marshall, K.J., Rainford, N., & Hall, J.E. (2016). A comprehensive technical package for the prevention of youth violence and associated risk behaviors.

Deaton, A., & Lubotsky, D. (2003). Mortality, Inequality and race in American cities and states. *Social Science & Medicine*, *56*, 1139–1153.

Department of Health and Human Services. *Report of the Surgeon General's Conference on Children's Mental Health: A National Action Agenda*; 2002. Available at: http://www.surgeongeneral.gov/topics/cmh/childreport.html.

Duncan, G. J., & Brooks-Gunn, J. (2000). Family poverty, welfare reform, and child development. *Child Development*, *71*(1), 188–196.

Eaton, W. W., Martins, S. S., Nestadt, G., Bienvenu, O. J., Clarke, D., & Alexandre, P. (2008). The burden of mental disorders. *Epidemiologic Reviews*, *30*(1), 1–14.

Egger, H. L., & Angold, A. (2006). Common emotional and behavioral disorders in preschool children: Presentation, nosology, and epidemiology. *Journal of Child Psychology and Psychiatry*, *47*(3-4), 313–337.

Fiscella, K., & Kitzman, H. (2009). Disparities in academic achievement and health: The intersection of child education and health policy. *Pediatrics*, *123*(3), 1073–1080.

Ford, J. D., Chapman, J., MACK, J. M., & Pearson, G. (2006). Pathways from traumatic child victimization to delinquency: Implications for juvenile and permanency court proceedings and decisions. *Juvenile and Family Court Journal*, *57*(1), 13–26.

Foster, J. D., Kuperminc, G. P., & Price, A. W. (2004). Gender differences in posttraumatic stress and related symptoms among inner-city minority youth exposed to community violence. *Journal of Youth and Adolescence*, *33*(1), 59–69.

Fowler, P. J., Tompsett, C. J., Braciszewski, J. M., Jacques-Tiura, A. J., & Baltes, B. B. (2009).). Community violence: A meta-analysis on the effect of exposure and mental health outcomes of children and adolescent. *s. Development and Psychopathology*, *21* (1), 227–259.

Frazier, S. L., Chacko, A., Van Gessel, C., O'Boyle, C., & Pelham, W. E. (2012). The summer treatment program meets the south side of Chicago: Bridging science and service in urban after-school programs. *Child and Adolescent Mental Health*, *17*(2), 86–92.

Frazier, S. L., Mehta, T. G., Atkins, M. S., Hur, K., & Rusch, D. (2013). Not just a walk in the park: Efficacy to effectiveness for after school programs in communities of concentrated urban poverty. *Administration and Policy in Mental Health and MentalHealth Services Research*, *40*(5), 406–418. Available from: https://doi.org/10.1007/s10488-012-0432-x.

Frick, P. J., & Nigg, J. T. (2012). Current issues in the diagnosis of attention deficit hyperactivity disorder, oppositional defiant disorder, and conduct disorder. *Annual Review of Clinical Psychology*, *8*, 77–107.

Gallagher, M. (2010). USDA defines food deserts. *Nutrition Digest*, *35*(3). Retrieved from: http://americannutritionassociation.org/newsletter/usda-defines-food-deserts.

Garland, A. F., Hough, R. L., McCabe, K. M., Yeh, M. A. Y., Wood, P. A., & Aarons, G. A. (2001). Prevalence of psychiatric disorders in youths across five sectors of care. *Journal of the American Academy of Child & Adolescent Psychiatry*, *40*(4), 409–418.

Gavine, A. J., Donnelly, P. D., & Williams, D. J. (2016). Effectiveness of universal school-based programs for prevention of violence in adolescents. *Psychology of Violence*, *6*(3), 390.

Gee, G. C., & Payne-Sturges, D. C. (2004). Environmental health disparities: A framework integrating psychosocial and environmental concepts. *Environmental Health Perspectives*, *112*, 1645–1653.

Gennetian, L., Darling, M., & Aber, J. L. (2016). Behavioral economics and developmental science: A new framework to support early childhood interventions. *Journal of Applied Research on Children: Informing Policy for Children at Risk*, *7*(2), Article 2.

Gorman-Smith, D., Henry, D. B., & Tolan, P. H. (2004). Exposure to community violence and violence perpetration: The protective effects of family functioning. *Journal of Clinical Child and Adolescent Psychology*, *33*, 439–449.

Gorman-Smith, D., & Tolan, P. (1998). The role of exposure to community violence and developmental problems among inner-city youth. *Development and Psychopathology*, *10*(1), 101–116.

Greenberg, M. T., Kusche, C. A., Cook, E. T., & Quamma, J. P. (1995). Promoting emotional competence in school-aged children: The effects of the PATHS curriculum. *Development and Psychopathology*, *7*(1), 117–136.

Greenberg, M., Lombardi, J., & Schumacher, R. (2000). *The child care and development block grant: An overview*. Washington, DC: The Center for Law and Social Policy.

Hamby, S., & Grych, J. (2013). Evidence-based interventions need to be more systematic, not more disruptive. *American Psychologist*, *68*, 476–477. Available from https://doi.org/10.1037/a0032884.

Hart, A., Gagnon, E., Eryigit-Madzwamuse, S., Cameron, J., Aranda, K., Rathbone, A., & Heaver, B. (2016). Uniting resilience research and practice with an inequalities approach. *SAGE Open*, *6*(4), 2158244016682477.

Hay, D. F. (2005). The beginnings of aggression in infancy. In R. E. Tremblay, W. W. Hartup, & J. Archer (Eds.), *Developmental Origins of Aggression* (pp. 107–132). New York: Guilford Press.

Heckman, J. J. (2006). Skill formation and the economics of investing in disadvantaged children. *Science*, *312*(5782), 1900–1902.

Herbst, C. M., & Tekin, E. (2010). Child care subsidies and child development. *Economics of Education Review*, *29*(4), 618–638.

Henry, D. B., Farrell, A. D., Schoeny, M. E., Tolan, P. H., & Dymnicki, A. B. (2011). Influence of school-level variables on aggression and associated attitudes of middle school students. *Journal of School Psychology*, *49*(5), 481–503.

Hernández, D. (2016). Affording housing at the expense of health: Exploring the housing and neighborhood strategies of poor families. *Journal of Family Issues*, *37*(7), 921–946. Available from: https://doi.org/10.1177/0192513X14530970.

Hernandez, D., & Suglla, S. (2016). *Housing as a social determinant of health*. Retrieved from: https://healthequity.globalpolicysolutions.org/wp-content/uploads/2016/12/Housing2.pdf.

Hessling, R., Schmidt, T., & Traxel, N. (2004). Floor effect. In M. S. Lewis-Beck, A. Bryman, & T. F. Liao (Eds.), *The SAGE Encyclopedia of Social science research methods* (pp. 391–392). Thousand Oaks, CA: Sage Publications, Inc.

Javdani, S., Sadeh, N., & Verona, E. (2011). Expanding our lens: Female pathways to antisocial behavior in adolescence and adulthood. *Clinical Psychology Review*, *31*(8), 1324–1348.

Javdani, S., Abdul-Adil, J., Suarez, L., Nichols, S. R., & Farmer, A. D. (2014). Gender differences in the effects of community violence on mental health outcomes in a sample of low-income youth receiving psychiatric care. *American Journal of Community Psychology*, *53*(3-4), 235–248.

Johnson, R. M., Kotch, J. B., Catellier, D. J., Winsor, J. R., Dufort, V., Hunter, W., & Amaya-Jackson, L. (2002). Adverse behavioral and emotional outcomes from child abuse and witnessed violence. *Child Maltreatment*, *7*(3), 179–186.

Kannampallil, T. G., Schauer, G. F., Cohen, T., & Patel, V. L. (2011). Considering complexity in healthcare systems. *Journal of Biomedical Informatics*, *44*(6), 943–947.

Keenan, K., & Wakschlag, L. S. (2002). Can a valid diagnosis of disruptive behavior disorder be made in preschool children? *American Journal of Psychiatry*, *159*(3), 351–358.

Kusche, C. A., & Greenberg, M. T. (1994). *The PATHS (Promoting alternative thinking strategies) curriculum. South Deerfield, MA: Channing-Bete.*

Lee, K., & Ludington, B. (2016). Head Start's Impact on Socio-Emotional Outcomes for Children Who Have Experienced Violence or Neighborhood Crime. *Journal of Family Violence*, *31*(4), 499–513.

Lochman, J. E., Powell, N. R., Clanton, N., & McElroy, H. K. (2006). Anger and Aggression. In G. G. Bear, & K. M. Minke (Eds.), *Children's needs III: Development, prevention, and intervention* (pp. 115–133). Washington, DC, US: National Association of School Psychologists.

Loeber, R., & Ahonen, L. (2014). What are the policy implications of our knowledge on serious, violent, and chronic offenders? *Criminology & Public Policy*, *13*(1), 117–125.

Lorion, R. P., & Saltzman, W. (1993). Children's exposure to community violence: Following a path from concern to research to action. *Psychiatry*, *56*(1), 55–65.

Love, J. M., Kisker, E. E., Ross, C., Raikes, H., Constantine, J., Boller, K., & Fuligni, A. S. (2005). The effectiveness of early head start for 3-year-old children and their parents: lessons for policy and programs. *Developmental Psychology*, *41*(6), 885.

Lynch, M., & Cicchetti, D. (1998). An ecological-transactional analysis of children and contexts: The longitudinal interplay among child maltreatment, community violence, and children's symptomatology. *Development and Psychopathology*, *10*(2), 235–257.

Margolin, G., & Gordis, E. B. (2000). The effects of family and community violence on children. *Annual review of psychology*, *51*(1), 445–479.

Kochanska, G., Coy, K. C., & Murray, K. T. (2001). The development of self-regulation in the first four years of life. *Child Development, 72*(4), 1091−1111.

Matthys, W., & Lochman, J. E. (2017). *Oppositional defiant disorder and conduct disorder in childhood*. John Wiley & Sons.

McGuire, T. G., & Miranda, J. (2008). New evidence regarding racial and ethnic disparities in mental health: Policy implications. *Health Affairs, 27*(2), 393−403.

Michigan Youth Violence Prevention Center. (2017). *Multi-level approach to youth violence prevention*. Retrieved from http://yvpc.sph.umich.edu/projects/multi-level-approach-to-youth-violence-prevention-2010-2015/

Miles, J., Espiritu, R. C., Horen, N., Sebian, J., & Waetzig, E. (2010). *A public health approach to children's mental health: A conceptual framework*. Washington, DC: Georgetown University Center for Child and Human Development, National Technical Assistance Center for Children's Mental Health.

Miller-Johnson, S., Sullivan, T. N., & Simon, T. R. (2004). Multisite Violence Prevention Project. Evaluating the impact of interventions in the multisite violence prevention study: Samples, procedures, and measures. *American Journal of Preventive Medicine, 26*(1), 48−61.

Morland, K., Wing, S., Diez Roux, A. V., & Poole, C. (2002). Neighborhood characteristics associated with the location of food stores and food service places. *American Journal of Preventive Medicine, 22*(1), 23−29.

Multisite Violence Prevention Project. (2008). Impact of a universal school-based violence prevention program on social-cognitive outcomes. *Prevention Science: The Official Journal of the Society for Prevention Research, 9*(4), 231−244.

Nadeem, E., Maslak, K., Chacko, A., & Hoagwood, K. E. (2010). Aligning research and policy on social-emotional and academic competence for young children. *Early Education and Development, 21*(5), 765−779.

National Center for Injury Prevention and Control: Division of Violence Prevention(NCIPC: DVP). (2014, August). *Essentials for childhood: Steps to create safe, stable, nurturing relationships and environments*. Retrieved from https://www.cdc.gov/violenceprevention/pdf/essentials_for_childhood_framework.pdf

National Center for Injury Prevention and Control: Division of Violence Prevention(NCIPC: DVP). (2016, August 30). *National centers for excellence in youth violence prevention*. Retrieved from https://www.cdc.gov/violenceprevention/ace/

National Information Center on Health Services Research and Health Care Technology (NICHSR). 2009. *Health Services and Sciences Research Resources (HSRR)*. Available from: http://wwwcf.nlm.nih.gov/ hsrr_search/index.cfm (accessed April 14, 2009).

National Scientific Council on the Developing Child (NSCDC). (2005). *Excessive stress disrupts the architecture of the developing brain. Working paper No. 3*. Boston, MA: Center on the Developing Child at Harvard University. Retrieved from http://developingchild.harvard.edu/resources/wp3/.

NICHD Early Child Care Research Network. (2001). Nonmaternal care and family factors in early development: An overview of the NICHD Study of Early Child Care. *Journal of Applied Developmental Psychology, 22*(5), 457−492.

Neville, F. G. (2015). Preventing violence through changing social norms. In P. Donnelly, & C. Ward (Eds.), *Oxford textbook of violence prevention: Epidemiology, evidence and policy* (pp. 239−244). Oxford: Oxford University Press.

Newcorn, J. H., Lalonde, M. M., & Leikauf, J. (2015). ODD and Conduct Disorder. *Psychiatry, Fourth Edition*, 1350−1366.

O'Donnell, D. A., Schwab-Stone, M. E., & Muyeed, A. Z. (2002). Multidimensional resilience in urban children exposed to community violence. *Child Development, 73*, 1265–1282.

Olfson, M., Marcus, S. C., Druss, B., Pincus, H. A., & Weissman, M. M. (2003). Parental depression, child mental health problems, and health care utilization. *Medical Care, 41* (6), 716–721.

Osofsky, J. D. (1995). The effect of exposure to violence on young children. *American Psychologist, 50*(9), 782.

Osofsky, J. D. (1997). Community and domestic violence exposure: Effects on development and psychopathology. In D. Cicchetti, & S. L. Toth (Eds.), *Rochester Symposium on Developmental Psychopathology: Vol. 8. Developmental perspectives on trauma: Theory, research, and intervention* (pp. 155–180).

Ozer, E. J., & Weinstein, R. S. (2004). Urban adolescents' exposure to community violence: The role of support, school safety, and social constraints in a school-based sample of boys and girls. *Journal of Clinical Child and Adolescent Psychology, 33*, 463–486.

Parke, R. D., & Slaby, R. G. (1983). The development of aggression. *Handbook of Child Psychology, 4*, 547–641.

Patterson, G. R., DeBaryshe, B. D., & Ramsey, E. (1989). A developmental perspective on antisocial behavior. *American Psychological Association, 44*(2), 329–335.

Peisner-Feinberg, E. S., Burchinal, M. R., Clifford, R. M., Culkin, M. L., Howes, C., Kagan, S. L., & Yazejian, N. (2001). The relation of preschool child-care quality to children's cognitive and social developmental trajectories through second grade. *Child development, 72*(5), 1534–1553.

Phillips, D., & Adams, G. (2001). Child care and our youngest children. *The future of children*, 35–51.

Plybon, L. E., & Kliewer, W. (2001). Neighborhood types and externalizing behavior in urban school-age children: Tests of direct, mediated, and moderated effects. *Journal of Child and Family Studies, 10*(4), 419–437.

Powell, L. M., Slater, S., Mirtcheva, D., Bao, Y., & Chaloupka, F. J. (2007). Food store availability and neighborhood characteristics in the United States. *Preventive Medicine, 44*, 189–195.

Pumariega, A. J., Rogers, K., & Rothe, E. (2005). Culturally competent systems of care for children's mental health: Advances and challenges. *Community Mental Health Journal, 41*(5), 539–555.

Raikes, H. H., & Love, J. M. (2002). Early Head Start: A dynamic new program for infants and toddlers and their families. *Infant Mental Health Journal, 23*(1-2), 1–13.

Reid, J. B., Eddy, J. M., Fetrow, R. A., & Stoolmiller, M. (1999). Description and immediate impacts of a preventive intervention for conduct problems. *American Journal of Community Psychology, 27*(4), 483–518.

Repetti, R. L., Taylor, S. E., & Seeman, T. E. (2002). Risky families: Family social environments and the mental and physical health of offspring. *Psychological Bulletin, 128*(2), 330.

Shonkoff, J. P., Garner, A. S., Siegel, B. S., Dobbins, M. I., Earls, M. F., McGuinn, L., … Committee on Early Childhood, Adoption, and Dependent Care. (2012). The lifelong effects of early childhood adversity and toxic stress. *Pediatrics, 129*(1), e232–e246.

Solari, C. D., & Mare, R. D. (2012). Housing crowding effects on children's wellbeing. *Social Science Research, 41*(2), 464–476. Available from: https://doi.org/10.1016/j.ssresearch.2011.09.012.

Sroufe, L. A. (1997). *Emotional development: The organization of emotional life in the early years*. New York: Cambridge University Press.

Steps to Success (STS). (2014, June). Steps to success (STS) annual progress report, June 2014. Retrieved from https://static1.squarespace.com/static/53139c60e4b0e81d1553864d/t/53c82031e4b0f6b1906c29e5/1405624369496/Steps + to + Success + Progress + Report + June + 2014.pdf

Stewart, P. W., Lonky, E., Reihman, J., Pagano, J., Gump, B. B., & Darvill, T. (2008). The relationship between prenatal PCB exposure and intelligence (IQ) in 9-year-old children. *Environmental Health Perspectives*, *116*(10), 1416.

Sterba, S., Egger, H. L., & Angold, A. (2007). Diagnostic specificity and nonspecificity in the dimensions of preschool psychopathology. *Journal of Child Psychology and Psychiatry*, *48*(10), 1005–1013.

Talge, N. M., Neal, C., & Glover, V. (2007). Antenatal maternal stress and long-term effects on child neurodevelopment: How and why?. *Journal of Child Psychology and Psychiatry*, *48*(3-4), 245–261.

Thelen & Smith. (2006). Dynamic systems theories. In W. Damon, & R. M. Lerner (Eds.), *Handbook of child psychology, Volume one: Theoretical models of human development* (6th ed.). New York: John Wiley & Sons, Inc.

Thomas, C. R. (2017). 5.3 Conduct Disorder, Violence, and the Treatment of Aggression. *Journal of the American Academy of Child & Adolescent Psychiatry*, *56*(10), S144.

Tremblay, R. E. (2010). Developmental origins of disruptive behaviour problems: The 'original sin' hypothesis, epigenetics and their consequences for prevention. *Journal of Child Psychology and Psychiatry*, *51*(4), 341–367.

United States Department of Agriculture, Food and Nutrition Services. (2017a). Supplemental Nutrition Assistance Program (SNAP). Retrieved from https://www.fns.usda.gov/snap/eligibility

United States Department of Agriculture, Food and Nutrition Services. (2017b). Women, Infants, and Children (WIC). Retrieved from https://www.fns.usda.gov/wic/women-infants-and-children-wic

United States Department of Agriculture, Food and Nutrition Services. (2017c). School Meals. Retrieved from https://www.fns.usda.gov/snap/eligible-food-items

Wakschlag, L. S., Briggs-Gowan, M. J., Carter, A. S., Hill, C., Danis, B., Keenan, K., … Leventhal, B. L. (2007). A developmental framework for distinguishing disruptive behavior from normative misbehavior in preschool children. *Journal of Child Psychology and Psychiatry*, *48*(10), 976–987.

Wakschlag, L. S., Briggs-Gowan, M. J., Choi, S. W., Nichols, S. R., Kestler, J., Burns, J. L., … Henry, D. (2014). Advancing a multidimensional, developmental spectrum approach to preschool disruptive behavior. *Journal of the American Academy of Child & Adolescent Psychiatry*, *53*(1), 82–96.

Wakschlag, L. S., Estabrook, R., Petitclerc, A., Henry, D., Burns, J. L., Perlman, S. B., … Briggs-Gowan, M. L. (2015). Clinical implications of a dimensional approach: The normal:abnormal spectrum of early irritability. *Journal of the American Academy of Child & Adolescent Psychiatry*, *54*(8), 626–634.

Wakschlag, L. S., Tolan, P. H., & Leventhal, B. L. (2010). Research review:'Ain't misbehavin': Towards a developmentally-specified nosology for preschool disruptive behavior. *Journal of Child Psychology and Psychiatry*, *51*(1), 3–22.

Walker, R. E., Keane, C. R., & Burke, J. G. (2010). Disparities and access to healthy food in the United States: A review of food deserts literature. *Health & Place, 16*, 876–884.

Webster-Stratton, C. (1998). Preventing conduct problems in Head Start children: strengthening parenting competencies. *Journal of consulting and clinical psychology*, *66*(5), 715.

Webster-Stratton, C., Reid, M. J., & Hammond, M. (2001). Preventing conduct problems, promoting social competence: A parent and teacher training partnership in Head Start. *Journal of clinical child psychology*, *30*(3), 283–302.

Webster-Stratton, C., & Reid, M. (2010). Adapting the Incredible Years, an evidence-based parenting programme, for families involved in the child welfare system. *Journal of Children's Services*, *5*(1), 25–42.

Weisz, J. R., & Kazdin, A. E. (Eds.), (2010). *Evidence-based psychotherapies for children and adolescents*. Guilford Press.

Weisz, J. R., Ugueto, A. M., Cheron, D. M., & Herren, J. (2013). Evidence-based youth psychotherapy in the mental health ecosystem. *Journal of Clinical Child & Adolescent Psychology*, *42*(2), 274–286.

Whitebook, M. (2003). Early education quality: Higher teacher qualifications for better living environments. A review of the literature.

Williams, D. J., Gavine, A. J., Ward, C. L., & Donnelly, P. D. (2015). What is evidence in violence prevention. In P. D. Donnelly, & C. L. Ward (Eds.), *Oxford textbook of violence prevention: Epidemiology, evidence and policy* (pp. 125–131). Oxford, UK: Oxford University Press.

Youngstrom, E., Weist, M. D., & Albus, K. E. (2003). Exploring violence exposure, stress, protective factors and behavioral problems among inner-city youth. *American Journal of Community Psychology*, *32*(1-2), 115–129.

Index

Note: Page numbers followed by "*f*" and "*t*" refer to figures and tables, respectively.

E

Made in the USA
Monee, IL
18 August 2021

75958851R00227